Bank Profitability

FINANCIAL STATEMENTS OF BANKS

2002 Edition

Rentabilité des banques

COMPTES DES BANQUES

OECD

ORGANISATION FOR ECONOMIC CO-OPERATION AND DEVELOPMENT

ORGANISATION FOR ECONOMIC CO-OPERATION AND DEVELOPMENT

Pursuant to Article 1 of the Convention signed in Paris on 14th December 1960, and which came into force on 30th September 1961, the Organisation for Economic Co-operation and Development (OECD) shall promote policies designed:

- to achieve the highest sustainable economic growth and employment and a rising standard of living in Member countries, while maintaining financial stability, and thus to contribute to the development of the world economy;
- to contribute to sound economic expansion in Member as well as non-member countries in the process of economic development; and
- to contribute to the expansion of world trade on a multilateral, non-discriminatory basis in accordance with international obligations.

The original Member countries of the OECD are Austria, Belgium, Canada, Denmark, France, Germany, Greece, Iceland, Ireland, Italy, Luxembourg, the Netherlands, Norway, Portugal, Spain, Sweden, Switzerland, Turkey, the United Kingdom and the United States. The following countries became Members subsequently through accession at the dates indicated hereafter: Japan (28th April 1964), Finland (28th January 1969), Australia (7th June 1971), New Zealand (29th May 1973), Mexico (18th May 1994), the Czech Republic (21st December 1995), Hungary (7th May 1996), Poland (22nd November 1996), Korea (12th December 1996) and the Slovak Republic (14th December 2000). The Commission of the European Communities takes part in the work of the OECD (Article 13 of the OECD Convention).

ORGANISATION DE COOPÉRATION ET DE DÉVELOPPEMENT ÉCONOMIQUES

En vertu de l'article 1er de la Convention signée le 14 décembre 1960, à Paris, et entrée en vigueur le 30 septembre 1961, l'Organisation de Coopération et de Développement Économiques (OCDE) a pour objectif de promouvoir des politiques visant :

- à réaliser la plus forte expansion de l'économie et de l'emploi et une progression du niveau de vie dans les pays Membres, tout en maintenant la stabilité financière, et à contribuer ainsi au développement de l'économie mondiale ;
- à contribuer à une saine expansion économique dans les pays Membres, ainsi que les pays non membres, en voie de développement économique ;
- à contribuer à l'expansion du commerce mondial sur une base multilatérale et non discriminatoire conformément aux obligations internationales.

Les pays Membres originaires de l'OCDE sont : l'Allemagne, l'Autriche, la Belgique, le Canada, le Danemark, l'Espagne, les États-Unis, la France, la Grèce, l'Irlande, l'Islande, l'Italie, le Luxembourg, la Norvège, les Pays-Bas, le Portugal, le Royaume-Uni, la Suède, la Suisse et la Turquie. Les pays suivants sont ultérieurement devenus Membres par adhésion aux dates indiquées ci-après : le Japon (28 avril 1964), la Finlande (28 janvier 1969), l'Australie (7 juin 1971), la Nouvelle-Zélande (29 mai 1973), le Mexique (18 mai 1994), la République tchèque (21 décembre 1995), la Hongrie (7 mai 1996), la Pologne (22 novembre 1996), la Corée (12 décembre 1996) et la République slovaque (14 décembre 2000). La Commission des Communautés européennes participe aux travaux de l'OCDE (article 13 de la Convention de l'OCDE).

FOREWORD

This publication provides information on financial statements of banks in all OECD Member countries. The coverage of banks in this volume is not the same in each country, though the objective is to include all institutions which conduct ordinary banking business, namely institutions which primarily take deposits from the public at large and provide finance for a wide range of purposes. Some supplementary information on the number of reporting banks, their branches and staff is also included. *Bank Profitability -- Methodological Notes* complement the series included in the present publication.

The institutional coverage of the tables has been largely dictated by the availability of data on income and expenditure accounts of banks. As a result of the reporting methods which are being used in OECD countries, the tables are not integrated in the system of national accounts. International comparisons in the field of income and expenditure accounts of banks are particularly difficult due to considerable differences in OECD countries as regards structural and regulatory features of national banking systems, accounting rules and practices, and reporting methods.

The standard framework used for presenting the statistics was modified following the recommendations of the Task Force on Bank Profitability. This publication was prepared by the Financial Statistics Unit but could not have been accomplished without the assistance of the members of the OECD Working Party on Financial Statistics and the national administrations which they represent. It is published on the responsibility of the Secretary-General of the OECD.

AVANT-PROPOS

Cet ouvrage présente les informations relatives aux comptes des banques dans tous les pays Membres de l'OCDE. La couverture des banques figurant dans ces statistiques n'est pas la même dans chaque pays, bien que l'objectif reste d'inclure toutes les institutions qui effectuent des opérations courantes de banque, c'est-à-dire qui reçoivent des dépôts du public et offrent des concours financiers à des fins très diverses. Des informations complémentaires sur le nombre de banques, celui de leurs succursales et de leurs salariés figurent également dans cet ouvrage. *La Rentabilité des banques -- Notes méthodologiques,* complètent les séries incluses dans la présente publication.

La couverture institutionnelle des tableaux a été largement dictée par la disponibilité des données sur les comptes de revenus et de dépenses des banques. Du fait des modes de communication des données en vigueur dans les pays de l'OCDE, ces tableaux ne sont pas intégrés dans le Système de comptabilité nationale. Les comparaisons internationales dans le domaine des comptes de revenus et de dépenses des banques sont particulièrement délicates étant donné les différences importantes qui existent entre les pays de l'OCDE en ce qui concerne la structure du système bancaire et la réglementation des banques, les règles et pratiques comptables et le système de communication des données.

Le cadre de référence utilisé pour la présentation des statistiques a été modifié suivant les recommandations du Groupe de projet sur la Rentabilité des banques. Cet ouvrage a été réalisé par l'unité des Statistiques financières, mais n'aurait pu être réalisé sans l'aide des membres du Groupe de travail de l'OCDE sur les statistiques financières et des administrations nationales qu'ils représentent. Cet ouvrage est publié sous la responsabilité du Secrétaire général de l'OCDE.

TABLE OF CONTENTS

Part II **GENERAL TABLES**[1]

---

1 .   a.   Structure of the Financial System

        b.   Resident/Non-resident and Domestic/Foreign Currency
             Classification of Bank Assets and Liabilities

Methodological country notes are published in the companion volume *Bank Profitability - Country Notes, 2003.*

CONVENTIONAL SIGNS

..	*Not available*
-	*Nil or negligible*
·	*Decimal point*

TABLE DES MATIÈRES

Partie II TABLEAUX GÉNÉRAUX[1]

---

1 . a. Structure du système financier

b. Résident/non résident et monnaie nationale/étrangère
classification de l'actif et du passif des banques

Les notes méthodologiques sont publiées dans le volume *Rentabilité des banques—Notes méthodologiques par pays, 2003.*

SIGNES CONVENTIONNELS

..	*Non disponible*
-	*Nul ou négligeable*
·	*Point décimal (sépare les unités des décimales)*

INTRODUCTION

The present volume provides statistics updating the earlier editions of *Bank Profitability -- Financial Statements of Banks.*

1. Standard framework for detailed statistics by country

National data are grouped and, where necessary, re-classified to fit as far as possible into the following standard framework of presentation.

Income statement

1. Interest income

This item generally includes income on interest-bearing assets, fee income related to lending operations, and dividend income on shares and participations. In some cases it may also include income on bonds calculated as the difference between the book value and the redemption value of bonds.

2. Interest expenses

This item generally includes interest paid on liabilities, fee expenses related to borrowing operations and may include in some cases the difference between the issue price on debt instruments and their par value.

3. Net interest income (item 1 minus item 2)

4. Non-interest income (net)

a. Fees and commissions receivable

b. Fees and commissions payable

c. Net profit or loss on financial operations

d. Other

This item is generally the net result of a number of different income and expense items (other than those included in items 1 and 2) such as the following: commissions received and paid in connection with payments services, securities transactions and related services (new issues, trading, portfolio management, safe-custody) and foreign exchange transactions in the banks own name and on behalf of clients. Other income and expenses resulting from special transactions which do not represent ordinary and regular banking business may also be included. Realised losses and gains on foreign-exchange operations and securities transactions are generally included as well.

5. *Gross income* (item 3 plus item 4)

6. *Operating expenses*

   a. Staff costs

   b. Property costs

   c. Other

This item includes all expenses relating to the ordinary and regular banking business other than those included in items 2 and 4, particularly salaries and other employee benefits, including transfers to pension reserves (staff costs), and expenses for property and equipment and related depreciation expenses. Taxes other than income or corporate taxes are also included.

7. *Net income* (item 5 minus item 6)

8. *Provisions (net)*

   a. Provisions on loans

   b. Provisions on securities

   c. Other

This item includes, in part or in full, charges for value adjustments in respect of loans, credits and securities, book gains from such adjustments, losses on loans and transfers to and from reserves for possible losses on such assets. Realised gains or losses from foreign exchange transactions and securities transactions are, however, generally included under *Non-interest income (net)* (item 4).

9. *Profit before tax* (item 7 minus item 8)

10. *Income tax*

11. *Profit after tax* (item 9 minus item 10)

12. *Distributed profit*

13. *Retained profit* (item 11 minus item 12)

Balance sheet

Assets

14. *Cash and balance with Central bank*

15. *Interbank deposits*

16. *Loans*

17. *Securities*

18. *Other assets*

Liabilities

19. *Capital and reserves*

20. *Borrowing from Central bank*

21. *Interbank deposits*

22. *Non-bank deposits*

23. *Bonds*

24. *Other liabilities*

Balance sheet total

25. *End-year total* (sum of items 14 to 18 or 19 to 24)

26. *Average total*

Method of calculation varies between countries. The majority is the average of two end-year totals. Others are based on 13-month averages.

Memorandum items

27. *Short-term securities* (included in item 17)

Following the definition used in the European System of Integrated Accounts (paragraph 539), short-term securities with an original maturity of usually up to 12 months, but with a maximum maturity of two years.

28. *Bonds* (included in item 17)

Following the definition of the European System of Integrated Accounts (paragraph 542), this item includes fixed or variable-interest rate securities with an original maturity of several years.

29. *Shares and participations* (included in item 17)

30. *Claims on non-residents* (included in items 15 to 18)

31. *Liabilities to non-residents* (included in items 21 to 24)

Capital Adequacy

32. *Tier 1 Capital*: paid up shared capital/common stocks, disclosed reserves

33. *Tier 2 Capital*: undisclosed reserves, asset revaluation reserves, general provision/general loan loss reserves, debt/equity capital instruments, subordinated term debt.

34. *Supervisory deductions*

35. *Total net capital resources* (item 32 plus item 33 minus item 34)

36. *Risk-weighted assets*

Supplementary information

37. *Number of institutions* (covered by the data)

38. *Number of branches* (covered by the data)

39. *Number of staff* ('000) (of the institutions covered by the data)

2. Standard presentations for general tables

Structure of the financial system
Year

	Number of institutions	Number of branches	Number of employees	Total assets or liabilities	Total financial assets	
				in national currency	in national currency	%
Central bank						
Other monetary institutions						
Commercial banks						
Foreign owned banks						
Savings banks						
Co-operative banks						
Other financial institutions						
Mortgage credit institutions						
Development credit institutions						
Finance companies						
Others						
Insurance institutions						
Insurance companies						
Pension funds and foundations						
Others						
All financial institutions						

Resident/non-resident and domestic/foreign currency classification of bank assets and liabilities

Year

in national currency

	Residents	Non-residents	Total
Assets			
Domestic currency			
Foreign currencies			
Total			
Liabilities			
Domestic currency			
Foreign currencies			
Total			

3.   *Methodological information*

In order to facilitate the interpretation and analysis of the data included in the present publication and to enable the user of the data to judge how cautiously the figures should be used for comparative purposes, methodological country notes provide detailed information[1] on the following:

- Institutional coverage, and the relative importance of the institutions covered as compared with the whole financial system;

- Geographical coverage and degree of consolidation indicating whether domestic or foreign financial or non-financial subsidiaries of the reporting banks are covered by the data and whether branches and/or subsidiaries of foreign banks are included;

- Structure of the banking system including information on the regulatory framework;

- Summary description of activities of banks: payment facilities, deposit business, lending business, savings instruments, money market business, security business, foreign exchange business, non-bank business.

- Explanations on individual items and reconciliation tables for income statement and balance sheet items giving detailed information on the way in which the data included in the present publication are derived from generally more detailed national data;

- Sources of data.

---

1. *Bank Profitability -- Methodological Country Notes*, OECD.

INTRODUCTION

Le présent volume fournit des statistiques mettant à jour les éditions antérieures de *Rentabilité des banques -- Comptes des banques.*

1.   Modèle de présentation des statistiques détaillées par pays

Les données communiquées par les pays ont été groupées et, lorsque nécessaire, reclassées afin de cadrer, autant que possible, avec le modèle de présentation ci-après.

Compte de résultats

1. Produits financiers

Ce poste comprend, en principe, les revenus des actifs porteurs d'intérêts, les commissions afférentes aux opérations de prêt, ainsi que les dividendes d'actions et titres de participation. Dans certains cas, il peut comprendre aussi les revenus d'obligations définis comme la différence entre la valeur comptable et la valeur de remboursement des titres.

2. Frais financiers

Ce poste comprend, en principe, les intérêts versés sur les éléments du passif et les commissions versées sur les opérations d'emprunt. Il peut comprendre aussi, dans certains cas, la différence entre la valeur d'émission des instruments de dette et leur valeur nominale.

3. Produits financiers nets (poste 1 moins poste 2)

4. Produits non financiers (nets)

    a. Frais et commissions à recevoir

    b. Frais et commissions à payer

    c. Profits ou pertes nets sur opérations financières

    d. Autres

Ce poste est en principe le résultat net d'un certain nombre de produits et frais différents (autres que ceux figurant aux postes 1 et 2) tels que : commissions reçues et versées en paiement de services, opérations sur titres et services y afférents (nouvelles émissions, transactions, gestion de portefeuille, garde de titres), et opérations de change effectuées par les banques pour leur propre compte ou pour celui de leurs clients. Figurent aussi à ce poste, les produits et les charges résultant d'opérations exceptionnelles et non des activités courantes des banques. Les gains et pertes de change réalisées et les plus-values et moins-values réalisées sur les opérations sur titres y figurent également.

5. *Résultat brut* (poste 3 plus poste 4)

6. *Frais d'exploitation*

    a. Dépenses en personnel

    b. Dépenses afférentes à l'immobilier

    c. Autres

Ce poste comprend toutes les dépenses afférentes aux activités courantes des banques (à l'exclusion de celles reprises aux postes 2 et 4), en particulier les salaires et autres avantages perçus par les salariés, y compris les dotations au fonds de pension (dépenses en personnel) et les charges afférentes aux terrains et immeubles et aux matériels, mobilier et installations ainsi que les amortissements. Sont aussi comptabilisés à ce poste les impôts autres que l'impôt sur le revenu ou les sociétés.

7. *Résultat net* (poste 5 moins poste 6)

8. *Provisions (nettes)*

    a. Provisions sur prêts

    b. Provisions sur titres

    c. Autres

Ce poste comprend, en partie ou en totalité, les charges pour ajustement de la valeur comptable des prêts, crédits et titres de placement, les plus-values comptables découlant de cet ajustement, les pertes sur prêts, les dotations aux provisions pour pertes éventuelles sur ces éléments d'actif et les reprises de provisions. En revanche, les gains ou pertes de change réalisés et les plus-values ou moins-values réalisées sur les opérations sur titres de placement figurent normalement au poste *Produits non financiers (nets)* (poste 4).

9. *Bénéfices avant impôt* (poste 7 moins poste 8)

10. *Impôt sur le revenu*

11. *Bénéfices après impôt* (poste 9 moins poste 10)

12. *Bénéfices distribués*

13. *Bénéfices mis en réserve* (poste 11 moins poste 12)

Bilan

Actif

    14. *Caisse et soldes auprès de la Banque centrale*

    15. *Dépôts interbancaires*

    16. *Prêts*

    17. *Valeurs mobilières*

    18. *Autres actifs*

Passif

    19. *Capital et réserves*

    20. *Emprunts auprès de la Banque centrale*

    21. *Dépôts interbancaires*

    22. *Dépôts non bancaires*

    23. *Obligations*

    24. *Autres engagements*

Total du bilan

    25. Total en fin d'exercice (somme des postes 14 à 18 ou 19 à 24)

    26. Total moyen

    Les méthodes de calcul varient selon les pays. La moyenne sur deux fins d'exercices constitue la majorité. Les autres sont basées sur des moyennes de 13 mois.

Pour mémoire

    27. *Titres à court terme* (comptabilisés au poste 17)

    Ce poste comprend, selon la définition du Système européen de comptes économiques intégrés (paragraphe 539), les titres dont l'échéance initiale est normalement fixée jusqu'à 12 mois, mais avec une échéance maximum de deux ans.

    28. *Obligations* (comptabilisées au poste 17)

    Ce poste comprend, selon la définition du Système européen de comptes économiques intégrés (paragraphe 542), les titres à revenu fixe ou variable avec une échéance initiale de plusieurs années.

29.*Actions et participations* (comptabilisées au poste 17)

30.*Créances sur des non résidents* (comptabilisées aux postes 15 à 18)

31.*Engagements envers des non résidents* (comptabilisés aux postes 21 à 24)

Solvabilité

32. *Fonds propres de base:* capital social libéré/actions ordinaires, réserves publiées.

33.*Fonds propres complémentaires:* réserves non publiées, réserves de réévaluation des actifs, provisions générales/réserves générales pour créances douteuses, instruments dette/capital, dette subordonnée à terme.

34. *Eléments à déduire des fonds propres*

35. *Total net des ressources en capital* (poste 32 plus poste 33 moins poste 34)

36. *Actifs pondérés des risques*

Renseignements complémentaires

35.*Nombre d'institutions* (prises en compte)

36.*Nombre de succursales* (prises en compte)

37.*Nombre de salariés* (en milliers) (des institutions prises en compte)

2. Modèle de présentation pour les tableaux généraux

Structure du système financier

Année

	Nombre d'institutions	Nombre de succursales	Nombres de salariés	Total des actifs ou des passifs	Total des actifs financiers	
				en monnaie nationale	en monnaie nationale	%
Banque centrale						
Autres institutions monétaires						
Banques commerciales						
Banques étrangères						
Caisses d'épargne						
Banques mutualistes						
Autres institutions financières						
Institutions de crédit hypothécaire						
Institutions de crédit de développement						
Sociétés financières						
Autres						
Institutions d'assurance						
Sociétés d'assurance						
Fonds de pension et fondations						
Autres						
Ensemble des institutions financières						

Résident/non résident et monnaie nationale/étrangère classification de l'actif et du passif des banques
Année

Monnaie nationale

	Résidents	Non résidents	Total
Actif			
Monnaie nationale			
Monnaies étrangères			
Total			
Passif			
Monnaie nationale			
Monnaies étrangères			
Total			

3. Informations méthodologiques

Pour faciliter l'interprétation et l'analyse des données reprises dans la présente publication et pour inciter l'utilisateur à être prudent dans l'utilisation des statistiques à des fins de comparaisons internationales, les notes méthodologiques[1] par pays apportent des précisions sur les points suivants :

- Les institutions sur lesquelles portent les statistiques et leur importance par rapport à l'ensemble du système financier;

- Le champ géographique et le degré de consolidation indiquant si les filiales financières ou non financières nationales ou étrangères des banques déclarantes sont couvertes par les données et si les succursales et/ou les filiales des banques étrangères sont incluses ;

- La structure du système bancaire, y compris des informations sur la réglementation;

- Une description succincte des activités des banques : facilités de paiement, opérations de dépôts, de prêts, instruments d'épargne, marché monétaire, opérations sur titre, change, activités non-bancaires;

- Des explications sur les postes et des tableaux de concordance des comptes de résultats et des bilans comprenant des renseignements précis sur la façon dont les bilans reproduits dans cette publication ont été construits à partir des données plus détaillées fournies par les pays;

- Les sources des données

---

1. *Rentabilité des banques -- Notes méthodologiques par pays*, OCDE.

Part I

STATISTICS ON FINANCIAL STATEMENTS OF BANKS

STATISTIQUES SUR LES COMPTES DES BANQUES

AUSTRALIA
All banks

Million Australian dollars

	1992	1993	1994	1995	1996	1997	1998	1999	2000	2001
INCOME STATEMENT										
1. Interest income	33653	29136	28844	34634	39089	39477	38960	39340	37836	37560
2. Interest expenses	23306	18300	16909	22031	25547	25930	25799	25280	26146	26365
3. Net interest income	10347	10836	11935	12603	13542	13546	13161	14060	11690	11196
4. Non-interest income (net)	8111	7762	8409	7024	8626	10101	11358	11579	12449	11748
a. Fees and commissions receivable	..	..	..	..	..	..	..	..	..	..
b. Fees and commissions payable	..	..	..	..	..	..	..	..	..	..
c. Net profits or loss on financial operations	..	..	..	..	..	..	..	..	..	..
d. Other	..	..	..	..	..	..	..	..	..	..
5. Gross income	18458	18598	20344	19627	22168	23647	24519	25639	24139	22944
6. Operating expenses	13635	12409	12854	12684	13708	15268	14971	15929	12546	11981
a. Staff costs	..	..	..	..	..	..	..	..	..	..
b. Property costs	..	..	..	..	..	..	..	..	..	..
c. Other	..	..	..	..	..	..	..	..	..	..
7. Net income	4823	6189	7490	6943	8460	8379	9548	9710	11593	10963
8. Provisions (net)	4900	2560	1437	836	571	693	1097	1046	702	1157
a. Provisions on loans	..	..	..	..	..	..	..	..	..	..
b. Provisions on securities	..	..	..	..	..	..	..	..	..	..
c. Other	..	..	..	..	..	..	..	..	..	..
9. Profit before tax	-77	3629	6053	6106	7889	7686	8451	8664	10891	9806
10. Income tax	336	1440	1703	1611	2040	1983	2143	2295	2082	1899
11. Profit after tax	-413	2189	4350	4495	5849	5703	6308	6369	8809	7907
12. Distributed profit	1627	2101	2790	3713	4509	5143	5185	6481	5262	5645
13. Retained profit	-2040	88	1560	782	1340	560	1123	-112	3547	2262
BALANCE SHEET										
Assets (2)										
14. Cash & balance with Central bank	4215	4363	4768	6467	9036	8185	8847	5090	3684	4965
15. Interbank deposits	34770	28707	24597	23675	31039	30775	21346	20111	27045	25474
16. Loans (1)	256501	271828	284599	298961	336345	380423	422881	460782	496901	420709
17. Securities (1)	40438	37524	38298	42567	40880	39972	39191	42497	41269	25289
18. Other assets (1)	118047	118955	113827	138356	160769	185206	212788	198936	271711	255067
Liabilities (2)										
19. Capital & reserves	45221	46779	48803	50583	61310	64483	70707	71779	103764	83913
20. Borrowing from Central bank	..	..	..	..	..	..	..	..	..	..
21. Interbank deposits	42222	35436	33052	32462	33935	32337	30124	34432	49924	54142
22. Non-bank deposits (1)	245237	260154	269323	285323	326443	366137	402455	421612	446188	383626
23. Bonds	..	..	..	..	..	..	..	..	..	..
24. Other liabilities	121294	119008	114911	141658	156382	181601	201796	199593	240857	209827
Balance sheet total										
25. End-year total (2)	453971	461377	466089	510026	578069	644559	705053	727416	840610	731504
26. Average total	443790	457674	463733	488058	544048	611314	674820	716248	784012	786057

AUSTRALIE
Ensemble des banques

Millions de dollars australiens

COMPTE DE RESULTATS
1. Produits financiers
2. Frais financiers
3. Produits financiers nets
4. Produits non financiers (nets)
   a. Frais et commissions à recevoir
   b. Frais et commissions à payer
   c. Profits ou pertes nets sur opérations financières
   d. Autres
5. Résultat brut
6. Frais d'exploitation
   a. Dépenses en personnel
   b. Dépenses en immobilier
   c. Autres
7. Résultat net
8. Provisions (nettes)
   a. Provisions sur prêts
   b. Provisions sur titres
   c. Autres
9. Bénéfices avant impôt
10. Impôt sur le revenu
11. Bénéfices après impôt
12. Bénéfices distribués
13. Bénéfices mis en réserve

BILAN

Actif (2)
14. Caisse & solde auprès de la Banque centrale
15. Dépôts interbancaires
16. Prêts (1)
17. Valeurs mobilières (1)
18. Autres actifs (1)

Passif (2)
19. Capital et réserves
20. Emprunts auprès de la Banque centrale
21. Dépôts interbancaires
22. Dépôts non bancaires (1)
23. Obligations
24. Autres engagements

Total du bilan
25. En fin d'exercice (2)
26. Moyen

AUSTRALIA
All banks

	1992	1993	1994	1995	1996	1997	1998	1999	2000	2001
Million Australian dollars										
Memorandum items										
27. Short-term securities	10212	9412	11262	10006	7773	7147	8431	6064	3495	1791
28. Bonds	16024	15621	15674	19824	19033	16693	13824	14766	12998	12402
29. Shares and participations (1)	..	..	..	..	..	..	..	..	..	..
30. Claims on non-residents	..	..	..	..	..	..	..	..	..	..
31. Liabilities to non-residents	..	..	..	..	..	..	..	..	..	..
Capital adequacy (3)										
32. Tier 1 Capital	28929	29708	33882	38650	40131	43001	44150	48613	50823	58032
33. Tier 2 Capital	13955	15014	14080	13709	14291	15979	19854	20094	26331	29079
34. Supervisory deductions	955	457	508	757	1452	3097	2960	3874	9105	7386
35. Total net capital resources	41929	44265	47454	51602	52970	55883	61044	64833	68049	79725
36. Risk-weighted assets	412080	409427	398071	427006	475804	543827	619665	619275	688856	766092
SUPPLEMENTARY INFORMATION										
37. Number of institutions	35	33	34	34	33	29	28	26	25	27
38. Number of branches (4)	6920	7059	6738	6633	6477	6083	5546	5287	4938	4700
39. Number of employees (x 1000)	..	..	..	..	..	..	..	..	..	..

AUSTRALIE
Ensemble des banques

Millions de dollars australiens	
Pour mémoire	
27. Titres à court terme	
28. Obligations	
29. Actions et participations (1)	
30. Créances sur des non-résidents	
31. Engagements envers des non-résidents	
Solvabilité (3)	
32. Fonds propres de base	
33. Fonds propres complémentaires	
34. Eléments à déduire des fonds propres	
35. Total net des ressources en capital	
36. Actifs pondérés des risques	
RENSEIGNEMENTS COMPLÉMENTAIRES	
37. Nombre d'institutions	
38. Nombre de succursales (4)	
39. Nombre de salariés (x 1000)	

1 Change in methodology.

2 1998 and 2000 : Following data revisions, discrepancies have occurred in the data set.

3 Capital adequacy data (items 32 through 36) are consolidated worldwide and include banks' domestic and overseas non-bank subsidiaries.

4 There is a break in the serie between 1996 to 1997.

Change in methodology:

. Introduction of revised statistical collection in 1990 resulted in reclassification of shares and participations from Securities (item 17) to Loans and Other Assets (item 16 and item 18).

. Until 1990, Non-bank deposits (item 22) were included under Other liabilities (item 24). This item includes a small proportion of interbank deposits.

. As from 1990, Shares and participations (item 29) are not separately available following the introduction of revised statistical collection.

1 Changement méthodologique.

2 Pour les années 1998 et 2000: Suite à des révisions, les données présentent des écarts.

3 Les données sur la solvabilité (poste 32 à poste 36) sont regroupées sur une base mondiale y compris les filiales non-bancaires dans le pays et à l'étranger.

4 Il y a une rupture de série entre 1996 et 1997.

Changement méthodologique :

. La reclassification des actions et participations du poste 17 Titres au poste 16 Prêts et poste 18 Autres actifs est consécutive à l'introduction en 1990 d'une révision de la collecte statistique.

. Jusqu'en 1990, les Dépôts non bancaires (poste 22) étaient inclus sous Autres engagements (poste 24). Ce poste inclut une petite partie des dépôts interbancaires.

. A partir de 1990, les Actions et participations (poste 29) ne sont plus disponibles séparément suite à l'introduction d'une révision de la collecte statistique.

AUSTRALIA
All banks

AUSTRALIE
Ensemble des banques

Per cent — *Pourcentage*

INCOME STATEMENT ANALYSIS — ANALYSE DU COMPTE DE RESULTATS

		1992	1993	1994	1995	1996	1997	1998	1999	2000	2001		
% of average balance sheet total												**% du total moyen du bilan**	
40.	Interest income	7.58	6.37	6.22	7.10	7.18	6.46	5.77	5.49	4.83	4.78	Produits financiers	40.
41.	Interest expenses	5.25	4.00	3.65	4.51	4.70	4.24	3.82	3.53	3.33	3.35	Frais financiers	41.
42.	Net interest income	2.33	2.37	2.57	2.58	2.49	2.22	1.95	1.96	1.49	1.42	Produits financiers nets	42.
43.	Non-interest income (net)	1.83	1.70	1.81	1.44	1.59	1.65	1.68	1.62	1.59	1.49	Produits non financiers (nets)	43.
	a. Fees and commissions receivable	..	..	..	..	..	..	..	..	..	..	a. Frais et commissions à recevoir	
	b. Fees and commissions payable	..	..	..	..	..	..	..	..	..	..	b. Frais et commissions à payer	
	c. Net profits or loss on financial operations	..	..	..	..	..	..	..	..	..	..	c. Profits ou pertes nets sur operations financières	
	d. Other	..	..	..	..	..	..	..	..	..	..	d. Autres	
44.	Gross income	4.16	4.06	4.39	4.02	4.07	3.87	3.63	3.58	3.08	2.92	Résultat brut	44.
45.	Operating expenses	3.07	2.71	2.77	2.60	2.52	2.50	2.22	2.22	1.60	1.52	Frais d'exploitation	45.
	a. Staff costs	..	..	..	..	..	..	..	..	..	..	a. Dépenses en personnel	
	b. Property costs	..	..	..	..	..	..	..	..	..	..	b. Dépenses en immobilier	
	c. Other	..	..	..	..	..	..	..	..	..	..	c. Autres	
46.	Net income	1.09	1.35	1.62	1.42	1.56	1.37	1.41	1.36	1.48	1.39	Résultat net	46.
47.	Provisions (net)	1.10	0.56	0.31	0.17	0.10	0.11	0.16	0.15	0.09	0.15	Provisions (nettes)	47.
	a. Provisions on loans	..	..	..	..	..	..	..	..	..	..	a. Provisions sur prêts	
	b. Provisions on securities	..	..	..	..	..	..	..	..	..	..	b. Provisions sur titres	
	c. Other	..	..	..	..	..	..	..	..	..	..	c. Autres	
48.	Profit before tax	-0.02	0.79	1.31	1.25	1.45	1.26	1.25	1.21	1.39	1.25	Bénéfices avant impôt	48.
49.	Income tax	0.08	0.31	0.37	0.33	0.37	0.32	0.32	0.32	0.27	0.24	Impôt sur le revenu	49.
50.	Profit after tax	-0.09	0.48	0.94	0.92	1.08	0.93	0.93	0.89	1.12	1.01	Bénéfices après impôt	50.
51.	Distributed profit	0.37	0.46	0.60	0.76	0.83	0.84	0.77	0.90	0.67	0.72	Bénéfices distribués	51.
52.	Retained profit	-0.46	0.02	0.34	0.16	0.25	0.09	0.17	-0.02	0.45	0.29	Bénéfices mis en réserve	52.
% of gross income												**% du total du résultat brut**	
53.	Net interest income	56.06	58.26	58.67	64.21	61.09	57.28	53.68	54.84	48.43	48.80	Produits financiers nets	53.
54.	Non-interest income (net)	43.94	41.74	41.33	35.79	38.91	42.72	46.32	45.16	51.57	51.20	Produits non financiers (nets)	54.
	a. Fees and commissions receivable											a. Frais et commissions à recevoir	
	b. Fees and commissions payable											b. Frais et commissions à payer	
	c. Net profits or loss on financial operations											c. Profits ou pertes nets sur operations financières	
	d. Other											d. Autres	
55.	Operating expenses	73.87	66.72	63.18	64.63	61.84	64.57	61.06	62.13	51.97	52.22	Frais d'exploitation	55.
	a. Staff costs											a. Dépenses en personnel	
	b. Property costs											b. Dépenses en immobilier	
	c. Other											c. Autres	
56.	Net income	26.13	33.28	36.82	35.37	38.16	35.43	38.94	37.87	48.03	47.78	Résultat net	56.
57.	Provisions (net)	26.55	13.76	7.06	4.26	2.58	2.93	4.47	4.08	2.91	5.04	Provisions (nettes)	57.
	a. Provisions on loans											a. Provisions sur prêts	
	b. Provisions on securities											b. Provisions sur titres	
	c. Other											c. Autres	
58.	Profit before tax	-0.42	19.51	29.75	31.11	35.59	32.50	34.47	33.79	45.12	42.74	Bénéfices avant impôt	58.
59.	Income tax	1.82	7.74	8.37	8.21	9.20	8.39	8.74	8.95	8.63	8.28	Impôt sur le revenu	59.
60.	Profit after tax	-2.24	11.77	21.38	22.90	26.38	24.12	25.73	24.84	36.49	34.46	Bénéfices après impôt	60.
% of net income												**% du total du résultat net**	
61.	Provisions (net)	101.60	41.36	19.19	12.04	6.75	8.27	11.49	10.77	6.06	10.55	Provisions (nettes)	61.
	a. Provisions on loans											a. Provisions sur prêts	
	b. Provisions on securities											b. Provisions sur titres	
	c. Other											c. Autres	
62.	Profit before tax	-1.60	58.64	80.81	87.94	93.25	91.73	88.51	89.23	93.94	89.45	Bénéfices avant impôt	62.
63.	Income tax	6.97	23.27	22.74	23.20	24.11	23.67	22.44	23.64	17.96	17.32	Impôt sur le revenu	63.
64.	Profit after tax	-8.56	35.37	58.08	64.74	69.14	68.06	66.07	65.59	75.99	72.12	Bénéfices après impôt	64.

AUSTRALIA
All banks

AUSTRALIE
Ensemble des banques

Per cent — *Pourcentage*

BALANCE SHEET ANALYSIS — **ANALYSE DU BILAN**

% of year-end balance sheet total — *% du total du bilan en fin d'exercice*

Assets — *Actif*

	1992	1993	1994	1995	1996	1997	1998	1999	2000	2001	
65. Cash & balance with Central bank	0.93	0.95	1.02	1.27	1.56	1.27	1.25	0.70	0.44	0.68	65. Caisse & solde auprès de la Banque centrale
66. Interbank deposits	7.66	6.22	5.28	4.64	5.37	4.77	3.03	2.76	3.22	3.48	66. Dépôts interbancaires
67. Loans	56.50	58.92	61.06	58.62	58.18	59.02	59.98	63.35	59.11	57.51	67. Prêts
68. Securities	8.91	8.13	8.22	8.35	7.07	6.20	5.56	5.84	4.91	3.46	68. Valeurs mobilières
69. Other assets	26.00	25.78	24.42	27.13	27.81	28.73	30.18	27.35	32.32	34.87	69. Autres actifs
Liabilities											***Passif***
70. Capital & reserves	9.96	10.14	10.47	9.92	10.61	10.00	10.03	9.87	12.34	11.47	70. Capital et réserves
71. Borrowing from Central bank	..	..	..	..	..	..	..	..	..	..	71. Emprunts auprès de la Banque centrale
72. Interbank deposits	9.30	7.68	7.09	6.36	5.87	5.02	4.27	4.73	5.94	7.40	72. Dépôts interbancaires
73. Non-bank deposits	54.02	56.39	57.78	55.94	56.47	56.80	57.08	57.96	53.08	52.44	73. Dépôts non bancaires
74. Bonds	..	..	..	..	..	..	..	..	..	..	74. Obligations
75. Other liabilities	26.72	25.79	24.65	27.77	27.05	28.17	28.62	27.44	28.65	28.68	75. Autres engagements
Memorandum items											***Pour mémoire***
76. Short-term securities	*2.25*	*2.04*	*2.42*	*1.96*	*1.34*	*1.11*	*1.20*	*0.83*	*0.42*	*0.24*	*76. Titres à court terme*
77. Bonds	*3.53*	*3.39*	*3.36*	*3.89*	*3.29*	*2.59*	*1.96*	*2.03*	*1.55*	*1.70*	*77. Obligations*
78. Shares and participations	*..*	*..*	*..*	*..*	*..*	*..*	*..*	*..*	*..*	*..*	*78. Actions et participations*
79. Claims on non-residents	*..*	*..*	*..*	*..*	*..*	*..*	*..*	*..*	*..*	*..*	*79. Créances sur des non-résidents*
80. Liabilities to non-residents	*..*	*..*	*..*	*..*	*..*	*..*	*..*	*..*	*..*	*..*	*80. Engagements envers des non-résidents*

* See notes on previous pages.　　　* Voir les notes en pages précédentes.

AUSTRIA

All banks

Million euros

AUTRICHE

Ensemble des banques

Millions d'euros

	1992	1993	1994	1995	1996	1997	1998	1999	2000	2001	
INCOME STATEMENT											**COMPTE DE RESULTATS**
1. Interest income	25852	24200	22956	24050	22022	22335	22708	22333	27413	26867	1. Produits financiers
2. Interest expenses	19908	17555	16126	17517	15388	15847	16375	16117	20759	19922	2. Frais financiers
3. Net interest income	5945	6645	6830	6534	6634	6488	6332	6216	6653	6945	3. Produits financiers nets
4. Non-interest income (net)	2980	2575	2755	4243	4619	4894	5691	5999	6697	6942	4. Produits non financiers (nets)
a. Fees and commissions receivable	*1879*	*2189*	*2382*	*2212*	*2463*	*2731*	*3041*	*3436*	*4088*	*4069*	*a. Frais et commissions à recevoir*
b. Fees and commissions payable	*429*	*463*	*502*	*450*	*503*	*589*	*647*	*782*	*996*	*1010*	*b. Frais et commissions à payer*
c. Net profits or loss on financial operations	*:*	*:*	*:*	*573*	*615*	*616*	*642*	*453*	*504*	*516*	*c. Profits ou pertes nets sur opérations financières*
d. Other	*:*	*:*	*:*	*1908*	*2045*	*2137*	*2655*	*2892*	*3102*	*3367*	*d. Autres*
5. Gross income	8925	9219	9584	10777	11253	11382	12023	12215	13350	13887	5. Résultat brut
6. Operating expenses	5710	5853	6239	7484	7781	7897	8164	8426	8928	9383	6. Frais d'exploitation
a. Staff costs	*3402*	*3441*	*3682*	*3941*	*4086*	*4157*	*4239*	*4356*	*4451*	*4646*	*a. Dépenses en personnel*
b. Property costs	*:*	*:*	*:*	*2182*	*2326*	*2421*	*2587*	*2687*	*2899*	*3132*	*b. Dépenses en immobilier*
c. Other	*:*	*:*	*:*	*1362*	*1369*	*1319*	*1338*	*1384*	*1578*	*1604*	*c. Autres*
7. Net income	3214	3366	3345	3292	3472	3485	3859	3789	4422	4504	7. Résultat net
8. Provisions (net)	2115	1837	1838	1685	1759	1655	1709	1552	1602	1389	8. Provisions (nettes)
a. Provisions on loans	*1298*	*1406*	*1320*	*1929*	*1864*	*1834*	*2241*	*1809*	*2045*	*2313*	*a. Provisions sur prêts*
b. Provisions on securities	*272*	*80*	*345*	*-244*	*-105*	*-179*	*-532*	*-257*	*-443*	*-923*	*b. Provisions sur titres*
c. Other	*:*	*:*	*:*	*:*	*:*	*:*	*:*	*:*	*:*	*:*	*c. Autres*
9. Profit before tax (1)	1099	1529	1508	1479	1712	1830	2150	2237	2820	3115	9. Bénéfices avant impôt (1)
10. Income tax	189	198	177	308	363	338	244	279	404	320	10. Impôt sur le revenu
11. Profit after tax	910	1330	1331	1171	1349	1492	1906	1959	2416	2796	11. Bénéfices après impôt
12. Distributed profit	:	:	:	:	:	:	:	:	:	:	12. Bénéfices distribués
13. Retained profit	:	:	:	:	:	:	:	:	:	:	13. Bénéfices mis en réserve
BALANCE SHEET											**BILAN**
Assets											**Actif**
14. Cash & balance with Central bank	6092	6294	6775	5625	6529	6329	6399	6022	6427	10515	14. Caisse & solde auprès de la Banque centrale
15. Interbank deposits	94739	104432	106983	118338	120092	122064	144361	152252	159981	173732	15. Dépôts interbancaires
16. Loans	172905	179292	186209	198885	209520	222502	236846	254572	274432	281720	16. Prêts
17. Securities	34642	39230	46435	55794	62963	69909	76396	93682	103305	97719	17. Valeurs mobilières
18. Other assets	21590	21521	22683	12242	12544	13567	14797	16787	18079	19748	18. Autres actifs
Liabilities											**Passif**
19. Capital & reserves	16029	17561	19162	18155	17826	19566	22680	24134	24894	27604	19. Capital et réserves
20. Borrowing from Central bank	40	43	100	13	22	59	321	5342	7235	2174	20. Emprunts auprès de la Banque centrale
21. Interbank deposits	98779	103070	107002	114693	123382	130709	156517	173624	179784	188560	21. Dépôts interbancaires
22. Non-bank deposits	147485	155855	165116	171801	177751	182511	191953	198216	207341	218861	22. Dépôts non bancaires
23. Bonds	53577	59230	61622	68008	70962	77503	82311	94030	111850	111547	23. Obligations
24. Other liabilities	14057	15009	16082	18214	21706	24024	25016	27968	31120	34688	24. Autres engagements
Balance sheet total											**Total du bilan**
25. End-year total	329968	350768	369085	390883	411649	434372	478799	523315	562224	583434	25. En fin d'exercice
26. Average total	320819	315081	359507	379389	400087	427691	465438	507527	553796	562476	26. Moyen

AUSTRIA
All banks

AUTRICHE
Ensemble des banques

Million euros

Millions d'euros

	1992	1993	1994	1995	1996	1997	1998	1999	2000	2001	
Memorandum items											***Pour mémoire***
27. Short-term securities	397	401	415	398	404	294	788	534	324	396	27. Titres à court terme
28. Bonds	26285	29715	35890	39750	44043	49004	50760	60350	67885	59167	28. Obligations
29. Shares and participations	9290	9727	10164	14927	16414	20612	24848	32798	35096	38156	29. Actions et participations
30. Claims on non-residents	66560	73574	75541	82113	91007	104924	111352	132693	159831	156424	30. Créances sur des non-résidents
31. Liabilities to non-residents	75943	78780	80697	86489	100260	118981	126210	148361	176782	172011	31. Engagements envers des non-résidents
Capital adequacy											***Solvabilité***
32. Tier 1 Capital	..	..	16097	17166	18488	20073	22805	23790	24652	27440	32. Fonds propres de base
33. Tier 2 Capital	..	..	6299	6659	7599	9634	9862	10769	12659	13492	33. Fonds propres complémentaires
34. Supervisory deductions	..	..	872	916	888	907	1252	1621	1453	1368	34. Eléments à déduire des fonds propres
35. Total net capital resources	..	..	21524	22909	25199	28799	31415	32938	35858	39564	35. Total net des ressources en capital
36. Risk-weighted assets	..	..	165178	173374	182972	197643	209509	225893	240612	260735	36. Actifs pondérés des risques
SUPPLEMENTARY INFORMATION											**RENSEIGNEMENTS COMPLÉMENTAIRES**
37. Number of institutions	1104	1063	1053	1041	1019	995	971	951	923	907	37. Nombre d'institutions
38. Number of branches	4667	4691	4683	4686	4694	4691	4576	4576	4556	4546	38. Nombre de succursales
39. Number of employees (x 1000)	70.0	69.0	71.0	71.0	71.0	71.0	69.0	70.0	69.0	70.0	39. Nombre de salariés (x 1000)

1 For 1995, Profit before tax (item 9) includes "extraordinary profit or loss (net)" in the amount of -128.2 million euros.

Notes

Average balance sheet totals (item 26) are based on twelve end-month data

1 Pour l'année 1995, les Bénéfices avant impôt (poste 9) comprennent des pertes ou profits extraordinaires (net) d'un montant de -128.2 millions d' euros.

Notes

La moyenne du total des actifs/passifs (poste 26) est basée sur douze données de fin de mois.

AUSTRIA
All banks

AUTRICHE
Ensemble des banques

Per cent — *Pourcentage*

INCOME STATEMENT ANALYSIS — **ANALYSE DU COMPTE DE RESULTATS**

	1992	1993	1994	1995	1996	1997	1998	1999	2000	2001	
% of average balance sheet total											**% du total moyen du bilan**
40. Interest income	8.06	7.68	6.39	6.34	5.50	5.22	4.88	4.40	4.95	4.78	40. Produits financiers
41. Interest expenses	6.21	5.57	4.49	4.62	3.85	3.71	3.52	3.18	3.75	3.54	41. Frais financiers
42. Net interest income	1.85	2.11	1.90	1.72	1.66	1.52	1.36	1.22	1.20	1.23	42. Produits financiers nets
43. Non-interest income (net)	0.93	0.82	0.77	1.12	1.15	1.14	1.22	1.18	1.21	1.23	43. Produits non financiers (nets)
a. Fees and commissions receivable	0.59	0.69	0.66	0.58	0.62	0.64	0.65	0.68	0.74	0.72	a. Frais et commissions à recevoir
b. Fees and commissions payable	0.13	0.15	0.14	0.12	0.13	0.14	0.14	0.15	0.18	0.18	b. Frais et commissions à payer
c. Net profits or loss on financial operations	..	..	..	0.15	0.15	0.14	0.14	0.09	0.09	0.09	c. Profits ou pertes nets sur opérations financières
d. Other	..	..	..	0.50	0.51	0.50	0.57	0.57	0.56	0.60	d. Autres
44. Gross income	2.78	2.93	2.67	2.84	2.81	2.66	2.58	2.41	2.41	2.47	44. Résultat brut
45. Operating expenses	1.78	1.86	1.74	1.97	1.94	1.85	1.75	1.66	1.61	1.67	45. Frais d'exploitation
a. Staff costs	1.06	1.09	1.02	1.04	1.02	0.97	0.91	0.86	0.80	0.83	a. Dépenses en personnel
b. Property costs	..	..	..	0.58	0.58	0.57	0.56	0.53	0.52	0.56	b. Dépenses en immobilier
c. Other	..	..	..	0.36	0.34	0.31	0.29	0.27	0.28	0.29	c. Autres
46. Net income	1.00	1.07	0.93	0.87	0.87	0.81	0.83	0.75	0.80	0.80	46. Résultat net
47. Provisions (net)	0.66	0.58	0.51	0.44	0.44	0.39	0.37	0.31	0.29	0.25	47. Provisions (nettes)
a. Provisions on loans	0.40	0.45	0.37	0.51	0.47	0.43	0.48	0.36	0.37	0.41	a. Provisions sur prêts
b. Provisions on securities	0.08	0.03	0.10	-0.06	-0.03	-0.04	-0.11	-0.05	-0.08	-0.16	b. Provisions sur titres
c. Other	..	..	..	..	..	..	..	..	..	..	c. Autres
48. Profit before tax	0.34	0.49	0.42	0.39	0.43	0.43	0.46	0.44	0.51	0.55	48. Bénéfices avant impôt
49. Income tax	0.06	0.06	0.05	0.08	0.09	0.08	0.05	0.05	0.07	0.06	49. Impôt sur le revenu
50. Profit after tax	0.28	0.42	0.37	0.31	0.34	0.35	0.41	0.39	0.44	0.50	50. Bénéfices après impôt
51. Distributed profit	..	..	..	..	..	..	..	..	..	..	51. Bénéfices distribués
52. Retained profit	..	..	..	..	..	..	..	..	..	..	52. Bénéfices mis en réserve
% of gross income											**% du total du résultat brut**
53. Net interest income	66.61	72.07	71.26	60.63	58.95	57.00	52.67	50.89	49.84	50.01	53. Produits financiers nets
54. Non-interest income (net)	33.39	27.93	28.74	39.37	41.05	43.00	47.33	49.11	50.16	49.99	54. Produits non financiers (nets)
a. Fees and commissions receivable	21.06	23.74	24.85	20.53	21.89	23.99	25.29	28.13	30.62	29.30	a. Frais et commissions à recevoir
b. Fees and commissions payable	4.81	5.03	5.24	4.18	4.47	5.18	5.38	6.41	7.46	7.27	b. Frais et commissions à payer
c. Net profits or loss on financial operations	..	..	..	5.32	5.46	5.41	5.34	3.71	3.77	3.72	c. Profits ou pertes nets sur opérations financières
d. Other	..	..	..	17.70	18.17	18.78	22.08	23.68	23.23	24.25	d. Autres
55. Operating expenses	63.98	63.49	65.10	69.45	69.15	69.38	67.90	68.98	66.88	67.56	55. Frais d'exploitation
a. Staff costs	38.12	37.32	38.42	36.57	36.31	36.53	35.26	35.66	33.34	33.46	a. Dépenses en personnel
b. Property costs	..	..	..	20.24	20.67	21.27	21.52	22.00	21.72	22.55	b. Dépenses en immobilier
c. Other	..	..	..	12.64	12.17	11.59	11.13	11.33	11.82	11.55	c. Autres
56. Net income	36.02	36.51	34.90	30.55	30.85	30.62	32.10	31.02	33.12	32.44	56. Résultat net
57. Provisions (net)	23.70	19.93	19.17	15.64	15.64	14.54	14.22	12.70	12.00	10.00	57. Provisions (nettes)
a. Provisions on loans	14.54	15.25	13.77	17.90	16.57	16.11	18.64	14.81	15.32	16.65	a. Provisions sur prêts
b. Provisions on securities	3.05	0.87	3.59	-2.26	-0.93	-1.57	-4.42	-2.11	-3.32	-6.65	b. Provisions sur titres
c. Other	..	..	..	..	..	..	..	..	..	..	c. Autres
58. Profit before tax	12.31	16.58	15.73	13.72	15.22	16.08	17.88	18.32	21.12	22.43	58. Bénéfices avant impôt
59. Income tax	2.12	2.15	1.85	2.86	3.23	2.97	2.03	2.28	3.02	2.30	59. Impôt sur le revenu
60. Profit after tax	10.20	14.43	13.89	10.86	11.99	13.11	15.85	16.04	18.10	20.13	60. Bénéfices après impôt
% of net income											**% du total du résultat net**
61. Provisions (net)	65.81	54.59	54.93	51.19	50.68	47.49	44.29	40.95	36.23	30.84	61. Provisions (nettes)
a. Provisions on loans	40.37	41.76	39.46	58.59	53.70	52.62	58.07	47.74	46.26	51.34	a. Provisions sur prêts
b. Provisions on securities	8.48	2.39	10.30	-7.41	-3.02	-5.13	-13.78	-6.79	-10.03	-20.50	b. Provisions sur titres
c. Other	..	..	..	..	..	..	..	..	..	..	c. Autres
62. Profit before tax	34.19	45.41	45.07	44.92	49.32	52.51	55.71	59.05	63.77	69.16	62. Bénéfices avant impôt
63. Income tax	5.88	5.88	5.29	9.37	10.46	9.71	6.33	7.35	9.13	7.10	63. Impôt sur le revenu
64. Profit after tax	28.31	39.53	39.78	35.56	38.86	42.80	49.38	51.70	54.64	62.06	64. Bénéfices après impôt

Per cent / *Pourcentage*

BALANCE SHEET ANALYSIS / **ANALYSE DU BILAN**

% of year-end balance sheet total / **% du total du bilan en fin d'exercice**

	1992	1993	1994	1995	1996	1997	1998	1999	2000	2001	
Assets											**Actif**
65. Cash & balance with Central bank	1.85	1.79	1.84	1.44	1.59	1.46	1.34	1.15	1.14	1.80	65. Caisse & solde auprès de la Banque centrale
66. Interbank deposits	28.71	29.77	28.99	30.27	29.17	28.10	30.15	29.09	28.45	29.78	66. Dépôts interbancaires
67. Loans	52.40	51.11	50.45	50.88	50.90	51.22	49.47	48.65	48.81	48.29	67. Prêts
68. Securities	10.50	11.18	12.58	14.27	15.30	16.09	15.96	17.90	18.37	16.75	68. Valeurs mobilières
69. Other assets	6.54	6.14	6.15	3.13	3.05	3.12	3.09	3.21	3.22	3.38	69. Autres actifs
Liabilities											**Passif**
70. Capital & reserves	4.86	5.01	5.19	4.64	4.33	4.50	4.74	4.61	4.43	4.73	70. Capital et réserves
71. Borrowing from Central bank	0.01	0.01	0.03	-	0.01	0.01	0.07	1.02	1.29	0.37	71. Emprunts auprès de la Banque centrale
72. Interbank deposits	29.94	29.38	28.99	29.34	29.97	30.09	32.69	33.18	31.98	32.32	72. Dépôts interbancaires
73. Non-bank deposits	44.70	44.43	44.74	43.95	43.18	42.02	40.09	37.88	36.88	37.51	73. Dépôts non bancaires
74. Bonds	16.24	16.89	16.70	17.40	17.24	17.84	17.19	17.97	19.89	19.12	74. Obligations
75. Other liabilities	4.26	4.28	4.36	4.66	5.27	5.53	5.22	5.34	5.54	5.95	75. Autres engagements
Memorandum items											***Pour mémoire***
76. Short-term securities	*0.12*	*0.11*	*0.11*	*0.10*	*0.10*	*0.07*	*0.16*	*0.10*	*0.06*	*0.07*	*76. Titres à court terme*
77. Bonds	*7.97*	*8.47*	*9.72*	*10.17*	*10.70*	*11.28*	*10.60*	*11.53*	*12.07*	*10.14*	*77. Obligations*
78. Shares and participations	*2.82*	*2.77*	*2.75*	*3.82*	*3.99*	*4.75*	*5.19*	*6.27*	*6.24*	*6.54*	*78. Actions et participations*
79. Claims on non-residents	*20.17*	*20.98*	*20.47*	*21.01*	*22.11*	*24.16*	*23.26*	*25.36*	*28.43*	*26.81*	*79. Créances sur des non-résidents*
80. Liabilities to non-residents	*23.02*	*22.46*	*21.86*	*22.13*	*24.36*	*27.39*	*26.36*	*28.35*	*31.44*	*29.48*	*80. Engagements envers des non-résidents*

* See notes on previous pages.

* Voir les notes en pages précédentes.

Million euros / *Millions d'euros*

INCOME STATEMENT (1) / COMPTE DE RESULTATS (1)

	1992	1993	1994	1995	1996	1997	1998	1999	2000	2001	
1. Interest income	49715	57388	52871	56603	54483	60352	59794	55764	73243	64238	1. Produits financiers
2. Interest expenses	42282	49938	45494	49012	46355	52381	51409	47268	65046	56015	2. Frais financiers
3. Net interest income	7432	7449	7377	7591	8128	7971	8385	8496	8197	8223	3. Produits financiers nets
4. Non-interest income (net)	2048	2977	2620	3131	3594	4699	5281	5250	8350	7822	4. Produits non financiers (nets)
a. Fees and commissions receivable	..	1405	1599	1469	1776	2131	2748	3162	4587	4117	a. Frais et commissions à recevoir
b. Fees and commissions payable	..	736	875	899	959	1014	1125	1387	2022	1744	b. Frais et commissions à payer
c. Net profits or loss on financial operations	..	1584	1291	1902	2317	2423	3391	2665	3335	3765	c. Profits ou pertes nets sur opérations financières
d. Other	..	724	605	660	459	1159	268	810	2450	1684	d. Autres
5. Gross income	9480	10426	9997	10722	11721	12670	13667	13746	16547	16045	5. Résultat brut
6. Operating expenses	6473	7075	7170	7249	7701	8100	8679	9149	9900	10105	6. Frais d'exploitation
a. Staff costs (2)	3270	4316	4362	4412	4629	4638	4811	4966	5207	5255	a. Dépenses en personnel (2)
b. Property costs	..	541	551	553	583	627	697	664	645	690	b. Dépenses en immobilier
c. Other	..	2218	2256	2283	2490	2835	3172	3519	4048	4160	c. Autres
7. Net income	3007	3352	2828	3474	4020	4570	4988	4597	6647	5940	7. Résultat net
8. Provisions (net)	1864	1329	838	1453	1436	1725	1678	1118	1011	1208	8. Provisions (nettes)
a. Provisions on loans (3)	..	1165	757	939	1051	672	178	786	704	871	a. Provisions sur prêts (3)
b. Provisions on securities (3)	..	-33	32	-4	-1	24	97	-22	199	139	b. Provisions sur titres (3)
c. Other (3)	..	150	89	500	363	900	1496	318	48	84	c. Autres (3)
9. Profit before tax	1143	2023	1989	2021	2584	2845	3310	3479	5637	4732	9. Bénéfices avant impôt
10. Income tax	430	595	624	741	862	978	1130	658	1281	874	10. Impôt sur le revenu
11. Profit after tax	713	1428	1365	1281	1723	1867	2180	2821	4356	3858	11. Bénéfices après impôt
12. Distributed profit (3)	..	655	709	687	894	942	1144	1746	2382	2619	12. Bénéfices distribués (3)
13. Retained profit (3)	..	602	526	520	795	932	792	908	1504	1238	13. Bénéfices mis en réserve (3)

BALANCE SHEET / BILAN

Assets / **Actif**

	1992	1993	1994	1995	1996	1997	1998	1999	2000	2001	
14. Cash & balance with Central bank	1064	990	1063	1129	1159	1420	7864	5557	8823	8250	14. Caisse & solde auprès de la Banque centrale
15. Interbank deposits	158108	183032	183789	202104	220468	231342	213217	207066	171207	195265	15. Dépôts interbancaires
16. Loans	176743	187877	196890	201716	213873	230391	239944	257727	291365	291627	16. Prêts
17. Securities	148426	160471	169325	179509	200731	229200	224041	248766	245024	268205	17. Valeurs mobilières
18. Other assets	22487	30573	28369	31631	34627	41627	42471	51651	61644	82981	18. Autres actifs

Liabilities / **Passif**

	1992	1993	1994	1995	1996	1997	1998	1999	2000	2001	
19. Capital & reserves	20055	14317	15030	15680	16917	18815	22432	23755	27525	30899	19. Capital et réserves
20. Borrowing from Central bank (2)	117	36	75	4	88	174	30	20	516	118	20. Emprunts auprès de la Banque centrale (2)
21. Interbank deposits	197835	223730	225661	250944	276394	295475	280645	289683	261888	269049	21. Dépôts interbancaires
22. Non-bank deposits	183698	185643	192344	204647	227618	255868	271997	288433	301447	344401	22. Dépôts non bancaires
23. Bonds (4)	76021	101118	105170	100857	100447	95430	89565	97233	102889	95057	23. Obligations (4)
24. Other liabilities	29102	38097	41157	43957	49394	58218	62867	71641	83798	106806	24. Autres engagements

Balance sheet total / **Total du bilan**

	1992	1993	1994	1995	1996	1997	1998	1999	2000	2001	
25. End-year total	506828	562942	579436	616088	670857	723981	727537	770767	778063	846329	25. En fin d'exercice
26. Average total (2)	490929	553756	581327	614886	665461	743459	748568	777987	812855	825876	26. Moyen (2)

BELGIUM
All banks

Million euros

BELGIQUE
Ensemble des banques

Millions d'euros

	1992	1993	1994	1995	1996	1997	1998	1999	2000	2001	
Memorandum items											**Pour mémoire**
27. Short-term securities (2)	21640	28518	37310	28570	27601	24890	23333	36895	24798	23096	27. Titres à court terme (2)
28. Bonds (2)	79364	124560	124633	141797	163073	182134	183959	190246	195459	217103	28. Obligations (2)
29. Shares and participations (2)	3164	7393	7383	9141	10058	12176	16749	21625	24767	28006	29. Actions et participations (2)
30. Claims on non-residents (2)	170466	218080	217859	238646	260923	311312	303091	352870	383742	435457	30. Créances sur des non-résidents (2)
31. Liabilities to non-residents (2)	193528	236327	244105	268026	290567	337922	331853	346715	370388	413897	31. Engagements envers des non-résidents (2)
Capital adequacy (3)											**Solvabilité (3)**
32. Tier 1 Capital	..	14172	14965	16082	17387	19486	24524	25783	29145	30625	32. Fonds propres de base
33. Tier 2 Capital	..	6659	7369	7946	9271	10680	11687	16470	19152	20772	33. Fonds propres complémentaires
34. Supervisory deductions	..	2676	2873	4255	4939	6728	10341	14791	18187	20776	34. Eléments à déduire des fonds propres
35. Total net capital resources	..	18155	19462	19772	21720	23437	25870	27462	30109	29921	35. Total net des ressources en capital
36. Risk-weighted assets	..	139799	141323	148755	158472	173512	189317	210090	219408	215499	36. Actifs pondérés des risques
SUPPLEMENTARY INFORMATION											**RENSEIGNEMENTS COMPLEMENTAIRES**
37. Number of institutions	121	150	147	143	140	131	119	117	118	112	37. Nombre d'institutions
38. Number of branches	16405	19888	19159	18304	17963	17259	15391	14503	13696	12173	38. Nombre de succursales
39. Number of employees (x 1000)	76.0	76.0	76.0	77.0	77.0	77.0	76.0	76.0	76.0	76.0	39. Nombre de salariés (x 1000)

1 The Income Statement reporting period is the fiscal year ending 30 June of the following year.

2 Change in methodology

3 The subitems (a., b., and c.) of item 8, Provisions (net), Distributed and Retained profit (items 12 and 13), and data on Capital adequacy (items 32 to 36) cover only credit institutions governed by Belgian law.

4 Bonds (item 23) includes CD's.

Notes

All banks: All credit institutions.

Change in methodology

- Up to 1992, Staff costs (item 6.a) and Short-term securities, Bonds, Shares and participations, Claims on non-residents, Liabilities to non-residents (items 27 through 31) cover only Commercial banks and Savings banks.

- Up to 1992, Borrowing from Central bank (item 20) covers only the Savings banks; and for the Commercial banks, Borrowing from Central bank is included under interbank deposits (item 21).

Beginning 1993, average balance sheet totals (item 26) are the average of monthly data within the calendar year.

1 La période couverte pour le Compte de résultats est l'année fiscale se terminant le 30 juin de l'année suivante.

2 Changement méthodologique

3 Seuls les établissements de crédit de droit belge sont inclus dans les sous-catégories (a., b., et c.) des Provisions (nettes) (poste 8), dans les Bénéfices distribués et Bénéfices mis en réserve (postes 12 et 13), et dans les données relatives à la Solvabilité (postes 32 à 36).

4 Les obligations (poste 23) comprennent les certificats de dépôt.

Notes

Ensemble des banques : Ensemble des établissements de crédit.

Changement méthodologique

- Jusqu'en 1992, seules les Banques commerciales et les Caisses d'épargne sont incluses dans les Dépenses en personnel (poste 6.a.), les Titres à court terme, les Obligations, les Actions et participations, les Créances sur des non-résidents et les Engagements envers des non-résidents (postes 27 à 31).

- Jusqu'en 1992, seules les Caisses d'épargne sont incluses dans les Emprunts auprès de la Banque centrale (poste 20) ; les Emprunts auprès de la Banque Centrale sont repris, pour les banques commerciales, sous la rubrique Dépôts interbancaires (poste 21).

A partir de 1993, la moyenne du total des actifs/passifs (poste 26) est la moyenne des données mensuelles de l'année calendrier.

Per cent — *Pourcentage*

INCOME STATEMENT ANALYSIS — **ANALYSE DU COMPTE DE RESULTATS**

	1992	1993	1994	1995	1996	1997	1998	1999	2000	2001	
% of average balance sheet total											**% du total moyen du bilan**
40. Interest income	10.13	10.36	9.09	9.21	8.19	8.12	7.99	7.17	9.01	7.78	40. Produits financiers
41. Interest expenses	8.61	9.02	7.83	7.97	6.97	7.05	6.87	6.08	8.00	6.78	41. Frais financiers
42. Net interest income	1.51	1.35	1.27	1.23	1.22	1.07	1.12	1.09	1.01	1.00	42. Produits financiers nets
43. Non-interest income (net)	0.42	0.54	0.45	0.51	0.54	0.63	0.71	0.67	1.03	0.95	43. Produits non financiers (nets)
a. Fees and commissions receivable	..	0.25	0.28	0.24	0.27	0.29	0.37	0.41	0.56	0.50	a. Frais et commissions à recevoir
b. Fees and commissions payable	..	0.13	0.15	0.15	0.14	0.14	0.15	0.18	0.25	0.21	b. Frais et commissions à payer
c. Net profits or loss on financial operations	..	0.29	0.22	0.31	0.35	0.33	0.45	0.34	0.41	0.46	c. Profits ou pertes nets sur opérations financières
d. Other	..	0.13	0.10	0.11	0.07	0.16	0.04	0.10	0.30	0.20	d. Autres
44. Gross income	1.93	1.88	1.72	1.74	1.76	1.70	1.83	1.77	2.04	1.94	44. Résultat brut
45. Operating expenses	1.32	1.28	1.23	1.18	1.16	1.09	1.16	1.18	1.22	1.22	45. Frais d'exploitation
a. Staff costs	0.67	0.78	0.75	0.72	0.70	0.62	0.64	0.64	0.64	0.64	a. Dépenses en personnel
b. Property costs	..	0.10	0.09	0.09	0.09	0.08	0.09	0.09	0.08	0.08	b. Dépenses en immobilier
c. Other	..	0.40	0.39	0.37	0.37	0.38	0.42	0.45	0.50	0.50	c. Autres
46. Net income	0.61	0.61	0.49	0.56	0.60	0.61	0.67	0.59	0.82	0.72	46. Résultat net
47. Provisions (net)	0.38	0.24	0.14	0.24	0.22	0.23	0.22	0.14	0.12	0.15	47. Provisions (nettes)
a. Provisions on loans	..	0.21	0.13	0.15	0.16	0.09	0.02	0.10	0.09	0.11	a. Provisions sur prêts
b. Provisions on securities	..	-0.01	0.01	-	-	-	0.01	-	0.02	0.02	b. Provisions sur titres
c. Other	..	0.03	0.02	0.08	0.05	0.12	0.20	0.04	0.01	0.01	c. Autres
48. Profit before tax	0.23	0.37	0.34	0.33	0.39	0.38	0.44	0.45	0.69	0.57	48. Bénéfices avant impôt
49. Income tax	0.09	0.11	0.11	0.12	0.13	0.13	0.15	0.08	0.16	0.11	49. Impôt sur le revenu
50. Profit after tax	0.15	0.26	0.23	0.21	0.26	0.25	0.29	0.36	0.54	0.47	50. Bénéfices après impôt
51. Distributed profit	..	0.12	0.12	0.11	0.13	0.13	0.15	0.22	0.29	0.32	51. Bénéfices distribués
52. Retained profit	..	0.11	0.09	0.08	0.12	0.13	0.11	0.12	0.19	0.15	52. Bénéfices mis en réserve
% of gross income											**% du total du résultat brut**
53. Net interest income	78.40	71.45	73.79	70.80	69.35	62.91	61.35	61.81	49.54	51.25	53. Produits financiers nets
54. Non-interest income (net)	21.60	28.55	26.21	29.20	30.66	37.09	38.64	38.19	50.46	48.75	54. Produits non financiers (nets)
a. Fees and commissions receivable	..	13.48	15.99	13.70	15.15	16.82	20.11	23.00	27.72	25.66	a. Frais et commissions à recevoir
b. Fees and commissions payable	..	7.06	8.75	8.38	8.18	8.00	8.23	10.09	12.22	10.87	b. Frais et commissions à payer
c. Net profits or loss on financial operations	..	15.19	12.91	17.74	19.77	19.12	24.81	19.39	20.15	23.47	c. Profits ou pertes nets sur opérations financières
d. Other	..	6.94	6.05	6.16	3.92	9.15	1.96	5.89	14.81	10.50	d. Autres
55. Operating expenses	68.28	67.86	71.72	67.61	65.70	63.93	63.50	66.56	59.83	62.98	55. Frais d'exploitation
a. Staff costs	34.49	41.40	43.63	41.15	39.49	36.61	35.20	36.13	31.47	32.75	a. Dépenses en personnel
b. Property costs	..	5.19	5.51	5.16	4.97	4.95	5.10	4.83	3.90	4.30	b. Dépenses en immobilier
c. Other	..	21.27	22.57	21.29	21.24	22.38	23.21	25.60	24.46	25.93	c. Autres
56. Net income	31.72	32.15	28.29	32.40	34.30	36.07	36.50	33.44	40.17	37.02	56. Résultat net
57. Provisions (net)	19.66	12.75	8.38	13.55	12.25	13.61	12.28	8.13	6.11	7.53	57. Provisions (nettes)
a. Provisions on loans	..	11.17	7.57	8.76	8.97	5.30	1.30	5.72	4.25	5.43	a. Provisions sur prêts
b. Provisions on securities	..	-0.32	0.32	-0.04	-0.01	0.19	0.71	-0.16	1.20	0.87	b. Provisions sur titres
c. Other	..	1.44	0.89	4.66	3.10	7.10	10.95	2.31	0.29	0.52	c. Autres
58. Profit before tax	12.06	19.40	19.90	18.85	22.05	22.45	24.22	25.31	34.07	29.49	58. Bénéfices avant impôt
59. Income tax	4.54	5.71	6.24	6.91	7.35	7.72	8.27	4.79	7.74	5.45	59. Impôt sur le revenu
60. Profit after tax	7.52	13.70	13.65	11.95	14.70	14.74	15.95	20.52	26.33	24.04	60. Bénéfices après impôt
% of net income											**% du total du résultat net**
61. Provisions (net)	61.99	39.65	29.63	41.82	35.72	37.75	33.64	24.32	15.21	20.34	61. Provisions (nettes)
a. Provisions on loans	..	34.76	26.77	27.03	26.14	14.70	3.57	17.10	10.59	14.66	a. Provisions sur prêts
b. Provisions on securities	..	-0.98	1.13	-0.12	-0.02	0.53	1.94	-0.48	2.99	2.34	b. Provisions sur titres
c. Other	..	4.47	3.15	14.39	9.03	19.69	29.99	6.92	0.72	1.41	c. Autres
62. Profit before tax	38.01	60.35	70.33	58.18	64.28	62.25	66.36	75.68	84.81	79.66	62. Bénéfices avant impôt
63. Income tax	14.30	17.75	22.07	21.33	21.44	21.40	22.65	14.31	19.27	14.71	63. Impôt sur le revenu
64. Profit after tax	23.71	42.60	48.27	36.87	42.86	40.85	43.70	61.37	65.53	64.95	64. Bénéfices après impôt

Per cent

BALANCE SHEET ANALYSIS

% of year-end balance sheet total

Assets

	1992	1993	1994	1995	1996	1997	1998	1999	2000	2001
65. Cash & balance with Central bank	0.21	0.18	0.18	0.18	0.17	0.20	1.08	0.72	1.13	0.97
66. Interbank deposits	31.20	32.51	31.72	32.80	32.86	31.95	29.31	26.86	22.00	23.07
67. Loans	34.87	33.37	33.98	32.74	31.88	31.82	32.98	33.44	37.45	34.46
68. Securities	29.29	28.51	29.22	29.14	29.92	30.28	30.79	32.28	31.49	31.69
69. Other assets	4.44	5.43	4.90	5.13	5.16	5.75	5.84	6.70	7.92	9.80
Liabilities										
70. Capital & reserves	3.96	2.54	2.59	2.55	2.52	2.60	3.08	3.08	3.54	3.65
71. Borrowing from Central bank	0.02	0.01	0.01	-	0.01	0.02	-	-	0.07	0.01
72. Interbank deposits	39.03	39.74	38.94	40.73	41.20	40.81	38.57	37.58	33.66	31.79
73. Non-bank deposits	36.24	32.98	33.20	33.22	33.93	35.34	37.39	37.42	38.74	40.69
74. Bonds	15.00	17.96	18.15	16.37	14.97	13.18	12.31	12.62	13.22	11.23
75. Other liabilities	5.74	6.77	7.10	7.13	7.36	8.04	8.64	9.29	10.77	12.62
Memorandum items										
76. Short-term securities	4.27	5.07	6.44	4.64	4.11	3.44	3.21	4.79	3.19	2.73
77. Bonds	15.66	22.13	21.51	23.02	24.31	25.16	25.29	24.68	25.12	25.65
78. Shares and participations	0.62	1.31	1.27	1.48	1.50	1.68	2.30	2.81	3.18	3.31
79. Claims on non-residents	33.63	38.74	37.60	38.74	38.89	43.00	41.66	45.78	49.32	51.45
80. Liabilities to non-residents	38.18	41.98	42.13	43.50	43.31	46.68	45.61	44.98	47.60	48.90

* See notes on previous pages.

Pourcentage

ANALYSE DU BILAN

% du total du bilan en fin d'exercice

Actif

65. Caisse & solde auprès de la Banque centrale
66. Dépôts interbancaires
67. Prêts
68. Valeurs mobilières
69. Autres actifs

Passif

70. Capital et réserves
71. Emprunts auprès de la Banque centrale
72. Dépôts interbancaires
73. Dépôts non bancaires
74. Obligations
75. Autres engagements

Pour mémoire

76. Titres à court terme
77. Obligations
78. Actions et participations
79. Créances sur des non-résidents
80. Engagements envers des non-résidents

* Voir les notes en pages précédentes.

BELGIUM
Large commercial banks

BELGIQUE
Grandes banques commerciales

Million euros / *Millions d'euros*

INCOME STATEMENT (1) / COMPTE DE RESULTATS (1)	1993	1994	1995	1996	1997	1998	1999	2000	2001
1. Interest income / *Produits financiers*	31759	30170	33724	33252	38056	40832	43519	59355	52403
2. Interest expenses / *Frais financiers*	26952	25118	28400	27636	32486	34904	38001	54158	47008
3. Net interest income / *Produits financiers nets*	4807	5051	5324	5616	5570	5928	5518	5197	5395
4. Non-interest income (net) / *Produits non financiers (nets)*	2262	1827	2142	2680	3429	3848	4218	6123	6175
a. Fees and commissions receivable / *Frais et commissions à recevoir*	976	1123	1037	1230	1517	1995	2148	2574	2166
b. Fees and commissions payable / *Frais et commissions à payer*	376	455	459	470	562	632	737	915	832
c. Net profits or loss on financial operations / *Profits ou pertes nets sur opérations financières*	1264	934	1379	1825	1854	2682	2381	3004	3277
d. Other / *Autres*	399	225	185	95	620	-198	426	1460	1565
5. Gross income / *Résultat brut*	7069	6878	7466	8296	8999	9776	9736	11320	11571
6. Operating expenses / *Frais d'exploitation*	4871	5005	5110	5425	5831	6268	6451	6756	6877
a. Staff costs / *Dépenses en personnel*	3198	3263	3308	3474	3512	3684	3695	3904	3912
b. Property costs / *Dépenses en immobilier*	397	410	421	450	495	548	498	484	516
c. Other / *Autres*	1277	1331	1381	1501	1824	2037	2258	2368	2450
7. Net income / *Résultat net*	2198	1873	2356	2871	3168	3507	3285	4564	4693
8. Provisions (net) / *Provisions (nettes)*	931	580	858	1001	1128	1255	916	698	743
a. Provisions on loans / *Provisions sur prêts*	812	519	453	739	434	-41	583	480	629
b. Provisions on securities / *Provisions sur titres*	-18	16	4	2	18	68	-30	151	98
c. Other / *Autres*	136	45	401	260	677	1228	363	67	16
9. Profit before tax / *Bénéfices avant impôt*	1267	1293	1498	1870	2040	2253	2369	3865	3950
10. Income tax / *Impôt sur le revenu*	327	429	492	597	655	805	323	611	535
11. Profit after tax / *Bénéfices après impôt*	940	864	1006	1272	1385	1447	2046	3254	3415
12. Distributed profit / *Bénéfices distribués*	477	499	516	686	615	894	1318	1963	2195
13. Retained profit / *Bénéfices mis en réserve*	464	365	490	586	770	553	728	1291	1220
BALANCE SHEET / BILAN									
Assets / Actif									
14. Cash & balance with Central bank / *Caisse & solde auprès de la Banque centrale*	749	788	835	867	1114	5918	3680	7050	6032
15. Interbank deposits / *Dépôts interbancaires*	75834	84347	103675	119275	126251	132653	152468	118372	146000
16. Loans / *Prêts*	127599	136154	145250	158412	177231	189133	203866	230599	228790
17. Securities / *Valeurs mobilières*	100686	107459	118469	134600	153928	161532	190202	191161	216767
18. Other assets / *Autres actifs*	17513	15775	18208	21019	30204	32991	43254	52377	74566
Liabilities / Passif									
19. Capital & reserves / *Capital et réserves*	9001	9558	10133	11202	13344	16791	18053	20851	23650
20. Borrowing from Central bank / *Emprunts auprès de la Banque centrale*	2	63	-	69	133	-	11	3	97
21. Interbank deposits / *Dépôts interbancaires*	88619	100558	129405	155624	168085	184064	226728	202954	219113
22. Non-bank deposits / *Dépôts non bancaires*	128866	134392	144468	161510	188468	197358	206440	218492	257052
23. Bonds (2) / *Obligations (2)*	72786	75041	74041	73821	76428	72938	80006	84239	76120
24. Other liabilities / *Autres engagements*	23107	24910	28389	31947	42270	51077	62232	73019	96123
Balance sheet total / Total du bilan									
25. End-year total / *En fin d'exercice*	322382	344523	386436	434172	488728	522227	593470	599559	672155
26. Average total / *Moyen*	318127	342145	374742	421618	487304	523968	587327	624707	651974

BELGIUM
Large commercial banks

Million euros

	1993	1994	1995	1996	1997	1998	1999	2000	2001
Memorandum items									
27. Short-term securities	16158	24437	21227	19615	16125	15210	29078	17851	14197
28. Bonds	78322	76802	89273	106411	127360	131666	141553	150524	177267
29. Shares and participations	6206	6220	7969	8574	10443	14655	19571	22786	25303
30. Claims on non-residents	104978	109624	133157	154701	194436	208123	283075	305888	362575
31. Liabilities to non-residents	115021	124265	154062	173749	214030	230804	277792	297357	348182
Capital adequacy									
32. Tier 1 Capital	9503	10104	10889	11982	14251	19030	20513	23451	24162
33. Tier 2 Capital	5215	5814	6491	7720	9140	10389	15335	17518	18307
34. Supervisory deductions	2389	2505	3790	4252	5887	9489	14059	17390	20181
35. Total net capital resources	12329	13413	13590	15450	17504	19930	21789	23579	22289
36. Risk-weighted assets	98976	99206	107573	116134	133609	150452	171221	175383	169095
SUPPLEMENTARY INFORMATION									
37. Number of institutions	7	7	7	7	7	6	5	5	5
38. Number of branches	..	..	..	..	..	..	..	..	..
39. Number of employees (x 1000)	..	..	..	..	..	..	..	..	..

1 The Income Statement reporting period is the fiscal year ending 30 June of the following year.

2 Bonds (item 23) includes CD's.

Notes

Large commercial banks: 7 large credit institutions governed by Belgian law.

Average balance sheet totals (item 26) are the average of monthly data within the calendar year.

BELGIQUE
Grandes banques commerciales

Millions d'euros

Pour mémoire
27. Titres à court terme
28. Obligations
29. Actions et participations
30. Créances sur des non-résidents
31. Engagements envers des non-résidents

Solvabilité
32. Fonds propres de base
33. Fonds propres complémentaires
34. Eléments à déduire des fonds propres
35. Total net des ressources en capital
36. Actifs pondérés des risques

RENSEIGNEMENTS COMPLEMENTAIRES
37. Nombre d'institutions
38. Nombre de succursales
39. Nombre de salariés (x 1000)

1 La période couverte pour le Compte de résultats est l'année fiscale se terminant le 30 juin de l'année suivante.

2 Les obligations (poste 23) comprennent les certificats de dépôt.

Notes

Grandes banques commerciales : 7 grands établissements de crédit de droit belge.

La moyenne du total des actifs/passifs (poste 26) est la moyenne des données mensuelles de l'année calendrier.

BELGIUM

Large commercial banks

Per cent

INCOME STATEMENT ANALYSIS

		1993	1994	1995	1996	1997	1998	1999	2000	2001
	% of average balance sheet total									
40.	Interest income	9.98	8.82	9.00	7.89	7.81	7.79	7.41	9.50	8.04
41.	Interest expenses	8.47	7.34	7.58	6.55	6.67	6.66	6.47	8.67	7.21
42.	Net interest income	1.51	1.48	1.42	1.33	1.14	1.13	0.94	0.83	0.83
43.	Non-interest income (net)	0.71	0.53	0.57	0.64	0.70	0.73	0.72	0.98	0.95
	a. Fees and commissions receivable	0.31	0.33	0.28	0.29	0.31	0.38	0.37	0.41	0.33
	b. Fees and commissions payable	0.12	0.13	0.12	0.11	0.12	0.12	0.13	0.15	0.13
	c. Net profits or loss on financial operations	0.40	0.27	0.37	0.43	0.38	0.51	0.41	0.48	0.50
	d. Other	0.13	0.07	0.05	0.02	0.13	-0.04	0.07	0.23	0.24
44.	Gross income	2.22	2.01	1.99	1.97	1.85	1.87	1.66	1.81	1.77
45.	Operating expenses	1.53	1.46	1.36	1.29	1.20	1.20	1.10	1.08	1.05
	a. Staff costs	1.01	0.95	0.88	0.82	0.72	0.70	0.63	0.62	0.60
	b. Property costs	0.12	0.12	0.11	0.11	0.10	0.10	0.08	0.08	0.08
	c. Other	0.40	0.39	0.37	0.36	0.37	0.39	0.38	0.38	0.38
46.	Net income	0.69	0.55	0.63	0.68	0.65	0.67	0.56	0.73	0.72
47.	Provisions (net)	0.29	0.17	0.23	0.24	0.23	0.24	0.16	0.11	0.11
	a. Provisions on loans	0.26	0.15	0.12	0.18	0.09	-0.01	0.10	0.08	0.10
	b. Provisions on securities	-0.01	-	-	-	-	0.01	-0.01	0.02	0.02
	c. Other	0.04	0.01	0.11	0.06	0.14	0.23	0.06	0.01	-
48.	Profit before tax	0.40	0.38	0.40	0.44	0.42	0.43	0.40	0.62	0.61
49.	Income tax	0.10	0.13	0.13	0.14	0.13	0.15	0.05	0.10	0.08
50.	Profit after tax	0.30	0.25	0.27	0.30	0.28	0.28	0.35	0.52	0.52
51.	Distributed profit	0.15	0.15	0.14	0.16	0.13	0.17	0.22	0.31	0.34
52.	Retained profit	0.15	0.11	0.13	0.14	0.16	0.11	0.12	0.21	0.19
	% of gross income									
53.	Net interest income	68.00	73.44	71.31	67.70	61.90	60.64	56.68	45.91	46.63
54.	Non-interest income (net)	32.00	26.56	28.69	32.30	38.10	39.36	43.32	54.09	53.37
	a. Fees and commissions receivable	13.81	16.33	13.89	14.83	16.86	20.41	22.06	22.74	18.72
	b. Fees and commissions payable	5.32	6.62	6.15	5.67	6.25	6.46	7.57	8.08	7.19
	c. Net profits or loss on financial operations	17.88	13.58	18.47	22.00	20.60	27.43	24.46	26.54	28.32
	d. Other	5.64	3.27	2.48	1.15	6.89	-2.03	4.38	12.90	13.53
55.	Operating expenses	68.91	72.77	68.44	65.39	64.80	64.12	66.26	59.68	59.43
	a. Staff costs	45.24	47.44	44.31	41.88	39.03	37.68	37.95	34.49	33.81
	b. Property costs	5.62	5.96	5.64	5.42	5.50	5.61	5.12	4.28	4.46
	c. Other	18.06	19.35	18.50	18.09	20.27	20.84	23.19	20.92	21.17
56.	Net income	31.09	27.23	31.56	34.61	35.20	35.87	33.74	40.32	40.56
57.	Provisions (net)	13.17	8.43	11.49	12.07	12.53	12.84	9.41	6.17	6.42
	a. Provisions on loans	11.49	7.55	6.07	8.91	4.82	-0.42	5.99	4.24	5.44
	b. Provisions on securities	-0.25	0.23	0.05	0.02	0.20	0.70	-0.31	1.33	0.85
	c. Other	1.92	0.65	5.37	3.13	7.52	12.56	3.73	0.59	0.14
58.	Profit before tax	17.92	18.80	20.06	22.54	22.67	23.05	24.33	34.14	34.14
59.	Income tax	4.63	6.24	6.59	7.20	7.28	8.23	3.32	5.40	4.62
60.	Profit after tax	13.30	12.56	13.47	15.33	15.39	14.80	21.01	28.75	29.51
	% of net income									
61.	Provisions (net)	42.36	30.97	36.42	34.87	35.61	35.79	27.88	15.29	15.83
	a. Provisions on loans	36.94	27.71	19.23	25.74	13.70	-1.17	17.75	10.52	13.40
	b. Provisions on securities	-0.82	0.85	0.17	0.07	0.57	1.94	-0.91	3.31	2.09
	c. Other	6.19	2.40	17.02	9.06	21.37	35.02	11.05	1.47	0.34
62.	Profit before tax	57.64	69.03	63.58	65.13	64.39	64.24	72.12	84.68	84.17
63.	Income tax	14.88	22.90	20.88	20.79	20.68	22.95	9.83	13.39	11.40
64.	Profit after tax	42.77	46.13	42.70	44.31	43.72	41.26	62.28	71.30	72.77

BELGIQUE

Grandes banques commerciales

Pourcentage

ANALYSE DU COMPTE DE RESULTATS

	% du total moyen du bilan
40.	Produits financiers
41.	Frais financiers
42.	Produits financiers nets
43.	Produits non financiers (nets)
	a. Frais et commissions à recevoir
	b. Frais et commissions à payer
	c. Profits ou pertes nets sur opérations financières
	d. Autres
44.	Résultat brut
45.	Frais d'exploitation
	a. Dépenses en personnel
	b. Dépenses en immobilier
	c. Autres
46.	Résultat net
47.	Provisions (nettes)
	a. Provisions sur prêts
	b. Provisions sur titres
	c. Autres
48.	Bénéfices avant impôt
49.	Impôt sur le revenu
50.	Bénéfices après impôt
51.	Bénéfices distribués
52.	Bénéfices mis en réserve
	% du total du résultat brut
53.	Produits financiers nets
54.	Produits non financiers (nets)
	a. Frais et commissions à recevoir
	b. Frais et commissions à payer
	c. Profits ou pertes nets sur opérations financières
	d. Autres
55.	Frais d'exploitation
	a. Dépenses en personnel
	b. Dépenses en immobilier
	c. Autres
56.	Résultat net
57.	Provisions (nettes)
	a. Provisions sur prêts
	b. Provisions sur titres
	c. Autres
58.	Bénéfices avant impôt
59.	Impôt sur le revenu
60.	Bénéfices après impôt
	% du total du résultat net
61.	Provisions (nettes)
	a. Provisions sur prêts
	b. Provisions sur titres
	c. Autres
62.	Bénéfices avant impôt
63.	Impôt sur le revenu
64.	Bénéfices après impôt

BELGIUM
Large commercial banks

Per cent

BALANCE SHEET ANALYSIS

% of year-end balance sheet total

Assets

	1993	1994	1995	1996	1997	1998	1999	2000	2001
65. Cash & balance with Central bank	0.23	0.23	0.22	0.20	0.23	1.13	0.62	1.18	0.90
66. Interbank deposits	23.52	24.48	26.83	27.47	25.83	25.40	25.69	19.74	21.72
67. Loans	39.58	39.52	37.59	36.49	36.26	36.22	34.35	38.46	34.04
68. Securities	31.23	31.19	30.66	31.00	31.50	30.93	32.05	31.88	32.25
69. Other assets	5.43	4.58	4.71	4.84	6.18	6.32	7.29	8.74	11.09
Liabilities									
70. Capital & reserves	2.79	2.77	2.62	2.58	2.73	3.22	3.04	3.48	3.52
71. Borrowing from Central bank	-	0.02	-	0.02	0.03	-	-	-	0.01
72. Interbank deposits	27.49	29.19	33.49	35.84	34.39	35.25	38.20	33.85	32.60
73. Non-bank deposits	39.97	39.01	37.38	37.20	38.56	37.79	34.79	36.44	38.24
74. Bonds	22.58	21.78	19.16	17.00	15.64	13.97	13.48	14.05	11.32
75. Other liabilities	7.17	7.23	7.35	7.36	8.65	9.78	10.49	12.18	14.30
Memorandum items									
76. Short-term securities	5.01	7.09	5.49	4.52	3.30	2.91	4.90	2.98	2.11
77. Bonds	24.29	22.29	23.10	24.51	26.06	25.21	23.85	25.11	26.37
78. Shares and participations	1.93	1.81	2.06	1.97	2.14	2.81	3.30	3.80	3.76
79. Claims on non-residents	32.56	31.82	34.46	35.63	39.78	39.85	47.70	51.02	53.94
80. Liabilities to non-residents	35.68	36.07	39.87	40.02	43.79	44.20	46.81	49.60	51.80

* See notes on previous pages.

BELGIQUE
Grandes banques commerciales

Pourcentage

ANALYSE DU BILAN

% du total du bilan en fin d'exercice

Actif

65. Caisse & solde auprès de la Banque centrale
66. Dépôts interbancaires
67. Prêts
68. Valeurs mobilières
69. Autres actifs

Passif

70. Capital et réserves
71. Emprunts auprès de la Banque centrale
72. Dépôts interbancaires
73. Dépôts non bancaires
74. Obligations
75. Autres engagements

Pour mémoire

76. Titres à court terme
77. Obligations
78. Actions et participations
79. Créances sur des non-résidents
80. Engagements envers des non-résidents

* Voir les notes en pages précédentes.

BELGIUM
Other commercial banks

Million euros

BELGIQUE
Autres banques commerciales

Millions d'euros

	1993	1994	1995	1996	1997	1998	1999	2000	2001	
INCOME STATEMENT (1)										**COMPTE DE RESULTATS (1)**
1. Interest income	15563	14632	15075	14479	13552	12435	8641	9281	9459	1. Produits financiers
2. Interest expenses	13770	12675	13136	12281	11539	10441	6160	6950	6979	2. Frais financiers
3. Net interest income	1793	1958	1939	2198	2012	1993	2481	2331	2479	3. Produits financiers nets
4. Non-interest income (net)	641	398	587	483	759	914	437	1089	1294	4. Produits non financiers (nets)
a. Fees and commissions receivable	290	345	321	379	423	531	738	1633	1608	a. Frais et commissions à recevoir
b. Fees and commissions payable	314	364	388	407	391	446	592	1032	842	b. Frais et commissions à payer
c. Net profits or loss on financial operations	564	280	434	415	463	687	232	313	447	c. Profits ou pertes nets sur opérations financières
d. Other	101	136	219	97	264	141	59	175	81	d. Autres
5. Gross income	2434	2356	2526	2681	2771	2908	2917	3420	3773	5. Résultat brut
6. Operating expenses	1614	1540	1557	1629	1592	1684	1929	2210	2726	6. Frais d'exploitation
a. Staff costs	910	885	890	927	885	880	1008	1005	1157	a. Dépenses en personnel
b. Property costs	122	115	109	110	112	128	143	137	150	b. Dépenses en immobilier
c. Other	583	540	558	592	594	676	778	1068	1419	c. Autres
7. Net income	820	816	969	1052	1179	1224	988	1210	1047	7. Résultat net
8. Provisions (net)	351	298	578	411	469	516	165	253	350	8. Provisions (nettes)
a. Provisions on loans	353	237	487	311	239	219	202	223	241	a. Provisions sur prêts
b. Provisions on securities	-15	16	-7	-3	6	30	8	48	42	b. Provisions sur titres
c. Other	14	45	99	103	224	268	-45	-19	67	c. Autres
9. Profit before tax	468	518	391	641	711	708	823	957	697	9. Bénéfices avant impôt
10. Income tax	152	146	190	225	222	219	214	325	255	10. Impôt sur le revenu
11. Profit after tax	316	371	201	416	489	489	609	632	441	11. Bénéfices après impôt
12. Distributed profit	178	210	172	207	327	250	428	419	424	12. Bénéfices distribués
13. Retained profit	138	162	29	209	162	239	181	213	18	13. Bénéfices mis en réserve
BALANCE SHEET										**BILAN**
Assets										*Actif*
14. Cash & balance with Central bank	237	266	286	289	303	1429	1293	1286	1843	14. Caisse & solde auprès de la Banque centrale
15. Interbank deposits	27721	25380	29375	31908	30292	24509	16345	21217	24728	15. Dépôts interbancaires
16. Loans	45455	48192	43696	43744	40181	39589	42369	46708	48354	16. Prêts
17. Securities	47498	52848	53611	57116	56653	56531	53673	48992	49049	17. Valeurs mobilières
18. Other assets	8603	7882	8828	8597	7400	6424	6575	7366	7247	18. Autres actifs
Liabilities										*Passif*
19. Capital & reserves	4531	4713	4917	5102	4891	4955	5014	5591	6508	19. Capital et réserves
20. Borrowing from Central bank	7	3	3	8	17	30	10	7	11	20. Emprunts auprès de la Banque centrale
21. Interbank deposits	42469	42703	44465	44616	47396	39031	24125	24613	27534	21. Dépôts interbancaires
22. Non-bank deposits	43952	46129	48627	53960	53506	58521	66289	67561	68754	22. Dépôts non bancaires
23. Bonds (2)	28197	30018	26780	26483	18863	16626	17152	18651	18937	23. Obligations (2)
24. Other liabilities	10358	11003	11005	11485	10155	9320	7666	9147	9477	24. Autres engagements
Balance sheet total										**Total du bilan**
25. End-year total	129514	134569	135796	141654	134829	128483	120256	125570	131221	25. En fin d'exercice
26. Average total	128828	135530	138292	143745	146726	132039	124154	119733	130229	26. Moyen

BELGIUM
Other commercial banks

BELGIQUE
Autres banques commerciales

Million euros / *Millions d'euros*

	1993	1994	1995	1996	1997	1998	1999	2000	2001		
Memorandum items											**Pour mémoire**
27. Short-term securities	7013	8246	5223	4939	6377	6223	7075	6478	8268	27.	Titres à court terme
28. Bonds	39341	43483	47261	50725	48588	48287	44734	40735	38612	28.	Obligations
29. Shares and participations	1145	1119	1127	1452	1688	2021	1865	1780	2169	29.	Actions et participations
30. Claims on non-residents	33889	35433	38652	39416	42652	36705	28753	40423	42842	30.	Créances sur des non-résidents
31. Liabilities to non-residents	31496	36544	38458	38338	38779	32745	19857	28506	31750	31.	Engagements envers des non-résidents
Capital adequacy											**Solvabilité**
32. Tier 1 Capital	4668	4861	5192	5405	5235	5495	5270	5694	6463	32.	Fonds propres de base
33. Tier 2 Capital	1444	1555	1455	1551	1539	1298	1134	1634	1765	33.	Fonds propres complémentaires
34. Supervisory deductions	287	368	465	686	841	852	731	797	596	34.	Eléments à déduire des fonds propres
35. Total net capital resources	5826	6049	6182	6270	5934	5941	5673	6531	7632	35.	Total net des ressources en capital
36. Risk-weighted assets	40823	42117	41182	42338	39903	38865	38869	44025	46405	36.	Actifs pondérés des risques
SUPPLEMENTARY INFORMATION											**RENSEIGNEMENTS COMPLEMENTAIRES**
37. Number of institutions	105	100	97	93	86	75	70	67	62	37.	Nombre d'institutions
38. Number of branches	..	..	..	..	..	..	..	..	..	38.	Nombre de succursales
39. Number of employees (x 1000)	..	..	..	..	..	..	..	..	..	39.	Nombre de salariés (x 1000)

1 The Income Statement reporting period is the fiscal year ending 30 June of the following year.

2 Bonds (item 23) includes CD's.

Notes

Other commercial banks: Other credit institutions governed by Belgian law.

Average balance sheet totals (item 26) are the average of monthly data within the calendar year.

1 La période couverte pour le Compte de résultats est l'année fiscale se terminant le 30 juin de l'année suivante.

2 Les obligations (poste 23) comprennent les certificats de dépôt.

Notes

Autres banques commerciales : Autres établissements de crédit de droit belge.

La moyenne du total des actifs/passifs (poste 26) est la moyenne des données mensuelles de l'année calendrier.

BELGIUM

Other commercial banks

BELGIQUE

Autres banques commerciales

Per cent / *Pourcentage*

No.		1993	1994	1995	1996	1997	1998	1999	2000	2001	
	INCOME STATEMENT ANALYSIS										**ANALYSE DU COMPTE DE RESULTATS**
	% of average balance sheet total										**% du total moyen du bilan**
40.	Interest income	12.08	10.80	10.90	10.07	9.24	9.42	6.96	7.75	7.26	Produits financiers
41.	Interest expenses	10.69	9.35	9.50	8.54	7.86	7.91	4.96	5.80	5.36	Frais financiers
42.	Net interest income	1.39	1.44	1.40	1.53	1.37	1.51	2.00	1.95	1.90	Produits financiers nets
43.	Non-interest income (net)	0.50	0.29	0.42	0.34	0.52	0.69	0.35	0.91	0.99	Produits non financiers (nets)
	a. Fees and commissions receivable	0.23	0.25	0.23	0.26	0.29	0.40	0.59	1.36	1.23	a. Frais et commissions à recevoir
	b. Fees and commissions payable	0.24	0.27	0.28	0.28	0.27	0.34	0.48	0.86	0.65	b. Frais et commissions à payer
	c. Net profits or loss on financial operations	0.44	0.21	0.31	0.29	0.32	0.52	0.19	0.26	0.34	c. Profits ou pertes nets sur opérations financières
	d. Other	0.08	0.10	0.16	0.07	0.18	0.11	0.05	0.15	0.06	d. Autres
44.	Gross income	1.89	1.74	1.83	1.87	1.89	2.20	2.35	2.86	2.90	Résultat brut
45.	Operating expenses	1.25	1.14	1.13	1.13	1.09	1.28	1.55	1.85	2.09	Frais d'exploitation
	a. Staff costs	0.71	0.65	0.64	0.64	0.60	0.67	0.81	0.84	0.89	a. Dépenses en personnel
	b. Property costs	0.09	0.08	0.08	0.08	0.08	0.10	0.12	0.11	0.12	b. Dépenses en immobilier
	c. Other	0.45	0.40	0.40	0.41	0.40	0.51	0.63	0.89	1.09	c. Autres
46.	Net income	0.64	0.60	0.70	0.73	0.80	0.93	0.80	1.01	0.80	Résultat net
47.	Provisions (net)	0.27	0.22	0.42	0.29	0.32	0.39	0.13	0.21	0.27	Provisions (nettes)
	a. Provisions on loans	0.27	0.17	0.35	0.22	0.16	0.17	0.16	0.19	0.19	a. Provisions sur prêts
	b. Provisions on securities	-0.01	0.01	-0.01	-	.	0.02	0.01	0.04	0.03	b. Provisions sur titres
	c. Other	0.01	0.03	0.07	0.07	0.15	0.20	-0.04	-0.02	0.05	c. Autres
48.	Profit before tax	0.36	0.38	0.28	0.45	0.48	0.54	0.66	0.80	0.54	Bénéfices avant impôt
49.	Income tax	0.12	0.11	0.14	0.16	0.15	0.17	0.17	0.27	0.20	Impôt sur le revenu
50.	Profit after tax	0.25	0.27	0.15	0.29	0.33	0.37	0.49	0.53	0.34	Bénéfices après impôt
51.	Distributed profit	0.14	0.15	0.12	0.14	0.22	0.19	0.34	0.35	0.33	Bénéfices distribués
52.	Retained profit	0.11	0.12	0.02	0.15	0.11	0.18	0.15	0.18	0.01	Bénéfices mis en réserve
	% of gross income										**% du total du résultat brut**
53.	Net interest income	73.66	83.11	76.76	81.98	72.61	68.54	85.05	68.16	65.70	Produits financiers nets
54.	Non-interest income (net)	26.34	16.89	23.24	18.02	27.39	31.43	14.98	31.84	34.30	Produits non financiers (nets)
	a. Fees and commissions receivable	11.91	14.64	12.71	14.14	15.27	18.26	25.30	47.75	42.62	a. Frais et commissions à recevoir
	b. Fees and commissions payable	12.90	15.45	15.36	15.18	14.11	15.34	20.29	30.18	22.32	b. Frais et commissions à payer
	c. Net profits or loss on financial operations	23.17	11.88	17.18	15.48	16.71	23.62	7.95	9.15	11.85	c. Profits ou pertes nets sur opérations financières
	d. Other	4.15	5.77	8.67	3.62	9.53	4.85	2.02	5.12	2.15	d. Autres
55.	Operating expenses	66.31	65.37	61.64	60.76	57.45	57.91	66.13	64.62	72.25	Frais d'exploitation
	a. Staff costs	37.39	37.56	35.23	34.58	31.94	30.26	34.56	29.39	30.67	a. Dépenses en personnel
	b. Property costs	5.01	4.88	4.32	4.10	4.04	4.40	4.90	4.01	3.98	b. Dépenses en immobilier
	c. Other	23.95	22.92	22.09	22.08	21.44	23.25	26.67	31.23	37.61	c. Autres
56.	Net income	33.69	34.63	38.36	39.24	42.55	42.09	33.87	35.38	27.75	Résultat net
57.	Provisions (net)	14.42	12.65	22.88	15.33	16.93	17.74	5.66	7.40	9.28	Provisions (nettes)
	a. Provisions on loans	14.50	10.06	19.28	11.60	8.63	7.53	6.92	6.52	6.39	a. Provisions sur prêts
	b. Provisions on securities	-0.62	0.68	-0.28	-0.11	0.22	1.03	0.27	1.40	1.11	b. Provisions sur titres
	c. Other	0.58	1.91	3.92	3.84	8.08	9.22	-1.54	-0.56	1.78	c. Autres
58.	Profit before tax	19.23	21.99	15.48	23.91	25.66	24.35	28.21	27.98	18.47	Bénéfices avant impôt
59.	Income tax	6.24	6.20	7.52	8.39	8.01	7.53	7.34	9.50	6.76	Impôt sur le revenu
60.	Profit after tax	12.98	15.75	7.96	15.52	17.65	16.82	20.88	18.48	11.69	Bénéfices après impôt
	% of net income										**% du total du résultat net**
61.	Provisions (net)	42.80	36.52	59.65	39.07	39.78	42.16	16.70	20.91	33.43	Provisions (nettes)
	a. Provisions on loans	43.05	29.04	50.26	29.56	20.27	17.89	20.45	18.43	23.02	a. Provisions sur prêts
	b. Provisions on securities	-1.83	1.96	-0.72	-0.29	0.51	2.45	0.81	3.97	4.01	b. Provisions sur titres
	c. Other	1.71	5.51	10.22	9.79	19.00	21.90	-4.55	-1.57	6.40	c. Autres
62.	Profit before tax	57.07	63.48	40.35	60.93	60.31	57.84	83.30	79.09	66.57	Bénéfices avant impôt
63.	Income tax	18.54	17.89	19.61	21.39	18.83	17.89	21.66	26.86	24.36	Impôt sur le revenu
64.	Profit after tax	38.54	45.47	20.74	39.54	41.48	39.95	61.64	52.23	42.12	Bénéfices après impôt

BELGIUM

Other commercial banks

Per cent

BALANCE SHEET ANALYSIS

% of year-end balance sheet total

	1993	1994	1995	1996	1997	1998	1999	2000	2001
Assets									
65. Cash & balance with Central bank	0.18	0.20	0.21	0.20	0.22	1.11	1.08	1.02	1.40
66. Interbank deposits	21.40	18.86	21.63	22.53	22.47	19.08	13.59	16.90	18.84
67. Loans	35.10	35.81	32.18	30.88	29.80	30.81	35.23	37.20	36.85
68. Securities	36.67	39.27	39.48	40.32	42.02	44.00	44.63	39.02	37.38
69. Other assets	6.64	5.86	6.50	6.07	5.49	5.00	5.47	5.87	5.52
Liabilities									
70. Capital & reserves	3.50	3.50	3.62	3.60	3.63	3.86	4.17	4.45	4.96
71. Borrowing from Central bank	0.01	-	-	0.01	0.01	0.02	0.01	0.01	0.01
72. Interbank deposits	32.79	31.73	32.74	31.50	35.15	30.38	20.06	19.60	20.98
73. Non-bank deposits	33.94	34.28	35.81	38.09	39.68	45.55	55.12	53.80	52.40
74. Bonds	21.77	22.31	19.72	18.70	13.99	12.94	14.26	14.85	14.43
75. Other liabilities	8.00	8.18	8.10	8.11	7.53	7.25	6.37	7.28	7.22
Memorandum items									
76. Short-term securities	5.41	6.13	3.85	3.49	4.73	4.84	5.88	5.16	6.30
77. Bonds	30.38	32.31	34.80	35.81	36.04	37.58	37.20	32.44	29.43
78. Shares and participations	0.88	0.83	0.83	1.03	1.25	1.57	1.55	1.42	1.65
79. Claims on non-residents	26.17	26.33	28.46	27.83	31.63	28.57	23.91	32.19	32.65
80. Liabilities to non-residents	24.32	27.16	28.32	27.06	28.76	25.49	16.51	22.70	24.20

* See notes on previous pages.

BELGIQUE

Autres banques commerciales

Pourcentage

ANALYSE DU BILAN

% du total du bilan en fin d'exercice

Actif
65. Caisse & solde auprès de la Banque centrale
66. Dépôts interbancaires
67. Prêts
68. Valeurs mobilières
69. Autres actifs

Passif
70. Capital et réserves
71. Emprunts auprès de la Banque centrale
72. Dépôts interbancaires
73. Dépôts non bancaires
74. Obligations
75. Autres engagements

Pour mémoire
76. Titres à court terme
77. Obligations
78. Actions et participations
79. Créances sur des non-résidents
80. Engagements envers des non-résidents

* Voir les notes en pages précédentes.

BELGIUM
Foreign commercial banks

Million euros

BELGIQUE
Banques commerciales étrangères

Millions d'euros

INCOME STATEMENT (1) / COMPTE DE RESULTATS (1)

		1993	1994	1995	1996	1997	1998	1999	2000	2001	
1.	Interest income	10066	8069	7804	6752	8744	6527	3604	4607	2376	Produits financiers
2.	Interest expenses	9216	7702	7476	6438	8355	6064	3107	3938	2028	Frais financiers
3.	Net interest income	849	368	328	314	389	464	497	669	348	Produits financiers nets
4.	Non-interest income (net)	74	396	403	431	511	519	596	1137	353	Produits non financiers (nets)
	a. Fees and commissions receivable	140	131	111	167	192	221	276	381	343	a. Frais et commissions à recevoir
	b. Fees and commissions payable	45	57	52	81	61	48	58	75	70	b. Frais et commissions à payer
	c. Net profits or loss on financial operations	-244	77	88	77	106	22	52	18	42	c. Profits ou pertes nets sur opérations financières
	d. Other	224	244	256	268	274	324	326	814	38	d. Autres
5.	Gross income	924	763	731	745	900	983	1093	1807	701	Résultat brut
6.	Operating expenses	590	625	582	647	678	727	769	933	501	Frais d'exploitation
	a. Staff costs	208	214	214	228	240	247	263	297	186	a. Dépenses en personnel
	b. Property costs	23	26	24	23	20	21	23	23	24	b. Dépenses en immobilier
	c. Other	358	385	344	397	418	459	483	612	291	c. Autres
7.	Net income	334	138	149	97	223	256	324	874	200	Résultat net
8.	Provisions (net)	47	-40	17	24	128	-93	35	59	114	Provisions (nettes)
	a. Provisions on loans	..	..	..	..	..	..	..	..	..	a. Provisions sur prêts
	b. Provisions on securities	..	..	..	..	..	..	..	..	..	b. Provisions sur titres
	c. Other	..	..	..	..	..	..	..	..	..	c. Autres
9.	Profit before tax	287	178	132	74	94	350	289	814	85	Bénéfices avant impôt
10.	Income tax	116	49	59	40	101	105	122	345	84	Impôt sur le revenu
11.	Profit after tax	171	129	74	34	-7	244	167	469	2	Bénéfices après impôt
12.	Distributed profit	..	..	..	..	..	..	..	..	..	Bénéfices distribués
13.	Retained profit	..	..	..	..	..	..	..	..	..	Bénéfices mis en réserve

BALANCE SHEET / BILAN

Assets / Actif

		1993	1994	1995	1996	1997	1998	1999	2000	2001	
14.	Cash & balance with Central bank	3	9	9	3	4	517	583	487	375	Caisse & solde auprès de la Banque centrale
15.	Interbank deposits	79478	74062	69054	69285	74799	56054	38252	31618	24537	Dépôts interbancaires
16.	Loans	14823	12543	12770	11716	12980	11222	11491	14059	14483	Prêts
17.	Securities	12286	9017	7428	9016	8620	5978	4891	4870	2389	Valeurs mobilières
18.	Other assets	4457	4712	4595	5011	4022	3056	1822	1900	1169	Autres actifs

Liabilities / Passif

		1993	1994	1995	1996	1997	1998	1999	2000	2001	
19.	Capital & reserves	786	759	631	613	580	687	689	1083	741	Capital et réserves
20.	Borrowing from Central bank	27	9	1	10	24	-	-	506	9	Emprunts auprès de la Banque centrale
21.	Interbank deposits	92642	82400	77073	76154	79994	57550	38829	34321	22402	Dépôts interbancaires
22.	Non-bank deposits	12825	11822	11552	12147	13894	16119	15704	15393	18596	Dépôts non bancaires
23.	Bonds (2)	135	111	36	144	139	-	75	-	1205	Obligations (2)
24.	Other liabilities	4632	5244	4563	5962	5793	2471	1743	1631	1205	Autres engagements
	Balance sheet total										**Total du bilan**
25.	End-year total	111047	100344	93856	95031	100424	76827	57040	52935	42953	En fin d'exercice
26.	Average total	106802	103652	101852	100098	109429	92561	66506	68415	43673	Moyen

BELGIUM
Foreign commercial banks

Million euros

	1993	1994	1995	1996	1997	1998	1999	2000	2001			
Memorandum items											**Pour mémoire**	
27. Short-term securities	5347	4626	2121	3047	2389	1900	743	469	631	27.	Titres à court terme	
28. Bonds	6897	4347	5264	5937	6187	4006	3959	4200	1223	28.	Obligations	
29. Shares and participations	42	44	44	32	44	73	189	201	535	29.	Actions et participations	
30. Claims on non-residents	79212	72802	66838	66805	74223	58263	41043	37431	30041	30.	Créances sur des non-résidents	
31. Liabilities to non-residents	89811	83296	75506	78480	85113	68304	49066	44525	33965	31.	Engagements envers des non-résidents	
Capital adequacy											**Solvabilité**	
32. Tier 1 Capital	..	..	..	..	..	..	..	..	..	32.	Fonds propres de base	
33. Tier 2 Capital	..	..	..	..	..	..	..	..	..	33.	Fonds propres complémentaires	
34. Supervisory deductions	..	..	..	..	..	..	..	..	..	34.	Eléments à déduire des fonds propres	
35. Total net capital resources	..	..	..	..	..	..	..	..	..	35.	Total net des ressources en capital	
36. Risk-weighted assets	..	..	..	..	..	..	..	..	..	36.	Actifs pondérés des risques	
SUPPLEMENTARY INFORMATION											**RENSEIGNEMENTS COMPLEMENTAIRES**	
37. Number of institutions	38	40	39	40	38	38	42	46	45	37.	Nombre d'institutions	
38. Number of branches	..	..	..	..	..	..	..	..	..	38.	Nombre de succursales	
39. Number of employees (x 1000)	..	..	..	..	..	..	..	..	..	39.	Nombre de salariés (x 1000)	

1 The Income Statement reporting period is the fiscal year ending 30 June of the following year.

2 Bonds (item 23) includes CD's.

Notes

Foreign commercial banks: Branches of credit institutions governed by foreign law.

Average balance sheet totals (item 26) are the average of monthly data within the calendar year.

BELGIQUE
Banques commerciales étrangères

Millions d'euros

1 La période couverte pour le Compte de résultats est l'année fiscale se terminant le 30 juin de l'année suivante.

2 Les obligations (poste 23) comprennent les certificats de dépôt.

Notes

Banques commerciales étrangères : Succursales d'établissements de crédit de droit étranger.

La moyenne du total des actifs/passifs (poste 26) est la moyenne des données mensuelles de l'année calendrier.

Per cent — *Pourcentage*

INCOME STATEMENT ANALYSIS — **ANALYSE DU COMPTE DE RESULTATS**

No.	English	French	1993	1994	1995	1996	1997	1998	1999	2000	2001
	% of average balance sheet total	**% du total moyen du bilan**									
40.	Interest income	Produits financiers	9.42	7.78	7.66	6.75	7.99	7.05	5.42	6.73	5.44
41.	Interest expenses	Frais financiers	8.63	7.43	7.34	6.43	7.64	6.55	4.67	5.76	4.64
42.	Net interest income	Produits financiers nets	0.79	0.36	0.32	0.31	0.36	0.50	0.75	0.98	0.80
43.	Non-interest income (net)	Produits non financiers (nets)	0.07	0.38	0.40	0.43	0.47	0.56	0.90	1.66	0.81
a.	Fees and commissions receivable	Frais et commissions à recevoir	0.13	0.13	0.11	0.17	0.18	0.24	0.42	0.56	0.79
b.	Fees and commissions payable	Frais et commissions à payer	0.04	0.05	0.05	0.08	0.06	0.05	0.09	0.11	0.16
c.	Net profits or loss on financial operations	Profits ou pertes nets sur opérations financières	-0.23	0.07	0.09	0.08	0.10	0.02	0.08	0.03	0.10
d.	Other	Autres	0.21	0.24	0.25	0.27	0.25	0.35	0.49	1.19	0.09
44.	Gross income	Résultat brut	0.87	0.74	0.72	0.74	0.82	1.06	1.64	2.64	1.61
45.	Operating expenses	Frais d'exploitation	0.55	0.60	0.57	0.65	0.62	0.79	1.16	1.36	1.15
a.	Staff costs	Dépenses en personnel	0.19	0.21	0.21	0.23	0.22	0.27	0.40	0.43	0.43
b.	Property costs	Dépenses en immobilier	0.02	0.03	0.02	0.02	0.02	0.02	0.03	0.03	0.05
c.	Other	Autres	0.34	0.37	0.34	0.40	0.38	0.50	0.73	0.89	0.67
46.	Net income	Résultat net	0.31	0.13	0.15	0.10	0.20	0.28	0.49	1.28	0.46
47.	Provisions (net)	Provisions (nettes)	0.04	-0.04	0.02	0.02	0.12	-0.10	0.05	0.09	0.26
a.	Provisions on loans	Provisions sur prêts	..	..	..	..	..	..	..	..	..
b.	Provisions on securities	Provisions sur titres	..	..	..	..	..	..	..	..	..
c.	Other	Autres	..	..	..	..	..	..	..	..	..
48.	Profit before tax	Bénéfices avant impôt	0.27	0.17	0.13	0.07	0.09	0.38	0.43	1.19	0.19
49.	Income tax	Impôt sur le revenu	0.11	0.05	0.06	0.04	0.09	0.11	0.18	0.50	0.19
50.	Profit after tax	Bénéfices après impôt	0.16	0.12	0.07	0.03	-0.01	0.26	0.25	0.69	-
51.	Distributed profit	Bénéfices distribués	..	..	..	..	..	..	..	..	..
52.	Retained profit	Bénéfices mis en réserve	..	..	..	..	..	..	..	..	..
	% of gross income	**% du total du résultat brut**									
53.	Net interest income	Produits financiers nets	91.88	48.23	44.87	42.15	43.22	47.20	45.47	37.02	49.64
54.	Non-interest income (net)	Produits non financiers (nets)	8.01	51.90	55.13	57.85	56.78	52.80	54.53	62.92	50.36
a.	Fees and commissions receivable	Frais et commissions à recevoir	15.15	17.17	15.18	22.42	21.33	22.48	25.25	21.08	48.93
b.	Fees and commissions payable	Frais et commissions à payer	4.87	7.47	7.11	10.87	6.78	4.88	5.31	4.15	9.99
c.	Net profits or loss on financial operations	Profits ou pertes nets sur opérations financières	-26.41	10.09	12.04	10.34	11.78	2.24	4.76	1.00	5.99
d.	Other	Autres	24.24	31.98	35.02	35.97	30.44	32.96	29.83	45.05	5.42
55.	Operating expenses	Frais d'exploitation	63.85	81.91	79.62	86.85	75.33	73.96	70.36	51.63	71.47
a.	Staff costs	Dépenses en personnel	22.51	28.05	29.27	30.60	26.67	25.13	24.06	16.44	26.53
b.	Property costs	Dépenses en immobilier	2.49	3.41	3.28	3.09	2.22	2.14	2.10	1.27	3.42
c.	Other	Autres	38.74	50.46	47.06	53.29	46.44	46.69	44.19	33.87	41.51
56.	Net income	Résultat net	36.15	18.09	20.38	13.02	24.78	26.04	29.64	48.37	28.53
57.	Provisions (net)	Provisions (nettes)	5.09	-5.24	2.33	3.22	14.22	-9.46	3.20	3.27	16.26
a.	Provisions on loans	Provisions sur prêts	..	..	..	..	..	..	..	..	..
b.	Provisions on securities	Provisions sur titres	..	..	..	..	..	..	..	..	..
c.	Other	Autres	..	..	..	..	..	..	..	..	..
58.	Profit before tax	Bénéfices avant impôt	31.06	23.33	18.06	9.93	10.44	35.61	26.44	45.05	12.13
59.	Income tax	Impôt sur le revenu	12.55	6.42	8.07	5.37	11.22	10.68	11.16	19.09	11.98
60.	Profit after tax	Bénéfices après impôt	18.51	16.91	10.12	4.56	-0.78	24.82	15.28	25.95	0.29
	% of net income	**% du total du résultat net**									
61.	Provisions (net)	Provisions (nettes)	14.07	-28.99	11.41	24.74	57.40	-36.33	10.80	6.75	57.00
a.	Provisions on loans	Provisions sur prêts	..	..	..	..	..	..	..	..	..
b.	Provisions on securities	Provisions sur titres	..	..	..	..	..	..	..	..	..
c.	Other	Autres	..	..	..	..	..	..	..	..	..
62.	Profit before tax	Bénéfices avant impôt	85.93	128.99	88.59	76.29	42.15	136.72	89.20	93.14	42.50
63.	Income tax	Impôt sur le revenu	34.73	35.51	39.60	41.24	45.29	41.02	37.65	39.47	42.00
64.	Profit after tax	Bénéfices après impôt	51.20	93.48	49.66	35.05	-3.14	95.31	51.54	53.66	1.00

BELGIUM
Foreign commercial banks

BELGIQUE
Banques commerciales étrangères

Per cent — *Pourcentage*

BALANCE SHEET ANALYSIS — **ANALYSE DU BILAN**

% of year-end balance sheet total — **% du total du bilan en fin d'exercice**

	1993	1994	1995	1996	1997	1998	1999	2000	2001	
Assets										**Actif**
65. Cash & balance with Central bank	-	0.01	0.01	-	-	0.67	1.02	0.92	0.87	65. Caisse & solde auprès de la Banque centrale
66. Interbank deposits	71.57	73.81	73.57	72.91	74.48	72.96	67.06	59.73	57.13	66. Dépôts interbancaires
67. Loans	13.35	12.50	13.61	12.33	12.93	14.61	20.15	26.56	33.72	67. Prêts
68. Securities	11.06	8.99	7.91	9.49	8.58	7.78	8.57	9.20	5.56	68. Valeurs mobilières
69. Other assets	4.01	4.70	4.90	5.27	4.01	3.98	3.19	3.59	2.72	69. Autres actifs
Liabilities										**Passif**
70. Capital & reserves	0.71	0.76	0.67	0.65	0.58	0.89	1.21	2.05	1.73	70. Capital et réserves
71. Borrowing from Central bank	0.02	0.01	-	0.01	0.02	-	-	0.96	0.02	71. Emprunts auprès de la Banque centrale
72. Interbank deposits	83.43	82.12	82.12	80.14	79.66	74.91	68.07	64.84	52.15	72. Dépôts interbancaires
73. Non-bank deposits	11.55	11.78	12.31	12.78	13.84	20.98	27.53	29.08	43.29	73. Dépôts non bancaires
74. Bonds	0.12	0.11	0.04	0.15	0.14	-	0.13	-	-	74. Obligations
75. Other liabilities	4.17	5.23	4.86	6.27	5.77	3.22	3.06	3.08	2.81	75. Autres engagements
Memorandum items										***Pour mémoire***
76. Short-term securities	4.82	4.61	2.26	3.21	2.38	2.47	1.30	0.89	1.47	76. Titres à court terme
77. Bonds	6.21	4.33	5.61	6.25	6.16	5.21	6.94	7.93	2.85	77. Obligations
78. Shares and participations	0.04	0.04	0.05	0.03	0.04	0.10	0.33	0.38	1.25	78. Actions et participations
79. Claims on non-residents	71.33	72.55	71.21	70.30	73.91	75.84	71.95	70.71	69.94	79. Créances sur des non-résidents
80. Liabilities to non-residents	80.88	83.01	80.45	82.58	84.75	88.91	86.02	84.11	79.07	80. Engagements envers des non-résidents

* See notes on previous pages.   * Voir les notes en pages précédentes.

CANADA
Commercial banks

Million Canadian dollars

CANADA
Banques commerciales

Millions de dollars canadiens

	2001	2000	1999	1998	1997	1996	1995	1994	1993	1992	
INCOME STATEMENT											**COMPTE DE RESULTATS**
1. Interest income	77256	79839	70664	71364	60147	58853	56376	44623	41878	44115	1. Produits financiers
2. Interest expenses	47528	55591	47599	48962	38347	37714	36854	25588	24122	27324	2. Frais financiers
3. Net interest income	29728	24248	23064	22402	21801	21139	19522	19035	17756	16791	3. Produits financiers nets
4. Non-interest income (net)	31170	31071	25339	20302	17828	12417	10395	10058	8419	7533	4. Produits non financiers (nets)
a. Fees and commissions receivable	:	:	:	:	:	:	:	:	:	:	a. Frais et commissions à recevoir
b. Fees and commissions payable	:	:	:	:	:	:	:	:	:	:	b. Frais et commissions à payer
c. Net profits or loss on financial operations	:	:	:	:	:	:	:	:	:	:	c. Profits ou pertes nets sur opérations financières
d. Other	:	:	:	:	:	:	:	:	:	:	d. Autres
5. Gross income	60898	55319	48404	42703	39629	33556	29917	29093	26175	24324	5. Résultat brut
6. Operating expenses	41529	36881	31815	28807	25385	21281	19041	18493	16713	15367	6. Frais d'exploitation
a. Staff costs	22652	20380	17436	15975	14044	11882	10500	10269	9250	8502	a. Dépenses en personnel
b. Property costs	7222	6303	6079	5413	4826	4210	3906	3650	:	:	b. Dépenses en immobilier
c. Other	11656	10199	8299	7418	6515	5189	4635	4575	:	:	c. Autres
7. Net income	19369	18438	16589	13897	14244	12275	10876	10600	9462	8957	7. Résultat net
8. Provisions (net)	7032	3748	2948	2453	1985	1950	2560	3469	4780	6035	8. Provisions (nettes)
a. Provisions on loans	7032	3748	2948	2453	1985	1950	2560	3469	4780	6035	a. Provisions sur prêts
b. Provisions on securities	:	:	:	:	:	:	:	:	:	:	b. Provisions sur titres
c. Other	:	:	:	:	:	:	:	:	:	:	c. Autres
9. Profit before tax	12336	14690	13641	11444	12259	10325	8316	7131	4682	2922	9. Bénéfices avant impôt
10. Income tax	2766	4654	4292	4101	4529	3867	3028	2744	1666	969	10. Impôt sur le revenu
11. Profit after tax	9570	10036	9349	7343	7730	6458	5288	4387	3016	1953	11. Bénéfices après impôt
12. Distributed profit	:	:	:	:	:	:	:	:	:	:	12. Bénéfices distribués
13. Retained profit	:	:	:	:	:	:	:	:	:	:	13. Bénéfices mis en réserve
BALANCE SHEET											**BILAN**
Assets											**Actif**
14. Cash & balance with Central bank	6043	4915	5331	4716	4385	5219	4381	4433	5179	5897	14. Caisse & solde auprès de la Banque centrale
15. Interbank deposits	70836	72372	81354	72528	86435	72336	75468	53801	38148	36007	15. Dépôts interbancaires
16. Loans	875701	815970	753445	752955	704624	607840	532732	501495	457155	421772	16. Prêts
17. Securities	363627	317606	274945	241177	193452	180259	157242	135128	115151	89920	17. Valeurs mobilières
18. Other assets	192037	140630	113548	157756	98997	35368	31609	28653	27208	22444	18. Autres actifs
Liabilities											**Passif**
19. Capital & reserves	80249	71537	63487	58485	51183	43817	41600	38635	35352	31899	19. Capital et réserves
20. Borrowing from Central bank	126	298	302	52	17	20	204	61	311	6	20. Emprunts auprès de la Banque centrale
21. Interbank deposits	130951	125889	135672	143576	133549	125943	113583	97693	81890	81352	21. Dépôts interbancaires
22. Non-bank deposits	901940	839666	729671	687118	629902	541763	516121	481651	445195	405925	22. Dépôts non bancaires
23. Bonds	27338	27181	23841	23919	22851	17695	16977	16208	15309	12376	23. Obligations
24. Other liabilities	367640	286922	275650	315982	250391	171784	112947	89262	64784	44482	24. Autres engagements
Balance sheet total											**Total du bilan**
25. End-year total	1508244	1351493	1228623	1229132	1087893	901022	801432	723510	642841	576040	25. En fin d'exercice
26. Average total	1429869	1290059	1228878	1158513	994458	851227	762471	683176	609441	548883	26. Moyen

CANADA
Commercial banks

Million Canadian dollars

	1992	1993	1994	1995	1996	1997	1998	1999	2000	2001			
Memorandum items												*Pour mémoire*	
27. Short-term securities	..	..	..	..	..	..	..	..	..	..	27.	Titres à court terme	
28. Bonds	..	..	..	..	..	..	..	..	..	..	28.	Obligations	
29. Shares and participations	..	..	..	..	..	..	..	..	..	..	29.	Actions et participations	
30. Claims on non-residents	..	..	..	..	..	..	..	..	..	..	30.	Créances sur des non-résidents	
31. Liabilities to non-residents	..	..	..	..	..	..	..	..	..	..	31.	Engagements envers des non-résidents	
Capital adequacy												**Solvabilité**	
32. Tier 1 Capital	..	..	..	..	..	..	..	..	..	..	32.	Fonds propres de base	
33. Tier 2 Capital	..	..	..	..	..	..	..	..	..	..	33.	Fonds propres complémentaires	
34. Supervisory deductions	..	..	..	..	..	..	..	..	..	..	34.	Eléments à déduire des fonds propres	
35. Total net capital resources	..	..	..	..	..	..	..	..	..	..	35.	Total net des ressources en capital	
36. Risk-weighted assets	..	..	..	..	..	..	..	..	..	..	36.	Actifs pondérés des risques	
SUPPLEMENTARY INFORMATION												**RENSEIGNEMENTS COMPLEMENTAIRES**	
37. Number of institutions	10	11	11	11	11	9	9	9	9	15	37.	Nombre d'institutions	
38. Number of branches	..	..	..	..	..	..	..	..	..	..	38.	Nombre de succursales	
39. Number of employees (x 1000)	..	..	..	..	..	..	..	..	..	..	39.	Nombre de salariés (x 1000)	

Notes

- The reporting period is the fiscal year ending 31 October.

CANADA
Banques commerciales

Millions de dollars canadiens

Notes

- La période couverte est l'exercice financier qui se termine le 31 octobre.

52

CANADA

Commercial banks / Banques commerciales

Per cent / Pourcentage

INCOME STATEMENT ANALYSIS / ANALYSE DU COMPTE DE RESULTATS

	Item	1992	1993	1994	1995	1996	1997	1998	1999	2000	2001
	% of average balance sheet total / % du total moyen du bilan										
40.	Interest income / Produits financiers	8.04	6.87	6.53	7.39	6.91	6.05	6.16	5.75	6.19	5.40
41.	Interest expenses / Frais financiers	4.98	3.96	3.75	4.83	4.43	3.86	4.23	3.87	4.31	3.32
42.	Net interest income / Produits financiers nets	3.06	2.91	2.79	2.56	2.48	2.19	1.93	1.88	1.88	2.08
43.	Non-interest income (net) / Produits non financiers (nets)	1.37	1.38	1.47	1.36	1.46	1.79	1.75	2.06	2.41	2.18
	a. Fees and commissions receivable / Frais et commissions à recevoir	:	:	:	:	:	:	:	:	:	:
	b. Fees and commissions payable / Frais et commissions à payer	:	:	:	:	:	:	:	:	:	:
	c. Net profits or loss on financial operations / Profits ou pertes nets sur opérations financières	:	:	:	:	:	:	:	:	:	:
	d. Other / Autres	:	:	:	:	:	:	:	:	:	:
44.	Gross income / Résultat brut	4.43	4.29	4.26	3.92	3.94	3.98	3.69	3.94	4.29	4.26
45.	Operating expenses / Frais d'exploitation	2.80	2.74	2.71	2.50	2.50	2.55	2.49	2.59	2.86	2.90
	a. Staff costs / Dépenses en personnel	1.55	1.52	1.50	1.38	1.40	1.41	1.38	1.42	1.58	1.58
	b. Property costs / Dépenses en immobilier	:	:	0.53	0.51	0.49	0.49	0.47	0.49	0.49	0.51
	c. Other / Autres	:	:	0.67	0.61	0.61	0.66	0.64	0.68	0.79	0.82
46.	Net income / Résultat net	1.63	1.55	1.55	1.43	1.44	1.43	1.20	1.35	1.43	1.35
47.	Provisions (net) / Provisions (nettes)	1.10	0.78	0.51	0.34	0.23	0.20	0.21	0.24	0.29	0.49
	a. Provisions on loans / Provisions sur prêts	1.10	0.78	0.51	0.34	0.23	0.20	0.21	0.24	0.29	0.49
	b. Provisions on securities / Provisions sur titres	:	:	:	:	:	:	:	:	:	:
	c. Other / Autres	:	:	:	:	:	:	:	:	:	:
48.	Profit before tax / Bénéfices avant impôt	0.53	0.77	1.04	1.09	1.21	1.23	0.99	1.11	1.14	0.86
49.	Income tax / Impôt sur le revenu	0.18	0.27	0.40	0.40	0.45	0.46	0.35	0.35	0.36	0.19
50.	Profit after tax / Bénéfices après impôt	0.36	0.49	0.64	0.69	0.76	0.78	0.63	0.76	0.78	0.67
51.	Distributed profit / Bénéfices distribués	:	:	:	:	:	:	:	:	:	:
52.	Retained profit / Bénéfices mis en réserve	:	:	:	:	:	:	:	:	:	:
	% of gross income / % du total du résultat brut										
53.	Net interest income / Produits financiers nets	69.03	67.84	65.43	65.25	63.00	55.01	52.46	47.65	43.83	48.82
54.	Non-interest income (net) / Produits non financiers (nets)	30.97	32.16	34.57	34.75	37.00	44.99	47.54	52.35	56.17	51.18
	a. Fees and commissions receivable / Frais et commissions à recevoir	:	:	:	:	:	:	:	:	:	:
	b. Fees and commissions payable / Frais et commissions à payer	:	:	:	:	:	:	:	:	:	:
	c. Net profits or loss on financial operations / Profits ou pertes nets sur opérations financières	:	:	:	:	:	:	:	:	:	:
	d. Other / Autres	:	:	:	:	:	:	:	:	:	:
55.	Operating expenses / Frais d'exploitation	63.18	63.85	63.57	63.65	63.42	64.06	67.46	65.73	66.67	68.19
	a. Staff costs / Dépenses en personnel	34.95	35.34	35.30	35.10	35.41	35.44	37.41	36.02	36.84	37.20
	b. Property costs / Dépenses en immobilier	:	:	12.55	13.06	12.55	12.18	12.68	12.56	11.39	11.86
	c. Other / Autres	:	:	15.73	15.49	15.46	16.44	17.37	17.15	18.44	19.14
56.	Net income / Résultat net	36.82	36.15	36.43	36.35	36.58	35.94	32.54	34.27	33.33	31.81
57.	Provisions (net) / Provisions (nettes)	24.81	18.26	11.92	8.56	5.81	5.01	5.74	6.09	6.78	11.55
	a. Provisions on loans / Provisions sur prêts	24.81	18.26	11.92	8.56	5.81	5.01	5.74	6.09	6.78	11.55
	b. Provisions on securities / Provisions sur titres	:	:	:	:	:	:	:	:	:	:
	c. Other / Autres	:	:	:	:	:	:	:	:	:	:
58.	Profit before tax / Bénéfices avant impôt	12.01	17.89	24.51	27.80	30.77	30.93	26.80	28.18	26.56	20.26
59.	Income tax / Impôt sur le revenu	3.98	6.36	9.43	10.12	11.52	11.43	9.60	8.87	8.41	4.54
60.	Profit after tax / Bénéfices après impôt	8.03	11.52	15.08	17.68	19.25	19.51	17.20	19.31	18.14	15.71
	% of net income / % du total du résultat net										
61.	Provisions (net) / Provisions (nettes)	67.38	50.52	32.73	23.54	15.89	13.94	17.65	17.77	20.33	36.31
	a. Provisions on loans / Provisions sur prêts	67.38	50.52	32.73	23.54	15.89	13.94	17.65	17.77	20.33	36.31
	b. Provisions on securities / Provisions sur titres	:	:	:	:	:	:	:	:	:	:
	c. Other / Autres	:	:	:	:	:	:	:	:	:	:
62.	Profit before tax / Bénéfices avant impôt	32.62	49.48	67.27	76.46	84.11	86.06	82.35	82.23	79.67	63.69
63.	Income tax / Impôt sur le revenu	10.82	17.61	25.89	27.84	31.50	31.80	29.51	25.87	25.24	14.28
64.	Profit after tax / Bénéfices après impôt	21.80	31.87	41.39	48.62	52.61	54.27	52.84	56.36	54.43	49.41

CANADA
Commercial banks

Per cent

BALANCE SHEET ANALYSIS

% of year-end balance sheet total

CANADA
Banques commerciales

Pourcentage

ANALYSE DU BILAN

% du total du bilan en fin d'exercice

	1992	1993	1994	1995	1996	1997	1998	1999	2000	2001		
Assets											**Actif**	
65. Cash & balance with Central bank	1.02	0.81	0.61	0.55	0.58	0.40	0.38	0.43	0.36	0.40	65.	Caisse & solde auprès de la Banque centrale
66. Interbank deposits	6.25	5.93	7.44	9.42	8.03	7.95	5.90	6.62	5.35	4.70	66.	Dépôts interbancaires
67. Loans	73.22	71.11	69.31	66.47	67.46	64.77	61.26	61.32	60.38	58.06	67.	Prêts
68. Securities	15.61	17.91	18.68	19.62	20.01	17.78	19.62	22.38	23.50	24.11	68.	Valeurs mobilières
69. Other assets	3.90	4.23	3.96	3.94	3.93	9.10	12.83	9.24	10.41	12.73	69.	Autres actifs
Liabilities											**Passif**	
70. Capital & reserves	5.54	5.50	5.34	5.19	4.86	4.70	4.76	5.17	5.29	5.32	70.	Capital et réserves
71. Borrowing from Central bank	-	0.05	0.01	0.03	-	-	-	0.02	0.02	0.01	71.	Emprunts auprès de la Banque centrale
72. Interbank deposits	14.12	12.74	13.50	14.17	13.98	12.28	11.68	11.04	9.31	8.68	72.	Dépôts interbancaires
73. Non-bank deposits	70.47	69.25	66.57	64.40	60.13	57.90	55.90	59.39	62.13	59.80	73.	Dépôts non bancaires
74. Bonds	2.15	2.38	2.24	2.12	1.96	2.10	1.95	1.94	2.01	1.81	74.	Obligations
75. Other liabilities	7.72	10.08	12.34	14.09	19.07	23.02	25.71	22.44	21.23	24.38	75.	Autres engagements
Memorandum items											**Pour mémoire**	
76. Short-term securities	..	..	..	..	..	..	..	..	..	..	76.	Titres à court terme
77. Bonds	..	..	..	..	..	..	..	..	..	..	77.	Obligations
78. Shares and participations	..	..	..	..	..	..	..	..	..	..	78.	Actions et participations
79. Claims on non-residents	..	..	..	..	..	..	..	..	..	..	79.	Créances sur des non-résidents
80. Liabilities to non-residents	..	..	..	..	..	..	..	..	..	..	80.	Engagements envers des non-résidents

* See notes on previous pages.

* Voir les notes en pages précédentes.

54

CANADA

Foreign commercial banks

Million Canadian dollars

CANADA

Banques commerciales étrangères

Millions de dollars canadiens

#	English	Français	1992	1993	1994	1995	1996	1997	1998	1999	2000	2001
	INCOME STATEMENT	**COMPTE DE RESULTATS**										
1.	Interest income	Produits financiers	3792	3515	3608	4927	4638	4534	5941	5637	5635	4089
2.	Interest expenses	Frais financiers	2908	2628	2580	3696	3243	3248	4485	4189	3896	2402
3.	Net interest income	Produits financiers nets	884	887	1028	1231	1395	1286	1456	1449	1739	1687
4.	Non-interest income (net)	Produits non financiers (nets)	787	884	935	769	884	1209	1327	1592	1945	2115
	a. Fees and commissions receivable	a. Frais et commissions à recevoir	..	..	..	..	..	..	..	..	..	..
	b. Fees and commissions payable	b. Frais et commissions à payer	..	..	..	..	..	..	..	..	..	..
	c. Net profits or loss on financial operations	c. Profits ou pertes nets sur opérations financières	..	..	..	..	..	..	..	..	..	..
	d. Other	d. Autres	..	..	..	..	..	..	..	..	..	..
5.	Gross income	Résultat brut	1671	1771	1963	2000	2279	2495	2783	3040	3684	3802
6.	Operating expenses	Frais d'exploitation	1168	1273	1311	1386	1572	1766	2060	2269	2502	2307
	a. Staff costs	a. Dépenses en personnel	434	478	515	541	661	723	823	926	1021	891
	b. Property costs	b. Dépenses en immobilier	..	..	181	195	221	225	277	286	292	275
	c. Other	c. Autres	..	..	615	650	690	818	960	1057	1188	1140
7.	Net income	Résultat net	503	498	652	614	707	729	723	772	1182	1496
8.	Provisions (net)	Provisions (nettes)	1102	628	451	241	197	95	384	229	562	506
	a. Provisions on loans	a. Provisions sur prêts	1102	628	451	241	197	95	384	229	562	506
	b. Provisions on securities	b. Provisions sur titres	..	..	..	..	..	..	..	..	..	..
	c. Other	c. Autres	..	..	..	..	..	..	..	..	..	..
9.	Profit before tax	Bénéfices avant impôt	-599	-130	201	373	510	634	338	543	620	990
10.	Income tax	Impôt sur le revenu	-212	13	150	163	214	255	122	250	349	358
11.	Profit after tax	Bénéfices après impôt	-386	-143	51	210	296	379	216	293	271	633
12.	Distributed profit	Bénéfices distribués	..	..	..	..	..	..	..	..	..	..
13.	Retained profit	Bénéfices mis en réserve	..	..	..	..	..	..	..	..	..	..
	BALANCE SHEET	**BILAN**										
	Assets	*Actif*										
14.	Cash & balance with Central bank	Caisse & solde auprès de la Banque centrale	103	162	204	228	190	257	306	268	255	323
15.	Interbank deposits	Dépôts interbancaires	8260	6230	8650	7450	7434	8707	6032	6628	5930	7205
16.	Loans	Prêts	36285	37245	39464	43983	46071	53406	56913	57277	58480	51321
17.	Securities	Valeurs mobilières	9221	12474	11170	11599	12186	14501	15242	15070	17347	12821
18.	Other assets	Autres actifs	1736	2722	2053	2959	7300	10527	16263	11334	12180	13511
	Liabilities	*Passif*										
19.	Capital & reserves	Capital et réserves	3697	3830	4012	4176	4255	4983	5812	6317	7568	6841
20.	Borrowing from Central bank	Emprunts auprès de la Banque centrale	-	-	-	-	-	-	-	-	-	-
21.	Interbank deposits	Dépôts interbancaires	17049	15202	18419	19746	15756	19821	18863	15584	13139	12985
22.	Non-bank deposits	Dépôts non bancaires	27680	30565	30942	33492	37580	40076	43174	42958	52064	46127
23.	Bonds	Obligations	1147	1155	1272	1552	1540	1651	1850	1617	1652	1314
24.	Other liabilities	Autres engagements	6032	8081	6896	7253	14050	20867	25057	24101	19769	17914
	Balance sheet total	**Total du bilan**										
25.	End-year total	En fin d'exercice	55605	58833	61541	66219	73181	87398	94756	90577	94192	85181
26.	Average total	Moyen	52846	57219	60187	63880	69700	80293	91080	90770	90488	89687

CANADA

Foreign commercial banks

Million Canadian dollars

	1992	1993	1994	1995	1996	1997	1998	1999	2000	2001
Memorandum items										
27. Short-term securities	..	..	..	..	..	..	..	..	..	
28. Bonds	..	..	..	..	..	..	..	..	..	
29. Shares and participations	..	..	..	..	..	..	..	..	..	
30. Claims on non-residents	..	..	..	..	..	..	..	..	..	
31. Liabilities to non-residents	..	..	..	..	..	..	..	..	..	
Capital adequacy										
32. Tier 1 Capital	..	..	..	..	..	..	..	..	..	
33. Tier 2 Capital	..	..	..	..	..	..	..	..	..	
34. Supervisory deductions	..	..	..	..	..	..	..	..	..	
35. Total net capital resources	..	..	..	..	..	..	..	..	..	
36. Risk-weighted assets	..	..	..	..	..	..	..	..	..	
SUPPLEMENTARY INFORMATION										
37. Number of institutions	56	56	53	50	50	45	45	44	44	33
38. Number of branches	..	..	..	..	..	..	..	..	..	
39. Number of employees (x 1000)	..	..	..	..	..	..	..	..	..	

Notes

The reporting period is the fiscal year ending 31st October.

CANADA

Banques commerciales étrangères

Millions de dollars canadiens

Pour mémoire	
27. Titres à court terme	
28. Obligations	
29. Actions et participations	
30. Créances sur des non-résidents	
31. Engagements envers des non-résidents	
Solvabilité	
32. Fonds propres de base	
33. Fonds propres complémentaires	
34. Eléments à déduire des fonds propres	
35. Total net des ressources en capital	
36. Actifs pondérés des risques	
RENSEIGNEMENTS COMPLÉMENTAIRES	
37. Nombre d'institutions	
38. Nombre de succursales	
39. Nombre de salariés (x 1000)	

Notes

La période couverte est l'exercice fiscale qui se termine le 31 octobre.

CANADA

Foreign commercial banks

Per cent

INCOME STATEMENT ANALYSIS

#	Item (EN / FR)	1992	1993	1994	1995	1996	1997	1998	1999	2000	2001
	% of average balance sheet total / % du total moyen du bilan										
40.	Interest income / Produits financiers	7.18	6.14	5.99	7.71	6.65	5.65	6.52	6.21	6.23	4.56
41.	Interest expenses / Frais financiers	5.50	4.59	4.29	5.79	4.65	4.05	4.92	4.61	4.31	2.68
42.	Net interest income / Produits financiers nets	1.67	1.55	1.71	1.93	2.00	1.60	1.60	1.60	1.92	1.88
43.	Non-interest income (net) / Produits non financiers (nets)	1.49	1.54	1.55	1.20	1.27	1.51	1.46	1.75	2.15	2.36
	a. Fees and commissions receivable / Frais et commissions à recevoir										
	b. Fees and commissions payable / Frais et commissions à payer										
	c. Net profits or loss on financial operations / Profits ou pertes nets sur opérations financières										
	d. Other / Autres										
44.	Gross income / Résultat brut	3.16	3.10	3.26	3.13	3.27	3.11	3.06	3.35	4.07	4.24
45.	Operating expenses / Frais d'exploitation	2.21	2.22	2.18	2.17	2.26	2.20	2.26	2.50	2.77	2.57
	a. Staff costs / Dépenses en personnel	0.82	0.84	0.86	0.85	0.95	0.90	0.90	1.02	1.13	0.99
	b. Property costs / Dépenses en immobilier	..	..	0.30	0.31	0.32	0.28	0.30	0.32	0.32	0.31
	c. Other / Autres	..	..	1.02	1.02	0.99	1.02	1.05	1.16	1.31	1.27
46.	Net income / Résultat net	0.95	0.87	1.08	0.96	1.01	0.91	0.79	0.85	1.31	1.67
47.	Provisions (net) / Provisions (nettes)	2.09	1.10	0.75	0.38	0.28	0.12	0.42	0.25	0.62	0.56
	a. Provisions on loans / Provisions sur prêts	2.09	1.10	0.75	0.38	0.28	0.12	0.42	0.25	0.62	0.56
	b. Provisions on securities / Provisions sur titres										
	c. Other / Autres										
48.	Profit before tax / Bénéfices avant impôt	-1.13	-0.23	0.33	0.58	0.73	0.79	0.37	0.60	0.69	1.10
49.	Income tax / Impôt sur le revenu	-0.40	0.02	0.25	0.26	0.31	0.32	0.13	0.28	0.39	0.40
50.	Profit after tax / Bénéfices après impôt	-0.73	-0.25	0.08	0.33	0.42	0.47	0.24	0.32	0.30	0.71
51.	Distributed profit / Bénéfices distribués										
52.	Retained profit / Bénéfices mis en réserve										
	% of gross income / % du total du résultat brut										
53.	Net interest income / Produits financiers nets	52.90	50.08	52.37	61.55	61.21	51.54	52.32	47.66	47.20	44.37
54.	Non-interest income (net) / Produits non financiers (nets)	47.10	49.92	47.63	38.45	38.79	48.46	47.68	52.37	52.80	55.63
	a. Fees and commissions receivable / Frais et commissions à recevoir										
	b. Fees and commissions payable / Frais et commissions à payer										
	c. Net profits or loss on financial operations / Profits ou pertes nets sur opérations financières										
	d. Other / Autres										
55.	Operating expenses / Frais d'exploitation	69.90	71.88	66.79	69.30	68.98	70.78	74.02	74.64	67.92	60.68
	a. Staff costs / Dépenses en personnel	25.97	26.99	26.24	27.05	29.00	28.98	29.57	30.46	27.71	23.44
	b. Property costs / Dépenses en immobilier	..	..	9.22	9.75	9.70	9.02	9.95	9.41	7.93	7.23
	c. Other / Autres	30.10	..	31.33	32.50	30.28	32.79	34.50	34.77	32.25	29.98
56.	Net income / Résultat net	30.10	28.12	33.21	30.70	31.02	29.22	25.98	25.39	32.08	39.35
57.	Provisions (net) / Provisions (nettes)	65.95	35.46	22.98	12.05	8.64	3.81	13.80	7.53	15.26	13.31
	a. Provisions on loans / Provisions sur prêts	65.95	35.46	22.98	12.05	8.64	3.81	13.80	7.53	15.26	13.31
	b. Provisions on securities / Provisions sur titres										
	c. Other / Autres										
58.	Profit before tax / Bénéfices avant impôt	-35.85	-7.34	10.24	18.65	22.38	25.41	12.15	17.86	16.83	26.04
59.	Income tax / Impôt sur le revenu	-12.69	0.73	7.64	8.15	9.39	10.22	4.38	8.22	9.47	9.42
60.	Profit after tax / Bénéfices après impôt	-23.10	-8.07	2.60	10.50	12.99	15.19	7.76	9.64	7.36	16.65
	% of net income / % du total du résultat net										
61.	Provisions (net) / Provisions (nettes)	219.09	126.10	69.17	39.25	27.86	13.03	53.11	29.66	47.55	33.82
	a. Provisions on loans / Provisions sur prêts	219.09	126.10	69.17	39.25	27.86	13.03	53.11	29.66	47.55	33.82
	b. Provisions on securities / Provisions sur titres										
	c. Other / Autres										
62.	Profit before tax / Bénéfices avant impôt	-119.09	-26.10	30.83	60.75	72.14	86.97	46.75	70.34	52.45	66.18
63.	Income tax / Impôt sur le revenu	-42.15	2.61	23.01	26.55	30.27	34.98	16.87	32.38	29.53	23.93
64.	Profit after tax / Bénéfices après impôt	-76.74	-28.71	7.82	34.20	41.87	51.99	29.88	37.95	22.93	42.31

CANADA
Foreign commercial banks

CANADA
Banques commerciales étrangères

Per cent	1992	1993	1994	1995	1996	1997	1998	1999	2000	2001		Pourcentage
BALANCE SHEET ANALYSIS												**ANALYSE DU BILAN**
% of year-end balance sheet total												**% du total du bilan en fin d'exercice**
Assets												**Actif**
65. Cash & balance with Central bank	0.19	0.28	0.33	0.34	0.26	0.29	0.32	0.30	0.27	0.38	65.	Caisse & solde auprès de la Banque centrale
66. Interbank deposits	14.85	10.59	14.06	11.25	10.16	9.96	6.37	7.32	6.30	8.46	66.	Dépôts interbancaires
67. Loans	65.25	63.31	64.13	66.42	62.95	61.11	60.06	63.24	62.09	60.25	67.	Prêts
68. Securities	16.58	21.20	18.15	17.52	16.65	16.59	16.09	16.64	18.42	15.05	68.	Valeurs mobilières
69. Other assets	3.12	4.63	3.34	4.47	9.98	12.04	17.16	12.51	12.93	15.86	69.	Autres actifs
Liabilities												**Passif**
70. Capital & reserves	6.65	6.51	6.52	6.31	5.81	5.70	6.13	6.97	8.03	8.03	70.	Capital et réserves
71. Borrowing from Central bank	-	-	-	-	-	-	-	-	-	-	71.	Emprunts auprès de la Banque centrale
72. Interbank deposits	30.66	25.84	29.93	29.82	21.53	22.68	19.91	17.21	13.95	15.24	72.	Dépôts interbancaires
73. Non-bank deposits	49.78	51.95	50.28	50.58	51.35	45.85	45.56	47.43	55.27	54.15	73.	Dépôts non bancaires
74. Bonds	2.06	1.96	2.07	2.34	2.10	1.89	1.95	1.79	1.75	1.54	74.	Obligations
75. Other liabilities	10.85	13.74	11.21	10.95	19.20	23.88	26.44	26.61	20.99	21.03	75.	Autres engagements
Memorandum items												**Pour mémoire**
76. Short-term securities	:	:	:	:	:	:	:	:	:	:	76.	Titres à court terme
77. Bonds	:	:	:	:	:	:	:	:	:	:	77.	Obligations
78. Shares and participations	:	:	:	:	:	:	:	:	:	:	78.	Actions et participations
79. Claims on non-residents	:	:	:	:	:	:	:	:	:	:	79.	Créances sur des non-résidents
80. Liabilities to non-residents	:	:	:	:	:	:	:	:	:	:	80.	Engagements envers des non-résidents

* See notes on previous pages.

* Voir les notes en pages précédentes.

58

CZECH REPUBLIC

All banks

REPUBLIQUE TCHEQUE

Ensemble des banques

Million Czech koruna / *Millions de couronnes tchèques*

	1993	1994	1995	1996	1997	1998	1999	2000	2001		
INCOME STATEMENT										**COMPTE DE RESULTATS**	
1. Interest income	133675	139901	143808	155260	188327	221437	159957	127067	114018	1. Produits financiers	
2. Interest expenses	85325	88669	96115	113059	141824	162520	108671	81544	71397	2. Frais financiers	
3. Net interest income	48350	51232	47692	42201	46503	58918	51286	45523	42621	3. Produits financiers nets	
4. Non-interest income (net)	66842	91521	116052	152645	238230	238805	270570	486255	70891	4. Produits non financiers (nets)	
a. Fees and commissions receivable	8283	9770	10655	13357	14028	17416	20082	23117	25810	a. Frais et commissions à recevoir	
b. Fees and commissions payable	717	889	1149	1550	1716	4344	5459	5652	4835	b. Frais et commissions à payer	
c. Net profits or loss on financial operations	9727	11142	15837	19164	27663	24442	24970	17311	28913	c. Net profits ou pertes nets sur opérations financières	
d. Other	49549	71498	90709	121674	198255	201297	230977	451479	21003	d. Autres	
5. Gross income	115192	142753	163745	194846	284733	297722	321856	531777	113512	5. Résultat brut	
6. Operating expenses	70850	103918	134072	188723	263175	291803	334327	555902	85280	6. Frais d'exploitation	
a. Staff costs	8519	11446	14138	16776	18285	18416	19887	20663	22326	a. Dépenses en personnel	
b. Property costs	14550	17836	22372	26025	28465	32411	31534	32559	33228	b. Dépenses en immobilier	
c. Other	47781	74636	97562	145922	216425	240976	282906	502680	29726	c. Autres	
7. Net income	44342	38835	29673	6123	21558	5919	-12471	-24125	28232	7. Résultat net	
8. Provisions (net)	36919	31591	23958	14533	27181	25030	25506	-24311	5290	8. Provisions (nettes)	
a. Provisions on loans	..	..	..	..	..	12373	25350	-2887	5031	a. Provisions sur prêts	
b. Provisions on securities	..	..	..	..	..	1524	-294	-7371	1423	b. Provisions sur titres	
c. Other	..	..	..	..	..	11133	450	-14053	-1163	c. Autres	
9. Profit before tax	7423	7244	5714	-8410	-5623	-19111	-37976	186	22942	9. Bénéfices avant impôt	
10. Income tax	3625	3492	3463	1542	798	2763	1264	-1498	5835	10. Impôt sur le revenu	
11. Profit after tax	3798	3752	2251	-9953	-6421	-21874	-39241	1684	17107	11. Bénéfices après impôt	
12. Distributed profit	..	2649	4496	12833	14660	62462	3472	..	..	12. Bénéfices distribués	
13. Retained profit	..	1103	-2245	-22786	-21081	-84336	-42713	1684	17107	13. Bénéfices mis en réserve	
BALANCE SHEET										**BILAN**	
Assets										**Actif**	
14. Cash & balance with Central bank	81620	91634	173211	170233	228254	296064	311176	324457	360381	14. Caisse & solde auprès de la Banque centrale	
15. Interbank deposits	279544	313736	328152	398807	485851	501149	576670	592138	561305	15. Dépôts interbancaires	
16. Loans	720392	838940	915706	982668	1053477	1028587	941988	953330	921808	16. Prêts	
17. Securities	109256	186627	346168	329832	347509	410967	487816	628740	743934	17. Valeurs mobilières	
18. Other assets	84960	107569	139802	221073	215743	200543	211677	218566	179431	18. Autres actifs	
Liabilities										**Passif**	
19. Capital & reserves	148914	195365	201686	204722	210104	226430	209466	222875	166385	19. Capital et réserves	
20. Borrowing from Central bank	77836	77783	74078	79934	97071	52843	33764	18342	4717	20. Emprunts auprès de la Banque centrale	
21. Interbank deposits	254535	306762	408997	486023	495723	504745	492029	488215	367130	21. Dépôts interbancaires	
22. Non-bank deposits	730724	857672	973065	1045616	1154228	1182199	1200467	1251733	1603535	22. Dépôts non bancaires	
23. Bonds	3784	27622	56159	63656	93140	92876	98906	102427	81038	23. Obligations	
24. Other liabilities	59979	73302	189057	222662	280568	378217	494695	633640	544054	24. Autres engagements	
Balance sheet total										**Total du bilan**	
25. End-year total	1275772	1538506	1903042	2102613	2330834	2437310	2529327	2717232	2766859	25. En fin d'exercice	
26. Average total	..	1407139	1572440	1704983	1830153	1931346	2016772	2104330	2177944	26. Moyen	

CZECH REPUBLIC

All banks

REPUBLIQUE TCHEQUE

Ensemble des banques

Million Czech koruna

	1993	1994	1995	1996	1997	1998	1999	2000	2001		*Millions de couronnes tchèques*
Memorandum items											***Pour mémoire***
27. Short-term securities	..	..	..	..	..	..	282456	345765	417843	27.	*Titres à court terme*
28. Bonds	..	..	..	..	..	..	133232	191638	235556	28.	*Obligations*
29. Shares and participations	..	..	..	..	..	..	65042	85220	65669	29.	*Actions et participations*
30. Claims on non-residents	103838	114918	138507	189366	309206	351055	487610	512813	591267	30.	*Créances sur des non-résidents*
31. Liabilities to non-residents	64176	95863	204386	265596	329758	324034	364028	336998	319586	31.	*Engagements envers des non-résidents*
Capital adequacy											***Solvabilité***
32. Tier 1 Capital	..	..	99584	107528	125430	147148	129892	109962	117661	32.	*Fonds propres de base*
33. Tier 2 Capital	..	..	14511	15672	19113	35019	36857	26551	25874	33.	*Fonds propres complémentaires*
34. Supervisory deductions	..	..	22969	21410	34542	55118	32987	12285	11222	34.	*Eléments à déduire des fonds propres*
35. Total net capital resources	..	..	91126	101790	110001	127049	133762	124228	132312	35.	*Total net des ressources en capital*
36. Risk-weighted assets	..	..	1022073	1047409	1139593	1065470	980372	774369	791540	36.	*Actifs pondérés des risques*
SUPPLEMENTARY INFORMATION											**RENSEIGNEMENTS COMPLEMENTAIRES**
37. Number of institutions	53	56	58	53	50	45	42	40	38	37.	*Nombre d'institutions*
38. Number of branches	1497	1462	3411	3172	2467	2220	2006	1809	1800	38.	*Nombre de succursales*
39. Number of employees (x 1000)	51.0	57.0	61.5	58.8	60.8	52.8	49.3	45.5	40.9	39.	*Nombre de salariés (x 1000)*

Per cent — *Pourcentage*

INCOME STATEMENT ANALYSIS — **ANALYSE DU COMPTE DE RESULTATS**

% of average balance sheet total — **% du total moyen du bilan**

		1993	1994	1995	1996	1997	1998	1999	2000	2001		
40.	Interest income	..	9.94	9.15	9.11	10.29	11.47	7.93	6.04	5.24	Produits financiers	40.
41.	Interest expenses	..	6.30	6.11	6.63	7.75	8.41	5.39	3.88	3.28	Frais financiers	41.
42.	Net interest income	..	3.64	3.03	2.48	2.54	3.05	2.54	2.16	1.96	Produits financiers nets	42.
43.	Non-interest income (net)	..	6.50	7.38	8.95	13.02	12.36	13.42	23.11	3.25	Produits non financiers (nets)	43.
	a. Fees and commissions receivable	..	0.69	0.68	0.78	0.77	0.90	1.00	1.10	1.19	a. Frais et commissions à recevoir	
	b. Fees and commissions payable	..	0.06	0.07	0.09	0.09	0.22	0.27	0.27	0.22	b. Frais et commissions à payer	
	c. Net profits or loss on financial operations	..	0.79	1.01	1.12	1.51	1.27	1.24	0.82	1.33	c. Profits ou pertes nets sur opérations financières	
	d. Other	..	5.08	5.77	7.14	10.83	10.42	11.45	21.45	0.96	d. Autres	
44.	Gross income	..	10.14	10.41	11.43	15.56	15.42	15.96	25.27	5.21	Résultat brut	44.
45.	Operating expenses	..	7.39	8.53	11.07	14.38	15.11	16.58	26.42	3.92	Frais d'exploitation	45.
	a. Staff costs	..	0.81	0.90	0.98	1.00	0.95	0.99	0.98	1.03	a. Dépenses en personnel	
	b. Property costs	..	1.27	1.42	1.53	1.56	1.68	1.56	1.55	1.53	b. Dépenses en immobilier	
	c. Other	..	5.30	6.20	8.56	11.83	12.48	14.03	23.89	1.36	c. Autres	
46.	Net income	..	2.76	1.89	0.36	1.18	0.31	-0.62	-1.15	1.30	Résultat net	46.
47.	Provisions (net)	..	2.25	1.52	0.85	1.49	1.30	1.26	-1.16	0.24	Provisions (nettes)	47.
	a. Provisions on loans	..	..	..	..	..	0.64	1.26	-0.14	0.23	a. Provisions sur prêts	
	b. Provisions on securities	..	..	..	..	..	0.08	-0.01	-0.35	0.07	b. Provisions sur titres	
	c. Other	..	..	..	..	..	0.58	0.02	-0.67	-0.05	c. Autres	
48.	Profit before tax	..	0.51	0.36	-0.49	-0.31	-0.99	-1.88	0.01	1.05	Bénéfices avant impôt	48.
49.	Income tax	..	0.25	0.22	0.09	0.04	0.14	0.06	-0.07	0.27	Impôt sur le revenu	49.
50.	Profit after tax	..	0.27	0.14	-0.58	-0.35	-1.13	-1.95	0.08	0.79	Bénéfices après impôt	50.
51.	Distributed profit	..	0.19	0.29	0.75	0.80	3.23	0.17			Bénéfices distribués	51.
52.	Retained profit	..	0.08	-0.14	-1.34	-1.15	-4.37	-2.12	0.08	0.79	Bénéfices mis en réserve	52.

% of gross income — **% du total du résultat brut**

		1993	1994	1995	1996	1997	1998	1999	2000	2001		
53.	Net interest income	41.97	35.89	29.13	21.66	16.33	19.79	15.93	8.56	37.55	Produits financiers nets	53.
54.	Non-interest income (net)	58.03	64.11	70.87	78.34	83.67	80.21	84.07	91.44	62.45	Produits non financiers (nets)	54.
	a. Fees and commissions receivable	7.19	6.84	6.51	6.86	4.93	5.85	6.24	4.35	22.74	a. Frais et commissions à recevoir	
	b. Fees and commissions payable	0.62	0.62	0.70	0.80	0.60	1.46	1.70	1.06	4.26	b. Frais et commissions à payer	
	c. Net profits or loss on financial operations	8.44	7.81	9.67	9.84	9.72	8.21	7.76	3.26	25.47	c. Profits ou pertes nets sur opérations financières	
	d. Other	43.01	50.09	55.40	62.45	69.63	67.61	71.76	84.90	18.50	d. Autres	
55.	Operating expenses	61.51	72.80	81.88	96.86	92.43	98.01	103.87	104.54	75.13	Frais d'exploitation	55.
	a. Staff costs	7.40	8.02	8.63	8.61	6.42	6.19	6.18	3.89	19.67	a. Dépenses en personnel	
	b. Property costs	12.63	12.49	13.66	13.36	10.00	10.89	9.80	6.12	29.27	b. Dépenses en immobilier	
	c. Other	41.48	52.28	59.58	74.89	76.01	80.94	87.90	94.53	26.19	c. Autres	
56.	Net income	38.49	27.20	18.12	3.14	7.57	1.99	-3.87	-4.54	24.87	Résultat net	56.
57.	Provisions (net)	32.05	22.13	14.63	7.46	9.55	8.41	7.92	-4.57	4.66	Provisions (nettes)	57.
	a. Provisions on loans	..	..	..	..	..	4.16	7.88	-0.54	4.43	a. Provisions sur prêts	
	b. Provisions on securities	..	..	..	..	..	0.51	-0.09	-1.39	1.25	b. Provisions sur titres	
	c. Other	..	..	..	..	..	3.74	0.14	-2.64	-1.02	c. Autres	
58.	Profit before tax	6.44	5.07	3.49	-4.32	-1.97	-6.42	-11.80	0.03	20.21	Bénéfices avant impôt	58.
59.	Income tax	3.15	2.45	2.11	0.79	0.28	0.93	0.39	-0.28	5.14	Impôt sur le revenu	59.
60.	Profit after tax	3.30	2.63	1.37	-5.11	-2.26	-7.35	-12.19	0.32	15.07	Bénéfices après impôt	60.

% of net income — **% du total du résultat net**

		1993	1994	1995	1996	1997	1998	1999	2000	2001		
61.	Provisions (net)	83.26	81.35	80.74	237.37	126.08	422.85	-204.52	100.77	18.74	Provisions (nettes)	61.
	a. Provisions on loans	..	..	..	..	..	209.03	-203.27	11.97	17.82	a. Provisions sur prêts	
	b. Provisions on securities	..	..	..	..	..	25.74	2.36	30.55	5.04	b. Provisions sur titres	
	c. Other	..	..	..	..	..	188.08	-3.61	58.25	-4.12	c. Autres	
62.	Profit before tax	16.74	18.65	19.26	-137.37	-26.08	-322.85	304.52	-0.77	81.26	Bénéfices avant impôt	62.
63.	Income tax	8.18	8.99	11.67	25.19	3.70	46.68	-10.14	6.21	20.67	Impôt sur le revenu	63.
64.	Profit after tax	8.57	9.66	7.59	-162.55	-29.79	-369.53	314.66	-6.98	60.59	Bénéfices après impôt	64.

CZECH REPUBLIC
All banks

REPUBLIQUE TCHEQUE
Ensemble des banques

Per cent / *Pourcentage*

	1993	1994	1995	1996	1997	1998	1999	2000	2001		
BALANCE SHEET ANALYSIS										**ANALYSE DU BILAN**	
% of year-end balance sheet total										**% du total du bilan en fin d'exercice**	
Assets										**Actif**	
65. Cash & balance with Central bank	6.40	5.96	9.10	8.10	9.79	12.15	12.30	11.94	13.02	65.	Caisse & solde auprès de la Banque centrale
66. Interbank deposits	21.91	20.39	17.24	18.97	20.84	20.56	22.80	21.79	20.29	66.	Dépôts interbancaires
67. Loans	56.47	54.53	48.12	46.74	45.20	42.20	37.24	35.08	33.32	67.	Prêts
68. Securities	8.56	12.13	18.19	15.69	14.91	16.86	19.29	23.14	26.89	68.	Valeurs mobilières
69. Other assets	6.66	6.99	7.35	10.51	9.26	8.23	8.37	8.04	6.48	69.	Autres actifs
Liabilities										**Passif**	
70. Capital & reserves	11.67	12.70	10.60	9.74	9.01	9.29	8.28	8.20	6.01	70.	Capital et réserves
71. Borrowing from Central bank	6.10	5.06	3.89	3.80	4.16	2.17	1.33	0.68	0.17	71.	Emprunts auprès de la Banque centrale
72. Interbank deposits	19.95	19.94	21.49	23.12	21.27	20.71	19.45	17.97	13.27	72.	Dépôts interbancaires
73. Non-bank deposits	57.28	55.75	51.13	49.73	49.52	48.50	47.46	46.07	57.96	73.	Dépôts non bancaires
74. Bonds	0.30	1.80	2.95	3.03	4.00	3.81	3.91	3.77	2.93	74.	Obligations
75. Other liabilities	4.70	4.76	9.93	10.59	12.04	15.52	19.56	23.32	19.66	75.	Autres engagements
Memorandum items										*Pour mémoire*	
76. Short-term securities	..	..	..	..	..	..	11.17	12.72	15.10	76.	Titres à court terme
77. Bonds	..	..	..	..	..	..	5.27	7.05	8.51	77.	Obligations
78. Shares and participations	..	..	..	..	..	..	2.57	3.14	2.37	78.	Actions et participations
79. Claims on non-residents	8.14	7.47	7.28	9.01	13.27	14.40	19.28	18.87	21.37	79.	Créances sur des non-résidents
80. Liabilities to non-residents	5.03	6.23	10.74	12.63	14.15	13.29	14.39	12.40	11.55	80.	Engagements envers des non-résidents

DENMARK
Commercial banks and savings banks

DANEMARK
Banques commerciales et caisses d'épargne

Million Danish kroner / *Millions de couronnes danoises*

		1992	1993	1994	1995	1996	1997[1]	1998	1999	2000	2001	
INCOME STATEMENT												**COMPTE DE RESULTATS**
1. Interest income		98915	96366	77135	69679	64411	67707	76298	74149	93353	98469	1. Produits financiers
2. Interest expenses		64453	59298	39070	40340	35937	39616	47698	44695	62185	63403	2. Frais financiers
3. Net interest income		34462	37068	38065	29339	28474	28091	28601	29453	31168	35067	3. Produits financiers nets
4. Non-interest income (net) (2)		-3984	9435	-5450	14289	13476	13078	16390	17880	24836	22745	4. Produits non financiers (nets) (2)
a. Fees and commissions receivable		..	..	..	7296	8361	9206	11006	12727	15662	14680	*a. Frais et commissions à recevoir*
b. Fees and commissions payable		..	..	..	837	850	1171	1430	1931	2535	2488	*b. Frais et commissions à payer*
c. Net profits or loss on financial operations		..	..	..	9071	6880	4801	4613	5183	10085	8891	*c. Profits ou pertes nets sur opérations financières*
d. Other		..	..	..	-1241	-915	242	2201	1901	1625	1662	*d. Autres*
5. Gross income		30478	46503	32615	43628	41950	41169	44991	47333	56004	57811	5. Résultat brut
6. Operating expenses		24800	23759	23650	23558	23860	24362	26894	29381	33346	30672	6. Frais d'exploitation
a. Staff costs		15141	14497	14627	14477	14234	14313	15546	16697	18314	18783	*a. Dépenses en personnel*
b. Property costs		..	..	..	..	..	..	..	..	..	..	*b. Dépenses en immobilier*
c. Other		..	..	..	..	..	..	..	..	..	..	*c. Autres*
7. Net income		5678	22744	8965	20070	18090	16807	18097	17952	22658	27139	7. Résultat net
8. Provisions (net)		17331	16651	8924	7042	5152	4088	4672	4399	4853	6957	8. Provisions (nettes)
a. Provisions on loans		15826	15108	7382	5542	3681	2556	2787	2641	3060	5173	*a. Provisions sur prêts*
b. Provisions on securities		..	..	..	..	..	..	..	..	..	..	*b. Provisions sur titres*
c. Other		..	..	..	..	..	..	..	..	..	..	*c. Autres*
9. Profit before tax		-11653	6093	41	13028	12940	12720	13425	13553	17805	20183	9. Bénéfices avant impôt
10. Income tax		189	2114	361	2261	2107	1178	2163	2479	3434	5082	10. Impôt sur le revenu
11. Profit after tax		-11842	3979	-320	10767	10832	11542	11262	11074	14371	15101	11. Bénéfices après impôt
12. Distributed profit		959	1141	1209	1980	2755	5225	5239	4733	10053	5882	12. Bénéfices distribués
13. Retained profit		-12801	2838	-1529	8787	8076	6317	6023	6341	4318	9219	13. Bénéfices mis en réserve
BALANCE SHEET												**BILAN**
Assets												**Actif**
14. Cash & balance with Central bank		20858	37790	34464	41365	53117	70830	68685	89788	65581	80255	14. Caisse & solde auprès de la Banque centrale
15. Interbank deposits		160419	252109	183329	194171	241301	229259	266474	252034	281918	278511	15. Dépôts interbancaires
16. Loans		479976	478311	433769	440765	493336	576629	609569	690388	778770	889122	16. Prêts
17. Securities		227649	231968	251488	294531	330256	353120	392652	411575	461323	565803	17. Valeurs mobilières
18. Other assets		48069	41620	42668	45959	45869	58731	119633	130993	157785	165731	18. Autres actifs
Liabilities												**Passif**
19. Capital & reserves		55379	57424	62246	70419	80197	84294	91931	95644	116841	122083	19. Capital et réserves
20. Borrowing from Central bank		34573	83646	64046	47805	38620	32361	52282	63377	52586	86927	20. Emprunts auprès de la Banque centrale
21. Interbank deposits		242967	249313	204647	236165	302124	341318	359656	364270	423333	485048	21. Dépôts interbancaires
22. Non-bank deposits		499060	558750	557310	566019	620185	670476	700624	755449	760035	806036	22. Dépôts non bancaires
23. Bonds		32761	22524	14051	20075	30143	51717	54437	94797	109826	201095	23. Obligations
24. Other liabilities		72231	70141	63418	76308	92610	108403	198083	201242	282756	278232	24. Autres engagements
Balance sheet total												**Total du bilan**
25. End-year total		936971	1041798	945718	1016791	1163879	1288570	1457013	1574779	1745377	1979421	25. En fin d'exercice
26. Average total		967878	943654	965284	924495	1053444	1206798	1378894	1581825	1726058	1801763	26. Moyen

DENMARK

Commercial banks and savings banks

Million Danish kroner

	1992	1993	1994	1995	1996	1997 [1]	1998	1999	2000	2001
Memorandum items										
27. Short-term securities (3)	73969	51710	67767	80905	67625	72899	..	..	..	..
28. Bonds	120665	142582	146079	171087	211053	217883	323902	329864	355624	467720
29. Shares and participations	33015	37676	37642	42539	51578	62338	68750	81711	105700	98083
30. Claims on non-residents	..	..	..	..	..	..	..	..	..	..
31. Liabilities to non-residents	..	..	..	..	..	..	..	..	..	..
Capital adequacy										
32. Tier 1 Capital	..	..	..	..	..	..	..	..	..	..
33. Tier 2 Capital	..	..	..	..	..	..	..	..	..	..
34. Supervisory deductions	..	..	..	..	..	..	..	..	..	..
35. Total net capital resources	..	..	..	..	..	..	..	..	..	..
36. Risk-weighted assets	..	..	..	..	..	..	..	..	..	..
SUPPLEMENTARY INFORMATION										
37. Number of institutions	113	112	113	114	117	92	95	97	99	99
38. Number of branches	2467	2340	2245	2215	2203	2178	2185	2188	2258	2103
39. Number of employees (x 1000)	52.0	50.0	49.0	47.0	44.0	43.0	43.0	43.0	43.0	44.0

1 Break in series. See change in methodology.

2 Non-interest income (net) (item 4) includes value adjustments on foreign currency assets and liabilities and on securities.

3 As from 1998, Short term securities are no longer available, they are included in Bonds

Notes

Average balance sheet totals (item 26) are based on day-to-day data

Change in methodology

As from 1997, the statistics cover domestic banks with a working capital of more than DKr 250 million (DKr 100 million through 1996).

DANEMARK

Banques commerciales et caisses d'épargne

Millions de couronnes danoises

Pour mémoire

27. Titres à court terme (3)
28. Obligations
29. Actions et participations
30. Créances sur des non-résidents
31. Engagements envers des non-résidents

Solvabilité

32. Fonds propres de base
33. Fonds propres complémentaires
34. Eléments à déduire des fonds propres
35. Total net des ressources en capital
36. Actifs pondérés des risques

RENSEIGNEMENTS COMPLEMENTAIRES

37. Nombre d'institutions
38. Nombre de succursales
39. Nombre de salariés (x 1000)

1 Rupture de séries. Voir changement méthodologique

2 Les Produits non financiers (nets) (poste 4) contiennent des ajustements en valeurs concernant les actifs/passifs en monnaies étrangères et les valeurs mobilières.

3 A partir de 1998, les Titres à court terme ne sont plus disponibles, ils sont inclus dans la rubrique des Obligations.

Notes

La moyenne du total des actifs/passifs (poste 26) est basée sur des données au jour le jour.

Changement méthodologique

A partir de 1997, les données fournies englobent toutes les banques danoises dotées d'un fonds de roulement de plus de KrD 250 millions (KrD 100 millions jusqu'en 1996 inclus).

DENMARK
Commercial banks and savings banks

DANEMARK
Banques commerciales et caisses d'épargne

Per cent	1992	1993	1994	1995	1996	1997[1]	1998	1999	2000	2001	Pourcentage
INCOME STATEMENT ANALYSIS											**ANALYSE DU COMPTE DE RESULTATS**
% of average balance sheet total											**% du total moyen du bilan**
40. Interest income	10.22	10.21	7.99	7.54	6.11	5.61	5.53	4.69	5.41	5.47	40. Produits financiers
41. Interest expenses	6.66	6.28	4.05	4.36	3.41	3.28	3.46	2.83	3.60	3.52	41. Frais financiers
42. Net interest income	3.56	3.93	3.94	3.17	2.70	2.33	2.07	1.86	1.81	1.95	42. Produits financiers nets
43. Non-interest income (net)	-0.41	1.00	-0.56	1.55	1.28	1.08	1.19	1.13	1.44	1.26	43. Produits non financiers (nets)
a. Fees and commissions receivable	..	..	..	0.79	0.79	0.76	0.80	0.80	0.91	0.81	a. Frais et commissions à recevoir
b. Fees and commissions payable	..	..	..	0.09	0.08	0.10	0.10	0.12	0.15	0.14	b. Frais et commissions à payer
c. Net profits or loss on financial operations	..	..	..	0.98	0.65	0.40	0.33	0.33	0.58	0.49	c. Profits ou pertes nets sur opérations financières
d. Other	..	..	..	-0.13	-0.09	0.02	0.16	0.12	0.09	0.09	d. Autres
44. Gross income	3.15	4.93	3.38	4.72	3.98	3.41	3.26	2.99	3.24	3.21	44. Résultat brut
45. Operating expenses	2.56	2.52	2.45	2.55	2.26	2.02	1.95	1.86	1.93	1.70	45. Frais d'exploitation
a. Staff costs	1.56	1.54	1.52	1.57	1.35	1.19	1.13	1.06	1.06	1.04	a. Dépenses en personnel
b. Property costs	..	..	..	..	..	..	..	..	..	..	b. Dépenses en immobilier
c. Other	..	..	..	..	..	..	..	..	..	..	c. Autres
46. Net income	0.59	2.41	0.93	2.17	1.72	1.39	1.31	1.13	1.31	1.51	46. Résultat net
47. Provisions (net)	1.79	1.76	0.92	0.76	0.49	0.34	0.34	0.28	0.28	0.39	47. Provisions (nettes)
a. Provisions on loans	1.64	1.60	0.76	0.60	0.35	0.21	0.20	0.17	0.18	0.29	a. Provisions sur prêts
b. Provisions on securities	..	..	..	..	..	..	..	..	..	..	b. Provisions sur titres
c. Other	..	..	..	..	..	..	..	..	..	..	c. Autres
48. Profit before tax	-1.20	0.65	0.00	1.41	1.23	1.05	0.97	0.86	1.03	1.12	48. Bénéfices avant impôt
49. Income tax	0.02	0.22	0.04	0.24	0.20	0.10	0.16	0.16	0.20	0.28	49. Impôt sur le revenu
50. Profit after tax	-1.22	0.42	-0.03	1.16	1.03	0.96	0.82	0.70	0.83	0.84	50. Bénéfices après impôt
51. Distributed profit	0.10	0.12	0.13	0.21	0.26	0.43	0.38	0.30	0.58	0.33	51. Bénéfices distribués
52. Retained profit	-1.32	0.30	-0.16	0.95	0.77	0.52	0.44	0.40	0.25	0.51	52. Bénéfices mis en réserve
% of gross income											**% du total du résultat brut**
53. Net interest income	113.07	79.71	116.71	67.25	67.88	68.23	63.57	62.23	55.65	60.66	53. Produits financiers nets
54. Non-interest income (net)	-13.07	20.29	-16.71	32.75	32.12	31.77	36.43	37.77	44.35	39.34	54. Produits non financiers (nets)
a. Fees and commissions receivable	..	..	..	16.72	19.93	22.36	24.46	26.89	27.97	25.39	a. Frais et commissions à recevoir
b. Fees and commissions payable	..	..	..	1.92	2.03	2.84	3.18	4.08	4.53	4.30	b. Frais et commissions à payer
c. Net profits or loss on financial operations	..	..	..	20.79	16.40	11.66	10.25	10.95	18.01	15.38	c. Profits ou pertes nets sur opérations financières
d. Other	..	..	..	-2.84	-2.18	0.59	4.89	4.02	2.90	2.87	d. Autres
55. Operating expenses	81.37	51.09	72.51	54.00	56.88	59.18	59.78	62.07	59.54	53.06	55. Frais d'exploitation
a. Staff costs	49.68	31.17	44.85	33.18	33.93	34.77	34.55	35.28	32.70	32.49	a. Dépenses en personnel
b. Property costs	..	..	..	..	..	..	..	..	..	..	b. Dépenses en immobilier
c. Other	..	..	..	..	..	..	..	..	..	..	c. Autres
56. Net income	18.63	48.91	27.49	46.00	43.12	40.82	40.22	37.93	40.46	46.94	56. Résultat net
57. Provisions (net)	56.86	35.81	27.36	16.14	12.28	9.93	10.38	9.29	8.67	12.03	57. Provisions (nettes)
a. Provisions on loans	51.93	32.49	22.63	12.70	8.77	6.21	6.19	5.58	5.46	8.95	a. Provisions sur prêts
b. Provisions on securities	..	..	..	..	..	..	..	..	..	..	b. Provisions sur titres
c. Other	..	..	..	..	..	..	..	..	..	..	c. Autres
58. Profit before tax	-38.23	13.10	0.13	29.86	30.85	30.90	29.84	28.63	31.79	34.91	58. Bénéfices avant impôt
59. Income tax	0.62	4.55	1.11	5.18	5.02	2.86	4.81	5.24	6.13	8.79	59. Impôt sur le revenu
60. Profit after tax	-38.85	8.56	-0.98	24.68	25.82	28.04	25.03	23.40	25.66	26.12	60. Bénéfices après impôt
% of net income											**% du total du résultat net**
61. Provisions (net)	305.23	73.21	99.54	35.09	28.48	24.32	25.82	24.50	21.42	25.63	61. Provisions (nettes)
a. Provisions on loans	278.72	66.43	82.34	27.61	20.35	15.21	15.40	14.71	13.51	19.06	a. Provisions sur prêts
b. Provisions on securities	..	..	..	..	..	..	..	..	..	..	b. Provisions sur titres
c. Other	..	..	..	..	..	..	..	..	..	..	c. Autres
62. Profit before tax	-205.23	26.79	0.46	64.91	71.53	75.68	74.18	75.50	78.58	74.37	62. Bénéfices avant impôt
63. Income tax	3.33	9.29	4.03	11.27	11.65	7.01	11.95	13.81	15.16	18.73	63. Impôt sur le revenu
64. Profit after tax	-208.56	17.49	-3.57	53.65	59.88	68.67	62.23	61.69	63.43	55.64	64. Bénéfices après impôt

DENMARK
Commercial banks and savings banks

DANEMARK
Banques commerciales et caisses d'épargne

Per cent / *Pourcentage*

BALANCE SHEET ANALYSIS / **ANALYSE DU BILAN**

% of year-end balance sheet total / **% du total du bilan en fin d'exercice**

	1992	1993	1994	1995	1996	1997 [1]	1998	1999	2000	2001	
Assets											**Actif**
65. Cash & balance with Central bank	2.23	3.63	3.64	4.07	4.56	5.50	4.71	5.70	3.76	4.05	65. Caisse & solde auprès de la Banque centrale
66. Interbank deposits	17.12	24.20	19.39	19.10	20.73	17.79	18.29	16.00	16.15	14.07	66. Dépôts interbancaires
67. Loans	51.23	45.91	45.87	43.35	42.39	44.75	41.84	43.84	44.62	44.92	67. Prêts
68. Securities	24.30	22.27	26.59	28.97	28.38	27.40	26.95	26.14	26.43	28.58	68. Valeurs mobilières
69. Other assets	5.13	4.00	4.51	4.52	3.94	4.56	8.21	8.32	9.04	8.37	69. Autres actifs
Liabilities											**Passif**
70. Capital & reserves	5.91	5.51	6.58	6.93	6.89	6.54	6.31	6.07	6.69	6.17	70. Capital et réserves
71. Borrowing from Central bank	3.69	8.03	6.77	4.70	3.32	2.51	3.59	4.02	3.01	4.39	71. Emprunts auprès de la Banque centrale
72. Interbank deposits	25.93	23.93	21.64	23.23	25.96	26.49	24.68	23.13	24.25	24.50	72. Dépôts interbancaires
73. Non-bank deposits	53.26	53.63	56.82	55.67	53.29	52.03	48.09	47.97	43.55	40.72	73. Dépôts non bancaires
74. Bonds	3.50	2.16	1.49	1.97	2.59	4.01	3.74	6.02	6.29	10.16	74. Obligations
75. Other liabilities	7.71	6.73	6.71	7.50	7.96	8.41	13.60	12.78	16.20	14.06	75. Autres engagements
Memorandum items											***Pour mémoire***
76. Short-term securities	*7.89*	*4.96*	*7.17*	*7.96*	*5.81*	*5.66*	*..*	*..*	*..*	*..*	*76. Titres à court terme*
77. Bonds	*12.88*	*13.69*	*15.45*	*16.83*	*18.13*	*16.91*	*22.23*	*20.95*	*20.38*	*23.63*	*77. Obligations*
78. Shares and participations	*3.52*	*3.62*	*3.98*	*4.18*	*4.43*	*4.84*	*4.72*	*5.19*	*6.06*	*4.96*	*78. Actions et participations*
79. Claims on non-residents	*..*	*..*	*..*	*..*	*..*	*..*	*..*	*..*	*..*	*..*	*79. Créances sur des non-résidents*
80. Liabilities to non-residents	*..*	*..*	*..*	*..*	*..*	*..*	*..*	*..*	*..*	*..*	*80. Engagements envers des non-résidents*

* See notes on previous pages.   * Voir les notes en pages précédentes.

FINLAND / FINLANDE

All banks / Ensemble des banques

Million euros / Million d'euros

		1992	1993	1994	1995	1996	1997	1998	1999	2000	2001		
INCOME STATEMENT													**COMPTE DE RESULTATS**
1.	Interest income	12238	9649	6931	6546	5172	4908	5053	4763	6343	7007	1.	Produits financiers
2.	Interest expenses	10691	7554	4957	4561	3322	2964	2939	2675	3830	4470	2.	Frais financiers
3.	Net interest income	1547	2096	1975	1985	1851	1943	2114	2088	2513	2537	3.	Produits financiers nets
4.	Non-interest income (net)	2286	2890	1740	1509	1814	1627	2179	1692	1910	4546	4.	Produits non financiers (nets)
	a. Fees and commissions receivable	..	..	..	..	..	..	..	..	..	..		a. Frais et commissions à recevoir
	b. Fees and commissions payable	..	..	..	..	..	..	..	..	..	..		b. Frais et commissions à payer
	c. Net profits or loss on financial operations	..	..	..	..	..	..	..	..	..	..		c. Profits ou pertes nets sur opérations financières
	d. Other	..	..	..	..	..	..	..	..	..	..		d. Autres
5.	Gross income	3833	4985	3715	3495	3664	3571	4292	3780	4424	7083	5.	Résultat brut
6.	Operating expenses	7299	6802	5197	3921	3246	2620	3702	2673	2517	2672	6.	Frais d'exploitation
	a. Staff costs	1337	1197	1145	959	985	775	848	884	936	1036		a. Dépenses en personnel
	b. Property costs	471	486	397	311	300	275	276	249	242	246		b. Dépenses en immobilier
	c. Other	5492	5120	3655	2651	1961	1570	2578	1540	1339	1390		c. Autres
7.	Net income	-3466	-1817	-1482	-426	418	951	591	1108	1906	4411	7.	Résultat net
8.	Provisions (net)	-74	-7	-40	-16	-26	10	-19	51	135	131	8.	Provisions (nettes)
	a. Provisions on loans	-44	15	-34	..	..	..	..	..	..	..		a. Provisions sur prêts
	b. Provisions on securities	-31	-23	-6	..	..	..	..	..	..	..		b. Provisions sur titres
	c. Other	..	..	-	..	..	..	..	..	..	..		c. Autres
9.	Profit before tax	-3392	-1810	-1442	-410	444	941	609	1057	1772	4280	9.	Bénéfices avant impôt
10.	Income tax	44	30	27	58	82	130	-61	144	462	136	10.	Impôt sur le revenu
11.	Profit after tax	-3436	-1840	-1469	-468	362	811	671	914	1310	4144	11.	Bénéfices après impôt
12.	Distributed profit	10	13	11	22	100	186	122	138	369	1198	12.	Bénéfices distribués
13.	Retained profit	-3446	-1853	-1480	-489	262	625	549	775	940	2946	13.	Bénéfices mis en réserve
BALANCE SHEET													**BILAN**
Assets													**Actif**
14.	Cash & balance with Central bank	4374	2256	1987	2904	1798	2429	2995	5458	3013	1476	14.	Caisse & solde auprès de la Banque centrale
15.	Interbank deposits	4358	8590	3371	3197	2977	3986	3613	3619	3827	4488	15.	Dépôts interbancaires
16.	Loans	78051	67231	58554	53938	54005	57161	66452	72658	84502	84895	16.	Prêts
17.	Securities	21178	26075	27496	28717	25228	24887	20744	21574	20142	27433	17.	Valeurs mobilières
18.	Other assets	19970	22677	23092	19685	21756	24673	19598	22070	26325	37140	18.	Autres actifs
Liabilities													**Passif**
19.	Capital & reserves	6940	6370	5718	5168	5577	6198	6182	6975	8028	6346	19.	Capital et réserves
20.	Borrowing from Central bank	1349	964	148	1295	2121	483	4	1514	454	1294	20.	Emprunts auprès de la Banque centrale
21.	Interbank deposits	3727	2867	3299	3510	3489	4370	3318	3601	3495	3747	21.	Dépôts interbancaires
22.	Non-bank deposits	66184	62586	60609	60942	59666	63958	65042	66738	71821	81881	22.	Dépôts non bancaires
23.	Bonds	12717	10959	10628	7631	5707	6407	5674	6167	10733	8567	23.	Obligations
24.	Other liabilities	37014	43083	34097	29894	29205	31720	33183	40384	43278	53597	24.	Autres engagements
Balance sheet total													**Total du bilan**
25.	End-year total	127931	126829	114500	108440	105764	113136	113403	125380	137809	155432	25.	En fin d'exercice
26.	Average total	128751	127380	120664	111470	107103	109450	113270	119392	131595	146623	26.	Moyen

Million euros

Million d'euros

	1992	1993	1994	1995	1996	1997	1998	1999	2000	2001		
Memorandum items												**Pour mémoire**
27. Short-term securities	7944	11202	14403	10906	8598	8920	8636	9681	9685	9661	27.	Titres à court terme
28. Bonds	10913	12535	10645	13477	12182	11757	9963	9815	8319	7019	28.	Obligations
29. Shares and participations	2321	2337	2449	4333	4449	4210	2145	2079	2139	10753	29.	Actions et participations
30. Claims on non-residents	19575	21648	18111	17658	21050	26476	23270	29280	40516	53765	30.	Créances sur des non-résidents
31. Liabilities to non-residents	35662	31211	24477	21443	20217	23492	20787	24715	38752	48863	31.	Engagements envers des non-résidents
Capital adequacy												**Solvabilité**
32. Tier 1 Capital	..	..	..	..	..	..	..	..	..	..	32.	Fonds propres de base
33. Tier 2 Capital	..	..	..	..	..	..	..	..	..	..	33.	Fonds propres complémentaires
34. Supervisory deductions	..	..	..	..	..	..	..	..	..	..	34.	Eléments à déduire des fonds propres
35. Total net capital resources	..	..	..	..	..	..	..	..	..	..	35.	Total net des ressources en capital
36. Risk-weighted assets	..	..	..	..	..	..	..	..	..	..	36.	Actifs pondérés des risques
SUPPLEMENTARY INFORMATION												**RENSEIGNEMENTS COMPLÉMENTAIRES**
37. Number of institutions	370	358	357	351	350	348	347	345	342	342	37.	Nombre d'institutions
38. Number of branches	2393	2200	1828	1612	1409	1306	1268	1209	1221	1282	38.	Nombre de succursales
39. Number of employees (x 1000)	39	36	34	31	27	26	24	24	25	25	39.	Nombre de salariés (x 1000)

Notes

. All banks include Commercial banks, Post office bank, Foreign commercia banks, Savings banks and Co-operative banks.

Notes

. L'Ensemble des banques comprend les Banques commerciales, la Banque postale, les Banques commerciales étrangères, les Caisses d'épargne et les Banques mutualistes.

68

FINLAND / FINLANDE
All banks / Ensemble des banques

Per cent / Pourcentage

INCOME STATEMENT ANALYSIS / ANALYSE DU COMPTE DE RESULTATS

		1992	1993	1994	1995	1996	1997	1998	1999	2000	2001	
% of average balance sheet total												**% du total moyen du bilan**
40.	Interest income	9.51	7.58	5.74	5.87	4.83	4.48	4.46	3.99	4.82	4.78	Produits financiers
41.	Interest expenses	8.30	5.93	4.11	4.09	3.10	2.71	2.59	2.24	2.91	3.05	Frais financiers
42.	Net interest income	1.20	1.65	1.64	1.78	1.73	1.78	1.87	1.75	1.91	1.73	Produits financiers nets
43.	Non-interest income (net)	1.78	2.27	1.44	1.35	1.69	1.49	1.92	1.42	1.45	3.10	Produits non financiers (nets)
	a. Fees and commissions receivable	:	:	:	:	:	:	:	:	:	:	a. Frais et commissions à recevoir
	b. Fees and commissions payable	:	:	:	:	:	:	:	:	:	:	b. Frais et commissions à payer
	c. Net profits or loss on financial operations	:	:	:	:	:	:	:	:	:	:	c. Profits ou pertes nets sur opérations financières
	d. Other	:	:	:	:	:	:	:	:	:	:	d. Autres
44.	Gross income	2.98	3.91	3.08	3.14	3.42	3.26	3.79	3.17	3.36	4.83	Résultat brut
45.	Operating expenses	5.67	5.34	4.31	3.52	3.03	2.39	3.27	2.24	1.91	1.82	Frais d'exploitation
	a. Staff costs	1.04	0.94	0.95	0.86	0.92	0.71	0.75	0.74	0.71	0.71	a. Dépenses en personnel
	b. Property costs	0.37	0.38	0.33	0.28	0.28	0.25	0.24	0.21	0.18	0.17	b. Dépenses en immobilier
	c. Other	4.27	4.02	3.03	2.38	1.83	1.43	2.28	1.29	1.02	0.95	c. Autres
46.	Net income	-2.69	-1.43	-1.23	-0.38	0.39	0.87	0.52	0.93	1.45	3.01	Résultat net
47.	Provisions (net)	-0.06	-0.01	-0.03	-0.01	-0.02	0.01	-0.02	0.04	0.10	0.09	Provisions (nettes)
	a. Provisions on loans	-0.03	0.01	-0.03								a. Provisions sur prêts
	b. Provisions on securities	-0.02	-0.02	-0.01								b. Provisions sur titres
	c. Other											c. Autres
48.	Profit before tax	-2.63	-1.42	-1.19	-0.37	0.41	0.86	0.54	0.89	1.35	2.92	Bénéfices avant impôt
49.	Income tax	0.03	0.02	0.02	0.05	0.08	0.12	-0.05	0.12	0.35	0.09	Impôt sur le revenu
50.	Profit after tax	-2.67	-1.44	-1.22	-0.42	0.34	0.74	0.59	0.77	1.00	2.83	Bénéfices après impôt
51.	Distributed profit	0.01	0.01	0.01	0.02	0.09	0.17	0.11	0.12	0.28	0.82	Bénéfices distribués
52.	Retained profit	-2.68	-1.45	-1.23	-0.44	0.24	0.57	0.48	0.65	0.71	2.01	Bénéfices mis en réserve
% of gross income												**% du total du résultat brut**
53.	Net interest income	40.37	42.04	53.15	56.81	50.50	54.43	49.24	55.23	56.81	35.82	Produits financiers nets
54.	Non-interest income (net)	59.63	57.96	46.85	43.19	49.50	45.57	50.76	44.77	43.19	64.18	Produits non financiers (nets)
	a. Fees and commissions receivable											a. Frais et commissions à recevoir
	b. Fees and commissions payable											b. Frais et commissions à payer
	c. Net profits or loss on financial operations											c. Profits ou pertes nets sur opérations financières
	d. Other											d. Autres
55.	Operating expenses	190.44	136.45	139.89	112.20	88.60	73.36	86.24	70.69	56.90	37.72	Frais d'exploitation
	a. Staff costs	34.87	24.01	30.83	27.45	26.88	21.70	19.76	23.39	21.16	14.63	a. Dépenses en personnel
	b. Property costs	12.28	9.74	10.69	8.89	8.19	7.70	6.42	6.58	5.47	3.47	b. Dépenses en immobilier
	c. Other	143.29	102.70	98.37	75.86	53.52	43.96	60.06	40.73	30.27	19.62	c. Autres
56.	Net income	-90.44	-36.45	-39.89	-12.20	11.40	26.64	13.76	29.31	43.10	62.28	Résultat net
57.	Provisions (net)	-1.94	-0.14	-1.09	-0.47	-0.72	0.28	-0.43	1.34	3.05	1.85	Provisions (nettes)
	a. Provisions on loans	-1.14	0.31	-0.92								a. Provisions sur prêts
	b. Provisions on securities	-0.80	-0.45	-0.17								b. Provisions sur titres
	c. Other											c. Autres
% of net income												**% du total du résultat net**
58.	Profit before tax	-88.50	-36.30	-38.80	-11.73	12.12	26.36	14.20	27.97	40.05	60.43	Bénéfices avant impôt
59.	Income tax	1.15	0.60	0.74	1.65	2.24	3.65	-1.43	3.80	10.44	1.92	Impôt sur le revenu
60.	Profit after tax	-89.65	-36.91	-39.54	-13.38	9.88	22.71	15.63	24.17	29.61	58.51	Bénéfices après impôt
% of net income												**% du total du résultat net**
61.	Provisions (net)	2.14	0.39	2.72	3.83	-6.28	1.04	-3.16	4.57	7.07	2.97	Provisions (nettes)
	a. Provisions on loans	1.26	-0.85	2.30								a. Provisions sur prêts
	b. Provisions on securities	0.88	1.24	0.42								b. Provisions sur titres
	c. Other											c. Autres
62.	Profit before tax	97.86	99.61	97.28	96.17	106.28	98.96	103.16	95.43	92.93	97.03	Bénéfices avant impôt
63.	Income tax	-1.28	-1.66	-1.85	-13.49	19.65	13.70	-10.39	12.96	24.23	3.08	Impôt sur le revenu
64.	Profit after tax	99.13	101.27	99.13	109.66	86.63	85.25	113.55	82.47	68.70	93.95	Bénéfices après impôt

FINLAND
All banks

Per cent

BALANCE SHEET ANALYSIS

% of year-end balance sheet total

FINLANDE
Ensemble des banques

Pourcentage

ANALYSE DU BILAN

% du total du bilan en fin d'exercice

	1992	1993	1994	1995	1996	1997	1998	1999	2000	2001	
Assets											**Actif**
65. Cash & balance with Central bank	3.42	1.78	1.74	2.68	1.70	2.15	2.64	4.35	2.19	0.95	65. Caisse & solde auprès de la Banque centrale
66. Interbank deposits	3.41	6.77	2.94	2.95	2.81	3.52	3.19	2.89	2.78	2.89	66. Dépôts interbancaires
67. Loans	61.01	53.01	51.14	49.74	51.06	50.52	58.60	57.95	61.32	54.62	67. Prêts
68. Securities	16.55	20.56	24.01	26.48	23.85	22.00	18.29	17.21	14.62	17.65	68. Valeurs mobilières
69. Other assets	15.61	17.88	20.17	18.15	20.57	21.81	17.28	17.60	19.10	23.89	69. Autres actifs
Liabilities											**Passif**
70. Capital & reserves	5.42	5.02	4.99	4.77	5.27	5.48	5.45	5.56	5.83	4.08	70. Capital et réserves
71. Borrowing from Central bank	1.05	0.76	0.13	1.19	2.01	0.43	-	1.21	0.33	0.83	71. Emprunts auprès de la Banque centrale
72. Interbank deposits	2.91	2.26	2.88	3.24	3.30	3.86	2.93	2.87	2.54	2.41	72. Dépôts interbancaires
73. Non-bank deposits	51.73	49.35	52.93	56.20	56.41	56.53	57.35	53.23	52.12	52.68	73. Dépôts non bancaires
74. Bonds	9.94	8.64	9.28	7.04	5.40	5.66	5.00	4.92	7.79	5.51	74. Obligations
75. Other liabilities	28.93	33.97	29.78	27.57	27.61	28.04	29.26	32.21	31.40	34.48	75. Autres engagements
Memorandum items											***Pour mémoire***
76. Short-term securities	6.21	8.83	12.58	10.06	8.13	7.88	7.62	7.72	7.03	6.22	76. Titres à court terme
77. Bonds	8.53	9.88	9.30	12.43	11.52	10.39	8.79	7.83	6.04	4.52	77. Obligations
78. Shares and participations	1.81	1.84	2.14	4.00	4.21	3.72	1.89	1.66	1.55	6.92	78. Actions et participations
79. Claims on non-residents	15.30	17.07	15.82	16.28	19.90	23.40	20.52	23.35	29.40	34.59	79. Créances sur des non-résidents
80. Liabilities to non-residents	27.88	24.61	21.38	19.77	19.12	20.76	18.33	19.71	28.12	31.44	80. Engagements envers des non-résidents

* See notes on previous pages.

* Voir les notes en pages précédentes.

FINLAND
Commercial banks

FINLANDE
Banques commerciales

Million euros / *Million d'euros*

	1992	1993	1994	1995	1996	1997	1998	1999	2000	2001	
INCOME STATEMENT											**COMPTE DE RESULTATS**
1. Interest income	8307	6511	4914	4559	3506	3393	3528	3295	4419	4952	1. Produits financiers
2. Interest expenses	7310	5280	3726	3403	2459	2230	2265	2044	2901	3488	2. Frais financiers
3. Net interest income	997	1231	1189	1156	1046	1164	1263	1251	1518	1464	3. Produits financiers nets
4. Non-interest income (net)	1214	1293	1259	1046	1246	1046	1256	1053	1275	3987	4. Produits non financiers (nets)
a. Fees and commissions receivable	:	:	:	:	:	:	:	:	:	:	a. Frais et commissions à recevoir
b. Fees and commissions payable	:	:	:	:	:	:	:	:	:	:	b. Frais et commissions à payer
c. Net profits or loss on financial operations	:	:	:	:	:	:	:	:	:	:	c. Profits ou pertes nets sur opérations financières
d. Other	:	:	:	:	:	:	:	:	:	:	d. Autres
5. Gross income	2211	2523	2448	2202	2293	2209	2519	2304	2793	5451	5. Résultat brut
6. Operating expenses	3859	4076	3474	2662	2045	1478	2322	1652	1507	1615	6. Frais d'exploitation
a. Staff costs	767	691	750	633	661	462	522	568	594	680	a. Dépenses en personnel
b. Property costs	177	212	222	178	176	154	151	129	124	126	b. Dépenses en immobilier
c. Other	2914	3173	2502	1851	1208	862	1649	955	788	809	c. Autres
7. Net income	-1647	-1553	-1027	-460	247	732	198	652	1286	3836	7. Résultat net
8. Provisions (net)	-10	3	-42	-21	-36	9	-19	-13	37	13	8. Provisions (nettes)
a. Provisions on loans	-8	7	-35	:	:	:	:	:	:	:	a. Provisions sur prêts
b. Provisions on securities	-2	-4	-7	:	:	:	:	:	:	:	b. Provisions sur titres
c. Other	-	-	:	:	:	:	:	:	:	:	c. Autres
9. Profit before tax	-1637	-1556	-985	-439	284	722	216	665	1249	3823	9. Bénéfices avant impôt
10. Income tax	21	7	3	16	31	66	-81	95	335	13	10. Impôt sur le revenu
11. Profit after tax	-1659	-1562	-988	-456	252	656	298	571	914	3810	11. Bénéfices après impôt
12. Distributed profit	5	10	11	17	93	176	111	126	353	1177	12. Bénéfices distribués
13. Retained profit	-1664	-1572	-998	-473	159	480	187	445	562	2633	13. Bénéfices mis en réserve
BALANCE SHEET											**BILAN**
Assets											**Actif**
14. Cash & balance with Central bank	1924	1563	1337	2270	1137	1783	2131	4885	2113	1104	14. Caisse & solde auprès de la Banque centrale
15. Interbank deposits	1385	769	701	272	549	1172	553	590	559	473	15. Dépôts interbancaires
16. Loans	51909	49285	41229	36987	37630	40078	44981	47938	57081	55503	16. Prêts
17. Securities	18416	23107	24096	22228	19931	20520	15623	16351	16716	23257	17. Valeurs mobilières
18. Other assets	14225	16856	16451	14709	15746	17108	16539	18174	23279	34874	18. Autres actifs
Liabilities											**Passif**
19. Capital & reserves	4583	4442	4099	3504	3750	4215	4046	4527	5072	2960	19. Capital et réserves
20. Borrowing from Central bank	914	911	102	934	2037	483	4	1064	454	1194	20. Emprunts auprès de la Banque centrale
21. Interbank deposits	3710	2768	3295	3478	3381	4187	2850	3075	2924	2958	21. Dépôts interbancaires
22. Non-bank deposits	42159	44836	42002	41018	40626	44433	44021	44527	48791	56437	22. Dépôts non bancaires
23. Bonds	9732	8137	8368	6271	4644	5524	4994	5592	10145	7931	23. Obligations
24. Other liabilities	26762	30488	25949	21262	20555	21818	23912	29151	32362	43731	24. Autres engagements
Balance sheet total											**Total du bilan**
25. End-year total	87860	91581	83815	76466	74993	80660	79828	87936	99748	115211	25. En fin d'exercice
26. Average total (1)	88693	89721	87698	80141	75730	77826	80244	83882	93842	107480	26. Moyen (1)

FINLAND

Commercial banks

Million euros

FINLANDE

Banques commerciales

Million d'euros

	1992	1993	1994	1995	1996	1997	1998	1999	2000	2001		
Memorandum items												**Pour mémoire**
27. Short-term securities	6588	9721	12367	7402	6092	6980	5945	6640	8059	8237	27.	Titres à court terme
28. Bonds	10020	11574	9774	10826	9744	9702	7948	8238	7157	5670	28.	Obligations
29. Shares and participations	1809	1812	1956	4000	4095	3839	1729	1473	1500	9350	29.	Actions et participations
30. Claims on non-residents	19241	21407	17481	15890	18544	22316	20617	25369	37447	51469	30.	Créances sur des non-résidents
31. Liabilities to non-residents	34615	30738	23914	19329	18622	21019	19100	22404	36861	46724	31.	Engagements envers des non-résidents
Capital adequacy												**Solvabilité**
32. Tier 1 Capital	..	..	..	..	..	..	..	..	..	..	32.	Fonds propres de base
33. Tier 2 Capital	..	..	..	..	..	..	..	..	..	..	33.	Fonds propres complémentaires
34. Supervisory deductions	..	..	..	..	..	..	..	..	..	..	34.	Eléments à déduire des fonds propres
35. Total net capital resources	..	..	..	..	..	..	..	..	..	..	35.	Total net des ressources en capital
36. Risk-weighted assets	..	..	..	..	..	..	..	..	..	..	36.	Actifs pondérés des risques
SUPPLEMENTARY INFORMATION												**RENSEIGNEMENTS COMPLEMENTAIRES**
37. Number of institutions	10	10	10	7	8	9	9	9	9	9	37.	Nombre d'institutions
38. Number of branches	860	1114	909	729	620	547	523	481	485	505	38.	Nombre de succursales
39. Number of employees (x 1000)	22	20	23	20	18	17	15	15	15	15	39.	Nombre de salariés (x 1000)

1 In 1998, Average total (item 26) is calculated as an average of following figures : end year total of Commercial Banks and Post Office bank 1997 and end-year total of commercial banks 1996, Post office bank was added to commercial bank during 1998.

Notes

. As from 1988, the Post office bank (Postipankki) is included under Commercial banks.

1 En 1998, le Total moyen (poste 26) est la moyenne des données suivantes: fins d'exercice des Banques commerciales et de la Banque postale de 1997 et la fin d'exercice des banques commerciales de 1998. La Banque postale étant comprise dans les Banques commerciales seulement durant l'année 1998.

Notes

. Depuis 1988, la Banque postale (Postipankki) est classée dans la catégorie Banques commerciales.

FINLAND

Commercial banks

Per cent

INCOME STATEMENT ANALYSIS

FINLANDE

Banques commerciales

Pourcentage

ANALYSE DU COMPTE DE RESULTATS

	1992	1993	1994	1995	1996	1997	1998	1999	2000	2001	
% of average balance sheet total											**% du total moyen du bilan**
40. Interest income	9.37	7.26	5.60	5.69	4.63	4.36	4.40	3.93	4.71	4.61	40. Produits financiers
41. Interest expenses	8.24	5.89	4.25	4.25	3.25	2.86	2.82	2.44	3.09	3.25	41. Frais financiers
42. Net interest income	1.12	1.37	1.36	1.44	1.38	1.50	1.57	1.49	1.62	1.36	42. Produits financiers nets
43. Non-interest income (net)	1.37	1.44	1.44	1.31	1.65	1.34	1.57	1.26	1.36	3.71	43. Produits non financiers (nets)
a. Fees and commissions receivable	..	..	..	..	..	..	..	..	..	..	*a. Frais et commissions à recevoir*
b. Fees and commissions payable											*b. Frais et commissions à payer*
c. Net profits or loss on financial operations											*c. Profits ou pertes nets sur opérations financières*
d. Other											*d. Autres*
44. Gross income	2.49	2.81	2.79	2.75	3.03	2.84	3.14	2.75	2.98	5.07	44. Résultat brut
45. Operating expenses	4.35	4.54	3.96	3.32	2.70	1.90	2.89	1.97	1.61	1.50	45. Frais d'exploitation
a. Staff costs	0.86	0.77	0.86	0.79	0.87	0.59	0.65	0.68	0.63	0.63	*a. Dépenses en personnel*
b. Property costs	0.20	0.24	0.25	0.22	0.23	0.20	0.19	0.15	0.13	0.12	*b. Dépenses en immobilier*
c. Other	3.29	3.54	2.85	2.31	1.60	1.11	2.05	1.14	0.84	0.75	*c. Autres*
46. Net income	-1.86	-1.73	-1.17	-0.57	0.33	0.94	0.25	0.78	1.37	3.57	46. Résultat net
47. Provisions (net)	-0.01	..	-0.05	-0.03	-0.05	0.01	-0.02	-0.02	0.04	0.01	47. Provisions (nettes)
a. Provisions on loans	-0.01	0.01	-0.04	..							*a. Provisions sur prêts*
b. Provisions on securities											*b. Provisions sur titres*
c. Other	-		-0.01								*c. Autres*
48. Profit before tax	-1.85	-1.73	-1.12	-0.55	0.37	0.93	0.27	0.79	1.33	3.56	48. Bénéfices avant impôt
49. Income tax	0.02	0.01	-	0.02	0.04	0.08	-0.10	0.11	0.36	0.01	49. Impôt sur le revenu
50. Profit after tax	-1.87	-1.74	-1.13	-0.57	0.33	0.84	0.37	0.68	0.97	3.54	50. Bénéfices après impôt
51. Distributed profit	0.01	0.01	0.01	0.02	0.12	0.23	0.14	0.15	0.38	1.10	51. Bénéfices distribués
52. Retained profit	-1.88	-1.75	-1.14	-0.59	0.21	0.62	0.23	0.53	0.60	2.45	52. Bénéfices mis en réserve
% of gross income											**% du total du résultat brut**
53. Net interest income	45.07	48.77	48.56	52.49	45.65	52.67	50.15	54.30	54.35	26.86	53. Produits financiers nets
54. Non-interest income (net)	54.93	51.23	51.44	47.51	54.35	47.33	49.85	45.70	45.65	73.14	54. Produits non financiers (nets)
a. Fees and commissions receivable											*a. Frais et commissions à recevoir*
b. Fees and commissions payable											*b. Frais et commissions à payer*
c. Net profits or loss on financial operations											*c. Profits ou pertes nets sur opérations financières*
d. Other											*d. Autres*
55. Operating expenses	174.50	161.53	141.95	120.88	89.22	66.88	92.14	71.70	53.95	29.63	55. Frais d'exploitation
a. Staff costs	34.68	27.38	30.66	28.75	28.84	20.90	20.70	24.66	21.27	12.47	*a. Dépenses en personnel*
b. Property costs	8.02	8.40	9.08	8.09	7.69	6.97	6.00	5.58	4.46	2.31	*b. Dépenses en immobilier*
c. Other	131.80	125.75	102.21	84.05	52.69	39.00	65.44	41.46	28.22	14.84	*c. Autres*
56. Net income	-74.50	-61.53	-41.95	-20.88	10.78	33.12	7.86	28.30	46.05	70.37	56. Résultat net
57. Provisions (net)	-0.45	0.13	-1.72	-0.93	-1.58	0.43	-0.73	-0.57	1.32	0.24	57. Provisions (nettes)
a. Provisions on loans	-0.36	0.29	-1.45								*a. Provisions sur prêts*
b. Provisions on securities											*b. Provisions sur titres*
c. Other	-0.09	-0.15	-0.27								*c. Autres*
58. Profit before tax	-74.05	-61.66	-40.23	-19.95	12.37	32.70	8.59	28.87	44.73	70.13	58. Bénéfices avant impôt
59. Income tax	0.97	0.26	0.12	0.75	1.36	2.99	-3.23	4.10	12.01	0.24	59. Impôt sur le revenu
60. Profit after tax	-75.02	-61.92	-40.36	-20.70	11.00	29.70	11.82	24.77	32.72	69.90	60. Bénéfices après impôt
% of net income											**% du total du résultat net**
61. Provisions (net)	0.60	-0.22	4.10	4.46	-14.69	1.29	-9.35	-2.01	2.88	0.34	61. Provisions (nettes)
a. Provisions on loans	0.48	-0.47	3.46								*a. Provisions sur prêts*
b. Provisions on securities	0.12	0.25	0.64								*b. Provisions sur titres*
c. Other											*c. Autres*
62. Profit before tax	99.40	100.22	95.90	95.54	114.69	98.71	109.35	102.01	97.12	99.66	62. Bénéfices avant impôt
63. Income tax	-1.30	-0.42	-0.30	-3.58	12.65	9.03	-41.12	14.50	26.07	0.34	63. Impôt sur le revenu
64. Profit after tax	100.69	100.64	96.20	99.12	102.04	89.68	150.46	87.52	71.05	99.32	64. Bénéfices après impôt

FINLAND

Commercial banks

FINLANDE

Banques commerciales

Per cent

BALANCE SHEET ANALYSIS

Pourcentage

ANALYSE DU BILAN

% of year-end balance sheet total — **% du total du bilan en fin d'exercice**

	1992	1993	1994	1995	1996	1997	1998	1999	2000	2001	
Assets											**Actif**
65. Cash & balance with Central bank	2.19	1.71	1.59	2.97	1.52	2.21	2.67	5.55	2.12	0.96	65. Caisse & solde auprès de la Banque centrale
66. Interbank deposits	1.58	0.84	0.84	0.36	0.73	1.45	0.69	0.67	0.56	0.41	66. Dépôts interbancaires
67. Loans	59.08	53.82	49.19	48.37	50.18	49.69	56.35	54.51	57.23	48.18	67. Prêts
68. Securities	20.96	25.23	28.75	29.07	26.58	25.44	19.57	18.59	16.76	20.19	68. Valeurs mobilières
69. Other assets	16.19	18.41	19.63	19.24	21.00	21.21	20.72	20.67	23.34	30.27	69. Autres actifs
Liabilities											**Passif**
70. Capital & reserves	5.22	4.85	4.89	4.58	5.00	5.23	5.07	5.15	5.09	2.57	70. Capital et réserves
71. Borrowing from Central bank	1.04	0.99	0.12	1.22	2.72	0.60	-	1.21	0.46	1.04	71. Emprunts auprès de la Banque centrale
72. Interbank deposits	4.22	3.02	3.93	4.55	4.51	5.19	3.57	3.50	2.93	2.57	72. Dépôts interbancaires
73. Non-bank deposits	47.98	48.96	50.11	53.64	54.17	55.09	55.15	50.64	48.91	48.99	73. Dépôts non bancaires
74. Bonds	11.08	8.88	9.98	8.20	6.19	6.85	6.26	6.36	10.17	6.88	74. Obligations
75. Other liabilities	30.46	33.29	30.96	27.81	27.41	27.05	29.96	33.15	32.44	37.96	75. Autres engagements
Memorandum items											**Pour mémoire**
76. Short-term securities	7.50	10.61	14.75	9.68	8.12	8.65	7.45	7.55	8.08	7.15	76. Titres à court terme
77. Bonds	11.40	12.64	11.66	14.16	12.99	12.03	9.96	9.37	7.18	4.92	77. Obligations
78. Shares and participations	2.06	1.98	2.33	5.23	5.46	4.76	2.17	1.68	1.50	8.12	78. Actions et participations
79. Claims on non-residents	21.90	23.38	20.86	20.78	24.73	27.67	25.83	28.85	37.54	44.67	79. Créances sur des non-résidents
80. Liabilities to non-residents	39.40	33.56	28.53	25.28	24.83	26.06	23.93	25.48	36.95	40.56	80. Engagements envers des non-résidents

* See notes on previous pages.

* Voir les notes en pages précédentes.

FINLAND
Foreign commercial banks

Million euros

FINLANDE
Banques commerciales étrangères

Million d'euros

		1992	1993	1994	1995	1996	1997	1998	1999	2000	2001		
INCOME STATEMENT													**COMPTE DE RESULTATS**
1.	Interest income	261	200	121	378	329	328	315	323	478	448	1.	Produits financiers
2.	Interest expenses	253	191	112	369	281	309	283	276	440	396	2.	Frais financiers
3.	Net interest income	8	9	9	9	48	19	32	46	38	52	3.	Produits financiers nets
4.	Non-interest income (net)	14	12	6	42	22	25	40	24	116	90	4.	Produits non financiers (nets)
	a. Fees and commissions receivable	..	..	..	..	..	..	..	..	..	..		a. Frais et commissions à recevoir
	b. Fees and commissions payable	..	..	..	..	..	..	..	..	..	..		b. Frais et commissions à payer
	c. Net profits or loss on financial operations	..	..	..	..	..	..	..	..	..	..		c. Profits ou pertes nets sur opérations financières
	d. Other	..	..	..	..	..	..	..	..	..	..		d. Autres
5.	Gross income	22	21	15	51	70	44	72	71	154	142	5.	Résultat brut
6.	Operating expenses	25	15	19	42	52	67	140	78	104	131	6.	Frais d'exploitation
	a. Staff costs	6	7	7	21	28	32	40	41	53	60		a. Dépenses en personnel
	b. Property costs	1	1	1	2	2	4	4	5	5	8		b. Dépenses en immobilier
	c. Other	17	8	11	19	22	31	95	33	46	63		c. Autres
7.	Net income	-3	6	-3	9	18	-23	-68	-8	49	11	7.	Résultat net
8.	Provisions (net)	7	-1	-2	-2	3	-5	1	16	19	21	8.	Provisions (nettes)
	a. Provisions on loans	1	-1	-	..	..	..	..	..	..	..		a. Provisions sur prêts
	b. Provisions on securities	6	-	-2	..	..	..	..	..	..	..		b. Provisions sur titres
	c. Other	-	-	-	..	..	..	..	..	..	..		c. Autres
9.	Profit before tax	-10	7	-2	11	15	-19	-69	-23	30	-10	9.	Bénéfices avant impôt
10.	Income tax	1	2	1	3	3	0	-1	1	23	13	10.	Impôt sur le revenu
11.	Profit after tax	-10	5	-2	8	12	-19	-67	-24	7	-23	11.	Bénéfices après impôt
12.	Distributed profit	-	-	-	-	-	-	-	-	-	-	12.	Bénéfices distribués
13.	Retained profit	-10	5	-2	8	12	-19	-67	-24	7	-23	13.	Bénéfices mis en réserve
BALANCE SHEET													**BILAN**
Assets													**Actif**
14.	Cash & balance with Central bank	18	7	14	27	60	52	213	156	420	67	14.	Caisse & solde auprès de la Banque centrale
15.	Interbank deposits	6	1	17	14	21	32	506	12	20	46	15.	Dépôts interbancaires
16.	Loans	319	64	60	920	713	1121	4255	5703	6845	6794	16.	Prêts
17.	Securities	805	745	1124	4168	2671	1785	2382	2782	1300	1672	17.	Valeurs mobilières
18.	Other assets	146	224	868	2148	3423	5185	873	1955	952	770	18.	Autres actifs
Liabilities													**Passif**
19.	Capital & reserves	20	25	2	11	9	-24	-58	11	81	112	19.	Capital et réserves
20.	Borrowing from Central bank	0	-	17	361	84	-	-	450	-	100	20.	Emprunts auprès de la Banque centrale
21.	Interbank deposits	-	85	2	32	2	6	7	3	0	15	21.	Dépôts interbancaires
22.	Non-bank deposits	48	245	541	873	479	440	1196	1340	1298	1859	22.	Dépôts non bancaires
23.	Bonds	-	-	-	-	-	-	8	8	10	52	23.	Obligations
24.	Other liabilities	1226	685	1521	6000	6314	7754	7076	8797	8149	7211	24.	Autres engagements
Balance sheet total													**Total du bilan**
25.	End-year total	1295	1041	2083	7277	6888	8176	8229	10608	9537	9349	25.	En fin d'exercice
26.	Average total	1251	1168	1562	4680	7083	7532	8202	9419	10073	9443	26.	Moyen

Million euros

Million d'euros

	1992	1993	1994	1995	1996	1997	1998	1999	2000	2001	
Memorandum items											***Pour mémoire***
27. Short-term securities	723	598	1124	2892	1935	1477	1743	2404	984	621	27. Titres à court terme
28. Bonds	81	146	-	1274	710	291	582	156	62	80	28. Obligations
29. Shares and participations	1	1	0	2	27	16	57	222	254	971	29. Actions et participations
30. Claims on non-residents	326	224	626	1756	2488	4120	2627	3809	3059	2277	30. Créances sur des non-résidents
31. Liabilities to non-residents	820	245	561	2112	1591	2461	1680	2299	1865	2120	31. Engagements envers des non-résidents
Capital adequacy											***Solvabilité***
32. Tier 1 Capital	..	..	..	..	..	..	..	..	..	..	32. Fonds propres de base
33. Tier 2 Capital	..	..	..	..	..	..	..	..	..	..	33. Fonds propres complémentaires
34. Supervisory deductions	..	..	..	..	..	..	..	..	..	..	34. Eléments à déduire des fonds propres
35. Total net capital resources	..	..	..	..	..	..	..	..	..	..	35. Total net des ressources en capital
36. Risk-weighted assets	..	..	..	..	..	..	..	..	..	..	36. Actifs pondérés des risques
SUPPLEMENTARY INFORMATION											**RENSEIGNEMENTS COMPLEMENTAIRES**
37. Number of institutions	4	4	4	4	4	5	6	7	6	7	37. Nombre d'institutions
38. Number of branches	-	-	-	5	9	12	14	15	19	62	38. Nombre de succursales
39. Number of employees (x 1000)	0.1	0.1	0.2	0.4	0.4	0.5	0.6	0.6	0.7	0.8	39. Nombre de salariés (x 1000)

FINLAND
Foreign commercial banks

FINLANDE
Banques commerciales étrangères

Per cent / *Pourcentage*

INCOME STATEMENT ANALYSIS / ANALYSE DU COMPTE DE RESULTATS

	1992	1993	1994	1995	1996	1997	1998	1999	2000	2001	
% of average balance sheet total											**% du total moyen du bilan**
40. Interest income	20.88	17.14	7.73	8.07	4.64	4.36	3.83	3.42	4.75	4.74	40. Produits financiers
41. Interest expenses	20.24	16.38	7.17	7.89	3.96	4.11	3.45	2.93	4.37	4.19	41. Frais financiers
42. Net interest income	0.64	0.76	0.56	0.18	0.68	0.25	0.39	0.49	0.38	0.55	42. Produits financiers nets
43. Non-interest income (net)	1.12	1.07	0.41	0.91	0.31	0.33	0.49	0.26	1.15	0.95	43. Produits non financiers (nets)
a. Fees and commissions receivable	..	..	..	..	..	..	..	..	..	..	a. Frais et commissions à recevoir
b. Fees and commissions payable	..	..	..	..	..	..	..	..	..	..	b. Frais et commissions à payer
c. Net profits or loss on financial operations	..	..	..	..	..	..	..	..	..	..	c. Profits ou pertes nets sur opérations financières
d. Other	..	..	..	..	..	..	..	..	..	..	d. Autres
44. Gross income	1.76	1.83	0.97	1.09	0.99	0.58	0.88	0.75	1.52	1.50	44. Résultat brut
45. Operating expenses	2.00	1.32	1.18	0.89	0.73	0.89	1.70	0.83	1.03	1.39	45. Frais d'exploitation
a. Staff costs	0.51	0.56	0.43	0.44	0.39	0.43	0.49	0.43	0.53	0.64	a. Dépenses en personnel
b. Property costs	0.11	0.09	0.05	0.05	0.03	0.05	0.05	0.05	0.05	0.08	b. Dépenses en immobilier
c. Other	1.38	0.68	0.70	0.40	0.31	0.41	1.16	0.35	0.45	0.67	c. Autres
46. Net income	-0.24	0.50	-0.22	0.20	0.25	-0.31	-0.83	-0.08	0.49	0.12	46. Résultat net
47. Provisions (net)	0.55	-0.07	-0.12	-0.04	0.05	-0.06	0.01	0.17	0.19	0.22	47. Provisions (nettes)
a. Provisions on loans	0.04	-0.07	0.01	..	..	..	..	..	..	..	a. Provisions sur prêts
b. Provisions on securities	0.51	-	-0.13	..	..	..	..	..	..	..	b. Provisions sur titres
c. Other											c. Autres
48. Profit before tax	-0.79	0.58	-0.10	0.23	0.21	-0.25	-0.84	-0.25	0.30	-0.11	48. Bénéfices avant impôt
49. Income tax	0.04	0.13	0.04	0.06	0.04	-	-0.01	0.01	0.23	0.14	49. Impôt sur le revenu
50. Profit after tax	-0.83	0.45	-0.14	0.18	0.16	-0.25	-0.82	-0.25	0.07	-0.24	50. Bénéfices après impôt
51. Distributed profit											51. Bénéfices distribués
52. Retained profit	-0.83	0.45	-0.14	0.18	0.16	-0.25	-0.82	-0.25	0.07	-0.24	52. Bénéfices mis en réserve
% of gross income											**% du total du résultat brut**
53. Net interest income	36.63	41.71	57.79	16.84	68.99	42.92	44.03	65.56	24.64	36.62	53. Produits financiers nets
54. Non-interest income (net)	63.37	58.29	42.21	83.16	31.01	57.08	55.97	34.44	75.35	63.38	54. Produits non financiers (nets)
a. Fees and commissions receivable	..	..	..	..	..	..	..	..	..	..	a. Frais et commissions à recevoir
b. Fees and commissions payable	..	..	..	..	..	..	..	..	..	..	b. Frais et commissions à payer
c. Net profits or loss on financial operations	..	..	..	..	..	..	..	..	..	..	c. Profits ou pertes nets sur opérations financières
d. Other	..	..	..	..	..	..	..	..	..	..	d. Autres
55. Operating expenses	113.75	72.43	122.19	81.85	74.27	152.48	194.37	110.69	67.80	92.25	55. Frais d'exploitation
a. Staff costs	29.01	30.71	44.45	40.60	39.66	73.94	56.21	57.72	34.50	42.25	a. Dépenses en personnel
b. Property costs	6.13	4.73	5.55	4.61	3.36	8.04	5.39	6.41	3.50	5.63	b. Dépenses en immobilier
c. Other	78.62	36.99	72.19	36.64	31.24	70.50	132.78	46.55	29.79	44.37	c. Autres
56. Net income	-13.75	27.57	-22.19	18.15	25.73	-52.48	-94.37	-10.69	32.20	7.75	56. Résultat net
57. Provisions (net)	31.32	-3.93	-12.22	-3.30	4.80	-10.34	1.17	22.09	12.38	14.79	57. Provisions (nettes)
a. Provisions on loans	2.27	-3.93	1.12	..	..	..	..	..	..	..	a. Provisions sur prêts
b. Provisions on securities	29.01	-	-13.34	..	..	..	..	..	..	..	b. Provisions sur titres
c. Other											c. Autres
58. Profit before tax	-45.03	31.51	-9.97	21.45	20.91	-42.14	-95.54	-32.78	19.82	-7.04	58. Bénéfices avant impôt
59. Income tax	2.27	7.07	4.43	5.28	4.33	0.77	-1.64	0.71	15.00	9.15	59. Impôt sur le revenu
60. Profit after tax	-47.34	24.39	-14.46	16.17	16.58	-42.92	-93.90	-33.48	4.82	-16.20	60. Bénéfices après impôt
% of net income											**% du total du résultat net**
61. Provisions (net)	-227.72	-14.26	55.06	-18.16	18.67	19.70	-1.24	-206.61	38.44	190.91	61. Provisions (nettes)
a. Provisions on loans	-16.50	-14.26	-5.06	..	..	..	..	..	..	..	a. Provisions sur prêts
b. Provisions on securities	-210.89	-	60.12	..	..	..	..	..	..	..	b. Provisions sur titres
c. Other											c. Autres
62. Profit before tax	327.39	114.26	44.94	118.16	81.28	80.30	101.24	306.61	61.56	-90.91	62. Bénéfices avant impôt
63. Income tax	-16.50	25.64	-19.94	29.08	16.83	-1.48	1.74	-6.61	46.59	118.18	63. Impôt sur le revenu
64. Profit after tax	344.22	88.46	65.18	89.08	64.44	81.77	99.50	313.21	14.96	-209.09	64. Bénéfices après impôt

FINLAND

Foreign commercial banks

FINLANDE

Banques commerciales étrangères

Per cent / *Pourcentage*

BALANCE SHEET ANALYSIS / **ANALYSE DU BILAN**

% of year-end balance sheet total / **% du total du bilan en fin d'exercice**

	1992	1993	1994	1995	1996	1997	1998	1999	2000	2001		
Assets												**Actif**
65. Cash & balance with Central bank	1.40	0.69	0.69	0.37	0.87	0.64	2.59	1.47	4.41	0.72	65.	Caisse & solde auprès de la Banque centrale
66. Interbank deposits	0.43	0.06	0.84	0.19	0.30	0.39	6.15	0.12	0.21	0.49	66.	Dépôts interbancaires
67. Loans	24.67	6.14	2.86	12.64	10.36	13.72	51.70	53.76	71.77	72.67	67.	Prêts
68. Securities	62.19	71.59	53.94	57.28	38.78	21.83	28.95	26.22	13.63	17.88	68.	Valeurs mobilières
69. Other assets	11.31	21.51	41.66	29.52	49.70	63.42	10.60	18.43	9.98	8.24	69.	Autres actifs
Liabilities												**Passif**
70. Capital & reserves	1.56	2.42	0.11	0.15	0.13	-0.30	-0.70	0.10	0.85	1.20	70.	Capital et réserves
71. Borrowing from Central bank	0.01	-	0.83	4.96	1.21	-	-	4.24	-	1.07	71.	Emprunts auprès de la Banque centrale
72. Interbank deposits	-	8.18	0.08	0.44	0.03	0.07	0.08	0.03	-	0.16	72.	Dépôts interbancaires
73. Non-bank deposits	3.73	23.56	25.96	12.00	6.96	5.38	14.54	12.64	13.61	19.88	73.	Dépôts non bancaires
74. Bonds	-	-	-	-	-	-	0.09	0.07	0.10	0.56	74.	Obligations
75. Other liabilities	94.70	65.84	73.02	82.45	91.67	94.85	85.99	82.92	85.44	77.13	75.	Autres engagements
Memorandum items												***Pour mémoire***
76. Short-term securities	55.86	57.47	53.93	39.74	28.09	18.07	21.19	22.66	10.32	6.64	76.	Titres à court terme
77. Bonds	6.22	13.99	-	17.51	10.30	3.56	7.07	1.47	0.65	0.86	77.	Obligations
78. Shares and participations	0.10	0.13	0.02	0.03	0.39	0.20	0.70	2.09	2.66	10.39	78.	Actions et participations
79. Claims on non-residents	25.20	21.51	30.05	24.13	36.12	50.39	31.93	35.91	32.08	24.36	79.	Créances sur des non-résidents
80. Liabilities to non-residents	63.33	23.56	26.91	29.03	23.10	30.10	20.41	21.67	19.55	22.68	80.	Engagements envers des non-résidents

FINLAND
Savings banks

Million euros

FINLANDE
Caisses d'épargne

Million d'euros

	1992	1993	1994[1]	1995	1996	1997	1998	1999	2000	2001	
INCOME STATEMENT											**COMPTE DE RESULTATS**
1. Interest income	1754	1280	449	236	220	220	245	248	320	365	1. Produits financiers
2. Interest expenses	1683	1042	403	109	86	74	81	87	116	146	2. Frais financiers
3. Net interest income	70	237	46	127	134	145	163	161	204	219	3. Produits financiers nets
4. Non-interest income (net)	536	1247	127	53	61	61	68	68	81	68	4. Produits non financiers (nets)
a. Fees and commissions receivable	:	:	:	:	:	:	:	:	:	:	*a. Frais et commissions à recevoir*
b. Fees and commissions payable	:	:	:	:	:	:	:	:	:	:	*b. Frais et commissions à payer*
c. Net profits or loss on financial operations	:	:	:	:	:	:	:	:	:	:	*c. Profits ou pertes nets sur opérations financières*
d. Other	:	:	:	:	:	:	:	:	:	:	*d. Autres*
5. Gross income	606	1485	174	180	195	206	232	229	285	287	5. Résultat brut
6. Operating expenses	2437	1411	376	154	158	156	172	167	180	184	6. Frais d'exploitation
a. Staff costs	*277*	*245*	*113*	*53*	*53*	*57*	*62*	*62*	*69*	*71*	*a. Dépenses en personnel*
b. Property costs	*190*	*170*	*74*	*28*	*26*	*24*	*26*	*26*	*24*	*23*	*b. Dépenses en immobilier*
c. Other	*1971*	*996*	*189*	*73*	*79*	*76*	*84*	*79*	*87*	*90*	*c. Autres*
7. Net income	-1830	74	-202	26	37	50	60	62	105	103	7. Résultat net
8. Provisions (net)	-62	3	2	3	4	4	10	13	22	29	8. Provisions (nettes)
a. Provisions on loans	*-44*	*3*	*3*	:	:	:	:	:	:	:	*a. Provisions sur prêts*
b. Provisions on securities	*-18*	*-*	*-1*	:	:	:	:	:	:	:	*b. Provisions sur titres*
c. Other	:	*-*	:	:	:	:	:	:	:	:	*c. Autres*
9. Profit before tax	-1768	71	-204	23	33	46	50	49	84	74	9. Bénéfices avant impôt
10. Income tax	3	1	2	5	7	9	10	10	19	22	10. Impôt sur le revenu
11. Profit after tax	-1771	69	-206	18	26	37	40	39	64	52	11. Bénéfices après impôt
12. Distributed profit	-	-	-	-	-	-	-	-	-	-	12. Bénéfices distribués
13. Retained profit	-1771	69	-206	18	26	37	40	39	64	52	13. Bénéfices mis en réserve
BALANCE SHEET											**BILAN**
Assets											**Actif**
14. Cash & balance with Central bank	1611	141	138	131	129	136	227	224	313	171	14. Caisse & solde auprès de la Banque centrale
15. Interbank deposits	1307	5467	285	237	181	232	250	369	278	484	15. Dépôts interbancaires
16. Loans	12424	2926	3046	2081	2364	2696	3211	3779	4191	4923	16. Prêts
17. Securities	826	1126	868	703	956	1032	1162	1074	852	1147	17. Valeurs mobilières
18. Other assets	3009	2787	3109	383	397	383	351	327	617	248	18. Autres actifs
Liabilities											**Passif**
19. Capital & reserves	1039	519	250	227	285	322	348	394	469	541	19. Capital et réserves
20. Borrowing from Central bank	355	53	29	-	-	-	-	-	-	-	20. Emprunts auprès de la Banque centrale
21. Interbank deposits	16	14	2	-	106	172	460	522	565	773	21. Dépôts interbancaires
22. Non-bank deposits	11220	2450	2720	2954	3244	3652	3982	4429	4605	4973	22. Dépôts non bancaires
23. Bonds	1331	1218	871	75	70	90	68	69	110	119	23. Obligations
24. Other liabilities	5216	8193	3573	278	321	244	342	360	502	567	24. Autres engagements
Balance sheet total											**Total du bilan**
25. End-year total	19177	12447	7446	3534	4027	4478	5201	5773	6251	6973	25. En fin d'exercice
26. Average total	19682	15812	9946	5490	3780	4253	4839	5487	6012	6612	26. Moyen

FINLAND

Savings banks

Million euros

	1992	1993	1994[1]	1995	1996	1997	1998	1999	2000	2001
Memorandum items										
27. Short-term securities	376	658	696	346	429	391	634	493	402	612
28. Bonds	217	245	-	321	488	610	495	548	418	494
29. Shares and participations	233	222	172	35	40	31	33	33	31	41
30. Claims on non-residents	7	16	3	12	17	40	25	102	10	14
31. Liabilities to non-residents	224	30	2	2	4	12	7	11	12	6
Capital adequacy										
32. Tier 1 Capital	..	..	..	..	..	..	..	..	..	..
33. Tier 2 Capital	..	..	..	..	..	..	..	..	..	..
34. Supervisory deductions	..	..	..	..	..	..	..	..	..	..
35. Total net capital resources	..	..	..	..	..	..	..	..	..	..
36. Risk-weighted assets	..	..	..	..	..	..	..	..	..	..
SUPPLEMENTARY INFORMATION										
37. Number of institutions	39	41	41	40	40	40	40	40	40	40
38. Number of branches	845	173	233	211	207	211	210	213	212	213
39. Number of employees (x 1000)	7.9	7.2	1.7	1.4	1.6	1.7	1.7	1.8	1.9	1.9

FINLANDE

Caisses d'épargne

Million d'euros

Pour mémoire
27. Titres à court terme
28. Obligations
29. Actions et participations
30. Créances sur des non-résidents
31. Engagements envers des non-résidents

Solvabilité
32. Fonds propres de base
33. Fonds propres complémentaires
34. Eléments à déduire des fonds propres
35. Total net des ressources en capital
36. Actifs pondérés des risques

RENSEIGNEMENTS COMPLEMENTAIRES
37. Nombre d'institutions
38. Nombre de succursales
39. Nombre de salariés (x 1000)

1 Break in series : In 1994, change in the composition of "Savings banks".

1 Rupture de séries : A partir de 1994, changement dans la composition
   des caisses d'épargne

80

FINLAND
Savings banks

FINLANDE
Caisses d'épargne

Per cent / *Pourcentage*

INCOME STATEMENT ANALYSIS / **ANALYSE DU COMPTE DE RESULTATS**

No.		1992	1993	1994¹	1995	1996	1997	1998	1999	2000	2001	
	% of average balance sheet total											**% du total moyen du bilan**
40.	Interest income	8.91	8.09	4.52	4.30	5.82	5.17	5.06	4.52	5.33	5.52	Produits financiers
41.	Interest expenses	8.55	6.59	4.05	1.99	2.27	1.74	1.68	1.58	1.93	2.21	Frais financiers
42.	Net interest income	0.36	1.50	0.47	2.32	3.55	3.42	3.38	2.94	3.40	3.31	Produits financiers nets
43.	Non-interest income (net)	2.72	7.89	1.28	0.97	1.61	1.43	1.41	1.24	1.35	1.03	Produits non financiers (nets)
	a. Fees and commissions receivable	:	:	:	:	:	:	:	:	:	:	a. Frais et commissions à recevoir
	b. Fees and commissions payable	:	:	:	:	:	:	:	:	:	:	b. Frais et commissions à payer
	c. Net profits or loss on financial operations	:	:	:	:	:	:	:	:	:	:	c. Profits ou pertes nets sur opérations financières
	d. Other	:	:	:	:	:	:	:	:	:	:	d. Autres
44.	Gross income	3.08	9.39	1.75	3.28	5.16	4.85	4.79	4.18	4.74	4.34	Résultat brut
45.	Operating expenses	12.38	8.93	3.78	2.81	4.17	3.67	3.54	3.04	2.99	2.78	Frais d'exploitation
	a. Staff costs	1.40	1.55	1.14	0.96	1.40	1.34	1.27	1.13	1.15	1.07	a. Dépenses en personnel
	b. Property costs	0.96	1.08	0.74	0.51	0.68	0.55	0.53	0.48	0.39	0.35	b. Dépenses en immobilier
	c. Other	10.01	6.30	1.90	1.34	2.10	1.78	1.74	1.43	1.45	1.36	c. Autres
46.	Net income	-9.30	0.46	-2.03	0.47	0.99	1.18	1.25	1.14	1.75	1.56	Résultat net
47.	Provisions (net)	-0.32	0.02	0.02	0.06	0.11	0.10	0.22	0.24	0.36	0.44	Provisions (nettes)
	a. Provisions on loans	-0.22	0.02	0.03	:	:	:	:	:	:	:	a. Provisions sur prêts
	b. Provisions on securities	-0.09	-	-0.01	:	:	:	:	:	:	:	b. Provisions sur titres
	c. Other	:	:	:	:	:	:	:	:	:	:	c. Autres
48.	Profit before tax	-8.98	0.45	-2.05	0.41	0.88	1.08	1.03	0.90	1.39	1.12	Bénéfices avant impôt
49.	Income tax	0.01	0.01	0.02	0.09	0.20	0.22	0.21	0.18	0.32	0.33	Impôt sur le revenu
50.	Profit after tax	-9.00	0.44	-2.07	0.32	0.69	0.87	0.82	0.72	1.07	0.79	Bénéfices après impôt
51.	Distributed profit	:	:	:	:	:	:	:	:	:	:	Bénéfices distribués
52.	Retained profit	-9.00	0.44	-2.07	0.32	0.69	0.87	0.82	0.72	1.07	0.79	Bénéfices mis en réserve
	% of gross income											**% du total du résultat brut**
53.	Net interest income	11.59	15.99	26.65	70.59	68.77	70.49	70.49	70.34	71.62	76.31	Produits financiers nets
54.	Non-interest income (net)	88.41	84.01	73.35	29.41	31.23	29.50	29.51	29.66	28.38	23.69	Produits non financiers (nets)
	a. Fees and commissions receivable	:	:	:	:	:	:	:	:	:	:	a. Frais et commissions à recevoir
	b. Fees and commissions payable	:	:	:	:	:	:	:	:	:	:	b. Frais et commissions à payer
	c. Net profits or loss on financial operations	:	:	:	:	:	:	:	:	:	:	c. Profits ou pertes nets sur opérations financières
	d. Other	:	:	:	:	:	:	:	:	:	:	d. Autres
55.	Operating expenses	401.80	95.05	216.57	85.53	80.84	75.71	73.97	72.76	63.13	64.11	Frais d'exploitation
	a. Staff costs	45.59	16.49	65.11	29.22	27.09	27.71	26.54	27.02	24.31	24.74	a. Dépenses en personnel
	b. Property costs	31.25	11.47	42.44	15.59	13.11	11.41	11.02	11.46	8.32	8.01	b. Dépenses en immobilier
	c. Other	324.96	67.08	109.01	40.71	40.64	36.59	36.40	34.29	30.50	31.36	c. Autres
56.	Net income	-301.80	4.95	-116.57	14.47	19.16	24.29	26.03	27.24	36.87	35.89	Résultat net
57.	Provisions (net)	-10.26	0.19	0.87	1.87	2.07	1.96	4.50	5.65	7.55	10.10	Provisions (nettes)
	a. Provisions on loans	-7.27	0.17	1.55	:	:	:	:	:	:	:	a. Provisions sur prêts
	b. Provisions on securities	-2.99	0.02	-0.68	:	:	:	:	:	:	:	b. Provisions sur titres
	c. Other	:	:	:	:	:	:	:	:	:	:	c. Autres
58.	Profit before tax	-291.54	4.76	-117.44	12.61	17.08	22.33	21.54	21.59	29.32	25.78	Bénéfices avant impôt
59.	Income tax	0.44	0.08	1.26	2.71	3.80	4.48	4.42	4.40	6.78	7.67	Impôt sur le revenu
60.	Profit after tax	-291.98	4.68	-118.70	9.90	13.29	17.85	17.11	17.18	22.54	18.12	Bénéfices après impôt
	% of net income											**% du total du résultat net**
61.	Provisions (net)	3.40	3.89	-0.75	12.89	10.82	8.06	17.27	20.75	20.48	28.16	Provisions (nettes)
	a. Provisions on loans	2.41	3.43	-1.33	:	:	:	:	:	:	:	a. Provisions sur prêts
	b. Provisions on securities	0.99	0.46	0.58	:	:	:	:	:	:	:	b. Provisions sur titres
	c. Other	:	:	:	:	:	:	:	:	:	:	c. Autres
62.	Profit before tax	96.60	96.11	100.75	87.11	89.18	91.94	82.73	79.25	79.52	71.84	Bénéfices avant impôt
63.	Income tax	-0.15	1.61	-1.08	18.72	19.82	18.46	16.99	16.17	18.40	21.36	Impôt sur le revenu
64.	Profit after tax	96.75	94.50	101.83	68.39	69.36	73.48	65.73	63.08	61.12	50.49	Bénéfices après impôt

FINLAND
Savings banks

FINLANDE
Caisses d'épargne

Per cent — *Pourcentage*

BALANCE SHEET ANALYSIS — **ANALYSE DU BILAN**

% of year-end balance sheet total — % du total du bilan en fin d'exercice

	1992	1993	1994¹	1995	1996	1997	1998	1999	2000	2001	
Assets											**Actif**
65. Cash & balance with Central bank	8.40	1.13	1.85	3.69	3.19	3.03	4.36	3.88	5.01	2.45	65. Caisse & solde auprés de la Banque centrale
66. Interbank deposits	6.82	43.92	3.82	6.70	4.50	5.19	4.81	6.38	4.45	6.94	66. Dépôts interbancaires
67. Loans	64.79	23.51	40.91	58.89	58.71	60.20	61.74	65.47	67.05	70.60	67. Prêts
68. Securities	4.31	9.04	11.66	19.89	23.75	23.04	22.34	18.61	13.63	16.45	68. Valeurs mobilières
69. Other assets	15.69	22.39	41.76	10.83	9.85	8.54	6.75	5.66	9.87	3.56	69. Autres actifs
Liabilities											**Passif**
70. Capital & reserves	5.42	4.17	3.36	6.43	7.08	7.18	6.70	6.82	7.50	7.76	70. Capital et réserves
71. Borrowing from Central bank	1.85	0.43	0.39	-	-	-	-	-	-	-	71. Emprunts auprés de la Banque centrale
72. Interbank deposits	0.08	0.11	0.03	-	2.64	3.84	8.85	9.03	9.04	11.09	72. Dépôts interbancaires
73. Non-bank deposits	58.51	19.69	36.53	83.58	80.57	81.54	76.58	76.72	73.67	71.32	73. Dépôts non bancaires
74. Bonds	6.94	9.78	11.70	2.13	1.73	2.00	1.31	1.19	1.76	1.71	74. Obligations
75. Other liabilities	27.20	65.82	47.98	7.86	7.98	5.44	6.57	6.24	8.03	8.13	75. Autres engagements
Memorandum items											***Pour mémoire***
76. Short-term securities	*1.96*	*5.29*	*9.35*	*9.80*	*10.65*	*8.73*	*12.20*	*8.54*	*6.43*	*8.78*	*76. Titres à court terme*
77. Bonds	*1.13*	*1.97*	*-*	*9.10*	*12.11*	*13.62*	*9.51*	*9.50*	*6.69*	*7.08*	*77. Obligations*
78. Shares and participations	*1.21*	*1.78*	*2.31*	*0.99*	*0.99*	*0.69*	*0.64*	*0.57*	*0.50*	*0.59*	*78. Actions et participations*
79. Claims on non-residents	*0.03*	*0.13*	*0.04*	*0.33*	*0.43*	*0.89*	*0.49*	*1.76*	*0.16*	*0.20*	*79. Créances sur des non-résidents*
80. Liabilities to non-residents	*1.17*	*0.24*	*0.03*	*0.05*	*0.10*	*0.26*	*0.13*	*0.20*	*0.20*	*0.09*	*80. Engagements envers des non-résidents*

* See notes on previous pages.   * Voir les notes en pages précédentes.

FINLAND
Co-operative banks

FINLANDE
Banques mutualistes

Million euros / *Million d'euros*

INCOME STATEMENT / COMPTE DE RESULTATS

	1992	1993	1994	1995	1996	1997	1998	1999	2000	2001	
1. Interest income	1917	1658	1447	1373	1117	967	965	897	1125	1242	1. Produits financiers
2. Interest expenses	1445	1040	716	679	496	351	310	268	372	440	2. Frais financiers
3. Net interest income	472	619	731	694	622	615	655	629	753	802	3. Produits financiers nets
4. Non-interest income (net)	521	337	348	368	485	496	814	547	439	401	4. Produits non financiers (nets)
a. Fees and commissions receivable	..	..	..	..	..	..	..	..	..	..	a. Frais et commissions à recevoir
b. Fees and commissions payable	..	..	..	..	..	..	..	..	..	..	b. Frais et commissions à payer
c. Net profits or loss on financial operations	..	..	..	..	..	..	..	..	..	..	c. Profits ou pertes nets sur opérations financières
d. Other	..	..	..	..	..	..	..	..	..	..	d. Autres
5. Gross income	993	956	1079	1061	1107	1111	1469	1176	1191	1203	5. Résultat brut
6. Operating expenses	978	1300	1328	1063	991	919	1069	776	726	742	6. Frais d'exploitation
a. Staff costs	287	255	275	253	243	224	225	213	219	225	a. Dépenses en personnel
b. Property costs	102	102	100	102	96	94	95	89	88	89	b. Dépenses en immobilier
c. Other	589	943	953	708	652	602	749	473	418	428	c. Autres
7. Net income	15	-344	-249	-2	115	192	400	401	465	461	7. Résultat net
8. Provisions (net)	-9	-12	2	3	3	1	-11	35	57	68	8. Provisions (nettes)
a. Provisions on loans	8	7	-2	..	..	..	..	..	..	..	a. Provisions sur prêts
b. Provisions on securities	-17	-19	4	..	..	..	..	..	..	..	b. Provisions sur titres
c. Other	..	..	-	..	..	..	..	..	..	..	c. Autres
9. Profit before tax	24	-331	-251	-4	113	191	412	366	408	393	9. Bénéfices avant impôt
10. Income tax	20	21	22	33	40	55	11	39	84	88	10. Impôt sur le revenu
11. Profit after tax	4	-352	-273	-38	72	137	401	327	324	305	11. Bénéfices après impôt
12. Distributed profit	5	3	0	5	6	10	11	13	17	21	12. Bénéfices distribués
13. Retained profit	-1	-356	-273	-42	66	127	390	315	307	284	13. Bénéfices mis en réserve

BALANCE SHEET / BILAN

Assets / Actif

	1992	1993	1994	1995	1996	1997	1998	1999	2000	2001	
14. Cash & balance with Central bank	821	545	498	476	473	458	424	193	167	134	14. Caisse & solde auprès de la Banque centrale
15. Interbank deposits	1660	2354	2368	2675	2226	2550	2304	2649	2970	3485	15. Dépôts interbancaires
16. Loans	13398	14956	14219	13950	13298	13266	14006	15238	16385	17675	16. Prêts
17. Securities	1130	1097	1408	1618	1669	1551	1577	1368	1274	1357	17. Valeurs mobilières
18. Other assets	2589	2809	2663	2445	2191	1998	1835	1614	1477	1248	18. Autres actifs

Liabilities / Passif

	1992	1993	1994	1995	1996	1997	1998	1999	2000	2001	
19. Capital & reserves	1298	1384	1367	1426	1534	1686	1846	2044	2406	2733	19. Capital et réserves
20. Borrowing from Central bank	80	-	-	-	-	-	-	-	-	-	20. Emprunts auprès de la Banque centrale
21. Interbank deposits	0	-	-	-	-	5	1	1	6	1	21. Dépôts interbancaires
22. Non-bank deposits	12756	15055	15346	16097	15316	15434	15842	16442	17127	18612	22. Dépôts non bancaires
23. Bonds	1655	1605	1389	1285	993	793	604	499	468	465	23. Obligations
24. Other liabilities	3810	3717	3054	2355	2014	1904	1853	2076	2266	2088	24. Autres engagements

Balance sheet total / Total du bilan

	1992	1993	1994	1995	1996	1997	1998	1999	2000	2001	
25. End-year total	19599	21760	21156	21163	19856	19822	20146	21062	22273	23899	25. En fin d'exercice
26. Average total	19125	20680	21458	21160	20510	19839	19984	20604	21668	23088	26. Moyen

FINLAND

Co-operative banks

FINLANDE

Banques mutualistes

Million euros   *Million d'euros*

	1992	1993	1994	1995	1996	1997	1998	1999	2000	2001	
Memorandum items											**Pour mémoire**
27. Short-term securities	256	225	216	266	142	72	313	144	240	191	27. Titres à court terme
28. Bonds	596	570	871	1055	1240	1154	939	873	681	775	28. Obligations
29. Shares and participations	278	302	320	297	287	324	326	351	353	391	29. Actions et participations
30. Claims on non-residents	1	1	1	1	0	1	1	0	0	5	30. Créances sur des non-résidents
31. Liabilities to non-residents	3	197	1	1	0	-	-	-	13	13	31. Engagements envers des non-résidents
Capital adequacy											**Solvabilité**
32. Tier 1 Capital	..	..	..	..	..	..	..	..	..	..	32. Fonds propres de base
33. Tier 2 Capital	..	..	..	..	..	..	..	..	..	..	33. Fonds propres complémentaires
34. Supervisory deductions	..	..	..	..	..	..	..	..	..	..	34. Eléments à déduire des fonds propres
35. Total net capital resources	..	..	..	..	..	..	..	..	..	..	35. Total net des ressources en capital
36. Risk-weighted assets	..	..	..	..	..	..	..	..	..	..	36. Actifs pondérés des risques
SUPPLEMENTARY INFORMATION											**RENSEIGNEMENTS COMPLEMENTAIRES**
37. Number of institutions	317	303	302	300	298	294	292	289	287	286	37. Nombre d'institutions
38. Number of branches	688	913	686	667	573	536	521	500	505	502	38. Nombre de succursales
39. Number of employees (x 1000)	8.7	8.7	9.1	8.6	7.4	7.0	6.8	6.7	6.7	6.9	39. Nombre de salariés (x 1000)

Per cent / *Pourcentage*	1992	1993	1994	1995	1996	1997	1998	1999	2000	2001	
INCOME STATEMENT ANALYSIS											**ANALYSE DU COMPTE DE RESULTATS**
% of average balance sheet total											**% du total moyen du bilan**
40. Interest income	10.02	8.02	6.74	6.49	5.45	4.87	4.83	4.35	5.19	5.38	40. Produits financiers
41. Interest expenses	7.55	5.03	3.34	3.21	2.42	1.77	1.55	1.30	1.72	1.91	41. Frais financiers
42. Net interest income	2.47	2.99	3.41	3.28	3.03	3.10	3.28	3.05	3.47	3.47	42. Produits financiers nets
43. Non-interest income (net)	2.72	1.63	1.62	1.74	2.36	2.50	4.07	2.66	2.02	1.74	43. Produits non financiers (nets)
a. Fees and commissions receivable	:	:	:	:	:	:	:	:	:	:	a. Frais et commissions à recevoir
b. Fees and commissions payable	:	:	:	:	:	:	:	:	:	:	b. Frais et commissions à payer
c. Net profits or loss on financial operations	:	:	:	:	:	:	:	:	:	:	c. Profits ou pertes nets sur opérations financières
d. Other	:	:	:	:	:	:	:	:	:	:	d. Autres
44. Gross income	5.19	4.62	5.03	5.02	5.40	5.60	7.35	5.71	5.50	5.21	44. Résultat brut
45. Operating expenses	5.12	6.28	6.19	5.03	4.83	4.63	5.35	3.76	3.35	3.21	45. Frais d'exploitation
a. Staff costs	1.50	1.23	1.28	1.20	1.19	1.13	1.12	1.04	1.01	0.97	a. Dépenses en personnel
b. Property costs	0.53	0.49	0.47	0.48	0.47	0.47	0.48	0.43	0.41	0.39	b. Dépenses en immobilier
c. Other	3.08	4.56	4.44	3.35	3.18	3.03	3.75	2.29	1.93	1.85	c. Autres
46. Net income	0.08	-1.66	-1.16	-0.01	0.56	0.97	2.00	1.95	2.15	2.00	46. Résultat net
47. Provisions (net)	-0.05	-0.06	0.01	0.01	0.01	0.01	-0.06	0.17	0.26	0.29	47. Provisions (nettes)
a. Provisions on loans	0.04	0.03	-0.01	:	:	:	:	:	:	:	a. Provisions sur prêts
b. Provisions on securities	-0.09	-0.09	0.02	:	:	:	:	:	:	:	b. Provisions sur titres
c. Other	:	:	:	:	:	:	:	:	:	:	c. Autres
48. Profit before tax	0.12	-1.60	-1.17	-0.02	0.55	0.96	2.06	1.78	1.88	1.70	48. Bénéfices avant impôt
49. Income tax	0.10	0.10	0.10	0.16	0.20	0.28	0.05	0.19	0.39	0.38	49. Impôt sur le revenu
50. Profit after tax	0.02	-1.70	-1.27	-0.18	0.35	0.69	2.00	1.59	1.49	1.32	50. Bénéfices après impôt
51. Distributed profit	0.02	0.02	:	0.02	0.03	0.05	0.05	0.06	0.08	0.09	51. Bénéfices distribués
52. Retained profit	-	-1.72	-1.27	-0.20	0.32	0.64	1.95	1.53	1.42	1.23	52. Bénéfices mis en réserve
% of gross income											**% du total du résultat brut**
53. Net interest income	47.54	64.72	67.77	65.35	56.19	55.38	44.59	53.50	63.18	66.67	53. Produits financiers nets
54. Non-interest income (net)	52.46	35.28	32.23	34.65	43.81	44.62	55.41	46.51	36.82	33.33	54. Produits non financiers (nets)
a. Fees and commissions receivable	:	:	:	:	:	:	:	:	:	:	a. Frais et commissions à recevoir
b. Fees and commissions payable	:	:	:	:	:	:	:	:	:	:	b. Frais et commissions à payer
c. Net profits or loss on financial operations	:	:	:	:	:	:	:	:	:	:	c. Profits ou pertes nets sur opérations financières
d. Other	:	:	:	:	:	:	:	:	:	:	d. Autres
55. Operating expenses	98.53	135.97	123.12	100.17	89.59	82.68	72.76	65.92	60.94	61.68	55. Frais d'exploitation
a. Staff costs	28.90	26.64	25.49	23.83	21.99	20.11	15.28	18.13	18.42	18.70	a. Dépenses en personnel
b. Property costs	10.30	10.70	9.31	9.63	8.68	8.43	6.47	7.61	7.43	7.40	b. Dépenses en immobilier
c. Other	59.33	98.63	88.32	66.71	58.92	54.14	51.01	40.19	35.09	35.58	c. Autres
56. Net income	1.47	-35.97	-23.12	-0.17	10.41	17.32	27.24	34.08	39.06	38.32	56. Résultat net
57. Provisions (net)	-0.91	-1.30	0.19	0.24	0.24	0.09	-0.78	2.99	4.80	5.65	57. Provisions (nettes)
a. Provisions on loans	0.78	0.69	-0.14	:	:	:	:	:	:	:	a. Provisions sur prêts
b. Provisions on securities	-1.69	-1.99	0.33	:	:	:	:	:	:	:	b. Provisions sur titres
c. Other	:	:	:	:	:	:	:	:	:	:	c. Autres
58. Profit before tax	2.39	-34.66	-23.31	-0.41	10.17	17.22	28.01	31.09	34.26	32.67	58. Bénéfices avant impôt
59. Income tax	1.98	2.18	2.00	3.15	3.65	4.92	0.74	3.27	7.07	7.32	59. Impôt sur le revenu
60. Profit after tax	0.41	-36.85	-25.30	-3.57	6.52	12.31	27.27	27.82	27.19	25.35	60. Bénéfices après impôt
% of net income											**% du total du résultat net**
61. Provisions (net)	-62.06	3.62	-0.81	-136.22	2.33	0.52	-2.86	8.77	12.29	14.75	61. Provisions (nettes)
a. Provisions on loans	52.90	-1.91	0.61	:	:	:	:	:	:	:	a. Provisions sur prêts
b. Provisions on securities	-114.97	5.53	-1.42	:	:	:	:	:	:	:	b. Provisions sur titres
c. Other	:	:	:	:	:	:	:	:	:	:	c. Autres
62. Profit before tax	162.06	96.38	100.81	236.22	97.67	99.48	102.86	91.23	87.71	85.25	62. Bénéfices avant impôt
63. Income tax	134.52	-6.07	-8.63	-1809.19	35.04	28.41	2.73	9.61	18.11	19.09	63. Impôt sur le revenu
64. Profit after tax	27.61	102.45	109.44	2045.41	62.62	71.07	100.12	81.63	69.61	66.16	64. Bénéfices après impôt

FINLAND
Co-operative banks

FINLANDE
Banques mutualistes

Per cent — *Pourcentage*

	1992	1993	1994	1995	1996	1997	1998	1999	2000	2001	
BALANCE SHEET ANALYSIS											**ANALYSE DU BILAN**
% of year-end balance sheet total											**% du total du bilan en fin d'exercice**
Assets											**Actif**
65. Cash & balance with Central bank	4.19	2.50	2.36	2.25	2.38	2.31	2.11	0.92	0.75	0.56	65. Caisse & solde auprès de la Banque centrale
66. Interbank deposits	8.47	10.82	11.19	12.64	11.21	12.86	11.44	12.58	13.33	14.58	66. Dépôts interbancaires
67. Loans	68.36	68.73	67.21	65.91	66.97	66.92	69.52	72.35	73.56	73.96	67. Prêts
68. Securities	5.77	5.04	6.65	7.65	8.41	7.82	7.83	6.49	5.72	5.68	68. Valeurs mobilières
69. Other assets	13.21	12.91	12.59	11.55	11.03	10.08	9.11	7.66	6.63	5.22	69. Autres actifs
Liabilities											**Passif**
70. Capital & reserves	6.62	6.36	6.46	6.74	7.72	8.50	9.16	9.71	10.80	11.44	70. Capital et réserves
71. Borrowing from Central bank	0.41	-	-	-	-	-	-	-	-	-	71. Emprunts auprès de la Banque centrale
72. Interbank deposits	-	-	-	-	-	0.03	0.01	-	0.03	-	72. Dépôts interbancaires
73. Non-bank deposits	65.09	69.19	72.54	76.06	77.14	77.86	78.64	78.06	76.90	77.88	73. Dépôts non bancaires
74. Bonds	8.44	7.37	6.57	6.07	5.00	4.00	3.00	2.37	2.10	1.95	74. Obligations
75. Other liabilities	19.44	17.08	14.44	11.13	10.14	9.61	9.20	9.86	10.17	8.74	75. Autres engagements
Memorandum items											***Pour mémoire***
76. *Short-term securities*	*1.31*	*1.03*	*1.02*	*1.26*	*0.71*	*0.36*	*1.55*	*0.69*	*1.08*	*0.80*	76. *Titres à court terme*
77. *Bonds*	*3.04*	*2.62*	*4.12*	*4.99*	*6.25*	*5.82*	*4.66*	*4.14*	*3.06*	*3.24*	77. *Obligations*
78. *Shares and participations*	*1.42*	*1.39*	*1.51*	*1.40*	*1.45*	*1.64*	*1.62*	*1.67*	*1.58*	*1.64*	78. *Actions et participations*
79. *Claims on non-residents*	*0.01*	-	-	-	-	-	-	-	-	*0.02*	79. *Créances sur des non-résidents*
80. *Liabilities to non-residents*	*0.02*	*0.91*	-	-	-	-	-	-	*0.06*	*0.05*	80. *Engagements envers des non-résidents*

FRANCE
All banks

Million euros

FRANCE
Ensemble des banques

Millions d'euros

	1992	1993	1994	1995	1996	1997	1998	1999	2000[1]	2001	
INCOME STATEMENT											**COMPTE DE RESULTATS**
1. Interest income	206478	217391	183966	202996	187238	190967	197841	186953	214093	226183	1. Produits financiers
2. Interest expenses	168148	181951	149309	169794	156247	162378	171305	157278	185266	197173	2. Frais financiers
3. Net interest income	38331	35440	34657	33202	30991	28589	26536	29675	28827	29010	3. Produits financiers nets
4. Non-interest income (net)	19825	25258	20929	27769	27537	32443	37925	37504	44876	49702	4. Produits non financiers (nets)
a. Fees and commissions receivable	..	14123	15074	13775	15633	17429	19177	21405	24678	26241	a. Frais et commissions à recevoir
b. Fees and commissions payable	..	4588	4703	4119	4778	4985	5421	5733	6732	7079	b. Frais et commissions à payer
c. Net profits or loss on financial operations	1195	8841	4528	7659	9784	11312	14391	12848	13476	15289	c. Profits ou pertes nets sur opérations financières
d. Other	18630	6881	6029	10453	6898	8687	9778	8984	13455	15251	d. Autres
5. Gross income	58155	60698	55585	60970	58528	61032	64460	67179	73703	78712	5. Résultat brut
6. Operating expenses	38862	39302	39620	40021	40913	41979	43621	45424	48651	48862	6. Frais d'exploitation
a. Staff costs	20641	21596	21441	21692	22250	22980	23497	24515	..	..	a. Dépenses en personnel
b. Property costs	2338	2205	2159	2236	2205	1998	2230	2289	2335	2467	b. Dépenses en immobilier
c. Other	15883	15500	16020	16093	16458	17001	17894	18620	-	-	c. Autres
7. Net income	19293	21396	15965	20950	17615	19053	20839	21755	25052	29851	7. Résultat net
8. Provisions (net)	12374	18124	15389	16604	11976	9634	8156	4367	5657	8214	8. Provisions (nettes)
a. Provisions on loans	7396	15819	13945	12942	10288	9445	9236	5505	..	..	a. Provisions sur prêts
b. Provisions on securities	2230	1665	1669	3044	1486	-301	-1673	-1893	..	..	b. Provisions sur titres
c. Other	2749	640	-225	617	202	490	593	755	1470	2290	c. Autres
9. Profit before tax	6919	3273	577	4346	5639	9419	12684	17388	19395	21636	9. Bénéfices avant impôt
10. Income tax	2660	2735	2101	2843	2781	2895	2104	4510	3793	4162	10. Impôt sur le revenu
11. Profit after tax	4259	538	-1524	1504	2858	6525	10580	12878	15602	17475	11. Bénéfices après impôt
12. Distributed profit	3094	3429	3184	3532	3935	4720	4945	6135	7419	8408	12. Bénéfices distribués
13. Retained profit	1165	-2891	-4709	-2029	-1076	1804	5635	6743	8183	9067	13. Bénéfices mis en réserve
BALANCE SHEET											**BILAN**
Assets											**Actif**
14. Cash & balance with Central bank	10369	5727	5312	5770	9043	8885	20670	30453	26773	41200	14. Caisse & solde auprès de la Banque centrale
15. Interbank deposits	936796	1003525	1005835	1053975	1102620	1149668	1112490	1190078	1132240	1278393	15. Dépôts interbancaires
16. Loans	1006972	1017906	1018571	1042656	1038587	1107340	1126577	1189563	1291884	1381852	16. Prêts
17. Securities	310188	369862	403350	442243	542118	609507	627854	727219	709908	764779	17. Valeurs mobilières
18. Other assets	217703	143438	146475	162788	170401	203080	233280	333270	352050	409354	18. Autres actifs
Liabilities											**Passif**
19. Capital & reserves	99870	114079	118120	119752	117964	123020	127763	161261	160529	183957	19. Capital et réserves
20. Borrowing from Central bank	30724	5420	3455	2245	3253	4878	5814	1214	3800	11638	20. Emprunts auprès de la Banque centrale
21. Interbank deposits	928989	984892	1011562	1044226	1141158	1195310	1201829	1325664	1292762	1350972	21. Dépôts interbancaires
22. Non-bank deposits	588864	650626	698455	762838	813088	916484	936045	960584	992622	1116408	22. Dépôts non bancaires
23. Bonds	574030	608552	576480	576136	528621	530364	511938	562793	605207	690901	23. Obligations
24. Other liabilities	259552	176887	171471	202234	258686	308423	337481	459067	457935	521701	24. Autres engagements
Balance sheet total											**Total du bilan**
25. End-year total	2482028	2540458	2579544	2707432	2862769	3078479	3120870	3470583	3512854	3875577	25. En fin d'exercice
26. Average total	2460243	2671721	2719228	2836093	3062720	3384220	3610139	3725634	2909820	3010905	26. Moyen

FRANCE

All banks

Million euros

	1992	1993	1994	1995	1996	1997	1998	1999	2000[1]	2001		*Millions d'euros*
Memorandum items												**Pour mémoire**
27. Short-term securities	..	..	..	..	..	..	..	..	..	..	27.	Titres à court terme
28. Bonds	..	189860	197445	205600	262531	286485	288837	317530	312269	350887	28.	Obligations
29. Shares and participations	..	76585	80247	82382	78764	83560	90178	124418	121909	146109	29.	Actions et participations
30. Claims on non-residents	642822	495967	477001	508436	542551	667502	662024	781553	787438	880964	30.	Créances sur des non-résidents
31. Liabilities to non-residents	639676	447277	466978	477145	527718	619552	627445	732996	820638	956726	31.	Engagements envers des non-résidents
Capital adequacy												**Solvabilité**
32. Tier 1 Capital	..	..	..	..	..	..	..	..	..	..	32.	Fonds propres de base
33. Tier 2 Capital	..	..	..	..	..	..	..	..	..	..	33.	Fonds propres complémentaires
34. Supervisory deductions	..	..	..	..	..	..	..	..	..	..	34.	Eléments à déduire des fonds propres
35. Total net capital resources	..	..	..	..	..	..	..	..	..	..	35.	Total net des ressources en capital
36. Risk-weighted assets	..	..	..	..	..	..	..	..	..	..	36.	Actifs pondérés des risques
SUPPLEMENTARY INFORMATION												**RENSEIGNEMENTS COMPLEMENTAIRES**
37. Number of institutions	1701	1635	1618	1453	1404	1288	1242	1168	1108	1067	37.	Nombre d'institutions
38. Number of branches	25357	26291	26200	26606	26303	26386	26689	26101	26231	25874	38.	Nombre de succursales
39. Number of employees (x 1000)	425.0	406.0	409.0	408.0	404.0	397.0	398.0	394.0	399.3	411.5	39.	Nombre de salariés (x 1000)

FRANCE

Ensemble des banques

1 Since the year 2000, the French financial institutions' accounts have been published and presented in a new format. Therefore, some information is no longer available.

Notes

. The corporate data -- presented for all financial institutions and for each of the main categories of banks -- covers the activities and results of the foreign branches of banks with headquarters in France but exclude subsidiaries outside France.

. Foreign-controlled banks operating in France, in the form of branches or subsidiaries, are dealt with the same way as banks under French control. However, branches of banks with headquarters in another European Union country are excluded.

. Average balance sheet totals (item 26) are based on the average of quarterly totals.

1 A partir de 2000, les comptes publiés par les établissements de crédit français présentent un nouveau format. En conséquence, certaines informations ne sont plus disponibles.

Notes

. Les données établies sur une base sociale -- ensemble des établissements de crédit et principales catégories juridiques -- incluent l'activité et les résultats des succursales à l'étranger dont le siège est en France L'activité et les résultats des filiales étrangères sont exclus.

. Les établissements sous contrôle étranger opérant en France, sous la forme de succursales ou de filiales, sont traités dans les mêmes conditions que les banques sous contrôle français. Toutefois, sont exclues de cette présentation les succursales d'établissements dont le siège est implanté dans un autre pays de l'Union Européenne.

. La moyenne du total des actifs/passifs (poste26) est basée sur la moyenne des totaux des situations trimestrielles.

Per cent · *Pourcentage*

	1992	1993	1994	1995	1996	1997	1998	1999	2000[1]	2001		
INCOME STATEMENT ANALYSIS												**ANALYSE DU COMPTE DE RESULTATS**
% of average balance sheet total												**% du total moyen du bilan**
40. Interest income	8.39	8.14	6.77	7.16	6.11	5.64	5.48	5.02	7.36	7.51	40.	Produits financiers
41. Interest expenses	6.83	6.81	5.49	5.99	5.10	4.80	4.75	4.22	6.37	6.55	41.	Frais financiers
42. Net interest income	1.56	1.33	1.27	1.17	1.01	0.84	0.74	0.80	0.99	0.96	42.	Produits financiers nets
43. Non-interest income (net)	0.81	0.95	0.77	0.98	0.90	0.96	1.05	1.01	1.54	1.65	43.	Produits non financiers (nets)
a. Fees and commissions receivable	..	*0.53*	*0.55*	*0.49*	*0.51*	*0.51*	*0.53*	*0.57*	*0.85*	*0.87*		*a. Frais et commissions à recevoir*
b. Fees and commissions payable		*0.17*	*0.17*	*0.15*	*0.16*	*0.15*	*0.15*	*0.15*	*0.23*	*0.24*		*b. Frais et commissions à payer*
c. Net profits or loss on financial operations	*0.05*	*0.33*	*0.17*	*0.27*	*0.32*	*0.33*	*0.40*	*0.34*	*0.46*	*0.51*		*c. Profits ou pertes nets sur opérations financières*
d. Other	*0.76*	*0.26*	*0.22*	*0.37*	*0.23*	*0.26*	*0.27*	*0.24*	*0.46*	*0.51*		*d. Autres*
44. Gross income	2.36	2.27	2.04	2.15	1.91	1.80	1.79	1.80	2.53	2.61	44.	Résultat brut
45. Operating expenses	1.58	1.47	1.46	1.41	1.34	1.24	1.21	1.22	1.67	1.62	45.	Frais d'exploitation
a. Staff costs	*0.84*	*0.81*	*0.79*	*0.76*	*0.73*	*0.68*	*0.65*	*0.66*				*a. Dépenses en personnel*
b. Property costs	*0.10*	*0.08*	*0.08*	*0.08*	*0.07*	*0.06*	*0.06*	*0.06*	*0.08*	*0.08*		*b. Dépenses en immobilier*
c. Other	*0.65*	*0.58*	*0.59*	*0.57*	*0.54*	*0.50*	*0.50*	*0.50*	*-*	*-*		*c. Autres*
46. Net income	0.78	0.80	0.59	0.74	0.58	0.56	0.58	0.58	0.86	0.99	46.	Résultat net
47. Provisions (net)	0.50	0.68	0.57	0.59	0.39	0.28	0.23	0.12	0.19	0.27	47.	Provisions (nettes)
a. Provisions on loans	*0.30*	*0.59*	*0.51*	*0.46*	*0.34*	*0.28*	*0.26*	*0.15*				*a. Provisions sur prêts*
b. Provisions on securities	*0.09*	*0.06*	*0.06*	*0.11*	*0.05*	*-0.01*	*-0.05*	*-0.05*				*b. Provisions sur titres*
c. Other	*0.11*	*0.02*	*-0.01*	*0.02*	*0.01*	*0.01*	*0.02*	*0.02*	*0.05*	*0.08*		*c. Autres*
48. Profit before tax	0.28	0.12	0.02	0.15	0.18	0.28	0.35	0.47	0.67	0.72	48.	Bénéfices avant impôt
49. Income tax	0.11	0.10	0.08	0.10	0.09	0.09	0.06	0.12	0.13	0.14	49.	Impôt sur le revenu
50. Profit after tax	0.17	0.02	-0.06	0.05	0.09	0.19	0.29	0.35	0.54	0.58	50.	Bénéfices après impôt
51. Distributed profit	0.13	0.13	0.12	0.12	0.13	0.14	0.14	0.16	0.25	0.28	51.	Bénéfices distribués
52. Retained profit	0.05	-0.11	-0.17	-0.07	-0.04	0.05	0.16	0.18	0.28	0.30	52.	Bénéfices mis en réserve
% of gross income												**% du total du résultat brut**
53. Net interest income	65.91	58.39	62.35	54.46	52.95	46.84	41.17	44.17	39.11	36.86	53.	Produits financiers nets
54. Non-interest income (net)	34.09	41.61	37.65	45.54	47.05	53.16	58.83	55.83	60.89	63.14	54.	Produits non financiers (nets)
a. Fees and commissions receivable	..	*23.27*	*27.12*	*22.59*	*26.71*	*28.56*	*29.75*	*31.86*	*33.48*	*33.34*		*a. Frais et commissions à recevoir*
b. Fees and commissions payable		*7.56*	*8.46*	*6.76*	*8.16*	*8.17*	*8.41*	*8.53*	*9.13*	*8.99*		*b. Frais et commissions à payer*
c. Net profits or loss on financial operations	*2.05*	*14.56*	*8.15*	*12.56*	*16.72*	*18.54*	*22.33*	*19.12*	*18.28*	*19.42*		*c. Profits ou pertes nets sur opérations financières*
d. Other	*32.04*	*11.34*	*10.85*	*17.14*	*11.79*	*14.23*	*15.17*	*13.37*	*18.26*	*19.38*		*d. Autres*
55. Operating expenses	66.82	64.75	71.28	65.64	69.90	68.78	67.67	67.62	66.01	62.08	55.	Frais d'exploitation
a. Staff costs	*35.49*	*35.58*	*38.57*	*35.58*	*38.02*	*37.65*	*36.45*	*36.49*				*a. Dépenses en personnel*
b. Property costs	*4.02*	*3.63*	*3.88*	*3.67*	*3.77*	*3.27*	*3.46*	*3.41*	*3.17*	*3.13*		*b. Dépenses en immobilier*
c. Other	*27.31*	*25.54*	*28.82*	*26.39*	*28.12*	*27.86*	*27.76*	*27.72*				*c. Autres*
56. Net income	33.18	35.25	28.72	34.36	30.10	31.22	32.33	32.38	33.99	37.92	56.	Résultat net
57. Provisions (net)	21.28	29.86	27.69	27.23	20.46	15.79	12.65	6.50	7.68	10.44	57.	Provisions (nettes)
a. Provisions on loans	*12.72*	*26.06*	*25.09*	*21.23*	*17.58*	*15.48*	*14.33*	*8.19*				*a. Provisions sur prêts*
b. Provisions on securities	*3.83*	*2.74*	*3.00*	*4.99*	*2.54*	*-0.49*	*-2.59*	*-2.82*				*b. Provisions sur titres*
c. Other	*4.73*	*1.05*	*-0.40*	*1.01*	*0.35*	*0.80*	*0.92*	*1.12*	*1.99*	*2.91*		*c. Autres*
58. Profit before tax	11.90	5.39	1.04	7.13	9.63	15.43	19.68	25.88	26.32	27.49	58.	Bénéfices avant impôt
59. Income tax	4.57	4.51	3.78	4.66	4.75	4.74	3.26	6.71	5.15	5.29	59.	Impôt sur le revenu
60. Profit after tax	7.32	0.89	-2.74	2.47	4.88	10.69	16.41	19.17	21.17	22.20	60.	Bénéfices après impôt
% of net income												**% du total du résultat net**
61. Provisions (net)	64.14	84.70	96.39	79.25	67.99	50.56	39.14	20.07	22.58	27.52	61.	Provisions (nettes)
a. Provisions on loans	*38.33*	*73.93*	*87.34*	*61.78*	*58.40*	*49.57*	*44.32*	*25.30*				*a. Provisions sur prêts*
b. Provisions on securities	*11.56*	*7.78*	*10.46*	*14.53*	*8.44*	*-1.58*	*-8.03*	*-8.70*				*b. Provisions sur titres*
c. Other	*14.25*	*2.99*	*-1.41*	*2.94*	*1.15*	*2.57*	*2.84*	*3.47*	*5.87*	*7.67*		*c. Autres*
62. Profit before tax	35.86	15.30	3.61	20.75	32.01	49.44	60.86	79.93	77.42	72.48	62.	Bénéfices avant impôt
63. Income tax	13.79	12.78	13.16	13.57	15.79	15.19	10.10	20.73	15.14	13.94	63.	Impôt sur le revenu
64. Profit after tax	22.07	2.51	-9.55	7.18	16.23	34.24	50.77	59.19	62.28	58.54	64.	Bénéfices après impôt

FRANCE

All banks

FRANCE

Ensemble des banques

Per cent / *Pourcentage*

BALANCE SHEET ANALYSIS — **ANALYSE DU BILAN**

% of year-end balance sheet total — **% du total du bilan en fin d'exercice**

	1992	1993	1994	1995	1996	1997	1998	1999	2000[1]	2001	
Assets											**Actif**
65. Cash & balance with Central bank	0.42	0.23	0.21	0.21	0.32	0.29	0.66	0.88	0.76	1.06	65. Caisse & solde auprès de la Banque centrale
66. Interbank deposits	37.74	39.50	38.99	38.93	38.52	37.35	35.65	34.29	32.23	32.99	66. Dépôts interbancaires
67. Loans	40.57	40.07	39.49	38.51	36.28	35.97	36.10	34.28	36.78	35.66	67. Prêts
68. Securities	12.50	14.56	15.64	16.33	18.94	19.80	20.12	20.95	20.21	19.73	68. Valeurs mobilières
69. Other assets	8.77	5.65	5.68	6.01	5.95	6.60	7.47	9.60	10.02	10.56	69. Autres actifs
Liabilities											**Passif**
70. Capital & reserves	4.02	4.49	4.58	4.42	4.12	4.00	4.09	4.65	4.57	4.75	70. Capital et réserves
71. Borrowing from Central bank	1.24	0.21	0.13	0.08	0.11	0.16	0.19	0.03	0.11	0.30	71. Emprunts auprès de la Banque centrale
72. Interbank deposits	37.43	38.77	39.21	38.57	39.86	38.83	38.51	38.20	36.80	34.86	72. Dépôts interbancaires
73. Non-bank deposits	23.73	25.61	27.08	28.18	28.40	29.77	29.99	27.68	28.26	28.81	73. Dépôts non bancaires
74. Bonds	23.13	23.95	22.35	21.28	18.47	17.23	16.40	16.22	17.23	17.83	74. Obligations
75. Other liabilities	10.46	6.96	6.65	7.47	9.04	10.02	10.81	13.23	13.04	13.46	75. Autres engagements
Memorandum items											***Pour mémoire***
76. Short-term securities	*..*	*..*	*..*	*..*	*..*	*..*	*..*	*..*	*..*	*..*	*76. Titres à court terme*
77. Bonds	*..*	*7.47*	*7.65*	*7.59*	*9.17*	*9.31*	*9.26*	*9.15*	*8.89*	*9.05*	*77. Obligations*
78. Shares and participations	*..*	*3.01*	*3.11*	*3.04*	*2.75*	*2.71*	*2.89*	*3.58*	*3.47*	*3.77*	*78. Actions et participations*
79. Claims on non-residents	*25.90*	*19.52*	*18.49*	*18.78*	*18.95*	*21.68*	*21.21*	*22.52*	*22.42*	*22.73*	*79. Créances sur des non-résidents*
80. Liabilities to non-residents	*25.77*	*17.61*	*18.10*	*17.62*	*18.43*	*20.13*	*20.10*	*21.12*	*23.36*	*24.69*	*80. Engagements envers des non-résidents*

* See notes on previous pages.

* Voir les notes en pages précédentes.

FRANCE
Commercial banks

Million euros

	1992	1993	1994	1995	1996	1997	1998	1999	2000[1]	2001
INCOME STATEMENT										
1. Interest income	101796	108978	85037	102053	93295	100954	109611	101202	129508	137925
2. Interest expenses	86559	94662	71199	89302	81236	89416	99649	89286	117287	125645
3. Net interest income	15237	14316	13838	12751	12059	11538	9962	11916	12222	12280
4. Non-interest income (net)	13096	16148	12755	15733	15156	19467	23413	24174	29660	31570
a. Fees and commissions receivable	..	7835	8375	7440	8545	9960	10939	12095	14053	15226
b. Fees and commissions payable	..	2013	2254	1819	2191	2452	2679	2739	3528	3907
c. Net profits or loss on financial operations	568	6506	3879	5549	6730	7957	9550	9839	10178	11927
d. Other	12527	3819	2756	4563	2072	4003	5603	4979	8957	8323
5. Gross income	28332	30464	26593	28484	27215	31005	33375	36090	41882	43850
6. Operating expenses	20529	21239	21236	21194	21807	23178	24193	25496	28187	28466
a. Staff costs	11782	12327	12119	12118	12479	13381	13680	14477	..	..
b. Property costs	1224	1176	1170	1145	1232	1129	1257	1299	1346	1453
c. Other	7523	7736	7948	7931	8095	8668	9256	9719	-	-
7. Net income	7803	9224	5357	7291	5408	7827	9182	10594	13695	15384
8. Provisions (net)	6962	9684	8226	5797	4828	5468	4977	1855	2717	3728
a. Provisions on loans	3944	8448	7024	3893	4287	6026	6492	2965	..	..
b. Provisions on securities	1294	1115	1650	1796	882	-482	-1467	-1239	..	..
c. Other	1724	121	-448	108	-341	-76	-48	129	611	137
9. Profit before tax	841	-459	-2869	1494	580	2359	4205	8739	10978	11656
10. Income tax	1004	693	633	709	640	498	-903	1558	1201	1337
11. Profit after tax	-163	-1153	-3501	785	-59	1861	5108	7181	9777	10319
12. Distributed profit	1088	1183	1066	1325	1878	2502	2814	3992	5050	5629
13. Retained profit	-1251	-2336	-4567	-541	-1937	-641	2294	3189	4727	4690
BALANCE SHEET										
Assets										
14. Cash & balance with Central bank	6482	3570	3269	3483	6600	6266	14089	21497	20172	31936
15. Interbank deposits	541590	565863	553183	569555	612233	652427	600783	647507	592733	691274
16. Loans	487385	483635	472153	488760	495561	565545	571352	592493	699774	752431
17. Securities	205564	252420	258668	269786	323210	399181	404396	495927	489336	538613
18. Other assets	131620	95863	97660	106403	110701	144039	172538	259811	290628	342828
Liabilities										
19. Capital & reserves	42107	46326	46992	46902	48058	51840	60146	86601	81283	90222
20. Borrowing from Central bank	27286	4122	2911	1857	2961	4674	5627	1033	3741	2166
21. Interbank deposits	552433	603216	608462	622358	674571	737449	707905	770668	735356	757310
22. Non-bank deposits	280115	304721	313980	341176	368794	435786	443241	457137	487568	587355
23. Bonds	319439	320107	296793	288363	280682	307686	297165	345565	420411	501941
24. Other liabilities	151260	122859	115794	137330	173239	230022	249075	356230	364284	418088
Balance sheet total										
25. End-year total	1372640	1401352	1384932	1437987	1548305	1767458	1763159	2017235	2092642	2357083
26. Average total	1307940	1534540	1553706	1585106	1717426	2045782	2292193	2415928	1610089	1609422

FRANCE
Banques commerciales

Millions d'euros

COMPTE DE RESULTATS
1. Produits financiers
2. Frais financiers
3. Produits financiers nets
4. Produits non financiers (nets)
   a. Frais et commissions à recevoir
   b. Frais et commissions à payer
   c. Profits ou pertes nets sur opérations financières
   d. Autres
5. Résultat brut
6. Frais d'exploitation
   a. Dépenses en personnel
   b. Dépenses en immobilier
   c. Autres
7. Résultat net
8. Provisions (nettes)
   a. Provisions sur prêts
   b. Provisions sur titres
   c. Autres
9. Bénéfices avant impôt
10. Impôt sur le revenu
11. Bénéfices après impôt
12. Bénéfices distribués
13. Bénéfices mis en réserve

BILAN

Actif
14. Caisse & solde auprès de la Banque centrale
15. Dépôts interbancaires
16. Prêts
17. Valeurs mobilières
18. Autres actifs

Passif
19. Capital et réserves
20. Emprunts auprès de la Banque centrale
21. Dépôts interbancaires
22. Dépôts non bancaires
23. Obligations
24. Autres engagements

Total du bilan
25. En fin d'exercice
26. Moyen

FRANCE

Commercial banks

Million euros

	1992	1993	1994	1995	1996	1997	1998	1999	2000[1]	2001
Memorandum items										
27. Short-term securities	..	..	..	..	..	..	..	..	..	..
28. Bonds	..	127735	124691	125135	162330	191116	190276	203183	199361	236741
29. Shares and participations	..	44658	47250	39594	40695	42083	53577	81612	78485	91146
30. Claims on non-residents	575546	414769	400475	421788	436639	543527	536184	641388	658945	754302
31. Liabilities to non-residents	589719	364109	377786	386297	419156	503271	508803	624159	730970	865860
Capital adequacy										
32. Tier 1 Capital	..	..	..	..	..	..	..	..	..	..
33. Tier 2 Capital	..	..	..	..	..	..	..	..	..	..
34. Supervisory deductions	..	..	..	..	..	..	..	..	..	..
35. Total net capital resources	..	..	..	..	..	..	..	..	..	..
36. Risk-weighted assets	..	..	..	..	..	..	..	..	..	..
SUPPLEMENTARY INFORMATION										
37. Number of institutions	409	415	421	413	400	398	383	362	360	355
38. Number of branches	10081	10451	10131	10320	10240	9983	10118	9794	9964	10065
39. Number of employees (x 1000)	232.0	219.0	218.0	214.0	209.0	208.0	207.0	202.0	205.0	212.1

1 Since the year 2000, the French financial institutions' accounts have been published and presented in a new format. Therefore, some information is no longer available.

Notes

. Average balance sheet totals (item 26) are based on the average of quarterly totals.

FRANCE

Banques commerciales

Millions d'euros

Pour mémoire
27. Titres à court terme
28. Obligations
29. Actions et participations
30. Créances sur des non-résidents
31. Engagements envers des non-résidents

Solvabilité
32. Fonds propres de base
33. Fonds propres complémentaires
34. Eléments à déduire des fonds propres
35. Total net des ressources en capital
36. Actifs pondérés des risques

RENSEIGNEMENTS COMPLEMENTAIRES
37. Nombre d'institutions
38. Nombre de succursales
39. Nombre de salariés (x 1000)

1 A partir de 2000, les comptes publiés par les établissements de crédit français présentent un nouveau format. En conséquence, certaines informations ne sont plus disponibles.

Notes

. La moyenne du total des actifs/passifs (poste26) est basée sur la moyenne des totaux des situations trimestrielles.

FRANCE
Commercial banks

FRANCE
Banques commerciales

FRANCE
Banques commerciales

Per cent / *Pourcentage*

INCOME STATEMENT ANALYSIS / **ANALYSE DU COMPTE DE RESULTATS**

Item	1992	1993	1994	1995	1996	1997	1998	1999	2000 [1]	2001	Rubrique
% of average balance sheet total											**% du total moyen du bilan**
40. Interest income	7.78	7.10	5.47	6.44	5.43	4.93	4.78	4.19	8.04	8.57	40. Produits financiers
41. Interest expenses	6.62	6.17	4.58	5.63	4.73	4.37	4.35	3.70	7.28	7.81	41. Frais financiers
42. Net interest income	1.16	0.93	0.89	0.80	0.70	0.56	0.43	0.49	0.76	0.76	42. Produits financiers nets
43. Non-interest income (net)	1.00	1.05	0.82	0.99	0.88	0.95	1.02	1.00	1.84	1.96	43. Produits non financiers (nets)
a. Fees and commissions receivable	..	0.51	0.54	0.47	0.50	0.49	0.48	0.50	0.87	0.95	*a. Frais et commissions à recevoir*
b. Fees and commissions payable	..	0.13	0.15	0.11	0.13	0.12	0.12	0.11	0.22	0.24	*b. Frais et commissions à payer*
c. Net profits or loss on financial operations	0.04	0.42	0.25	0.35	0.39	0.39	0.42	0.41	0.63	0.74	*c. Profits ou pertes nets sur opérations financières*
d. Other	0.96	0.25	0.18	0.29	0.12	0.20	0.24	0.21	0.56	0.52	*d. Autres*
44. Gross income	2.17	1.99	1.71	1.80	1.58	1.52	1.46	1.49	2.60	2.72	44. Résultat brut
45. Operating expenses	1.57	1.38	1.37	1.34	1.27	1.13	1.06	1.06	1.75	1.77	45. Frais d'exploitation
a. Staff costs	0.90	0.80	0.78	0.76	0.73	0.65	0.60	0.60	..	..	*a. Dépenses en personnel*
b. Property costs	0.09	0.08	0.08	0.07	0.07	0.06	0.05	0.05	0.08	0.09	*b. Dépenses en immobilier*
c. Other	0.58	0.50	0.51	0.50	0.47	0.42	0.40	0.40	..	..	*c. Autres*
46. Net income	0.60	0.60	0.34	0.46	0.31	0.38	0.40	0.44	0.85	0.96	46. Résultat net
47. Provisions (net)	0.53	0.63	0.53	0.37	0.28	0.27	0.22	0.08	0.17	0.23	47. Provisions (nettes)
a. Provisions on loans	0.30	0.55	0.45	0.25	0.25	0.29	0.28	0.12	..	..	*a. Provisions sur prêts*
b. Provisions on securities	0.10	0.07	0.11	0.11	0.05	-0.02	-0.06	-0.05	..	..	*b. Provisions sur titres*
c. Other	0.13	0.01	-0.03	0.01	-0.02	..	..	0.01	0.04	0.01	*c. Autres*
48. Profit before tax	0.06	-0.03	-0.18	0.09	0.03	0.12	0.18	0.36	0.68	0.72	48. Bénéfices avant impôt
49. Income tax	0.08	0.05	0.04	0.04	0.04	0.02	-0.04	0.06	0.07	0.08	49. Impôt sur le revenu
50. Profit after tax	-0.01	-0.08	-0.23	0.05	-	0.09	0.22	0.30	0.61	0.64	50. Bénéfices après impôt
51. Distributed profit	0.08	0.08	0.07	0.08	0.11	0.12	0.12	0.17	0.31	0.35	51. Bénéfices distribués
52. Retained profit	-0.10	-0.15	-0.29	-0.03	-0.11	-0.03	0.10	0.13	0.29	0.29	52. Bénéfices mis en réserve
% of gross income											**% du total du résultat brut**
53. Net interest income	53.78	46.99	52.04	44.77	44.31	37.21	29.85	33.02	29.18	28.00	53. Produits financiers nets
54. Non-interest income (net)	46.22	53.01	47.96	55.23	55.69	62.79	70.15	66.98	70.82	72.00	54. Produits non financiers (nets)
a. Fees and commissions receivable	..	25.72	31.49	26.12	31.40	32.12	32.78	33.51	33.55	34.72	*a. Frais et commissions à recevoir*
b. Fees and commissions payable	..	6.61	8.47	6.39	8.05	7.91	8.03	7.59	8.42	8.91	*b. Frais et commissions à payer*
c. Net profits or loss on financial operations	2.01	21.36	14.59	19.48	24.73	25.66	28.61	27.26	24.30	27.20	*c. Profits ou pertes nets sur opérations financières*
d. Other	44.22	12.54	10.36	16.02	7.61	12.91	16.79	13.80	21.39	18.98	*d. Autres*
55. Operating expenses	72.46	69.72	79.86	74.40	80.13	74.76	72.49	70.65	67.30	64.92	55. Frais d'exploitation
a. Staff costs	41.58	40.46	45.57	42.54	45.85	43.16	40.99	40.11	..	..	*a. Dépenses en personnel*
b. Property costs	4.32	3.86	4.40	4.02	4.53	3.64	3.77	3.60	3.21	3.31	*b. Dépenses en immobilier*
c. Other	26.55	25.40	29.89	27.84	29.75	27.96	27.73	26.93	..	..	*c. Autres*
56. Net income	27.54	30.28	20.14	25.60	19.87	25.24	27.51	29.35	32.70	35.08	56. Résultat net
57. Provisions (net)	24.57	31.79	30.93	20.35	17.74	17.64	14.91	5.14	6.49	8.50	57. Provisions (nettes)
a. Provisions on loans	13.92	27.73	26.41	13.67	15.75	19.44	19.45	8.22	..	..	*a. Provisions sur prêts*
b. Provisions on securities	4.57	3.66	6.20	6.30	3.24	-1.55	-4.40	-3.43	..	..	*b. Provisions sur titres*
c. Other	6.08	0.40	-1.69	0.38	-1.25	-0.24	-0.14	0.36	1.46	0.31	*c. Autres*
58. Profit before tax	2.97	-1.51	-10.79	5.25	2.13	7.61	12.60	24.21	26.21	26.58	58. Bénéfices avant impôt
59. Income tax	3.54	2.28	2.38	2.49	2.35	1.61	-2.71	4.32	2.87	3.05	59. Impôt sur le revenu
60. Profit after tax	-0.58	-3.78	-13.17	2.76	-0.22	6.00	15.31	19.90	23.34	23.53	60. Bénéfices après impôt
% of net income											**% du total du résultat net**
61. Provisions (net)	89.22	104.98	153.56	79.51	89.27	69.86	54.20	17.51	19.84	24.23	61. Provisions (nettes)
a. Provisions on loans	50.55	91.58	131.12	53.40	79.27	76.99	70.71	27.99	..	..	*a. Provisions sur prêts*
b. Provisions on securities	16.58	12.09	30.80	24.63	16.30	-6.15	-15.98	-11.69	..	..	*b. Provisions sur titres*
c. Other	22.09	1.31	-8.37	1.48	-6.31	-0.97	-0.53	1.22	4.46	0.89	*c. Autres*
62. Profit before tax	10.78	-4.98	-53.56	20.49	10.73	30.14	45.80	82.49	80.16	75.77	62. Bénéfices avant impôt
63. Income tax	12.87	7.52	11.81	9.73	11.82	6.36	-9.84	14.70	8.77	8.69	63. Impôt sur le revenu
64. Profit after tax	-2.09	-12.50	-65.37	10.76	-1.10	23.78	55.64	67.79	71.39	67.08	64. Bénéfices après impôt

FRANCE
Commercial banks

FRANCE
Banques commerciales

Per cent — *Pourcentage*

BALANCE SHEET ANALYSIS — **ANALYSE DU BILAN**

% of year-end balance sheet total — **% du total du bilan en fin d'exercice**

	1992	1993	1994	1995	1996	1997	1998	1999	2000[1]	2001	
Assets											**Actif**
65. Cash & balance with Central bank	0.47	0.25	0.24	0.24	0.43	0.35	0.80	1.07	0.96	1.35	65. Caisse & solde auprès de la Banque centrale
66. Interbank deposits	39.46	40.38	39.94	39.61	39.54	36.91	34.07	32.10	28.32	29.33	66. Dépôts interbancaires
67. Loans	35.51	34.51	34.09	33.99	32.01	32.00	32.41	29.37	33.44	31.92	67. Prêts
68. Securities	14.98	18.01	18.68	18.76	20.88	22.59	22.94	24.58	23.38	22.85	68. Valeurs mobilières
69. Other assets	9.59	6.84	7.05	7.40	7.15	8.15	9.79	12.88	13.89	14.54	69. Autres actifs
Liabilities											**Passif**
70. Capital & reserves	3.07	3.31	3.39	3.26	3.10	2.93	3.41	4.29	3.88	3.83	70. Capital et réserves
71. Borrowing from Central bank	1.99	0.29	0.21	0.13	0.19	0.26	0.32	0.05	0.18	0.09	71. Emprunts auprès de la Banque centrale
72. Interbank deposits	40.25	43.05	43.93	43.28	43.57	41.72	40.15	38.20	35.14	32.13	72. Dépôts interbancaires
73. Non-bank deposits	20.41	21.74	22.67	23.73	23.82	24.66	25.14	22.66	23.30	24.92	73. Dépôts non bancaires
74. Bonds	23.27	22.84	21.43	20.05	18.13	17.41	16.85	17.13	20.09	21.30	74. Obligations
75. Other liabilities	11.02	8.77	8.36	9.55	11.19	13.01	14.13	17.66	17.41	17.74	75. Autres engagements
Memorandum items											***Pour mémoire***
76. Short-term securities	..	..	..	..	..	..	..	..	..		*76. Titres à court terme*
77. Bonds	..	9.12	9.00	8.70	10.48	10.81	10.79	10.07	9.53	10.04	*77. Obligations*
78. Shares and participations	..	3.19	3.41	2.75	2.63	2.38	3.04	4.05	3.75	3.87	*78. Actions et participations*
79. Claims on non-residents	41.93	29.60	28.92	29.33	28.20	30.75	30.41	31.80	31.49	32.00	*79. Créances sur des non-résidents*
80. Liabilities to non-residents	42.96	25.98	27.28	26.86	27.07	28.47	28.86	30.94	34.93	36.73	*80. Engagements envers des non-résidents*

* See notes on previous pages.

* Voir les notes en pages précédentes.

FRANCE

Large commercial banks

FRANCE

Grandes banques commerciales

Million euros — *Millions d'euros*

		1992	1993	1994	1995	1996	1997	1998	1999	2000[1]	2001[2]	
INCOME STATEMENT												**COMPTE DE RESULTATS**
1. Interest income		88740	85983	70162	73226	69616	76260	82026	73951	108034	121122	1. Produits financiers
2. Interest expenses		70248	72117	56246	60211	57936	65278	73080	64225	98539	111137	2. Frais financiers
3. Net interest income		18492	13866	13916	13015	11679	10982	8946	9725	9495	9985	3. Produits financiers nets
4. Non-interest income (net)		7719	13125	10649	10898	13503	17617	20608	20779	33803	38554	4. Produits non financiers (nets)
a. Fees and commissions receivable		..	6885	8214	7093	8148	9688	11208	11577	17494	18072	a. Frais et commissions à recevoir
b. Fees and commissions payable		..	1510	1949	1486	1821	2483	2937	2720	4441	6193	b. Frais et commissions à payer
c. Net profits or loss on financial operations		..	6220	3024	3824	5906	8087	10330	10341	14162	16986	c. Profits ou pertes nets sur opérations financières
d. Other		..	1530	1360	1468	1270	2325	2007	1581	6587	9689	d. Autres
5. Gross income		26211	26991	24566	23913	25182	28599	29554	30504	43297	48539	5. Résultat brut
6. Operating expenses		18130	19068	19111	18889	19402	20860	22088	21385	28038	31375	6. Frais d'exploitation
a. Staff costs		10282	11219	11008	10869	11253	12236	12809	12577	..	..	a. Dépenses en personnel
b. Property costs		1354	1268	1270	1357	1338	1413	1471	1353	1765	2519	b. Dépenses en immobilier
c. Other		6493	6581	6832	6663	6810	7211	7808	7455	..	-	c. Autres
7. Net income		8082	7923	5455	5025	5780	7739	7465	9119	15260	17165	7. Résultat net
8. Provisions (net)		6174	6601	4909	3303	2126	2932	3408	879	2600	3544	8. Provisions (nettes)
a. Provisions on loans		..	7087	6006	3424	3336	4522	5448	2630	..	..	a. Provisions sur prêts
b. Provisions on securities		..	-483	-692	-136	-897	-1611	-1978	-1743	..	..	b. Provisions sur titres
c. Other		..	-3	-405	15	-313	21	-62	-7	65	18	c. Autres
9. Profit before tax		1907	1322	546	1721	3654	4807	4057	8240	12659	13621	9. Bénéfices avant impôt
10. Income tax		713	951	989	939	1088	1109	1463	2769	3431	3996	10. Impôt sur le revenu
11. Profit after tax		1194	372	-443	783	2566	3698	2594	5470	9229	9625	11. Bénéfices après impôt
12. Distributed profit		684	-24	-911	263	2030	2992	2232	4911	8388	8611	12. Bénéfices distribués
13. Retained profit		510	396	468	520	537	705	362	559	841	1014	13. Bénéfices mis en réserve
BALANCE SHEET												**BILAN**
Assets												**Actif**
14. Cash & balance with Central bank		6520	5297	4457	3971	6046	6094	12431	18378	5331	-	14. Caisse & solde auprès de la Banque centrale
15. Interbank deposits		247775	277717	254968	258063	270175	301960	287587	280613	320237	629457	15. Dépôts interbancaires
16. Loans		449352	453224	436818	438139	461445	502407	505262	575904	619550	687065	16. Prêts
17. Securities		161824	204895	199070	216987	270768	313001	325267	401620	453623	583397	17. Valeurs mobilières
18. Other assets		113199	87971	81266	91895	96779	127510	154607	269288	237754	290824	18. Autres actifs
Liabilities												**Passif**
19. Capital & reserves		23830	37913	36981	35253	35680	38117	40778	47692	46111	62930	19. Capital et réserves
20. Borrowing from Central bank		21040	6418	3936	2440	3383	4652	5581	1062	193	-	20. Emprunts auprès de la Banque centrale
21. Interbank deposits		300651	361862	350465	362826	395619	440380	410809	430314	406843	486243	21. Dépôts interbancaires
22. Non-bank deposits		288013	306751	305513	315212	342916	378728	414869	418529	445688	695790	22. Dépôts non bancaires
23. Bonds		212389	214248	187964	177340	173230	190174	173625	278434	306783	364315	23. Obligations
24. Other liabilities		132749	101911	91721	115984	154385	198921	239492	369775	430877	581465	24. Autres engagements
Balance sheet total												**Total du bilan**
25. End-year total		978671	1029104	976579	1009055	1105213	1250971	1285154	1545805	1636495	2190743	25. En fin d'exercice
26. Average total		919060	1003888	1002842	992817	1057134	1178092	1268063	1415479	..	-	26. Moyen

FRANCE
Large commercial banks

Million euros

	1992	1993	1994	1995	1996	1997	1998	1999	2000[1]	2001[2]
Memorandum items										
27. Short-term securities	..	..	..	..	..	..	..	..	..	..
28. Bonds	..	120972	110400	119364	142105	148297	148898	167316	..	..
29. Shares and participations	25812	27779	27369	19503	19230	18784	18075	18967	..	..
30. Claims on non-residents	..	..	..	..	..	..	..	..	..	..
31. Liabilities to non-residents	..	..	..	..	..	..	..	..	..	..
Capital adequacy										
32. Tier 1 Capital	..	..	..	..	..	..	..	..	..	..
33. Tier 2 Capital	..	..	..	..	..	..	..	..	..	..
34. Supervisory deductions	..	..	..	..	..	..	..	..	..	..
35. Total net capital resources	..	..	..	..	..	..	..	..	..	..
36. Risk-weighted assets	..	..	..	..	..	..	..	..	..	..
SUPPLEMENTARY INFORMATION										
37. Number of institutions	5	5	5	5	5	5	5	5	5	5
38. Number of branches	..	..	..	..	..	..	..	..	..	..
39. Number of employees (x 1000)	..	..	..	..	..	..	..	..	..	..

1 Since the year 2000, the French financial institutions' accounts have been published and presented in a new format. Therefore, some information is no longer available.

2 Break in series : sample of large commercial banks composed of five banks has been modified.

Notes

. The consolidated data for large commercial banks cover all subsidiaries and branches including non-financial agencies, in France and abroad. Accordingly, they are not comparable with the corporate data for commercial banks.

FRANCE
Grandes banques commerciales

Millions d'euros

Pour mémoire
27. Titres à court terme
28. Obligations
29. Actions et participations
30. Créances sur des non-résidents
31. Engagements envers des non-résidents

Solvabilité
32. Fonds propres de base
33. Fonds propres complémentaires
34. Eléments à déduire des fonds propres
35. Total net des ressources en capital
36. Actifs pondérés des risques

RENSEIGNEMENTS COMPLÉMENTAIRES
37. Nombre d'institutions
38. Nombre de succursales
39. Nombre de salariés (x 1000)

1 A partir de 2000, les comptes publiés par les établissements de crédit français présentent un nouveau format. En conséquence, certaines informations ne sont plus disponibles.

2 Rupture de séries : la composition de l'échantillon des grandes banques commerciales, constitué de cinq banques, a été modifié.

Notes

. Les données consolidées des Grandes banques commerciales incluent l'ensemble des succursales et filiales, y compris les établissements non financiers, installées en France et à l'étranger. Ces données ne sont donc pas comparables avec les données de la catégories des Banques commerciales.

FRANCE
Large commercial banks

FRANCE
Grandes banques commerciales

Per cent — *Pourcentage*

INCOME STATEMENT ANALYSIS — **ANALYSE DU COMPTE DE RESULTATS**

	1992	1993	1994	1995	1996	1997	1998	1999	2000[1]	2001[2]		
% of average balance sheet total												**% du total moyen du bilan**
40. Interest income	9.66	8.56	7.00	7.38	6.59	6.47	6.47	5.22	..	..	40.	Produits financiers
41. Interest expenses	7.64	7.18	5.61	6.06	5.48	5.54	5.76	4.54	..	..	41.	Frais financiers
42. Net interest income	2.01	1.38	1.39	1.31	1.10	0.93	0.71	0.69	..	..	42.	Produits financiers nets
43. Non-interest income (net)	0.84	1.31	1.06	1.10	1.28	1.50	1.63	1.47	..	..	43.	Produits non financiers (nets)
a. Fees and commissions receivable	..	0.69	0.82	0.71	0.77	0.82	0.88	0.82	..	..		a. Frais et commissions à recevoir
b. Fees and commissions payable	..	0.15	0.19	0.15	0.17	0.21	0.23	0.19	..	..		b. Frais et commissions à payer
c. Net profits or loss on financial operations	..	0.62	0.30	0.39	0.56	0.69	0.81	0.73	..	..		c. Profits ou pertes nets sur opérations financières
d. Other	..	0.15	0.14	0.15	0.12	0.20	0.16	0.11	..	..		d. Autres
44. Gross income	2.85	2.69	2.45	2.41	2.38	2.43	2.33	2.16	..	..	44.	Résultat brut
45. Operating expenses	1.97	1.90	1.91	1.90	1.84	1.77	1.74	1.51	..	..	45.	Frais d'exploitation
a. Staff costs	1.12	1.12	1.10	1.09	1.06	1.04	1.01	0.89	..	..		a. Dépenses en personnel
b. Property costs	0.15	0.13	0.13	0.14	0.13	0.12	0.12	0.10	..	..		b. Dépenses en immobilier
c. Other	0.71	0.66	0.68	0.67	0.64	0.61	0.62	0.53	..	..		c. Autres
46. Net income	0.88	0.79	0.54	0.51	0.55	0.66	0.59	0.64	..	..	46.	Résultat net
47. Provisions (net)	0.67	0.66	0.49	0.33	0.20	0.25	0.27	0.06	..	..	47.	Provisions (nettes)
a. Provisions on loans	..	0.71	0.60	0.34	0.32	0.38	0.43	0.19	..	..		a. Provisions sur prêts
b. Provisions on securities	..	-0.05	-0.07	-0.01	-0.08	-0.14	-0.16	-0.12	..	..		b. Provisions sur titres
c. Other	..	..	-0.04	..	-0.03	..	..	..	..	..		c. Autres
48. Profit before tax	0.21	0.13	0.05	0.17	0.35	0.41	0.32	0.58	..	..	48.	Bénéfices avant impôt
49. Income tax	0.08	0.09	0.10	0.09	0.10	0.09	0.12	0.20	..	..	49.	Impôt sur le revenu
50. Profit after tax	0.13	0.04	-0.04	0.08	0.24	0.31	0.20	0.39	..	..	50.	Bénéfices après impôt
51. Distributed profit	0.07	-	-0.09	0.03	0.19	0.25	0.18	0.35	..	..	51.	Bénéfices distribués
52. Retained profit	0.06	0.04	0.05	0.05	0.05	0.06	0.03	0.04	..	..	52.	Bénéfices mis en réserve
% of gross income												**% du total du résultat brut**
53. Net interest income	70.55	51.37	56.65	54.43	46.38	38.40	30.27	31.88	21.93	20.57	53.	Produits financiers nets
54. Non-interest income (net)	29.45	48.63	43.35	45.57	53.62	61.60	69.73	68.12	78.07	79.43	54.	Produits non financiers (nets)
a. Fees and commissions receivable	..	25.51	33.44	29.66	32.36	33.88	37.92	37.95	40.40	37.23		a. Frais et commissions à recevoir
b. Fees and commissions payable	..	5.59	7.93	6.21	7.23	8.68	9.94	8.92	10.26	12.76		b. Frais et commissions à payer
c. Net profits or loss on financial operations	..	23.04	12.31	15.99	23.45	28.28	34.95	33.90	32.71	34.99		c. Profits ou pertes nets sur opérations financières
d. Other	..	5.67	5.53	6.14	5.04	8.13	6.79	5.18	15.21	19.96		d. Autres
55. Operating expenses	69.17	70.65	77.80	78.99	77.05	72.94	74.74	70.11	64.76	64.64	55.	Frais d'exploitation
a. Staff costs	39.23	41.57	44.81	45.45	44.69	42.78	43.34	41.23	..	..		a. Dépenses en personnel
b. Property costs	5.17	4.70	5.17	5.67	5.31	4.94	4.98	4.44	4.08	5.19		b. Dépenses en immobilier
c. Other	24.77	24.38	27.81	27.86	27.04	25.21	26.42	24.44	..	..		c. Autres
56. Net income	30.83	29.35	22.20	21.01	22.95	27.06	25.26	29.89	35.24	35.36	56.	Résultat net
57. Provisions (net)	23.56	24.45	19.98	13.81	8.44	10.25	11.53	2.88	6.01	7.30	57.	Provisions (nettes)
a. Provisions on loans	..	26.26	24.45	14.32	13.25	15.81	18.44	8.62	..	..		a. Provisions sur prêts
b. Provisions on securities	..	-1.79	-2.82	-0.57	-3.56	-5.63	-6.69	-5.72	..	..		b. Provisions sur titres
c. Other	..	-0.01	-1.65	0.06	-1.24	0.07	-0.21	-0.02	0.15	0.04		c. Autres
58. Profit before tax	7.28	4.90	2.22	7.20	14.51	16.81	13.73	27.01	29.24	28.06	58.	Bénéfices avant impôt
59. Income tax	2.72	3.52	4.03	3.93	4.32	3.88	4.95	9.08	7.92	8.23	59.	Impôt sur le revenu
60. Profit after tax	4.56	1.38	-1.80	3.27	10.19	12.93	8.78	17.93	21.31	19.83	60.	Bénéfices après impôt
% of net income												**% du total du résultat net**
61. Provisions (net)	76.40	83.31	89.99	65.74	36.78	37.89	45.66	9.64	17.04	20.65	61.	Provisions (nettes)
a. Provisions on loans	..	89.45	110.10	68.15	57.71	58.43	72.98	28.84	..	..		a. Provisions sur prêts
b. Provisions on securities	..	-6.10	-12.69	-2.72	-15.52	-20.81	-26.50	-19.12	..	..		b. Provisions sur titres
c. Other	..	-0.03	-7.42	0.30	-5.41	0.27	-0.83	-0.08	0.43	0.10		c. Autres
62. Profit before tax	23.60	16.69	10.01	34.26	63.22	62.11	54.34	90.36	82.96	79.35	62.	Bénéfices avant impôt
63. Income tax	8.82	12.00	18.13	18.68	18.82	14.33	19.60	30.37	22.48	23.28	63.	Impôt sur le revenu
64. Profit after tax	14.78	4.69	-8.12	15.58	44.40	47.78	34.75	59.99	60.48	56.07	64.	Bénéfices après impôt

FRANCE

Large commercial banks

Per cent

BALANCE SHEET ANALYSIS

% of year-end balance sheet total

	1992	1993	1994	1995	1996	1997	1998	1999	2000[1]	2001[2]
Assets										
65. Cash & balance with Central bank	0.67	0.51	0.46	0.39	0.55	0.49	0.97	1.19	0.33	-
66. Interbank deposits	25.32	26.99	26.11	25.57	24.45	24.14	22.38	18.15	19.57	28.73
67. Loans	45.91	44.04	44.73	43.42	41.75	40.16	39.32	37.26	37.86	31.36
68. Securities	16.54	19.91	20.38	21.50	24.50	25.02	25.31	25.98	27.72	26.63
69. Other assets	11.57	8.55	8.32	9.11	8.76	10.19	12.03	17.42	14.53	13.28
Liabilities										
70. Capital & reserves	2.43	3.68	3.79	3.49	3.23	3.05	3.17	3.09	2.82	2.87
71. Borrowing from Central bank	2.15	0.62	0.40	0.24	0.31	0.37	0.43	0.07	0.01	-
72. Interbank deposits	30.72	35.16	35.89	35.96	35.80	35.20	31.97	27.84	24.86	22.20
73. Non-bank deposits	29.43	29.81	31.28	31.24	31.03	30.27	32.28	27.08	27.23	31.76
74. Bonds	21.70	20.82	19.25	17.57	15.67	15.20	13.51	18.01	18.75	16.63
75. Other liabilities	13.56	9.90	9.39	11.49	13.97	15.90	18.64	23.92	26.33	26.54
Memorandum items										
76. Short-term securities	..	..	..	..	..	..	..	..	..	..
77. Bonds	..	11.76	11.30	11.83	12.86	11.85	11.59	10.82	..	..
78. Shares and participations	2.64	2.70	2.80	1.93	1.74	1.50	1.41	1.23	..	..
79. Claims on non-residents	..	..	..	..	..	..	..	..	..	..
80. Liabilities to non-residents	..	..	..	..	..	..	..	..	..	..

* See notes on previous pages.

FRANCE

Grandes banques commerciales

Pourcentage

ANALYSE DU BILAN

% du total du bilan en fin d'exercice

Actif

65. Caisse & solde auprès de la Banque centrale
66. Dépôts interbancaires
67. Prêts
68. Valeurs mobilières
69. Autres actifs

Passif

70. Capital et réserves
71. Emprunts auprès de la Banque centrale
72. Dépôts interbancaires
73. Dépôts non bancaires
74. Obligations
75. Autres engagements

Pour mémoire

76. Titres à court terme
77. Obligations
78. Actions et participations
79. Créances sur des non-résidents
80. Engagements envers des non-résidents

* Voir les notes en pages précédentes.

FRANCE
Savings banks

FRANCE
Caisses d'épargne

Million euros / *Millions d'euros*

	1992	1993	1994	1995	1996	1997	1998	1999	2000[1]	2001	
INCOME STATEMENT											**COMPTE DE RESULTATS**
1. Interest income	9508	9427	9403	10284	9918	10064	10319	10048	..		1. Produits financiers
2. Interest expenses	6271	6335	6574	7216	6900	7167	7298	6993	..		2. Frais financiers
3. Net interest income	3237	3092	2829	3068	3018	2897	3021	3055	..		3. Produits financiers nets
4. Non-interest income (net)	583	945	698	1039	999	1149	1337	1381	..		4. Produits non financiers (nets)
a. Fees and commissions receivable	*..*	*733*	*844*	*686*	*804*	*976*	*1112*	*1414*	*..*		*a. Frais et commissions à recevoir*
b. Fees and commissions payable	*..*	*177*	*185*	*199*	*213*	*221*	*254*	*314*	*..*		*b. Frais et commissions à payer*
c. Net profits or loss on financial operations	*83*	*201*	*-161*	*391*	*297*	*283*	*307*	*259*	*..*		*c. Profits ou pertes nets sur opérations financières*
d. Other	*501*	*188*	*200*	*161*	*111*	*111*	*172*	*22*	*..*		*d. Autres*
5. Gross income	3820	4037	3528	4107	4017	4046	4358	4436	..		5. Résultat brut
6. Operating expenses	2944	3063	3123	3250	3298	3347	3427	3446	..		6. Frais d'exploitation
a. Staff costs	*1642*	*1744*	*1763*	*1856*	*1884*	*1912*	*1963*	*1994*	*..*		*a. Dépenses en personnel*
b. Property costs	*204*	*224*	*229*	*237*	*230*	*232*	*237*	*225*	*..*		*b. Dépenses en immobilier*
c. Other	*1098*	*1095*	*1131*	*1157*	*1183*	*1204*	*1227*	*1226*	*..*		*c. Autres*
7. Net income	876	974	404	857	720	699	931	991	..		7. Résultat net
8. Provisions (net)	339	399	174	356	212	241	261	191	..		8. Provisions (nettes)
a. Provisions on loans	*248*	*250*	*158*	*121*	*117*	*127*	*91*	*88*	*..*		*a. Provisions sur prêts*
b. Provisions on securities	*-4*	*-11*	*-6*	*-2*	*-26*	*-8*	*-6*	*-12*	*..*		*b. Provisions sur titres*
c. Other	*95*	*160*	*22*	*237*	*121*	*123*	*177*	*115*	*..*		*c. Autres*
9. Profit before tax	538	574	230	500	508	457	670	800	..		9. Bénéfices avant impôt
10. Income tax	218	304	30	279	254	209	361	408	..		10. Impôt sur le revenu
11. Profit after tax	319	270	201	221	254	248	309	392	..		11. Bénéfices après impôt
12. Distributed profit	-	-	-	-	-	-	-	-			12. Bénéfices distribués
13. Retained profit	319	270	201	221	254	248	309	392	..		13. Bénéfices mis en réserve
BALANCE SHEET											**BILAN**
Assets											**Actif**
14. Cash & balance with Central bank	469	399	419	444	460	525	557	660	..		14. Caisse & solde auprès de la Banque centrale
15. Interbank deposits	73728	71375	75225	84836	82822	91485	98763	103243	..		15. Dépôts interbancaires
16. Loans	43282	45537	48894	51062	54994	59232	63896	70680	..		16. Prêts
17. Securities	11787	17801	21340	22937	29148	31433	32791	36853	..		17. Valeurs mobilières
18. Other assets	8382	6472	7238	8582	8887	9709	9657	9821	..		18. Autres actifs
Liabilities											**Passif**
19. Capital & reserves	5705	6287	6585	7000	7337	7453	6736	8590	..		19. Capital et réserves
20. Borrowing from Central bank	97	55	18	12	10	10	5	3	..		20. Emprunts auprès de la Banque centrale
21. Interbank deposits	7276	5146	14578	15354	17972	24596	33560	45371	..		21. Dépôts interbancaires
22. Non-bank deposits	110321	118130	127911	140787	146487	155893	159456	159652	..		22. Dépôts non bancaires
23. Bonds	6807	9366	1382	1437	812	537	735	1513	..		23. Obligations
24. Other liabilities	7442	2599	2643	3271	3693	3896	5172	6127	..		24. Autres engagements
Balance sheet total											**Total du bilan**
25. End-year total	137648	141584	153116	167862	176310	192384	205664	221257	..		25. En fin d'exercice
26. Average total	139152	139475	145593	158826	170806	182881	197672	212204	..		26. Moyen

99

FRANCE

Savings banks

Million euros

FRANCE

Caisses d'épargne

Millions d'euros

	1992	1993	1994	1995	1996	1997	1998	1999	2000[1]	2001			
Memorandum items													***Pour mémoire***
27. Short-term securities	..	..	..	..		..	..	..	..	..	27.	*Titres à court terme*	
28. Bonds	..	12007	15104	15784	20318	22778	23388	25158	..	..	28.	*Obligations*	
29. Shares and participations	..	597	681	663	831	945	1299	2840	..	..	29.	*Actions et participations*	
30. Claims on non-residents	3	385	837	1438	2809	4802	8401	11024	..	..	30.	*Créances sur des non-résidents*	
31. Liabilities to non-residents	2	47	46	48	76	144	249	340	..	..	31.	*Engagements envers des non-résidents*	
Capital adequacy													***Solvabilité***
32. Tier 1 Capital	..	..	..	..	..	..	..	..	..	..	32.	*Fonds propres de base*	
33. Tier 2 Capital	..	..	..	..	..	..	..	..	..	..	33.	*Fonds propres complémentaires*	
34. Supervisory deductions	..	..	..	..	..	..	..	..	..	..	34.	*Eléments à déduire des fonds propres*	
35. Total net capital resources	..	..	..	..	..	..	..	..	..	..	35.	*Total net des ressources en capital*	
36. Risk-weighted assets	..	..	..	..	..	..	..	..	..	..	36.	*Actifs pondérés des risques*	
SUPPLEMENTARY INFORMATION													**RENSEIGNEMENTS COMPLEMENTAIRES**
37. Number of institutions	36	35	35	35	34	34	34	34	..	..	37.	*Nombre d'institutions*	
38. Number of branches	4411	4308	4200	4226	4214	4270	4265	4240	..	..	38.	*Nombre de succursales*	
39. Number of employees (x 1000)	36.0	36.0	36.0	36.0	36.0	36.0	36.0	35.0			39.	*Nombre de salariés (x 1000)*	

1 Starting 1st January 2000, Savings banks adopted the co-operative banks status. The data are for now on reported in the co-operative banks category.

Notes

. Average balance sheet totals (item 26) are based on the average of quarterly totals.

1 Depuis le 1er janvier 2000, les caisses d'épargne ont le statut de banques mutualistes. Aussi, les données sont désormais comprises dans les banques mutualistes.

Notes

. La moyenne du total des actifs/passifs (poste26) est basée sur la moyenne des totaux des situations trimestrielles.

FRANCE
Savings banks

FRANCE
Caisses d'épargne

Per cent — *Pourcentage*

INCOME STATEMENT ANALYSIS — ANALYSE DU COMPTE DE RESULTATS

		1992	1993	1994	1995	1996	1997	1998	1999	2000¹	2001	
	% of average balance sheet total											**% du total moyen du bilan**
40.	Interest income	6.83	6.76	6.46	6.47	5.81	5.50	5.22	4.74	..		Produits financiers
41.	Interest expenses	4.51	4.54	4.52	4.54	4.04	3.92	3.69	3.30	..		Frais financiers
42.	Net interest income	2.33	2.22	1.94	1.93	1.77	1.58	1.53	1.44	..		Produits financiers nets
43.	Non-interest income (net)	0.42	0.68	0.48	0.65	0.58	0.63	0.68	0.65	..		Produits non financiers (nets)
	a. Fees and commissions receivable	..	0.53	0.58	0.43	0.47	0.53	0.56	0.67	..		a. Frais et commissions à recevoir
	b. Fees and commissions payable		0.13	0.13	0.13	0.12	0.12	0.13	0.15			b. Frais et commissions à payer
	c. Net profits or loss on financial operations	0.06	0.14	-0.11	0.25	0.17	0.15	0.16	0.12			c. Profits ou pertes nets sur opérations financières
	d. Other	0.36	0.14	0.14	0.10	0.07	0.06	0.09	0.01			d. Autres
44.	Gross income	2.75	2.89	2.42	2.59	2.35	2.21	2.20	2.09	..		Résultat brut
45.	Operating expenses	2.12	2.20	2.15	2.05	1.93	1.83	1.73	1.62	..		Frais d'exploitation
	a. Staff costs	1.18	1.25	1.21	1.17	1.10	1.05	0.99	0.94			a. Dépenses en personnel
	b. Property costs	0.15	0.16	0.16	0.15	0.13	0.13	0.12	0.11			b. Dépenses en immobilier
	c. Other	0.79	0.78	0.78	0.73	0.69	0.66	0.62	0.58			c. Autres
46.	Net income	0.63	0.70	0.28	0.54	0.42	0.38	0.47	0.47	..		Résultat net
47.	Provisions (net)	0.24	0.29	0.12	0.22	0.12	0.13	0.13	0.09	..		Provisions (nettes)
	a. Provisions on loans	0.18	0.18	0.11	0.08	0.07	0.07	0.05	0.04			a. Provisions sur prêts
	b. Provisions on securities	-	-0.01	-	-	-0.01	-	-	-0.01			b. Provisions sur titres
	c. Other	0.07	0.11	0.02	0.15	0.07	0.07	0.09	0.05			c. Autres
48.	Profit before tax	0.39	0.41	0.16	0.32	0.30	0.25	0.34	0.38	..		Bénéfices avant impôt
49.	Income tax	0.16	0.22	0.02	0.18	0.15	0.11	0.18	0.19	..		Impôt sur le revenu
50.	Profit after tax	0.23	0.19	0.14	0.14	0.15	0.14	0.16	0.18	..		Bénéfices après impôt
51.	Distributed profit	-	-	-	-	-	-	-	-			Bénéfices distribués
52.	Retained profit	0.23	0.19	0.14	0.14	0.15	0.14	0.16	0.18	..		Bénéfices mis en réserve
	% of gross income											**% du total du résultat brut**
53.	Net interest income	84.73	76.60	80.20	74.70	75.13	71.61	69.31	68.87	..		Produits financiers nets
54.	Non-interest income (net)	15.27	23.40	19.80	25.30	24.87	28.39	30.69	31.13	..		Produits non financiers (nets)
	a. Fees and commissions receivable	..	18.16	23.94	16.70	20.03	24.13	25.52	31.86	..		a. Frais et commissions à recevoir
	b. Fees and commissions payable		4.40	5.23	4.84	5.30	5.46	5.82	7.07			b. Frais et commissions à payer
	c. Net profits or loss on financial operations	2.17	4.97	-4.57	9.52	7.38	6.99	7.03	5.84			c. Profits ou pertes nets sur opérations financières
	d. Other	13.11	4.67	5.66	3.92	2.77	2.74	3.95	0.50			d. Autres
55.	Operating expenses	77.07	75.88	88.53	79.14	82.08	82.74	78.63	77.67	..		Frais d'exploitation
	a. Staff costs	42.99	43.20	49.98	45.19	46.90	47.25	45.03	44.95			a. Dépenses en personnel
	b. Property costs	5.33	5.56	6.50	5.78	5.73	5.72	5.44	5.08			b. Dépenses en immobilier
	c. Other	28.75	27.12	32.06	28.17	29.45	29.76	28.16	27.64			c. Autres
56.	Net income	22.93	24.12	11.47	20.86	17.92	17.27	21.37	22.33	..		Résultat net
57.	Provisions (net)	8.86	9.89	4.94	8.68	5.28	5.97	6.00	4.30	..		Provisions (nettes)
	a. Provisions on loans	6.49	6.19	4.48	2.95	2.90	3.13	2.08	1.98			a. Provisions sur prêts
	b. Provisions on securities	-0.12	-0.28	-0.18	-0.05	-0.64	-0.20	-0.13	-0.27			b. Provisions sur titres
	c. Other	2.49	3.97	0.64	5.78	3.01	3.04	4.05	2.59			c. Autres
58.	Profit before tax	14.07	14.23	6.53	12.19	12.64	11.29	15.38	18.03	..		Bénéfices avant impôt
59.	Income tax	5.72	7.53	0.84	6.80	6.32	5.17	8.28	9.20	..		Impôt sur le revenu
60.	Profit after tax	8.35	6.70	5.69	5.38	6.32	6.12	7.09	8.83	..		Bénéfices après impôt
	% of net income											**% du total du résultat net**
61.	Provisions (net)	38.65	41.01	43.05	41.58	29.46	34.57	28.05	19.25	..		Provisions (nettes)
	a. Provisions on loans	28.31	25.67	39.09	14.15	16.20	18.14	9.72	8.85			a. Provisions sur prêts
	b. Provisions on securities	-0.50	-1.14	-1.58	-0.25	-3.56	-1.13	-0.62	-1.22			b. Provisions sur titres
	c. Other	10.86	16.47	5.54	27.69	16.82	17.59	18.95	11.62			c. Autres
62.	Profit before tax	61.35	58.99	56.95	58.42	70.54	65.41	71.95	80.75	..		Bénéfices avant impôt
63.	Income tax	24.93	31.21	7.31	32.62	35.27	29.97	38.76	41.20	..		Impôt sur le revenu
64.	Profit after tax	36.42	27.77	49.64	25.80	35.27	35.46	33.19	39.55	..		Bénéfices après impôt

FRANCE
Savings banks

Per cent

BALANCE SHEET ANALYSIS

% of year-end balance sheet total

	1992	1993	1994	1995	1996	1997	1998	1999	2000[1]	2001
Assets										
65. Cash & balance with Central bank	0.34	0.28	0.27	0.26	0.26	0.27	0.27	0.30	..	
66. Interbank deposits	53.56	50.41	49.13	50.54	46.97	47.55	48.02	46.66	..	
67. Loans	31.44	32.16	31.93	30.42	31.19	30.79	31.07	31.94	..	
68. Securities	8.56	12.57	13.94	13.66	16.53	16.34	15.94	16.66	..	
69. Other assets	6.09	4.57	4.73	5.11	5.04	5.05	4.70	4.44	..	
Liabilities										
70. Capital & reserves	4.14	4.44	4.30	4.17	4.16	3.87	3.28	3.88	..	
71. Borrowing from Central bank	0.07	0.04	0.01	0.01	0.01	0.01		-	..	
72. Interbank deposits	5.29	3.63	9.52	9.15	10.19	12.78	16.32	20.51	..	
73. Non-bank deposits	80.15	83.44	83.54	83.87	83.08	81.03	77.53	72.16	..	
74. Bonds	4.95	6.62	0.90	0.86	0.46	0.28	0.36	0.68	..	
75. Other liabilities	5.41	1.84	1.73	1.95	2.09	2.02	2.51	2.77	..	
Memorandum items										
76. Short-term securities	..	..	..	..	..	..	..	..	..	
77. Bonds	..	8.48	9.86	9.40	11.52	11.84	11.37	11.37	..	
78. Shares and participations	..	0.42	0.44	0.39	0.47	0.49	0.63	1.28	..	
79. Claims on non-residents	-	0.27	0.55	0.86	1.59	2.50	4.09	4.98	..	
80. Liabilities to non-residents	-	0.03	0.03	0.03	0.04	0.08	0.12	0.15	..	

* See notes on previous pages.

FRANCE
Caisses d'épargne

Pourcentage

ANALYSE DU BILAN

% du total du bilan en fin d'exercice

Actif
65. Caisse & solde auprès de la Banque centrale
66. Dépôts interbancaires
67. Prêts
68. Valeurs mobilières
69. Autres actifs

Passif
70. Capital et réserves
71. Emprunts auprès de la Banque centrale
72. Dépôts interbancaires
73. Dépôts non bancaires
74. Obligations
75. Autres engagements

Pour mémoire
76. Titres à court terme
77. Obligations
78. Actions et participations
79. Créances sur des non-résidents
80. Engagements envers des non-résidents

* Voir les notes en pages précédentes.

FRANCE
Co-operative banks

FRANCE
Banques mutualistes

Million euros / *Millions d'euros*

	Item (EN)	Poste (FR)	1992	1993	1994	1995	1996	1997	1998	1999	2000[1]	2001
	INCOME STATEMENT	**COMPTE DE RESULTATS**										
1.	Interest income	Produits financiers	44238	46155	41280	44014	41120	38547	38702	37153	48598	48806
2.	Interest expenses	Frais financiers	31665	34462	30541	33270	31407	29614	30590	27480	36445	35458
3.	Net interest income	Produits financiers nets	12573	11693	10738	10744	9713	8934	8112	9673	12153	13347
4.	Non-interest income (net)	Produits non financiers (nets)	2076	4128	4287	5024	6149	7159	8544	6880	10294	11976
	a. Fees and commissions receivable	a. Frais et commissions à recevoir	..	3885	4146	4164	4620	5084	5612	6203	8783	9229
	b. Fees and commissions payable	b. Frais et commissions à payer	..	1648	1576	1554	1803	1906	2080	2197	2742	2682
	c. Net profits or loss on financial operations	c. Profits ou pertes nets sur opérations financières	220	813	457	1190	2255	2322	3436	1476	1918	852
	d. Other	d. Autres	1856	1078	1260	1225	1077	1658	1576	1397	2335	4577
5.	Gross income	Résultat brut	14649	15821	15026	15768	15862	16092	16656	16553	22447	25324
6.	Operating expenses	Frais d'exploitation	10076	10009	10176	10397	10593	10639	10876	10875	15093	15206
	a. Staff costs	a. Dépenses en personnel	5285	5413	5502	5657	5762	5798	5929	5994	..	..
	b. Property costs	b. Dépenses en immobilier	538	531	534	520	530	551	552	560	789	803
	c. Other	c. Autres	4252	4064	4140	4221	4300	4290	4396	4320	-	-
7.	Net income	Résultat net	4573	5812	4850	5371	5269	5453	5780	5678	7354	10118
8.	Provisions (net)	Provisions (nettes)	2393	3571	2804	2662	2425	2030	1741	1446	1980	3399
	a. Provisions on loans	a. Provisions sur prêts	1348	3198	2522	2137	1867	1507	1381	1341	..	..
	b. Provisions on securities	b. Provisions sur titres	116	87	9	130	159	135	-24	-277	..	..
	c. Other	c. Autres	930	285	273	395	399	389	384	383	806	1928
9.	Profit before tax	Bénéfices avant impôt	2180	2242	2046	2709	2844	3423	4039	4232	5374	6719
10.	Income tax	Impôt sur le revenu	803	968	787	1251	1229	1477	1712	1675	1871	2039
11.	Profit after tax	Bénéfices après impôt	1378	1274	1258	1458	1615	1946	2328	2557	3503	4680
12.	Distributed profit	Bénéfices distribués	390	369	404	417	451	592	611	722	889	1077
13.	Retained profit	Bénéfices mis en réserve	988	905	855	1041	1164	1355	1717	1835	2614	3602
	BALANCE SHEET	**BILAN**										
	Assets	**Actif**										
14.	Cash & balance with Central bank	Caisse & solde auprès de la Banque centrale	2285	1343	1356	1446	1667	1861	5559	7573	6212	6999
15.	Interbank deposits	Dépôts interbancaires	234146	267188	277638	304945	301114	293231	297158	306501	421175	421912
16.	Loans	Prêts	212457	212890	215044	220825	234566	243353	260872	287090	390581	412860
17.	Securities	Valeurs mobilières	40897	43742	60186	75764	97543	98406	106174	98429	127134	127476
18.	Other assets	Autres actifs	45498	24767	26100	29085	32307	29653	31353	31810	41729	45777
	Liabilities	**Passif**										
19.	Capital & reserves	Capital et réserves	20024	20741	22368	24495	27218	29616	34253	37985	51506	65296
20.	Borrowing from Central bank	Emprunts auprès de la Banque centrale	3078	113	95	142	152	71	123	116	22	30
21.	Interbank deposits	Dépôts interbancaires	210102	221484	232348	250429	263777	250417	261773	274912	336278	327372
22.	Non-bank deposits	Dépôts non bancaires	189880	218136	238774	268512	283970	301440	314654	328219	486304	507970
23.	Bonds	Obligations	68752	71212	68852	66843	63299	60435	59606	59966	73114	70456
24.	Other liabilities	Autres engagements	43446	18243	17888	21643	28781	24524	30708	30205	39607	43900
	Balance sheet total	**Total du bilan**										
25.	End-year total	En fin d'exercice	535283	549929	580325	632065	667197	666503	701117	731404	986831	1015023
26.	Average total	Moyen	532052	553128	576300	628658	669722	683383	685009	712128	965210	982895

FRANCE
Co-operative banks

Million euros

	1992	1993	1994	1995	1996	1997	1998	1999	2000¹	2001
Memorandum items										
27. Short-term securities	..	..	..	..	..	..	..	..	..	..
28. Bonds	..	22972	27701	30473	36980	31484	27322	27019	51314	48832
29. Shares and participations	..	8771	9702	11143	14929	16948	21601	26570	32297	43327
30. Claims on non-residents	49995	46267	41887	49812	52141	55235	51717	44133	58102	59799
31. Liabilities to non-residents	36822	25600	26585	26903	33972	32790	29406	25496	29526	26058
Capital adequacy										
32. Tier 1 Capital	..	..	..	..	..	..	..	..	..	..
33. Tier 2 Capital	..	..	..	..	..	..	..	..	..	..
34. Supervisory deductions	..	..	..	..	..	..	..	..	..	..
35. Total net capital resources	..	..	..	..	..	..	..	..	..	..
36. Risk-weighted assets	..	..	..	..	..	..	..	..	..	..
SUPPLEMENTARY INFORMATION										
37. Number of institutions	158	150	144	136	133	131	128	125	157	151
38. Number of branches	10704	9903	10082	10113	10242	10365	10428	10361	14451	14427
39. Number of employees (x 1000)	122.0	115.0	120.0	122.0	123.0	123.0	124.0	125.0	163.7	168.6

Notes

1 Since the year 2000, the French financial institutions' accounts have been published and presented in a new format. Therefore, some information is no longer available.

1 Savings banks data are included in co-operative banks, from 2000.

Notes

. Average balance sheet totals (item 26) are based on the average of quarterly totals.

FRANCE
Banques mutualistes

Millions d'euros

Pour mémoire

27. Titres à court terme
28. Obligations
29. Actions et participations
30. Créances sur des non-résidents
31. Engagements envers des non-résidents

Solvabilité

32. Fonds propres de base
33. Fonds propres complémentaires
34. Eléments à déduire des fonds propres
35. Total net des ressources en capital
36. Actifs pondérés des risques

RENSEIGNEMENTS COMPLÉMENTAIRES

37. Nombre d'institutions
38. Nombre de succursales
39. Nombre de salariés (x 1000)

1 A partir de 2000, les comptes publiés par les établissements de crédit français présentent un nouveau format. En conséquence, certaines informations ne sont plus disponibles.

1 A partir de 2000, les données des caisses d'épargne sont comprises dans la catégorie des banques mutualistes.

Notes

. La moyenne du total des actifs/passifs (poste26) est basée sur la moyenne des totaux des situations trimestrielles.

FRANCE

Co-operative banks

FRANCE

Banques mutualistes

Per cent — *Pourcentage*

INCOME STATEMENT ANALYSIS — **ANALYSE DU COMPTE DE RESULTATS**

No.	Item (English)	Élément (Français)	1992	1993	1994	1995	1996	1997	1998	1999	2000[1]	2001
	% of average balance sheet total	**% du total moyen du bilan**										
40.	Interest income	Produits financiers	8.31	8.34	7.16	7.00	6.14	5.64	5.65	5.22	5.03	4.97
41.	Interest expenses	Frais financiers	5.95	6.23	5.30	5.29	4.69	4.33	4.47	3.86	3.78	3.61
42.	Net interest income	Produits financiers nets	2.36	2.11	1.86	1.71	1.45	1.31	1.18	1.36	1.26	1.36
43.	Non-interest income (net)	Produits non financiers (nets)	0.39	0.75	0.74	0.80	0.92	1.05	1.25	0.97	1.07	1.22
	a. Fees and commissions receivable	a. Frais et commissions à recevoir	..	0.70	0.72	0.66	0.69	0.74	0.82	0.87	0.91	0.94
	b. Fees and commissions payable	b. Frais et commissions à payer	0.04	0.30	0.27	0.25	0.27	0.28	0.30	0.31	0.28	0.27
	c. Net profits or loss on financial operations	c. Profits ou pertes nets sur opérations financières		0.15	0.08	0.19	0.34	0.34	0.50	0.21	0.20	0.09
	d. Other	d. Autres	0.35	0.19	0.22	0.19	0.16	0.24	0.23	0.20	0.24	0.47
44.	Gross income	Résultat brut	2.75	2.86	2.61	2.51	2.37	2.35	2.43	2.32	2.33	2.58
45.	Operating expenses	Frais d'exploitation	1.89	1.81	1.77	1.65	1.58	1.56	1.59	1.53	1.56	1.55
	a. Staff costs	a. Dépenses en personnel	0.99	0.98	0.95	0.90	0.86	0.85	0.87	0.84	..	..
	b. Property costs	b. Dépenses en immobilier	0.10	0.10	0.09	0.08	0.08	0.08	0.08	0.08	0.08	0.08
	c. Other	c. Autres	0.80	0.73	0.72	0.67	0.64	0.63	0.64	0.61	-	-
46.	Net income	Résultat net	0.86	1.05	0.84	0.85	0.79	0.80	0.84	0.80	0.76	1.03
47.	Provisions (net)	Provisions (nettes)	0.45	0.65	0.49	0.42	0.36	0.30	0.25	0.20	0.21	0.35
	a. Provisions on loans	a. Provisions sur prêts	0.25	0.58	0.44	0.34	0.28	0.22	0.20	0.19	..	..
	b. Provisions on securities	b. Provisions sur titres	0.02	0.02	-	0.02	0.02	0.02	-	-0.04	..	..
	c. Other	c. Autres	0.17	0.05	0.05	0.06	0.06	0.06	0.06	0.05	0.08	0.20
48.	Profit before tax	Bénéfices avant impôt	0.41	0.41	0.35	0.43	0.42	0.50	0.59	0.59	0.56	0.68
49.	Income tax	Impôt sur le revenu	0.15	0.18	0.14	0.20	0.18	0.22	0.25	0.24	0.19	0.21
50.	Profit after tax	Bénéfices après impôt	0.26	0.23	0.22	0.23	0.24	0.28	0.34	0.36	0.36	0.48
51.	Distributed profit	Bénéfices distribués	0.07	0.07	0.07	0.07	0.07	0.09	0.09	0.10	0.09	0.11
52.	Retained profit	Bénéfices mis en réserve	0.19	0.16	0.15	0.17	0.17	0.20	0.25	0.26	0.27	0.37
	% of gross income	**% du total du résultat brut**										
53.	Net interest income	Produits financiers nets	85.83	73.91	71.47	68.14	61.24	55.51	48.70	58.44	54.14	52.70
54.	Non-interest income (net)	Produits non financiers (nets)	14.17	26.09	28.53	31.86	38.76	44.48	51.30	41.56	45.86	47.29
	a. Fees and commissions receivable	a. Frais et commissions à recevoir	..	24.55	27.59	26.40	29.13	31.60	33.69	37.47	39.13	36.44
	b. Fees and commissions payable	b. Frais et commissions à payer	..	10.41	10.49	9.85	11.37	11.84	12.49	13.27	12.22	10.59
	c. Net profits or loss on financial operations	c. Profits ou pertes nets sur opérations financières	1.50	5.14	3.04	7.55	14.21	14.43	20.63	8.92	8.54	3.36
	d. Other	d. Autres	12.67	6.82	8.39	7.77	6.79	10.31	9.46	8.44	10.40	18.07
55.	Operating expenses	Frais d'exploitation	68.78	63.26	67.73	65.94	66.78	66.11	65.30	65.70	67.24	60.05
	a. Staff costs	a. Dépenses en personnel	36.08	34.22	36.62	35.88	36.33	36.03	35.59	36.21	..	..
	b. Property costs	b. Dépenses en immobilier	3.67	3.36	3.56	3.30	3.34	3.42	3.31	3.38	3.51	3.17
	c. Other	c. Autres	29.02	25.69	27.55	26.77	27.11	26.66	26.39	26.10	..	..
56.	Net income	Résultat net	31.22	36.74	32.27	34.06	33.22	33.89	34.70	34.30	32.76	39.95
57.	Provisions (net)	Provisions (nettes)	16.33	22.57	18.66	16.88	15.29	12.62	10.45	8.74	8.82	13.42
	a. Provisions on loans	a. Provisions sur prêts	9.20	20.22	16.78	13.55	11.77	9.36	8.29	8.10	..	..
	b. Provisions on securities	b. Provisions sur titres	0.79	0.55	0.06	0.82	1.01	0.84	-0.14	-1.68	..	..
	c. Other	c. Autres	6.35	1.80	1.82	2.51	2.51	2.42	2.30	2.31	3.59	7.61
58.	Profit before tax	Bénéfices avant impôt	14.89	14.17	13.62	17.18	17.93	21.27	24.25	25.57	23.94	26.53
59.	Income tax	Impôt sur le revenu	5.48	6.12	5.24	7.93	7.75	9.18	10.28	10.12	8.33	8.05
60.	Profit after tax	Bénéfices après impôt	9.40	8.05	8.38	9.25	10.18	12.09	13.97	15.45	15.61	18.48
	% of net income	**% du total du résultat net**										
61.	Provisions (net)	Provisions (nettes)	52.32	61.43	57.81	49.56	46.02	37.23	30.12	25.47	26.93	33.59
	a. Provisions on loans	a. Provisions sur prêts	29.47	55.03	52.00	39.78	35.43	27.62	23.89	23.62	..	..
	b. Provisions on securities	b. Provisions sur titres	2.53	1.50	0.18	2.42	3.03	2.47	-0.41	-4.88	..	..
	c. Other	c. Autres	20.33	4.90	5.63	7.35	7.56	7.14	6.64	6.74	10.96	19.06
62.	Profit before tax	Bénéfices avant impôt	47.68	38.57	42.19	50.44	53.98	62.77	69.89	74.53	73.07	66.41
63.	Income tax	Impôt sur le revenu	17.56	16.66	16.24	23.30	23.33	27.09	29.62	29.50	25.44	20.15
64.	Profit after tax	Bénéfices après impôt	30.12	21.91	25.95	27.14	30.65	35.68	40.27	45.03	47.63	46.25

FRANCE
Co-operative banks

FRANCE
Banques mutualistes

Per cent

Pourcentage

BALANCE SHEET ANALYSIS

ANALYSE DU BILAN

% of year-end balance sheet total

% du total du bilan en fin d'exercice

	1992	1993	1994	1995	1996	1997	1998	1999	2000[1]	2001	
Assets											**Actif**
65. Cash & balance with Central bank	0.43	0.24	0.23	0.23	0.25	0.28	0.79	1.04	0.63	0.69	65. Caisse & solde auprès de la Banque centrale
66. Interbank deposits	43.74	48.59	47.84	48.25	45.13	44.00	42.38	41.91	42.68	41.57	66. Dépôts interbancaires
67. Loans	39.69	38.71	37.06	34.94	35.16	36.51	37.21	39.25	39.58	40.67	67. Prêts
68. Securities	7.64	7.95	10.37	11.99	14.62	14.76	15.14	13.46	12.88	12.56	68. Valeurs mobilières
69. Other assets	8.50	4.50	4.50	4.60	4.84	4.45	4.47	4.35	4.23	4.51	69. Autres actifs
Liabilities											**Passif**
70. Capital & reserves	3.74	3.77	3.85	3.88	4.08	4.44	4.89	5.19	5.22	6.43	70. Capital et réserves
71. Borrowing from Central bank	0.58	0.02	0.02	0.02	0.02	0.01	0.02	0.02	-	-	71. Emprunts auprès de la Banque centrale
72. Interbank deposits	39.25	40.28	40.04	39.62	39.54	37.57	37.34	37.59	34.08	32.25	72. Dépôts interbancaires
73. Non-bank deposits	35.47	39.67	41.14	42.48	42.56	45.23	44.88	44.88	49.28	50.05	73. Dépôts non bancaires
74. Bonds	12.84	12.95	11.86	10.58	9.49	9.07	8.50	8.20	7.41	6.94	74. Obligations
75. Other liabilities	8.12	3.32	3.08	3.42	4.31	3.68	4.38	4.13	4.01	4.33	75. Autres engagements
Memorandum items											***Pour mémoire***
76. Short-term securities	..	..	..	..	..	..	..	..	..	..	76. Titres à court terme
77. Bonds	..	4.18	4.77	4.82	5.54	4.72	3.90	3.69	5.20	4.81	77. Obligations
78. Shares and participations	..	1.59	1.67	1.76	2.24	2.54	3.08	3.63	3.27	4.27	78. Actions et participations
79. Claims on non-residents	9.34	8.41	7.22	7.88	7.81	8.29	7.38	6.03	5.89	5.89	79. Créances sur des non-résidents
80. Liabilities to non-residents	6.88	4.66	4.58	4.26	5.09	4.92	4.19	3.49	2.99	2.57	80. Engagements envers des non-résidents

* See notes on previous pages.

* Voir les notes en pages précédentes.

FRANCE
Other banks

Million euros

FRANCE
Autres banques

Millions d'euros

INCOME STATEMENT / COMPTE DE RESULTATS	1992	1993	1994	1995	1996	1997	1998	1999	2000[1]	2001
1. Interest income / Produits financiers	50936	52831	48246	46645	42905	41401	39210	38550	35986	39453
2. Interest expenses / Frais financiers	43652	46492	40994	40006	36705	36181	33769	33519	31534	36070
3. Net interest income / Produits financiers nets	7284	6339	7251	6639	6200	5220	5441	5031	4452	3383
4. Non-interest income (net) / Produits non financiers (nets)	4070	4037	3188	5973	5234	4668	4630	5069	4922	6156
a. Fees and commissions receivable / Frais et commissions à recevoir	..	1671	1709	1486	1664	1408	1514	1694	1842	1785
b. Fees and commissions payable / Frais et commissions à payer	..	750	689	547	570	406	409	484	462	490
c. Net profits or loss on financial operations / Profits ou pertes nets sur opérations financières	324	1321	354	529	503	751	1099	1273	1380	2510
d. Other / Autres	3746	1795	1814	4504	3637	2915	2426	2585	2162	2351
5. Gross income / Résultat brut	11354	10376	10439	12611	11434	9889	10071	10100	9374	9539
6. Operating expenses / Frais d'exploitation	5313	4991	5084	5180	5216	4815	5125	5608	5371	5190
a. Staff costs / Dépenses en personnel	1931	2112	2057	2061	2124	1889	1926	2050	..	..
b. Property costs / Dépenses en immobilier	372	274	225	334	213	87	184	204	200	211
c. Other / Autres	3010	2605	2802	2785	2879	2839	3015	3354	-	-
7. Net income / Résultat net	6041	5386	5355	7432	6218	5074	4946	4492	4003	4349
8. Provisions (net) / Provisions (nettes)	2681	4470	4185	7789	4511	1894	1177	875	960	1087
a. Provisions on loans / Provisions sur prêts	1856	3923	4241	6791	4017	1786	1273	1111	..	..
b. Provisions on securities / Provisions sur titres	825	473	17	1121	470	54	-176	-365	..	..
c. Other / Autres	1	74	-72	-123	24	54	80	129	53	225
9. Profit before tax / Bénéfices avant impôt	3360	916	1169	-357	1707	3180	3769	3617	3043	3261
10. Income tax / Impôt sur le revenu	635	769	651	603	658	711	935	870	722	785
11. Profit after tax / Bénéfices après impôt	2725	147	518	-960	1049	2470	2834	2748	2321	2476
12. Distributed profit / Bénéfices distribués	1617	1877	1715	1790	1606	1626	1520	1421	1479	1701
13. Retained profit / Bénéfices mis en réserve	1109	-1730	-1197	-2750	-558	843	1315	1327	842	775

BALANCE SHEET / BILAN	1992	1993	1994	1995	1996	1997	1998	1999	2000[1]	2001
Assets / Actif										
14. Cash & balance with Central bank / Caisse & solde auprès de la Banque centrale	1133	415	268	397	316	233	465	723	389	2265
15. Interbank deposits / Dépôts interbancaires	87331	99099	99789	94638	106451	112525	115785	132826	118332	165207
16. Loans / Prêts	263849	275844	282480	282009	253466	239210	230457	239300	201529	216561
17. Securities / Valeurs mobilières	51940	55898	63156	73755	92216	80488	84493	96011	93437	98690
18. Other assets / Autres actifs	32204	16337	15477	18719	18507	19678	19731	31828	19693	20748
Liabilities / Passif										
19. Capital & reserves / Capital et réserves	32034	40725	42176	41355	35351	34111	26628	28084	27740	28439
20. Borrowing from Central bank / Emprunts auprès de la Banque centrale	262	1131	431	233	130	124	59	62	36	9442
21. Interbank deposits / Dépôts interbancaires	159179	155046	156174	156085	184837	182848	198591	234713	221128	266290
22. Non-bank deposits / Dépôts non bancaires	8548	9638	17790	12362	13838	23364	18694	15576	18751	21083
23. Bonds / Obligations	179031	207867	209457	219492	183828	161706	154432	155749	111681	118504
24. Other liabilities / Autres engagements	57404	33187	35143	39991	52973	49981	52526	66505	54044	59713
Balance sheet total / Total du bilan										
25. End-year total / En fin d'exercice	436457	447594	461171	469518	470957	452134	450930	500688	433380	503471
26. Average total / Moyen	481098	444277	333865	463502	504765	472175	435266	385374	334521	418587

Million euros

	1992	1993	1994	1995	1996	1997	1998	1999	2000[1]	2001
Memorandum items										
27. Short-term securities	..	..	..	..	..	..	..	..	..	..
28. Bonds	..	27145	29948	34209	42903	41108	47851	62171	61594	65314
29. Shares and participations	..	22559	22614	30982	22310	23583	13702	13396	11127	11636
30. Claims on non-residents	17278	34545	33803	35398	50961	63939	65721	85008	70391	66863
31. Liabilities to non-residents	13133	57522	62561	63897	74514	83346	88988	83001	60141	64808
Capital adequacy										
32. Tier 1 Capital	..	..	..	..	..	..	..	..	..	..
33. Tier 2 Capital	..	..	..	..	..	..	..	..	..	..
34. Supervisory deductions	..	..	..	..	..	..	..	..	..	..
35. Total net capital resources	..	..	..	..	..	..	..	..	..	..
36. Risk-weighted assets	..	..	..	..	..	..	..	..	..	..
SUPPLEMENTARY INFORMATION										
37. Number of institutions	1098	1035	1018	869	837	725	692	647	591	561
38. Number of branches	161	1629	1768	1947	1607	1768	1878	1706	1816	1382
39. Number of employees (x 1000)	35.0	36.0	36.0	36.0	37.0	30.0	32.0	31.0	30.6	30.9

1 Since the year 2000, the French financial institutions' accounts have been published and presented in a new format. Therefore, some information is no longer available.

Notes

. Other banks include municipal credit institutions, finance companies and specialised financial institutions.

. Average balance sheet totals (item 26) are based on the average of quarterly totals.

Millions d'euros

Pour mémoire
27. Titres à court terme
28. Obligations
29. Actions et participations
30. Créances sur des non-résidents
31. Engagements envers des non-résidents

Solvabilité
32. Fonds propres de base
33. Fonds propres complémentaires
34. Eléments à déduire des fonds propres
35. Total net des ressources en capital
36. Actifs pondérés des risques

RENSEIGNEMENTS COMPLEMENTAIRES
37. Nombre d'institutions
38. Nombre de succursales
39. Nombre de salariés (x 1000)

1 A partir de 2000, les comptes publiés par les établissements de crédit français présentent un nouveau format. En conséquence, certaines informations ne sont plus disponibles.

Notes

. La catégorie "autres banques" comprend les caisses de credit municipal, les sociétés financières et les institutions financières spécialisées

. La moyenne du total des actifs/passifs (poste26) est basée sur la moyenne des totaux des situations trimestrielles.

FRANCE
Other banks

FRANCE
Autres banques

Per cent / *Pourcentage*

INCOME STATEMENT ANALYSIS / **ANALYSE DU COMPTE DE RESULTATS**

No.		1992	1993	1994	1995	1996	1997	1998	1999	2000[1]	2001	
	% of average balance sheet total											**% du total moyen du bilan**
40.	Interest income	10.59	11.89	14.45	10.06	8.50	8.77	9.01	10.00	10.76	9.43	Produits financiers
41.	Interest expenses	9.07	10.46	12.28	8.63	7.27	7.66	7.76	8.70	9.43	8.62	Frais financiers
42.	Net interest income	1.51	1.43	2.17	1.43	1.23	1.11	1.25	1.31	1.33	0.81	Produits financiers nets
43.	Non-interest income (net)	0.85	0.91	0.95	1.29	1.04	0.99	1.06	1.32	1.47	1.47	Produits non financiers (nets)
	a. Fees and commissions receivable	..	0.38	0.51	0.32	0.33	0.30	0.35	0.44	0.55	0.43	a. Frais et commissions à recevoir
	b. Fees and commissions payable	..	0.17	0.21	0.12	0.11	0.09	0.09	0.13	0.14	0.12	b. Frais et commissions à payer
	c. Net profits or loss on financial operations	0.07	0.30	0.11	0.11	0.10	0.16	0.25	0.33	0.41	0.60	c. Profits ou pertes nets sur opérations financières
	d. Other	0.78	0.40	0.54	0.97	0.72	0.62	0.56	0.67	0.65	0.56	d. Autres
44.	Gross income	2.36	2.34	3.13	2.72	2.27	2.09	2.31	2.62	2.80	2.28	Résultat brut
45.	Operating expenses	1.10	1.12	1.52	1.12	1.03	1.02	1.18	1.46	1.61	1.24	Frais d'exploitation
	a. Staff costs	0.40	0.48	0.62	0.44	0.42	0.40	0.44	0.53	..	..	a. Dépenses en personnel
	b. Property costs	0.08	0.06	0.07	0.07	0.04	0.02	0.04	0.05	0.06	0.05	b. Dépenses en immobilier
	c. Other	0.63	0.59	0.84	0.60	0.57	0.60	0.69	0.87	..	..	c. Autres
46.	Net income	1.26	1.21	1.60	1.60	1.23	1.07	1.14	1.17	1.20	1.04	Résultat net
47.	Provisions (net)	0.56	1.01	1.25	1.68	0.89	0.40	0.27	0.23	0.29	0.26	Provisions (nettes)
	a. Provisions on loans	0.39	0.88	1.27	1.47	0.80	0.38	0.29	0.29	..	..	a. Provisions sur prêts
	b. Provisions on securities	0.17	0.11	0.01	0.24	0.09	0.01	-0.04	-0.09	..	..	b. Provisions sur titres
	c. Other	..	0.02	-0.02	-0.03	..	0.01	0.02	0.03	0.02	0.05	c. Autres
48.	Profit before tax	0.70	0.21	0.35	-0.08	0.34	0.67	0.87	0.94	0.91	0.78	Bénéfices avant impôt
49.	Income tax	0.13	0.17	0.20	0.13	0.13	0.15	0.21	0.23	0.22	0.19	Impôt sur le revenu
50.	Profit after tax	0.57	0.03	0.16	-0.21	0.21	0.52	0.65	0.71	0.69	0.59	Bénéfices après impôt
51.	Distributed profit	0.34	0.42	0.51	0.39	0.32	0.34	0.35	0.37	0.44	0.41	Bénéfices distribués
52.	Retained profit	0.23	-0.39	-0.36	-0.59	-0.11	0.18	0.30	0.34	0.25	0.19	Bénéfices mis en réserve
	% of gross income											**% du total du résultat brut**
53.	Net interest income	64.15	61.09	69.46	52.64	54.23	52.79	54.03	49.81	47.49	35.46	Produits financiers nets
54.	Non-interest income (net)	35.85	38.91	30.54	47.36	45.77	47.21	45.97	50.19	52.50	64.54	Produits non financiers (nets)
	a. Fees and commissions receivable	..	16.10	16.37	11.78	14.55	14.24	15.03	16.78	19.65	18.71	a. Frais et commissions à recevoir
	b. Fees and commissions payable	..	7.22	6.60	4.34	4.99	4.10	4.06	4.79	4.93	5.14	b. Frais et commissions à payer
	c. Net profits or loss on financial operations	2.86	12.73	3.39	4.19	4.40	7.60	10.91	12.61	14.72	26.31	c. Profits ou pertes nets sur opérations financières
	d. Other	32.99	17.30	17.38	35.72	31.81	29.47	24.09	25.60	23.07	24.65	d. Autres
55.	Operating expenses	46.79	48.10	48.70	41.07	45.62	48.69	50.89	55.52	57.30	54.41	Frais d'exploitation
	a. Staff costs	17.01	20.35	19.71	16.34	18.57	19.10	19.12	20.29	..	..	a. Dépenses en personnel
	b. Property costs	3.28	2.64	2.16	2.65	1.86	0.88	1.83	2.02	2.13	2.21	b. Dépenses en immobilier
	c. Other	26.51	25.11	26.84	22.08	25.18	28.71	29.94	33.21	..	..	c. Autres
56.	Net income	53.21	51.90	51.30	58.93	54.38	51.31	49.11	44.48	42.70	45.59	Résultat net
57.	Provisions (net)	23.61	43.08	40.10	61.76	39.45	19.15	11.69	8.66	10.24	11.40	Provisions (nettes)
	a. Provisions on loans	16.34	37.81	40.63	53.85	35.13	18.06	12.64	11.00	..	..	a. Provisions sur prêts
	b. Provisions on securities	7.26	4.56	0.16	8.88	4.11	0.54	-1.75	-3.61	..	..	b. Provisions sur titres
	c. Other	0.01	0.71	-0.69	-0.97	0.21	0.55	0.80	1.27	0.56	2.36	c. Autres
58.	Profit before tax	29.59	8.83	11.20	-2.83	14.93	32.16	37.42	35.82	32.46	34.19	Bénéfices avant impôt
59.	Income tax	5.59	7.42	6.24	4.78	5.76	7.19	9.28	8.61	7.70	8.23	Impôt sur le revenu
60.	Profit after tax	24.00	1.41	4.96	-7.61	9.17	24.97	28.14	27.20	24.76	25.96	Bénéfices après impôt
	% of net income											**% du total du résultat net**
61.	Provisions (net)	44.38	82.99	78.16	104.81	72.55	37.32	23.79	19.47	23.98	24.99	Provisions (nettes)
	a. Provisions on loans	30.72	72.84	79.20	91.38	64.61	35.19	25.73	24.73	..	..	a. Provisions sur prêts
	b. Provisions on securities	13.65	8.79	0.32	15.08	7.56	1.06	-3.56	-8.11	..	..	b. Provisions sur titres
	c. Other	0.01	1.37	-1.35	-1.65	0.38	1.07	1.63	2.86	1.32	5.17	c. Autres
62.	Profit before tax	55.62	17.01	21.84	-4.81	27.45	62.68	76.21	80.53	76.02	74.98	Bénéfices avant impôt
63.	Income tax	10.51	14.29	12.17	8.11	10.59	14.01	18.90	19.36	18.03	18.05	Impôt sur le revenu
64.	Profit after tax	45.12	2.72	9.67	-12.92	16.86	48.67	57.31	61.17	58.00	56.93	Bénéfices après impôt

FRANCE
Other banks

FRANCE
Autres banques

Per cent — *Pourcentage*

BALANCE SHEET ANALYSIS — **ANALYSE DU BILAN**

% of year-end balance sheet total — **% du total du bilan en fin d'exercice**

	1992	1993	1994	1995	1996	1997	1998	1999	2000[1]	2001		
Assets												**Actif**
65. Cash & balance with Central bank	0.26	0.09	0.06	0.08	0.07	0.05	0.10	0.14	0.09	0.45	65.	Caisse & solde auprès de la Banque centrale
66. Interbank deposits	20.01	22.14	21.64	20.16	22.60	24.89	25.68	26.53	27.30	32.81	66.	Dépôts interbancaires
67. Loans	60.45	61.63	61.25	60.06	53.82	52.91	51.11	47.79	46.50	43.01	67.	Prêts
68. Securities	11.90	12.49	13.69	15.71	19.58	17.80	18.74	19.18	21.56	19.60	68.	Valeurs mobilières
69. Other assets	7.38	3.65	3.36	3.99	3.93	4.35	4.38	6.36	4.54	4.12	69.	Autres actifs
Liabilities												**Passif**
70. Capital & reserves	7.34	9.10	9.15	8.81	7.51	7.54	5.91	5.61	6.40	5.65	70.	Capital et réserves
71. Borrowing from Central bank	0.06	0.25	0.09	0.05	0.03	0.03	0.01	0.01	0.01	1.88	71.	Emprunts auprès de la Banque centrale
72. Interbank deposits	36.47	34.64	33.86	33.24	39.25	40.44	44.04	46.88	51.02	52.89	72.	Dépôts interbancaires
73. Non-bank deposits	1.96	2.15	3.86	2.63	2.94	5.17	4.15	3.11	4.33	4.19	73.	Dépôts non bancaires
74. Bonds	41.02	46.44	45.42	46.75	39.03	35.77	34.25	31.11	25.77	23.54	74.	Obligations
75. Other liabilities	13.15	7.41	7.62	8.52	11.25	11.05	11.65	13.28	12.47	11.86	75.	Autres engagements
Memorandum items												***Pour mémoire***
76. Short-term securities	..	..	..	..	..	..	..	..	..	..	76.	Titres à court terme
77. Bonds	..	6.06	6.49	7.29	9.11	9.09	10.61	12.42	14.21	12.97	77.	Obligations
78. Shares and participations	..	5.04	4.90	6.60	4.74	5.22	3.04	2.68	2.57	2.31	78.	Actions et participations
79. Claims on non-residents	3.96	7.72	7.33	7.54	10.82	14.14	14.57	16.98	16.24	13.28	79.	Créances sur des non-résidents
80. Liabilities to non-residents	3.01	12.85	13.57	13.61	15.82	18.43	19.73	16.58	13.88	12.87	80.	Engagements envers des non-résidents

* See notes on previous pages. — * Voir les notes en pages précédentes.

GERMANY

All banks

Million euros

ALLEMAGNE

Ensemble des banques

Million d'euros

INCOME STATEMENT / COMPTE DE RESULTATS	1992	1993[1]	1994	1995	1996	1997	1998	1999	2000	2001	
1. Interest income	182512	196361	195370	201017	206892	219688	234442	250171	295127	303899	1. Produits financiers
2. Interest expenses	136420	141425	133262	139442	142104	153464	167608	179508	224956	231406	2. Frais financiers
3. Net interest income	46091	54936	62109	61575	64788	66224	66834	70663	70171	72493	3. Produits financiers nets
4. Non-interest income (net) (2)	14444	17040	14782	16336	17203	20435	36856	29456	39213	39990	4. Produits non financiers (nets) (2)
a. Fees and commissions receivable	..	14199	14559	14496	16000	18857	21214	26064	33049	30457	a. Frais et commissions à recevoir
b. Fees and commissions payable	..	1357	1404	1465	1765	2133	2879	3775	5199	5362	b. Frais et commissions à payer
c. Net profits or loss on financial operations	..	3401	220	2197	2004	2596	3425	3436	6275	5346	c. Profits ou pertes nets sur opérations financières
d. Other	..	797	1407	1109	964	1114	15096	3731	5088	9549	d. Autres
5. Gross income	60535	71976	76891	77912	81992	86659	103690	100119	109384	112483	5. Résultat brut
6. Operating expenses	39066	44906	46750	49743	52272	55551	59726	67845	75150	78560	6. Frais d'exploitation
a. Staff costs	24696	27584	28464	30055	31030	32142	33776	37170	40708	41718	a. Dépenses en personnel
b. Property costs (3)	..	..	..	..	..	..	..	..	..	..	b. Dépenses en immobilier (3)
c. Other	..	17322	18287	19688	21242	23409	25949	30675	34442	36842	c. Autres
7. Net income	21470	27070	30141	28169	29720	31108	43964	32274	34234	33923	7. Résultat net
8. Provisions (net)	8858	11945	15292	10972	11604	13179	13689	14004	17128	21986	8. Provisions (nettes)
a. Provisions on loans	8641	11781	14515	10718	11333	12901	13440	13476	15522	20283	a. Provisions sur prêts
b. Provisions on securities (4)	..	..	..	..	..	..	..	..	..	..	b. Provisions sur titres (4)
c. Other	..	164	777	254	272	277	250	528	1606	1703	c. Autres
9. Profit before tax	12612	15125	14849	17197	18116	17929	30275	18270	17106	11937	9. Bénéfices avant impôt
10. Income tax	7805	8341	7217	8987	9546	9166	14782	8023	6184	3269	10. Impôt sur le revenu
11. Profit after tax	4806	6784	7632	8209	8570	8764	15493	10247	10922	8668	11. Bénéfices après impôt
12. Distributed profit	3335	4454	4808	5310	5519	5838	7942	6916	7798	4825	12. Bénéfices distribués
13. Retained profit	1472	2330	2824	2899	3050	2925	7551	3331	3124	3843	13. Bénéfices mis en réserve
BALANCE SHEET											**BILAN**
Assets											**Actif**
14. Cash & balance with Central bank	52108	48574	39535	40835	42689	42937	46552	63902	66485	70904	14. Caisse & solde auprès de la Banque centrale
15. Interbank deposits	515723	616546	633977	715037	811754	914499	1016637	1093303	1171942	1295505	15. Dépôts interbancaires
16. Loans	1326730	1528203	1635065	1781348	1938466	2109053	2259088	2397906	2627567	2718858	16. Prêts
17. Securities	385497	523434	592259	642157	740071	869456	1008188	1125920	1278645	1370407	17. Valeurs mobilières
18. Other assets	57913	70398	70622	82656	88697	107789	135403	252287	280822	258907	18. Autres actifs
Liabilities											**Passif**
19. Capital & reserves	95817	111285	126035	136846	147203	164460	174206	197860	217704	233163	19. Capital et réserves
20. Borrowing from Central bank	78070	118290	101461	96997	100986	102897	99890	76113	113606	96614	20. Emprunts auprès de la Banque centrale
21. Interbank deposits	562504	637010	730606	855431	962109	1128400	1317764	1381820	1524043	1624321	21. Dépôts interbancaires
22. Non-bank deposits	1203824	1423367	1457365	1535149	1680091	1823835	1953201	2152577	2303467	2451818	22. Dépôts non bancaires
23. Bonds	299863	368223	428795	487409	555622	599357	655560	830990	941421	1003147	23. Obligations
24. Other liabilities	97892	128980	127196	150200	175664	224786	265247	293958	325220	305518	24. Autres engagements
Balance sheet total											**Total du bilan**
25. End-year total	2337971	2787155	2971458	3262032	3621676	4043735	4465868	4933318	5425461	5714581	25. En fin d'exercice
26. Average total	2229197	2588051	2843213	3042710	3421884	3838263	4288903	4767324	5356909	5648060	26. Moyen

GERMANY
All banks

Million euros

	1992	1993[1]	1994	1995	1996	1997	1998	1999	2000	2001
Memorandum items										
27. Short-term securities	68575	87574	75786	80388	101777	133749	144996	102629	119380	127115
28. Bonds	254589	356152	424993	450727	511436	586594	665255	783003	859341	922380
29. Shares and participations	62332	79709	91479	111041	126858	149114	197937	240288	299924	320912
30. Claims on non-residents	373538	477595	474717	554996	702514	925463	1097410	1235930	1544223	1813573
31. Liabilities to non-residents	271279	294999	354574	436626	536048	753758	916680	1057328	1275242	1432904
Capital adequacy										
32. Tier 1 Capital	..	..	..	..	..	..	..	..	..	..
33. Tier 2 Capital	..	..	..	..	..	..	..	..	..	..
34. Supervisory deductions	..	..	..	..	..	..	..	..	..	..
35. Total net capital resources	..	..	..	..	..	..	..	..	..	..
36. Risk-weighted assets	..	..	..	..	..	..	..	..	..	..
SUPPLEMENTARY INFORMATION										
37. Number of institutions	3517	3769	3613	3500	3392	3284	3111	2833	2575	2370
38. Number of branches	39295	44922	44436	44012	43585	43013	41680	40934	39327	37259
39. Number of employees (x 1000)	709	717	724	724	716	718	718	723	725	717

1 Break in series due to change in methodology.

2 Non-interest income (item 4), in the national definition, excluding items 4.c and 4.d.

3 Property costs (item 6.b.) included under Other operating expenses (item 6.c.).

4 Provisions on securities (item 8.b.) included under Provisions on loans (item 8.a).

Notes

. Average balance sheet totals (item 26) are based on twelve end-month data.

Change in methodology

. As from 1993, data include eastern German credit institutions and are in accordance with the new accounting regulations.

ALLEMAGNE
Ensemble des banques

Million d'euros

Pour mémoire

27. Titres à court terme
28. Obligations
29. Actions et participations
30. Créances sur des non-résidents
31. Engagements envers des non-résidents

Solvabilité

32. Fonds propres de base
33. Fonds propres complémentaires
34. Eléments à déduire des fonds propres
35. Total net des ressources en capital
36. Actifs pondérés des risques

RENSEIGNEMENTS COMPLEMENTAIRES

37. Nombre d'institutions
38. Nombre de succursales
39. Nombre de salariés (x 1000)

1 Rupture dans les séries suite au changement méthodologique.

2 Produits non financiers (nets) (poste 4), suivant la définition nationale, non compris les rubriques 4.c et 4.d.

3 Les Dépenses en immobilier (poste 6.b.), sont incluses sous Autres frais d'exploitation (poste 6.c.).

4 Les Provisions sur titres (poste 8.b.) sont incluses sous Provisions sur prêts (poste 8.a).

Notes

. La moyenne du total des actifs/passifs (poste 26) est basée sur douze données de fin de mois.

Changement méthodologique

. Depuis 1993, les données comprennent les organismes de crédit d'Allemagne orientale et sont conformes aux nouvelles règles de comptabilité.

GERMANY
All banks

ALLEMAGNE
Ensemble des banques

Per cent — *Pourcentage*

INCOME STATEMENT ANALYSIS — **ANALYSE DU COMPTE DE RESULTATS**

		1992	1993[1]	1994	1995	1996	1997	1998	1999	2000	2001		
	% of average balance sheet total												**% du total moyen du bilan**
40.	Interest income	8.19	7.59	6.87	6.61	6.05	5.72	5.47	5.25	5.51	5.38	40.	Produits financiers
41.	Interest expenses	6.12	5.46	4.69	4.58	4.15	4.00	3.91	3.77	4.20	4.10	41.	Frais financiers
42.	Net interest income	2.07	2.12	2.18	2.02	1.89	1.73	1.56	1.48	1.31	1.28	42.	Produits financiers nets
43.	Non-interest income (net)	0.65	0.66	0.52	0.54	0.50	0.53	0.86	0.62	0.73	0.71	43.	Produits non financiers (nets)
	a. Fees and commissions receivable	..	0.55	0.51	0.48	0.47	0.49	0.49	0.55	0.62	0.54		a. Frais et commissions à recevoir
	b. Fees and commissions payable	..	0.05	0.05	0.05	0.05	0.06	0.07	0.08	0.10	0.09		b. Frais et commissions à payer
	c. Net profits or loss on financial operations	..	0.13	0.01	0.07	0.06	0.07	0.08	0.07	0.12	0.09		c. Profits ou pertes nets sur opérations financières
	d. Other	..	0.03	0.05	0.04	0.03	0.03	0.35	0.08	0.09	0.17		d. Autres
44.	Gross income	2.72	2.78	2.70	2.56	2.40	2.26	2.42	2.10	2.04	1.99	44.	Résultat brut
45.	Operating expenses	1.75	1.74	1.64	1.63	1.53	1.45	1.39	1.42	1.40	1.39	45.	Frais d'exploitation
	a. Staff costs	1.11	1.07	1.00	0.99	0.91	0.84	0.79	0.78	0.76	0.74		a. Dépenses en personnel
	b. Property costs	..	..	..	..	..	..	..	..	..	..		b. Dépenses en immobilier
	c. Other	..	0.67	0.64	0.65	0.62	0.61	0.61	0.64	0.64	0.65		c. Autres
46.	Net income	0.96	1.05	1.06	0.93	0.87	0.81	1.03	0.68	0.64	0.60	46.	Résultat net
47.	Provisions (net)	0.40	0.46	0.54	0.36	0.34	0.34	0.32	0.29	0.32	0.39	47.	Provisions (nettes)
	a. Provisions on loans	0.39	0.46	0.51	0.35	0.33	0.34	0.31	0.28	0.29	0.36		a. Provisions sur prêts
	b. Provisions on securities	..	..	..	..	..	..	..	..	..	..		b. Provisions sur titres
	c. Other	..	0.01	0.03	0.01	0.01	0.01	0.01	0.01	0.03	0.03		c. Autres
48.	Profit before tax	0.57	0.58	0.52	0.57	0.53	0.47	0.71	0.38	0.32	0.21	48.	Bénéfices avant impôt
49.	Income tax	0.35	0.32	0.25	0.30	0.28	0.24	0.34	0.17	0.12	0.06	49.	Impôt sur le revenu
50.	Profit after tax	0.22	0.26	0.27	0.27	0.25	0.23	0.36	0.21	0.20	0.15	50.	Bénéfices après impôt
51.	Distributed profit	0.15	0.17	0.17	0.17	0.16	0.15	0.19	0.15	0.15	0.09	51.	Bénéfices distribués
52.	Retained profit	0.07	0.09	0.10	0.10	0.09	0.08	0.18	0.07	0.06	0.07	52.	Bénéfices mis en réserve
	% of gross income												**% du total du résultat brut**
53.	Net interest income	76.14	76.33	80.77	79.03	79.02	76.42	64.46	70.58	64.15	64.45	53.	Produits financiers nets
54.	Non-interest income (net)	23.86	23.67	19.23	20.97	20.98	23.58	35.54	29.42	35.85	35.55	54.	Produits non financiers (nets)
	a. Fees and commissions receivable	..	19.73	18.93	18.61	19.51	21.76	20.46	26.03	30.21	27.08		a. Frais et commissions à recevoir
	b. Fees and commissions payable	..	1.89	1.83	1.88	2.15	2.46	2.78	3.77	4.75	4.77		b. Frais et commissions à payer
	c. Net profits or loss on financial operations	..	4.73	0.29	2.82	2.44	3.00	3.30	3.43	5.74	4.75		c. Profits ou pertes nets sur opérations financières
	d. Other	..	1.11	1.83	1.42	1.18	1.29	14.56	3.73	4.65	8.49		d. Autres
55.	Operating expenses	64.53	62.39	60.80	63.85	63.75	64.10	57.60	67.76	68.70	69.84	55.	Frais d'exploitation
	a. Staff costs	40.80	38.32	37.02	38.58	37.84	37.09	32.57	37.13	37.22	37.09		a. Dépenses en personnel
	b. Property costs	..	..	..	..	..	..	..	..	..	..		b. Dépenses en immobilier
	c. Other	..	24.07	23.76	25.27	25.91	27.01	25.03	30.64	31.49	32.75		c. Autres
56.	Net income	35.47	37.61	39.20	36.15	36.25	35.90	42.40	32.24	31.30	30.16	56.	Résultat net
57.	Provisions (net)	14.63	16.60	19.89	14.08	14.15	15.21	13.20	13.99	15.66	19.55	57.	Provisions (nettes)
	a. Provisions on loans	14.27	16.37	18.88	13.76	13.82	14.89	12.96	13.46	14.19	18.03		a. Provisions sur prêts
	b. Provisions on securities	..	..	..	..	..	..	..	..	..	..		b. Provisions sur titres
	c. Other	..	0.23	1.01	0.33	0.33	0.32	0.24	0.53	1.47	1.51		c. Autres
58.	Profit before tax	20.83	21.01	19.31	22.07	22.09	20.69	29.20	18.25	15.64	10.61	58.	Bénéfices avant impôt
59.	Income tax	12.89	11.59	9.39	11.54	11.64	10.58	14.26	8.01	5.65	2.91	59.	Impôt sur le revenu
60.	Profit after tax	7.94	9.43	9.93	10.54	10.45	10.11	14.94	10.23	9.99	7.71	60.	Bénéfices après impôt
	% of net income												**% du total du résultat net**
61.	Provisions (net)	41.26	44.13	50.73	38.95	39.05	42.36	31.14	43.39	50.03	64.81	61.	Provisions (nettes)
	a. Provisions on loans	40.25	43.52	48.16	38.05	38.13	41.47	30.57	41.75	45.34	59.79		a. Provisions sur prêts
	b. Provisions on securities	..	..	..	..	..	..	..	..	..	..		b. Provisions sur titres
	c. Other	..	0.61	2.58	0.90	0.91	0.89	0.57	1.64	4.69	5.02		c. Autres
62.	Profit before tax	58.74	55.87	49.27	61.05	60.95	57.64	68.86	56.61	49.97	35.19	62.	Bénéfices avant impôt
63.	Income tax	36.36	30.81	23.95	31.91	32.12	29.46	33.62	24.86	18.06	9.64	63.	Impôt sur le revenu
64.	Profit after tax	22.39	25.06	25.32	29.14	28.84	28.17	35.24	31.75	31.90	25.55	64.	Bénéfices après impôt

GERMANY
All banks

ALLEMAGNE
Ensemble des banques

Per cent — *Pourcentage*

BALANCE SHEET ANALYSIS — **ANALYSE DU BILAN**

% of year-end balance sheet total — **% du total du bilan en fin d'exercice**

	1992	1993[1]	1994	1995	1996	1997	1998	1999	2000	2001	
Assets											**Actif**
65. Cash & balance with Central bank	2.23	1.74	1.33	1.25	1.18	1.06	1.04	1.30	1.23	1.24	65. Caisse & solde auprès de la Banque centrale
66. Interbank deposits	22.06	22.12	21.34	21.92	22.41	22.62	22.76	22.16	21.60	22.67	66. Dépôts interbancaires
67. Loans	56.75	54.83	55.03	54.61	53.52	52.16	50.59	48.61	48.43	47.58	67. Prêts
68. Securities	16.49	18.78	19.93	19.69	20.43	21.50	22.58	22.82	23.57	23.98	68. Valeurs mobilières
69. Other assets	2.48	2.53	2.38	2.53	2.45	2.67	3.03	5.11	5.18	4.53	69. Autres actifs
Liabilities											**Passif**
70. Capital & reserves	4.10	3.99	4.24	4.20	4.06	4.07	3.90	4.01	4.01	4.08	70. Capital et réserves
71. Borrowing from Central bank	3.34	4.24	3.41	2.97	2.79	2.54	2.24	1.54	2.09	1.69	71. Emprunts auprès de la Banque centrale
72. Interbank deposits	24.06	22.86	24.59	26.22	26.57	27.90	29.51	28.01	28.09	28.42	72. Dépôts interbancaires
73. Non-bank deposits	51.49	51.07	49.05	47.06	46.39	45.10	43.74	43.63	42.46	42.90	73. Dépôts non bancaires
74. Bonds	12.83	13.21	14.43	14.94	15.34	14.82	14.68	16.84	17.35	17.55	74. Obligations
75. Other liabilities	4.19	4.63	4.28	4.60	4.85	5.56	5.94	5.96	5.99	5.35	75. Autres engagements
Memorandum items											***Pour mémoire***
76. Short-term securities	2.93	3.14	2.55	2.46	2.81	3.31	3.25	2.08	2.20	2.22	76. Titres à court terme
77. Bonds	10.89	12.78	14.30	13.82	14.12	14.51	14.90	15.87	15.84	16.14	77. Obligations
78. Shares and participations	2.67	2.86	3.08	3.40	3.50	3.69	4.43	4.87	5.53	5.62	78. Actions et participations
79. Claims on non-residents	15.98	17.14	15.98	17.01	19.40	22.89	24.57	25.05	28.46	31.74	79. Créances sur des non-résidents
80. Liabilities to non-residents	11.60	10.58	11.93	13.39	14.80	18.64	20.53	21.43	23.50	25.07	80. Engagements envers des non-résidents

* See notes on previous pages. — * Voir les notes en pages précédentes.

GERMANY
Commercial banks

Million euros

ALLEMAGNE
Banques commerciales

Million d'euros

	1992	1993[1]	1994	1995	1996	1997	1998	1999	2000	2001	
INCOME STATEMENT											**COMPTE DE RESULTATS**
1. Interest income	64012	65557	63036	64718	67415	73218	80127	88921	115872	119425	1. Produits financiers
2. Interest expenses	47087	46614	42339	44635	45970	50673	56888	63298	90321	92359	2. Frais financiers
3. Net interest income	16925	18942	20697	20083	21445	22544	23239	25623	25551	27066	3. Produits financiers nets
4. Non-interest income (net) (2)	7534	8682	7060	7871	8834	10157	23151	19089	24088	25650	4. Produits non financiers (nets) (2)
a. Fees and commissions receivable	..	7366	7125	6984	7990	10062	11650	14475	19542	18511	a. Frais et commissions à recevoir
b. Fees and commissions payable	..	750	797	829	1044	1291	1815	1903	2787	3355	b. Frais et commissions à payer
c. Net profits or loss on financial operations	..	2010	70	1129	1029	1287	2038	2511	5203	4691	c. Profits ou pertes nets sur opérations financières
d. Other	..	55	662	588	859	99	11278	4006	2130	5803	d. Autres
5. Gross income	24459	27625	27758	27954	30279	32701	46390	44712	49639	52716	5. Résultat brut
6. Operating expenses	15569	16886	17705	18658	19868	21787	24226	30606	36466	38753	6. Frais d'exploitation
a. Staff costs	9695	10457	10710	11217	11636	12276	13181	15738	18478	19087	a. Dépenses en personnel
b. Property costs (3)	..	-	-	-	-	..	..	..	..	..	b. Dépenses en immobilier (3)
c. Other	..	6429	6994	7441	8232	9511	11045	14868	17988	19666	c. Autres
7. Net income	8890	10739	10053	9297	10411	10914	22164	14106	13173	13963	7. Résultat net
8. Provisions (net)	5273	6006	4897	4122	4630	5377	5240	7344	6871	9801	8. Provisions (nettes)
a. Provisions on loans	5136	5900	4843	3933	4462	5238	5066	7184	5851	8683	a. Provisions sur prêts
b. Provisions on securities (4)	..	..	..	..	..	..	..	..	..	..	b. Provisions sur titres (4)
c. Other	..	106	53	189	168	139	174	160	1020	1118	c. Autres
9. Profit before tax	3617	4733	5156	5175	5781	5537	16924	6762	6302	4162	9. Bénéfices avant impôt
10. Income tax	1954	1894	1883	1701	2197	1715	7540	1855	682	402	10. Impôt sur le revenu
11. Profit after tax	1663	2839	3274	3474	3584	3822	9384	4907	5620	3760	11. Bénéfices après impôt
12. Distributed profit	1480	2160	2340	2595	2777	3005	4918	3713	4481	1721	12. Bénéfices distribués
13. Retained profit	184	679	934	879	807	817	4466	1194	1139	2039	13. Bénéfices mis en réserve
BALANCE SHEET											**BILAN**
Assets											*Actif*
14. Cash & balance with Central bank	19834	18102	12811	13537	15317	16016	19074	29238	30166	27220	14. Caisse & solde auprès de la Banque centrale
15. Interbank deposits	176747	200757	219617	241072	277512	317470	354346	358114	420783	515849	15. Dépôts interbancaires
16. Loans	479740	539483	565129	627557	701462	782757	848395	905843	1077198	1138913	16. Prêts
17. Securities	105257	151678	161261	185809	224093	285659	346529	393500	483121	524012	17. Valeurs mobilières
18. Other assets	17821	21577	19567	25886	27491	34239	50934	114974	136189	131563	18. Autres actifs
Liabilities											*Passif*
19. Capital & reserves	42043	46709	54233	58506	61634	69481	70354	82274	94320	99306	19. Capital et réserves
20. Borrowing from Central bank	28684	50631	37971	37381	35841	33705	34078	19815	34802	54215	20. Emprunts auprès de la Banque centrale
21. Interbank deposits	212649	225938	278999	330918	365705	421704	500620	498695	598420	677928	21. Dépôts interbancaires
22. Non-bank deposits	401028	452774	434451	456102	527963	603886	644347	771263	911251	970003	22. Dépôts non bancaires
23. Bonds	72572	100272	120787	142779	170517	188724	221433	290748	341201	377522	23. Obligations
24. Other liabilities	42423	55272	51945	68175	84216	118640	148445	138874	167463	158583	24. Autres engagements
Balance sheet total											**Total du bilan**
25. End-year total	799398	931596	978386	1093860	1245876	1436141	1619278	1801669	2147457	2337557	25. En fin d'exercice
26. Average total	764826	867712	947276	1012874	1174819	1363362	1588848	1769718	2167739	2325961	26. Moyen

GERMANY

Commercial banks

ALLEMAGNE

Banques commerciales

Million euros

	1992	1993[1]	1994	1995	1996	1997	1998	1999	2000	2001		*Million d'euros*
Memorandum items												**Pour mémoire**
27. Short-term securities	20398	31823	24955	29363	39117	62070	67662	60984	61809	60249	27.	Titres à court terme
28. Bonds	50502	77740	91059	103673	124002	154985	183158	214892	262642	298955	28.	Obligations
29. Shares and participations	34357	42115	45247	52772	60974	68604	95709	117624	158670	164808	29.	Actions et participations
30. Claims on non-residents	223677	282516	304748	350509	433722	573589	667063	706227	945102	1139382	30.	Créances sur des non-résidents
31. Liabilities to non-residents	190841	210123	245724	300808	362512	488645	569343	628562	809309	930195	31.	Engagements envers des non-résidents
Capital adequacy												**Solvabilité**
32. Tier 1 Capital	..	..	..	..	..	..	..	..	..	..	32.	Fonds propres de base
33. Tier 2 Capital	..	..	..	..	..	..	..	..	..	..	33.	Fonds propres complémentaires
34. Supervisory deductions	..	..	..	..	..	..	..	..	..	..	34.	Eléments à déduire des fonds propres
35. Total net capital resources	..	..	..	..	..	..	..	..	..	..	35.	Total net des ressources en capital
36. Risk-weighted assets	..	..	..	..	..	..	..	..	..	..	36.	Actifs pondérés des risques
SUPPLEMENTARY INFORMATION												**RENSEIGNEMENTS COMPLEMENTAIRES**
37. Number of institutions	276	270	273	266	258	249	244	203	204	199	37.	Nombre d'institutions
38. Number of branches	6394	7331	7303	7260	7235	7030	6758	6795	6440	5563	38.	Nombre de succursales
39. Number of employees (x 1000)	223	221	220	218	213	216	217	222	221	215	39.	Nombre de salariés (x 1000)

1 Break in series due to change in methodology

2 Non-interest income (item 4), in the national definition, excluding items 4.c and 4.d.

3 Property costs (item 6.b.) included under Other operating expenses (item 6.c.).

4 Provisions on securities (item 8.b.) included under Provisions on loans (item 8.a)

Notes

. Average balance sheet totals (item 26) are based on twelve end-month data.

Change in methodology

. As from 1993, data include eastern German credit institutions and are ir accordance with the new accounting regulations.

1 Rupture de série suite au changement méthodologique

2 Produits non financiers (nets) (poste 4), suivant la définition nationale, non compris les rubriques 4.c et 4.d.

3 Les Dépenses en immobilier (poste 6.b.) sont incluses sous Autres frais d'exploitation (poste 6.c.).

4 Les Provisions sur titres (poste 8.b.) sont incluses sous Provisions sur prêts (poste 8.a).

Notes

. La moyenne du total des actifs/passifs (poste 26) est basée sur douze données de fin de mois.

Changement méthodologique

. Depuis 1993, les données comprennent les organismes de crédit d'Allemagne orientale et sont conformes aux nouvelles règles de comptabilité.

GERMANY
Commercial banks

ALLEMAGNE
Banques commerciales

Per cent — *Pourcentage*

INCOME STATEMENT ANALYSIS — **ANALYSE DU COMPTE DE RESULTATS**

	1992	1993[1]	1994	1995	1996	1997	1998	1999	2000	2001	
% of average balance sheet total											**% du total moyen du bilan**
40. Interest income	8.37	7.56	6.65	6.39	5.74	5.37	5.04	5.02	5.35	5.13	40. Produits financiers
41. Interest expenses	6.16	5.37	4.47	4.41	3.91	3.72	3.58	3.58	4.17	3.97	41. Frais financiers
42. Net interest income	2.21	2.18	2.18	1.98	1.83	1.65	1.46	1.45	1.18	1.16	42. Produits financiers nets
43. Non-interest income (net)	0.99	1.00	0.75	0.78	0.75	0.74	1.46	1.08	1.11	1.10	43. Produits non financiers (nets)
a. Fees and commissions receivable	..	0.85	0.75	0.69	0.68	0.74	0.73	0.82	0.90	0.80	*a. Frais et commissions à recevoir*
b. Fees and commissions payable	..	0.09	0.08	0.08	0.09	0.09	0.11	0.11	0.13	0.14	*b. Frais et commissions à payer*
c. Net profits or loss on financial operations	..	0.23	0.01	0.11	0.09	0.09	0.13	0.14	0.24	0.20	*c. Profits ou pertes nets sur opérations financières*
d. Other	..	0.01	0.07	0.06	0.07	0.01	0.71	0.23	0.10	0.25	*d. Autres*
44. Gross income	3.20	3.18	2.93	2.76	2.58	2.40	2.92	2.53	2.29	2.27	44. Résultat brut
45. Operating expenses	2.04	1.95	1.87	1.84	1.69	1.60	1.52	1.73	1.68	1.67	45. Frais d'exploitation
a. Staff costs	1.27	1.21	1.13	1.11	0.99	0.90	0.83	0.89	0.85	0.82	*a. Dépenses en personnel*
b. Property costs	..	..	-	-	-	-	-	-	-	-	*b. Dépenses en immobilier*
c. Other	..	0.74	0.74	0.73	0.70	0.70	0.70	0.84	0.83	0.85	*c. Autres*
46. Net income	1.16	1.24	1.06	0.92	0.89	0.80	1.39	0.80	0.61	0.60	46. Résultat net
47. Provisions (net)	0.69	0.69	0.52	0.41	0.39	0.39	0.33	0.41	0.32	0.42	47. Provisions (nettes)
a. Provisions on loans	0.67	0.68	0.51	0.39	0.38	0.38	0.32	0.41	0.27	0.37	*a. Provisions sur prêts*
b. Provisions on securities	..	..	..	..	..	..	..	..	..	..	*b. Provisions sur titres*
c. Other	..	0.01	0.01	0.02	0.01	0.01	0.01	0.01	0.05	0.05	*c. Autres*
48. Profit before tax	0.47	0.55	0.54	0.51	0.49	0.41	1.07	0.38	0.29	0.18	48. Bénéfices avant impôt
49. Income tax	0.26	0.22	0.20	0.17	0.19	0.13	0.47	0.10	0.03	0.02	49. Impôt sur le revenu
50. Profit after tax	0.22	0.33	0.35	0.34	0.31	0.28	0.59	0.28	0.26	0.16	50. Bénéfices après impôt
51. Distributed profit	0.19	0.25	0.25	0.26	0.24	0.22	0.31	0.21	0.21	0.07	51. Bénéfices distribués
52. Retained profit	0.02	0.08	0.10	0.09	0.07	0.06	0.28	0.07	0.05	0.09	52. Bénéfices mis en réserve
% of gross income											**% du total du résultat brut**
53. Net interest income	69.20	68.57	74.56	71.84	70.82	68.94	50.10	57.31	51.47	51.34	53. Produits financiers nets
54. Non-interest income (net)	30.80	31.43	25.44	28.16	29.18	31.06	49.90	42.69	48.53	48.66	54. Produits non financiers (nets)
a. Fees and commissions receivable	..	26.67	25.67	24.98	26.39	30.77	25.11	32.37	39.37	35.11	*a. Frais et commissions à recevoir*
b. Fees and commissions payable	..	2.71	2.87	2.97	3.45	3.95	3.91	4.26	5.61	6.36	*b. Frais et commissions à payer*
c. Net profits or loss on financial operations	..	7.28	0.25	4.04	3.40	3.94	4.39	5.62	10.48	8.90	*c. Profits ou pertes nets sur opérations financières*
d. Other	..	0.20	2.39	2.10	2.84	0.30	24.31	8.96	4.29	11.01	*d. Autres*
55. Operating expenses	63.65	61.13	63.78	66.74	65.62	66.62	52.22	68.45	73.46	73.51	55. Frais d'exploitation
a. Staff costs	39.64	37.85	38.58	40.13	38.43	37.54	28.41	35.20	37.22	36.21	*a. Dépenses en personnel*
b. Property costs	..	..	-	-	-	-	-	-	-	-	*b. Dépenses en immobilier*
c. Other	..	23.27	25.20	26.62	27.19	29.08	23.81	33.25	36.24	37.31	*c. Autres*
56. Net income	36.35	38.87	36.22	33.26	34.38	33.38	47.78	31.55	26.54	26.49	56. Résultat net
57. Provisions (net)	21.56	21.74	17.64	14.75	15.29	16.44	11.29	16.43	13.84	18.59	57. Provisions (nettes)
a. Provisions on loans	21.00	21.36	17.45	14.07	14.74	16.02	10.92	16.07	11.79	16.47	*a. Provisions sur prêts*
b. Provisions on securities	..	..	..	..	..	..	..	..	..	..	*b. Provisions sur titres*
c. Other	..	0.38	0.19	0.68	0.56	0.43	0.37	0.36	2.05	2.12	*c. Autres*
58. Profit before tax	14.79	17.13	18.58	18.51	19.09	16.93	36.48	15.12	12.70	7.90	58. Bénéfices avant impôt
59. Income tax	7.99	6.86	6.78	6.09	7.26	5.25	16.25	4.15	1.37	0.76	59. Impôt sur le revenu
60. Profit after tax	6.80	10.28	11.79	12.43	11.84	11.69	20.23	10.97	11.32	7.13	60. Bénéfices après impôt
% of net income											**% du total du résultat net**
61. Provisions (net)	59.31	55.93	48.71	44.34	44.47	49.26	23.64	52.06	52.16	70.19	61. Provisions (nettes)
a. Provisions on loans	57.78	54.94	48.18	42.30	42.86	47.99	22.86	50.93	44.42	62.19	*a. Provisions sur prêts*
b. Provisions on securities	..	..	..	..	..	..	..	..	..	..	*b. Provisions sur titres*
c. Other	..	0.99	0.53	2.03	1.62	1.27	0.78	1.13	7.74	8.01	*c. Autres*
62. Profit before tax	40.69	44.07	51.29	55.66	55.53	50.74	76.36	47.94	47.84	29.81	62. Bénéfices avant impôt
63. Income tax	21.98	17.64	18.73	18.30	21.10	15.72	34.02	13.15	5.18	2.88	63. Impôt sur le revenu
64. Profit after tax	18.71	26.43	32.57	37.36	34.42	35.02	42.34	34.79	42.66	26.93	64. Bénéfices après impôt

GERMANY
Commercial banks

ALLEMAGNE
Banques commerciales

Per cent	1992	1993[1]	1994	1995	1996	1997	1998	1999	2000	2001		Pourcentage
BALANCE SHEET ANALYSIS												**ANALYSE DU BILAN**
% of year-end balance sheet total												**% du total du bilan en fin d'exercice**
Assets												**Actif**
65. Cash & balance with Central bank	2.48	1.94	1.31	1.24	1.23	1.12	1.18	1.62	1.40	1.16		65. Caisse & solde auprès de la Banque centrale
66. Interbank deposits	22.11	21.55	22.45	22.04	22.27	22.11	21.88	19.88	19.59	22.07		66. Dépôts interbancaires
67. Loans	60.01	57.91	57.76	57.37	56.30	54.50	52.39	50.28	50.16	48.72		67. Prêts
68. Securities	13.17	16.28	16.48	16.99	17.99	19.89	21.40	21.84	22.50	22.42		68. Valeurs mobilières
69. Other assets	2.23	2.32	2.00	2.37	2.21	2.38	3.15	6.38	6.34	5.63		69. Autres actifs
Liabilities												**Passif**
70. Capital & reserves	5.26	5.01	5.54	5.35	4.95	4.84	4.34	4.57	4.39	4.25		70. Capital et réserves
71. Borrowing from Central bank	3.59	5.43	3.88	3.42	2.88	2.35	2.10	1.10	1.62	2.32		71. Emprunts auprès de la Banque centrale
72. Interbank deposits	26.60	24.25	28.52	30.25	29.35	29.36	30.92	27.68	27.87	29.00		72. Dépôts interbancaires
73. Non-bank deposits	50.17	48.60	44.40	41.70	42.38	42.05	39.79	42.81	42.43	41.50		73. Dépôts non bancaires
74. Bonds	9.08	10.76	12.35	13.05	13.69	13.14	13.67	16.14	15.89	16.15		74. Obligations
75. Other liabilities	5.31	5.93	5.31	6.23	6.76	8.26	9.17	7.71	7.80	6.78		75. Autres engagements
Memorandum items												**Pour mémoire**
76. Short-term securities	2.55	3.42	2.55	2.68	3.14	4.32	4.18	3.38	2.88	2.58		76. Titres à court terme
77. Bonds	6.32	8.34	9.31	9.48	9.95	10.79	11.31	11.93	12.23	12.79		77. Obligations
78. Shares and participations	4.30	4.52	4.62	4.82	4.89	4.78	5.91	6.53	7.39	7.05		78. Actions et participations
79. Claims on non-residents	27.98	30.33	31.15	32.04	34.81	39.94	41.20	39.20	44.01	48.74		79. Créances sur des non-résidents
80. Liabilities to non-residents	23.87	22.56	25.12	27.50	29.10	34.02	35.16	34.89	37.69	39.79		80. Engagements envers des non-résidents

* See notes on previous pages.

* Voir les notes en pages précédentes.

GERMANY
Large commercial banks

Million euros

ALLEMAGNE
Grandes banques commerciales

Million d'euros

	1992	1993[1]	1994	1995	1996	1997	1998	1999[2]	2000	2001	
INCOME STATEMENT											**COMPTE DE RESULTATS**
1. Interest income	28489	28680	26510	28314	30344	33848	39260	60389	79073	81187	1. Produits financiers
2. Interest expenses	19733	19364	16970	19333	20741	23603	28328	46038	64899	66460	2. Frais financiers
3. Net interest income	8756	9316	9540	8981	9603	10245	10932	14351	14174	14727	3. Produits financiers nets
4. Non-interest income (net) (3)	4195	4921	3991	4628	5155	6005	15976	12676	16446	19336	4. Produits non financiers (nets) (3)
a. Fees and commissions receivable	..	4222	3928	3843	4465	5671	6705	8869	11251	11134	a. Frais et commissions à recevoir
b. Fees and commissions payable	..	188	220	269	372	444	869	961	1046	1680	b. Frais et commissions à payer
c. Net profits or loss on financial operations	..	1011	-26	548	590	876	749	2151	4761	4882	c. Profits ou pertes nets sur opérations financières
d. Other	..	-124	309	506	473	-99	9391	2617	1480	5000	d. Autres
5. Gross income	12951	14237	13530	13609	14758	16249	26908	27027	30620	34063	5. Résultat brut
6. Operating expenses	8194	8730	9091	9539	10321	11644	13122	18652	22770	24505	6. Frais d'exploitation
a. Staff costs	5306	5678	5785	6047	6359	6829	7550	10049	12182	12688	a. Dépenses en personnel
b. Property costs (4)	..	..	..	..	..	..	..	..	..	..	b. Dépenses en immobilier (4)
c. Other	..	3052	3306	3492	3963	4814	5572	8603	10588	11817	c. Autres
7. Net income	4756	5507	4440	4070	4437	4606	13786	8375	7850	9558	7. Résultat net
8. Provisions (net)	2261	3258	1982	1900	1640	2661	2322	5478	4669	6607	8. Provisions (nettes)
a. Provisions on loans	2156	3200	1982	1789	1548	2625	2211	5429	4092	6099	a. Provisions sur prêts
b. Provisions on securities (5)	..	58	-	112	92	36	111	49	577	508	b. Provisions sur titres (5)
c. Other	..	..	..	..	..	..	..	..	..	..	c. Autres
9. Profit before tax	2495	2249	2457	2169	2797	1945	11464	2897	3181	2951	9. Bénéfices avant impôt
10. Income tax	1022	872	859	427	949	510	5882	350	-443	-438	10. Impôt sur le revenu
11. Profit after tax	1473	1377	1598	1742	1848	1435	5582	2547	3624	3389	11. Bénéfices après impôt
12. Distributed profit	811	853	1010	1032	1106	1230	2777	1945	2299	2235	12. Bénéfices distribués
13. Retained profit	662	524	588	711	741	205	2805	602	1325	1154	13. Bénéfices mis en réserve
BALANCE SHEET											**BILAN**
Assets											**Actif**
14. Cash & balance with Central bank	10970	10704	7462	7899	9673	11110	10418	17385	22166	18280	14. Caisse & solde auprès de la Banque centrale
15. Interbank deposits	88710	94681	112957	124061	139550	162999	204564	218903	265321	362247	15. Dépôts interbancaires
16. Loans	214048	228777	234132	273537	318902	381172	431161	635869	763164	810421	16. Prêts
17. Securities	47503	71653	74691	93631	112491	154832	214984	279552	330036	369689	17. Valeurs mobilières
18. Other assets	5502	7404	6183	6311	7306	12296	27983	84369	99052	95817	18. Autres actifs
Liabilities											**Passif**
19. Capital & reserves	19459	21536	23747	25830	28259	33312	34442	54401	62952	65672	19. Capital et réserves
20. Borrowing from Central bank	9421	10670	13580	12974	10678	11056	17147	2275	13446	29162	20. Emprunts auprès de la Banque centrale
21. Interbank deposits	89676	92965	126416	160321	177875	220845	300391	338237	416385	496201	21. Dépôts interbancaires
22. Non-bank deposits	216590	241978	220832	241888	291871	348839	368100	492213	607542	650129	22. Dépôts non bancaires
23. Bonds	14435	25020	30081	38801	45837	50476	76486	255665	266400	307209	23. Obligations
24. Other liabilities	17151	21051	20768	25625	33402	57881	92544	93287	113014	108081	24. Autres engagements
Balance sheet total											**Total du bilan**
25. End-year total	366732	413219	435425	505439	587922	722409	889110	1236078	1479739	1656454	25. En fin d'exercice
26. Average total	355032	393064	424331	466173	562105	685187	851586	1246031	1508019	1653158	26. Moyen

GERMANY

Large commercial banks

ALLEMAGNE

Grandes banques commerciales

Million euros — *Million d'euros*

	1992	1993[1]	1994	1995	1996	1997	1998	1999[2]	2000	2001		
Memorandum items												***Pour mémoire***
27. Short-term securities	7950	14644	13656	18268	23576	42395	49126	51449	49920	49610	27.	*Titres à court terme*
28. Bonds	17193	30295	34060	43491	54651	73267	103156	140274	156358	185243	28.	*Obligations*
29. Shares and participations	22360	26714	26975	31872	34264	39170	62702	87829	123758	134836	29.	*Actions et participations*
30. Claims on non-residents	131867	159296	179766	225037	282297	387575	488044	587472	787081	966953	30.	*Créances sur des non-résidents*
31. Liabilities to non-residents	118735	129253	156175	203496	253372	354226	432893	538559	703663	817844	31.	*Engagements envers des non-résidents*
Capital adequacy												***Solvabilité***
32. Tier 1 Capital	..	..	..	..	..	..	..	..	..	..	32.	*Fonds propres de base*
33. Tier 2 Capital	..	..	..	..	..	..	..	..	..	..	33.	*Fonds propres complémentaires*
34. Supervisory deductions	..	..	..	..	..	..	..	..	..	..	34.	*Eléments à déduire des fonds propres*
35. Total net capital resources	..	..	..	..	..	..	..	..	..	..	35.	*Total net des ressources en capital*
36. Risk-weighted assets	..	..	..	..	..	..	..	..	..	..	36.	*Actifs pondérés des risques*
SUPPLEMENTARY INFORMATION												**RENSEIGNEMENTS COMPLÉMENTAIRES**
37. Number of institutions	4	3	3	3	3	3	3	4	4	4	37.	*Nombre d'institutions*
38. Number of branches	3036	3598	3621	3624	3579	3553	4353	3114	2873	2369	38.	*Nombre de succursales*
39. Number of employees (x 1000)	..	..	..	..	..	..	..	..	..	..	39.	*Nombre de salariés (x 1000)*

1 Break in series due to change in methodology

2 As from 1999, the group of large commercial banks was extended tc four institutions. In plus, some banks which were formerly classified as "banks with special functions" had been re-classified

3 Non-interest income (item 4), in the national definition, excluding items 4.c and 4.d.

4 Property costs (item 6.b.) included under Other operating expenses (item 6.c.).

5 Provisions on securities (item 8.b.) included under Provisions on loans (item 8.a)

Notes

. Large commercial banks are a sub-group of Commercial banks

. Average balance sheet totals (item 26) are based on twelve end-montr data.

Change in methodology

. As from 1993, data include eastern German credit institutions and are ir accordance with the new accounting regulations.

1 Rupture de serie, suite au changement méthodologique.

2 A partir de 1999, l'échantillon des Grandes banques commerciales a été agrandi à quatre institutions. En outre, certaines banques auparavant classifiées parmi les "banques à fonctions spéciales" ont été reclassifiées parmi les banques commerciales

3 Produits non financiers (nets) (poste 4), suivant la définition nationale, non compris les rubriques 4.c et 4.d.

4 Les Dépenses en immobilier (poste 6.b.) sont incluses sous Autres frais d'exploitation (poste 6.c).

5 Les Provisions sur titres (poste 8.b.) sont incluses sous Provisions sur prêts (poste 8.a).

Notes

. Les Grandes banques commerciales sont un sous-groupe des Banques commerciales.

. La moyenne du total des actifs/passifs (poste 26) est basée sur douze données de fin de mois.

Changement méthodologique

. Depuis 1993, les données comprennent les organismes de crédit d'Allemagne orientale et sont conformes aux nouvelles règles de comptabilité.

GERMANY
Large commercial banks

ALLEMAGNE
Grandes banques commerciales

Per cent — *Pourcentage*

INCOME STATEMENT ANALYSIS — ANALYSE DU COMPTE DE RESULTATS

#		1992	1993[1]	1994	1995	1996	1997	1998	1999[2]	2000	2001	Libellé
	% of average balance sheet total											**% du total moyen du bilan**
40.	Interest income	8.02	7.30	6.25	6.07	5.40	4.94	4.61	4.85	5.24	4.91	Produits financiers
41.	Interest expenses	5.56	4.93	4.00	4.15	3.69	3.44	3.33	3.69	4.30	4.02	Frais financiers
42.	Net interest income	2.47	2.37	2.25	1.93	1.71	1.50	1.28	1.15	0.94	0.89	Produits financiers nets
43.	Non-interest income (net)	1.18	1.25	0.94	0.99	0.92	0.88	1.88	1.02	1.09	1.17	Produits non financiers (nets)
	a. Fees and commissions receivable	..	*1.07*	*0.93*	*0.82*	*0.79*	*0.83*	*0.79*	*0.71*	*0.75*	*0.67*	*a. Frais et commissions à recevoir*
	b. Fees and commissions payable	..	*0.05*	*0.05*	*0.06*	*0.07*	*0.06*	*0.10*	*0.08*	*0.07*	*0.10*	*b. Frais et commissions à payer*
	c. Net profits or loss on financial operations	..	*0.26*	*-0.01*	*0.12*	*0.10*	*0.13*	*0.09*	*0.17*	*0.32*	*0.30*	*c. Profits ou pertes nets sur opérations financières*
	d. Other	..	*-0.03*	*0.07*	*0.11*	*0.08*	*-0.01*	*1.10*	*0.21*	*0.10*	*0.30*	*d. Autres*
44.	Gross income	3.65	3.62	3.19	2.92	2.63	2.37	3.16	2.17	2.03	2.06	Résultat brut
45.	Operating expenses	2.31	2.22	2.14	2.05	1.84	1.70	1.54	1.50	1.51	1.48	Frais d'exploitation
	a. Staff costs	*1.49*	*1.44*	*1.36*	*1.30*	*1.13*	*1.00*	*0.89*	*0.81*	*0.81*	*0.77*	*a. Dépenses en personnel*
	b. Property costs											*b. Dépenses en immobilier*
	c. Other	..	*0.78*	*0.78*	*0.75*	*0.70*	*0.70*	*0.65*	*0.69*	*0.70*	*0.71*	*c. Autres*
46.	Net income	1.34	1.40	1.05	0.87	0.79	0.67	1.62	0.67	0.52	0.58	Résultat net
47.	Provisions (net)	0.64	0.83	0.47	0.41	0.29	0.39	0.27	0.44	0.31	0.40	Provisions (nettes)
	a. Provisions on loans	*0.61*	*0.81*	*0.47*	*0.38*	*0.28*	*0.38*	*0.26*	*0.44*	*0.27*	*0.37*	*a. Provisions sur prêts*
	b. Provisions on securities											*b. Provisions sur titres*
	c. Other	..	*0.01*	..	*0.02*	*0.02*	*0.01*	*0.01*	..	*0.04*	*0.03*	*c. Autres*
48.	Profit before tax	0.70	0.57	0.58	0.47	0.50	0.28	1.35	0.23	0.21	0.18	Bénéfices avant impôt
49.	Income tax	0.29	0.22	0.20	0.09	0.17	0.07	0.69	0.03	-0.03	-0.03	Impôt sur le revenu
50.	Profit after tax	0.41	0.35	0.38	0.37	0.33	0.21	0.66	0.20	0.24	0.21	Bénéfices après impôt
51.	Distributed profit	0.23	0.22	0.24	0.22	0.20	0.18	0.33	0.16	0.15	0.14	Bénéfices distribués
52.	Retained profit	0.19	0.13	0.14	0.15	0.13	0.03	0.33	0.05	0.09	0.07	Bénéfices mis en réserve
	% of gross income											**% du total du résultat brut**
53.	Net interest income	67.61	65.43	70.51	65.99	65.07	63.05	40.63	53.10	46.29	43.23	Produits financiers nets
54.	Non-interest income (net)	32.39	34.57	29.49	34.01	34.93	36.95	59.37	46.90	53.71	56.77	Produits non financiers (nets)
	a. Fees and commissions receivable	..	*29.66*	*29.03*	*28.24*	*30.25*	*34.90*	*24.92*	*32.82*	*36.74*	*32.69*	*a. Frais et commissions à recevoir*
	b. Fees and commissions payable	..	*1.32*	*1.63*	*1.98*	*2.52*	*2.73*	*3.23*	*3.56*	*3.42*	*4.93*	*b. Frais et commissions à payer*
	c. Net profits or loss on financial operations	..	*7.10*	*-0.19*	*4.02*	*4.00*	*5.39*	*2.78*	*7.96*	*15.55*	*14.33*	*c. Profits ou pertes nets sur opérations financières*
	d. Other	..	*-0.87*	*2.28*	*3.72*	*3.20*	*-0.61*	*34.90*	*9.68*	*4.83*	*14.68*	*d. Autres*
55.	Operating expenses	63.28	61.32	67.19	70.09	69.94	71.66	48.77	69.01	74.36	71.94	Frais d'exploitation
	a. Staff costs	*40.97*	*39.88*	*42.75*	*44.43*	*43.09*	*42.03*	*28.06*	*37.18*	*39.78*	*37.25*	*a. Dépenses en personnel*
	b. Property costs											*b. Dépenses en immobilier*
	c. Other	..	*21.44*	*24.43*	*25.66*	*26.85*	*29.63*	*20.71*	*31.83*	*34.58*	*34.69*	*c. Autres*
56.	Net income	36.72	38.68	32.81	29.91	30.06	28.34	51.23	30.99	25.64	28.06	Résultat net
57.	Provisions (net)	17.46	22.88	14.65	13.96	11.11	16.37	8.63	20.27	15.25	19.40	Provisions (nettes)
	a. Provisions on loans	*16.65*	*22.48*	*14.65*	*13.14*	*10.49*	*16.15*	*8.22*	*20.09*	*13.36*	*17.91*	*a. Provisions sur prêts*
	b. Provisions on securities											*b. Provisions sur titres*
	c. Other	..	*0.41*	..	*0.82*	*0.62*	*0.22*	*0.41*	*0.18*	*1.88*	*1.49*	*c. Autres*
58.	Profit before tax	19.26	15.80	18.16	15.94	18.95	11.97	42.61	10.72	10.39	8.66	Bénéfices avant impôt
59.	Income tax	7.89	6.13	6.35	3.14	6.43	3.14	21.86	1.30	-1.45	-1.29	Impôt sur le revenu
60.	Profit after tax	11.37	9.67	11.81	12.80	12.52	8.83	20.75	9.42	11.84	9.95	Bénéfices après impôt
	% of net income											**% du total du résultat net**
61.	Provisions (net)	47.55	59.16	44.65	46.70	36.96	57.77	16.84	65.41	59.48	69.13	Provisions (nettes)
	a. Provisions on loans	*45.33*	*58.11*	*44.65*	*43.94*	*34.89*	*56.99*	*16.04*	*64.82*	*52.13*	*63.81*	*a. Provisions sur prêts*
	b. Provisions on securities											*b. Provisions sur titres*
	c. Other	..	*1.05*	..	*2.75*	*2.06*	*0.78*	*0.80*	*0.59*	*7.35*	*5.31*	*c. Autres*
62.	Profit before tax	52.45	40.84	55.35	53.30	63.04	42.23	83.16	34.59	40.52	30.87	Bénéfices avant impôt
63.	Income tax	21.49	15.84	19.35	10.49	21.40	11.08	42.67	4.18	-5.64	-4.58	Impôt sur le revenu
64.	Profit after tax	30.96	25.00	36.00	42.81	41.65	31.15	40.49	30.41	46.17	35.46	Bénéfices après impôt

GERMANY
Large commercial banks

ALLEMAGNE
Grandes banques commerciales

Per cent — *Pourcentage*

BALANCE SHEET ANALYSIS — **ANALYSE DU BILAN**

% of year-end balance sheet total — % du total du bilan en fin d'exercice

	1992	1993[1]	1994	1995	1996	1997	1998	1999[2]	2000	2001	
Assets											**Actif**
65. Cash & balance with Central bank	2.99	2.59	1.71	1.56	1.65	1.54	1.17	1.41	1.50	1.10	65. Caisse & solde auprès de la Banque centrale
66. Interbank deposits	24.19	22.91	25.94	24.55	23.74	22.56	23.01	17.71	17.93	21.87	66. Dépôts interbancaires
67. Loans	58.37	55.36	53.77	54.12	54.24	52.76	48.49	51.44	51.57	48.93	67. Prêts
68. Securities	12.95	17.34	17.15	18.52	19.13	21.43	24.18	22.62	22.30	22.32	68. Valeurs mobilières
69. Other assets	1.50	1.79	1.42	1.25	1.24	1.70	3.15	6.83	6.69	5.78	69. Autres actifs
Liabilities											**Passif**
70. Capital & reserves	5.31	5.21	5.45	5.11	4.81	4.61	3.87	4.40	4.25	3.96	70. Capital et réserves
71. Borrowing from Central bank	2.57	2.58	3.12	2.57	1.82	1.53	1.93	0.18	0.91	1.76	71. Emprunts auprès de la Banque centrale
72. Interbank deposits	24.45	22.50	29.03	31.72	30.25	30.57	33.79	27.36	28.14	29.96	72. Dépôts interbancaires
73. Non-bank deposits	59.06	58.56	50.72	47.86	49.64	48.29	41.40	39.82	41.06	39.25	73. Dépôts non bancaires
74. Bonds	3.94	6.05	6.91	7.68	7.80	6.99	8.60	20.68	18.00	18.55	74. Obligations
75. Other liabilities	4.68	5.09	4.77	5.07	5.68	8.01	10.41	7.55	7.64	6.52	75. Autres engagements
Memorandum items											**Pour mémoire**
76. Short-term securities	2.17	3.54	3.14	3.61	4.01	5.87	5.53	4.16	3.37	2.99	76. Titres à court terme
77. Bonds	4.69	7.33	7.82	8.60	9.30	10.14	11.60	11.35	10.57	11.18	77. Obligations
78. Shares and participations	6.10	6.46	6.20	6.31	5.83	5.42	7.05	7.11	8.36	8.14	78. Actions et participations
79. Claims on non-residents	35.96	38.55	41.29	44.52	48.02	53.65	54.89	47.53	53.19	58.37	79. Créances sur des non-résidents
80. Liabilities to non-residents	32.38	31.28	35.87	40.26	43.10	49.03	48.69	43.57	47.55	49.37	80. Engagements envers des non-résidents

* See notes on previous pages.

* Voir les notes en pages précédentes.

GERMANY / ALLEMAGNE

Regional giro institutions / Organismes régionaux de compensation

Million euros / Million d'euros

#	Item (EN)	1992	1993[1]	1994	1995	1996	1997	1998	1999	2000	2001	Item (FR)
	INCOME STATEMENT											**COMPTE DE RESULTATS**
1.	Interest income	39257	41941	43846	46540	50170	56040	61698	71683	84761	87500	Produits financiers
2.	Interest expenses	35863	37942	38724	41498	44317	49685	54736	63292	76375	77981	Frais financiers
3.	Net interest income	3394	3999	5123	5041	5853	6355	6961	8391	8386	9519	Produits financiers nets
4.	Non-interest income (net) (2)	1026	1381	710	1150	938	1751	3468	2344	3038	2850	Produits non financiers (nets) (2)
	a. Fees and commissions receivable	..	844	932	941	1068	1338	1468	2431	3185	2831	a. Frais et commissions à recevoir
	b. Fees and commissions payable	..	213	204	209	255	323	407	993	1242	1086	b. Frais et commissions à payer
	c. Net profits or loss on financial operations	..	523	-33	399	327	537	730	384	680	573	c. Profits ou pertes nets sur opérations financières
	d. Other	..	228	14	19	-202	198	1677	522	415	532	d. Autres
5.	Gross income	4420	5380	5832	6191	6791	8106	10429	10735	11424	12369	Résultat brut
6.	Operating expenses	2589	2824	3052	3366	3695	4119	4497	5925	6479	7255	Frais d'exploitation
	a. Staff costs	1646	1739	1782	1988	2133	2267	2372	3023	3364	3613	a. Dépenses en personnel
	b. Property costs (3)	..	..	..	..	..	..	..	..	..	..	b. Dépenses en immobilier (3)
	c. Other	..	1085	1270	1378	1562	1852	2125	2902	3115	3642	c. Autres
7.	Net income	1831	2555	2780	2825	3096	3986	5932	4810	4945	5114	Résultat net
8.	Provisions (net)	906	1227	1443	1126	1309	1560	3027	1566	2102	3277	Provisions (nettes)
	a. Provisions on loans	868	1226	1358	1113	1253	1546	2989	1566	1765	3181	a. Provisions sur prêts
	b. Provisions on securities (4)	..	1	85	13	56	15	39	-	337	96	b. Provisions sur titres (4)
	c. Other											c. Autres
9.	Profit before tax	925	1329	1337	1699	1787	2426	2905	3244	2843	1837	Bénéfices avant impôt
10.	Income tax	455	679	570	788	664	1115	1328	1435	1371	296	Impôt sur le revenu
11.	Profit after tax	471	650	766	911	1123	1311	1577	1809	1472	1541	Bénéfices après impôt
12.	Distributed profit	222	257	281	323	443	440	708	852	843	904	Bénéfices distribués
13.	Retained profit	249	393	485	588	680	871	869	957	629	637	Bénéfices mis en réserve
	BALANCE SHEET											**BILAN**
	Assets											**Actif**
14.	Cash & balance with Central bank	2739	2838	1657	2022	2378	1967	2231	3870	4873	6412	Caisse & solde auprès de la Banque centrale
15.	Interbank deposits	188647	221897	235583	272865	327053	380360	423706	497959	519456	536560	Dépôts interbancaires
16.	Loans	267771	321455	344072	370339	402646	448746	484193	549520	578463	596748	Prêts
17.	Securities	80955	103088	114935	132810	157255	193110	239162	308834	351447	394207	Valeurs mobilières
18.	Other assets	10317	15764	17105	21222	23178	33034	41834	83250	89096	69900	Autres actifs
	Liabilities											**Passif**
19.	Capital & reserves	15260	18584	20855	22818	25423	29787	34521	42608	46923	54040	Capital et réserves
20.	Borrowing from Central bank	16275	34400	23524	22745	24768	24726	21676	22835	29109	20764	Emprunts auprès de la Banque centrale
21.	Interbank deposits	189726	214556	228337	269553	315131	389803	456138	501186	520899	530415	Dépôts interbancaires
22.	Non-bank deposits	133337	158415	177346	194941	233320	257752	295711	366304	384070	419751	Dépôts non bancaires
23.	Bonds	176136	210402	236131	259942	287611	305544	325063	425297	474238	506832	Obligations
24.	Other liabilities	19695	28684	27159	29258	36258	49605	58018	85203	88096	72025	Autres engagements
	Balance sheet total											**Total du bilan**
25.	End-year total	550429	665041	713352	799258	912511	1057217	1191126	1443433	1543335	1603827	En fin d'exercice
26.	Average total	522462	610622	675572	736712	850108	983397	1114848	1358039	1506853	1599339	Moyen

123

GERMANY

Regional giro institutions

Million euros

ALLEMAGNE

Organismes régionaux de compensation

Million d'euros

	1992	1993[1]	1994	1995	1996	1997	1998	1999	2000	2001		
Memorandum items												**Pour mémoire**
27. Short-term securities	21489	20400	15003	13361	19905	26910	37776	35325	47696	58568	27.	Titres à court terme
28. Bonds	49861	70733	85506	99957	115541	142977	173160	242537	267094	294849	28.	Obligations
29. Shares and participations	9605	11955	14426	19492	21809	23223	28227	30972	36657	40790	29.	Actions et participations
30. Claims on non-residents	126767	155580	145517	165781	224287	305092	370280	464812	512447	566773	30.	Créances sur des non-résidents
31. Liabilities to non-residents	68690	68785	89732	114325	148360	228898	294005	377373	399751	434463	31.	Engagements envers des non-résidents
Capital adequacy												**Solvabilité**
32. Tier 1 Capital	..	..	..	..	..	..	..	..	..	..	32.	Fonds propres de base
33. Tier 2 Capital	..	..	..	..	..	..	..	..	..	..	33.	Fonds propres complémentaires
34. Supervisory deductions	..	..	..	..	..	..	..	..	..	..	34.	Eléments à déduire des fonds propres
35. Total net capital resources	..	..	..	..	..	..	..	..	..	..	35.	Total net des ressources en capital
36. Risk-weighted assets	..	..	..	..	..	..	..	..	..	..	36.	Actifs pondérés des risques
SUPPLEMENTARY INFORMATION												**RENSEIGNEMENTS COMPLEMENTAIRES**
37. Number of institutions	12	13	13	13	13	13	13	13	13	13	37.	Nombre d'institutions
38. Number of branches	329	436	433	433	436	428	430	655	638	603	38.	Nombre de succursales
39. Number of employees (x 1000)	32	34	33	33	34	34	34	41	42	43	39.	Nombre de salariés (x 1000)

1 Break in series due to change in methodology

2 Non-interest income (item 4), in the national definition, excluding items 4.c and 4.d.

3 Property costs (item 6.b.) included under Other operating expenses (item 6.c.).

4 Provisions on securities (item 8.b.) included under Provisions on loans (item 8.a)

Notes

. Average balance sheet totals (item 26) are based on twelve end-month data.

Change in methodology

. As from 1993, data include eastern German credit institutions and are in accordance with the new accounting regulations.

1 Rupture de serie, suite au changement méthodologique.

2 Produits non financiers (nets) (poste 4), suivant la définition nationale, non compris les rubriques 4.c et 4.d.

3 Les Dépenses en immobilier (poste 6.b.) sont incluses sous Autres frais d'exploitation (poste 6.c).

4 Les Provisions sur titres (poste 8.b.) sont incluses sous Provisions sur prêts (poste 8.a).

Notes

. La moyenne du total des actifs/passifs (poste 26) est basée sur douze données de fin de mois.

Changement méthodologique

. Depuis 1993, les données comprennent les organismes de crédit d'Allemagne orientale et sont conformes aux nouvelles règles de comptabilité.

GERMANY

Regional giro institutions

ALLEMAGNE

Organismes régionaux de compensation

Per cent / *Pourcentage*

INCOME STATEMENT ANALYSIS / **ANALYSE DU COMPTE DE RESULTATS**

	1992	1993[1]	1994	1995	1996	1997	1998	1999	2000	2001	
% of average balance sheet total											**% du total moyen du bilan**
40. Interest income	7.51	6.87	6.49	6.32	5.90	5.70	5.53	5.28	5.63	5.47	40. Produits financiers
41. Interest expenses	6.86	6.21	5.73	5.63	5.21	5.05	4.91	4.66	5.07	4.88	41. Frais financiers
42. Net interest income	0.65	0.65	0.76	0.68	0.69	0.65	0.62	0.62	0.56	0.60	42. Produits financiers nets
43. Non-interest income (net)	0.20	0.23	0.11	0.16	0.11	0.18	0.31	0.17	0.20	0.18	43. Produits non financiers (nets)
a. Fees and commissions receivable	*..*	*0.14*	*0.14*	*0.13*	*0.13*	*0.14*	*0.13*	*0.18*	*0.21*	*0.18*	*a. Frais et commissions à recevoir*
b. Fees and commissions payable	*..*	*0.03*	*0.03*	*0.03*	*0.03*	*0.03*	*0.04*	*0.07*	*0.08*	*0.07*	*b. Frais et commissions à payer*
c. Net profits or loss on financial operations	*..*	*0.09*	*-*	*0.05*	*0.04*	*0.05*	*0.07*	*0.03*	*0.05*	*0.04*	*c. Profits ou pertes nets sur opérations financières*
d. Other	*..*	*0.04*	*-*	*-*	*-0.02*	*0.02*	*0.15*	*0.04*	*0.03*	*0.03*	*d. Autres*
44. Gross income	0.85	0.88	0.86	0.84	0.80	0.82	0.94	0.79	0.76	0.77	44. Résultat brut
45. Operating expenses	0.50	0.46	0.45	0.46	0.43	0.42	0.40	0.44	0.43	0.45	45. Frais d'exploitation
a. Staff costs	*0.32*	*0.28*	*0.26*	*0.27*	*0.25*	*0.23*	*0.21*	*0.22*	*0.22*	*0.23*	*a. Dépenses en personnel*
b. Property costs	*..*	*..*	*..*	*..*	*..*	*..*	*..*	*..*	*..*	*..*	*b. Dépenses en immobilier*
c. Other	*..*	*0.18*	*0.19*	*0.19*	*0.18*	*0.19*	*0.19*	*0.21*	*0.21*	*0.23*	*c. Autres*
46. Net income	0.35	0.42	0.41	0.38	0.36	0.41	0.53	0.35	0.33	0.32	46. Résultat net
47. Provisions (net)	0.17	0.20	0.21	0.15	0.15	0.16	0.27	0.12	0.14	0.20	47. Provisions (nettes)
a. Provisions on loans	*0.17*	*0.20*	*0.20*	*0.15*	*0.15*	*0.16*	*0.27*	*0.12*	*0.12*	*0.20*	*a. Provisions sur prêts*
b. Provisions on securities	*..*	*..*	*..*	*..*	*..*	*..*	*..*	*..*	*..*	*..*	*b. Provisions sur titres*
c. Other	*..*	*..*	*0.01*	*-*	*0.01*	*..*	*..*	*..*	*0.02*	*0.01*	*c. Autres*
48. Profit before tax	0.18	0.22	0.20	0.23	0.21	0.25	0.26	0.24	0.19	0.11	48. Bénéfices avant impôt
49. Income tax	0.09	0.11	0.08	0.11	0.08	0.11	0.12	0.11	0.09	0.02	49. Impôt sur le revenu
50. Profit after tax	0.09	0.11	0.11	0.12	0.13	0.13	0.14	0.13	0.10	0.10	50. Bénéfices après impôt
51. Distributed profit	0.04	0.04	0.04	0.04	0.05	0.04	0.06	0.06	0.06	0.06	51. Bénéfices distribués
52. Retained profit	0.05	0.06	0.07	0.08	0.08	0.09	0.08	0.07	0.04	0.04	52. Bénéfices mis en réserve
% of gross income											**% du total du résultat brut**
53. Net interest income	76.79	74.33	87.83	81.43	86.19	78.40	66.75	78.16	73.41	76.96	53. Produits financiers nets
54. Non-interest income (net)	23.21	25.67	12.17	18.57	13.81	21.60	33.25	21.84	26.59	23.04	54. Produits non financiers (nets)
a. Fees and commissions receivable	*..*	*15.68*	*15.98*	*15.20*	*15.73*	*16.51*	*14.08*	*22.65*	*27.88*	*22.89*	*a. Frais et commissions à recevoir*
b. Fees and commissions payable	*..*	*3.95*	*3.50*	*3.38*	*3.76*	*3.99*	*3.90*	*9.25*	*10.87*	*8.78*	*b. Frais et commissions à payer*
c. Net profits or loss on financial operations	*..*	*9.71*	*-0.56*	*6.44*	*-2.98*	*6.63*	*7.00*	*3.58*	*5.95*	*4.63*	*c. Profits ou pertes nets sur opérations financières*
d. Other	*..*	*4.23*	*0.25*	*0.31*	*0.83*	*2.45*	*16.08*	*4.86*	*3.63*	*4.30*	*d. Autres*
55. Operating expenses	58.57	52.50	52.34	54.36	54.41	50.82	43.12	55.19	56.71	58.65	55. Frais d'exploitation
a. Staff costs	*37.25*	*32.32*	*30.56*	*32.11*	*31.41*	*27.97*	*22.75*	*28.16*	*29.45*	*29.21*	*a. Dépenses en personnel*
b. Property costs	*..*	*..*	*..*	*..*	*..*	*..*	*..*	*..*	*..*	*..*	*b. Dépenses en immobilier*
c. Other	*..*	*20.18*	*21.78*	*22.26*	*23.00*	*22.85*	*20.37*	*27.03*	*27.27*	*29.44*	*c. Autres*
56. Net income	41.43	47.50	47.66	45.64	45.59	49.18	56.88	44.81	43.29	41.35	56. Résultat net
57. Provisions (net)	20.49	22.80	24.75	18.19	19.27	19.25	29.03	14.59	18.40	26.49	57. Provisions (nettes)
a. Provisions on loans	*19.63*	*22.79*	*23.28*	*17.98*	*18.45*	*19.07*	*28.65*	*14.59*	*15.45*	*25.72*	*a. Provisions sur prêts*
b. Provisions on securities	*..*	*..*	*..*	*..*	*..*	*..*	*..*	*..*	*..*	*..*	*b. Provisions sur titres*
c. Other	*..*	*0.01*	*1.46*	*0.21*	*0.83*	*0.18*	*0.37*	*..*	*2.95*	*0.78*	*c. Autres*
58. Profit before tax	20.94	24.70	22.92	27.44	26.31	29.92	27.85	30.22	24.89	14.85	58. Bénéfices avant impôt
59. Income tax	10.28	12.62	9.77	12.73	9.78	13.75	12.73	13.37	12.00	2.39	59. Impôt sur le revenu
60. Profit after tax	10.65	12.08	13.14	14.71	16.53	16.17	15.12	16.85	12.89	12.46	60. Bénéfices après impôt
% of net income											**% du total du résultat net**
61. Provisions (net)	49.46	48.00	51.92	39.87	42.28	39.15	51.03	32.56	42.51	64.08	61. Provisions (nettes)
a. Provisions on loans	*47.39*	*47.98*	*48.85*	*39.40*	*40.46*	*38.78*	*50.38*	*32.56*	*35.69*	*62.20*	*a. Provisions sur prêts*
b. Provisions on securities	*..*	*..*	*..*	*..*	*..*	*..*	*..*	*..*	*..*	*..*	*b. Provisions sur titres*
c. Other	*..*	*0.02*	*3.07*	*0.47*	*1.82*	*0.37*	*0.66*	*..*	*6.81*	*1.88*	*c. Autres*
62. Profit before tax	50.54	52.00	48.08	60.13	57.72	60.85	48.97	67.44	57.49	35.92	62. Bénéfices avant impôt
63. Income tax	24.83	26.57	20.51	27.90	21.45	27.96	22.38	29.83	27.72	5.79	63. Impôt sur le revenu
64. Profit after tax	25.72	25.43	27.57	32.23	36.27	32.89	26.58	37.61	29.77	30.13	64. Bénéfices après impôt

GERMANY

Regional giro institutions

ALLEMAGNE

Organismes régionaux de compensation

Per cent — *Pourcentage*

BALANCE SHEET ANALYSIS — **ANALYSE DU BILAN**

% of year-end balance sheet total — % du total du bilan en fin d'exercice

	1992	1993¹	1994	1995	1996	1997	1998	1999	2000	2001	
Assets											**Actif**
65. Cash & balance with Central bank	0.50	0.43	0.23	0.25	0.26	0.19	0.19	0.27	0.32	0.40	65. Caisse & solde auprès de la Banque centrale
66. Interbank deposits	34.27	33.37	33.02	34.14	35.84	35.98	35.57	34.50	33.66	33.45	66. Dépôts interbancaires
67. Loans	48.65	48.34	48.23	46.34	44.13	42.45	40.65	38.07	37.48	37.21	67. Prêts
68. Securities	14.71	15.50	16.11	16.62	17.23	18.27	20.08	21.40	22.77	24.58	68. Valeurs mobilières
69. Other assets	1.87	2.37	2.40	2.66	2.54	3.12	3.51	5.77	5.77	4.36	69. Autres actifs
Liabilities											**Passif**
70. Capital & reserves	2.77	2.79	2.92	2.85	2.79	2.82	2.90	2.95	3.04	3.37	70. Capital et réserves
71. Borrowing from Central bank	2.96	5.17	3.30	2.85	2.71	2.34	1.82	1.58	1.89	1.29	71. Emprunts auprès de la Banque centrale
72. Interbank deposits	34.47	32.26	32.01	33.73	34.53	36.87	38.29	34.72	33.75	33.07	72. Dépôts interbancaires
73. Non-bank deposits	24.22	23.82	24.86	24.39	24.47	24.38	24.83	25.38	24.89	26.17	73. Dépôts non bancaires
74. Bonds	32.00	31.64	33.10	32.52	31.52	28.90	27.29	29.46	30.73	31.60	74. Obligations
75. Other liabilities	3.58	4.31	3.81	3.66	3.97	4.69	4.87	5.90	5.71	4.49	75. Autres engagements
Memorandum items											***Pour mémoire***
76. *Short-term securities*	*3.90*	*3.07*	*2.10*	*1.67*	*2.18*	*2.55*	*3.17*	*2.45*	*3.09*	*3.65*	76. *Titres à court terme*
77. *Bonds*	*9.06*	*10.64*	*11.99*	*12.51*	*12.66*	*13.52*	*14.54*	*16.80*	*17.31*	*18.38*	77. *Obligations*
78. *Shares and participations*	*1.74*	*1.80*	*2.02*	*2.44*	*2.39*	*2.20*	*2.37*	*2.15*	*2.38*	*2.54*	78. *Actions et participations*
79. *Claims on non-residents*	*23.03*	*23.39*	*20.40*	*20.74*	*24.58*	*28.86*	*31.09*	*32.20*	*33.20*	*35.34*	79. *Créances sur des non-résidents*
80. *Liabilities to non-residents*	*12.48*	*10.34*	*12.58*	*14.30*	*16.26*	*21.65*	*24.68*	*26.14*	*25.90*	*27.09*	80. *Engagements envers des non-résidents*

* See notes on previous pages. — * Voir les notes en pages précédentes.

GERMANY
Savings banks

ALLEMAGNE
Caisse d'épargne

Million euros / *Million d'euros*

	1992	1993¹	1994	1995	1996	1997	1998	1999	2000	2001	
INCOME STATEMENT											**COMPTE DE RESULTATS**
1. Interest income	43530	50960	51271	52057	52055	52473	53384	51228	52774	54435	1. Produits financiers
2. Interest expenses	28344	31491	29233	29817	29119	29765	31179	28965	31248	32859	2. Frais financiers
3. Net interest income	15186	19469	22038	22241	22936	22709	22205	22263	21526	21576	3. Produits financiers nets
4. Non-interest income (net) (2)	3152	3770	3489	3927	3760	4580	5075	3503	6264	6070	4. Produits non financiers (nets) (2)
a. Fees and commissions receivable	..	3307	3623	3691	3857	4104	4449	4868	5355	5010	a. Frais et commissions à recevoir
b. Fees and commissions payable	..	106	106	115	130	169	196	231	303	274	b. Frais et commissions à payer
c. Net profits or loss on financial operations	..	548	105	366	359	490	468	236	150	-11	c. Profits ou pertes nets sur opérations financières
d. Other	..	21	-133	-15	-326	155	354	-1370	1062	1345	d. Autres
5. Gross income	18337	23239	25526	26168	26696	27289	27280	25766	27790	27646	5. Résultat brut
6. Operating expenses	11755	14642	14949	15993	16584	17130	18022	18012	18335	18659	6. Frais d'exploitation
a. Staff costs	7690	9064	9350	9863	10117	10284	10797	10784	10993	11059	a. Dépenses en personnel
b. Property costs (3)	..	..	..	..	..	..	..	..	..	..	b. Dépenses en immobilier (3)
c. Other	..	5578	5599	6130	6466	6847	7224	7228	7342	7600	c. Autres
7. Net income	6582	8597	10578	10175	10112	10158	9259	7754	9455	8987	7. Résultat net
8. Provisions (net)	1773	3056	5615	3879	3697	3919	3115	2349	4423	5314	8. Provisions (nettes)
a. Provisions on loans	1762	3005	5160	3859	3686	3886	3098	2186	4306	4978	a. Provisions sur prêts
b. Provisions on securities (4)	..	..	..	..	..	..	..	..	..	..	b. Provisions sur titres (4)
c. Other	..	51	454	20	10	33	16	163	117	336	c. Autres
9. Profit before tax	4810	5541	4963	6296	6416	6239	6144	5405	5032	3673	9. Bénéfices avant impôt
10. Income tax	3311	3582	2894	4066	4189	4095	3896	3227	2770	1651	10. Impôt sur le revenu
11. Profit after tax	1499	1959	2069	2229	2227	2144	2249	2178	2262	2022	11. Bénéfices après impôt
12. Distributed profit	882	1160	1240	1315	1275	1305	1318	1305	1286	1197	12. Bénéfices distribués
13. Retained profit	617	799	829	915	952	839	931	873	976	825	13. Bénéfices mis en réserve
BALANCE SHEET											**BILAN**
Assets											**Actif**
14. Cash & balance with Central bank	17337	17209	14691	14947	14257	14267	14274	18771	18732	21933	14. Caisse & solde auprès de la Banque centrale
15. Interbank deposits	47195	69427	56039	65218	67686	73220	77768	73864	73137	79563	15. Dépôts interbancaires
16. Loans	350478	409499	444426	475987	505017	529229	556538	558936	578906	594613	16. Prêts
17. Securities	117938	164796	195642	197598	212838	226667	243537	246860	256488	262614	17. Valeurs mobilières
18. Other assets	16858	19605	19387	20066	21039	21803	22540	27281	26974	27074	18. Autres actifs
Liabilities											**Passif**
19. Capital & reserves	20951	25331	27671	29900	32272	34686	36922	38139	40266	42672	19. Capital et réserves
20. Borrowing from Central bank	19467	21845	24154	22726	24607	28158	29094	21919	32854	17452	20. Emprunts auprès de la Banque centrale
21. Interbank deposits	60520	81276	101703	116777	129860	146290	163928	185500	201247	211235	21. Dépôts interbancaires
22. Non-bank deposits	396435	491194	507842	529111	554144	573606	600366	595382	591162	625781	22. Dépôts non bancaires
23. Bonds	30054	32651	39388	44711	48118	49951	50310	45998	47480	45992	23. Obligations
24. Other liabilities	22378	27637	29427	30591	31837	32494	34037	38774	41228	42665	24. Autres engagements
Balance sheet total											**Total du bilan**
25. End-year total	549805	680535	730185	773816	820838	865184	914656	925712	954237	985797	25. En fin d'exercice
26. Average total	526369	640808	699261	735390	787037	835946	881761	896501	922381	948723	26. Moyen

GERMANY
Savings banks

ALLEMAGNE
Caisse d'épargne

Million euros — *Million d'euros*

	1992	1993[1]	1994	1995	1996	1997	1998	1999	2000	2001		
Memorandum items												***Pour mémoire***
27. Short-term securities	11372	14922	17239	18792	21513	20371	18760	2729	3498	2932	27.	*Titres à court terme*
28. Bonds	94939	133304	156887	153197	161520	167085	174169	185155	184703	186964	28.	*Obligations*
29. Shares and participations	11627	16570	21516	25610	29806	39211	50607	58976	68287	72718	29.	*Actions et participations*
30. Claims on non-residents	8989	13793	12272	12791	14151	14453	17021	18147	23663	30007	30.	*Créances sur des non-résidents*
31. Liabilities to non-residents	5625	7278	7508	8020	8548	10863	12903	11892	13813	14353	31.	*Engagements envers des non-résidents*
Capital adequacy												***Solvabilité***
32. Tier 1 Capital	..	..	..	..	..	..	..	..	..	..	32.	*Fonds propres de base*
33. Tier 2 Capital	..	..	..	..	..	..	..	..	..	..	33.	*Fonds propres complémentaires*
34. Supervisory deductions	..	..	..	..	..	..	..	..	..	..	34.	*Eléments à déduire des fonds propres*
35. Total net capital resources	..	..	..	..	..	..	..	..	..	..	35.	*Total net des ressources en capital*
36. Risk-weighted assets	..	..	..	..	..	..	..	..	..	..	36.	*Actifs pondérés des risques*
SUPPLEMENTARY INFORMATION												**RENSEIGNEMENTS COMPLÉMENTAIRES**
37. Number of institutions	542	704	657	626	607	598	594	578	562	537	37.	*Nombre d'institutions*
38. Number of branches	16923	19510	19271	19071	18895	18751	18327	17667	16892	16491	38.	*Nombre de succursales*
39. Number of employees (x 1000)	284	288	291	290	288	289	288	282	283	282	39.	*Nombre de salariés (x 1000)*

1 Break in series due to change in methodology

2 Non-interest income (item 4), in the national definition, excluding items 4.c and 4.d.

3 Property costs (item 6.b.) included under Other operating expenses (item 6.c.).

4 Provisions on securities (item 8.b.) included under Provisions on loans (item 8.a)

Notes

. Average balance sheet totals (item 26) are based on twelve end-month data.

Change in methodology

. As from 1993, data include eastern German credit institutions and are in accordance with the new accounting regulations.

1 Rupture de serie, suite au changement méthodologique.

2 Produits non financiers (nets) (poste 4), suivant la définition nationale, non compris les rubriques 4.c et 4.d.

3 Les Dépenses en immobilier (poste 6.b.) sont incluses sous Autres frais d'exploitation (poste 6.c).

4 Les Provisions sur titres (poste 8.b.) sont incluses sous Provisions sur prêts (poste 8.a).

Notes

. La moyenne du total des actifs/passifs (poste 26) est basée sur douze données de fin de mois.

Changement méthodologique

. Depuis 1993, les données comprennent les organismes de crédit d'Allemagne orientale et sont conformes aux nouvelles règles de comptabilité.

GERMANY
Savings banks

ALLEMAGNE
Caisse d'épargne

Per cent — *Pourcentage*

INCOME STATEMENT ANALYSIS — ANALYSE DU COMPTE DE RESULTATS

		1992	1993[1]	1994	1995	1996	1997	1998	1999	2000	2001
	% of average balance sheet total — **% du total moyen du bilan**										
40.	Interest income — Produits financiers	8.27	7.95	7.33	7.08	6.61	6.28	6.05	5.71	5.72	5.74
41.	Interest expenses — Frais financiers	5.38	4.91	4.18	4.05	3.70	3.56	3.54	3.23	3.39	3.46
42.	Net interest income — Produits financiers nets	2.89	3.04	3.15	3.02	2.91	2.72	2.52	2.48	2.33	2.27
43.	Non-interest income (net) — Produits non financiers (nets)	0.60	0.59	0.50	0.53	0.48	0.55	0.58	0.39	0.68	0.64
	a. Fees and commissions receivable — Frais et commissions à recevoir	..	0.52	0.52	0.50	0.49	0.49	0.50	0.54	0.58	0.53
	b. Fees and commissions payable — Frais et commissions à payer	..	0.02	0.02	0.02	0.02	0.02	0.02	0.03	0.03	0.03
	c. Net profits or loss on financial operations — Profits ou pertes nets sur opérations financières	..	0.09	0.01	0.05	0.05	0.06	0.05	0.03	0.02	0.03
	d. Other — Autres	..	..	-0.02	-	-0.04	0.02	0.04	-0.15	0.12	0.14
44.	Gross income — Résultat brut	3.48	3.63	3.65	3.56	3.39	3.26	3.09	2.87	3.01	2.91
45.	Operating expenses — Frais d'exploitation	2.23	2.28	2.14	2.17	2.11	2.05	2.04	2.01	1.99	1.97
	a. Staff costs — Dépenses en personnel	1.46	1.41	1.34	1.34	1.29	1.23	1.22	1.20	1.19	1.17
	b. Property costs — Dépenses en immobilier	..									
	c. Other — Autres	..	0.87	0.80	0.83	0.82	0.82	0.82	0.81	0.80	0.80
46.	Net income — Résultat net	1.25	1.34	1.51	1.38	1.28	1.22	1.05	0.86	1.03	0.95
47.	Provisions (net) — Provisions (nettes)	0.34	0.48	0.80	0.53	0.47	0.47	0.35	0.26	0.48	0.56
	a. Provisions on loans — Provisions sur prêts	0.33	0.47	0.74	0.52	0.47	0.46	0.35	0.24	0.47	0.52
	b. Provisions on securities — Provisions sur titres	..									
	c. Other — Autres	..	0.01	0.06	..	..	..	..	0.02	0.01	0.04
48.	Profit before tax — Bénéfices avant impôt	0.91	0.86	0.71	0.86	0.82	0.75	0.70	0.60	0.55	0.39
49.	Income tax — Impôt sur le revenu	0.63	0.56	0.41	0.55	0.53	0.49	0.44	0.36	0.30	0.17
50.	Profit after tax — Bénéfices après impôt	0.28	0.31	0.30	0.30	0.28	0.26	0.26	0.24	0.25	0.21
51.	Distributed profit — Bénéfices distribués	0.17	0.18	0.18	0.18	0.16	0.16	0.15	0.15	0.14	0.13
52.	Retained profit — Bénéfices mis en réserve	0.12	0.12	0.12	0.12	0.12	0.10	0.11	0.10	0.11	0.09
	% of gross income — **% du total du résultat brut**										
53.	Net interest income — Produits financiers nets	82.81	83.78	86.33	84.99	85.92	83.22	81.40	86.40	77.46	78.04
54.	Non-interest income (net) — Produits non financiers (nets)	17.19	16.22	13.67	15.01	14.08	16.78	18.60	13.60	22.54	21.96
	a. Fees and commissions receivable — Frais et commissions à recevoir	..	14.23	14.19	14.11	14.45	15.04	16.31	18.89	19.27	18.12
	b. Fees and commissions payable — Frais et commissions à payer	..	0.46	0.42	0.44	0.49	0.62	0.72	0.90	1.09	0.99
	c. Net profits or loss on financial operations — Profits ou pertes nets sur opérations financières	..	2.36	0.41	1.40	1.35	1.79	1.72	0.92	0.54	-0.04
	d. Other — Autres	..	0.09	-0.52	-0.06	-1.22	0.57	1.30	-5.32	3.82	4.87
55.	Operating expenses — Frais d'exploitation	64.10	63.01	58.56	61.12	62.12	62.77	66.06	69.91	65.98	67.49
	a. Staff costs — Dépenses en personnel	41.94	39.00	36.63	37.69	37.90	37.68	39.58	41.85	39.56	40.00
	b. Property costs — Dépenses en immobilier	..									
	c. Other — Autres	..	24.00	21.93	23.43	24.22	25.09	26.48	28.05	26.42	27.49
56.	Net income — Résultat net	35.90	36.99	41.44	38.88	37.88	37.23	33.94	30.09	34.02	32.51
57.	Provisions (net) — Provisions (nettes)	9.67	13.15	22.00	14.82	13.85	14.36	11.42	9.12	15.92	19.22
	a. Provisions on loans — Provisions sur prêts	9.61	12.93	20.22	14.75	13.81	14.24	11.36	8.48	15.49	18.01
	b. Provisions on securities — Provisions sur titres	..									
	c. Other — Autres	..	0.22	1.78	0.08	0.04	0.12	0.06	0.63	0.42	1.22
58.	Profit before tax — Bénéfices avant impôt	26.23	23.84	19.44	24.06	24.03	22.86	22.52	20.98	18.11	13.29
59.	Income tax — Impôt sur le revenu	18.05	15.41	11.34	15.54	15.69	15.01	14.28	12.52	9.97	5.97
60.	Profit after tax — Bénéfices après impôt	8.18	8.43	8.10	8.52	8.34	7.86	8.24	8.45	8.14	7.31
	% of net income — **% du total du résultat net**										
61.	Provisions (net) — Provisions (nettes)	26.93	35.55	53.08	38.13	36.56	38.58	33.64	30.29	46.78	59.13
	a. Provisions on loans — Provisions sur prêts	26.77	34.96	48.79	37.92	36.45	38.25	33.46	28.19	45.54	55.39
	b. Provisions on securities — Provisions sur titres	..									
	c. Other — Autres	..	0.59	4.29	0.20	0.10	0.33	0.18	2.10	1.24	3.74
62.	Profit before tax — Bénéfices avant impôt	73.07	64.45	46.92	61.87	63.44	61.42	66.36	69.71	53.22	40.87
63.	Income tax — Impôt sur le revenu	50.30	41.67	27.36	39.96	41.42	40.32	42.07	41.62	29.30	18.37
64.	Profit after tax — Bénéfices après impôt	22.77	22.78	19.56	21.91	22.02	21.10	24.29	28.09	23.92	22.50

GERMANY
Savings banks

ALLEMAGNE
Caisse d'épargne

Per cent — *Pourcentage*

	1992	1993[1]	1994	1995	1996	1997	1998	1999	2000	2001		ANALYSE DU BILAN
BALANCE SHEET ANALYSIS												**% du total du bilan en fin d'exercice**
% of year-end balance sheet total												
Assets												**Actif**
65. Cash & balance with Central bank	3.15	2.53	2.01	1.93	1.74	1.65	1.56	2.03	1.96	2.22		65. Caisse & solde auprès de la Banque centrale
66. Interbank deposits	8.58	10.20	7.67	8.43	8.25	8.46	8.50	7.98	7.66	8.07		66. Dépôts interbancaires
67. Loans	63.75	60.17	60.86	61.51	61.52	61.17	60.85	60.38	60.67	60.32		67. Prêts
68. Securities	21.45	24.22	26.79	25.54	25.93	26.20	26.63	26.67	26.88	26.64		68. Valeurs mobilières
69. Other assets	3.07	2.88	2.66	2.59	2.56	2.52	2.46	2.95	2.83	2.75		69. Autres actifs
Liabilities												**Passif**
70. Capital & reserves	3.81	3.72	3.79	3.86	3.93	4.01	4.04	4.12	4.22	4.33		70. Capital et réserves
71. Borrowing from Central bank	3.54	3.21	3.31	2.94	3.00	3.25	3.18	2.37	3.44	1.77		71. Emprunts auprès de la Banque centrale
72. Interbank deposits	11.01	11.94	13.93	15.09	15.82	16.91	17.92	20.04	21.09	21.43		72. Dépôts interbancaires
73. Non-bank deposits	72.10	72.27	69.55	68.38	67.51	66.30	65.64	64.32	61.95	63.48		73. Dépôts non bancaires
74. Bonds	5.47	4.80	5.39	5.78	5.86	5.77	5.50	4.97	4.98	4.67		74. Obligations
75. Other liabilities	4.07	4.06	4.03	3.95	3.88	3.76	3.72	4.19	4.32	4.33		75. Autres engagements
Memorandum items												**Pour mémoire**
76. Short-term securities	2.07	2.19	2.36	2.43	2.62	2.35	2.05	0.29	0.37	0.30		76. Titres à court terme
77. Bonds	17.27	19.59	21.49	19.80	19.68	19.31	19.04	20.00	19.36	18.97		77. Obligations
78. Shares and participations	2.11	2.43	2.95	3.31	3.63	4.53	5.53	6.37	7.16	7.38		78. Actions et participations
79. Claims on non-residents	1.63	2.03	1.68	1.65	1.72	1.67	1.86	1.96	2.48	3.04		79. Créances sur des non-résidents
80. Liabilities to non-residents	1.02	1.07	1.03	1.04	1.04	1.26	1.41	1.28	1.45	1.46		80. Engagements envers des non-résidents

* See notes on previous pages.

* Voir les notes en pages précédentes.

GERMANY — ALLEMAGNE

Regional institutions of co-operative banks — Institutions régionales des banques mutualistes

Million euros — Million d'euros

		1992	1993[1]	1994	1995	1996	1997	1998	1999	2000	2001	
INCOME STATEMENT												**COMPTE DE RESULTATS**
1.	Interest income	8231	7940	7593	7133	7114	7954	9108	9008	11800	11769	1. Produits financiers
2.	Interest expenses	7483	7001	6068	6005	5980	6723	7615	7688	9979	10289	2. Frais financiers
3.	Net interest income	749	939	1526	1127	1134	1230	1493	1320	1821	1480	3. Produits financiers nets
4.	Non-interest income (net) (2)	299	387	680	410	529	552	1424	684	1445	910	4. Produits non financiers (nets) (2)
	a. Fees and commissions receivable	..	411	398	414	463	517	571	710	979	647	a. Frais et commissions à recevoir
	b. Fees and commissions payable	..	138	129	131	134	129	183	315	480	293	b. Frais et commissions à payer
	c. Net profits or loss on financial operations	..	154	93	153	152	176	95	256	219	132	c. Profits ou pertes nets sur opérations financières
	d. Other	..	-41	318	-26	48	-13	941	33	727	424	d. Autres
5.	Gross income	1048	1326	2205	1537	1663	1782	2917	2004	3266	2390	5. Résultat brut
6.	Operating expenses	687	745	781	835	887	987	1121	1224	1323	1316	6. Frais d'exploitation
	a. Staff costs	370	393	410	433	439	490	523	563	621	614	a. Dépenses en personnel
	b. Property costs (3)	..	..	..	..	..	..	..	..	..	..	b. Dépenses en immobilier (3)
	c. Other	..	352	371	402	447	497	598	661	702	702	c. Autres
7.	Net income	360	581	1424	703	777	795	1797	780	1943	1074	7. Résultat net
8.	Provisions (net)	125	358	865	173	132	233	376	432	1108	772	8. Provisions (nettes)
	a. Provisions on loans	97	357	865	171	119	184	372	365	1108	772	a. Provisions sur prêts
	b. Provisions on securities (4)	..	1	1	2	13	50	4	67	-	-	b. Provisions sur titres (4)
	c. Other	..	..	..	..	..	..	..	..	..	..	c. Autres
9.	Profit before tax	236	223	559	530	645	561	1420	348	835	302	9. Bénéfices avant impôt
10.	Income tax	133	133	278	265	292	307	270	107	265	115	10. Impôt sur le revenu
11.	Profit after tax	102	90	282	264	352	254	1150	241	570	187	11. Bénéfices après impôt
12.	Distributed profit	40	47	95	161	94	159	120	138	105	79	12. Bénéfices distribués
13.	Retained profit	62	43	187	103	259	96	1030	103	465	108	13. Bénéfices mis en réserve
BALANCE SHEET												**BILAN**
Assets												**Actif**
14.	Cash & balance with Central bank	1075	611	510	881	569	699	1708	890	933	952	14. Caisse & solde auprès de la Banque centrale
15.	Interbank deposits	54491	60260	65597	72043	74992	77421	91021	93911	97730	95700	15. Dépôts interbancaires
16.	Loans	29661	29167	29889	34342	40111	44485	51199	60270	60127	52026	16. Prêts
17.	Securities	20408	25344	27069	32210	44227	57279	66128	63693	77620	74491	17. Valeurs mobilières
18.	Other assets	2035	1987	2334	2563	3495	4993	5644	8302	9823	11860	18. Autres actifs
Liabilities												**Passif**
19.	Capital & reserves	4034	4353	4780	5161	5544	6515	7180	8662	8958	9297	19. Capital et réserves
20.	Borrowing from Central bank	5243	4207	7465	5889	7039	6893	7013	6989	10118	125	20. Emprunts auprès de la Banque centrale
21.	Interbank deposits	75910	81914	79889	90793	98821	112469	131423	124169	129162	129893	21. Dépôts interbancaires
22.	Non-bank deposits	9729	11221	13019	14296	17887	20941	29278	35086	41456	42066	22. Dépôts non bancaires
23.	Bonds	9736	10916	14818	18060	25908	29174	31550	40093	47812	41610	23. Obligations
24.	Other liabilities	3017	4760	5428	7840	8194	8885	9257	12067	8727	12038	24. Autres engagements
Balance sheet total												**Total du bilan**
25.	End-year total	107669	117370	125399	142039	163394	184878	215701	227066	246233	235029	25. En fin d'exercice
26.	Average total	96345	102327	117856	127175	148836	171407	197433	219046	234249	239709	26. Moyen

GERMANY

Regional institutions of co-operative banks

Million euros — *Million d'euros*

	1992	1993[1]	1994	1995	1996	1997	1998	1999	2000	2001	
Memorandum items											**Pour mémoire**
27. Short-term securities	6034	7377	5573	5185	7431	9907	9548	2226	4710	3294	27. Titres à court terme
28. Bonds	10623	13569	16814	19873	29412	38514	45923	47130	57617	53835	28. Obligations
29. Shares and participations	3751	4398	4682	7151	7385	8858	10657	14337	15293	17362	29. Actions et participations
30. Claims on non-residents	14173	17771	18178	18073	22643	24214	34773	37259	50636	59409	30. Créances sur des non-résidents
31. Liabilities to non-residents	4089	4137	6049	6964	8973	16621	30110	27464	39485	40393	31. Engagements envers des non-résidents
Capital adequacy											**Solvabilité**
32. Tier 1 Capital	..	..	..	..	..	..	..	..	..	..	32. Fonds propres de base
33. Tier 2 Capital	..	..	..	..	..	..	..	..	..	..	33. Fonds propres complémentaires
34. Supervisory deductions	..	..	..	..	..	..	..	..	..	..	34. Eléments à déduire des fonds propres
35. Total net capital resources	..	..	..	..	..	..	..	..	..	..	35. Total net des ressources en capital
36. Risk-weighted assets	..	..	..	..	..	..	..	..	..	..	36. Actifs pondérés des risques
SUPPLEMENTARY INFORMATION											**RENSEIGNEMENTS COMPLÉMENTAIRES**
37. Number of institutions	4	4	4	4	4	4	4	4	4	2	37. Nombre d'institutions
38. Number of branches	31	46	46	43	42	42	26	24	25	18	38. Nombre de succursales
39. Number of employees (x 1000)	7	7	7	7	7	7	7	7	7	7	39. Nombre de salariés (x 1000)

1 Break in series due to change in methodology

2 Non-interest income (item 4), in the national definition, excluding items 4.c and 4.d.

3 Property costs (item 6.b.) included under Other operating expenses (item 6.c.).

4 Provisions on securities (item 8.b.) included under Provisions on loans (item 8.a)

Notes

. Average balance sheet totals (item 26) are based on twelve end-month data.

Change in methodology

. As from 1993, data include eastern German credit institutions and are in accordance with the new accounting regulations.

1 Rupture de serie, suite au changement méthodologique.

2 Produits non financiers (nets) (poste 4), suivant la définition nationale, non compris les rubriques 4.c et 4.d.

3 Les Dépenses en immobilier (poste 6.b.) sont incluses sous Autres frais d'exploitation (poste 6.c).

4 Les Provisions sur titres (poste 8.b.) sont incluses sous Provisions sur prêts (poste 8.a).

Notes

. La moyenne du total des actifs/passifs (poste 26) est basée sur douze données de fin de mois.

Changement méthodologique

. Depuis 1993, les données comprennent les organismes de crédit d'Allemagne orientale et sont conformes aux nouvelles règles de comptabilité.

GERMANY

Regional institutions of co-operative banks

ALLEMAGNE

Institutions régionales des banques mutualistes

Per cent / *Pourcentage*

INCOME STATEMENT ANALYSIS / ANALYSE DU COMPTE DE RESULTATS

% of average balance sheet total / **% du total moyen du bilan**

#	Item (EN)	Item (FR)	1992	1993[1]	1994	1995	1996	1997	1998	1999	2000	2001
40.	Interest income	Produits financiers	8.54	7.76	6.44	5.61	4.78	4.64	4.61	4.11	5.04	4.91
41.	Interest expenses	Frais financiers	7.77	6.84	5.15	4.72	4.02	3.92	3.86	3.51	4.26	4.29
42.	Net interest income	Produits financiers nets	0.78	0.92	1.29	0.89	0.76	0.72	0.76	0.60	0.78	0.62
43.	Non-interest income (net)	Produits non financiers (nets)	0.31	0.38	0.58	0.32	0.36	0.32	0.72	0.31	0.62	0.38
a.	*Fees and commissions receivable*	*Frais et commissions à recevoir*		0.40	0.34	0.33	0.31	0.30	0.29	0.32	0.42	0.27
b.	*Fees and commissions payable*	*Frais et commissions à payer*		0.13	0.11	0.10	0.09	0.08	0.09	0.14	0.20	0.12
c.	*Net profits or loss on financial operations*	*Net profits ou pertes nets sur opérations financières*		0.15	0.08	0.12	0.10	0.10	0.05	0.12	0.09	0.06
d.	*Other*	*Autres*		-0.04	0.27	-0.02	0.03	-0.01	0.48	0.02	0.31	0.18
44.	Gross income	Résultat brut	1.09	1.30	1.87	1.21	1.12	1.04	1.48	0.91	1.39	1.00
45.	Operating expenses	Frais d'exploitation	0.71	0.73	0.66	0.66	0.60	0.58	0.57	0.56	0.56	0.55
a.	*Staff costs*	*Dépenses en personnel*	0.38	0.38	0.35	0.34	0.30	0.29	0.26	0.26	0.27	0.26
b.	*Property costs*	*Dépenses en immobilier*										
c.	*Other*	*Autres*		0.34	0.31	0.32	0.30	0.29	0.30	0.30	0.30	0.29
46.	Net income	Résultat net	0.37	0.57	1.21	0.55	0.52	0.46	0.91	0.36	0.83	0.45
47.	Provisions (net)	Provisions (nettes)	0.13	0.35	0.73	0.14	0.09	0.14	0.19	0.20	0.47	0.32
a.	*Provisions on loans*	*Provisions sur prêts*	0.10	0.35	0.73	0.13	0.08	0.11	0.19	0.17	0.47	0.32
b.	*Provisions on securities*	*Provisions sur titres*										
c.	*Other*	*Autres*					0.01	0.03		0.03		
48.	Profit before tax	Bénéfices avant impôt	0.24	0.22	0.47	0.42	0.43	0.33	0.72	0.16	0.36	0.13
49.	Income tax	Impôt sur le revenu	0.14	0.13	0.24	0.21	0.20	0.18	0.14	0.05	0.11	0.05
50.	Profit after tax	Bénéfices après impôt	0.11	0.09	0.24	0.21	0.24	0.15	0.58	0.11	0.24	0.08
51.	Distributed profit	Bénéfices distribués	0.04	0.05	0.08	0.13	0.06	0.09	0.06	0.06	0.04	0.03
52.	Retained profit	Bénéfices mis en réserve	0.06	0.04	0.16	0.08	0.17	0.06	0.52	0.05	0.20	0.05

% of gross income / **% du total du résultat brut**

#	Item (EN)	Item (FR)	1992	1993[1]	1994	1995	1996	1997	1998	1999	2000	2001
53.	Net interest income	Produits financiers nets	71.45	70.84	69.19	73.33	68.18	69.04	51.19	65.87	55.76	61.92
54.	Non-interest income (net)	Produits non financiers (nets)	28.55	29.16	30.81	26.67	31.82	30.96	48.81	34.13	44.24	38.08
a.	*Fees and commissions receivable*	*Frais et commissions à recevoir*		31.01	18.04	26.94	27.85	29.04	19.58	35.43	29.98	27.07
b.	*Fees and commissions payable*	*Frais et commissions à payer*		10.37	5.84	8.51	8.05	7.23	6.27	15.72	14.70	12.26
c.	*Net profits or loss on financial operations*	*Profits ou pertes nets sur opérations financières*		11.61	4.22	9.94	9.16	9.87	3.26	12.77	6.71	5.52
d.	*Other*	*Autres*		-3.08	14.40	-1.70	2.86	-0.72	32.25	1.65	22.26	17.74
55.	Operating expenses	Frais d'exploitation	65.59	56.19	35.40	54.31	53.30	55.41	38.42	61.08	40.51	55.06
a.	*Staff costs*	*Dépenses en personnel*	35.29	29.66	18.57	28.17	26.41	27.49	17.91	28.09	19.01	25.69
b.	*Property costs*	*Dépenses en immobilier*										
c.	*Other*	*Autres*		26.53	16.83	26.14	26.90	27.92	20.50	32.98	21.49	29.37
56.	Net income	Résultat net	34.41	43.81	64.60	45.69	46.70	44.59	61.58	38.92	59.49	44.94
57.	Provisions (net)	Provisions (nettes)	11.91	27.00	39.23	11.24	7.93	13.08	12.90	21.56	33.93	32.30
a.	*Provisions on loans*	*Provisions sur prêts*	9.22	26.92	39.21	11.14	7.13	10.30	12.76	18.21	33.93	32.30
b.	*Provisions on securities*	*Provisions sur titres*										
c.	*Other*	*Autres*		0.08	0.02	0.10	0.80	2.78	0.14	3.34		
58.	Profit before tax	Bénéfices avant impôt	22.50	16.81	25.37	34.45	38.76	31.51	48.69	17.37	25.57	12.64
59.	Income tax	Impôt sur le revenu	12.74	10.03	12.59	17.26	17.58	17.25	9.27	5.34	8.11	4.81
60.	Profit after tax	Bénéfices après impôt	9.76	6.79	12.78	17.19	21.18	14.26	39.41	12.03	17.45	7.82

% of net income / **% du total du résultat net**

#	Item (EN)	Item (FR)	1992	1993[1]	1994	1995	1996	1997	1998	1999	2000	2001
61.	Provisions (net)	Provisions (nettes)	34.61	61.62	60.73	24.60	16.98	29.34	20.94	55.38	57.03	71.88
a.	*Provisions on loans*	*Provisions sur prêts*	26.81	61.44	60.70	24.38	15.27	23.10	20.72	46.79	57.03	71.88
b.	*Provisions on securities*	*Provisions sur titres*										
c.	*Other*	*Autres*		0.18	0.04	0.22	1.71	6.24	0.23	8.59		
62.	Profit before tax	Bénéfices avant impôt	65.39	38.38	39.27	75.40	83.02	70.66	79.06	44.62	42.97	28.12
63.	Income tax	Impôt sur le revenu	37.02	22.89	19.49	37.77	37.66	38.67	15.05	13.72	13.64	10.71
64.	Profit after tax	Bénéfices après impôt	28.37	15.49	19.78	37.63	45.36	31.98	64.00	30.90	29.34	17.41

GERMANY — ALLEMAGNE

Regional institutions of co-operative banks — **Institutions régionales des banques mutualistes**

Per cent — *Pourcentage*

BALANCE SHEET ANALYSIS — **ANALYSE DU BILAN**
% of year-end balance sheet total — **% du total du bilan en fin d'exercice**

	1992	1993[1]	1994	1995	1996	1997	1998	1999	2000	2001	
Assets											**Actif**
65. Cash & balance with Central bank	1.00	0.52	0.41	0.62	0.35	0.38	0.79	0.39	0.38	0.41	65. Caisse & solde auprès de la Banque centrale
66. Interbank deposits	50.61	51.34	52.31	50.72	45.90	41.88	42.20	41.36	39.69	40.72	66. Dépôts interbancaires
67. Loans	27.55	24.85	23.83	24.18	24.55	24.06	23.74	26.54	24.42	22.14	67. Prêts
68. Securities	18.95	21.59	21.59	22.68	27.07	30.98	30.66	28.05	31.52	31.69	68. Valeurs mobilières
69. Other assets	1.89	1.69	1.86	1.80	2.14	2.70	2.62	3.66	3.99	5.05	69. Autres actifs
Liabilities											**Passif**
70. Capital & reserves	3.75	3.71	3.81	3.63	3.39	3.52	3.33	3.81	3.64	3.96	70. Capital et réserves
71. Borrowing from Central bank	4.87	3.58	5.95	4.15	4.31	3.73	3.25	3.08	4.11	0.05	71. Emprunts auprès de la Banque centrale
72. Interbank deposits	70.50	69.79	63.71	63.92	60.48	60.83	60.93	54.68	52.46	55.27	72. Dépôts interbancaires
73. Non-bank deposits	9.04	9.56	10.38	10.07	10.95	11.33	13.57	15.45	16.84	17.90	73. Dépôts non bancaires
74. Bonds	9.04	9.30	11.82	12.72	15.86	15.78	14.63	17.66	19.42	17.70	74. Obligations
75. Other liabilities	2.80	4.06	4.33	5.52	5.01	4.81	4.29	5.31	3.54	5.12	75. Autres engagements
Memorandum items											***Pour mémoire***
76. Short-term securities	5.60	6.29	4.44	3.65	4.55	5.36	4.43	0.98	1.91	1.40	76. Titres à court terme
77. Bonds	9.87	11.56	13.41	13.99	18.00	20.83	21.29	20.76	23.40	22.91	77. Obligations
78. Shares and participations	3.48	3.75	3.73	5.03	4.52	4.79	4.94	6.31	6.21	7.39	78. Actions et participations
79. Claims on non-residents	13.16	15.14	14.50	12.72	13.86	13.10	16.12	16.41	20.56	25.28	79. Créances sur des non-résidents
80. Liabilities to non-residents	3.80	3.52	4.82	4.90	5.49	8.99	13.96	12.10	16.04	17.19	80. Engagements envers des non-résidents

* See notes on previous pages.   * Voir les notes en pages précédentes.

GERMANY

Co-operative banks

ALLEMAGNE

Banques mutualistes

Million euros / *Million d'euros*

INCOME STATEMENT / COMPTE DE RESULTATS	1992	1993[1]	1994	1995	1996	1997	1998	1999	2000	2001
1. Interest income / 1. Produits financiers	27481	29963	29624	30570	30139	30003	30125	29331	29920	30770
2. Interest expenses / 2. Frais financiers	17643	18376	16899	17487	16719	16618	17191	16265	17033	17918
3. Net interest income / 3. Produits financiers nets	9838	11587	12726	13083	13420	13386	12934	13066	12887	12852
4. Non-interest income (net) (2) / 4. Produits non financiers (nets) (2)	2434	2820	2844	2978	3142	3396	3739	3836	4378	4510
a. Fees and commissions receivable / a. Frais et commissions à recevoir	..	2271	2481	2466	2622	2836	3076	3580	3988	3458
b. Fees and commissions payable / b. Frais et commissions à payer	..	152	168	182	201	221	278	333	387	354
c. Net profits or loss on financial operations / c. Profits ou pertes nets sur opérations financières	..	167	-15	150	136	106	95	49	23	-39
d. Other / d. Autres	..	534	546	543	585	674	846	540	754	1445
5. Gross income / 5. Résultat brut	12272	14407	15570	16061	16562	16782	16673	16902	17265	17362
6. Operating expenses / 6. Frais d'exploitation	8465	9808	10264	10892	11238	11527	11860	12078	12547	12577
a. Staff costs / a. Dépenses en personnel	5295	5930	6212	6554	6704	6825	6903	7062	7252	7345
b. Property costs (3) / b. Dépenses en immobilier (3)	..	..	..	..	..	..	..	..	..	..
c. Other / c. Autres	..	3878	4053	4337	4534	4701	4957	5016	5295	5232
7. Net income / 7. Résultat net	3806	4599	5306	5169	5324	5255	4813	4824	4718	4785
8. Provisions (net) / 8. Provisions (nettes)	782	1299	2472	1671	1837	2089	1931	2313	2624	2822
a. Provisions on loans / a. Provisions sur prêts	778	1293	2289	1642	1813	2049	1915	2175	2492	2669
b. Provisions on securities (4) / b. Provisions sur titres (4)	..	6	184	30	24	40	16	138	132	153
c. Other / c. Autres	..	..	..	..	..	..	..	..	..	..
9. Profit before tax / 9. Bénéfices avant impôt	3024	3299	2834	3498	3488	3166	2882	2511	2094	1963
10. Income tax / 10. Impôt sur le revenu	1953	2052	1593	2166	2203	1933	1748	1399	1096	805
11. Profit after tax / 11. Bénéfices après impôt	1071	1247	1241	1331	1284	1233	1134	1112	998	1158
12. Distributed profit / 12. Bénéfices distribués	711	831	852	917	932	930	879	908	1083	924
13. Retained profit / 13. Bénéfices mis en réserve	360	416	389	414	353	303	255	204	-85	234
BALANCE SHEET / BILAN										
Assets / Actif										
14. Cash & balance with Central bank / 14. Caisse & solde auprès de la Banque centrale	11124	9814	9865	9448	10168	9989	9265	11133	11781	14387
15. Interbank deposits / 15. Dépôts interbancaires	50765	64205	57141	63839	64510	66028	69796	69455	60836	67833
16. Loans / 16. Prêts	202113	228599	251549	273122	289229	303837	318764	323337	332873	336558
17. Securities / 17. Valeurs mobilières	61077	78529	93351	93731	101657	106742	112832	113033	109969	115083
18. Other assets / 18. Autres actifs	10850	11465	12229	12920	13495	13720	14451	18480	18740	18510
Liabilities / Passif										
19. Capital & reserves / 19. Capital et réserves	13529	16307	18497	20461	22329	23991	25229	26177	27237	27848
20. Borrowing from Central bank / 20. Emprunts auprès de la Banque centrale	8401	7207	8347	8256	8731	9415	8028	4555	6723	4058
21. Interbank deposits / 21. Dépôts interbancaires	25462	33325	41678	47390	52592	58134	65656	72270	74315	74850
22. Non-bank deposits / 22. Dépôts non bancaires	266621	309164	324708	340699	356778	367650	383500	384542	375528	394217
23. Bonds / 23. Obligations	11366	13983	17670	21917	23468	25963	27204	28854	30690	31191
24. Other liabilities / 24. Autres engagements	10551	12627	13236	14336	15160	15162	15491	19040	19706	20207
Balance sheet total / Total du bilan										
25. End-year total / 25. En fin d'exercice	335930	392613	424136	453059	479059	500315	525108	535438	534199	552371
26. Average total / 26. Moyen	319195	366581	403248	430559	461084	484151	506013	524020	525687	534337

GERMANY
Co-operative banks

ALLEMAGNE
Banques mutualistes

Million euros / *Million d'euros*

	1992	1993[1]	1994	1995	1996	1997	1998	1999	2000	2001		
Memorandum items												**Pour mémoire**
27. Short-term securities	9324	13052	13016	13688	13812	14491	11249	1365	1667	2072	27.	Titres à court terme
28. Bonds	48754	60806	74726	74027	80961	83033	88845	93289	87285	87777	28.	Obligations
29. Shares and participations	3000	4671	5608	6016	6885	9218	12737	18379	21017	25234	29.	Actions et participations
30. Claims on non-residents	3878	7935	7806	7842	7711	8115	8274	9485	12375	18002	30.	Créances sur non-résidents
31. Liabilities to non-residents	3573	4676	5562	6508	7656	8731	10318	12037	12884	13500	31.	Engagements envers des non-résidents
Capital adequacy												**Solvabilité**
32. Tier 1 Capital	:	:	:	:	:	:	:	:	:	:	32.	Fonds propres de base
33. Tier 2 Capital	:	:	:	:	:	:	:	:	:	:	33.	Fonds propres complémentaires
34. Supervisory deductions	:	:	:	:	:	:	:	:	:	:	34.	Eléments à déduire des fonds propres
35. Total net capital resources	:	:	:	:	:	:	:	:	:	:	35.	Total net des ressources en capital
36. Risk-weighted assets	:	:	:	:	:	:	:	:	:	:	36.	Actifs pondérés des risques
SUPPLEMENTARY INFORMATION												**RENSEIGNEMENTS COMPLÉMENTAIRES**
37. Number of institutions	2683	2778	2666	2591	2510	2420	2256	2035	1792	1619	37.	Nombre d'institutions
38. Number of branches	15618	17599	17383	17205	16977	16762	16139	15793	15332	14584	38.	Nombre de succursales
39. Number of employees (x 1000)	163	167	173	176	174	172	172	171	171	170	39.	Nombre de salariés (x 1000)

1 Break in series due to change in methodology

2 Non-interest income (item 4), in the national definition, excluding items 4.c and 4.d.

3 Property costs (item 6.b.) included under Other operating expenses (item 6.c.)

4 Provisions on securities (item 8.b.) included under Provisions on loans (item 8.a)

Notes

. Average balance sheet totals (item 26) are based on twelve end-month data.

Change in methodology

. As from 1993, data include eastern German credit institutions and are in accordance with the new accounting regulations.

1 Rupture de serie, suite au changement méthodologique.

2 Produits non financiers (nets) (poste 4), suivant la définition nationale, non compris les rubriques 4.c et 4.d.

3 Les Dépenses en immobilier (poste 6.b.) sont incluses sous Autres frais d'exploitation (poste 6.c).

4 Les Provisions sur titres (poste 8.b.) sont incluses sous Provisions sur prêts (poste 8.a).

Notes

. La moyenne du total des actifs/passifs (poste 26) est basée sur douze données de fin de mois.

Changement méthodologique

. Depuis 1993, les données comprennent les organismes de crédit d'Allemagne orientale et sont conformes aux nouvelles règles de comptabilité

GERMANY
Co-operative banks

ALLEMAGNE
Banques mutualistes

Per cent — *Pourcentage*

INCOME STATEMENT ANALYSIS — **ANALYSE DU COMPTE DE RESULTATS**

	English	1992	1993¹	1994	1995	1996	1997	1998	1999	2000	2001		French
	% of average balance sheet total												**% du total moyen du bilan**
40.	Interest income	8.61	8.17	7.35	7.10	6.54	6.20	5.95	5.60	5.69	5.76	40.	Produits financiers
41.	Interest expenses	5.53	5.01	4.19	4.06	3.63	3.43	3.40	3.10	3.24	3.35	41.	Frais financiers
42.	Net interest income	3.08	3.16	3.16	3.04	2.91	2.76	2.56	2.49	2.45	2.41	42.	Produits financiers nets
43.	Non-interest income (net)	0.76	0.77	0.71	0.69	0.68	0.70	0.74	0.73	0.83	0.84	43.	Produits non financiers (nets)
	a. Fees and commissions receivable	..	0.62	0.62	0.57	0.57	0.59	0.61	0.68	0.76	0.65		*a. Frais et commissions à recevoir*
	b. Fees and commissions payable	..	0.04	0.04	0.04	0.04	0.05	0.05	0.06	0.07	0.07		*b. Frais et commissions à payer*
	c. Net profits or loss on financial operations	..	0.05	-	0.03	0.03	0.02	0.02	0.01	..	-0.01		*c. Profits ou pertes nets sur opérations financières*
	d. Other	..	0.15	0.14	0.13	0.13	0.14	0.17	0.10	0.14	0.27		*d. Autres*
44.	Gross income	3.84	3.93	3.86	3.73	3.59	3.47	3.29	3.23	3.28	3.25	44.	Résultat brut
45.	Operating expenses	2.65	2.68	2.55	2.53	2.44	2.38	2.34	2.30	2.39	2.35	45.	Frais d'exploitation
	a. Staff costs	1.66	1.62	1.54	1.52	1.45	1.41	1.36	1.35	1.38	1.37		*a. Dépenses en personnel*
	b. Property costs												*b. Dépenses en immobilier*
	c. Other	..	1.06	1.00	1.01	0.98	0.97	0.98	0.96	1.01	0.98		*c. Autres*
46.	Net income	1.19	1.25	1.32	1.20	1.15	1.09	0.95	0.92	0.90	0.90	46.	Résultat net
47.	Provisions (net)	0.25	0.35	0.61	0.39	0.40	0.43	0.38	0.44	0.50	0.53	47.	Provisions (nettes)
	a. Provisions on loans	0.24	0.35	0.57	0.38	0.39	0.42	0.38	0.42	0.47	0.50		*a. Provisions sur prêts*
	b. Provisions on securities												*b. Provisions sur titres*
	c. Other	..	..	0.05	0.01	0.01	0.01	-	0.03	0.03	0.03		*c. Autres*
48.	Profit before tax	0.95	0.90	0.70	0.81	0.76	0.65	0.57	0.48	0.40	0.37	48.	Bénéfices avant impôt
49.	Income tax	0.61	0.56	0.39	0.50	0.48	0.40	0.35	0.27	0.21	0.15	49.	Impôt sur le revenu
50.	Profit after tax	0.34	0.34	0.31	0.31	0.28	0.25	0.22	0.21	0.19	0.22	50.	Bénéfices après impôt
51.	Distributed profit	0.22	0.23	0.21	0.21	0.20	0.19	0.17	0.17	0.21	0.17	51.	Bénéfices distribués
52.	Retained profit	0.11	0.11	0.10	0.10	0.08	0.06	0.05	0.04	-0.02	0.04	52.	Bénéfices mis en réserve
	% of gross income												**% du total du résultat brut**
53.	Net interest income	80.17	80.43	81.73	81.46	81.03	79.76	77.58	77.30	74.64	74.02	53.	Produits financiers nets
54.	Non-interest income (net)	19.83	19.57	18.27	18.54	18.97	20.24	22.42	22.70	25.36	25.98	54.	Produits non financiers (nets)
	a. Fees and commissions receivable	..	15.76	15.93	15.35	15.83	16.90	18.45	21.18	23.10	19.92		*a. Frais et commissions à recevoir*
	b. Fees and commissions payable	..	1.05	1.08	1.13	1.22	1.32	1.67	1.97	2.24	2.04		*b. Frais et commissions à payer*
	c. Net profits or loss on financial operations	..	1.16	-0.10	0.94	0.82	0.63	0.57	0.29	0.13	-0.22		*c. Profits ou pertes nets sur opérations financières*
	d. Other	..	3.71	3.51	3.38	3.53	4.02	5.08	3.19	4.37	8.32		*d. Autres*
55.	Operating expenses	68.98	68.08	65.92	67.81	67.85	68.69	71.13	71.46	72.67	72.44	55.	Frais d'exploitation
	a. Staff costs	43.15	41.16	39.90	40.81	40.48	40.67	41.40	41.78	42.00	42.31		*a. Dépenses en personnel*
	b. Property costs												*b. Dépenses en immobilier*
	c. Other	..	26.92	26.03	27.01	27.38	28.01	29.73	29.68	30.67	30.13		*c. Autres*
56.	Net income	31.02	31.92	34.08	32.19	32.15	31.31	28.87	28.54	27.33	27.56	56.	Résultat net
57.	Provisions (net)	6.37	9.02	15.88	10.41	11.09	12.45	11.58	13.68	15.20	16.25	57.	Provisions (nettes)
	a. Provisions on loans	6.34	8.98	14.70	10.22	10.95	12.21	11.48	12.87	14.43	15.37		*a. Provisions sur prêts*
	b. Provisions on securities												*b. Provisions sur titres*
	c. Other	..	0.04	1.18	0.18	0.14	0.24	0.10	0.82	0.76	0.88		*c. Autres*
58.	Profit before tax	24.64	22.90	18.20	21.78	21.06	18.87	17.28	14.86	12.13	11.31	58.	Bénéfices avant impôt
59.	Income tax	15.92	14.25	10.23	13.49	13.30	11.52	10.48	8.28	6.35	4.64	59.	Impôt sur le revenu
60.	Profit after tax	8.72	8.66	7.97	8.29	7.75	7.35	6.80	6.58	5.78	6.67	60.	Bénéfices après impôt
	% of net income												**% du total du résultat net**
61.	Provisions (net)	20.55	28.25	46.59	32.33	34.50	39.75	40.13	47.95	55.62	58.98	61.	Provisions (nettes)
	a. Provisions on loans	20.45	28.12	43.13	31.76	34.05	38.99	39.79	45.09	52.82	55.78		*a. Provisions sur prêts*
	b. Provisions on securities												*b. Provisions sur titres*
	c. Other	..	0.13	3.46	0.57	0.44	0.77	0.34	2.86	2.80	3.20		*c. Autres*
62.	Profit before tax	79.45	71.75	53.41	67.67	65.50	60.25	59.87	52.05	44.38	41.02	62.	Bénéfices avant impôt
63.	Income tax	51.32	44.63	30.02	41.91	41.38	36.79	36.32	29.00	23.23	16.82	63.	Impôt sur le revenu
64.	Profit after tax	28.13	27.12	23.39	25.76	24.12	23.46	23.55	23.05	21.15	24.20	64.	Bénéfices après impôt

Per cent

Pourcentage

BALANCE SHEET ANALYSIS

ANALYSE DU BILAN

% of year-end balance sheet total

% du total du bilan en fin d'exercice

	1992	1993[1]	1994	1995	1996	1997	1998	1999	2000	2001		
Assets												**Actif**
65. Cash & balance with Central bank	3.31	2.50	2.33	2.09	2.12	2.00	1.76	2.08	2.21	2.60	65.	Caisse & solde auprès de la Banque centrale
66. Interbank deposits	15.11	16.35	13.47	14.09	13.47	13.20	13.29	12.97	11.39	12.28	66.	Dépôts interbancaires
67. Loans	60.17	58.22	59.31	60.28	60.37	60.73	60.70	60.39	62.31	60.93	67.	Prêts
68. Securities	18.18	20.00	22.01	20.69	21.22	21.33	21.49	21.11	20.59	20.83	68.	Valeurs mobilières
69. Other assets	3.23	2.92	2.88	2.85	2.82	2.74	2.75	3.45	3.51	3.35	69.	Autres actifs
Liabilities												**Passif**
70. Capital & reserves	4.03	4.15	4.36	4.52	4.66	4.80	4.80	4.89	5.10	5.04	70.	Capital et réserves
71. Borrowing from Central bank	2.50	1.84	1.97	1.82	1.82	1.88	1.53	0.85	1.26	0.73	71.	Emprunts auprès de la Banque centrale
72. Interbank deposits	7.58	8.49	9.83	10.46	10.98	11.62	12.50	13.50	13.91	13.55	72.	Dépôts interbancaires
73. Non-bank deposits	79.37	78.75	76.56	75.20	74.47	73.48	73.03	71.82	70.30	71.37	73.	Dépôts non bancaires
74. Bonds	3.38	3.56	4.17	4.84	4.90	5.19	5.18	5.39	5.75	5.65	74.	Obligations
75. Other liabilities	3.14	3.22	3.12	3.16	3.16	3.03	2.95	3.56	3.69	3.66	75.	Autres engagements
Memorandum items												***Pour mémoire***
76. *Short-term securities*	*2.78*	*3.32*	*3.07*	*3.02*	*2.88*	*2.90*	*2.14*	*0.25*	*0.31*	*0.38*	*76.*	*Titres à court terme*
77. *Bonds*	*14.51*	*15.49*	*17.62*	*16.34*	*16.90*	*16.60*	*16.92*	*17.42*	*16.34*	*15.89*	*77.*	*Obligations*
78. *Shares and participations*	*0.89*	*1.19*	*1.32*	*1.33*	*1.44*	*1.84*	*2.43*	*3.43*	*3.93*	*4.57*	*78.*	*Actions et participations*
79. *Claims on non-residents*	*1.15*	*2.02*	*1.84*	*1.73*	*1.61*	*1.62*	*1.58*	*1.77*	*2.32*	*3.26*	*79.*	*Créances sur des non-résidents*
80. *Liabilities to non-residents*	*1.06*	*1.19*	*1.31*	*1.44*	*1.60*	*1.75*	*1.96*	*2.25*	*2.41*	*2.44*	*80.*	*Engagements envers des non-résidents*

* See notes on previous pages.

* *Voir les notes en pages précédentes.*

GREECE

Commercial banks

GRECE

Banques commerciales

Million euros / *Million d'euros*

	1992	1993	1994	1995	1996	1997	1998	1999	2000[2]	2001		
INCOME STATEMENT												**COMPTE DE RESULTATS**
1. Interest income	4206	4665	5347	5170	5650	6022	7699	8493	10794	8675	1.	Produits financiers
2. Interest expenses	3682	4061	4758	4184	4564	4581	5765	5975	7363	4786	2.	Frais financiers
3. Net interest income	524	604	589	986	1086	1441	1935	2517	3432	3889	3.	Produits financiers nets
4. Non-interest income (net)	719	840	1233	1012	1214	1410	1536	3484	2754	2191	4.	Produits non financiers (nets)
a. Fees and commissions receivable	388	456	661	593	676	716	772	1224	1220	935	a.	Frais et commissions à recevoir
b. Fees and commissions payable	4	14	21	33	36	61	83	78	262	239	b.	Frais et commissions à payer
c. Net profits or loss on financial operations	236	271	360	222	407	494	522	2154	1336	836	c.	Profits ou pertes nets sur opérations financières
d. Other (1)	98	128	233	230	168	262	325	184	460	660	d.	Autres (1)
5. Gross income	1242	1444	1822	1998	2300	2851	3470	6001	6186	6080	5.	Résultat brut
6. Operating expenses	758	906	1084	1284	1569	1801	2056	2497	3296	3551	6.	Frais d'exploitation
a. Staff costs	543	629	762	893	1082	1194	1343	1527	1971	2074	a.	Dépenses en personnel
b. Property costs	54	62	74	101	120	144	183	229	380	442	b.	Dépenses en immobilier
c. Other	162	215	248	290	368	464	530	742	945	1035	c.	Autres
7. Net income	484	538	738	714	730	1049	1415	3503	2890	2529	7.	Résultat net
8. Provisions (net)	105	131	170	122	299	414	457	672	510	510	8.	Provisions (nettes)
a. Provisions on loans	97	130	163	110	286	395	419	596	477	482	a.	Provisions sur prêts
b. Provisions on securities	2	-	1	-	1	6	8	2	22	8	b.	Provisions sur titres
c. Other	7	1	6	11	12	13	29	74	11	20	c.	Autres
9. Profit before tax	379	407	568	592	431	635	958	2831	2380	2019	9.	Bénéfices avant impôt
10. Income tax	123	135	160	169	163	189	356	587	611	564	10.	Impôt sur le revenu
11. Profit after tax	255	272	408	423	268	447	602	2244	1769	1455	11.	Bénéfices après impôt
12. Distributed profit	124	159	217	239	149	257	408	681	795	804	12.	Bénéfices distribués
13. Retained profit	131	113	191	185	119	190	194	1563	973	651	13.	Bénéfices mis en réserve
BALANCE SHEET												**BILAN**
Assets												**Actif**
14. Cash & balance with Central bank	6326	7310	8328	10932	10339	12293	12519	16314	16670	10086	14.	Caisse & solde auprès de la Banque centrale
15. Interbank deposits	2338	3231	5008	5694	6191	9367	8830	9705	13023	14471	15.	Dépôts interbancaires
16. Loans	8625	9857	11323	14049	18379	22190	30050	37915	60702	72373	16.	Prêts
17. Securities	13034	15133	16110	17442	19083	22688	27725	35789	42453	48204	17.	Valeurs mobilières
18. Other assets	5231	5924	4222	1946	4307	3024	3723	3918	5761	6682	18.	Autres actifs
Liabilities												**Passif**
19. Capital & reserves	1639	1887	2191	2425	2607	3548	4954	10246	12390	14095	19.	Capital et réserves
20. Borrowing from Central bank	73	77	66	728	413	2047	1947	2482	691	72	20.	Emprunts auprès de la Banque centrale
21. Interbank deposits	779	1161	2759	4452	3594	4845	3252	5512	10707	9689	21.	Dépôts interbancaires
22. Non-bank deposits	27683	32557	33806	36786	43852	54846	64476	70137	88098	97532	22.	Dépôts non bancaires
23. Bonds	350	353	352	352	303	253	500	237	140	127	23.	Obligations
24. Other liabilities	5028	5421	5817	5321	7532	4022	7718	15027	26584	30303	24.	Autres engagements
Balance sheet total	35553	41455	44991	50064	58299	69562	82846	103641	138610	151817		**Total du bilan**
25. End-year total	35553	41455	44991	50064	58299	69562	82846	103641	138610	151817	25.	En fin d'exercice
26. Average total	32813	38516	43219	47102	54773	63931	79896	93244	127817	145654	26.	Moyen

GREECE
Commercial banks

Million euros	1992	1993	1994	1995	1996	1997	1998	1999	2000[2]	2001
Memorandum items										
27. Short-term securities	2248	688	995	1227	352	760	309	295	283	176
28. Bonds	9374	12786	12854	13994	15873	19729	24109	30101	33620	38599
29. Shares and participations	1412	1659	2261	2221	2858	2200	3306	5393	8550	9430
30. Claims on non-residents	..	..	..	..	..	..	..	..	..	..
31. Liabilities to non-residents	..	..	..	..	..	..	..	..	..	..
Capital adequacy										
32. Tier 1 Capital	..	..	..	..	..	..	..	..	..	..
33. Tier 2 Capital	..	..	..	..	..	..	..	..	..	..
34. Supervisory deductions	..	..	..	..	..	..	..	..	..	..
35. Total net capital resources	..	..	..	2345	2684	3675	4806	10373	10531	11058
36. Risk-weighted assets	..	..	..	17748	25731	33202	40187	56939	74281	88149
SUPPLEMENTARY INFORMATION										
37. Number of institutions	19	20	19	18	20	19	19	16	17	20
38. Number of branches	1154	1200	1244	1469	1599	1788	2048	2070	2670	2766
39. Number of employees (x 1000)	37	38	40	40	43	44	46	47	53	52

1 Other non-interest income (item 4.d) inclduesdividend income on shares and participation.

2 Break in series in 2000 : the composition of commercial banks and large commercial banks has been modified.

Notes

Commercial banks are incorporated in Greece.

GREECE
Banques commerciales

Million d'euros

Pour mémoire

27. Titres à court terme
28. Obligations
29. Actions et participations
30. Créances sur des non-résidents
31. Engagements envers des non-résidents

Solvabilité

32. Fonds propres de base
33. Fonds propres complémentaires
34. Eléments à déduire des fonds propres
35. Total net des ressources en capital
36. Actifs pondérés des risques

RENSEIGNEMENTS COMPLEMENTAIRES

37. Nombre d'institutions
38. Nombre de succursales
39. Nombre de salariés (x 1000)

1 Les Autres produits non financiers (poste 4.d) incluent les revenus de dividendes d'actions et de participations.

2 Rupture de série en 2000 : La composition des catégories de banques commerciales et des grandes banques commerciales a changé.

Notes

Les banques commerciales sont celles de droit grec.

GREECE
Commercial banks

GREECE
Banques commerciales

Per cent — *Pourcentage*

INCOME STATEMENT ANALYSIS — ANALYSE DU COMPTE DE RESULTATS

% of average balance sheet total — % du total moyen du bilan

	English	1992	1993	1994	1995	1996	1997	1998	1999	2000[2]	2001	French
40.	Interest income	12.82	12.11	12.37	10.98	10.32	9.42	9.64	9.11	8.44	5.96	Produits financiers
41.	Interest expenses	11.22	10.54	11.01	8.88	8.33	7.17	7.22	6.41	5.76	3.29	Frais financiers
42.	Net interest income	1.60	1.57	1.36	2.09	1.98	2.25	2.42	2.70	2.69	2.67	Produits financiers nets
43.	Non-interest income (net)	2.19	2.18	2.85	2.15	2.22	2.21	1.92	3.74	2.15	1.50	Produits non financiers (nets)
	a. Fees and commissions receivable	*1.18*	*1.18*	*1.53*	*1.26*	*1.23*	*1.12*	*0.97*	*1.31*	*0.95*	*0.64*	*a. Frais et commissions à recevoir*
	b. Fees and commissions payable	*0.01*	*0.04*	*0.05*	*0.07*	*0.07*	*0.10*	*0.10*	*0.08*	*0.20*	*0.16*	*b. Frais et commissions à payer*
	c. Net profits or loss on financial operations	*0.72*	*0.70*	*0.83*	*0.47*	*0.74*	*0.77*	*0.65*	*2.31*	*1.05*	*0.57*	*c. Profits ou pertes nets sur opérations financières*
	d. Other	*0.30*	*0.33*	*0.54*	*0.49*	*0.31*	*0.41*	*0.41*	*0.20*	*0.36*	*0.45*	*d. Autres*
44.	Gross income	3.79	3.75	4.22	4.24	4.20	4.46	4.34	6.44	4.84	4.17	Résultat brut
45.	Operating expenses	2.31	2.35	2.51	2.73	2.86	2.82	2.57	2.68	2.58	2.44	Frais d'exploitation
	a. Staff costs	*1.65*	*1.63*	*1.76*	*1.90*	*1.98*	*1.87*	*1.68*	*1.64*	*1.54*	*1.42*	*a. Dépenses en personnel*
	b. Property costs	*0.16*	*0.16*	*0.17*	*0.21*	*0.22*	*0.23*	*0.23*	*0.25*	*0.30*	*0.30*	*b. Dépenses en immobilier*
	c. Other	*0.49*	*0.56*	*0.57*	*0.62*	*0.67*	*0.73*	*0.66*	*0.80*	*0.74*	*0.71*	*c. Autres*
46.	Net income	1.48	1.40	1.71	1.52	1.33	1.64	1.77	3.76	2.26	1.74	Résultat net
47.	Provisions (net)	0.32	0.34	0.39	0.26	0.55	0.65	0.57	0.72	0.40	0.35	Provisions (nettes)
	a. Provisions on loans	*0.30*	*0.34*	*0.38*	*0.23*	*0.52*	*0.62*	*0.52*	*0.64*	*0.37*	*0.33*	*a. Provisions sur prêts*
	b. Provisions on securities	*0.01*	*-*	*-*	*-*	*-*	*0.01*	*0.01*	*-*	*0.02*	*0.01*	*b. Provisions sur titres*
	c. Other	*0.02*	*-*	*0.01*	*0.02*	*0.02*	*0.02*	*0.04*	*0.08*	*0.01*	*0.01*	*c. Autres*
48.	Profit before tax	1.16	1.06	1.31	1.26	0.79	0.99	1.20	3.04	1.86	1.39	Bénéfices avant impôt
49.	Income tax	0.37	0.35	0.37	0.36	0.30	0.30	0.45	0.63	0.48	0.39	Impôt sur le revenu
50.	Profit after tax	0.78	0.71	0.94	0.90	0.49	0.70	0.75	2.41	1.38	1.00	Bénéfices après impôt
51.	Distributed profit	0.38	0.41	0.50	0.51	0.27	0.40	0.51	0.73	0.62	0.55	Bénéfices distribués
52.	Retained profit	0.40	0.29	0.44	0.39	0.22	0.30	0.24	1.68	0.76	0.45	Bénéfices mis en réserve

% of gross income — % du total du résultat brut

	English	1992	1993	1994	1995	1996	1997	1998	1999	2000[2]	2001	French
53.	Net interest income	42.19	41.83	32.33	49.35	47.22	50.54	55.76	41.94	55.48	63.96	Produits financiers nets
54.	Non-interest income (net)	57.89	58.17	67.67	50.65	52.78	49.46	44.27	58.06	44.52	36.04	Produits non financiers (nets)
	a. Fees and commissions receivable	*31.24*	*31.58*	*36.28*	*29.68*	*29.39*	*25.11*	*22.25*	*20.40*	*19.72*	*15.38*	*a. Frais et commissions à recevoir*
	b. Fees and commissions payable	*0.32*	*0.97*	*1.15*	*1.65*	*1.57*	*2.14*	*2.39*	*1.30*	*4.24*	*3.93*	*b. Frais et commissions à payer*
	c. Net profits or loss on financial operations	*19.00*	*18.77*	*19.76*	*11.11*	*17.70*	*17.33*	*15.04*	*35.89*	*21.60*	*13.75*	*c. Profits ou pertes nets sur opérations financières*
	d. Other	*7.89*	*8.86*	*12.79*	*11.51*	*7.30*	*9.19*	*9.37*	*3.07*	*7.44*	*10.86*	*d. Autres*
55.	Operating expenses	61.03	62.74	59.50	64.26	68.22	63.17	59.25	41.61	53.28	58.40	Frais d'exploitation
	a. Staff costs	*43.72*	*43.56*	*41.82*	*44.69*	*47.04*	*41.88*	*38.70*	*25.45*	*31.86*	*34.11*	*a. Dépenses en personnel*
	b. Property costs	*4.35*	*4.29*	*4.06*	*5.06*	*5.22*	*5.05*	*5.27*	*3.82*	*6.14*	*7.27*	*b. Dépenses en immobilier*
	c. Other	*13.04*	*14.89*	*13.61*	*14.51*	*16.00*	*16.27*	*15.27*	*12.36*	*15.28*	*17.02*	*c. Autres*
56.	Net income	38.97	37.26	40.50	35.74	31.74	36.79	40.78	58.37	46.72	41.60	Résultat net
57.	Provisions (net)	8.45	9.07	9.33	6.11	13.00	14.52	13.17	11.20	8.24	8.39	Provisions (nettes)
	a. Provisions on loans	*7.81*	*9.00*	*8.95*	*5.51*	*12.43*	*13.85*	*12.07*	*9.93*	*7.71*	*7.93*	*a. Provisions sur prêts*
	b. Provisions on securities	*0.16*	*-*	*0.05*	*-*	*0.04*	*0.21*	*0.23*	*0.03*	*0.36*	*0.13*	*b. Provisions sur titres*
	c. Other	*0.56*	*0.07*	*0.33*	*0.55*	*0.52*	*0.46*	*0.84*	*1.23*	*0.18*	*0.33*	*c. Autres*
58.	Profit before tax	30.52	28.19	31.17	29.63	18.74	22.27	27.61	47.18	38.47	33.21	Bénéfices avant impôt
59.	Income tax	9.90	9.35	8.78	8.46	7.09	6.63	10.26	9.78	9.88	9.28	Impôt sur le revenu
60.	Profit after tax	20.53	18.84	22.39	21.17	11.65	15.68	17.35	37.39	28.60	23.93	Bénéfices après impôt

% of net income — % du total du résultat net

	English	1992	1993	1994	1995	1996	1997	1998	1999	2000[2]	2001	French
61.	Provisions (net)	21.69	24.35	23.04	17.09	40.96	39.47	32.30	19.18	17.65	20.17	Provisions (nettes)
	a. Provisions on loans	*20.04*	*24.16*	*22.09*	*15.41*	*39.18*	*37.65*	*29.61*	*17.01*	*16.51*	*19.06*	*a. Provisions sur prêts*
	b. Provisions on securities	*0.41*	*-*	*0.14*	*-*	*1.64*	*0.57*	*0.57*	*0.06*	*0.76*	*0.32*	*b. Provisions sur titres*
	c. Other	*1.45*	*0.19*	*0.81*	*1.54*	*-*	*1.24*	*2.05*	*2.11*	*0.38*	*0.79*	*c. Autres*
62.	Profit before tax	78.31	75.65	76.96	82.91	59.04	60.53	67.70	80.82	82.35	79.83	Bénéfices avant impôt
63.	Income tax	25.41	25.09	21.68	23.67	22.33	18.02	25.16	16.76	21.14	22.30	Impôt sur le revenu
64.	Profit after tax	52.69	50.56	55.28	59.24	36.71	42.61	42.54	64.06	61.21	57.53	Bénéfices après impôt

GREECE
Commercial banks

GRECE
Banques commerciales

Per cent — *Pourcentage*

BALANCE SHEET ANALYSIS — **ANALYSE DU BILAN**

% of year-end balance sheet total — **% du total du bilan en fin d'exercice**

	1992	1993	1994	1995	1996	1997	1998	1999	2000[2]	2001	
Assets											**Actif**
65. Cash & balance with Central bank	17.79	17.63	18.51	21.84	17.73	17.67	15.11	15.74	12.03	6.64	65. Caisse & solde auprès de la Banque centrale
66. Interbank deposits	6.58	7.79	11.13	11.37	10.62	13.47	10.66	9.36	9.40	9.53	66. Dépôts interbancaires
67. Loans	24.26	23.78	25.17	28.06	31.53	31.90	36.27	36.58	43.79	47.67	67. Prêts
68. Securities	36.66	36.50	35.81	34.84	32.73	32.62	33.47	34.53	30.63	31.75	68. Valeurs mobilières
69. Other assets	14.71	14.29	9.38	3.89	7.39	4.35	4.49	3.78	4.16	4.40	69. Autres actifs
Liabilities											**Passif**
70. Capital & reserves	4.61	4.55	4.87	4.84	4.47	5.10	5.98	9.89	8.94	9.28	70. Capital et réserves
71. Borrowing from Central bank	0.21	0.19	0.15	1.45	0.71	2.94	2.35	2.39	0.50	0.05	71. Emprunts auprès de la Banque centrale
72. Interbank deposits	2.19	2.80	6.13	8.89	6.16	6.97	3.93	5.32	7.72	6.38	72. Dépôts interbancaires
73. Non-bank deposits	77.86	78.54	75.14	73.48	75.22	78.84	77.83	67.67	63.56	64.24	73. Dépôts non bancaires
74. Bonds	0.98	0.85	0.78	0.70	0.52	0.36	0.60	0.23	0.10	0.08	74. Obligations
75. Other liabilities	14.14	13.08	12.93	10.63	12.92	5.78	9.32	14.50	19.18	19.96	75. Autres engagements
Memorandum items											*Pour mémoire*
76. Short-term securities	*6.32*	*1.66*	*2.21*	*2.45*	*0.60*	*1.09*	*0.37*	*0.28*	*0.20*	*0.12*	*76. Titres à court terme*
77. Bonds	*26.37*	*30.84*	*28.57*	*27.95*	*27.23*	*28.36*	*29.10*	*29.04*	*24.26*	*25.42*	*77. Obligations*
78. Shares and participations	*3.97*	*4.00*	*5.03*	*4.44*	*4.90*	*3.16*	*3.99*	*5.20*	*6.17*	*6.21*	*78. Actions et participations*
79. Claims on non-residents	:	:	:	:	:	:	:	:	:	:	*79. Créances sur des non-résidents*
80. Liabilities to non-residents	:	:	:	:	:	:	:	:	:	:	*80. Engagements envers des non-résidents*

* See notes on previous pages. * Voir les notes en pages précédentes.

142

GREECE
Large commercial banks

GREECE
Grandes banques commerciales

Million euros / Million d'euros	1992	1993	1994	1995	1996	1997	1998	1999	2000[2]	2001	
INCOME STATEMENT											**COMPTE DE RESULTATS**
1. Interest income	3532	3815	4229	4148	4426	4696	5972	6460	9466	7243	1. Produits financiers
2. Interest expenses	3185	3403	3878	3458	3681	3733	4653	4677	6536	4241	2. Frais financiers
3. Net interest income	348	412	351	691	745	963	1319	1782	2930	3001	3. Produits financiers nets
4. Non-interest income (net)	577	656	1026	783	885	1066	1225	2401	2338	2178	4. Produits non financiers (nets)
a. Fees and commissions receivable	305	341	532	463	488	496	523	752	1011	810	a. Frais et commissions à recevoir
b. Fees and commissions payable	4	13	18	28	30	55	68	33	235	211	b. Frais et commissions à payer
c. Net profits or loss on financial operations	183	213	302	147	253	440	494	1641	1215	968	c. Profits ou pertes nets sur opérations financières
d. Other (1)	93	116	210	202	174	186	276	41	347	610	d. Autres (1)
5. Gross income	925	1068	1377	1474	1631	2029	2545	4183	5268	5179	5. Résultat brut
6. Operating expenses	584	684	809	977	1144	1299	1510	1706	2743	2893	6. Frais d'exploitation
a. Staff costs	434	493	593	708	823	895	1027	1140	1707	1758	a. Dépenses en personnel
b. Property costs	34	39	48	71	79	94	128	144	309	349	b. Dépenses en immobilier
c. Other	116	151	167	198	243	309	355	422	727	786	c. Autres
7. Net income	341	384	568	497	486	730	1034	2478	2525	2286	7. Résultat net
8. Provisions (net)	72	89	130	81	238	350	361	353	413	394	8. Provisions (nettes)
a. Provisions on loans	71	88	130	80	236	336	346	294	388	378	a. Provisions sur prêts
b. Provisions on securities	-	-	-	-	-	6	-	-	-	-	b. Provisions sur titres
c. Other	1	1	-	1	2	8	15	59	17	16	c. Autres
9. Profit before tax	269	295	438	415	248	380	673	2124	2112	1892	9. Bénéfices avant impôt
10. Income tax	79	89	113	115	94	106	250	350	547	514	10. Impôt sur le revenu
11. Profit after tax	190	206	325	300	155	274	423	1774	1566	1378	11. Bénéfices après impôt
12. Distributed profit	87	117	166	178	91	179	287	388	719	736	12. Bénéfices distribués
13. Retained profit	103	89	160	122	64	95	136	1386	846	642	13. Bénéfices mis en réserve
BALANCE SHEET											**BILAN**
Assets											*Actif*
14. Cash & balance with Central bank	5616	6478	6980	9037	8435	10233	10316	12534	14677	7429	14. Caisse & solde auprès de la Banque centrale
15. Interbank deposits	1710	2371	3105	3933	4694	6505	4877	4146	10611	11268	15. Dépôts interbancaires
16. Loans	6731	7602	8563	10748	13215	16025	21527	27135	51508	60279	16. Prêts
17. Securities	11220	13427	14445	15806	16772	19751	23660	28215	36882	42691	17. Valeurs mobilières
18. Other assets	4731	4762	3639	1649	3419	2533	2645	2562	4473	6517	18. Autres actifs
Liabilities											*Passif*
19. Capital & reserves	1198	1401	1722	1843	1778	2451	2957	5744	9877	10004	19. Capital et réserves
20. Borrowing from Central bank	4	4	2	651	253	1037	1555	2040	547	71	20. Emprunts auprès de la Banque centrale
21. Interbank deposits	526	849	2362	3716	2545	3321	2174	3539	8502	7324	21. Dépôts interbancaires
22. Non-bank deposits	23529	27359	27683	30761	34831	43704	50444	53791	77038	83934	22. Dépôts non bancaires
23. Bonds	350	350	350	350	303	253	500	237	135	127	23. Obligations
24. Other liabilities	4401	4679	4612	3852	6826	4281	5395	9240	22050	26726	24. Autres engagements
Balance sheet total											**Total du bilan**
25. End-year total	30008	34641	36731	41173	46536	55047	63024	74592	118151	128185	25. En fin d'exercice
26. Average total	27804	32326	35686	38952	43854	50792	62727	68808	110390	123583	26. Moyen

GREECE

Large commercial banks

Million euros

	1992	1993	1994	1995	1996	1997	1998	1999	2000[2]	2001
Memorandum items										
27. Short-term securities	1485	472	829	896	215	674	243	197	68	160
28. Bonds	8560	11400	11517	12819	14028	17079	20785	24505	29763	34360
29. Shares and participations	1175	1555	2099	2091	2529	1998	2632	3513	7051	8171
30. Claims on non-residents	..	..	..	..	..	..	..	..	..	..
31. Liabilities to non-residents	..	..	..	..	..	..	..	..	..	..
Capital adequacy										
32. Tier 1 Capital	..	..	..	..	..	..	..	..	..	..
33. Tier 2 Capital	..	..	..	..	..	..	..	..	..	..
34. Supervisory deductions	..	..	..	..	..	..	..	..	..	..
35. Total net capital resources	..	..	1657	1733	1959	2706	3151	6028	8534	8972
36. Risk-weighted assets	..	..	11362	13615	19692	24728	27908	38546	61737	72541
SUPPLEMENTARY INFORMATION										
37. Number of institutions	4	4	4	4	4	4	4	4	5	5
38. Number of branches	824	843	856	1100	1128	1268	1425	1430	2191	2200
39. Number of employees (x 1000)	28	28	29	31	31	31	33	32	44	42

1 Other non-interest income (item 4.d) includes dividend income on shares and participations.

2 Break in series in 2000 : the composition of commercial banks and large commercial banks has been modified.

Notes

• Large commercial banks are a sub-group of Commercial banks.

GRECE

Grandes banques commerciales

Million d'euros

Pour mémoire

27. Titres à court terme
28. Obligations
29. Actions et participations
30. Créances sur des non-résidents
31. Engagements envers des non-résidents

Solvabilité

32. Fonds propres de base
33. Fonds propres complémentaires
34. Eléments à déduire des fonds propres
35. Total net des ressources en capital
36. Actifs pondérés des risques

RENSEIGNEMENTS COMPLÉMENTAIRES

37. Nombre d'institutions
38. Nombre de succursales
39. Nombre de salariés (x 1000)

1 Les Autres produits non financier (poste 4.d.) incluent les revenus de dividendes d'actions et de participations.

2 Rupture de série en 2000 : La composition des catégories de banques commerciales et des grandes banques commerciales a changé.

Notes

• Les Grandes banques commerciales sont un sous-groupe des Banques commerciales.

GREECE

Large commercial banks

GREECE

Grandes banques commerciales

Per cent / *Pourcentage*

INCOME STATEMENT ANALYSIS / *ANALYSE DU COMPTE DE RESULTATS*

% of average balance sheet total / *% du total moyen du bilan*

	1992	1993	1994	1995	1996	1997	1998	1999	2000[2]	2001	
40. Interest income	12.70	11.80	11.85	10.65	10.09	9.25	9.52	9.39	8.58	5.86	*Produits financiers*
41. Interest expenses	11.46	10.53	10.87	8.88	8.39	7.35	7.42	6.80	5.92	3.43	*Frais financiers*
42. Net interest income	1.25	1.27	0.98	1.77	1.70	1.90	2.10	2.59	2.65	2.43	*Produits financiers nets*
43. Non-interest income (net)	2.08	2.03	2.88	2.01	2.02	2.10	1.95	3.49	2.12	1.76	*Produits non financiers (nets)*
a. Fees and commissions receivable	1.10	1.05	1.49	1.19	1.11	0.98	0.83	1.09	0.92	0.66	*a. Frais et commissions à recevoir*
b. Fees and commissions payable	0.01	0.04	0.05	0.07	0.07	0.11	0.11	0.05	0.21	0.17	*b. Frais et commissions à payer*
c. Net profits or loss on financial operations	0.66	0.66	0.85	0.38	0.58	0.87	0.79	2.38	1.10	0.78	*c. Profits ou pertes nets sur opérations financières*
d. Other	0.33	0.36	0.59	0.52	0.40	0.37	0.44	0.06	0.31	0.49	*d. Autres*
44. Gross income	3.33	3.30	3.86	3.78	3.72	3.99	4.06	6.08	4.77	4.19	*Résultat brut*
45. Operating expenses	2.10	2.12	2.27	2.51	2.61	2.56	2.41	2.48	2.48	2.34	*Frais d'exploitation*
a. Staff costs	1.56	1.53	1.66	1.82	1.88	1.76	1.64	1.66	1.55	1.42	*a. Dépenses en personnel*
b. Property costs	0.12	0.12	0.13	0.18	0.18	0.19	0.20	0.21	0.28	0.28	*b. Dépenses en immobilier*
c. Other	0.42	0.47	0.47	0.51	0.55	0.61	0.57	0.61	0.66	0.64	*c. Autres*
46. Net income	1.23	1.19	1.59	1.28	1.11	1.44	1.65	3.60	2.29	1.85	*Résultat net*
47. Provisions (net)	0.26	0.28	0.36	0.21	0.54	0.69	0.58	0.51	0.37	0.32	*Provisions (nettes)*
a. Provisions on loans	0.26	0.27	0.36	0.21	0.54	0.66	0.55	0.43	0.35	0.31	*a. Provisions sur prêts*
b. Provisions on securities						0.01	0.02	0.09	0.02	0.01	*b. Provisions sur titres*
c. Other						0.02			0.01		*c. Autres*
48. Profit before tax	0.97	0.91	1.23	1.07	0.57	0.75	1.07	3.09	1.91	1.53	*Bénéfices avant impôt*
49. Income tax	0.28	0.28	0.32	0.30	0.21	0.21	0.40	0.51	0.50	0.42	*Impôt sur le revenu*
50. Profit after tax	0.68	0.64	0.91	0.77	0.35	0.54	0.67	2.58	1.42	1.12	*Bénéfices après impôt*
51. Distributed profit	0.31	0.36	0.47	0.46	0.21	0.35	0.46	0.56	0.65	0.60	*Bénéfices distribués*
52. Retained profit	0.37	0.28	0.45	0.31	0.15	0.19	0.22	2.01	0.77	0.52	*Bénéfices mis en réserve*

% of gross income / *% du total du résultat brut*

	1992	1993	1994	1995	1996	1997	1998	1999	2000[2]	2001	
53. Net interest income	37.62	38.58	25.49	46.88	45.68	47.46	51.83	42.60	55.62	57.95	*Produits financiers nets*
54. Non-interest income (net)	62.38	61.42	74.51	53.12	54.26	52.54	48.13	57.40	44.38	42.05	*Produits non financiers (nets)*
a. Fees and commissions receivable	32.97	31.93	38.63	31.41	29.92	24.45	20.55	17.98	19.19	15.64	*a. Frais et commissions à recevoir*
b. Fees and commissions payable	0.43	1.22	1.31	1.90	1.84	2.71	2.67	0.79	4.46	4.07	*b. Frais et commissions à payer*
c. Net profits or loss on financial operations	19.78	19.94	21.93	9.97	15.51	21.69	19.41	39.23	23.06	18.69	*c. Profits ou pertes nets sur opérations financières*
d. Other	10.05	10.86	15.25	13.70	10.67	9.17	10.84	0.98	6.59	11.78	*d. Autres*
55. Operating expenses	63.14	64.04	58.75	66.28	70.14	64.02	59.33	40.78	52.07	55.86	*Frais d'exploitation*
a. Staff costs	46.92	46.16	43.06	48.03	50.46	44.11	40.35	27.25	32.40	33.94	*a. Dépenses en personnel*
b. Property costs	3.68	3.65	3.49	4.82	4.84	4.63	5.03	3.44	5.87	6.74	*b. Dépenses en immobilier*
c. Other	12.54	14.14	12.13	13.43	14.90	15.23	13.95	10.09	13.80	15.18	*c. Autres*
56. Net income	36.86	35.96	41.25	33.72	29.80	35.98	40.63	59.24	47.93	44.14	*Résultat net*
57. Provisions (net)	7.78	8.33	9.44	5.50	14.59	17.25	14.18	8.44	7.84	7.61	*Provisions (nettes)*
a. Provisions on loans	7.68	8.24	9.44	5.43	14.47	16.56	13.60	7.03	7.37	7.30	*a. Provisions sur prêts*
b. Provisions on securities						0.30	0.59	1.41	0.32	0.31	*b. Provisions sur titres*
c. Other	0.11	0.09		0.07	0.12	0.39			0.15		*c. Autres*
58. Profit before tax	29.08	27.62	31.81	28.15	15.21	18.73	26.44	50.78	40.09	36.53	*Bénéfices avant impôt*
59. Income tax	8.54	8.33	8.21	7.80	5.76	5.22	9.82	8.37	10.38	9.92	*Impôt sur le revenu*
60. Profit after tax	20.54	19.29	23.60	20.35	9.50	13.50	16.62	42.41	29.73	26.61	*Bénéfices après impôt*

% of net income / *% du total du résultat net*

	1992	1993	1994	1995	1996	1997	1998	1999	2000[2]	2001	
61. Provisions (net)	21.11	23.18	22.89	16.30	48.97	47.95	34.91	14.25	16.36	17.24	*Provisions (nettes)*
a. Provisions on loans	20.82	22.92	22.89	16.10	48.56	46.03	33.46	11.86	15.37	16.54	*a. Provisions sur prêts*
b. Provisions on securities						0.82	1.45	2.38	0.67	0.70	*b. Provisions sur titres*
c. Other	0.29	0.26		0.20	0.41	1.10			0.32		*c. Autres*
62. Profit before tax	78.89	76.82	77.11	83.50	51.03	52.05	65.09	85.71	83.64	82.76	*Bénéfices avant impôt*
63. Income tax	23.17	23.18	19.89	23.14	19.34	14.52	24.18	14.12	21.66	22.48	*Impôt sur le revenu*
64. Profit after tax	55.72	53.65	57.22	60.36	31.89	37.53	40.91	71.59	62.02	60.28	*Bénéfices après impôt*

GREECE

Large commercial banks

Per cent

BALANCE SHEET ANALYSIS

% of year-end balance sheet total

	1992	1993	1994	1995	1996	1997	1998	1999	2000[2]	2001
Assets										
65. Cash & balance with Central bank	18.72	18.70	19.00	21.95	18.13	18.59	16.37	16.80	12.42	5.80
66. Interbank deposits	5.70	6.84	8.45	9.55	10.09	11.82	7.74	5.56	8.98	8.79
67. Loans	22.43	21.95	23.31	26.10	28.40	29.11	34.16	36.38	43.60	47.03
68. Securities	37.39	38.76	39.33	38.39	36.04	35.88	37.54	37.83	31.22	33.30
69. Other assets	15.77	13.75	9.91	4.01	7.35	4.60	4.20	3.43	3.79	5.08
Liabilities										
70. Capital & reserves	3.99	4.04	4.69	4.48	3.82	4.45	4.69	7.70	8.36	7.80
71. Borrowing from Central bank	0.01	0.01	0.01	1.58	0.54	1.88	2.47	2.73	0.46	0.06
72. Interbank deposits	1.75	2.45	6.43	9.03	5.47	6.03	3.45	4.74	7.20	5.71
73. Non-bank deposits	78.41	78.98	75.37	74.71	74.85	79.39	80.04	72.11	65.20	65.48
74. Bonds	1.17	1.01	0.95	0.85	0.65	0.46	0.79	0.32	0.11	0.10
75. Other liabilities	14.67	13.51	12.56	9.36	14.67	7.78	8.56	12.39	18.66	20.85
Memorandum items										
76. Short-term securities	*4.95*	*1.36*	*2.26*	*2.18*	*0.46*	*1.22*	*0.39*	*0.26*	*0.06*	*0.12*
77. Bonds	*28.53*	*32.91*	*31.35*	*31.13*	*30.14*	*31.03*	*32.98*	*32.85*	*25.19*	*26.81*
78. Shares and participations	*3.92*	*4.49*	*5.71*	*5.08*	*5.43*	*3.63*	*4.18*	*4.71*	*5.97*	*6.37*
79. Claims on non-residents	*..*	*..*	*..*	*..*	*..*	*..*	*..*	*..*	*..*	*..*
80. Liabilities to non-residents	*..*	*..*	*..*	*..*	*..*	*..*	*..*	*..*	*..*	*..*

* See notes on previous pages.

GRECE

Grandes banques commerciales

Pourcentage

ANALYSE DU BILAN

% du total du bilan en fin d'exercice

Actif

65. Caisse & solde auprès de la Banque centrale
66. Dépôts interbancaires
67. Prêts
68. Valeurs mobilières
69. Autres actifs

Passif

70. Capital et réserves
71. Emprunts auprès de la Banque centrale
72. Dépôts interbancaires
73. Dépôts non bancaires
74. Obligations
75. Autres engagements

Pour mémoire

76. Titres à court terme
77. Obligations
78. Actions et participations
79. Créances sur des non-résidents
80. Engagements envers des non-résidents

* Voir les notes en pages précédentes.

HUNGARY / HONGRIE

Commercial banks / Banques commerciales

Million forints / Millions de forints

	English / Français	1994	1995	1996	1997	1998	1999	2000	2001
	INCOME STATEMENT / COMPTE DE RESULTATS								
1.	Interest income / Produits financiers	444205	607483	665689	780603	931768	873314	791692	839931
2.	Interest expenses / Frais financiers	297092	424429	470004	562593	661492	596552	481473	477347
3.	Net interest income / Produits financiers nets	147113	183054	195685	218010	270276	276762	310219	362584
4.	Non-interest income (net) / Produits non financiers (nets)	38580	89986	60310	12284	-250700	25774	88231	57951
	a. Fees and commissions receivable / Frais et commissions à recevoir	43274	52956	50747	62259	75812	88655	109273	145425
	b. Fees and commissions payable / Frais et commissions à payer	16760	20888	13759	20369	23593	27896	30338	42033
	c. Net profits or loss on financial operations / Profits ou pertes nets sur opérations financières	25590	27169	42017	40794	-34420	19590	62637	171575
	d. Other / Autres	-13524	30749	-18695	-70400	-268499	-54575	-53341	-217016
5.	Gross income / Résultat brut	185693	273040	255995	230294	19576	302536	398450	420535
6.	Operating expenses / Frais d'exploitation	96696	124118	148170	194374	241668	271043	294138	329292
	a. Staff costs / Dépenses en personnel	46868	56629	67007	81255	98796	106740	117619	136620
	b. Property costs / Dépenses en immobilier	14721	19357	26258	35633	47522	61867	70356	72060
	c. Other / Autres	35107	48132	54905	77486	95350	102436	106163	120612
7.	Net income / Résultat net	88997	148922	107825	35920	-222092	31493	104312	91243
8.	Provisions (net) / Provisions (nettes)	-31537	-67964	-24214	11881	98384	3514	1769	38123
	a. Provisions on loans / Provisions sur prêts	:	:	:	:	:	:	:	16060
	b. Provisions on securities / Provisions sur titres	:	:	:	:	:	:	:	22191
	c. Other / Autres	:	:	:	:	:	:	:	-128
9.	Profit before tax (1) / Bénéfices avant impôt (1)	21792	53707	77556	47013	-131303	36983	96760	148107
10.	Income tax / Impôt sur le revenu	9531	11944	16142	15131	12615	12980	19331	26046
11.	Profit after tax / Bénéfices après impôt	12261	41763	61414	31882	-143918	24003	77429	122061
12.	Distributed profit (2) / Bénéfices distribués (2)	8400	13296	18366	15284	17224	16187	18525	25586
13.	Retained profit / Bénéfices mis en réserve	-6797	17676	34812	18551	-159301	3478	53054	88991
	BALANCE SHEET / BILAN								
	Assets (3) / Actif (3)								
14.	Cash & balance with Central bank / Caisse & solde auprès de la Banque centrale	565570	769045	710801	1420229	1237318	1565749	1443839	1172106
15.	Interbank deposits / Dépôts interbancaires	331649	449656	822164	732241	790192	812531	772883	992003
16.	Loans / Prêts	1370161	1501974	1650039	2138117	2703358	3343794	4407229	5231807
17.	Securities / Valeurs mobilières	745239	792317	1060940	1082966	1631856	1395793	1561011	1885631
18.	Other assets (4) / Autres actifs (4)	276430	338814	381738	385213	365522	369500	376996	431248
	Liabilities / Passif								
19.	Capital & reserves (5) / Capital et réserves (5)	233840	314181	390435	536609	644474	723135	878595	1010807
20.	Borrowing from Central bank / Emprunts auprès de la Banque centrale	400538	300564	226516	182035	175572	123733	91146	44297
21.	Interbank deposits / Dépôts interbancaires	203513	276842	451133	864452	1241468	1162844	1373921	1477306
22.	Non-bank deposits / Dépôts non bancaires	1775556	2144025	2583907	3260794	3986233	4669507	5370807	6064029
23.	Bonds / Obligations	204608	286889	361024	322343	90767	109652	136023	269032
24.	Other liabilities / Autres engagements	254263	370967	475301	487156	421685	559952	577079	633882
	Balance sheet total / Total du bilan								
25.	End-year total / En fin d'exercice	3072318	3693468	4488316	5653389	6560199	7348823	8427571	9499353
26.	Average total (6) / Moyen (6)	2689706	3388252	3973635	4875677	5998644	6782272	7866137	8798497

Commercial banks

Million forints

	1994	1995	1996	1997	1998	1999	2000	2001		
Memorandum items										***Pour mémoire***
27. Short-term securities	..	..	..	..	..	..	..	..	27.	Titres à court terme
28. Bonds	638583	652592	905819	844025	1386009	1151152	1290278	1518737	28.	Obligations
29. Shares and participations	106656	139725	155121	238941	245847	244641	270733	366894	29.	Actions et participations
30. Claims on non-residents	..	..	..	..	656997	832241	727417	1120106	30.	Créances sur des non-résidents
31. Liabilities to non-residents	337945	511740	647436	920909	1206051	1398697	1596852	1671331	31.	Engagements envers des non-résidents
Capital adequacy										***Solvabilité***
32. Tier 1 Capital	209474	295794	377188	411345	458372	508073	665362	906999	32.	Fonds propres de base
33. Tier 2 Capital	33665	51567	65616	92093	113483	124801	127408	118928	33.	Fonds propres complémentaires
34. Supervisory deductions	37073	40575	61976	41381	23343	43235	51639	134467	34.	Eléments à déduire des fonds propres
35. Total net capital resources	206066	306786	380828	462057	548512	589639	741131	891460	35.	Total net des ressources en capital
36. Risk-weighted assets	1316844	1657272	2147913	2885496	3358288	3931156	4873164	5700006	36.	Actifs pondérés des risques
SUPPLEMENTARY INFORMATION										**RENSEIGNEMENTS COMPLEMENTAIRES**
37. Number of institutions	43	43	42	45	44	43	42	41	37.	Nombre d'institutions
38. Number of branches	..	1279	1181	1166	1117	1172	1131	1125	38.	Nombre de succursales
39. Number of employees (x 1000)	36	35	33	32	30	28	27	26	39.	Nombre de salariés (x 1000)

Banques commerciales

Millions de forints

1 Profit before tax (item 9) includes extraordinary profits/losses in the amount of million Ft -35515 in 1994, million Ft -27245 in 1995, million Ft -6054 in 1996, and million Ft 1047 in 1997.

2 Distributed profit (item 12) also includes the distributed profit paid from retained profit.

3 The assets include gross values, therefore the sum may not correspond to the end-year total (item 25).

4 Other assets (item 18) includes the provisions on loans, on interest, and on investments.

5 Capital and reserves (item 19) does not include the provisions generated on future and contingent liabilities, on exchange rate risk and on exchange rate loss.

6 Average balance sheet totals (item 26) are based on twelve end-month data.

1 Les Bénéfices avant impôt (poste 9) comprennent des bénéfices/pertes extraordinaires d'un montant de -35515 millions de Ft en 1994, -27245 millions de Ft en 1995, -6054 millions de Ft en 1996, et 1047 millions de Ft en 1997.

2 Les Bénéfices distribués (poste 12) prennent également en compte les bénéfices distribués payés à partir des bénéfices mis en réserve.

3 Les actifs présentés contiennent des valeurs brutes, c'est pourquoi la somme ne correspond pas au total du bilan en fin d'exercice (poste 25)

4 Autres actifs (poste 18) incluent les provisions sur les prêts, sur l'intérêt, et sur les investissements.

5 Capital et réserves (poste 19) ne comprend pas les provisions sur les dettes futures et imprévues, sur le risque de change et sur les pertes de change.

6 La moyenne du total des actifs/passifs (poste 26) est basée sur douze données de fin de mois.

HUNGARY / HONGRIE

Commercial banks / Banques commerciales

Per cent / *Pourcentage*

INCOME STATEMENT ANALYSIS / ANALYSE DU COMPTE DE RESULTATS

	English	French	1994	1995	1996	1997	1998	1999	2000	2001
	% of average balance sheet total	**% du total moyen du bilan**								
40.	Interest income	Produits financiers	16.52	17.93	16.75	16.01	15.53	12.88	10.06	9.55
41.	Interest expenses	Frais financiers	11.05	12.53	11.83	11.54	11.03	8.80	6.12	5.43
42.	Net interest income	Produits financiers nets	5.47	5.40	4.92	4.47	4.51	4.08	3.94	4.12
43.	Non-interest income (net)	Produits non financiers (nets)	1.43	2.66	1.52	0.25	-4.18	0.38	1.12	0.66
	a. Fees and commissions receivable	*a. Frais et commissions à recevoir*	*1.61*	*1.56*	*1.28*	*1.28*	*1.26*	*1.31*	*1.39*	*1.65*
	b. Fees and commissions payable	*b. Frais et commissions à payer*	*0.62*	*0.62*	*0.35*	*0.42*	*0.39*	*0.41*	*0.39*	*0.48*
	c. Net profits or loss on financial operations	*c. Profits ou pertes nets sur opérations financières*	*0.95*	*0.80*	*1.06*	*0.84*	*-0.57*	*0.29*	*0.80*	*1.95*
	d. Other	*d. Autres*	*-0.50*	*0.91*	*-0.47*	*-1.44*	*-4.48*	*-0.80*	*-0.68*	*-2.47*
44.	Gross income	Résultat brut	6.90	8.06	6.44	4.72	0.33	4.46	5.07	4.78
45.	Operating expenses	Frais d'exploitation	3.60	3.66	3.73	3.99	4.03	4.00	3.74	3.74
	a. Staff costs	*a. Dépenses en personnel*	*1.74*	*1.67*	*1.69*	*1.67*	*1.65*	*1.57*	*1.50*	*1.55*
	b. Property costs	*b. Dépenses en immobilier*	*0.55*	*0.57*	*0.66*	*0.73*	*0.79*	*0.91*	*0.89*	*0.82*
	c. Other	*c. Autres*	*1.31*	*1.42*	*1.38*	*1.59*	*1.59*	*1.51*	*1.35*	*1.37*
46.	Net income	Résultat net	3.31	4.40	2.71	0.74	-3.70	0.46	1.33	1.04
47.	Provisions (net)	Provisions (nettes)	-1.17	-2.01	-0.61	0.24	1.64	0.05	0.02	0.43
	a. Provisions on loans	*a. Provisions sur prêts*	:	:	:	:	:	:	:	*0.18*
	b. Provisions on securities	*b. Provisions sur titres*	:	:	:	:	:	:	:	*0.25*
	c. Other	*c. Autres*								
48.	Profit before tax	Bénéfices avant impôt	0.81	1.59	1.95	0.96	-2.19	0.55	1.23	1.68
49.	Income tax	Impôt sur le revenu	0.35	0.35	0.41	0.31	0.21	0.19	0.25	0.30
50.	Profit after tax	Bénéfices après impôt	0.46	1.23	1.55	0.65	-2.40	0.35	0.98	1.39
51.	Distributed profit	Bénéfices distribués	0.31	0.39	0.46	0.31	0.29	0.24	0.24	0.29
52.	Retained profit	Bénéfices mis en réserve	-0.25	0.52	0.88	0.38	-2.66	0.05	0.67	1.01
	% of gross income	**% du total du résultat brut**								
53.	Net interest income	Produits financiers nets	79.22	67.04	76.44	94.67	1380.65	91.48	77.86	86.22
54.	Non-interest income (net)	Produits non financiers (nets)	20.78	32.96	23.56	5.33	-1280.65	8.52	22.14	13.78
	a. Fees and commissions receivable	*a. Frais et commissions à recevoir*	*23.30*	*19.39*	*19.82*	*27.03*	*387.27*	*29.30*	*27.42*	*34.58*
	b. Fees and commissions payable	*b. Frais et commissions à payer*	*9.03*	*7.65*	*5.37*	*8.84*	*120.52*	*9.22*	*7.61*	*10.00*
	c. Net profits or loss on financial operations	*c. Profits ou pertes nets sur opérations financières*	*13.78*	*9.95*	*16.41*	*17.71*	*-175.83*	*6.48*	*15.72*	*40.80*
	d. Other	*d. Autres*	*-7.28*	*11.26*	*-7.30*	*-30.57*	*-1371.57*	*-18.04*	*-13.39*	*-51.60*
55.	Operating expenses	Frais d'exploitation	52.07	45.46	57.88	84.40	1234.51	89.59	73.82	78.30
	a. Staff costs	*a. Dépenses en personnel*	*25.24*	*20.74*	*26.18*	*35.28*	*504.68*	*35.28*	*29.52*	*32.49*
	b. Property costs	*b. Dépenses en immobilier*	*7.93*	*7.09*	*10.26*	*15.47*	*242.76*	*20.45*	*17.66*	*17.14*
	c. Other	*c. Autres*	*18.91*	*17.63*	*21.45*	*33.65*	*487.08*	*33.86*	*26.64*	*28.68*
56.	Net income	Résultat net	47.93	54.54	42.12	15.60	-1134.51	10.41	26.18	21.70
57.	Provisions (net)	Provisions (nettes)	-16.98	-24.89	-9.46	5.16	502.57	1.16	0.44	9.07
	a. Provisions on loans	*a. Provisions sur prêts*	:	:	:	:	:	:	:	*3.82*
	b. Provisions on securities	*b. Provisions sur titres*	:	:	:	:	:	:	:	*5.28*
	c. Other	*c. Autres*	:	:	:	:	:	:	:	*-0.03*
58.	Profit before tax	Bénéfices avant impôt	11.74	19.67	30.30	20.41	-670.73	12.22	24.28	35.22
59.	Income tax	Impôt sur le revenu	5.13	4.37	6.31	6.57	64.44	4.29	4.85	6.19
60.	Profit after tax	Bénéfices après impôt	6.60	15.30	23.99	13.84	-735.18	7.93	19.43	29.03
	% of net income	**% du total du résultat net**								
61.	Provisions (net)	Provisions (nettes)	-35.44	-45.64	-22.46	33.08	-44.30	11.16	1.70	41.78
	a. Provisions on loans	*a. Provisions sur prêts*	:	:	:	:	:	:	:	*17.60*
	b. Provisions on securities	*b. Provisions sur titres*	:	:	:	:	:	:	:	*24.32*
	c. Other	*c. Autres*	:	:	:	:	:	:	:	*-0.14*
62.	Profit before tax	Bénéfices avant impôt	24.49	36.06	71.93	130.88	59.12	117.43	92.76	162.32
63.	Income tax	Impôt sur le revenu	10.71	8.02	14.97	42.12	-5.68	41.22	18.53	28.55
64.	Profit after tax	Bénéfices après impôt	13.78	28.04	56.96	88.76	64.80	76.22	74.23	133.78

HUNGARY

Commercial banks

HONGRIE

Banques commerciales

Per cent — *Pourcentage*

BALANCE SHEET ANALYSIS — **ANALYSE DU BILAN**

% of year-end balance sheet total — **% du total du bilan en fin d'exercice**

	1994	1995	1996	1997	1998	1999	2000	2001	
Assets									**Actif**
65. Cash & balance with Central bank	18.41	20.82	15.84	25.12	18.86	21.31	17.13	12.34	65. Caisse & solde auprès de la Banque centrale
66. Interbank deposits	10.79	12.17	18.32	12.95	12.05	11.06	9.17	10.44	66. Dépôts interbancaires
67. Loans	44.60	40.67	36.76	37.82	41.21	45.50	52.30	55.08	67. Prêts
68. Securities	24.26	21.45	23.64	19.16	24.88	18.99	18.52	19.85	68. Valeurs mobilières
69. Other assets	9.00	9.17	8.51	6.81	5.57	5.03	4.47	4.54	69. Autres actifs
Liabilities									**Passif**
70. Capital & reserves	7.61	8.51	8.70	9.49	9.82	9.84	10.43	10.64	70. Capital et réserves
71. Borrowing from Central bank	13.04	8.14	5.05	3.22	2.68	1.68	1.08	0.47	71. Emprunts auprès de la Banque centrale
72. Interbank deposits	6.62	7.50	10.05	15.29	18.92	15.82	16.30	15.55	72. Dépôts interbancaires
73. Non-bank deposits	57.79	58.05	57.57	57.68	60.76	63.54	63.73	63.84	73. Dépôts non bancaires
74. Bonds	6.66	7.77	8.04	5.70	1.38	1.49	1.61	2.83	74. Obligations
75. Other liabilities	8.28	10.04	10.59	8.62	6.43	7.62	6.85	6.67	75. Autres engagements
Memorandum items									***Pour mémoire***
76. Short-term securities	*..*	*..*	*..*	*..*	*..*	*..*	*..*	*..*	*76. Titres à court terme*
77. Bonds	*20.79*	*17.67*	*20.18*	*14.93*	*21.13*	*15.66*	*15.31*	*15.99*	*77. Obligations*
78. Shares and participations	*3.47*	*3.78*	*3.46*	*4.23*	*3.75*	*3.33*	*3.21*	*3.86*	*78. Actions et participations*
79. Claims on non-residents	*..*	*..*	*..*	*..*	*10.01*	*11.32*	*8.63*	*11.79*	*79. Créances sur des non-résidents*
80. Liabilities to non-residents	*11.00*	*13.86*	*14.42*	*16.29*	*18.38*	*19.03*	*18.95*	*17.59*	*80. Engagements envers des non-résidents*

* See notes on previous pages. — * Voir les notes en pages précédentes.

ICELAND

Commercial banks and savings banks

ISLANDE

Banques commerciales et caisses d'épargne

Million Icelandic krónur / *Millions de couronnes islandaises*

	1992	1993	1994	1995¹	1996	1997	1998	1999	2000	2001	
INCOME STATEMENT											**COMPTE DE RESULTATS**
1. Interest income	26546	27916	22455	23772	25956	29901	34044	50721	75214	103414	1. Produits financiers
2. Interest expenses	14572	15366	10490	12024	13747	16674	19854	32946	53267	73609	2. Frais financiers
3. Net interest income	11974	12550	11965	11748	12209	13227	14190	17776	21947	29804	3. Produits financiers nets
4. Non-interest income (net)	4583	5334	6147	5449	6445	7328	9438	12457	13670	10154	4. Produits non financiers (nets)
a. Fees and commissions receivable	4235	4591	5004	4490	4805	5297	5890	7326	9932	12740	a. Frais et commissions à recevoir
b. Fees and commissions payable				225	407	474	742	1121	2327	2302	b. Frais et commissions à payer
c. Net profits or loss on financial operations	-134	474	435	392	795	1188	2503	2297	-1064	-1098	c. Profits ou pertes nets sur opérations financières
d. Other	482	269	708	792	1252	1317	1787	3955	7129	813	d. Autres
5. Gross income	16557	17884	18112	17197	18654	20555	23628	30232	35617	39959	5. Résultat brut
6. Operating expenses	12425	11584	12169	12483	12926	14232	16366	19104	22470	25171	6. Frais d'exploitation
a. Staff costs	6021	5727	5907	6506	6568	7331	8589	9663	11280	13016	a. Dépenses en personnel
b. Property costs (2)	1793	1692	1871	1910	832	5922	6573	7803	9523	10062	b. Dépenses en immobilier (2)
c. Other	4611	4165	4391	4067	5526	979	1204	1639	1667	2093	c. Autres
7. Net income	4132	6300	5943	4714	5728	6323	7262	11128	13148	14788	7. Résultat net
8. Provisions (net)	6802	6047	4715	2918	2959	2429	3032	3961	6132	8481	8. Provisions (nettes)
a. Provisions on loans	6802	6047	4715	2918	2959	2429	3032	3961	4575	8445	a. Provisions sur prêts
b. Provisions on securities		-	-	-	-	-	-	-	-	-	b. Provisions sur titres
c. Other		-	-	-	-	-	-	-	1557	37	c. Autres
9. Profit before tax	-2670	253	1228	1796	2769	3894	4231	7167	7016	6307	9. Bénéfices avant impôt
10. Income tax	97	421	480	527	741	982	547	1218	1953	-376	10. Impôt sur le revenu
11. Profit after tax	-2767	-168	748	1269	2028	2912	3684	5949	5063	6683	11. Bénéfices après impôt
12. Distributed profit	189	97	159	184	287	352	333	1183	2724	1340	12. Bénéfices distribués
13. Retained profit	-2956	-265	589	1085	1741	2560	3350	4766	2340	5343	13. Bénéfices mis en réserve
BALANCE SHEET											**BILAN**
Assets											**Actif**
14. Cash & balance with Central bank	14642	11901	11740	10570	13721	15634	14451	26756	26824	22078	14. Caisse & solde auprès de la Banque centrale
15. Interbank deposits	6211	10799	11511	14947	20818	37134	54758	67781	93728	118954	15. Dépôts interbancaires
16. Loans	185216	191021	194164	197695	219625	246502	320247	391148	593733	697605	16. Prêts
17. Securities	27861	31678	23456	26804	35153	47631	72398	99477	116220	148936	17. Valeurs mobilières
18. Other assets	11135	11462	10520	13243	13418	13587	14776	16380	31747	26413	18. Autres actifs
Liabilities											**Passif**
19. Capital & reserves	16718	19025	19885	20982	24157	26458	33127	40057	55272	68284	19. Capital et réserves
20. Borrowing from Central bank	2520	1599	3107	4841	1878	6494	19600	29511	36825	50020	20. Emprunts auprès de la Banque centrale
21. Interbank deposits	2404	1812	2147	8077	11381	16374	23574	32209	31771	40442	21. Dépôts interbancaires
22. Non-bank deposits	147998	157888	160736	164356	175401	191521	220580	260334	288659	333264	22. Dépôts non bancaires
23. Bonds	20666	22549	22273	23537	31027	42430	53213	61110	169067	197602	23. Obligations
24. Other liabilities	54759	53988	43243	41466	58891	77209	126536	178321	280658	324374	24. Autres engagements
Balance sheet total											**Total du bilan**
25. End-year total	245065	256861	251391	263258	302735	360486	476630	601543	862252	1013986	25. En fin d'exercice
26. Average total	241283	250963	254126	257325	282997	331611	418558	539086	731897	938119	26. Moyen

ICELAND

Commercial banks and savings banks

ISLANDE

Banques commerciales et caisses d'épargne

Million Icelandic krónur

Millions de couronnes islandaises

	1992	1993	1994	1995¹	1996	1997	1998	1999	2000	2001	
Memorandum items											**Pour mémoire**
27. Short-term securities	8361	7202	2191	6324	9058	5549	3235	5740	1635	10492	27. Titres à court terme
28. Bonds	15500	20453	17127	15695	19354	31831	54044	63872	65473	74677	28. Obligations
29. Shares and participations	4000	4023	4138	4785	6741	10251	15118	29864	49112	63769	29. Actions et participations
30. Claims on non-residents	4524	6812	8105	5213	6951	15320	10570	16169	22453	33360	30. Créances sur des non-résidents
31. Liabilities to non-residents	43769	43126	31843	27938	27845	69577	106951	162227	348659	415920	31. Engagements envers des non-résidents
Capital adequacy											**Solvabilité**
32. Tier 1 Capital	16718	19025	19885	20982	24157	26458	33076	40057	55272	68287	32. Fonds propres de base
33. Tier 2 Capital	1291	2680	2497	2120	3460	4374	6588	11889	18708	32980	33. Fonds propres complémentaires
34. Supervisory deductions	2327	2271	2313	2020	2748	3563	5218	7668	8552	8419	34. Eléments à déduire des fonds propres
35. Total net capital resources	15682	19434	20069	21082	24869	27232	34446	44278	65427	92848	35. Total net des ressources en capital
36. Risk-weighted assets	175718	182206	177710	183292	218778	259020	339960	423388	631488	742465	36. Actifs pondérés des risques
SUPPLEMENTARY INFORMATION											**RENSEIGNEMENTS COMPLEMENTAIRES**
37. Number of institutions	36	34	33	33	33	31	30	29	29	28	37. Nombre d'institutions
38. Number of branches	178	174	176	179	182	182	187	184	180	180	38. Nombre de succursales
39. Number of employees (x 1000)	3	3	3	3	3	3	3	3	3	3	39. Nombre de salariés (x 1000)

1 Break in series in 1995 due to new accounting regulations.

2 The breakdown of Property costs and Other operating expenses (items 6.b. and 6.c.) is estimated for the years 1995 and 1996.

Notes

. Includes all commercial banks and savings banks operating in Iceland. The figures are based on non-consolidated accounts.

1 Rupture dans les séries en 1995 suite aux nouvelles règles de comptabilité.

2 La ventilation des rubriques Dépenses en immobilier et Autres frais d'exploitation (poste 6.b. et poste 6.c.) est une estimation pour les années 1995 et 1996.

Notes

. Comprend toutes les banques commerciales et les caisses d'épargne en activité en Islande. Les chiffres sont basées sur des comptes non consolidés.

ICELAND
Commercial banks and savings banks

Per cent / *Pourcentage*

No.		1992	1993	1994	1995[1]	1996	1997	1998	1999	2000	2001	
	INCOME STATEMENT ANALYSIS											**ANALYSE DU COMPTE DE RESULTATS**
	% of average balance sheet total											**% du total moyen du bilan**
40.	Interest income	11.00	11.12	8.84	9.24	9.17	9.02	8.13	9.41	10.28	11.02	Produits financiers
41.	Interest expenses	6.04	6.12	4.13	4.67	4.86	5.03	4.74	6.11	7.28	7.85	Frais financiers
42.	Net interest income	4.96	5.00	4.71	4.57	4.31	3.99	3.39	3.30	3.00	3.18	Produits financiers nets
43.	Non-interest income (net)	1.90	2.13	2.42	2.12	2.28	2.21	2.25	2.31	1.87	1.08	Produits non financiers (nets)
	a. Fees and commissions receivable	*1.76*	*1.83*	*1.97*	*1.74*	*1.70*	*1.60*	*1.41*	*1.36*	*1.36*	*1.36*	*a. Frais et commissions à recevoir*
	b. Fees and commissions payable					*0.14*	*0.14*	*0.18*	*0.21*	*0.32*	*0.25*	*b. Frais et commissions à payer*
	c. Net profits or loss on financial operations	*-0.06*	*0.19*	*0.17*	*0.09*	*0.28*	*0.36*	*0.60*	*0.43*	*-0.15*	*-0.12*	*c. Profits ou pertes nets sur opérations financières*
	d. Other	*0.20*	*0.11*	*0.28*	*0.31*	*0.44*	*0.40*	*0.43*	*0.73*	*0.97*	*0.09*	*d. Autres*
44.	Gross income	6.86	7.13	7.13	6.68	6.59	6.20	5.65	5.61	4.87	4.26	Résultat brut
45.	Operating expenses	5.15	4.62	4.79	4.85	4.57	4.29	3.91	3.54	3.07	2.68	Frais d'exploitation
	a. Staff costs	*2.50*	*2.28*	*2.32*	*2.53*	*2.32*	*2.21*	*2.05*	*1.79*	*1.54*	*1.39*	*a. Dépenses en personnel*
	b. Property costs	*0.74*	*0.67*	*0.74*	*0.74*	*0.29*	*1.79*	*1.57*	*1.45*	*1.30*	*1.07*	*b. Dépenses en immobilier*
	c. Other	*1.91*	*1.66*	*1.73*	*1.58*	*1.95*	*0.30*	*0.29*	*0.30*	*0.23*	*0.22*	*c. Autres*
46.	Net income	1.71	2.51	2.34	1.83	2.02	1.91	1.74	2.06	1.80	1.58	Résultat net
47.	Provisions (net)	2.82	2.41	1.86	1.13	1.05	0.73	0.72	0.73	0.84	0.90	Provisions (nettes)
	a. Provisions on loans	*2.82*	*2.41*	*1.86*	*1.13*	*1.05*	*0.73*	*0.72*	*0.73*	*0.63*	*0.90*	*a. Provisions sur prêts*
	b. Provisions on securities											*b. Provisions sur titres*
	c. Other									*0.21*		*c. Autres*
48.	Profit before tax	-1.11	0.10	0.48	0.70	0.98	1.17	1.01	1.33	0.96	0.67	Bénéfices avant impôt
49.	Income tax	0.04	0.17	0.19	0.20	0.26	0.30	0.13	0.23	0.27	-0.04	Impôt sur le revenu
50.	Profit after tax	-1.15	-0.07	0.29	0.49	0.72	0.88	0.88	1.10	0.69	0.71	Bénéfices après impôt
51.	Distributed profit	0.08	0.04	0.06	0.07	0.10	0.11	0.08	0.22	0.37	0.14	Bénéfices distribués
52.	Retained profit	-1.23	-0.11	0.23	0.42	0.62	0.77	0.80	0.88	0.32	0.57	Bénéfices mis en réserve
	% of gross income											**% du total du résultat brut**
53.	Net interest income	72.32	70.17	66.06	68.31	65.45	64.35	60.06	58.80	61.62	74.59	Produits financiers nets
54.	Non-interest income (net)	27.68	29.83	33.94	31.69	34.55	35.65	39.94	41.20	38.38	25.41	Produits non financiers (nets)
	a. Fees and commissions receivable	*25.58*	*25.67*	*27.63*	*26.11*	*25.76*	*25.77*	*24.93*	*24.23*	*27.89*	*31.88*	*a. Frais et commissions à recevoir*
	b. Fees and commissions payable					*2.18*	*2.31*	*3.14*	*3.71*	*6.53*	*5.76*	*b. Frais et commissions à payer*
	c. Net profits or loss on financial operations	*-0.81*	*2.65*	*2.40*	*1.31*	*4.26*	*5.78*	*10.59*	*7.60*	*-2.99*	*-2.75*	*c. Profits ou pertes nets sur opérations financières*
	d. Other	*2.91*	*1.50*	*3.91*	*4.61*	*6.71*	*6.41*	*7.56*	*13.08*	*20.02*	*2.03*	*d. Autres*
55.	Operating expenses	75.04	64.77	67.19	72.59	69.29	69.24	69.27	63.19	63.09	62.99	Frais d'exploitation
	a. Staff costs	*36.37*	*32.02*	*32.61*	*37.83*	*35.21*	*35.67*	*36.35*	*31.96*	*31.67*	*32.57*	*a. Dépenses en personnel*
	b. Property costs	*10.83*	*9.46*	*10.33*	*11.11*	*4.46*	*28.81*	*27.82*	*25.81*	*26.74*	*25.18*	*b. Dépenses en immobilier*
	c. Other	*27.85*	*23.29*	*24.24*	*23.65*	*29.62*	*4.76*	*5.10*	*5.42*	*4.68*	*5.24*	*c. Autres*
56.	Net income	24.96	35.23	32.81	27.41	30.71	30.76	30.73	36.81	36.91	37.01	Résultat net
57.	Provisions (net)	41.08	33.81	26.03	16.97	15.86	11.82	12.83	13.10	17.22	21.22	Provisions (nettes)
	a. Provisions on loans	*41.08*	*33.81*	*26.03*	*16.97*	*15.86*	*11.82*	*12.83*	*13.10*	*12.84*	*21.13*	*a. Provisions sur prêts*
	b. Provisions on securities											*b. Provisions sur titres*
	c. Other									*4.37*	*0.09*	*c. Autres*
58.	Profit before tax	-16.13	1.41	6.78	10.44	14.84	18.94	17.91	23.71	19.70	15.78	Bénéfices avant impôt
59.	Income tax	0.59	2.35	2.65	3.06	3.97	4.78	2.32	4.03	5.48	-0.94	Impôt sur le revenu
60.	Profit after tax	-16.71	-0.94	4.13	7.38	10.87	14.17	15.59	19.68	14.22	16.72	Bénéfices après impôt
	% of net income											**% du total du résultat net**
61.	Provisions (net)	164.62	95.98	79.34	61.90	51.66	38.42	41.75	35.59	46.64	57.35	Provisions (nettes)
	a. Provisions on loans	*164.62*	*95.98*	*79.34*	*61.90*	*51.66*	*38.42*	*41.75*	*35.59*	*34.80*	*57.11*	*a. Provisions sur prêts*
	b. Provisions on securities											*b. Provisions sur titres*
	c. Other									*11.84*	*0.25*	*c. Autres*
62.	Profit before tax	-64.62	4.02	20.66	38.10	48.34	61.58	58.26	64.41	53.36	42.65	Bénéfices avant impôt
63.	Income tax	2.35	6.68	8.08	11.18	12.94	15.53	7.53	10.95	14.85	-2.54	Impôt sur le revenu
64.	Profit after tax	-66.97	-2.67	12.59	26.92	35.41	46.05	50.73	53.46	38.51	45.19	Bénéfices après impôt

ICELAND

Commercial banks and savings banks

ISLANDE

Banques commerciales et caisses d'épargne

Per cent — *Pourcentage*

	1992	1993	1994	1995¹	1996	1997	1998	1999	2000	2001		
BALANCE SHEET ANALYSIS												**ANALYSE DU BILAN**
% of year-end balance sheet total												**% du total du bilan en fin d'exercice**
Assets												**Actif**
65. Cash & balance with Central bank	5.97	4.63	4.67	4.02	4.53	4.34	3.03	4.45	3.11	2.18	65.	Caisse & solde auprès de la Banque centrale
66. Interbank deposits	2.53	4.20	4.58	5.68	6.88	10.30	11.49	11.27	10.87	11.73	66.	Dépôts interbancaires
67. Loans	75.58	74.37	77.24	75.10	72.55	68.38	67.19	65.02	68.86	68.80	67.	Prêts
68. Securities	11.37	12.33	9.33	10.18	11.61	13.21	15.19	16.54	13.48	14.69	68.	Valeurs mobilières
69. Other assets	4.54	4.46	4.18	5.03	4.43	3.77	3.10	2.72	6.58	2.60	69.	Autres actifs
Liabilities												**Passif**
70. Capital & reserves	6.82	7.41	7.91	7.97	7.98	7.34	6.95	6.66	6.41	6.73	70.	Capital et réserves
71. Borrowing from Central bank	1.03	0.62	1.24	1.84	0.62	1.80	4.11	4.91	4.27	4.93	71.	Emprunts auprès de la Banque centrale
72. Interbank deposits	0.98	0.71	0.85	3.07	3.76	4.54	4.95	5.35	3.68	3.99	72.	Dépôts interbancaires
73. Non-bank deposits	60.39	61.47	63.94	62.43	57.94	53.13	46.28	43.28	33.48	32.87	73.	Dépôts non bancaires
74. Bonds	8.43	8.78	8.86	8.94	10.25	11.77	11.16	10.16	19.61	19.49	74.	Obligations
75. Other liabilities	22.34	21.02	17.20	15.75	19.45	21.42	26.55	29.64	32.55	31.99	75.	Autres engagements
Memorandum items												*Pour mémoire*
76. *Short-term securities*	*3.41*	*2.80*	*0.87*	*2.40*	*2.99*	*1.54*	*0.68*	*0.95*	*0.19*	*1.03*	*76.*	*Titres à court terme*
77. *Bonds*	*6.32*	*7.96*	*6.81*	*5.96*	*6.39*	*8.83*	*11.34*	*10.62*	*7.59*	*7.36*	*77.*	*Obligations*
78. *Shares and participations*	*1.63*	*1.57*	*1.65*	*1.82*	*2.23*	*2.84*	*3.17*	*4.96*	*5.70*	*6.29*	*78.*	*Actions et participations*
79. *Claims on non-residents*	*1.85*	*2.65*	*3.22*	*1.98*	*2.30*	*4.25*	*2.22*	*2.69*	*2.60*	*3.29*	*79.*	*Créances sur des non-résidents*
80. *Liabilities to non-residents*	*17.86*	*16.79*	*12.67*	*10.61*	*9.20*	*19.30*	*22.44*	*26.97*	*40.44*	*41.02*	*80.*	*Engagements envers des non-résidents*

* See notes on previous pages.

* Voir les notes en pages précédentes.

154

IRELAND
All banks

IRLANDE
Ensemble des banques

Million euros — *Millions d'euros*

	1995	1996	1997	1998	1999	2000	2001	
INCOME STATEMENT								**COMPTE DE RESULTATS**
1. Interest income	5509	6085	9183	12408	15761	22060	23945	1. Produits financiers
2. Interest expenses	3364	3880	6457	9150	11076	16635	17816	2. Frais financiers
3. Net interest income	2144	2205	2726	3258	4684	5425	6129	3. Produits financiers nets
4. Non-interest income (net)	911	1044	1393	1919	2751	3444	3180	4. Produits non financiers (nets)
a. Fees and commissions receivable	*733*	*800*	*1062*	*1352*	*2126*	*2566*	*2908*	*a. Frais et commissions à recevoir*
b. Fees and commissions payable	*69*	*80*	*113*	*161*	*304*	*317*	*409*	*b. Frais et commissions à payer*
c. Net profits or loss on financial operations	*114*	*120*	*165*	*295*	*429*	*517*	*-174*	*c. Profits ou pertes nets sur opérations financières*
d. Other	*133*	*204*	*279*	*433*	*501*	*679*	*854*	*d. Autres*
5. Gross income	3055	3249	4119	5177	7436	8869	9309	5. Résultat brut
6. Operating expenses	1811	1871	2402	2690	3842	4446	5183	6. Frais d'exploitation
a. Staff costs	*1065*	*1090*	*1328*	*1495*	*2065*	*2455*	*1839*	*a. Dépenses en personnel*
b. Property costs	*128*	*142*	*174*	*228*	*336*	*358*	*565*	*b. Dépenses en immobilier*
c. Other	*618*	*639*	*900*	*967*	*1441*	*1633*	*2779*	*c. Autres*
7. Net income	1244	1378	1718	2487	3593	4423	4126	7. Résultat net
8. Provisions (net)	117	115	157	213	267	406	635	8. Provisions (nettes)
a. Provisions on loans	*115*	*114*	*155*	*206*	*266*	*404*	*635*	*a. Provisions sur prêts*
b. Provisions on securities	*2*	*-*	*2*	*2*	*1*	*2*	*1*	*b. Provisions sur titres*
c. Other	*-*	*1*	*1*	*5*	*-*	*-*	*-*	*c. Autres*
9. Profit before tax (1)	1082	1269	1684	2487	3479	4172	3480	9. Bénéfices avant impôt (1)
10. Income tax	309	364	450	649	804	1016	520	10. Impôt sur le revenu
11. Profit after tax	773	905	1235	1839	2675	3157	2960	11. Bénéfices après impôt
12. Distributed profit	296	331	415	641	854	1139	1113	12. Bénéfices distribués
13. Retained profit (2)	431	553	709	1045	1907	1895	1515	13. Bénéfices mis en réserve (2)
BALANCE SHEET								**BILAN**
Assets								**Actif**
14. Cash & balance with Central bank	472	530	682	1519	2359	2507	3748	14. Caisse & solde auprès de la Banque centrale
15. Interbank deposits	14951	17585	27722	33471	51337	59206	66789	15. Dépôts interbancaires
16. Loans	43954	51878	85872	99999	156500	181732	213589	16. Prêts
17. Securities	14944	18149	30035	43279	69617	82382	101193	17. Valeurs mobilières
18. Other assets (3)	5487	6438	11073	13526	38009	44346	45300	18. Autres actifs (3)
Liabilities								**Passif**
19. Capital & reserves	5347	6319	8842	11536	19269	23332	28320	19. Capital et réserves
20. Borrowing from Central bank	-	-	-	-	-	-	-	20. Emprunts auprès de la Banque centrale
21. Interbank deposits	17999	22855	41344	58180	93280	113100	134538	21. Dépôts interbancaires
22. Non-bank deposits	44876	49061	75622	83658	127660	145161	166730	22. Dépôts non bancaires
23. Bonds	6071	9295	17876	22031	36381	45255	55096	23. Obligations
24. Other liabilities	5516	7050	11700	16389	41232	43325	45935	24. Autres engagements
Balance sheet total								**Total du bilan**
25. End-year total	79809	94580	155383	191793	317822	370173	430618	25. En fin d'exercice
26. Average total	72154	87194	124982	173588	254808	343998	400395	26. Moyen

IRELAND
All banks

IRLANDE
Ensemble des banques

Million euros / *Millions d'euros*

	1995	1996	1997	1998	1999	2000	2001		
Memorandum items									**Pour mémoire**
27. Short-term securities	3794	1392	4147	4845	7510	9259	11797	27.	Titres à court terme
28. Bonds	10973	16323	24770	37685	61431	72052	87879	28.	Obligations
29. Shares and participations	177	434	1118	749	672	1031	1359	29.	Actions et participations
30. Claims on non-residents	40922	53254	92372	115389	192626	267544	280727	30.	Créances sur des non-résidents
31. Liabilities to non-residents	42270	53618	81934	108142	180019	246122	259155	31.	Engagements envers des non-résidents
Capital adequacy									**Solvabilité**
32. Tier 1 Capital	5141	6211	8086	10923	19442	23138	27931	32.	Fonds propres de base
33. Tier 2 Capital	1714	2226	3232	3636	6390	7958	9734	33.	Fonds propres complémentaires
34. Supervisory deductions	201	349	673	657	423	4677	5619	34.	Eléments à déduire des fonds propres
35. Total net capital resources	6654	8088	10644	13902	21611	26419	32046	35.	Total net des ressources en capital
36. Risk-weighted assets	47909	58222	81601	98764	159144	193558	231387	36.	Actifs pondérés des risques
SUPPLEMENTARY INFORMATION									**RENSEIGNEMENTS COMPLÉMENTAIRES**
37. Number of institutions	44	48	52	56	56	54	55	37.	Nombre d'institutions
38. Number of branches (4)	1300	1517	942	1026	977	880	970	38.	Nombre de succursales (4)
39. Number of employees (x 1000) (4)	33	32	33	34	38	35	41	39.	Nombre de salariés (x 1000) (4)

1 Profit before tax (item 9) is adjusted by (+) Income from Associate and (-) Exceptional items.

2 Retained profit (item 13) has been adjusted to include (+) Transfer from reserves and (-) Minority interest/Transfers to reserves/Non-equity dividends.

3 Other assets (item 18) and Other liabilities (item 24) include long-term assurance assets/liabilities attributable to policyholders.

4 The figures submitted for credit institutions are based on consolidated data therefore the figures for staff and branches include subsidiaries of Irish credit institutions located inside and outside the State. Figures submitted before 1999 were completed on a best efforts basis only.

Notes

. All figures are based on the published annual accounts of the credit institutions covered.

. "All banks" comprises the following categories of credit institutions :
  - branches and subsidiaries of Irish-authorised credit institutions
  - branches of non-EEA credit institutions
  - Subsidiaries of internation banks
  - building societies
  - One state-owned credit institutions.

1 La rubrique Bénéfices avant impot (poste 9) est corrigée par (+) Revenu d'entreprises associées et (-) Eléments exceptionnels.

2 Les Bénéfices mis en réserve (poste 13) a été ajusté pour prendre en compte (+) les transferts provenant des réserves et (-) intérêt minoritaires/Dotations aux réserves. Rémunération de titres hors actions.

3 Les Autres actifs (poste 18) et autres engagements (poste 24) comprennent les actifs/engagements d'assurance à long terme attribuables aux détenteurs de police.

4 Les données fournies pour les établissements de crédit sont basées sur des données consolidées; Ainsi les données pour le personnel et les succursales incluent les succursales des établissements de crédit irlandaises localisées à l'intérieur et à l'extérieur de l'Etat. Les données présentées avant 1999 étaient estimées.

Notes

. Toutes les données se réfèrent aux comptes annuels publiés par les établissements de crédit couverts.

. La catégorie "ensemble des banques" comprend les établissements de crédits suivants:
  - succursales et filiales d'établissements de crédit irlandais agréés.
  - succursales irlandaises d'établissements de crédit de pays non membres de l'IEEE
  - filiales irlandaises de banques internationales.
  - Caisse de crédit hypothécaire
  - un établissement de crédit public

IRELAND
All banks

IRLANDE
Ensemble des banques

Per cent / *Pourcentage*

INCOME STATEMENT ANALYSIS / **ANALYSE DU COMPTE DE RESULTATS**

	1995	1996	1997	1998	1999	2000	2001	
% of average balance sheet total								**% du total moyen du bilan**
40. Interest income	7.63	6.98	7.35	7.15	6.19	6.41	5.98	40. Produits financiers
41. Interest expenses	4.66	4.45	5.17	5.27	4.35	4.84	4.45	41. Frais financiers
42. Net interest income	2.97	2.53	2.18	1.88	1.84	1.58	1.53	42. Produits financiers nets
43. Non-interest income (net)	1.26	1.20	1.11	1.11	1.08	1.00	0.79	43. Produits non financiers (nets)
a. Fees and commissions receivable	*1.02*	*0.92*	*0.85*	*0.78*	*0.83*	*0.75*	*0.73*	*a. Frais et commissions à recevoir*
b. Fees and commissions payable	*0.10*	*0.09*	*0.09*	*0.09*	*0.12*	*0.09*	*0.10*	*b. Frais et commissions à payer*
c. Net profits or loss on financial operations	*0.16*	*0.14*	*0.13*	*0.17*	*0.17*	*0.15*	*-0.04*	*c. Profits ou pertes nets sur opérations financières*
d. Other	*0.18*	*0.23*	*0.22*	*0.25*	*0.20*	*0.20*	*0.21*	*d. Autres*
44. Gross income	4.23	3.73	3.30	2.98	2.92	2.58	2.33	44. Résultat brut
45. Operating expenses	2.51	2.15	1.92	1.55	1.51	1.29	1.29	45. Frais d'exploitation
a. Staff costs	*1.48*	*1.25*	*1.06*	*0.86*	*0.81*	*0.71*	*0.46*	*a. Dépenses en personnel*
b. Property costs	*0.18*	*0.16*	*0.14*	*0.13*	*0.13*	*0.10*	*0.14*	*b. Dépenses en immobilier*
c. Other	*0.86*	*0.73*	*0.72*	*0.56*	*0.57*	*0.47*	*0.69*	*c. Autres*
46. Net income	1.72	1.58	1.37	1.43	1.41	1.29	1.03	46. Résultat net
47. Provisions (net)	0.16	0.13	0.13	0.12	0.10	0.12	0.16	47. Provisions (nettes)
a. Provisions on loans	*0.16*	*0.13*	*0.12*	*0.12*	*0.10*	*0.12*	*0.16*	*a. Provisions sur prêts*
b. Provisions on securities	-	-	-	-	-	-	-	*b. Provisions sur titres*
c. Other								*c. Autres*
48. Profit before tax	1.50	1.46	1.35	1.43	1.37	1.21	0.87	48. Bénéfices avant impôt
49. Income tax	0.43	0.42	0.36	0.37	0.32	0.30	0.13	49. Impôt sur le revenu
50. Profit after tax	1.07	1.04	0.99	1.06	1.05	0.92	0.74	50. Bénéfices après impôt
51. Distributed profit	0.41	0.38	0.33	0.37	0.34	0.33	0.28	51. Bénéfices distribués
52. Retained profit	0.60	0.63	0.57	0.60	0.75	0.55	0.38	52. Bénéfices mis en réserve
% of gross income								**% du total du résultat brut**
53. Net interest income	70.19	67.87	66.17	62.94	63.00	61.16	65.84	53. Produits financiers nets
54. Non-interest income (net)	29.81	32.13	33.82	37.06	37.00	38.84	34.16	54. Produits non financiers (nets)
a. Fees and commissions receivable	*24.00*	*24.62*	*25.79*	*26.11*	*28.59*	*28.93*	*31.24*	*a. Frais et commissions à recevoir*
b. Fees and commissions payable	*2.26*	*2.47*	*2.74*	*3.10*	*4.08*	*3.58*	*4.40*	*b. Frais et commissions à payer*
c. Net profits or loss on financial operations	*3.71*	*3.69*	*4.01*	*5.70*	*5.77*	*5.83*	*-1.87*	*c. Profits ou pertes nets sur opérations financières*
d. Other	*4.36*	*6.28*	*6.77*	*8.36*	*6.73*	*7.65*	*9.17*	*d. Autres*
55. Operating expenses	59.27	57.60	58.31	51.96	51.67	50.13	55.68	55. Frais d'exploitation
a. Staff costs	*34.86*	*33.56*	*32.23*	*28.89*	*27.77*	*27.69*	*19.75*	*a. Dépenses en personnel*
b. Property costs	*4.19*	*4.38*	*4.23*	*4.40*	*4.52*	*4.04*	*6.07*	*b. Dépenses en immobilier*
c. Other	*20.22*	*19.66*	*21.85*	*18.68*	*19.38*	*18.41*	*29.86*	*c. Autres*
56. Net income	40.73	42.40	41.69	48.04	48.33	49.87	44.32	56. Résultat net
57. Provisions (net)	3.82	3.55	3.81	4.12	3.59	4.57	6.83	57. Provisions (nettes)
a. Provisions on loans	*3.76*	*3.50*	*3.76*	*3.98*	*3.58*	*4.55*	*6.82*	*a. Provisions sur prêts*
b. Provisions on securities	*0.06*	*0.01*	*0.04*	*0.04*	*0.02*	*0.02*	*0.01*	*b. Provisions sur titres*
c. Other	-	*0.04*	*0.02*	*0.10*	-	-	-	*c. Autres*
58. Profit before tax	35.42	39.05	40.89	48.04	46.79	47.05	37.38	58. Bénéfices avant impôt
59. Income tax	10.11	11.21	10.91	12.53	10.81	11.45	5.58	59. Impôt sur le revenu
60. Profit after tax	25.31	27.84	29.98	35.51	35.97	35.59	31.80	60. Bénéfices après impôt
% of net income								**% du total du résultat net**
61. Provisions (net)	9.38	8.36	9.14	8.58	7.44	9.17	15.40	61. Provisions (nettes)
a. Provisions on loans	*9.24*	*8.25*	*9.01*	*8.29*	*7.41*	*9.13*	*15.38*	*a. Provisions sur prêts*
b. Provisions on securities	*0.14*	*0.01*	*0.09*	*0.09*	*0.03*	*0.04*	*0.02*	*b. Provisions sur titres*
c. Other	-	*0.10*	*0.05*	*0.20*	-	-	-	*c. Autres*
62. Profit before tax	86.97	92.10	98.07	100.00	96.81	94.34	84.34	62. Bénéfices avant impôt
63. Income tax	24.83	26.44	26.17	26.08	22.37	22.97	12.60	63. Impôt sur le revenu
64. Profit after tax	62.13	65.66	71.90	73.93	74.44	71.38	71.74	64. Bénéfices après impôt

IRELAND
All banks

IRLANDE
Ensemble des banques

Per cent — *Pourcentage*

BALANCE SHEET ANALYSIS — **ANALYSE DU BILAN**

% of year-end balance sheet total — **% du total du bilan en fin d'exercice**

	1995	1996	1997	1998	1999	2000	2001	
Assets								**Actif**
65. Cash & balance with Central bank	0.59	0.56	0.44	0.79	0.74	0.68	0.87	65. Caisse & solde auprès de la Banque centrale
66. Interbank deposits	18.73	18.59	17.84	17.45	16.15	15.99	15.51	66. Dépôts interbancaires
67. Loans	55.07	54.85	55.26	52.14	49.24	49.09	49.60	67. Prêts
68. Securities	18.73	19.19	19.33	22.57	21.90	22.26	23.50	68. Valeurs mobilières
69. Other assets	6.88	6.81	7.13	7.05	11.96	11.98	10.52	69. Autres actifs
Liabilities								**Passif**
70. Capital & reserves	6.70	6.68	5.69	6.01	6.06	6.30	6.58	70. Capital et réserves
71. Borrowing from Central bank	-	-	-	-	-	-	-	71. Emprunts auprès de la Banque centrale
72. Interbank deposits	22.55	24.16	26.61	30.33	29.35	30.55	31.24	72. Dépôts interbancaires
73. Non-bank deposits	56.23	51.87	48.67	43.62	40.17	39.21	38.72	73. Dépôts non bancaires
74. Bonds	7.61	9.83	11.50	11.49	11.45	12.23	12.79	74. Obligations
75. Other liabilities	6.91	7.45	7.53	8.54	12.97	11.70	10.67	75. Autres engagements
Memorandum items								*Pour mémoire*
76. Short-term securities	*4.75*	*1.47*	*2.67*	*2.53*	*2.36*	*2.50*	*2.74*	*76. Titres à court terme*
77. Bonds	*13.75*	*17.26*	*15.94*	*19.65*	*19.33*	*19.46*	*20.41*	*77. Obligations*
78. Shares and participations	*0.22*	*0.46*	*0.72*	*0.39*	*0.21*	*0.28*	*0.32*	*78. Actions et participations*
79. Claims on non-residents	*51.28*	*56.31*	*59.45*	*60.16*	*60.61*	*72.28*	*65.19*	*79. Créances sur des non-résidents*
80. Liabilities to non-residents	*52.96*	*56.69*	*52.73*	*56.38*	*56.64*	*66.49*	*60.18*	*80. Engagements envers des non-résidents*

* See notes on previous pages.

* Voir les notes en pages précédentes.

Million euros — *Millions d'euros*

	1992	1993	1994	1995	1996	1997	1998	1999	2000	2001	
INCOME STATEMENT											**COMPTE DE RESULTATS**
1. Interest income	104712	113221	100504	112206	110925	99050	89202	73441	89229	100299	1. Produits financiers
2. Interest expenses	68276	75935	65265	73728	72866	63064	52756	36657	46991	51358	2. Frais financiers
3. Net interest income	36436	37287	35239	38478	38059	35986	36446	36784	42237	48942	3. Produits financiers nets
4. Non-interest income (net)	7449	13277	9968	9484	12275	14315	19591	21455	23814	20806	4. Produits non financiers (nets)
a. Fees and commissions receivable	4854	5179	5526	5093	5778	7965	11936	14419	17694	16351	a. Frais et commissions à recevoir
b. Fees and commissions payable	3482	2108	1357	1276	1431	1647	2025	2259	3111	3453	b. Frais et commissions à payer
c. Net profits or loss on financial operations	1100	181	-148	-328	-385	319	907	2016	1479	22	c. Profits ou pertes nets sur opérations financières
d. Other	4977	10025	5947	5995	8312	7678	8773	7279	7752	7887	d. Autres
5. Gross income	43884	50564	45207	47962	50334	50300	56037	58239	66052	69748	5. Résultat brut
6. Operating expenses	28802	30742	30939	32446	33583	34580	34184	35343	36972	38533	6. Frais d'exploitation
a. Staff costs	18373	19352	19989	20556	21486	21480	20730	20738	20917	21146	a. Dépenses en personnel
b. Property costs	8464	9011	8945	9493	9693	10628	11263	12331	13703	15047	b. Dépenses en immobilier
c. Other	1965	2380	2005	2397	2403	2472	2191	2274	2353	2340	c. Autres
7. Net income	15082	19822	14267	15516	16751	15720	21852	22896	29079	31214	7. Résultat net
8. Provisions (net)	6930	9288	10186	9989	9138	10142	7534	6478	6398	12492	8. Provisions (nettes)
a. Provisions on loans	5381	8748	6393	8812	6621	8483	7147	7114	6282	6977	a. Provisions sur prêts
b. Provisions on securities	1693	8	3496	-135	-409	-358	141	1905	466	952	b. Provisions sur titres
c. Other	-145	533	297	1313	2925	2017	245	-2541	-350	4563	c. Autres
9. Profit before tax	8152	10534	4081	5527	7614	5578	14319	16419	22681	18723	9. Bénéfices avant impôt
10. Income tax	4053	6746	2947	4360	4361	4186	6737	6490	8598	7429	10. Impôt sur le revenu
11. Profit after tax	4099	3787	1134	1167	3253	1392	7582	9929	14083	11294	11. Bénéfices après impôt
12. Distributed profit	1862	1749	1443	1746	2116	2318	4005	6047	7727	7428	12. Bénéfices distribués
13. Retained profit	2237	2039	-309	-579	1136	-925	3577	3882	6356	3866	13. Bénéfices mis en réserve
BALANCE SHEET											**BILAN**
Assets											**Actif**
14. Cash & balance with Central bank	68369	56280	48122	41118	42168	45462	11960	14788	14106	27396	14. Caisse & solde auprès de la Banque centrale
15. Interbank deposits	87041	96114	91999	88670	102805	109531	113356	127337	169280	155225	15. Dépôts interbancaires
16. Loans	526759	550362	558902	579133	583989	632519	676935	750849	857356	923053	16. Prêts
17. Securities	184316	198537	220306	202319	219507	203988	209181	196244	167825	157694	17. Valeurs mobilières
18. Other assets	355048	410176	423613	472876	510172	566458	596346	628847	687200	692808	18. Autres actifs
Liabilities											**Passif**
19. Capital & reserves	82948	87470	93891	93502	95507	100961	108702	118434	128986	133625	19. Capital et réserves
20. Borrowing from Central bank	4632	1421	1478	4135	988	1487	1075	475	156	617	20. Emprunts auprès de la Banque centrale
21. Interbank deposits	83569	94646	90079	89607	103784	111180	114489	124448	159670	148022	21. Dépôts interbancaires
22. Non-bank deposits	470261	508882	512708	518969	529044	491504	491361	504254	506903	535325	22. Dépôts non bancaires
23. Bonds	86174	100395	112157	111878	145808	204543	240406	253731	271107	294643	23. Obligations
24. Other liabilities	493948	518655	532628	566026	583511	648282	651743	716722	828944	843943	24. Autres engagements
Balance sheet total											**Total du bilan**
25. End-year total	1221533	1311469	1342942	1384117	1458642	1557958	1607776	1718063	1895767	1956176	25. En fin d'exercice
26. Average total	1103603	1222991	1287122	1314462	1369996	1469435	1573573	1633222	1786479	1889169	26. Moyen

ITALY / ITALIE

All banks / Ensemble des banques

Million euros / Millions d'euros

	1992	1993	1994	1995	1996	1997	1998	1999	2000	2001	
Memorandum items											**Pour mémoire**
27. Short-term securities	16835	39948	37370	24258	28525	17382	25035	17356	7845	12010	27. Titres à court terme
28. Bonds	167480	158589	182936	178061	190981	186605	184146	178888	159980	145684	28. Obligations
29. Shares and participations	21785	22725	26318	26911	29956	33618	44036	58124	68748	69701	29. Actions et participations
30. Claims on non-residents	87157	121646	109341	124285	157487	168792	176579	167916	172580	158770	30. Créances sur des non-résidents
31. Liabilities to non-residents	194301	198838	203828	187351	191813	216477	224471	246002	293114	299686	31. Engagements envers des non-résidents
Capital adequacy											**Solvabilité**
32. Tier 1 Capital	75729	82003	83952	85158	87190	92764	104204	115007	124143	131127	32. Fonds propres de base
33. Tier 2 Capital	17008	16687	15467	18946	19161	20368	25891	30870	40581	46050	33. Fonds propres complémentaires
34. Supervisory deductions	3446	3077	3230	3715	3160	3319	3466	3541	4200	5769	34. Eléments à déduire des fonds propres
35. Total net capital resources	89291	95613	96189	100389	103191	109814	126629	142335	160524	171407	35. Total net des ressources en capital
36. Risk-weighted assets	737871	740085	743057	797017	794388	864591	939278	1047233	1181523	1226673	36. Actifs pondérés des risques
SUPPLEMENTARY INFORMATION											**RENSEIGNEMENTS COMPLEMENTAIRES**
37. Number of institutions	1088	1051	977	959	917	916	901	861	828	821	37. Nombre d'institutions
38. Number of branches	19784	21297	22433	23370	24103	25170	26195	27135	28178	29259	38. Nombre de succursales
39. Number of employees (x 1000)	357	361	360	360	350	346	343	341	344	344	39. Nombre de salariés (x 1000)

Notes

. "All banks" comprises the following categories of banks:
 - Limited company banks
 - Co-operative banks
 - Main mutual banks
 - Central credit institutions
 - Branches of foreign banks

. Average balance sheet totals (item 26) are a weighted average of monthly data.

Notes

. "L'Ensemble des banques" regroupe les catégories suivantes:
 - Banques société anonyme
 - Banques mutualistes
 - Mutuelles principales
 - institutions centrales de crédit
 - Succursales de Banques étrangères

. La moyenne du total des actifs/passifs (poste 26) est une moyenne pondérée des données mensuelles.

ITALY
All banks

ITALIE
Ensemble des banques

Per cent / *Pourcentage*

INCOME STATEMENT ANALYSIS / **ANALYSE DU COMPTE DE RESULTATS**

		1992	1993	1994	1995	1996	1997	1998	1999	2000	2001	
	% of average balance sheet total											**% du total moyen du bilan**
40.	Interest income	9.49	9.26	7.81	8.54	8.10	6.74	5.67	4.50	4.99	5.31	Produits financiers
41.	Interest expenses	6.19	6.21	5.07	5.61	5.32	4.29	3.35	2.24	2.63	2.72	Frais financiers
42.	Net interest income	3.30	3.05	2.74	2.93	2.78	2.45	2.32	2.25	2.36	2.59	Produits financiers nets
43.	Non-interest income (net)	0.67	1.09	0.77	0.72	0.90	0.97	1.25	1.31	1.33	1.10	Produits non financiers (nets)
	a. Fees and commissions receivable	0.44	0.42	0.43	0.39	0.42	0.54	0.76	0.88	0.99	0.87	*a. Frais et commissions à recevoir*
	b. Fees and commissions payable	0.32	0.17	0.11	0.10	0.10	0.11	0.13	0.14	0.17	0.18	*b. Frais et commissions à payer*
	c. Net profits or loss on financial operations	0.10	0.01	-0.01	-0.02	-0.03	0.02	0.06	0.12	0.08	0.00	*c. Profits ou pertes nets sur opérations financières*
	d. Other	0.45	0.82	0.46	0.46	0.61	0.52	0.56	0.45	0.43	0.42	*d. Autres*
44.	Gross income	3.98	4.13	3.51	3.65	3.67	3.42	3.56	3.57	3.70	3.69	Résultat brut
45.	Operating expenses	2.61	2.51	2.40	2.47	2.45	2.35	2.17	2.16	2.07	2.04	Frais d'exploitation
	a. Staff costs	1.66	1.58	1.55	1.56	1.57	1.46	1.32	1.27	1.17	1.12	*a. Dépenses en personnel*
	b. Property costs	0.77	0.74	0.69	0.72	0.71	0.72	0.72	0.76	0.77	0.80	*b. Dépenses en immobilier*
	c. Other	0.18	0.19	0.16	0.18	0.18	0.17	0.14	0.14	0.13	0.12	*c. Autres*
46.	Net income	1.37	1.62	1.11	1.18	1.22	1.07	1.39	1.40	1.63	1.65	Résultat net
47.	Provisions (net)	0.63	0.76	0.79	0.76	0.67	0.69	0.48	0.40	0.36	0.66	Provisions (nettes)
	a. Provisions on loans	0.49	0.72	0.50	0.67	0.48	0.58	0.45	0.44	0.35	0.37	*a. Provisions sur prêts*
	b. Provisions on securities	0.15	0.00	0.27	-0.01	-0.03	-0.02	0.01	0.12	0.03	0.05	*b. Provisions sur titres*
	c. Other	-0.01	0.04	0.02	0.10	0.21	0.14	0.02	-0.16	-0.02	0.24	*c. Autres*
48.	Profit before tax	0.74	0.86	0.32	0.42	0.56	0.38	0.91	1.01	1.27	0.99	Bénéfices avant impôt
49.	Income tax	0.37	0.55	0.23	0.33	0.32	0.28	0.43	0.40	0.48	0.39	Impôt sur le revenu
50.	Profit after tax	0.37	0.31	0.09	0.09	0.24	0.09	0.48	0.61	0.79	0.60	Bénéfices après impôt
51.	Distributed profit	0.17	0.14	0.11	0.13	0.15	0.16	0.25	0.37	0.43	0.39	Bénéfices distribués
52.	Retained profit	0.20	0.17	-0.02	-0.04	0.08	-0.06	0.23	0.24	0.36	0.20	Bénéfices mis en réserve
	% of gross income											**% du total du résultat brut**
53.	Net interest income	83.03	73.74	77.95	80.23	75.61	71.54	65.04	63.16	63.95	70.17	Produits financiers nets
54.	Non-interest income (net)	16.97	26.26	22.05	19.77	24.39	28.46	34.96	36.84	36.05	29.83	Produits non financiers (nets)
	a. Fees and commissions receivable	11.06	10.24	12.22	10.62	11.48	15.83	21.30	24.76	26.79	23.44	*a. Frais et commissions à recevoir*
	b. Fees and commissions payable	7.93	4.17	3.00	2.66	2.84	3.27	3.61	3.88	4.71	4.95	*b. Frais et commissions à payer*
	c. Net profits or loss on financial operations	2.51	0.36	-0.33	-0.68	-0.76	0.63	1.62	3.46	2.24	0.03	*c. Profits ou pertes nets sur opérations financières*
	d. Other	11.34	19.83	13.16	12.50	16.51	15.26	15.66	12.50	11.74	11.31	*d. Autres*
55.	Operating expenses	65.63	60.80	68.44	67.65	66.72	68.75	61.00	60.69	55.97	55.25	Frais d'exploitation
	a. Staff costs	41.87	38.27	44.22	42.86	42.69	42.70	36.99	35.61	31.67	30.32	*a. Dépenses en personnel*
	b. Property costs	19.29	17.82	19.79	19.79	19.26	21.13	20.10	21.17	20.75	21.57	*b. Dépenses en immobilier*
	c. Other	4.48	4.71	4.44	5.00	4.77	4.91	3.91	3.90	3.56	3.35	*c. Autres*
56.	Net income	34.37	39.20	31.56	32.35	33.28	31.25	39.00	39.31	44.02	44.75	Résultat net
57.	Provisions (net)	15.79	18.37	22.53	20.83	18.15	20.16	13.44	11.12	9.69	17.91	Provisions (nettes)
	a. Provisions on loans	12.26	17.30	14.14	18.37	13.15	16.86	12.75	12.22	9.51	10.00	*a. Provisions sur prêts*
	b. Provisions on securities	3.86	0.02	7.73	-0.28	-0.81	-0.71	0.25	3.27	0.71	1.36	*b. Provisions sur titres*
	c. Other	-0.33	1.05	0.66	2.74	5.81	4.01	0.44	-4.36	-0.53	6.54	*c. Autres*
58.	Profit before tax	18.58	20.83	9.03	11.52	15.13	11.09	25.55	28.19	34.34	26.84	Bénéfices avant impôt
59.	Income tax	9.24	13.34	6.52	9.09	8.66	8.32	12.02	11.14	13.02	10.65	Impôt sur le revenu
60.	Profit after tax	9.34	7.49	2.51	2.43	6.46	2.77	13.53	17.05	21.32	16.19	Bénéfices après impôt
	% of net income											**% du total du résultat net**
61.	Provisions (net)	45.95	46.86	71.40	64.38	54.55	64.52	34.48	28.29	22.00	40.02	Provisions (nettes)
	a. Provisions on loans	35.68	44.13	44.81	56.79	39.53	53.96	32.71	31.07	21.60	22.35	*a. Provisions sur prêts*
	b. Provisions on securities	11.23	0.04	24.50	-0.87	-2.44	-2.28	0.65	8.32	1.60	3.05	*b. Provisions sur titres*
	c. Other	-0.96	2.69	2.08	8.46	17.46	12.83	1.12	-11.10	-1.20	14.62	*c. Autres*
62.	Profit before tax	54.05	53.14	28.60	35.62	45.45	35.48	65.53	71.71	78.00	59.98	Bénéfices avant impôt
63.	Income tax	26.87	34.03	20.66	28.10	26.03	26.63	30.83	28.35	29.57	23.80	Impôt sur le revenu
64.	Profit after tax	27.18	19.11	7.95	7.52	19.42	8.85	34.70	43.37	48.43	36.18	Bénéfices après impôt

ITALY
All banks

ITALIE
Ensemble des banques

Per cent

Pourcentage

BALANCE SHEET ANALYSIS

ANALYSE DU BILAN

% of year-end balance sheet total

% du total du bilan en fin d'exercice

	1992	1993	1994	1995	1996	1997	1998	1999	2000	2001		
Assets												**Actif**
65. Cash & balance with Central bank	5.60	4.29	3.58	2.97	2.89	2.92	0.74	0.86	0.74	1.40	65.	Caisse & solde auprès de la Banque centrale
66. Interbank deposits	7.13	7.33	6.85	6.41	7.05	7.03	7.05	7.41	8.93	7.94	66.	Dépôts interbancaires
67. Loans	43.12	41.97	41.62	41.84	40.04	40.60	42.10	43.70	45.22	47.19	67.	Prêts
68. Securities	15.09	15.14	16.40	14.62	15.05	13.09	13.01	11.42	8.85	8.06	68.	Valeurs mobilières
69. Other assets	29.07	31.28	31.54	34.16	34.98	36.36	37.09	36.60	36.25	35.42	69.	Autres actifs
Liabilities												**Passif**
70. Capital & reserves	6.79	6.67	6.99	6.76	6.55	6.48	6.76	6.89	6.80	6.83	70.	Capital et réserves
71. Borrowing from Central bank	0.38	0.11	0.11	0.30	0.07	0.10	0.07	0.03	0.01	0.03	71.	Emprunts auprès de la Banque centrale
72. Interbank deposits	6.84	7.22	6.71	6.47	7.12	7.14	7.12	7.24	8.42	7.57	72.	Dépôts interbancaires
73. Non-bank deposits	38.50	38.80	38.18	37.49	36.27	31.55	30.56	29.35	26.74	27.37	73.	Dépôts non bancaires
74. Bonds	7.05	7.66	8.35	8.08	10.00	13.13	14.95	14.77	14.30	15.06	74.	Obligations
75. Other liabilities	40.44	39.55	39.66	40.89	40.00	41.61	40.54	41.72	43.73	43.14	75.	Autres engagements
Memorandum items												***Pour mémoire***
76. *Short-term securities*	*1.38*	*3.05*	*2.78*	*1.75*	*1.96*	*1.12*	*1.56*	*1.01*	*0.41*	*0.61*	76.	*Titres à court terme*
77. *Bonds*	*13.71*	*12.09*	*13.62*	*12.86*	*13.09*	*11.98*	*11.45*	*10.41*	*8.44*	*7.45*	77.	*Obligations*
78. *Shares and participations*	*1.78*	*1.73*	*1.96*	*1.94*	*2.05*	*2.16*	*2.74*	*3.38*	*3.63*	*3.56*	78.	*Actions et participations*
79. *Claims on non-residents*	*7.14*	*9.28*	*8.14*	*8.98*	*10.80*	*10.83*	*10.98*	*9.77*	*9.10*	*8.12*	79.	*Créances sur des non-résidents*
80. *Liabilities to non-residents*	*15.91*	*15.16*	*15.18*	*13.54*	*13.15*	*13.89*	*13.96*	*14.32*	*15.46*	*15.32*	80.	*Engagements envers des non-résidents*

* See notes on previous pages.

* Voir les notes en pages précédentes.

JAPAN
Commercial banks

JAPON
Banques commerciales

100 million yen — *100 millions de yen*

English	1992	1993	1994	1995	1996	1997	1998	1999	2000	2001	Français
INCOME STATEMENT											**COMPTE DE RESULTATS**
1. Interest income	360912	301478	281579	278801	245896	210308	182495	158060	138605	122907	1. Produits financiers
2. Interest expenses	269818	214466	189919	178634	148361	118791	92585	67542	50567	33345	2. Frais financiers
3. Net interest income	91094	87012	91660	100168	97535	91517	89910	90518	88037	89561	3. Produits financiers nets
4. Non-interest income (net)	3489	2702	-2945	1992	-5229	5865	-17397	12702	-1483	-32178	4. Produits non financiers (nets)
a. Fees and commissions receivable	..	..	..	14968	14989	15083	14762	15122	16241	16515	a. Frais et commissions à recevoir
b. Fees and commissions payable	..	..	..	5489	5550	5657	5648	5486	5602	6024	b. Frais et commissions à payer
c. Net profits or loss on financial operations	..	..	..	-7316	-15143	-8111	-31438	3837	-8644	-41435	c. Profits ou pertes nets sur opérations financières
d. Other	..	..	..	-170	475	4550	4927	-771	-3478	-1234	d. Autres
5. Gross income	94583	89714	88716	102160	92305	97382	72513	103220	86553	57382	5. Résultat brut
6. Operating expenses	66294	67111	67730	67977	70006	69376	66563	64348	63156	61163	6. Frais d'exploitation
a. Staff costs	34624	35312	35507	35628	35146	34888	32611	31253	30228	28852	a. Dépenses en personnel
b. Property costs	..	..	..	28478	31172	30471	30397	29828	29743	29259	b. Dépenses en immobilier
c. Other	..	..	..	3869	3686	4014	3552	3265	3183	3050	c. Autres
7. Net income	28289	22603	20986	34183	22299	28006	5950	38872	23396	-3781	7. Résultat net
8. Provisions (net)	9612	9739	13054	45842	19931	62804	57143	20928	25292	41285	8. Provisions (nettes)
a. Provisions on loans	9329	9550	13019	45760	19753	65317	57143	20928	25292	41285	a. Provisions sur prêts
b. Provisions on securities (1)	283	189	35	82	177	-2513	-	-	-	-	b. Provisions sur titres (1)
c. Other	-	-	-	-	-	-	-	-	-	-	c. Autres
9. Profit before tax	18677	12864	7932	-11659	2367	-34798	-51193	17944	-1895	-45066	9. Bénéfices avant impôt
10. Income tax	11084	6137	5849	10980	2303	5391	5908	6753	4694	2605	10. Impôt sur le revenu
11. Profit after tax	7593	6727	2083	-22639	64	-40189	-57101	11191	-6590	-47672	11. Bénéfices après impôt
12. Distributed profit	1706	1685	1756	1446	1727	1903	1549	1874	1823	1290	12. Bénéfices distribués
13. Retained profit	5887	5042	327	-24085	-1663	-42092	-58650	9317	-8413	-48962	13. Bénéfices mis en réserve
BALANCE SHEET											**BILAN**
Assets											*Actif*
14. Cash & balance with Central bank (2)	710380	737768	679009	596516	520874	413237	258788	331781	351921	418493	14. Caisse & solde auprès de la Banque centrale (2)
15. Interbank deposits (3)	..	..	..	..	..	..	..	..	..	..	15. Dépôts interbancaires (3)
16. Loans	4538361	4520965	4520184	4653040	4714569	4564309	4346872	4193352	4184902	4046328	16. Prêts
17. Securities (4)	960568	952841	983659	998309	1012661	994871	977638	1133855	1492236	1316082	17. Valeurs mobilières (4)
18. Other assets (4)	786390	711979	705356	713139	772029	992493	966325	694230	905961	744546	18. Autres actifs (4)
Liabilities											*Passif*
19. Capital & reserves	253907	258587	258042	233091	238884	196544	286027	297446	313729	254440	19. Capital et réserves
20. Borrowing from Central bank	39738	39515	28183	8244	6231	47702	8475	10582	4674	2991	20. Emprunts auprès de la Banque centrale
21. Interbank deposits	..	..	..	..	..	..	..	..	..	..	21. Dépôts interbancaires
22. Non-bank deposits	5357468	5363045	5394567	5412819	5421534	5221281	4954774	4951358	5157922	5099196	22. Dépôts non bancaires
23. Bonds	56566	54374	58466	70157	70111	64559	55507	53082	40081	28468	23. Obligations
24. Other liabilities	1288020	1208032	1148950	1236692	1283375	1434824	1244840	1040750	1418612	1140353	24. Autres engagements
Balance sheet total											**Total du bilan**
25. End-year total	6995699	6923553	6888208	6961003	7020135	6964910	6549623	6353218	6935020	6525451	25. En fin d'exercice
26. Average total	7221216	6959626	6905881	6924606	6990569	6992522	6757266	6451420	6644119	6730236	26. Moyen

JAPAN — Commercial banks / JAPON — Banques commerciales

100 million yen / 100 millions de yen

	1992	1993	1994	1995	1996	1997	1998	1999	2000	2001		
Memorandum items												**Pour mémoire**
27. Short-term securities	..	..	..	..	..	..	..	..	..	..	27.	Titres à court terme
28. Bonds	..	..	..	..	..	..	..	..	..	..	28.	Obligations
29. Shares and participations	258058	271948	300249	323250	329416	332399	326334	339629	348370	271466	29.	Actions et participations
30. Claims on non-residents	..	..	..	..	..	..	..	..	..	..	30.	Créances sur des non-résidents
31. Liabilities to non-residents	..	..	..	..	..	..	..	..	..	..	31.	Engagements envers des non-résidents
Capital adequacy												**Solvabilité**
32. Tier 1 Capital	..	..	..	238614	245248	255955	214798	202737	200507	156953	32.	Fonds propres de base
33. Tier 2 Capital	..	..	..	195991	187011	211711	160292	154746	145446	126511	33.	Fonds propres complémentaires
34. Supervisory deductions	..	..	..	-	-	130	4508	4892	6734	6870	34.	Eléments à déduire des fonds propres
35. Total net capital resources	..	..	..	434605	432260	467537	370581	352591	339218	276594	35.	Total net des ressources en capital
36. Risk-weighted assets	..	..	..	4699002	4710222	4853411	3159242	2875580	2918450	2506024	36.	Actifs pondérés des risques
SUPPLEMENTARY INFORMATION												**RENSEIGNEMENTS COMPLÉMENTAIRES**
37. Number of institutions	141	140	140	139	136	136	130	127	127	124	37.	Nombre d'institutions
38. Number of branches	14782	14804	14823	14693	14567	14395	13817	13341	13342	13016	38.	Nombre de succursales
39. Number of employees (x 1000)	412	417	414	400	383	367	350	335	324	306	39.	Nombre de salariés (x 1000)

1 In 1997, the main components of Provisions on securities (item 8.b) were abolished in the Japanese accounting system. The 1997 figure represents the outflow of the assets of this item. As from then, the amount for this item will be negligible.

2 Cash and balance with Central bank (item 14) is included under Interbank deposits (item 15).

3 Interbank deposits (item 21) are included under Non-bank deposits (item 22).

4 1998 to 2000 : data are based on the summation of both current cost basis and book value basis.

Notes

. The category commercial banks correponds to the term Ordinary banks, used in Japanese publications.

. Data relate to fiscal years ending 31st March.

1 En 1997, les principales composantes des Provisions sur titres (poste 8.b) ont été supprimées du système de comptabilité japonais. Le montant publié pour l'année 1997 correspond à la sortie des actifs de ce poste. Par la suite, ce montant sera négligeable.

2 Caisse et solde auprès de la Banque centrale (poste 14) est inclus sous Dépôts interbancaires (poste 15).

3 Les Dépôts interbancaires (poste 21) sont inclus sous Dépôts non bancaires (poste 22).

4 1998 à 2000 : les données sont basées sur la somme des couts actuels et de la valeur comptable.

Notes

. La catégorie des banques commerciales correspond au terme "ordinary banks" (Banques ordinaires) utilisé dans les publications japonaises.

. Les données portent sur l'exercice financier qui se termine le 31 mars

JAPAN

Commercial banks

Per cent

INCOME STATEMENT ANALYSIS

JAPON

Banques commerciales

Pourcentage

ANALYSE DU COMPTE DE RESULTATS

#	Item	1992	1993	1994	1995	1996	1997	1998	1999	2000	2001	Rubrique
	% of average balance sheet total											**% du total moyen du bilan**
40.	Interest income	5.00	4.33	4.08	4.03	3.52	3.01	2.70	2.45	2.09	1.83	Produits financiers
41.	Interest expenses	3.74	3.08	2.75	2.58	2.12	1.70	1.37	1.05	0.76	0.50	Frais financiers
42.	Net interest income	1.26	1.25	1.33	1.45	1.40	1.31	1.33	1.40	1.33	1.33	Produits financiers nets
43.	Non-interest income (net)	0.05	0.04	-0.04	0.03	-0.07	0.08	-0.26	0.20	-0.02	-0.48	Produits non financiers (nets)
	a. Fees and commissions receivable	..	..	..	0.22	0.21	0.22	0.22	0.23	0.24	0.25	*a. Frais et commissions à recevoir*
	b. Fees and commissions payable	..	..	..	0.08	0.08	0.08	0.08	0.09	0.08	0.09	*b. Frais et commissions à payer*
	c. Net profits or loss on financial operations	..	..	..	-0.11	-0.22	-0.12	-0.47	0.06	-0.13	-0.62	*c. Profits ou pertes nets sur opérations financières*
	d. Other	..	..	..	-	0.01	0.07	0.07	-0.01	-0.05	-0.02	*d. Autres*
44.	Gross income	1.31	1.29	1.28	1.48	1.32	1.39	1.07	1.60	1.30	0.85	Résultat brut
45.	Operating expenses	0.92	0.96	0.98	0.98	1.00	0.99	0.99	1.00	0.95	0.91	Frais d'exploitation
	a. Staff costs	0.48	0.51	0.51	0.51	0.50	0.50	0.48	0.48	0.45	0.43	*a. Dépenses en personnel*
	b. Property costs	..	..	..	0.41	0.45	0.44	0.45	0.46	0.45	0.43	*b. Dépenses en immobilier*
	c. Other	..	..	..	0.06	0.05	0.06	0.05	0.05	0.05	0.05	*c. Autres*
46.	Net income	0.39	0.32	0.30	0.49	0.32	0.40	0.09	0.60	0.35	-0.06	Résultat net
47.	Provisions (net)	0.13	0.14	0.19	0.66	0.29	0.90	0.85	0.32	0.38	0.61	Provisions (nettes)
	a. Provisions on loans	0.13	0.14	0.19	0.66	0.28	0.93	0.85	0.32	0.38	0.61	*a. Provisions sur prêts*
	b. Provisions on securities						-0.04					*b. Provisions sur titres*
	c. Other											*c. Autres*
48.	Profit before tax	0.26	0.18	0.11	-0.17	0.03	-0.50	-0.76	0.28	-0.03	-0.67	Bénéfices avant impôt
49.	Income tax	0.15	0.09	0.08	0.16	0.03	0.08	0.09	0.10	0.07	0.04	Impôt sur le revenu
50.	Profit after tax	0.11	0.10	0.03	-0.33	-	-0.57	-0.85	0.17	-0.10	-0.71	Bénéfices après impôt
51.	Distributed profit	0.02	0.02	0.03	0.02	0.02	0.03	0.02	0.03	0.03	0.02	Bénéfices distribués
52.	Retained profit	0.08	0.07	-	-0.35	-0.02	-0.60	-0.87	0.14	-0.13	-0.73	Bénéfices mis en réserve
	% of gross income											**% du total du résultat brut**
53.	Net interest income	96.31	96.99	103.32	98.05	105.67	93.98	123.99	87.69	101.71	156.08	Produits financiers nets
54.	Non-interest income (net)	3.69	3.01	-3.32	1.95	-5.66	6.02	-23.99	12.31	-1.71	-56.08	Produits non financiers (nets)
	a. Fees and commissions receivable	..	..	..	14.65	16.24	15.49	20.36	14.65	18.76	28.78	*a. Frais et commissions à recevoir*
	b. Fees and commissions payable	..	..	..	5.37	6.01	5.81	7.79	5.31	6.47	10.50	*b. Frais et commissions à payer*
	c. Net profits or loss on financial operations	..	..	..	-7.16	-16.41	-8.33	-43.35	3.72	-9.99	-72.21	*c. Profits ou pertes nets sur opérations financières*
	d. Other	..	..	..	-0.17	0.51	4.67	6.79	-0.75	-4.02	-2.15	*d. Autres*
55.	Operating expenses	70.09	74.81	76.34	66.54	75.84	71.24	91.79	62.34	72.97	106.59	Frais d'exploitation
	a. Staff costs	36.61	39.36	40.02	34.87	38.08	35.83	44.97	30.28	34.92	50.28	*a. Dépenses en personnel*
	b. Property costs	..	..	..	27.88	33.77	31.29	41.92	28.90	34.36	50.99	*b. Dépenses en immobilier*
	c. Other	..	..	..	3.79	3.99	4.12	4.90	3.16	3.68	5.32	*c. Autres*
56.	Net income	29.91	25.19	23.66	33.46	24.16	28.76	8.21	37.66	27.03	-6.59	Résultat net
57.	Provisions (net)	10.16	10.86	14.71	44.87	21.59	64.49	78.80	20.28	29.22	71.95	Provisions (nettes)
	a. Provisions on loans	9.86	10.64	14.67	44.79	21.40	67.07	78.80	20.28	29.22	71.95	*a. Provisions sur prêts*
	b. Provisions on securities	0.30	0.21	0.04	0.08	0.19	-2.58	..				*b. Provisions sur titres*
	c. Other											*c. Autres*
58.	Profit before tax	19.75	14.34	8.94	-11.41	2.56	-35.73	-70.60	17.38	-2.19	-78.54	Bénéfices avant impôt
59.	Income tax	11.72	6.84	6.59	10.75	2.49	5.54	8.15	6.54	5.42	4.54	Impôt sur le revenu
60.	Profit after tax	8.03	7.50	2.35	-22.16	0.07	-41.27	-78.75	10.84	-7.61	-83.08	Bénéfices après impôt
	% of net income											**% du total du résultat net**
61.	Provisions (net)	33.98	43.09	62.20	134.11	89.38	224.25	960.39	53.84	108.10	-1091.91	Provisions (nettes)
	a. Provisions on loans	32.98	42.25	62.04	133.87	88.58	233.23	960.39	53.84	108.10	-1091.91	*a. Provisions sur prêts*
	b. Provisions on securities	1.00	0.84	0.17	0.24	0.79	-8.97	..	..	..	..	*b. Provisions sur titres*
	c. Other											*c. Autres*
62.	Profit before tax	66.02	56.91	37.80	-34.11	10.61	-124.25	-860.39	46.16	-8.10	1191.91	Bénéfices avant impôt
63.	Income tax	39.18	27.15	27.87	32.12	10.33	19.25	99.29	17.37	20.06	-68.90	Impôt sur le revenu
64.	Profit after tax	26.84	29.76	9.93	-66.23	0.29	-143.50	-959.68	28.79	-28.17	1260.83	Bénéfices après impôt

JAPAN
Commercial banks

JAPON
Banques commerciales

Per cent	1992	1993	1994	1995	1996	1997	1998	1999	2000	2001	Pourcentage
BALANCE SHEET ANALYSIS											**ANALYSE DU BILAN**
% of year-end balance sheet total											**% du total du bilan en fin d'exercice**
Assets											**Actif**
65. Cash & balance with Central bank	..	..	..	..	..	..	..	..	..	..	65. Caisse & solde auprès de la Banque centrale
66. Interbank deposits	10.15	10.66	9.86	8.57	7.42	5.93	3.95	5.22	5.07	6.41	66. Dépôts interbancaires
67. Loans	64.87	65.30	65.62	66.84	67.16	65.53	66.37	66.00	60.34	62.01	67. Prêts
68. Securities	13.73	13.76	14.28	14.34	14.43	14.28	14.93	17.85	21.52	20.17	68. Valeurs mobilières
69. Other assets	11.24	10.28	10.24	10.24	11.00	14.25	14.75	10.93	13.06	11.41	69. Autres actifs
Liabilities											**Passif**
70. Capital & reserves	3.63	3.73	3.75	3.35	3.40	2.82	4.37	4.68	4.52	3.90	70. Capital et réserves
71. Borrowing from Central bank	0.57	0.57	0.41	0.12	0.09	0.68	0.13	0.17	0.07	0.05	71. Emprunts auprès de la Banque centrale
72. Interbank deposits	..	..	..	..	..	..	..	..	..	..	72. Dépôts interbancaires
73. Non-bank deposits	76.58	77.46	78.32	77.76	77.23	74.97	75.65	77.93	74.38	78.14	73. Dépôts non bancaires
74. Bonds	0.81	0.79	0.85	1.01	1.00	0.93	0.85	0.84	0.58	0.44	74. Obligations
75. Other liabilities	18.41	17.45	16.68	17.77	18.28	20.60	19.01	16.38	20.46	17.48	75. Autres engagements
Memorandum items											**Pour mémoire**
76. Short-term securities	..	..	..	..	..	..	..	..	..	..	76. Titres à court terme
77. Bonds	..	..	..	..	..	..	..	..	..	..	77. Obligations
78. Shares and participations	3.69	3.93	4.36	4.64	4.69	4.77	4.98	5.35	5.02	4.16	78. Actions et participations
79. Claims on non-residents	..	..	..	..	..	..	..	..	..	..	79. Créances sur des non-résidents
80. Liabilities to non-residents	..	..	..	..	..	..	..	..	..	..	80. Engagements envers des non-résidents

* See notes on previous pages.

* Voir les notes en pages précédentes.

JAPAN
Large commercial banks

JAPON
Grandes banques commerciales

100 million yen / 100 millions de yen

INCOME STATEMENT / COMPTE DE RESULTATS	1992	1993	1994	1995	1996	1997	1998	1999	2000	2001	(Français)
1. Interest income	226675	188626	177263	187678	167869	136417	117069	98656	81426	70105	1. Produits financiers
2. Interest expenses	180932	145110	135250	136670	119912	94233	74485	55123	39220	25775	2. Frais financiers
3. Net interest income	45743	43516	42013	51009	47956	42184	42584	43533	42206	44329	3. Produits financiers nets
4. Non-interest income (net)	2807	548	-241	-1394	-3559	4926	-20207	10006	-1372	-24782	4. Produits non financiers (nets)
a. Fees and commissions receivable	..	..	..	9471	9369	9322	8999	9149	10023	9980	*a. Frais et commissions à recevoir*
b. Fees and commissions payable	..	..	..	3068	3089	3251	3342	3167	3189	3468	*b. Frais et commissions à payer*
c. Net profits or loss on financial operations	..	..	..	-9205	-10210	-6090	-29083	3992	-6881	-31175	*c. Profits ou pertes nets sur opérations financières*
d. Other	..	..	..	1408	369	4945	3219	32	-1324	-119	*d. Autres*
5. Gross income	48550	44064	41772	49614	44396	47110	22377	53539	40834	19546	5. Résultat brut
6. Operating expenses	31779	32023	32239	32336	33380	32450	31697	30444	29297	27812	6. Frais d'exploitation
a. Staff costs	14970	15140	15135	15161	15000	14601	13707	12982	12218	11332	*a. Dépenses en personnel*
b. Property costs	..	..	..	15099	16407	15752	16194	15881	15566	15048	*b. Dépenses en immobilier*
c. Other	..	..	..	2076	1973	2096	1794	1579	1511	1431	*c. Autres*
7. Net income	16771	12041	9533	17278	11015	14660	-9320	23095	11537	-8265	7. Résultat net
8. Provisions (net)	7368	6438	8884	30706	10774	42957	31071	8884	11770	27326	8. Provisions (nettes)
a. Provisions on loans	7114	6316	8809	30645	10622	44538	31071	8884	11770	27326	*a. Provisions sur prêts*
b. Provisions on securities (1)	254	122	75	61	151	-1581	..	..	..	..	*b. Provisions sur titres (1)*
c. Other	..	..	..	..	..	..	..	..	..	..	*c. Autres*
9. Profit before tax	9403	5603	649	-13428	240	-28297	-40391	14211	-233	-35592	9. Bénéfices avant impôt
10. Income tax	5727	2418	1343	4091	718	1503	1660	2719	1333	308	10. Impôt sur le revenu
11. Profit after tax	3676	3185	-693	-17518	-477	-29800	-42051	11492	-1566	-35900	11. Bénéfices après impôt
12. Distributed profit	1113	1105	1130	887	1128	1323	1017	1263	1192	657	12. Bénéfices distribués
13. Retained profit	2563	2080	-1823	-18405	-1606	-31123	-43068	10229	-2759	-36558	13. Bénéfices mis en réserve
BALANCE SHEET / BILAN											
Assets / Actif											
14. Cash & balance with Central bank (2)	556503	568884	517242	450130	396230	309679	165191	217997	253662	284241	14. Caisse & solde auprès de la Banque centrale (2)
15. Interbank deposits (3)	513673	504841	531647	537436	542816	556199	529281	608602	887108	738196	15. Dépôts interbancaires (3)
16. Loans	2743890	2703186	2670535	2771343	2834197	2656555	2487497	2414691	2384195	2252403	16. Prêts
17. Securities	546982	481154	473919	504433	566710	749765	713763	543384	746653	586613	17. Valeurs mobilières
18. Other assets	..	..	..	..	..	..	..	..	..	..	18. Autres actifs
Liabilities / Passif											
19. Capital & reserves	149928	152224	149560	131435	134346	103308	177092	180903	180006	132551	19. Capital et réserves
20. Borrowing from Central bank	34859	34790	23605	1011	1013	43994	5895	3265	4176	1494	20. Emprunts auprès de la Banque centrale
21. Interbank deposits	54181	52944	57213	69287	68974	63033	54178	49005	37187	24784	21. Dépôts interbancaires
22. Non-bank deposits	3087810	3060102	3034603	3069487	3073519	2888778	2641230	2645596	2779185	2706103	22. Dépôts non bancaires
23. Bonds	..	..	..	..	..	..	..	..	..	..	23. Obligations
24. Other liabilities	1034270	958005	928363	992122	1062102	1173085	1017339	905906	1271066	996521	24. Autres engagements
Balance sheet total / Total du bilan											
25. End-year total	4361048	4258065	4193343	4263342	4339954	4272198	3895734	3784675	4271620	3861455	25. En fin d'exercice
26. Average total	4555351	4309557	4225704	4228342	4301648	4306076	4083966	3840204	4028147	4066537	26. Moyen

JAPAN
Large commercial banks

JAPON
Grandes banques commerciales

100 million yen / *100 millions de yen*

	1992	1993	1994	1995	1996	1997	1998	1999	2000	2001	
Memorandum items											***Pour mémoire***
27. Short-term securities	..	..	..	..	..	..	..	..	..	..	27. *Titres à court terme*
28. Bonds	..	..	..	..	..	..	..	..	..	..	28. *Obligations*
29. Shares and participations	200637	211988	238626	256135	262972	267007	264648	278442	274578	211805	29. *Actions et participations*
30. Claims on non-residents	..	..	..	..	..	..	..	..	..	..	30. *Créances sur des non-résidents*
31. Liabilities to non-residents	..	..	..	..	..	..	..	..	..	..	31. *Engagements envers des non-résidents*
Capital adequacy											***Solvabilité***
32. Tier 1 Capital	..	..	..	150245	155033	143886	176668	170223	167618	128435	32. *Fonds propres de base*
33. Tier 2 Capital	..	..	..	146837	147093	139724	145174	141161	132448	116203	33. *Fonds propres complémentaires*
34. Supervisory deductions	..	..	..	..	-	100	4473	4857	6683	6810	34. *Eléments à déduire des fonds propres*
35. Total net capital resources	..	..	..	297081	302127	283510	317369	306527	293383	237802	35. *Total net des ressources en capital*
36. Risk-weighted assets	..	..	..	3286754	3351642	3061973	2659444	2476239	2513165	2151057	36. *Actifs pondérés des risques*
SUPPLEMENTARY INFORMATION											**RENSEIGNEMENTS COMPLEMENTAIRES**
37. Number of institutions	11	11	11	11	10	9	9	9	9	7	37. *Nombre d'institutions*
38. Number of branches	3293	3238	3224	3199	3174	2955	2807	2684	2556	2472	38. *Nombre de succursales*
39. Number of employees (x 1000)	157	158	155	149	139	129	124	119	113	105	39. *Nombre de salariés (x 1000)*

1 In 1997, the main components of Provisions on securities (item 8.b) were abolished in the Japanese accounting system. The 1997 figure represents the outflow of the assets of this item. As from then, the amount for this item will be negligible.

2 Cash and balance with Central bank (item 14) is included under Interbank deposits (item 15).

3 Interbank deposits (item 21) are included under Non-bank deposits (item 22)

Notes

· The term Large commercial banks corresponds to the term City banks used in Japanese publications. Data are based on the annual publication of the Federation of Bankers Associations of Japan "Analysis of Financial Statements of All Banks".

· Data relate to fiscal years ending 31st March.

1 En 1997, les principales composantes des Provisions sur titres (poste 8.b) ont été supprimées du système de comptabilité japonais. Le montant publié pour l'année 1997 correspond à la sortie des actifs de ce poste. Par la suite, ce montant sera négligeable.

2 Caisse et solde auprès de la Banque centrale (poste 14) est inclus sous Dépôts interbancaires (poste 15).

3 Les Dépôts interbancaires (poste 21) sont inclus sous Dépôts non bancaires (poste 22).

Notes

· Le terme, Grandes banques commerciales correspond au terme City banks utilisé dans les publications japonaises. Ces données sont extraites d'une publication annuelle de la Fédération des associations de banquiers du Japon "Analysis of Financial Statements of All Banks".

· Les données portent sur l'exercice financier qui se termine le 31 mars

168

JAPAN

Large commercial banks

JAPON

Grandes banques commerciales

Per cent / *Pourcentage*

INCOME STATEMENT ANALYSIS / **ANALYSE DU COMPTE DE RESULTATS**

#	Item (English)	Poste (Français)	1992	1993	1994	1995	1996	1997	1998	1999	2000	2001
	% of average balance sheet total	**% du total moyen du bilan**										
40.	Interest income	Produits financiers	4.98	4.38	4.19	4.44	3.90	3.17	2.87	2.57	2.02	1.72
41.	Interest expenses	Frais financiers	3.97	3.37	3.20	3.23	2.79	2.19	1.82	1.44	0.97	0.63
42.	Net interest income	Produits financiers nets	1.00	1.01	0.99	1.21	1.11	0.98	1.04	1.13	1.05	1.09
43.	Non-interest income (net)	Produits non financiers (nets)	0.06	0.01	-0.01	-0.03	-0.08	0.11	-0.49	0.26	-0.03	-0.61
	a. Fees and commissions receivable	*Frais et commissions à recevoir*	..	..	..	0.22	0.22	0.22	0.22	0.24	0.25	0.25
	b. Fees and commissions payable	*Frais et commissions à payer*	..	..	..	0.07	0.07	0.08	0.08	0.08	0.08	0.09
	c. Net profits or loss on financial operations	*Profits ou pertes nets sur opérations financières*	..	..	..	-0.22	-0.24	-0.14	-0.71	0.10	-0.17	-0.77
	d. Other	*Autres*	..	..	..	0.03	0.01	0.11	0.08	..	-0.03	..
44.	Gross income	Résultat brut	1.07	1.02	0.99	1.17	1.03	1.09	0.55	1.39	1.01	0.48
45.	Operating expenses	Frais d'exploitation	0.70	0.74	0.76	0.76	0.78	0.75	0.78	0.79	0.73	0.68
	a. Staff costs	*Dépenses en personnel*	0.33	0.35	0.36	0.36	0.35	0.34	0.34	0.34	0.30	0.28
	b. Property costs	*Dépenses en immobilier*	..	..	..	0.36	0.38	0.37	0.40	0.41	0.39	0.37
	c. Other	*Autres*	..	..	..	0.05	0.05	0.05	0.04	0.04	0.04	0.04
46.	Net income	Résultat net	0.37	0.28	0.23	0.41	0.26	0.34	-0.23	0.60	0.29	-0.20
47.	Provisions (net)	Provisions (nettes)	0.16	0.15	0.21	0.73	0.25	1.00	0.76	0.23	0.29	0.67
	a. Provisions on loans	*Provisions sur prêts*	0.16	0.15	0.21	0.72	0.25	1.03	0.76	0.23	0.29	0.67
	b. Provisions on securities	*Provisions sur titres*	0.01	..	..	..	..	..	..	..	..	..
	c. Other	*Autres*	..	..	..	..	..	-0.04	..	..	..	..
48.	Profit before tax	Bénéfices avant impôt	0.21	0.13	0.02	-0.32	0.01	-0.66	-0.99	0.37	-0.01	-0.88
49.	Income tax	Impôt sur le revenu	0.13	0.06	0.03	0.10	0.02	0.03	0.04	0.07	0.03	0.01
50.	Profit after tax	Bénéfices après impôt	0.08	0.07	-0.02	-0.41	-0.01	-0.69	-1.03	0.30	-0.04	-0.88
51.	Distributed profit	Bénéfices distribués	0.02	0.03	0.03	0.02	0.03	0.03	0.02	0.03	0.03	0.02
52.	Retained profit	Bénéfices mis en réserve	0.06	0.05	-0.04	-0.44	-0.04	-0.72	-1.05	0.27	-0.07	-0.90
	% of gross income	**% du total du résultat brut**										
53.	Net interest income	Produits financiers nets	94.22	98.76	100.58	102.81	108.02	89.54	190.30	81.31	103.36	226.79
54.	Non-interest income (net)	Produits non financiers (nets)	5.78	1.24	-0.58	-2.81	-8.02	10.46	-90.30	18.69	-3.36	-126.79
	a. Fees and commissions receivable	*Frais et commissions à recevoir*	..	..	..	19.09	21.10	19.79	40.22	17.09	24.55	51.06
	b. Fees and commissions payable	*Frais et commissions à payer*	..	..	..	6.18	6.96	6.90	14.93	5.92	7.81	17.74
	c. Net profits or loss on financial operations	*Profits ou pertes nets sur opérations financières*	..	..	..	-18.55	-23.00	-12.93	-129.97	7.46	-16.85	-159.50
	d. Other	*Autres*	..	..	..	2.84	0.83	10.50	14.39	0.06	-3.24	-0.61
55.	Operating expenses	Frais d'exploitation	65.46	72.67	77.18	65.18	75.19	68.88	141.65	56.86	71.75	142.29
	a. Staff costs	*Dépenses en personnel*	30.83	34.36	36.23	30.56	33.79	30.99	61.25	24.25	29.92	57.98
	b. Property costs	*Dépenses en immobilier*	..	..	..	30.43	36.96	33.44	72.37	29.66	38.12	76.99
	c. Other	*Autres*	..	..	..	4.18	4.44	4.45	8.02	2.95	3.70	7.32
56.	Net income	Résultat net	34.54	27.33	22.82	34.82	24.81	31.12	-41.65	43.14	28.25	-42.28
57.	Provisions (net)	Provisions (nettes)	15.18	14.61	21.27	61.89	24.27	91.18	138.85	16.59	28.82	139.80
	a. Provisions on loans	*Provisions sur prêts*	14.65	14.33	21.09	61.77	23.93	94.54	138.85	16.59	28.82	139.80
	b. Provisions on securities	*Provisions sur titres*	0.52	0.28	0.18	0.12	0.34	-3.36	..	..	..	..
	c. Other	*Autres*	..	..	..	..	..	..	..	..	..	..
58.	Profit before tax	Bénéfices avant impôt	19.37	12.72	1.55	-27.06	0.54	-60.07	-180.50	26.54	-0.57	-182.09
59.	Income tax	Impôt sur le revenu	11.80	5.49	3.22	8.25	1.62	3.19	7.42	5.08	3.26	1.58
60.	Profit after tax	Bénéfices après impôt	7.57	7.23	-1.66	-35.31	-1.07	-63.26	-187.92	21.46	-3.84	-183.67
	% of net income	**% du total du résultat net**										
61.	Provisions (net)	Provisions (nettes)	43.93	53.47	93.19	177.72	97.81	293.02	-333.38	38.47	102.02	-330.62
	a. Provisions on loans	*Provisions sur prêts*	42.42	52.45	92.41	177.36	96.43	303.81	-333.38	38.47	102.02	-330.62
	b. Provisions on securities	*Provisions sur titres*	1.51	1.01	0.79	0.35	1.37	-10.78	..	..	..	..
	c. Other	*Autres*	..	..	..	..	..	..	..	..	..	..
62.	Profit before tax	Bénéfices avant impôt	56.07	46.53	6.81	-77.72	2.18	-193.02	433.38	61.53	-2.02	430.64
63.	Income tax	Impôt sur le revenu	34.15	20.08	14.09	23.68	6.52	10.25	-17.81	11.77	11.55	-3.73
64.	Profit after tax	Bénéfices après impôt	21.92	26.45	-7.27	-101.39	-4.33	-203.27	451.19	49.76	-13.57	434.36

JAPAN
Large commercial banks

Per cent

BALANCE SHEET ANALYSIS

% of year-end balance sheet total

	1992	1993	1994	1995	1996	1997	1998	1999	2000	2001
Assets										
65. Cash & balance with Central bank	..	..	..	..	..	..	..	..	..	..
66. Interbank deposits	12.76	13.36	12.33	10.56	9.13	7.25	4.24	5.76	5.94	7.36
67. Loans	62.92	63.48	63.69	65.00	65.30	62.18	63.85	63.80	55.81	58.33
68. Securities	11.78	11.86	12.68	12.61	12.51	13.02	13.59	16.08	20.77	19.12
69. Other assets	12.54	11.30	11.30	11.83	13.06	17.55	18.32	14.36	17.48	15.19
Liabilities										
70. Capital & reserves	3.44	3.57	3.57	3.08	3.10	2.42	4.55	4.78	4.21	3.43
71. Borrowing from Central bank	0.80	0.82	0.56	0.02	0.02	1.03	0.15	0.09	0.10	0.04
72. Interbank deposits	..	..	..	..	..	..	..	..	..	..
73. Non-bank deposits	70.80	71.87	72.37	72.00	70.82	67.62	67.80	69.90	65.06	70.08
74. Bonds	1.24	1.24	1.36	1.63	1.59	1.48	1.39	1.29	0.87	0.64
75. Other liabilities	23.72	22.50	22.14	23.27	24.47	27.46	26.11	23.94	29.76	25.81
Memorandum items										
76. Short-term securities	..	..	..	..	..	..	..	..	..	..
77. Bonds	..	..	..	..	..	..	..	..	..	..
78. Shares and participations	4.60	4.98	5.69	6.01	6.06	6.25	6.79	7.36	6.43	5.49
79. Claims on non-residents	..	..	..	..	..	..	..	..	..	..
80. Liabilities to non-residents	..	..	..	..	..	..	..	..	..	..

* See notes on previous pages.

JAPON
Grandes banques commerciales

Pourcentage

ANALYSE DU BILAN

% du total du bilan en fin d'exercice

Actif
- 65. Caisse & solde auprés de la Banque centrale
- 66. Dépôts interbancaires
- 67. Prêts
- 68. Valeurs mobilières
- 69. Autres actifs

Passif
- 70. Capital et réserves
- 71. Emprunts auprès de la Banque centrale
- 72. Dépôts interbancaires
- 73. Dépôts non bancaires
- 74. Obligations
- 75. Autres engagements

Pour mémoire
- 76. Titres à court terme
- 77. Obligations
- 78. Actions et participations
- 79. Créances sur des non-résidents
- 80. Engagements envers des non-résidents

* Voir les notes en pages précédentes.

170

Billion won — *Milliards de won*

	1992	1993	1994	1995	1996	1997	1998	1999	2000	2001	
INCOME STATEMENT											**COMPTE DE RESULTATS**
1. Interest income	10471	10110	12309	18322	21756	31892	37943	35017	38579	32458	1. Produits financiers
2. Interest expenses	7383	6983	8882	13402	15696	24075	31166	25971	29012	22997	2. Frais financiers
3. Net interest income	3088	3127	3427	4920	6060	7817	6777	9047	9567	9461	3. Produits financiers nets
4. Non-interest income (net)	2248	2869	4906	4420	4359	2689	-3868	-680	4852	6304	4. Produits non financiers (nets)
a. Fees and commissions receivable	*1251*	*1552*	*2481*	*2249*	*2281*	*10299*	*13266*	*8210*	*8795*	*9390*	*a. Frais et commissions à recevoir*
b. Fees and commissions payable	*184*	*176*	*238*	*373*	*650*	*8039*	*11849*	*5292*	*6635*	*7200*	*b. Frais et commissions à payer*
c. Net profits or loss on financial operations	*1140*	*1453*	*2408*	*2354*	*2569*	*2697*	*615*	*444*	*1069*	*3959*	*c. Profits ou pertes nets sur opérations financières*
d. Other	*42*	*40*	*255*	*189*	*159*	*-2268*	*-5900*	*-4042*	*1623*	*155*	*d. Autres*
5. Gross income	5336	5996	8333	9340	10418	10506	2909	8367	14419	15765	5. Résultat brut
6. Operating expenses	3177	3650	4363	6033	6982	8094	7587	6446	6868	6542	6. Frais d'exploitation
a. Staff costs	*2221*	*2595*	*3187*	*4229*	*4964*	*5609*	*5596*	*2886*	*3026*	*2773*	*a. Dépenses en personnel*
b. Property costs	*955*	*1054*	*1175*	*1804*	*2018*	*2485*	*1991*	*3560*	*3843*	*3769*	*b. Dépenses en immobilier*
c. Other	-	-	-	-	-	-	-	-	-	-	*c. Autres*
7. Net income	2160	2346	3970	3307	3436	2412	-4678	1922	7551	9223	7. Résultat net
8. Provisions (net)	943	1023	2372	2320	2342	6193	7780	7487	9855	5412	8. Provisions (nettes)
a. Provisions on loans	*788*	*996*	*2127*	*1758*	*1548*	*3511*	*8067*	*7487*	*9855*	*5412*	*a. Provisions sur prêts*
b. Provisions on securities	*96*	*-33*	*184*	*544*	*895*	*2759*	*-126*	*-*	*-*	*-*	*b. Provisions sur titres*
c. Other	*59*	*61*	*61*	*18*	*-101*	*-78*	*-161*	*-*	*-*	*-*	*c. Autres*
9. Profit before tax	1217	1323	1598	987	1094	-3781	-12458	-5566	-2304	3811	9. Bénéfices avant impôt
10. Income tax	286	434	550	119	247	139	52	430	536	239	10. Impôt sur le revenu
11. Profit after tax	932	889	1048	868	847	-3920	-12511	-5996	-2841	3572	11. Bénéfices après impôt
12. Distributed profit	371	301	346	296	367	96	126	240	447	531	12. Bénéfices distribués
13. Retained profit	560	588	703	571	480	-4016	-12637	-6236	-3287	3041	13. Bénéfices mis en réserve
BALANCE SHEET											**BILAN**
Assets											**Actif**
14. Cash & balance with Central bank	21872	18804	19758	23126	24180	18540	17470	19658	19256	21638	14. Caisse & solde auprès de la Banque centrale
15. Interbank deposits	5669	7083	8905	12296	15343	18084	12590	12496	11064	5372	15. Dépôts interbancaires
16. Loans	80871	88381	106470	136722	163458	225690	190985	225020	265778	296754	16. Prêts
17. Securities	19066	23408	30931	42294	52291	73769	105041	125564	130153	139080	17. Valeurs mobilières
18. Other assets	24544	28289	34487	45553	56889	84855	94362	69700	90307	95304	18. Autres actifs
Liabilities											**Passif**
19. Capital & reserves	13014	13978	16416	18618	20106	18046	15831	21415	21620	25777	19. Capital et réserves
20. Borrowing from Central bank	13636	12719	10525	8769	5274	9838	11597	7183	6245	8589	20. Emprunts auprès de la Banque centrale
21. Interbank deposits	120	967	1871	3112	2747	2843	2090	1210	1589	517	21. Dépôts interbancaires
22. Non-bank deposits	88247	98934	118869	157822	184125	252100	252971	286611	348813	391165	22. Dépôts non bancaires
23. Bonds	793	679	1035	3227	8817	21913	17402	20709	24669	27404	23. Obligations
24. Other liabilities	36212	38688	51835	68444	91093	116198	120557	115310	113622	104696	24. Autres engagements
Balance sheet total											**Total du bilan**
25. End-year total	152022	165965	200551	259992	312161	420938	420448	452438	516559	558148	25. En fin d'exercice
26. Average total	130383	144080	169499	225579	269207	370844	396574	421691	495433	468872	26. Moyen

KOREA
Commercial banks

COREE
Banques commerciales

Billion won

Milliards de won

	1992	1993	1994	1995	1996	1997	1998	1999	2000	2001		
Memorandum items												***Pour mémoire***
27. Short-term securities	..	..	..	..	..	..	..	..	..	..	27.	Titres à court terme
28. Bonds	..	..	..	..	..	..	..	..	..	..	28.	Obligations
29. Shares and participations	2734	3606	6268	8531	9136	10187	..	..	..	..	29.	Actions et participations
30. Claims on non-residents	..	..	..	..	..	..	..	..	..	..	30.	Créances sur des non-résidents
31. Liabilities to non-residents	..	..	..	..	..	..	..	..	..	..	31.	Engagements envers des non-résidents
Capital adequacy												***Solvabilité***
32. Tier 1 Capital	..	14912	17063	19339	20632	13893	14368	19840	20717	24906	32.	Fonds propres de base
33. Tier 2 Capital	..	2747	3162	3340	5238	11177	9969	11936	14102	15212	33.	Fonds propres complémentaires
34. Supervisory deductions	..	39	46	117	129	165	164	140	100	169	34.	Eléments à déduire des fonds propres
35. Total net capital resources	..	17620	20179	22563	25741	24905	24173	31636	34718	39949	35.	Total net des ressources en capital
36. Risk-weighted assets	..	160167	190033	241932	281496	353750	293744	292072	329563	369674	36.	Actifs pondérés des risques
SUPPLEMENTARY INFORMATION												**RENSEIGNEMENTS COMPLEMENTAIRES**
37. Number of institutions	24	24	24	25	25	26	20	17	17	15	37.	Nombre d'institutions
38. Number of branches	3029	3381	3750	4632	5185	6077	5132	4844	4770	4753	38.	Nombre de succursales
39. Number of employees (x 1000)	88	88	87	103	104	114	76	75	71	68	39.	Nombre de salariés (x 1000)

Notes

Commercial banks: nation-wide commercial banks and regional banks.

Average balance sheet totals (item 26) are based on daily data

Notes

Les Banques commerciales : les banques commerciales nationales et les banques régionales.

La moyenne du total des actifs/passifs (poste 26) est basée sur des données journalières.

172

KOREA
Commercial banks

COREE
Banques commerciales

Per cent — *Pourcentage*

INCOME STATEMENT ANALYSIS — **ANALYSE DU COMPTE DE RESULTATS**

	1992	1993	1994	1995	1996	1997	1998	1999	2000	2001	
% of average balance sheet total											**% du total moyen du bilan**
40. Interest income	8.03	7.02	7.26	8.12	8.08	8.60	9.57	8.30	7.79	6.92	40. Produits financiers
41. Interest expenses	5.66	4.85	5.24	5.94	5.83	6.49	7.86	6.16	5.86	4.90	41. Frais financiers
42. Net interest income	2.37	2.17	2.02	2.18	2.25	2.11	1.71	2.15	1.93	2.02	42. Produits financiers nets
43. Non-interest income (net)	1.72	1.99	2.89	1.96	1.62	0.73	-0.98	-0.16	0.98	1.34	43. Produits non financiers (nets)
a. Fees and commissions receivable	*0.96*	*1.08*	*1.46*	*1.00*	*0.85*	*2.78*	*3.35*	*1.95*	*1.78*	*2.00*	*a. Frais et commissions à recevoir*
b. Fees and commissions payable	*0.14*	*0.12*	*0.14*	*0.17*	*0.24*	*2.17*	*2.99*	*1.25*	*1.34*	*1.54*	*b. Frais et commissions à payer*
c. Net profits or loss on financial operations	*0.87*	*1.01*	*1.42*	*1.04*	*0.95*	*0.73*	*0.16*	*0.11*	*0.22*	*0.84*	*c. Profits ou pertes nets sur opérations financières*
d. Other	*0.03*	*0.03*	*0.15*	*0.08*	*0.06*	*-0.61*	*-1.49*	*-0.96*	*0.33*	*0.03*	*d. Autres*
44. Gross income	4.09	4.16	4.92	4.14	3.87	2.83	0.73	1.98	2.91	3.36	44. Résultat brut
45. Operating expenses	2.44	2.53	2.57	2.67	2.59	2.18	1.91	1.53	1.39	1.40	45. Frais d'exploitation
a. Staff costs	*1.70*	*1.80*	*1.88*	*1.87*	*1.84*	*1.51*	*1.41*	*0.68*	*0.61*	*0.59*	*a. Dépenses en personnel*
b. Property costs	*0.73*	*0.73*	*0.69*	*0.80*	*0.75*	*0.67*	*0.50*	*0.84*	*0.78*	*0.80*	*b. Dépenses en immobilier*
c. Other	*-*	*-*	*-*	*-*	*-*	*-*	*-*	*-*	*-*	*-*	*c. Autres*
46. Net income	1.66	1.63	2.34	1.47	1.28	0.65	-1.18	0.46	1.52	1.97	46. Résultat net
47. Provisions (net)	0.72	0.71	1.40	1.03	0.87	1.67	1.96	1.78	1.99	1.15	47. Provisions (nettes)
a. Provisions on loans	*0.60*	*0.69*	*1.26*	*0.78*	*0.57*	*0.95*	*2.03*	*1.78*	*1.99*	*1.15*	*a. Provisions sur prêts*
b. Provisions on securities	*0.07*	*-0.02*	*0.11*	*0.24*	*0.33*	*0.74*	*-0.03*	*-*	*-*	*-*	*b. Provisions sur titres*
c. Other	*0.05*	*0.04*	*0.04*	*0.01*	*-0.04*	*-0.02*	*-0.04*	*-*	*-*	*-*	*c. Autres*
48. Profit before tax	0.93	0.92	0.94	0.44	0.41	-1.02	-3.14	-1.32	-0.47	0.81	48. Bénéfices avant impôt
49. Income tax	0.22	0.30	0.32	0.05	0.09	0.04	0.01	0.10	0.11	0.05	49. Impôt sur le revenu
50. Profit after tax	0.71	0.62	0.62	0.38	0.31	-1.06	-3.15	-1.42	-0.57	0.76	50. Bénéfices après impôt
51. Distributed profit	0.28	0.21	0.20	0.13	0.14	0.03	0.03	0.06	0.09	0.11	51. Bénéfices distribués
52. Retained profit	0.43	0.41	0.41	0.25	0.18	-1.08	-3.19	-1.48	-0.66	0.65	52. Bénéfices mis en réserve
% of gross income											**% du total du résultat brut**
53. Net interest income	57.87	52.15	41.12	52.68	58.16	74.41	232.94	108.13	66.35	60.01	53. Produits financiers nets
54. Non-interest income (net)	42.13	47.85	58.88	47.32	41.84	25.59	-132.94	-8.13	33.65	39.99	54. Produits non financiers (nets)
a. Fees and commissions receivable	*23.44*	*25.88*	*29.77*	*24.08*	*21.89*	*98.03*	*455.98*	*98.12*	*61.00*	*59.56*	*a. Frais et commissions à recevoir*
b. Fees and commissions payable	*3.45*	*2.93*	*2.86*	*3.99*	*6.24*	*76.52*	*407.27*	*63.25*	*46.02*	*45.67*	*b. Frais et commissions à payer*
c. Net profits or loss on financial operations	*21.36*	*24.24*	*28.90*	*25.20*	*24.66*	*25.67*	*21.13*	*5.31*	*7.41*	*25.11*	*c. Profits ou pertes nets sur opérations financières*
d. Other	*0.78*	*0.67*	*3.06*	*2.02*	*1.52*	*-21.59*	*-202.79*	*-48.31*	*11.26*	*0.98*	*d. Autres*
55. Operating expenses	59.53	60.87	52.36	64.60	67.02	77.04	260.79	77.04	47.63	41.50	55. Frais d'exploitation
a. Staff costs	*41.63*	*43.29*	*38.25*	*45.28*	*47.65*	*53.39*	*192.34*	*34.49*	*20.99*	*17.59*	*a. Dépenses en personnel*
b. Property costs	*17.90*	*17.59*	*14.10*	*19.32*	*19.37*	*23.65*	*68.44*	*42.55*	*26.65*	*23.91*	*b. Dépenses en immobilier*
c. Other	*-*	*-*	*-*	*-*	*-*	*-*	*-*	*-*	*-*	*-*	*c. Autres*
56. Net income	40.47	39.13	47.64	35.40	32.98	22.96	-160.78	22.97	52.37	58.50	56. Résultat net
57. Provisions (net)	17.66	17.07	28.46	24.84	22.48	58.94	267.42	89.48	68.35	34.33	57. Provisions (nettes)
a. Provisions on loans	*14.76*	*16.60*	*25.53*	*18.82*	*14.86*	*33.42*	*277.26*	*89.48*	*68.35*	*34.33*	*a. Provisions sur prêts*
b. Provisions on securities	*1.79*	*-0.55*	*2.20*	*5.82*	*8.59*	*26.27*	*-4.32*	*-*	*-*	*-*	*b. Provisions sur titres*
c. Other	*1.11*	*1.02*	*0.73*	*0.19*	*-0.97*	*-0.74*	*-5.52*	*-*	*-*	*-*	*c. Autres*
58. Profit before tax	22.81	22.06	19.18	10.57	10.50	-35.99	-428.21	-66.52	-15.98	24.17	58. Bénéfices avant impôt
59. Income tax	5.35	7.23	6.60	1.28	2.37	1.32	1.80	5.14	3.72	1.52	59. Impôt sur le revenu
60. Profit after tax	17.46	14.83	12.58	9.29	8.13	-37.31	-430.01	-71.66	-19.70	22.66	60. Bénéfices après impôt
% of net income											**% du total du résultat net**
61. Provisions (net)	43.64	43.62	59.74	70.15	68.16	256.75	-166.33	389.54	130.51	58.68	61. Provisions (nettes)
a. Provisions on loans	*36.47*	*42.43*	*53.58*	*53.16*	*45.04*	*145.58*	*-172.45*	*389.54*	*130.51*	*58.68*	*a. Provisions sur prêts*
b. Provisions on securities	*4.43*	*-1.41*	*4.62*	*16.44*	*26.05*	*114.40*	*2.69*	*-*	*-*	*-*	*b. Provisions sur titres*
c. Other	*2.74*	*2.60*	*1.53*	*0.55*	*-2.93*	*-3.23*	*3.43*	*-*	*-*	*-*	*c. Autres*
62. Profit before tax	56.36	56.38	40.26	29.85	31.84	-156.75	266.33	-289.59	-30.51	41.32	62. Bénéfices avant impôt
63. Income tax	13.22	18.48	13.86	3.60	7.19	5.77	-1.12	22.37	7.10	2.59	63. Impôt sur le revenu
64. Profit after tax	43.13	37.89	26.40	26.24	24.65	-162.52	267.45	-311.97	-37.62	38.73	64. Bénéfices après impôt

KOREA
Commercial banks

COREE
Banques commerciales

Per cent — *Pourcentage*

BALANCE SHEET ANALYSIS — **ANALYSE DU BILAN**

% of year-end balance sheet total — % du total du bilan en fin d'exercice

	1992	1993	1994	1995	1996	1997	1998	1999	2000	2001	
Assets											**Actif**
65. Cash & balance with Central bank	14.39	11.33	9.85	8.89	7.75	4.40	4.15	4.34	3.73	3.88	65. Caisse & solde auprès de la Banque centrale
66. Interbank deposits	3.73	4.27	4.44	4.73	4.92	4.30	2.99	2.76	2.14	0.96	66. Dépôts interbancaires
67. Loans	53.20	53.25	53.09	52.59	52.36	53.62	45.42	49.73	51.45	53.17	67. Prêts
68. Securities	12.54	14.10	15.42	16.27	16.75	17.52	24.98	27.75	25.20	24.92	68. Valeurs mobilières
69. Other assets	16.15	17.05	17.20	17.52	18.22	20.16	22.44	15.41	17.48	17.08	69. Autres actifs
Liabilities											**Passif**
70. Capital & reserves	8.56	8.42	8.19	7.16	6.44	4.29	3.77	4.73	4.19	4.62	70. Capital et réserves
71. Borrowing from Central bank	8.97	7.66	5.25	3.37	1.69	2.34	2.76	1.59	1.21	1.54	71. Emprunts auprès de la Banque centrale
72. Interbank deposits	0.08	0.58	0.93	1.20	0.88	0.68	0.50	0.27	0.31	0.09	72. Dépôts interbancaires
73. Non-bank deposits	58.05	59.61	59.27	60.70	58.98	59.89	60.17	63.35	67.53	70.08	73. Dépôts non bancaires
74. Bonds	0.52	0.41	0.52	1.24	2.82	5.21	4.14	4.58	4.78	4.91	74. Obligations
75. Other liabilities	23.82	23.31	25.85	26.33	29.18	27.60	28.67	25.49	22.00	18.76	75. Autres engagements
Memorandum items											*Pour mémoire*
76. Short-term securities	..	..	..	..	..	..	..	..	..	..	76. Titres à court terme
77. Bonds	..	..	..	..	..	..	..	..	..	..	77. Obligations
78. Shares and participations	1.80	2.17	3.13	3.28	2.93	2.42	..	..	..	..	78. Actions et participations
79. Claims on non-residents	..	..	..	..	..	..	..	..	..	..	79. Créances sur des non-résidents
80. Liabilities to non-residents	..	..	..	..	..	..	..	..	..	..	80. Engagements envers des non-résidents

* See notes on previous pages.

* Voir les notes en pages précédentes.

174

KOREA
Foreign commercial banks

COREE
Banques commerciales étrangères

Billion won / *Milliards de won*

	1992	1993	1994	1995	1996	1997	1998	1999	2000	2001	
INCOME STATEMENT											**COMPTE DE RESULTATS**
1. Interest income	1084	995	1171	1568	1717	2386	2768	1960	2491	2491	1. Produits financiers
2. Interest expenses	749	697	810	1162	1187	1753	1638	1247	1755	1755	2. Frais financiers
3. Net interest income	335	298	361	405	530	634	1129	713	735	646	3. Produits financiers nets
4. Non-interest income (net)	205	196	183	202	311	1672	-73	328	678	649	4. Produits non financiers (nets)
a. Fees and commissions receivable	196	185	193	235	908	4391	5701	8040	11341	17975	a. Frais et commissions à recevoir
b. Fees and commissions payable	5	5	36	67	637	2737	5786	7727	10699	17418	b. Frais et commissions à payer
c. Net profits or loss on financial operations	10	15	22	37	37	27	24	50	33	94	c. Profits ou pertes nets sur opérations financières
d. Other	2	1	4	-3	3	-8	-12	-36	4	-2	d. Autres
5. Gross income	540	494	544	607	841	2306	1057	1040	1413	1295	5. Résultat brut
6. Operating expenses	192	211	221	245	291	321	331	352	417	501	6. Frais d'exploitation
a. Staff costs	:	:	:	:	:	:	161	160	186	228	a. Dépenses en personnel
b. Property costs	:	:	:	:	:	:	170	192	231	272	b. Dépenses en immobilier
c. Other	:	:	:	:	:	:	-	-	-	-	c. Autres
7. Net income	348	283	323	362	550	1984	726	688	997	794	7. Résultat net
8. Provisions (net)	44	33	18	62	72	212	17	242	29	46	8. Provisions (nettes)
a. Provisions on loans	44	33	18	53	70	146	:	:	:	:	a. Provisions sur prêts
b. Provisions on securities	-	-	-	0	0	66	:	:	:	:	b. Provisions sur titres
c. Other	-	-	-	9	2	-	:	:	:	:	c. Autres
9. Profit before tax	304	250	304	300	478	1773	709	446	967	748	9. Bénéfices avant impôt
10. Income tax	108	86	98	64	112	551	200	122	286	218	10. Impôt sur le revenu
11. Profit after tax	196	164	206	235	366	1222	509	324	681	531	11. Bénéfices après impôt
12. Distributed profit	:	:	:	:	:	:	:	:	:	:	12. Bénéfices distribués
13. Retained profit	:	:	:	:	:	:	:	:	:	:	13. Bénéfices mis en réserve
BALANCE SHEET											**BILAN**
Assets											*Actif*
14. Cash & balance with Central bank	45	43	23	43	70	161	129	270	156	14	14. Caisse & solde auprès de la Banque centrale
15. Interbank deposits	577	561	655	1563	2018	3477	1276	1714	2243	168	15. Dépôts interbancaires
16. Loans	6279	5213	5972	11156	15400	24484	10495	9928	12079	1104	16. Prêts
17. Securities	482	893	931	2045	2602	6904	5417	7375	10792	1383	17. Valeurs mobilières
18. Other assets	4162	4627	5691	4584	3902	11110	11924	9262	20963	2015	18. Autres actifs
Liabilities											*Passif*
19. Capital & reserves	1560	1750	1957	2610	3251	4272	3181	3027	3533	324	19. Capital et réserves
20. Borrowing from Central bank	27	34	3	2	2	-	3	-	-	-	20. Emprunts auprès de la Banque centrale
21. Interbank deposits	-	-	-	606	353	979	696	816	1246	113	21. Dépôts interbancaires
22. Non-bank deposits	1712	1583	1757	1587	1652	3218	4653	5024	9104	1027	22. Dépôts non bancaires
23. Bonds	-	-	-	-	-	-	-	-	-	-	23. Obligations
24. Other liabilities	8246	7969	9554	14586	18736	37668	20708	19683	32350	3220	24. Autres engagements
Balance sheet total											**Total du bilan**
25. End-year total	11545	11336	13271	19390	23992	46137	29241	28550	46233	4683	25. En fin d'exercice
26. Average total	12737	13551	14807	19026	22722	33141	29183	29435	40435	4964	26. Moyen

175

KOREA

Foreign commercial banks

Billion won	1992	1993	1994	1995	1996	1997	1998	1999	2000	2001
Memorandum items										
27. Short-term securities	..	..	..	..	..	..	..	..	..	..
28. Bonds	..	..	..	..	..	..	..	..	..	..
29. Shares and participations	4	5	72	9	3	18	..	..	..	..
30. Claims on non-residents	..	..	..	..	..	..	..	..	..	..
31. Liabilities to non-residents	..	..	..	..	..	..	..	..	..	..
Capital adequacy										
32. Tier 1 Capital	..	1727	1900	2584	3180	4263	..	..	..	..
33. Tier 2 Capital	..	149	149	144	189	1804	..	..	..	..
34. Supervisory deductions	..	-	-	-	-	-	..	..	..	..
35. Total net capital resources	..	1876	2049	2728	3369	6066	..	..	..	..
36. Risk-weighted assets	..	10669	12322	14966	19271	30561	..	..	..	..
SUPPLEMENTARY INFORMATION										
37. Number of institutions	51	52	52	52	48	53	51	46	43	42
38. Number of branches	73	74	72	71	67	68	66	62	62	62
39. Number of employees (x 1000)	3	3	3	3	3	3	3	2	3	3

COREE

Banques commerciales étrangères

Milliards de won

Pour mémoire
27. Titres à court terme
28. Obligations
29. Actions et participations
30. Créances sur des non-résidents
31. Engagements envers des non-résidents

Solvabilité
32. Fonds propres de base
33. Fonds propres complémentaires
34. Eléments à déduire des fonds propres
35. Total net des ressources en capital
36. Actifs pondérés des risques

RENSEIGNEMENTS COMPLEMENTAIRES
37. Nombre d'institutions
38. Nombre de succursales
39. Nombre de salariés (x 1000)

Notes

Foreign commercial banks: domestic branches of foreign commercial banks.

Average balance sheet totals (item 26) are based on daily data.

Notes

Les Banques commerciales étrangères : les succursales nationales des banques commerciales étrangères.

La moyenne du total des actifs/passifs (poste 26) est basée sur des données journalières.

KOREA
Foreign commercial banks

COREE
Banques commerciales étrangères

Per cent — *Pourcentage*

INCOME STATEMENT ANALYSIS — **ANALYSE DU COMPTE DE RESULTATS**

No.	Item (EN)	1992	1993	1994	1995	1996	1997	1998	1999	2000	2001	Libellé (FR)	No.
	% of average balance sheet total											**% du total moyen du bilan**	
40.	Interest income	8.51	7.34	7.91	8.24	7.56	7.20	9.48	6.66	6.16	50.18	Produits financiers	40.
41.	Interest expenses	5.88	5.14	5.47	6.11	5.22	5.29	5.61	4.24	4.34	35.35	Frais financiers	41.
42.	Net interest income	2.63	2.20	2.44	2.13	2.33	1.91	3.87	2.42	1.82	13.01	Produits financiers nets	42.
43.	Non-interest income (net)	1.61	1.45	1.24	1.06	1.37	5.05	-0.25	1.11	1.68	13.07	Produits non financiers (nets)	43.
	a. Fees and commissions receivable	1.54	1.36	1.30	1.24	4.00	13.25	19.53	27.31	28.05	362.11	a. Frais et commissions à recevoir	
	b. Fees and commissions payable	0.04	0.04	0.24	0.35	2.80	8.26	19.83	26.25	26.46	350.89	b. Frais et commissions à payer	
	c. Net profits or loss on financial operations	0.08	0.11	0.15	0.19	0.16	0.08	0.08	0.17	0.08	1.89	c. Profits ou pertes nets sur opérations financières	
	d. Other	0.02	0.01	0.03	-0.02	0.01	-0.03	-0.04	-0.12	0.01	-0.04	d. Autres	
44.	Gross income	4.24	3.64	3.67	3.19	3.70	6.96	3.62	3.53	3.49	26.09	Résultat brut	44.
45.	Operating expenses	1.50	1.56	1.49	1.29	1.28	0.97	1.13	1.20	1.03	10.09	Frais d'exploitation	45.
	a. Staff costs	:	:	:	:	:	:	0.55	0.54	0.46	4.59	a. Dépenses en personnel	
	b. Property costs	:	:	:	:	:	:	0.58	0.65	0.57	5.48	b. Dépenses en immobilier	
	c. Other											c. Autres	
46.	Net income	2.73	2.09	2.18	1.90	2.42	5.99	2.49	2.34	2.47	16.00	Résultat net	46.
47.	Provisions (net)	0.35	0.24	0.12	0.33	0.32	0.64	0.06	0.82	0.07	0.93	Provisions (nettes)	47.
	a. Provisions on loans	0.35	0.24	0.12	0.28	0.31	0.44	:	:	:	:	a. Provisions sur prêts	
	b. Provisions on securities							:	:	:	:	b. Provisions sur titres	
	c. Other	-	-	-	0.05	0.01	0.20	:	:	:	:	c. Autres	
48.	Profit before tax	2.38	1.85	2.05	1.57	2.10	5.35	2.43	1.52	2.39	15.07	Bénéfices avant impôt	48.
49.	Income tax	0.85	0.64	0.66	0.34	0.49	1.66	0.69	0.41	0.71	4.39	Impôt sur le revenu	49.
50.	Profit after tax	1.54	1.21	1.39	1.24	1.61	3.69	1.74	1.10	1.68	10.70	Bénéfices après impôt	50.
51.	Distributed profit											Bénéfices distribués	51.
52.	Retained profit	:	:	:	:	:	:	:	:	:	:	Bénéfices mis en réserve	52.
	% of gross income											**% du total du résultat brut**	
53.	Net interest income	62.12	60.30	66.35	66.78	63.05	27.48	106.87	68.56	52.02	49.88	Produits financiers nets	53.
54.	Non-interest income (net)	37.90	39.70	33.65	33.22	36.95	72.52	-6.87	31.54	47.98	50.12	Produits non financiers (nets)	54.
	a. Fees and commissions receivable	36.40	37.43	35.49	38.74	107.93	190.45	539.44	773.08	802.62	1388.03	a. Frais et commissions à recevoir	
	b. Fees and commissions payable	0.83	1.03	6.57	11.09	75.73	118.72	547.51	742.98	757.18	1345.02	b. Frais et commissions à payer	
	c. Net profits or loss on financial operations	1.93	3.08	4.03	6.06	4.45	1.15	2.31	4.81	2.34	7.26	c. Profits ou pertes nets sur opérations financières	
	d. Other	0.41	0.22	0.70	-0.49	0.31	-0.36	-1.11	-3.46	0.28	-0.15	d. Autres	
55.	Operating expenses	35.51	42.72	40.66	40.41	34.58	13.94	31.31	33.85	29.51	38.69	Frais d'exploitation	55.
	a. Staff costs	:	:	:	:	:	:	15.24	15.38	13.16	17.61	a. Dépenses en personnel	
	b. Property costs	:	:	:	:	:	:	16.07	18.46	16.35	21.00	b. Dépenses en immobilier	
	c. Other											c. Autres	
56.	Net income	64.49	57.26	59.34	59.59	65.42	86.06	68.69	66.15	70.56	61.31	Résultat net	56.
57.	Provisions (net)	8.21	6.59	3.39	10.28	8.61	9.19	1.61	23.27	2.05	3.55	Provisions (nettes)	57.
	a. Provisions on loans	8.21	6.59	3.39	8.80	8.27	6.31	:	:	:	:	a. Provisions sur prêts	
	b. Provisions on securities					0.05		:	:	:	:	b. Provisions sur titres	
	c. Other	-	-	-	1.48	0.29	2.87	:	:	:	:	c. Autres	
58.	Profit before tax	56.28	50.68	55.95	49.33	56.82	76.87	67.08	42.88	68.44	57.76	Bénéfices avant impôt	58.
59.	Income tax	20.03	17.47	18.05	10.61	13.29	23.89	18.93	11.73	20.24	16.83	Impôt sur le revenu	59.
60.	Profit after tax	36.25	33.23	37.90	38.71	43.53	52.99	48.15	31.15	48.20	41.00	Bénéfices après impôt	60.
	% of net income											**% du total du résultat net**	
61.	Provisions (net)	12.73	11.50	5.71	17.25	13.15	10.67	2.34	35.17	2.91	5.79	Provisions (nettes)	61.
	a. Provisions on loans	12.73	11.50	5.71	14.76	12.65	7.34	:	:	:	:	a. Provisions sur prêts	
	b. Provisions on securities					0.05		:	:	:	:	b. Provisions sur titres	
	c. Other	-	-	-	2.49	0.44	3.34	:	:	:	:	c. Autres	
62.	Profit before tax	87.27	88.50	94.29	82.78	86.85	89.33	97.66	64.83	96.99	94.21	Bénéfices avant impôt	62.
63.	Income tax	31.06	30.50	30.42	17.80	20.31	27.76	27.55	17.73	28.69	27.46	Impôt sur le revenu	63.
64.	Profit after tax	56.21	58.03	63.88	64.95	66.53	61.57	70.11	47.09	68.30	66.88	Bénéfices après impôt	64.

KOREA
Foreign commercial banks

COREE
Banques commerciales étrangères

Per cent / *Pourcentage*

BALANCE SHEET ANALYSIS / **ANALYSE DU BILAN**

% of year-end balance sheet total / **% du total du bilan en fin d'exercice**

Assets / **Actif**

	1992	1993	1994	1995	1996	1997	1998	1999	2000	2001	
65. Cash & balance with Central bank	0.39	0.38	0.17	0.22	0.29	0.35	0.44	0.95	0.34	0.30	65. Caisse & solde auprès de la Banque centrale
66. Interbank deposits	5.00	4.95	4.94	8.06	8.41	7.54	4.36	6.00	4.85	3.59	66. Dépôts interbancaires
67. Loans	54.39	45.99	45.00	57.54	64.19	53.07	35.89	34.77	26.13	23.57	67. Prêts
68. Securities	4.17	7.88	7.01	10.54	10.84	14.97	18.52	25.83	23.34	29.53	68. Valeurs mobilières
69. Other assets	36.05	40.81	42.88	23.64	16.26	24.08	40.78	32.44	45.34	43.03	69. Autres actifs
Liabilities											**Passif**
70. Capital & reserves	13.51	15.44	14.74	13.46	13.55	9.26	10.88	10.60	7.64	6.92	70. Capital et réserves
71. Borrowing from Central bank	0.23	0.30	0.02	0.01	0.01	-	0.01	-	-	-	71. Emprunts auprès de la Banque centrale
72. Interbank deposits	-	-	-	3.13	1.47	2.12	2.38	2.86	2.70	2.41	72. Dépôts interbancaires
73. Non-bank deposits	14.83	13.97	13.24	8.18	6.88	6.98	15.91	17.60	19.69	21.93	73. Dépôts non bancaires
74. Bonds	-	-	-	-	-	-	-	-	-	-	74. Obligations
75. Other liabilities	71.43	70.29	71.99	75.22	78.09	81.64	70.82	68.94	69.97	68.76	75. Autres engagements
Memorandum items											***Pour mémoire***
76. Short-term securities	..	..	..	..	..	..	..	..	..	..	*76. Titres à court terme*
77. Bonds	..	..	..	..	..	..	..	..	..	..	*77. Obligations*
78. Shares and participations	0.03	0.04	0.54	0.05	0.01	0.04	..	..	..	..	*78. Actions et participations*
79. Claims on non-residents	..	..	..	..	..	..	..	..	..	..	*79. Créances sur des non-résidents*
80. Liabilities to non-residents	..	..	..	..	..	..	..	..	..	..	*80. Engagements envers des non-résidents*

* See notes on previous pages.   * Voir les notes en pages précédentes.

LUXEMBOURG

Commercial banks

Million euros

	1992	1993	1994	1995	1996	1997	1998	1999	2000	2001
INCOME STATEMENT										
1. Interest income	34109	32393	28999	33556	30985	33935	38436	37539	51628	52790
2. Interest expenses	31212	29462	25902	30408	27809	30775	35299	34140	47925	48332
3. Net interest income	2898	2932	3098	3148	3177	3160	3137	3399	3703	4458
4. Non-interest income (net)	1194	1917	1533	1659	1970	2579	3864	3274	4325	3693
a. Fees and commissions receivable	..	..	..	..	..	..	..	..	..	..
b. Fees and commissions payable	..	..	..	..	..	..	..	..	..	..
c. Net profits or loss on financial operations	..	..	..	..	..	..	..	..	..	..
d. Other	..	..	..	..	..	..	..	..	..	..
5. Gross income	4092	4849	4630	4807	5146	5739	7001	6673	8028	8151
6. Operating expenses	1611	1841	2082	2237	2393	2517	2752	3072	3618	3807
a. Staff costs	838	946	1103	1150	1205	1265	1321	1483	1716	1804
b. Property costs	..	..	..	..	..	..	..	..	..	..
c. Other	..	..	..	..	..	..	..	..	..	..
7. Net income	2480	3008	2548	2570	2753	3222	4249	3601	4410	4344
8. Provisions (net)	1368	1020	349	297	131	537	1046	651	888	719
a. Provisions on loans	..	..	..	..	..	..	..	..	..	..
b. Provisions on securities	..	..	..	..	..	..	..	..	..	..
c. Other	..	..	..	..	..	..	..	..	..	..
9. Profit before tax	1112	1987	2200	2273	2622	2685	3203	2950	3522	3625
10. Income tax	409	635	650	761	907	903	722	898	969	833
11. Profit after tax	704	1352	1549	1512	1715	1782	2482	2052	2553	2792
12. Distributed profit	..	..	..	..	..	..	..	..	..	..
13. Retained profit	..	..	..	..	..	..	..	..	..	..
BALANCE SHEET										
Assets										
14. Cash & balance with Central bank	626	3435	1484	834	1025	936	890	5218	6736	7103
15. Interbank deposits	211072	232006	263032	265497	265853	281170	287078	289442	311632	344495
16. Loans	88252	88517	80745	85995	88123	96773	98220	117233	131271	150719
17. Securities	33874	58974	76316	86116	104531	116462	129022	152758	155954	168577
18. Other assets	23738	14217	16430	17031	17819	21229	25675	33808	42156	50106
Liabilities										
19. Capital & reserves	9973	10516	10516	11395	11768	11761	12987	15042	17172	19595
20. Borrowing from Central bank	..	..	..	..	..	..	..	..	..	..
21. Interbank deposits	156379	174257	198132	213701	220047	240873	256786	295896	290297	334904
22. Non-bank deposits	151777	175379	185590	179131	187889	194185	191471	193825	226932	231734
23. Bonds	16936	16979	21435	28059	34748	42811	40782	48879	59360	73045
24. Other liabilities	22498	20018	22334	23186	22899	26941	38860	44816	53988	61722
Balance sheet total										
25. End-year total	357563	397148	438007	455472	477351	516571	540886	598459	647749	721000
26. Average total	343117	383002	414241	446883	466746	503700	550007	567408	630064	685944

LUXEMBOURG

Banques commerciales

Millions d'euros

COMPTE DE RESULTATS

1. Produits financiers
2. Frais financiers
3. Produits financiers nets
4. Produits non financiers (nets)
   a. Frais et commissions à recevoir
   b. Frais et commissions à payer
   c. Profits ou pertes nets sur opérations financières
   d. Autres
5. Résultat brut
6. Frais d'exploitation
   a. Dépenses en personnel
   b. Dépenses en immobilier
   c. Autres
7. Résultat net
8. Provisions (nettes)
   a. Provisions sur prêts
   b. Provisions sur titres
   c. Autres
9. Bénéfices avant impôt
10. Impôt sur le revenu
11. Bénéfices après impôt
12. Bénéfices distribués
13. Bénéfices mis en réserve

BILAN

Actif

14. Caisse & solde auprès de la Banque centrale
15. Dépôts interbancaires
16. Prêts
17. Valeurs mobilières
18. Autres actifs

Passif

19. Capital et réserves
20. Emprunts auprès de la Banque centrale
21. Dépôts interbancaires
22. Dépôts non bancaires
23. Obligations
24. Autres engagements

Total du bilan

25. En fin d'exercice
26. Moyen

179

LUXEMBOURG
Commercial banks

Million euros

LUXEMBOURG
Banques commerciales

Millions d'euros

	1992	1993	1994	1995	1996	1997	1998	1999	2000	2001	
Memorandum items											**Pour mémoire**
27. Short-term securities	..	..	..	..	..	..	..	..	..	..	27. Titres à court terme
28. Bonds	17355	..	..	..	..	..	..	..	..	..	28. Obligations
29. Shares and participations	2216	1960	2415	1359	2592	2442	4262	5661	7518	10396	29. Actions et participations
30. Claims on non-residents	311452	330422	358340	368102	396714	431837	460347	502858	..	..	30. Créances sur des non-résidents
31. Liabilities to non-residents	286537	297020	319688	329569	345991	370534	403584	423626	..	..	31. Engagements envers des non-résidents
Capital adequacy											**Solvabilité**
32. Tier 1 Capital	..	..	..	..	..	..	..	..	..	..	32. Fonds propres de base
33. Tier 2 Capital	..	..	..	..	..	..	..	..	..	..	33. Fonds propres complémentaires
34. Supervisory deductions	..	..	..	..	..	..	..	..	..	..	34. Eléments à déduire des fonds propres
35. Total net capital resources	..	..	..	..	..	..	..	..	..	..	35. Total net des ressources en capital
36. Risk-weighted assets	..	..	..	..	..	..	..	..	..	..	36. Actifs pondérés des risques
SUPPLEMENTARY INFORMATION											**RENSEIGNEMENTS COMPLEMENTAIRES**
37. Number of institutions	213	218	222	220	221	215	209	210	202	189	37. Nombre d'institutions
38. Number of branches	303	306	367	356	..	..	..	..	..	..	38. Nombre de succursales
39. Number of employees (x 1000)	16	17	18	18	19	19	20	21	23	24	39. Nombre de salariés (x 1000)

Notes

. Average balance sheet totals (item 26) are based on thirteen end-month data

Notes

. La moyenne du total des actifs/passifs (poste 26) est basée sur treize données de fin de mois.

LUXEMBOURG
Commercial banks

LUXEMBOURG
Banques commerciales

Per cent — *Pourcentage*

INCOME STATEMENT ANALYSIS — **ANALYSE DU COMPTE DE RESULTATS**

		1992	1993	1994	1995	1996	1997	1998	1999	2000	2001
% of average balance sheet total	**% du total moyen du bilan**										
40. Interest income	Produits financiers	9.94	8.46	7.00	7.51	6.64	6.74	6.99	6.62	8.19	7.70
41. Interest expenses	Frais financiers	9.10	7.69	6.25	6.80	5.96	6.11	6.42	6.02	7.61	7.05
42. Net interest income	Produits financiers nets	0.84	0.77	0.75	0.70	0.68	0.63	0.57	0.60	0.59	0.65
43. Non-interest income (net)	Produits non financiers (nets)	0.35	0.50	0.37	0.37	0.42	0.51	0.70	0.58	0.69	0.54
a. Fees and commissions receivable	a. Frais et commissions à recevoir	:	:	:	:	:	:	:	:	:	:
b. Fees and commissions payable	b. Frais et commissions à payer	:	:	:	:	:	:	:	:	:	:
c. Net profits or loss on financial operations	c. Profits ou pertes nets sur opérations financières	:	:	:	:	:	:	:	:	:	:
d. Other	d. Autres	:	:	:	:	:	:	:	:	:	:
44. Gross income	Résultat brut	1.19	1.27	1.12	1.08	1.10	1.14	1.27	1.18	1.27	1.19
45. Operating expenses	Frais d'exploitation	0.47	0.48	0.50	0.50	0.51	0.50	0.50	0.54	0.57	0.56
a. Staff costs	a. Dépenses en personnel	0.24	0.25	0.27	0.26	0.26	0.25	0.24	0.26	0.27	0.26
b. Property costs	b. Dépenses en immobilier	:	:	:	:	:	:	:	:	:	:
c. Other	c. Autres	:	:	:	:	:	:	:	:	:	:
46. Net income	Résultat net	0.72	0.79	0.62	0.58	0.59	0.64	0.77	0.63	0.70	0.63
47. Provisions (net)	Provisions (nettes)	0.40	0.27	0.08	0.07	0.03	0.11	0.19	0.11	0.14	0.10
a. Provisions on loans	a. Provisions sur prêts	:	:	:	:	:	:	:	:	:	:
b. Provisions on securities	b. Provisions sur titres	:	:	:	:	:	:	:	:	:	:
c. Other	c. Autres	:	:	:	:	:	:	:	:	:	:
48. Profit before tax	Bénéfices avant impôt	0.32	0.52	0.53	0.51	0.56	0.53	0.58	0.52	0.56	0.53
49. Income tax	Impôt sur le revenu	0.12	0.17	0.16	0.17	0.19	0.18	0.13	0.16	0.15	0.12
50. Profit after tax	Bénéfices après impôt	0.21	0.35	0.37	0.34	0.37	0.35	0.45	0.36	0.41	0.41
51. Distributed profit	Bénéfices distribués	:	:	:	:	:	:	:	:	:	:
52. Retained profit	Bénéfices mis en réserve	:	:	:	:	:	:	:	:	:	:
% of gross income	**% du total du résultat brut**										
53. Net interest income	Produits financiers nets	70.81	60.46	66.90	65.48	61.72	55.05	44.81	50.94	46.13	54.69
54. Non-interest income (net)	Produits non financiers (nets)	29.19	39.54	33.10	34.52	38.28	44.95	55.19	49.06	53.87	45.31
a. Fees and commissions receivable	a. Frais et commissions à recevoir	:	:	:	:	:	:	:	:	:	:
b. Fees and commissions payable	b. Frais et commissions à payer	:	:	:	:	:	:	:	:	:	:
c. Net profits or loss on financial operations	c. Profits ou pertes nets sur opérations financières	:	:	:	:	:	:	:	:	:	:
d. Other	d. Autres	:	:	:	:	:	:	:	:	:	:
55. Operating expenses	Frais d'exploitation	39.38	37.97	44.96	46.54	46.51	43.86	39.31	46.04	45.07	46.71
a. Staff costs	a. Dépenses en personnel	20.49	19.51	23.82	23.92	23.41	22.05	18.87	22.22	21.38	22.13
b. Property costs	b. Dépenses en immobilier	:	:	:	:	:	:	:	:	:	:
c. Other	c. Autres	:	:	:	:	:	:	:	:	:	:
56. Net income	Résultat net	60.62	62.03	55.04	53.46	53.49	56.14	60.69	53.96	54.93	53.29
57. Provisions (net)	Provisions (nettes)	33.43	21.04	7.53	6.18	2.55	9.36	14.94	9.76	11.06	8.82
a. Provisions on loans	a. Provisions sur prêts	:	:	:	:	:	:	:	:	:	:
b. Provisions on securities	b. Provisions sur titres	:	:	:	:	:	:	:	:	:	:
c. Other	c. Autres	:	:	:	:	:	:	:	:	:	:
58. Profit before tax	Bénéfices avant impôt	27.19	40.99	47.50	47.28	50.94	46.78	45.76	44.21	43.87	44.47
59. Income tax	Impôt sur le revenu	10.00	13.11	14.04	15.84	17.62	15.73	10.31	13.46	12.07	10.22
60. Profit after tax	Bénéfices après impôt	17.19	27.88	33.46	31.44	33.33	31.05	35.45	30.75	31.80	34.25
% of net income	**% du total du résultat net**										
61. Provisions (net)	Provisions (nettes)	55.15	33.92	13.69	11.55	4.77	16.67	24.61	18.08	20.14	16.55
a. Provisions on loans	a. Provisions sur prêts	:	:	:	:	:	:	:	:	:	:
b. Provisions on securities	b. Provisions sur titres	:	:	:	:	:	:	:	:	:	:
c. Other	c. Autres	:	:	:	:	:	:	:	:	:	:
62. Profit before tax	Bénéfices avant impôt	44.85	66.08	86.31	88.45	95.23	83.33	75.39	81.92	79.86	83.45
63. Income tax	Impôt sur le revenu	16.49	21.13	25.51	29.63	32.93	28.02	16.98	24.94	21.97	19.18
64. Profit after tax	Bénéfices après impôt	28.36	44.95	60.80	58.82	62.30	55.31	58.41	56.98	57.89	64.27

LUXEMBOURG

Commercial banks

Per cent

BALANCE SHEET ANALYSIS

% of year-end balance sheet total	1992	1993	1994	1995	1996	1997	1998	1999	2000	2001
Assets										
65. Cash & balance with Central bank	0.18	0.86	0.34	0.18	0.21	0.18	0.16	0.87	1.04	0.99
66. Interbank deposits	59.03	58.42	60.05	58.29	55.69	54.43	53.08	48.36	48.11	47.78
67. Loans	24.68	22.29	18.43	18.88	18.46	18.73	18.16	19.59	20.27	20.90
68. Securities	9.47	14.85	17.42	18.91	21.90	22.55	23.85	25.53	24.08	23.38
69. Other assets	6.64	3.58	3.75	3.74	3.73	4.11	4.75	5.65	6.51	6.95
Liabilities										
70. Capital & reserves	2.79	2.65	2.40	2.50	2.47	2.28	2.40	2.51	2.65	2.72
71. Borrowing from Central bank	..	..	..	..	..	..	..	..	..	..
72. Interbank deposits	43.73	43.88	45.23	46.92	46.10	46.63	47.48	49.44	44.82	46.45
73. Non-bank deposits	42.45	44.16	42.37	39.33	39.36	37.59	35.40	32.39	35.03	32.14
74. Bonds	4.74	4.28	4.89	6.16	7.28	8.29	7.54	8.17	9.16	10.13
75. Other liabilities	6.29	5.04	5.10	5.09	4.80	5.22	7.18	7.49	8.33	8.56
Memorandum items										
76. *Short-term securities*	*4.85*	..	..	..	..	..	..	..	..	..
77. *Bonds*	..	..	..	..	..	..	..	..	..	..
78. *Shares and participations*	*0.62*	*0.49*	*0.55*	*0.30*	*0.54*	*0.47*	*0.79*	*0.95*	*1.16*	*1.44*
79. *Claims on non-residents*	*87.10*	*83.20*	*81.81*	*80.82*	*83.11*	*83.60*	*85.11*	*84.03*	*..*	*..*
80. *Liabilities to non-residents*	*80.14*	*74.79*	*72.99*	*72.36*	*72.48*	*71.73*	*74.62*	*70.79*	*..*	*..*

* See notes on previous pages.

LUXEMBOURG

Banques commerciales

Pourcentage

ANALYSE DU BILAN

% du total du bilan en fin d'exercice

Actif

65. Caisse & solde auprès de la Banque centrale
66. Dépôts interbancaires
67. Prêts
68. Valeurs mobilières
69. Autres actifs

Passif

70. Capital et réserves
71. Emprunts auprès de la Banque centrale
72. Dépôts interbancaires
73. Dépôts non bancaires
74. Obligations
75. Autres engagements

Pour mémoire

76. *Titres à court terme*
77. *Obligations*
78. *Actions et participations*
79. *Créances sur des non-résidents*
80. *Engagements envers des non-résidents*

* Voir les notes en pages précédentes.

MEXICO
Commercial banks

MEXIQUE
Banques commerciales

Million pesos / *Millions de pesos*

	1992	1993	1994	1995	1996	1997[1]	1998	1999	2000	2001	
INCOME STATEMENT											**COMPTE DE RESULTATS**
1. Interest income (2)	73980	92987	104325	311439	244677	207028	284926	322242	296253	244757	1. Produits financiers (2)
2. Interest expenses (2)	50532	63501	72931	266830	209147	165082	225710	251196	221660	171155	2. Frais financiers (2)
3. Net interest income (2)	23449	29486	31394	44609	35530	41946	59216	71047	74593	73602	3. Produits financiers nets (2)
4. Non-interest income (net) (2)	7031	9502	8673	17070	28593	25130	16797	43399	29553	29608	4. Produits non financiers (nets) (2)
a. Fees and commissions receivable	*2482*	*3183*	*4070*	*9856*	*6625*	*9836*	*13748*	*17718*	*24573*	*28570*	*a. Frais et commissions à recevoir*
b. Fees and commissions payable	*538*	*742*	*893*	*1897*	*1677*				*3971*	*5462*	*b. Frais et commissions à payer*
c. Net profits or loss on financial operations	*5879*	*6458*	*4786*	*9182*	*22542*	*9689*	*5658*	*22168*	*7690*	*12884*	*c. Profits ou pertes nets sur opérations financières*
d. Other	*792*	*604*	*709*	*71*	*1103*	*5605*	*-2608*	*3514*	*1262*	*-6363*	*d. Autres*
5. Gross income	30480	38988	40067	61679	64123	67077	76014	114446	104147	103211	5. Résultat brut
6. Operating expenses	18045	21534	25720	32919	40828	49149	57691	69031	74028	68702	6. Frais d'exploitation
a. Staff costs	*8626*	*10661*	*12301*	*13330*	*15953*	*21452*	*23767*	*26921*	*33939*	*28673*	*a. Dépenses en personnel*
b. Property costs	*8816*	*10176*	*11859*	*17750*	*22595*	*25011*	*29502*	*36920*	*36301*	*36884*	*b. Dépenses en immobilier*
c. Other	*603*	*697*	*1560*	*1838*	*2280*	*2686*	*4421*	*5190*	*3788*	*3144*	*c. Autres*
7. Net income	12435	17454	14347	28760	23295	17929	18323	45414	30119	34509	7. Résultat net
8. Provisions (net)	3502	6885	9619	24668	29998	16482	16608	32976	13854	17601	8. Provisions (nettes)
a. Provisions on loans	*3502*	*6885*	*9619*	*24668*	*29998*	*16482*	*16608*	*32976*	*13854*	*17601*	*a. Provisions sur prêts*
b. Provisions on securities											*b. Provisions sur titres*
c. Other											*c. Autres*
9. Profit before tax	8933	10569	4728	4092	-6704	1447	1715	12438	16265	16908	9. Bénéfices avant impôt
10. Income tax	2414	2160	1048	781	615	665	-4817	3067	2816	4544	10. Impôt sur le revenu
11. Profit after tax	6519	8409	3680	3312	-7318	782	6532	9371	13449	12365	11. Bénéfices après impôt
12. Distributed profit	691	624	254	187	180	100	-	-	-	-	12. Bénéfices distribués
13. Retained profit	5828	7785	3427	3125	-7498	681	6532	9371	13449	12365	13. Bénéfices mis en réserve
BALANCE SHEET											**BILAN**
Assets											**Actif**
14. Cash & balance with Central bank	6945	5850	9529	11912	16186	21093	36611	73338	41728	60319	14. Caisse & solde auprès de la Banque centrale
15. Interbank deposits (2) (3)	4056	5284	7646	24128	24169	71584	100763	124991	174400	226815	15. Dépôts interbancaires (2) (3)
16. Loans	263654	321495	444600	607548	699242	745549	814831	819007	878053	858650	16. Prêts
17. Securities	75691	93243	153306	187239	245179	148103	155229	219425	203417	272525	17. Valeurs mobilières
18. Other assets	64787	84933	112334	115830	190945	61635	144022	140424	180722	166550	18. Autres actifs
Liabilities											**Passif**
19. Capital & reserves	26028	33712	40035	64580	70743	84196	103999	109687	141381	149256	19. Capital et réserves
20. Borrowing from Central bank	4576	5294	6837	13051	19831	18659	1710	36672	74444	42617	20. Emprunts auprès de la Banque centrale
21. Interbank deposits (4)	33204	43843	104165	154807	122260	148848	202147	203969	175192	159423	21. Dépôts interbancaires (4)
22. Non-bank deposits	314100	386315	479618	593050	793182	730903	875713	965175	977937	1125993	22. Dépôts non bancaires
23. Bonds (5)											23. Obligations (5)
24. Other liabilities	37224	41642	96761	121170	169706	65358	67888	61682	109367	107569	24. Autres engagements
Balance sheet total											**Total du bilan**
25. End-year total	415132	510805	727415	946657	1175722	1047963	1251456	1377185	1478321	1584859	25. En fin d'exercice
26. Average total	384804	462968	619110	837036	1061190	1111842	1149709	1314320	1427753	1531590	26. Moyen

MEXICO
Commercial banks

MEXIQUE
Banques commerciales

Million pesos / *Millions de pesos*

	1992	1993	1994	1995	1996	1997[1]	1998	1999	2000	2001
Memorandum items / **Pour mémoire**										
27. Short-term securities / Titres à court terme	..	..	..	..	..	..	..	..	..	..
28. Bonds / Obligations	..	..	..	..	..	..	..	..	..	..
29. Shares and participations / Actions et participations	4164	5762	12815	21802	24788	21847	15377	21670	28020	19931
30. Claims on non-residents / Créances sur des non-résidents	..	..	..	..	..	..	..	..	..	..
31. Liabilities to non-residents / Engagements envers des non-résidents	..	..	..	..	..	..	..	..	..	..
Capital adequacy / **Solvabilité**										
32. Tier 1 Capital / Fonds propres de base	..	..	30613	48169	56660	66558	72571	99505	104566	115297
33. Tier 2 Capital / Fonds propres complémentaires	..	..	20707	32387	32745	34963	40004	35062	19292	20548
34. Supervisory deductions / Eléments à déduire des fonds propres			..	-	-					
35. Total net capital resources / Total net des ressources en capital	31008	39897	51320	80555	89405	101521	112575	134567	123858	135846
36. Risk-weighted assets / Actifs pondérés des risques	337507	411476	523231	666146	684399	746944	830524	829637	896882	923147
SUPPLEMENTARY INFORMATION / **RENSEIGNEMENTS COMPLEMENTAIRES**										
37. Number of institutions / Nombre d'institutions	13	14	26	42	41	39	39	38	36	32
38. Number of branches / Nombre de succursales	3535	3763	4338	4806	6264	6411	6563	6891	7039	6511
39. Number of employees (x 1000) / Nombre de salariés (x 1000)	139	131	127	121	131	121	119	115	110	100

1 Break in series in 1997 due to new accounting regulations. — Rupture dans les séries en 1997 suite aux nouvelles règles de comptabilité

2 Change in methodology — Changement méthodologique.

3 Interbank deposits as assets (item 15) includes deposits in domestic and foreign banks. — Les Dépôts interbancaires sous la rubrique de l'actif (poste 15) incluent les dépôts dans les banques domestiques et étrangères.

4 Interbank deposits as liabilities (item 21) includes deposits and loans in domestic and foreign banks. — Les Dépôts interbancaires sous la rubrique du passif (poste 21) incluent les dépôts et les prêts dans les banques domestiques et étrangères.

5 Bonds (item 23) is included under Capital and reserves (item 19). — Les Obligations (poste 23) sont incluses sous Capital et réserves (poste 19).

Change in methodology — **Changement méthodologique**

. Beginning 1991 the composition of Interest income, Interest expenses, Net interest income and Non-interest income(net) (items 1 to 4) is consistent with the country's methodology and shows the same financial margins as in national publications. — A compter de 1991, la composition des Produits financiers, Frais financiers, Produits financiers (nets) et Produits non financiers (nets) (postes 1 à 4) sont conformes à la méthodologie du pays et font apparaître la même marge financière que les publications nationales

. Until 1991, the sub-items (a., b., c. and d.) of Non-interest income (item 4) are included under Interest income or Interest expenses (item 1 or 2). — Jusqu'en 1991, les sous-catégories (a., b., c. et d.), des Produits non financiers (poste 4) sont incluses sous la rubrique Produits financiers ou la rubrique Frais financiers (poste 1 ou poste 2).

. Until 1990, Interbank deposits (item 15) is included under Cash and balance with Central bank (item 14). — Jusqu'en 1990, les Dépôts interbancaires (poste 15) sont inclus sous la rubrique Caisse et solde auprès de la Banque centrale (poste 14).

Notes

. Due to their special situation as a result of mergers and acquisitions, the following banks are excluded from the coverage: Inverlat, Union, Cremi, Oriente, Obrero, and Interestatal. Banpais and Centro are excluded from the coverage until 1997. Beginning 1996, Sureste, Promotor del Norte and Anahuac are also excluded. — Compte tenu de leur situation spéciale à la suite de fusions et acquisitions, les banques suivantes sont exclues du champ de couverture : Inverlat, Union, Cremi, Oriente, Obrero et Interestatal. Banpais et Centro sont exclues jusqu'en 1997. A compter de 1996, Sureste, Capital, Promotor del Norte et Anahuac sont également exclues.

MEXICO
Commercial banks

MEXIQUE
Banques commerciales

Per cent / *Pourcentage*

INCOME STATEMENT ANALYSIS / ANALYSE DU COMPTE DE RESULTATS

		1992	1993	1994	1995	1996	1997[1]	1998	1999	2000	2001	
	% of average balance sheet total											**% du total moyen du bilan**
40.	Interest income	19.23	20.08	16.85	37.21	23.06	18.62	24.78	24.52	20.75	15.98	Produits financiers
41.	Interest expenses	13.13	13.72	11.78	31.88	19.71	14.85	19.63	19.11	15.53	11.17	Frais financiers
42.	Net interest income	6.09	6.37	5.07	5.33	3.35	3.77	5.15	5.41	5.22	4.81	Produits financiers nets
43.	Non-interest income (net)	1.83	2.05	1.40	2.04	2.69	2.26	1.46	3.30	2.07	1.93	Produits non financiers (nets)
	a. Fees and commissions receivable	0.65	0.69	0.66	1.18	0.62	0.88	1.20	1.35	1.72	1.87	a. Frais et commissions à recevoir
	b. Fees and commissions payable	0.14	0.16	0.14	0.23	0.16	..	..	..	0.28	0.36	b. Frais et commissions à payer
	c. Net profits or loss on financial operations	1.53	1.39	0.77	1.10	2.12	0.87	0.49	1.69	0.54	0.84	c. Profits ou pertes nets sur opérations financières
	d. Other	0.21	0.13	0.11	0.01	0.10	0.50	-0.23	0.27	0.09	-0.42	d. Autres
44.	Gross income	7.92	8.42	6.47	7.37	6.04	6.03	6.61	8.71	7.29	6.74	Résultat brut
45.	Operating expenses	4.69	4.65	4.15	3.93	3.85	4.42	5.02	5.25	5.18	4.49	Frais d'exploitation
	a. Staff costs	2.24	2.30	1.99	1.59	1.50	1.93	2.07	2.05	2.38	1.87	a. Dépenses en personnel
	b. Property costs	2.29	2.20	1.92	2.12	2.13	2.25	2.57	2.81	2.54	2.41	b. Dépenses en immobilier
	c. Other	0.16	0.15	0.25	0.22	0.21	0.24	0.38	0.39	0.27	0.21	c. Autres
46.	Net income	3.23	3.77	2.32	3.44	2.20	1.61	1.59	3.46	2.11	2.25	Résultat net
47.	Provisions (net)	0.91	1.49	1.55	2.95	2.83	1.48	1.44	2.51	0.97	1.15	Provisions (nettes)
	a. Provisions on loans	0.91	1.49	1.55	2.95	2.83	1.48	1.44	2.51	0.97	1.15	a. Provisions sur prêts
	b. Provisions on securities	-	-	-	-	-	-	-	-	-	-	b. Provisions sur titres
	c. Other											c. Autres
48.	Profit before tax	2.32	2.28	0.76	0.49	-0.63	0.13	0.15	0.95	1.14	1.10	Bénéfices avant impôt
49.	Income tax	0.63	0.47	0.17	0.09	0.06	0.06	-0.42	0.23	0.20	0.30	Impôt sur le revenu
50.	Profit after tax	1.69	1.82	0.59	0.40	-0.69	0.07	0.57	0.71	0.94	0.81	Bénéfices après impôt
51.	Distributed profit	0.18	0.13	0.04	0.02	0.02	0.01					Bénéfices distribués
52.	Retained profit	1.51	1.68	0.55	0.37	-0.71	0.06	0.57	0.71	0.94	0.81	Bénéfices mis en réserve
	% of gross income											**% du total du résultat brut**
53.	Net interest income	76.93	75.63	78.35	72.32	55.41	62.53	77.90	62.08	71.62	71.31	Produits financiers nets
54.	Non-interest income (net)	23.07	24.37	21.65	27.68	44.59	37.46	22.10	37.92	28.38	28.69	Produits non financiers (nets)
	a. Fees and commissions receivable	8.14	8.16	10.16	15.98	10.33	14.66	18.09	15.48	23.59	27.68	a. Frais et commissions à recevoir
	b. Fees and commissions payable	1.77	1.90	2.23	3.08	2.62	..	..	..	3.81	5.29	b. Frais et commissions à payer
	c. Net profits or loss on financial operations	19.29	16.56	11.94	14.89	35.15	14.44	7.44	19.37	7.38	12.48	c. Profits ou pertes nets sur opérations financières
	d. Other	2.60	1.55	1.77	0.12	1.72	8.36	-3.43	3.07	1.21	-6.18	d. Autres
55.	Operating expenses	59.20	55.23	64.19	53.37	63.67	73.27	75.90	60.32	71.08	66.56	Frais d'exploitation
	a. Staff costs	28.30	27.34	30.70	21.61	24.88	31.98	31.27	23.52	32.59	27.78	a. Dépenses en personnel
	b. Property costs	28.92	26.10	29.60	28.78	35.24	37.29	38.81	32.26	34.86	35.74	b. Dépenses en immobilier
	c. Other	1.98	1.79	3.89	2.98	3.56	4.00	5.82	4.53	3.64	3.05	c. Autres
56.	Net income	40.80	44.77	35.81	46.63	36.33	26.73	24.10	39.68	28.92	33.44	Résultat net
57.	Provisions (net)	11.49	17.66	24.01	39.99	46.78	24.57	21.85	28.81	13.30	17.05	Provisions (nettes)
	a. Provisions on loans	11.49	17.66	24.01	39.99	46.78	24.57	21.85	28.81	13.30	17.05	a. Provisions sur prêts
	b. Provisions on securities											b. Provisions sur titres
	c. Other											c. Autres
58.	Profit before tax	29.31	27.11	11.80	6.63	-10.45	2.16	2.26	10.87	15.62	16.38	Bénéfices avant impôt
59.	Income tax	7.92	5.54	2.62	1.27	0.96	0.99	-6.34	2.68	2.70	4.40	Impôt sur le revenu
60.	Profit after tax	21.39	21.57	9.18	5.37	-11.41	1.17	8.59	8.19	12.91	11.98	Bénéfices après impôt
	% of net income											**% du total du résultat net**
61.	Provisions (net)	28.16	39.45	67.05	85.77	128.77	91.93	90.64	72.61	46.00	51.00	Provisions (nettes)
	a. Provisions on loans	28.16	39.45	67.05	85.77	128.77	91.93	90.64	72.61	46.00	51.00	a. Provisions sur prêts
	b. Provisions on securities											b. Provisions sur titres
	c. Other											c. Autres
62.	Profit before tax	71.84	60.55	32.95	14.23	-28.78	8.07	9.36	27.39	54.00	49.00	Bénéfices avant impôt
63.	Income tax	19.41	12.38	7.30	2.72	2.64	3.71	-26.29	6.75	9.35	13.17	Impôt sur le revenu
64.	Profit after tax	52.42	48.18	25.65	11.52	-31.41	4.36	35.65	20.63	44.65	35.83	Bénéfices après impôt

MEXICO
Commercial banks

MEXIQUE
Banques commerciales

Per cent — *Pourcentage*

	1992	1993	1994	1995	1996	1997[1]	1998	1999	2000	2001	
BALANCE SHEET ANALYSIS											**ANALYSE DU BILAN**
% of year-end balance sheet total											**% du total du bilan en fin d'exercice**
Assets											**Actif**
65. Cash & balance with Central bank	1.67	1.15	1.31	1.26	1.38	2.01	2.93	5.33	2.82	3.81	65. Caisse & solde auprès de la Banque centrale
66. Interbank deposits	0.98	1.03	1.05	2.55	2.06	6.83	8.05	9.08	11.80	14.31	66. Dépôts interbancaires
67. Loans	63.51	62.94	61.12	64.18	59.47	71.14	65.11	59.47	59.40	54.18	67. Prêts
68. Securities	18.23	18.25	21.08	19.78	20.85	14.13	12.40	15.93	13.76	17.20	68. Valeurs mobilières
69. Other assets	15.61	16.63	15.44	12.24	16.24	5.88	11.51	10.20	12.22	10.51	69. Autres actifs
Liabilities											**Passif**
70. Capital & reserves	6.27	6.60	5.50	6.82	6.02	8.03	8.31	7.96	9.56	9.42	70. Capital et réserves
71. Borrowing from Central bank	1.10	1.04	0.94	1.38	1.69	1.78	0.14	2.66	5.04	2.69	71. Emprunts auprès de la Banque centrale
72. Interbank deposits	8.00	8.58	14.32	16.35	10.40	14.20	16.15	14.81	11.85	10.06	72. Dépôts interbancaires
73. Non-bank deposits	75.66	75.63	65.93	62.65	67.46	69.75	69.98	70.08	66.15	71.05	73. Dépôts non bancaires
74. Bonds	..	..	..	..	..	..	..	..	..	..	74. Obligations
75. Other liabilities	8.97	8.15	13.30	12.80	14.43	6.24	5.42	4.48	7.40	6.79	75. Autres engagements
Memorandum items											***Pour mémoire***
76. Short-term securities	..	..	..	..	..	..	..	..	..	..	*76. Titres à court terme*
77. Bonds	..	..	..	..	..	..	..	..	..	..	*77. Obligations*
78. Shares and participations	*1.00*	*1.13*	*1.76*	*2.30*	*2.11*	*2.08*	*1.23*	*1.57*	*1.90*	*1.26*	*78. Actions et participations*
79. Claims on non-residents	..	..	..	..	..	..	..	..	..	..	*79. Créances sur des non-résidents*
80. Liabilities to non-residents	..	..	..	..	..	..	..	..	..	..	*80. Engagements envers des non-résidents*

* See notes on previous pages.

* Voir les notes en pages précédentes.

186

NETHERLANDS

All banks

Million euros

PAYS-BAS

Ensemble des banques

Millions d'euros

		1992	1993	1994	1995	1996	1997	1998	1999	2000	2001	
INCOME STATEMENT (1)												**COMPTE DE RESULTATS (1)**
1. Interest income		..	45226	42996	45642	48245	57533	74276	82318	99407	99562	1. Produits financiers
2. Interest expenses		..	34416	31137	33374	34501	41510	55266	60326	76020	74660	2. Frais financiers
3. Net interest income		10081	10810	11859	12268	13744	16023	19010	21991	23387	24902	3. Produits financiers nets
4. Non-interest income (net)		4144	5504	4772	6117	7707	10494	12796	16284	20769	20755	4. Produits non financiers (nets)
a. Fees and commissions receivable		..	..	..	..	..	..	..	..	14535	13011	a. Frais et commissions à recevoir
b. Fees and commissions payable		..	..	..	..	..	..	..	..	1725	1566	b. Frais et commissions à payer
c. Net profits or loss on financial operations		970	1245	609	1277	1710	2224	2208	3202	4002	3478	c. Profits ou pertes nets sur opérations financières
d. Other		508	947	562	717	959	1033	1536	3070	3957	5832	d. Autres
5. Gross income		14225	16314	16631	18386	21451	26518	31805	38275	44156	45657	5. Résultat brut
6. Operating expenses		9563	10859	11152	12372	14433	18353	22513	25994	31130	31787	6. Frais d'exploitation
a. Staff costs		5557	6023	6165	6831	7788	9772	12472	14694	17476	18415	a. Dépenses en personnel
b. Property costs		710	1114	907	949	1057	1319	1744	1945	2189	2017	b. Dépenses en immobilier
c. Other		3297	3722	4080	4593	5588	7262	8297	9355	11465	11355	c. Autres
7. Net income		4662	5455	5479	6014	7018	8165	9293	12282	13026	13870	7. Résultat net
8. Provisions (net)		1490	1418	1101	1076	1316	1661	2619	2136	1831	3552	8. Provisions (nettes)
a. Provisions on loans		..	1347	1100	1059	1333	1343	2500	1840	1630	3220	a. Provisions sur prêts
b. Provisions on securities		..	69	1	16	-13	-18	98	35	-35	96	b. Provisions sur titres
c. Other		..	2	-	1	-4	336	20	261	237	236	c. Autres
9. Profit before tax		3172	4037	4378	4938	5702	6504	6673	10145	11194	10318	9. Bénéfices avant impôt
10. Income tax		901	1213	1279	1488	1521	1787	1904	2774	3127	2303	10. Impôt sur le revenu
11. Profit after tax		2271	2823	3098	3450	4181	4717	4769	7371	8067	8015	11. Bénéfices après impôt
12. Distributed profit		..	..	..	..	..	..	..	..	..	..	12. Bénéfices distribués
13. Retained profit		..	..	..	..	..	..	..	..	..	..	13. Bénéfices mis en réserve
BALANCE SHEET												**BILAN**
Assets												**Actif**
14. Cash & balance with Central bank		13362	16406	8072	3272	3655	9857	9301	16242	16671	33359	14. Caisse & solde auprès de la Banque centrale
15. Interbank deposits		120534	127233	126687	132841	130286	148209	171321	148285	186619	201317	15. Dépôts interbancaires
16. Loans		358376	388594	378299	412874	475137	582701	684849	824266	964988	1033476	16. Prêts
17. Securities		63389	71802	88949	104041	137117	200518	294790	317165	377031	408480	17. Valeurs mobilières
18. Other assets		14076	14879	25128	29027	35215	43371	53447	66348	75873	85280	18. Autres actifs
Liabilities												**Passif**
19. Capital & reserves		22897	25426	28855	31221	35651	41631	46651	56666	65137	67730	19. Capital et réserves
20. Borrowing from Central bank		3016	1841	3741	4519	7252	5112	8453	9443	8896	3394	20. Emprunts auprès de la Banque centrale
21. Interbank deposits		134757	149387	140144	150641	177864	228310	289237	280006	363646	381216	21. Dépôts interbancaires
22. Non-bank deposits		263640	280792	335938	355959	390765	465936	557609	629814	730674	817263	22. Dépôts non bancaires
23. Bonds		76554	84080	75496	87078	107111	141083	174979	239114	263886	305391	23. Obligations
24. Other liabilities		68873	77389	42961	52637	62768	102584	136779	157262	188942	186917	24. Autres engagements
Balance sheet total												**Total du bilan**
25. End-year total		569737	618914	627135	682055	781411	984656	1213708	1372306	1621182	1761912	25. En fin d'exercice
26. Average total		549799	594326	623024	654595	731733	883034	1099182	1293007	1496744	1691547	26. Moyen

NETHERLANDS

All banks

Million euros

Millions d'euros

	1992	1993	1994	1995	1996	1997	1998	1999	2000	2001		
Memorandum items												**Pour mémoire**
27. Short-term securities	10101	11101	5980	8531	9081	16923	16309	22381	24447	23995	27.	Titres à court terme
28. Bonds	50159	57575	76677	86145	115188	161752	246803	249330	288234	327506	28.	Obligations
29. Shares and participations	3130	3127	6292	9365	12849	21843	31678	45454	64351	56980	29.	Actions et participations
30. Claims on non-residents	155986	172407	:	:	:	:	:	:	:	:	30.	Créances sur des non-résidents
31. Liabilities to non-residents	135585	149025	:	:	:	:	:	:	:	:	31.	Engagements envers des non-résidents
Capital adequacy												**Solvabilité**
32. Tier 1 Capital	23396	25767	27507	29987	33860	44186	49501	57896	65020	68444	32.	Fonds propres de base
33. Tier 2 Capital	11345	12585	13145	14091	16436	15386	16755	19655	22175	25328	33.	Fonds propres complémentaires
34. Supervisory deductions	444	461	582	573	622	689	820	1248	2851	2329	34.	Eléments à déduire des fonds propres
35. Total net capital resources	34297	37891	40069	43505	49675	58883	65436	76303	84345	91442	35.	Total net des ressources en capital
36. Risk-weighted assets	297569	309489	334935	367055	445647	525856	590527	702685	789499	853460	36.	Actifs pondérés des risques
SUPPLEMENTARY INFORMATION												**RENSEIGNEMENTS COMPLEMENTAIRES**
37. Number of institutions	177	175	173	174	172	169	162	85	87	84	37.	Nombre d'institutions
38. Number of branches	7518	7167	7269	6729	6822	7032	6792	6245	5968	..	38.	Nombre de succursales
39. Number of employees (x 1000)	120	115	109	111	116	120	129	147	154	..	39.	Nombre de salariés (x 1000)

1 Break in series in 1993 due to change in methodology

Change in methodology

. As from 1993, the reporting system underlying the income statement has been adapted to legal changes.

Notes

. As from 1989, data cover universal banks, banks organised on a co-operative basis, savings banks, mortgage banks, other capital market institutions and security credit institutions. Data for previous years include only the first two banking groups.

. As from 1986, the data include the Postbank.

1 Rupture de séries en 1993, suite à un chagement méthodologique.

Changement méthodologique

. A partir de 1993, le règlement en vigueur sur lequel repose le compte de résultats a été adapté en fonction des modifications législatives.

Notes

. A partir de 1989, les données concernent les banques universelles, les banques organisées en mutuelles, les caisses d'épargne, les banques hypothécaires, les autres institutions du marché financier et les institutions des titres de crédit. Les données pour les années précédentes n'incluent que les deux premiers groupes bancaires.

. A compter de 1986, les données incluent la Banque postale.

NETHERLANDS

All banks

Per cent — *Pourcentage*

INCOME STATEMENT ANALYSIS — ANALYSE DU COMPTE DE RESULTATS

	1992	1993	1994	1995	1996	1997	1998	1999	2000	2001	
% of average balance sheet total											**% du total moyen du bilan**
40. Interest income	..	7.61	6.90	6.97	6.59	6.52	6.76	6.37	6.64	5.89	40. Produits financiers
41. Interest expenses	..	5.79	5.00	5.10	4.72	4.70	5.03	4.67	5.08	4.41	41. Frais financiers
42. Net interest income	1.83	1.82	1.90	1.87	1.88	1.81	1.73	1.70	1.56	1.47	42. Produits financiers nets
43. Non-interest income (net)	0.75	0.93	0.77	0.93	1.05	1.19	1.16	1.26	1.39	1.23	43. Produits non financiers (nets)
a. Fees and commissions receivable	..	..	..	..	..	..	..	..	*0.97*	*0.77*	*a. Frais et commissions à recevoir*
b. Fees and commissions payable	..	..	..	..	..	..	..	..	*0.12*	*0.09*	*b. Frais et commissions à payer*
c. Net profits or loss on financial operations	*0.18*	*0.21*	*0.10*	*0.20*	*0.23*	*0.25*	*0.20*	*0.25*	*0.27*	*0.21*	*c. Profits ou pertes nets sur opérations financières*
d. Other	*0.09*	*0.16*	*0.09*	*0.11*	*0.13*	*0.12*	*0.14*	*0.24*	*0.26*	*0.34*	*d. Autres*
44. Gross income	2.59	2.74	2.67	2.81	2.93	3.00	2.89	2.96	2.95	2.70	44. Résultat brut
45. Operating expenses	1.74	1.83	1.79	1.89	1.97	2.08	2.05	2.01	2.08	1.88	45. Frais d'exploitation
a. Staff costs	*1.01*	*1.01*	*0.99*	*1.04*	*1.06*	*1.11*	*1.13*	*1.14*	*1.17*	*1.09*	*a. Dépenses en personnel*
b. Property costs	*0.13*	*0.19*	*0.15*	*0.14*	*0.14*	*0.15*	*0.16*	*0.15*	*0.15*	*0.12*	*b. Dépenses en immobilier*
c. Other	*0.60*	*0.63*	*0.65*	*0.70*	*0.76*	*0.82*	*0.75*	*0.72*	*0.77*	*0.67*	*c. Autres*
46. Net income	0.85	0.92	0.88	0.92	0.96	0.92	0.85	0.95	0.87	0.82	46. Résultat net
47. Provisions (net)	0.27	0.24	0.18	0.16	0.18	0.19	0.24	0.17	0.12	0.21	47. Provisions (nettes)
a. Provisions on loans	..	*0.23*	*0.18*	*0.16*	*0.18*	*0.15*	*0.23*	*0.14*	*0.11*	*0.19*	*a. Provisions sur prêts*
b. Provisions on securities	..	*0.01*	..	..	-	..	*0.01*	..	..	*0.01*	*b. Provisions sur titres*
c. Other	..	..	..	..	..	*0.04*	..	*0.02*	*0.02*	*0.01*	*c. Autres*
48. Profit before tax	0.58	0.68	0.70	0.75	0.78	0.74	0.61	0.78	0.75	0.61	48. Bénéfices avant impôt
49. Income tax	0.16	0.20	0.21	0.23	0.21	0.20	0.17	0.21	0.21	0.14	49. Impôt sur le revenu
50. Profit after tax	0.41	0.48	0.50	0.53	0.57	0.53	0.43	0.57	0.54	0.47	50. Bénéfices après impôt
51. Distributed profit	..	..	..	..	..	..	..	..	..	..	51. Bénéfices distribués
52. Retained profit	..	..	..	..	..	..	..	..	..	..	52. Bénéfices mis en réserve
% of gross income											**% du total du résultat brut**
53. Net interest income	70.87	66.26	71.30	66.73	64.07	60.43	59.77	57.45	52.97	54.54	53. Produits financiers nets
54. Non-interest income (net)	29.13	33.74	28.70	33.27	35.93	39.57	40.23	42.55	47.03	45.46	54. Produits non financiers (nets)
a. Fees and commissions receivable	..	..	..	..	..	..	..	..	*32.92*	*28.50*	*a. Frais et commissions à recevoir*
b. Fees and commissions payable	..	..	..	..	..	..	..	..	*3.91*	*3.43*	*b. Frais et commissions à payer*
c. Net profits or loss on financial operations	*6.82*	*7.63*	*3.66*	*6.95*	*7.97*	*8.39*	*6.94*	*8.37*	*9.06*	*7.62*	*c. Profits ou pertes nets sur opérations financières*
d. Other	*3.57*	*5.80*	*3.38*	*3.90*	*4.47*	*3.90*	*4.83*	*8.02*	*8.96*	*12.77*	*d. Autres*
55. Operating expenses	67.23	66.56	67.06	67.29	67.28	69.21	70.78	67.91	70.50	69.62	55. Frais d'exploitation
a. Staff costs	*39.06*	*36.92*	*37.07*	*37.15*	*36.30*	*36.85*	*39.21*	*38.39*	*39.58*	*40.33*	*a. Dépenses en personnel*
b. Property costs	*4.99*	*6.83*	*5.45*	*5.16*	*4.93*	*4.97*	*5.48*	*5.08*	*4.96*	*4.42*	*b. Dépenses en immobilier*
c. Other	*23.18*	*22.81*	*24.53*	*24.98*	*26.05*	*27.39*	*26.09*	*24.44*	*25.96*	*24.87*	*c. Autres*
56. Net income	32.77	33.44	32.94	32.71	32.72	30.79	29.22	32.09	29.50	30.38	56. Résultat net
57. Provisions (net)	10.47	8.69	6.62	5.85	6.14	6.26	8.23	5.58	4.15	7.78	57. Provisions (nettes)
a. Provisions on loans	..	*8.26*	*6.61*	*5.76*	*6.21*	*5.06*	*7.86*	*4.81*	*3.69*	*7.05*	*a. Provisions sur prêts*
b. Provisions on securities	..	*0.43*	*0.01*	*0.09*	*-0.06*	*-0.07*	*0.31*	*0.09*	*-0.08*	*0.21*	*b. Provisions sur titres*
c. Other	..	*0.01*	..	..	*-0.02*	*1.27*	*0.06*	*0.68*	*0.54*	*0.52*	*c. Autres*
58. Profit before tax	22.30	24.74	26.32	26.86	26.58	24.53	20.98	26.51	25.35	22.60	58. Bénéfices avant impôt
59. Income tax	6.33	7.44	7.69	8.09	7.09	6.74	5.99	7.25	7.08	5.04	59. Impôt sur le revenu
60. Profit after tax	15.97	17.31	18.63	18.76	19.49	17.79	15.00	19.26	18.27	17.56	60. Bénéfices après impôt
% of net income											**% du total du résultat net**
61. Provisions (net)	31.96	26.00	20.10	17.89	18.76	20.34	28.18	17.40	14.06	25.61	61. Provisions (nettes)
a. Provisions on loans	..	*24.69*	*20.07*	*17.61*	*18.99*	*16.45*	*26.90*	*14.98*	*12.51*	*23.21*	*a. Provisions sur prêts*
b. Provisions on securities	..	*1.27*	*0.02*	*0.26*	*-0.18*	*-0.22*	*1.06*	*0.29*	*-0.27*	*0.69*	*b. Provisions sur titres*
c. Other	..	*0.03*	*0.01*	*0.02*	*-0.05*	*4.12*	*0.22*	*2.13*	*1.82*	*1.70*	*c. Autres*
62. Profit before tax	68.04	74.00	79.90	82.11	81.24	79.66	71.81	82.60	85.94	74.39	62. Bénéfices avant impôt
63. Income tax	19.32	22.24	23.35	24.74	21.67	21.89	20.49	22.59	24.01	16.60	63. Impôt sur le revenu
64. Profit after tax	48.72	51.76	56.55	57.36	59.58	57.77	51.32	60.02	61.93	57.79	64. Bénéfices après impôt

NETHERLANDS
All banks

PAYS-BAS
Ensemble des banques

Per cent — *Pourcentage*

BALANCE SHEET ANALYSIS — **ANALYSE DU BILAN**

% of year-end balance sheet total — **% du total du bilan en fin d'exercice**

	1992	1993	1994	1995	1996	1997	1998	1999	2000	2001	
Assets											**Actif**
65. Cash & balance with Central bank	2.35	2.65	1.29	0.48	0.47	1.00	0.77	1.18	1.03	1.89	65. Caisse & solde auprès de la Banque centrale
66. Interbank deposits	21.16	20.56	20.20	19.48	16.67	15.05	14.12	10.81	11.51	11.43	66. Dépôts interbancaires
67. Loans	62.90	62.79	60.32	60.53	60.81	59.18	56.43	60.06	59.52	58.66	67. Prêts
68. Securities	11.13	11.60	14.18	15.25	17.55	20.36	24.29	23.11	23.26	23.18	68. Valeurs mobilières
69. Other assets	2.47	2.40	4.01	4.26	4.51	4.40	4.40	4.83	4.68	4.84	69. Autres actifs
Liabilities											**Passif**
70. Capital & reserves	4.02	4.11	4.60	4.58	4.56	4.23	3.84	4.13	4.02	3.84	70. Capital et réserves
71. Borrowing from Central bank	0.53	0.30	0.60	0.66	0.93	0.52	0.70	0.69	0.55	0.19	71. Emprunts auprès de la Banque centrale
72. Interbank deposits	23.65	24.14	22.35	22.09	22.76	23.19	23.83	20.40	22.43	21.64	72. Dépôts interbancaires
73. Non-bank deposits	46.27	45.37	53.57	52.19	50.01	47.32	45.94	45.89	45.07	46.39	73. Dépôts non bancaires
74. Bonds	13.44	13.59	12.04	12.77	13.71	14.33	14.42	17.42	16.28	17.33	74. Obligations
75. Other liabilities	12.09	12.50	6.85	7.72	8.03	10.42	11.27	11.46	11.65	10.61	75. Autres engagements
Memorandum items											***Pour mémoire***
76. Short-term securities	1.77	1.79	0.95	1.25	1.16	1.72	1.34	1.63	1.51	1.36	76. Titres à court terme
77. Bonds	8.80	9.30	12.23	12.63	14.74	16.43	20.33	18.17	17.78	18.59	77. Obligations
78. Shares and participations	0.55	0.51	1.00	1.37	1.64	2.22	2.61	3.31	3.97	3.23	78. Actions et participations
79. Claims on non-residents	27.38	27.86	..	..	..	..	..	..	..	..	79. Créances sur des non-résidents
80. Liabilities to non-residents	23.80	24.08	..	..	..	..	..	..	..	..	80. Engagements envers des non-résidents

* See notes on previous pages.   * Voir les notes en pages précédentes.

NEW ZEALAND / NOUVELLE-ZELANDE

All banks / **Ensemble des banques**

Million New Zealand dollars / *Millions de dollars de Nouvelle-Zélande*

		1992	1993	1994	1995	1996	1997	1998	1999	2000	2001
INCOME STATEMENT	**COMPTE DE RESULTATS**										
1. Interest income	1. Produits financiers	7276	6625	6845	9365	10697	10466	11482	9244	11718	12384
2. Interest expenses	2. Frais financiers	4810	4289	4383	6579	7870	7375	8290	5937	8191	8473
3. Net interest income	3. Produits financiers nets	2466	2336	2462	2786	2827	3090	3193	3307	3527	3911
4. Non-interest income (net)	4. Produits non financiers (nets)	1331	1496	1406	1592	1682	1778	1863	1985	2140	2265
a. Fees and commissions receivable	a. Frais et commissions à recevoir	:	:	:	:	:	:	:	:	:	:
b. Fees and commissions payable	b. Frais et commissions à payer	:	:	:	:	:	:	:	:	:	:
c. Net profits or loss on financial operations	c. Profits ou pertes nets sur opérations financières	:	:	:	:	:	:	:	:	:	:
d. Other	d. Autres	:	:	:	:	:	:	:	:	:	:
5. Gross income	5. Résultat brut	3797	3832	3868	4378	4509	4868	5056	5292	5667	6176
6. Operating expenses	6. Frais d'exploitation	2701	2739	2716	2910	3091	3157	3112	2948	3113	2999
a. Staff costs	a. Dépenses en personnel	:	:	:	:	:	:	:	:	:	:
b. Property costs	b. Dépenses en immobilier	:	:	:	:	:	:	:	:	:	:
c. Other	c. Autres	:	:	:	:	:	:	:	:	:	:
7. Net income	7. Résultat net	1096	1093	1152	1468	1418	1711	1945	2343	2554	3177
8. Provisions (net)	8. Provisions (nettes)	523	53	-97	-9	-43	88	201	144	127	191
a. Provisions on loans	a. Provisions sur prêts	:	:	:	:	:	:	:	:	:	:
b. Provisions on securities	b. Provisions sur titres	:	:	:	:	:	:	:	:	:	:
c. Other	c. Autres	:	:	:	:	:	:	:	:	:	:
9. Profit before tax	9. Bénéfices avant impôt	573	1040	1249	1477	1461	1623	1743	2199	2427	2986
10. Income tax	10. Impôt sur le revenu	260	339	410	462	445	505	507	566	606	799
11. Profit after tax	11. Bénéfices après impôt	313	701	839	1015	1016	1118	1236	1633	1821	2187
12. Distributed profit	12. Bénéfices distribués	357	199	627	528	1010	399	913	1354	845	1001
13. Retained profit	13. Bénéfices mis en réserve	-44	502	212	487	6	719	323	279	976	1186
BALANCE SHEET (1)	**BILAN (1)**										
Assets	**Actif**										
14. Cash & balance with Central bank	14. Caisse & solde auprès de la Banque centrale	459	462	474	529	1154	1488	2182	2194	1948	1737
15. Interbank deposits	15. Dépôts interbancaires	8916	7872	7431	8846	4957	3563	6020	4130	5046	6589
16. Loans	16. Prêts	54730	59393	68898	79793	89660	98916	107021	121239	130636	142982
17. Securities	17. Valeurs mobilières	16229	14704	11046	10059	12394	13838	14724	17864	17159	17356
18. Other assets	18. Autres actifs	2945	2862	4134	4065	10436	12359	11721	13012	25360	20899
Liabilities	**Passif**										
19. Capital & reserves	19. Capital et réserves	3571	4093	4420	4887	4364	6289	6925	8290	9523	10718
20. Borrowing from Central bank (2)	20. Emprunts auprès de la Banque centrale (2)	:	:	:	:	:	:	:	:	:	:
21. Interbank deposits (2)	21. Dépôts interbancaires (2)	:	:	:	:	:	:	:	:	:	:
22. Non-bank deposits (2)	22. Dépôts non bancaires (2)	77514	78997	84183	94017	93915	100641	126411	142206	159713	171031
23. Bonds (2)	23. Obligations (2)	:	:	:	:	:	:	:	:	:	:
24. Other liabilities	24. Autres engagements	2194	2204	3380	4388	20321	23234	8333	7943	10913	7813
Balance sheet total	**Total du bilan**										
25. End-year total	25. En fin d'exercice	83279	85293	91984	103292	118601	130164	141668	158439	180148	189563
26. Average total	26. Moyen	84404	84286	88513	97660	112040	121548	127963	150191	168300	190686

NEW ZEALAND
All banks

NOUVELLE-ZELANDE
Ensemble des banques

Million New Zealand dollars — *Millions de dollars de Nouvelle-Zélande*

	1992	1993	1994	1995	1996	1997	1998	1999	2000	2001	
Memorandum items											**Pour mémoire**
27. Short-term securities	..	..	..	..	..	..	..	..	..	..	27. Titres à court terme
28. Bonds	..	..	..	..	..	..	..	..	..	..	28. Obligations
29. Shares and participations	1409	1484	450	592	729	415	501	304	317	512	29. Actions et participations
30. Claims on non-residents	1014	3513	1669	2224	3982	2324	5333	9152	15737	21485	30. Créances sur non-résidents
31. Liabilities to non-residents	16443	16442	18486	21912	23640	29054	33990	45967	55563	63566	31. Engagements envers des non-résidents
Capital adequacy											**Solvabilité**
32. Tier 1 Capital	2965	3473	3855	4379	3838	4282	4804	5039	5919	6284	32. Fonds propres de base
33. Tier 2 Capital	..	..	..	..	..	..	2131	2294	2538	2605	33. Fonds propres complémentaires
34. Supervisory deductions	..	..	..	..	..	..	25	1	-		34. Eléments à déduire des fonds propres
35. Total net capital resources	4319	4841	5222	5962	5951	6502	6911	7332	8456	8889	35. Total net des ressources en capital
36. Risk-weighted assets	43646	45005	49757	56929	56649	61728	65750	71065	75198	82369	36. Actifs pondérés des risques
SUPPLEMENTARY INFORMATION											**RENSEIGNEMENTS COMPLEMENTAIRES**
37. Number of institutions	20	18	15	15	17	18	18	17	18	17	37. Nombre d'institutions
38. Number of branches	..	..	..	..	..	..	..	..	..	..	38. Nombre de succursales
39. Number of employees (x 1000)	..	..	..	..	..	..	..	..	..	..	39. Nombre de salariés (x 1000)

1 Change in methodology

2 Borrowing from Central bank (item 20), Interbank deposits (item 21), and Bonds (item 23) are included under Non-bank deposits (item 22).

Change in methodology

As from 1996, due to new reporting requirements, balance-sheet data are not directly comparable with earlier figures.

Notes

Average balance sheet totals (item 26) are the average of beginning and end-year assets, adjusted for take-overs and mergers during the year

1 Changement méthodologique

2 Les Emprunts auprès de la Banque centrale (poste 20), les Dépôts interbancaires (poste 21), et les Obligations (poste 23) sont inclus sous Dépôts non bancaires (poste 22).

Changement méthodologique

A partir de 1996, suite aux révisions du règlement en vigueur, les données du bilan ne sont pas directement comparables avec celles des années précédentes.

Notes

La moyenne du total des actifs/passifs (poste 26) est la moyenne des actifs du début et de la fin d'année, ajustée en considérant les fusions et acquisitions en cours d'année.

NEW ZEALAND

All banks

Per cent

INCOME STATEMENT ANALYSIS

NOUVELLE-ZELANDE

Ensemble des banques

Pourcentage

ANALYSE DU COMPTE DE RESULTATS

		1992	1993	1994	1995	1996	1997	1998	1999	2000	2001	
	% of average balance sheet total											**% du total moyen du bilan**
40.	Interest income	8.62	7.86	7.73	9.59	9.55	8.61	8.97	6.15	6.96	6.49	40. Produits financiers
41.	Interest expenses	5.70	5.09	4.95	6.74	7.02	6.07	6.48	3.95	4.87	4.44	41. Frais financiers
42.	Net interest income	2.92	2.77	2.78	2.85	2.52	2.54	2.50	2.20	2.10	2.05	42. Produits financiers nets
43.	Non-interest income (net)	1.58	1.77	1.59	1.63	1.50	1.46	1.46	1.32	1.27	1.19	43. Produits non financiers (nets)
	a. Fees and commissions receivable	:	:	:	:	:	:	:	:	:	:	a. Frais et commissions à recevoir
	b. Fees and commissions payable	:	:	:	:	:	:	:	:	:	:	b. Frais et commissions à payer
	c. Net profits or loss on financial operations	:	:	:	:	:	:	:	:	:	:	c. Profits ou pertes nets sur opérations financières
	d. Other	:	:	:	:	:	:	:	:	:	:	d. Autres
44.	Gross income	4.50	4.55	4.37	4.48	4.02	4.01	3.95	3.52	3.37	3.24	44. Résultat brut
45.	Operating expenses	3.20	3.25	3.07	2.98	2.76	2.60	2.43	1.96	1.85	1.57	45. Frais d'exploitation
	a. Staff costs	:	:	:	:	:	:	:	:	:	:	a. Dépenses en personnel
	b. Property costs	:	:	:	:	:	:	:	:	:	:	b. Dépenses en immobilier
	c. Other	:	:	:	:	:	:	:	:	:	:	c. Autres
46.	Net income	1.30	1.30	1.30	1.50	1.27	1.41	1.52	1.56	1.52	1.67	46. Résultat net
47.	Provisions (net)	0.62	0.06	-0.11	-0.01	-0.04	0.07	0.16	0.10	0.08	0.10	47. Provisions (nettes)
	a. Provisions on loans	:	:	:	:	:	:	:	:	:	:	a. Provisions sur prêts
	b. Provisions on securities	:	:	:	:	:	:	:	:	:	:	b. Provisions sur titres
	c. Other	:	:	:	:	:	:	:	:	:	:	c. Autres
48.	Profit before tax	0.68	1.23	1.41	1.51	1.30	1.34	1.36	1.46	1.44	1.57	48. Bénéfices avant impôt
49.	Income tax	0.31	0.40	0.46	0.47	0.40	0.42	0.40	0.38	0.36	0.42	49. Impôt sur le revenu
50.	Profit after tax	0.37	0.83	0.95	1.04	0.91	0.92	0.97	1.09	1.08	1.15	50. Bénéfices après impôt
51.	Distributed profit	0.42	0.24	0.71	0.54	0.90	0.33	0.71	0.90	0.50	0.53	51. Bénéfices distribués
52.	Retained profit	-0.05	0.60	0.24	0.50	0.01	0.59	0.25	0.19	0.58	0.62	52. Bénéfices mis en réserve
	% of gross income											**% du total du résultat brut**
53.	Net interest income	64.95	60.96	63.65	63.64	62.70	63.48	63.15	62.49	62.24	63.33	53. Produits financiers nets
54.	Non-interest income (net)	35.05	39.04	36.35	36.36	37.30	36.52	36.85	37.51	37.76	36.67	54. Produits non financiers (nets)
	a. Fees and commissions receivable	:	:	:	:	:	:	:	:	:	:	a. Frais et commissions à recevoir
	b. Fees and commissions payable	:	:	:	:	:	:	:	:	:	:	b. Frais et commissions à payer
	c. Net profits or loss on financial operations	:	:	:	:	:	:	:	:	:	:	c. Profits ou pertes nets sur opérations financières
	d. Other	:	:	:	:	:	:	:	:	:	:	d. Autres
55.	Operating expenses	71.14	71.48	70.22	66.47	68.55	64.85	61.55	55.71	54.94	48.55	55. Frais d'exploitation
	a. Staff costs	:	:	:	:	:	:	:	:	:	:	a. Dépenses en personnel
	b. Property costs	:	:	:	:	:	:	:	:	:	:	b. Dépenses en immobilier
	c. Other	:	:	:	:	:	:	:	:	:	:	c. Autres
56.	Net income	28.86	28.52	29.78	33.53	31.45	35.15	38.47	44.27	45.06	51.45	56. Résultat net
57.	Provisions (net)	13.77	1.38	-2.51	-0.21	-0.95	1.81	3.98	2.72	2.24	3.09	57. Provisions (nettes)
	a. Provisions on loans	:	:	:	:	:	:	:	:	:	:	a. Provisions sur prêts
	b. Provisions on securities	:	:	:	:	:	:	:	:	:	:	b. Provisions sur titres
	c. Other	:	:	:	:	:	:	:	:	:	:	c. Autres
58.	Profit before tax	15.09	27.14	32.29	33.74	32.40	33.34	34.47	41.55	42.83	48.35	58. Bénéfices avant impôt
59.	Income tax	6.85	8.85	10.60	10.55	9.87	10.37	10.03	10.70	10.70	12.94	59. Impôt sur le revenu
60.	Profit after tax	8.24	18.29	21.69	23.18	22.53	22.97	24.45	30.86	32.13	35.42	60. Bénéfices après impôt
	% of net income											**% du total du résultat net**
61.	Provisions (net)	47.72	4.85	-8.42	-0.61	-3.03	5.14	10.33	6.15	4.96	6.01	61. Provisions (nettes)
	a. Provisions on loans	:	:	:	:	:	:	:	:	:	:	a. Provisions sur prêts
	b. Provisions on securities	:	:	:	:	:	:	:	:	:	:	b. Provisions sur titres
	c. Other	:	:	:	:	:	:	:	:	:	:	c. Autres
62.	Profit before tax	52.28	95.15	108.42	100.61	103.03	94.86	89.61	93.85	95.04	93.99	62. Bénéfices avant impôt
63.	Income tax	23.72	31.02	35.59	31.47	31.38	29.51	26.07	24.16	23.74	25.15	63. Impôt sur le revenu
64.	Profit after tax	28.56	64.14	72.83	69.14	71.65	65.34	63.55	69.70	71.29	68.84	64. Bénéfices après impôt

NEW ZEALAND

All banks

NOUVELLE-ZELANDE

Ensemble des banques

Per cent — *Pourcentage*

	1992	1993	1994	1995	1996	1997	1998	1999	2000	2001	
BALANCE SHEET ANALYSIS											**ANALYSE DU BILAN**
% of year-end balance sheet total											**% du total du bilan en fin d'exercice**
Assets											**Actif**
65. Cash & balance with Central bank	0.55	0.54	0.52	0.51	0.97	1.14	1.54	1.38	1.08	0.92	65. Caisse & solde auprès de la Banque centrale
66. Interbank deposits	10.71	9.23	8.08	8.56	4.18	2.74	4.25	2.61	2.80	3.48	66. Dépôts interbancaires
67. Loans	65.72	69.63	74.90	77.25	75.60	75.99	75.54	76.52	72.52	75.43	67. Prêts
68. Securities	19.49	17.24	12.01	9.74	10.45	10.63	10.39	11.28	9.52	9.16	68. Valeurs mobilières
69. Other assets	3.54	3.36	4.49	3.94	8.80	9.49	8.27	8.21	14.08	11.02	69. Autres actifs
Liabilities											**Passif**
70. Capital & reserves	4.29	4.80	4.81	4.73	3.68	4.83	4.89	5.23	5.29	5.65	70. Capital et réserves
71. Borrowing from Central bank	..	..	..	..	..	..	..	..	..	..	71. Emprunts auprès de la Banque centrale
72. Interbank deposits	..	..	..	..	..	..	..	..	..	..	72. Dépôts interbancaires
73. Non-bank deposits	93.08	92.62	91.52	91.02	79.19	77.32	89.23	89.75	88.66	90.22	73. Dépôts non bancaires
74. Bonds	..	..	..	..	..	..	..	..	..	..	74. Obligations
75. Other liabilities	2.63	2.58	3.67	4.25	17.13	17.85	5.88	5.01	6.06	4.12	75. Autres engagements
Memorandum items											***Pour mémoire***
76. Short-term securities	..	..	..	..	..	..	..	..	..	..	*76. Titres à court terme*
77. Bonds	..	..	..	..	..	..	..	..	..	..	*77. Obligations*
78. Shares and participations	*1.69*	*1.74*	*0.49*	*0.57*	*0.61*	*0.32*	*0.35*	*0.19*	*0.18*	*0.27*	*78. Actions et participations*
79. Claims on non-residents	*1.22*	*4.12*	*1.81*	*2.15*	*3.36*	*1.79*	*3.76*	*5.78*	*8.74*	*11.33*	*79. Créances sur des non-résidents*
80. Liabilities to non-residents	*19.74*	*19.28*	*20.10*	*21.21*	*19.93*	*22.32*	*23.99*	*29.01*	*30.84*	*33.53*	*80. Engagements envers des non-résidents*

* See notes on previous pages. * Voir les notes en pages précédentes.

NORWAY
All banks

NORVEGE
Ensemble des banques

Million Norwegian kroner / Millions de couronnes norvégiennes

INCOME STATEMENT / COMPTE DE RESULTATS

	1992	1993	1994	1995	1996	1997	1998	1999	2000	2001
1. Interest income / Produits financiers	67670	58660	51286	52543	53452	52678	69410	80706	94306	112402
2. Interest expenses / Frais financiers	46937	35813	27693	30079	30524	29654	44008	53627	64136	79363
3. Net interest income / Produits financiers nets	20733	22847	23593	22464	22929	23024	25402	27079	30170	33039
4. Non-interest income (net) / Produits non financiers (nets)	5555	8776	5522	7940	8069	8951	7904	9441	12136	11561
a. Fees and commissions receivable / Frais et commissions à recevoir	3411	3613	4848	5310	6150	7047	7304	7031	8619	9521
b. Fees and commissions payable / Frais et commissions à payer	23	30	37	93	791	1091	1364	1331	1547	2097
c. Net profits or loss on financial operations / Profits ou pertes nets sur opérations financières	1354	4278	-200	1851	1774	2192	1109	3065	2851	1967
d. Other / Autres	813	916	912	873	937	803	854	675	2212	2169
5. Gross income / Résultat brut	26288	31623	29115	30405	30998	31975	33306	36520	42306	44600
6. Operating expenses (1) / Frais d'exploitation (1)	15859	15942	19149	21047	21539	22042	22659	21647	25188	27090
a. Staff costs / Dépenses en personnel	7868	7762	8386	9128	9794	10766	11350	11381	12940	13761
b. Property costs / Dépenses en immobilier	1669	1471	1440	1449	1574	1579	1720	1644	1909	2144
c. Other / Autres	6322	6707	9322	10469	10172	9697	9589	8622	10340	11185
7. Net income / Résultat net	10429	15681	9966	9358	9459	9933	10646	14873	17118	17510
8. Provisions (net) (1) / Provisions (nettes) (1)	11670	8822	1124	-792	-1015	-152	1091	645	-587	4302
a. Provisions on loans / Provisions sur prêts	11691	7336	674	-908	-593	-153	1600	1201	2104	4119
b. Provisions on securities / Provisions sur titres					4	1	32	-	-	10
c. Other / Autres					-425		-541	-556	-2690	173
9. Profit before tax / Bénéfices avant impôt	-1241	6859	8842	10150	10473	10085	9555	14229	17705	13208
10. Income tax / Impôt sur le revenu	404	917	1168	1263	1598	1670	1647	2680	4274	2232
11. Profit after tax / Bénéfices après impôt	-1645	5942	7674	8885	8875	8415	7907	11549	13430	10976
12. Distributed profit / Bénéfices distribués	122	619	2392	2925	3280	3061	3187	6199	6162	7678
13. Retained profit / Bénéfices mis en réserve	-1767	5323	5282	5961	5595	5354	4720	5350	7268	3298

BALANCE SHEET / BILAN

Assets / Actif

	1992	1993	1994	1995	1996	1997	1998	1999	2000	2001
14. Cash & balance with Central bank / Caisse & solde auprès de la Banque centrale	4890	3151	4738	5489	28658	17707	12704	38614	27524	29264
15. Interbank deposits / Dépôts interbancaires	41658	24142	27165	21658	27536	28758	39063	39109	65136	58702
16. Loans / Prêts	468575	461766	540180	552986	632189	750049	839673	923055	1054490	1160342
17. Securities / Valeurs mobilières	67493	69792	91316	97289	118495	118777	122563	109206	116012	129479
18. Other assets / Autres actifs	28094	27578	31781	30934	36341	36812	42535	65204	71360	73648

Liabilities / Passif

	1992	1993	1994	1995	1996	1997	1998	1999	2000	2001
19. Capital & reserves / Capital et réserves	21512	33909	45089	51675	58594	65196	72988	83903	93690	98116
20. Borrowing from Central bank / Emprunts auprès de la Banque centrale	39111	16973	5207	10348	474	7835	16952	25885	21299	15779
21. Interbank deposits / Dépôts interbancaires	48480	38323	37937	38566	98250	127156	115936	125730	144251	150987
22. Non-bank deposits / Dépôts non bancaires	409667	402294	506342	497032	534554	541436	575030	644890	706817	778672
23. Bonds / Obligations	64784	64575	61379	60542	78821	121132	168047	168060	212434	245193
24. Other liabilities / Autres engagements	27155	30356	39224	50192	72526	89348	106685	126712	156032	162688

Balance sheet total / Total du bilan

	1992	1993	1994	1995	1996	1997	1998	1999	2000	2001
25. End-year total / En fin d'exercice	610710	586431	695179	708356	843219	952103	1056538	1175187	1334522	1451435
26. Average total / Moyen	591255	611885	710384	705150	786264	908096	1023623	1130006	1263448	1409535

NORWAY

All banks

Million Norwegian kroner

NORVEGE

Ensemble des banques

Millions de couronnes norvégiennes

	1992	1993	1994	1995	1996	1997	1998	1999	2000	2001		
Memorandum items												**Pour mémoire**
27. Short-term securities	5420	10216	28603	33057	42873	41270	28792	41326	22788	21357	27.	Titres à court terme
28. Bonds	52360	48806	50183	50357	57260	54401	69365	54647	76339	88796	28.	Obligations
29. Shares and participations	9713	10770	12529	13875	18362	23106	24406	13232	16885	19326	29.	Actions et participations
30. Claims on non-residents	79515	50114	49911	47724	60458	69617	92046	101201	137220	137705	30.	Créances sur des non-résidents
31. Liabilities to non-residents	75435	70414	60255	57556	123234	183545	221588	254784	322065	351802	31.	Engagements envers des non-résidents
Capital adequacy												**Solvabilité**
32. Tier 1 Capital	28908	39831	44833	51559	58427	64389	71289	76166	85001	93697	32.	Fonds propres de base
33. Tier 2 Capital	18221	23277	21553	17487	18854	21754	22972	23200	28831	30207	33.	Fonds propres complémentaires
34. Supervisory deductions	321	122	181	639	636	2043	1399	1071	959	2134	34.	Eléments à déduire des fonds propres
35. Total net capital resources	46808	62986	66206	68408	76645	84100	92863	98295	112873	121770	35.	Total net des ressources en capital
36. Risk-weighted assets	475552	469712	472039	509119	592319	692261	762316	818093	931145	967188	36.	Actifs pondérés des risques
SUPPLEMENTARY INFORMATION												**RENSEIGNEMENTS COMPLEMENTAIRES**
37. Number of institutions	155	153	152	153	153	154	154	152	152	151	37.	Nombre d'institutions
38. Number of branches	1593	1561	1570	1593	1622	1586	1542	1535	1273	1390	38.	Nombre de succursales
39. Number of employees (x 1000)	27	26	27	25	25	25	25	24	23	23	39.	Nombre de salariés (x 1000)

1 Change in methodology

Change in methodology

. Average balance sheet totals (item 26) are based on thirteen end-month data.

Notes

. All banks include Commercial banks and Savings banks.

. Due to methodological changes, write-downs are included under Operating expenses (item 6) and not under Provisions (net) (item 8) in the 1991 data.

1 Changement méthodologique

Changement méthodologique

. La moyenne du total des actifs/passifs (poste 26) est basée sur treize données de fin de mois.

Notes

. L'Ensemble des banques comprend les Banques commerciales et les Caisses d'épargne.

. Suite aux changements méthodologiques, les dévaluations sont incluses sous la rubrique Frais d'exploitation (poste 6) et non sous la rubrique Provisions (nettes) (poste 8) pour les données de 1991.

NORWAY
All banks

NORVEGE
Ensemble des banques

Per cent — *Pourcentage*

INCOME STATEMENT ANALYSIS — **ANALYSE DU COMPTE DE RESULTATS**

	Item (EN)	1992	1993	1994	1995	1996	1997	1998	1999	2000	2001	Item (FR)
	% of average balance sheet total											**% du total moyen du bilan**
40.	Interest income	11.45	9.59	7.22	7.45	6.80	5.80	6.78	7.14	7.46	7.97	Produits financiers
41.	Interest expenses	7.94	5.85	3.90	4.27	3.88	3.27	4.30	4.75	5.08	5.63	Frais financiers
42.	Net interest income	3.51	3.73	3.32	3.19	2.92	2.54	2.48	2.40	2.39	2.34	Produits financiers nets
43.	Non-interest income (net)	0.94	1.43	0.78	1.13	1.03	0.99	0.77	0.84	0.96	0.82	Produits non financiers (nets)
	a. Fees and commissions receivable	0.58	0.59	0.68	0.75	0.78	0.78	0.71	0.62	0.68	0.68	a. Frais et commissions à recevoir
	b. Fees and commissions payable	-	-	0.01	0.01	0.10	0.12	0.13	0.12	0.12	0.15	b. Frais et commissions à payer
	c. Net profits or loss on financial operations	0.23	0.70	-0.03	0.26	0.23	0.24	0.11	0.27	0.23	0.14	c. Profits ou pertes nets sur opérations financières
	d. Other	0.14	0.15	0.13	0.12	0.12	0.09	0.08	0.06	0.18	0.15	d. Autres
44.	Gross income	4.45	5.17	4.10	4.31	3.94	3.52	3.25	3.23	3.35	3.16	Résultat brut
45.	Operating expenses	2.68	2.61	2.70	2.98	2.74	2.43	2.21	1.92	1.99	1.92	Frais d'exploitation
	a. Staff costs	1.33	1.27	1.18	1.29	1.25	1.19	1.11	1.01	1.02	0.98	a. Dépenses en personnel
	b. Property costs	0.28	0.24	0.20	0.21	0.20	0.17	0.17	0.15	0.15	0.15	b. Dépenses en immobilier
	c. Other	1.07	1.10	1.31	1.48	1.29	1.07	0.94	0.76	0.82	0.79	c. Autres
46.	Net income	1.76	2.56	1.40	1.33	1.20	1.09	1.04	1.32	1.35	1.24	Résultat net
47.	Provisions (net)	1.97	1.44	0.16	-0.11	-0.13	-0.02	0.11	0.06	-0.05	0.31	Provisions (nettes)
	a. Provisions on loans	1.98	1.20	0.09	-0.13	-0.08	-0.02	0.16	0.11	0.17	0.29	a. Provisions sur prêts
	b. Provisions on securities	..	..	..	..	..	..	..	..	..	..	b. Provisions sur titres
	c. Other	..	..	..	..	-0.05	..	-0.05	-0.05	-0.21	0.01	c. Autres
48.	Profit before tax	-0.21	1.12	1.24	1.44	1.33	1.11	0.93	1.26	1.40	0.94	Bénéfices avant impôt
49.	Income tax	0.07	0.15	0.16	0.18	0.20	0.18	0.16	0.24	0.34	0.16	Impôt sur le revenu
50.	Profit after tax	-0.28	0.97	1.08	1.26	1.13	0.93	0.77	1.02	1.06	0.78	Bénéfices après impôt
51.	Distributed profit	0.02	0.10	0.34	0.41	0.42	0.34	0.31	0.55	0.49	0.54	Bénéfices distribués
52.	Retained profit	-0.30	0.87	0.74	0.85	0.71	0.59	0.46	0.47	0.58	0.23	Bénéfices mis en réserve
	% of gross income											**% du total du résultat brut**
53.	Net interest income	78.87	72.25	81.03	73.88	73.97	72.01	76.27	74.15	71.31	74.08	Produits financiers nets
54.	Non-interest income (net)	21.13	27.75	18.97	26.11	26.03	27.99	23.73	25.85	28.69	25.92	Produits non financiers (nets)
	a. Fees and commissions receivable	12.98	11.43	16.65	17.46	19.84	22.04	21.93	19.25	20.37	21.35	a. Frais et commissions à recevoir
	b. Fees and commissions payable	0.09	0.09	0.13	0.31	2.55	3.41	4.10	3.64	3.66	4.70	b. Frais et commissions à payer
	c. Net profits or loss on financial operations	5.15	13.53	-0.69	6.09	5.72	6.86	3.33	8.39	6.74	4.41	c. Profits ou pertes nets sur opérations financières
	d. Other	3.09	2.90	3.13	2.87	3.02	2.51	2.56	1.85	5.23	4.86	d. Autres
55.	Operating expenses	60.33	50.41	65.77	69.22	69.49	68.94	68.03	59.27	59.54	60.74	Frais d'exploitation
	a. Staff costs	29.93	24.55	28.80	30.02	31.60	33.67	34.08	31.16	30.59	30.85	a. Dépenses en personnel
	b. Property costs	6.35	4.65	4.95	4.77	5.08	4.94	5.16	4.50	4.51	4.81	b. Dépenses en immobilier
	c. Other	24.05	21.21	32.02	34.43	32.82	30.33	28.79	23.61	24.44	25.08	c. Autres
56.	Net income	39.67	49.59	34.23	30.78	30.51	31.06	31.96	40.73	40.46	39.26	Résultat net
57.	Provisions (net)	44.39	27.90	3.86	-2.60	-3.27	-0.48	3.28	1.77	-1.39	9.65	Provisions (nettes)
	a. Provisions on loans	44.47	23.20	2.31	-2.99	-1.91	-0.48	4.80	3.29	4.97	9.24	a. Provisions sur prêts
	b. Provisions on securities	..	..	..	..	..	..	..	..	..	..	b. Provisions sur titres
	c. Other	..	..	..	0.01	-1.37	..	0.10	-1.52	-6.36	0.39	c. Autres
58.	Profit before tax	-4.72	21.69	30.37	33.38	33.79	31.54	28.69	38.96	41.85	29.61	Bénéfices avant impôt
59.	Income tax	1.54	2.90	4.01	4.15	5.16	5.22	4.95	7.34	10.10	5.00	Impôt sur le revenu
60.	Profit after tax	-6.26	18.79	26.36	29.22	28.63	26.32	23.74	31.62	31.74	24.61	Bénéfices après impôt
	% of net income											**% du total du résultat net**
61.	Provisions (net)	111.90	56.26	11.28	-8.46	-10.73	-1.53	10.25	4.34	-3.43	24.57	Provisions (nettes)
	a. Provisions on loans	112.10	46.78	6.76	-9.70	-6.27	-1.54	15.03	8.08	12.29	23.52	a. Provisions sur prêts
	b. Provisions on securities	..	..	..	..	0.04	..	0.30	..	..	0.06	b. Provisions sur titres
	c. Other	..	..	..	..	-4.49	0.01	-5.08	-3.74	-15.71	0.99	c. Autres
62.	Profit before tax	-11.90	43.74	88.72	108.46	110.72	101.53	89.75	95.67	103.43	75.43	Bénéfices avant impôt
63.	Income tax	3.87	5.85	11.72	13.50	16.89	16.81	15.47	18.02	24.97	12.75	Impôt sur le revenu
64.	Profit after tax	-15.77	37.89	77.00	94.95	93.83	84.72	74.27	77.65	78.46	62.68	Bénéfices après impôt

NORWAY

All banks

NORVEGE

Ensemble des banques

Per cent / *Pourcentage*

BALANCE SHEET ANALYSIS / **ANALYSE DU BILAN**

% of year-end balance sheet total / **% du total du bilan en fin d'exercice**

	1992	1993	1994	1995	1996	1997	1998	1999	2000	2001		
Assets												**Actif**
65. Cash & balance with Central bank	0.80	0.54	0.68	0.77	3.40	1.86	1.20	3.29	2.06	2.02	65.	Caisse & solde auprès de la Banque centrale
66. Interbank deposits	6.82	4.12	3.91	3.06	3.27	3.02	3.70	3.33	4.88	4.04	66.	Dépôts interbancaires
67. Loans	76.73	78.74	77.70	78.07	74.97	78.78	79.47	78.55	79.02	79.94	67.	Prêts
68. Securities	11.05	11.90	13.14	13.73	14.05	12.48	11.60	9.29	8.69	8.92	68.	Valeurs mobilières
69. Other assets	4.60	4.70	4.57	4.37	4.31	3.87	4.03	5.55	5.35	5.07	69.	Autres actifs
Liabilities												**Passif**
70. Capital & reserves	3.52	5.78	6.49	7.30	6.95	6.85	6.91	7.14	7.02	6.76	70.	Capital et réserves
71. Borrowing from Central bank	6.40	2.89	0.75	1.46	0.06	0.82	1.60	2.20	1.60	1.09	71.	Emprunts auprès de la Banque centrale
72. Interbank deposits	7.94	6.53	5.46	5.44	11.65	13.36	10.97	10.70	10.81	10.40	72.	Dépôts interbancaires
73. Non-bank deposits	67.08	68.60	72.84	70.17	63.39	56.87	54.43	54.88	52.96	53.65	73.	Dépôts non bancaires
74. Bonds	10.61	11.01	8.83	8.55	9.35	12.72	15.99	14.30	15.92	16.89	74.	Obligations
75. Other liabilities	4.45	5.18	5.64	7.09	8.60	9.38	10.10	10.78	11.69	11.21	75.	Autres engagements
Memorandum items												***Pour mémoire***
76. Short-term securities	*0.89*	*1.74*	*4.11*	*4.67*	*5.08*	*4.33*	*2.73*	*3.52*	*1.71*	*1.47*	*76.*	*Titres à court terme*
77. Bonds	*8.57*	*8.32*	*7.22*	*7.11*	*6.79*	*5.71*	*6.57*	*4.65*	*5.72*	*6.12*	*77.*	*Obligations*
78. Shares and participations	*1.59*	*1.84*	*1.80*	*1.96*	*2.18*	*2.43*	*2.31*	*1.13*	*1.27*	*1.33*	*78.*	*Actions et participations*
79. Claims on non-residents	*13.02*	*8.55*	*7.18*	*6.74*	*7.17*	*7.31*	*8.71*	*8.61*	*10.28*	*9.49*	*79.*	*Créances sur des non-résidents*
80. Liabilities to non-residents	*12.35*	*12.01*	*8.67*	*8.13*	*14.61*	*19.28*	*20.97*	*21.68*	*24.13*	*24.24*	*80.*	*Engagements envers des non-résidents*

* See notes on previous pages.   * Voir les notes en pages précédentes.

198

NORWAY
Commercial banks

NORVEGE
Banques commerciales

Million Norwegian kroner / *Millions de couronnes norvégiennes*

	1992	1993	1994	1995	1996	1997	1998	1999	2000	2001	
INCOME STATEMENT											**COMPTE DE RESULTATS**
1. Interest income	38821	32757	30524	31116	31933	32159	42351	45709	53487	62961	1. Produits financiers
2. Interest expenses	28587	21644	17761	19291	19444	19737	28556	32373	38507	46442	2. Frais financiers
3. Net interest income	10234	11113	12763	11825	12490	12423	13795	13337	14981	16519	3. Produits financiers nets
4. Non-interest income (net)	3850	5433	4375	5419	5646	6213	5557	5781	8706	8183	4. Produits non financiers (nets)
a. Fees and commissions receivable	*2133*	*2204*	*3224*	*3530*	*4026*	*4491*	*4588*	*3983*	*5020*	*5597*	*a. Frais et commissions à recevoir*
b. Fees and commissions payable	*1*	*4*	*1*	*50*	*334*	*534*	*775*	*669*	*762*	*1171*	*b. Frais et commissions à payer*
c. Net profits or loss on financial operations	*1132*	*2559*	*468*	*1295*	*1278*	*1693*	*1123*	*2003*	*2410*	*1769*	*c. Profits ou pertes nets sur opérations financières*
d. Other	*587*	*674*	*684*	*645*	*677*	*562*	*620*	*464*	*2038*	*1988*	*d. Autres*
5. Gross income	14084	16546	17138	17244	18136	18635	19352	19118	23686	24702	5. Résultat brut
6. Operating expenses (1)	8659	8602	11556	12930	13210	13597	13969	11917	14713	15705	6. Frais d'exploitation (1)
a. Staff costs	*4348*	*4392*	*4822*	*5354*	*5975*	*6568*	*7008*	*6506*	*7702*	*8153*	*a. Dépenses en personnel*
b. Property costs	*1036*	*897*	*925*	*936*	*994*	*946*	*1026*	*925*	*1065*	*1219*	*b. Dépenses en immobilier*
c. Other	*3275*	*3312*	*5809*	*6640*	*6242*	*6084*	*5934*	*4486*	*5946*	*6333*	*c. Autres*
7. Net income	5425	7944	5582	4314	4926	5038	5383	7201	8973	8997	7. Résultat net
8. Provisions (net) (1)	9842	6082	328	-1183	-1111	-404	661	164	739	2957	8. Provisions (nettes) (1)
a. Provisions on loans	*7800*	*4836*	*-209*	*-1343*	*-837*	*-446*	*833*	*179*	*878*	*2451*	*a. Provisions sur prêts*
b. Provisions on securities	*..*	*..*	*..*	*..*	*1*	*-*	*32*	*-*	*-*	*-*	*b. Provisions sur titres*
c. Other	*..*	*..*	*..*	*..*	*-274*	*42*	*-204*	*-15*	*-140*	*506*	*c. Autres*
9. Profit before tax	-4417	1862	5254	5497	6036	5442	4722	7037	8234	6040	9. Bénéfices avant impôt
10. Income tax	77	262	387	267	412	385	315	1082	1797	244	10. Impôt sur le revenu
11. Profit after tax	-4494	1600	4867	5230	5624	5057	4407	5955	6437	5796	11. Bénéfices après impôt
12. Distributed profit	105	199	1742	2107	2394	2074	2062	4836	4603	6208	12. Bénéfices distribués
13. Retained profit	-4599	1401	3125	3123	3231	2983	2346	1119	1834	-412	13. Bénéfices mis en réserve
BALANCE SHEET											**BILAN**
Assets											**Actif**
14. Cash & balance with Central bank	2535	1079	2284	2819	23791	11595	7618	26766	18091	20604	14. Caisse & solde auprès de la Banque centrale
15. Interbank deposits	36086	20082	21321	18022	21960	21452	29276	32566	54142	48780	15. Dépôts interbancaires
16. Loans	273155	256624	320973	313773	360542	438371	494219	506796	572814	620206	16. Prêts
17. Securities	40519	39824	62728	66804	88288	89760	88641	71169	75928	82499	17. Valeurs mobilières
18. Other assets	19628	19644	23115	22649	29074	28908	33402	49481	53426	54163	18. Autres actifs
Liabilities											**Passif**
19. Capital & reserves	8167	15163	24365	28270	32593	36580	39494	45205	49383	49661	19. Capital et réserves
20. Borrowing from Central bank	28544	8261	2437	5478	327	6198	10549	19877	18721	10445	20. Emprunts auprès de la Banque centrale
21. Interbank deposits	38093	32779	31852	30899	80080	95619	82799	79301	101568	112125	21. Dépôts interbancaires
22. Non-bank deposits	219812	205032	297843	280974	304504	306566	323752	354896	383235	423124	22. Dépôts non bancaires
23. Bonds	56546	54837	47468	46149	58449	86380	120935	111430	128419	135322	23. Obligations
24. Other liabilities	20761	21183	26456	32296	47701	58744	75629	76068	93076	95575	24. Autres engagements
Balance sheet total											**Total du bilan**
25. End-year total	371923	337255	430421	424067	523654	590086	653157	686777	774401	826252	25. En fin d'exercice
26. Average total	349682	360924	448808	428449	483790	567615	639918	686388	740548	812781	26. Moyen

NORWAY
Commercial banks

NORVEGE
Banques commerciales

Million Norwegian kroner / *Millions de couronnes norvégiennes*

	1992	1993	1994	1995	1996	1997	1998	1999	2000	2001	
Memorandum items											**Pour mémoire**
27. Short-term securities	3807	6933	23287	25106	32984	33575	20505	24972	16283	17384	27. Titres à court terme
28. Bonds	29839	26335	31517	33457	42806	40572	51483	38230	50580	54582	28. Obligations
29. Shares and participations	6872	6556	7924	8241	12498	15614	16653	7967	9065	10533	29. Actions et participations
30. Claims on non-residents	73447	45567	42583	42717	54218	61225	81450	89952	124582	120144	30. Créances sur des non-résidents
31. Liabilities to non-residents	66734	60748	50439	48909	107755	146927	176625	185422	236114	252413	31. Engagements envers des non-résidents
Capital adequacy											**Solvabilité**
32. Tier 1 Capital	13353	20080	24008	28139	32530	35917	38041	38417	42509	46981	32. Fonds propres de base
33. Tier 2 Capital	13706	17484	14461	11506	12293	14164	15052	14477	17521	17960	33. Fonds propres complémentaires
34. Supervisory deductions	116	88	42	337	256	1113	815	612	422	1476	34. Eléments à déduire des fonds propres
35. Total net capital resources	26943	37476	38427	39308	44567	48968	52278	52283	59609	63465	35. Total net des ressources en capital
36. Risk-weighted assets	312264	302948	296395	319997	379733	447813	478384	480845	541926	543440	36. Actifs pondérés des risques
SUPPLEMENTARY INFORMATION											**RENSEIGNEMENTS COMPLEMENTAIRES**
37. Number of institutions	21	20	20	20	20	21	21	22	22	22	37. Nombre d'institutions
38. Number of branches	488	451	480	469	462	470	468	466	411	388	38. Nombre de succursales
39. Number of employees (x 1000)	13	13	15	14	14	14	14	13	12	12	39. Nombre de salariés (x 1000)

1 Change in methodology

1 Changement méthodologique.

Notes

Notes

. Average balance sheet totals (item 26) are based on thirteen end-month data.

. La moyenne du total des actifs/passifs (poste 26) est basée sur treize données de fin de mois.

. As from 1994, data for the Postal Saving bank (Postbanken) are inluded under Commercial banks.

. Depuis 1994, les données de la banque postale (Postbanken) sont comprises dans la catégorie Banques commerciales.

Change in methodology

Changement méthodologique

. Due to methodological changes, write-downs are included under Operating expenses (item 6) and not under Provisions (net) (item 8' in the 1991 data.

. Suite aux changements méthodologiques, les dévaluations sont incluses sous la rubrique Frais d'exploitation (poste 6) et non sous la rubrique Provisions (nettes) (poste 8) pour les données de 1991.

NORWAY
Commercial banks

NORVEGE
Banques commerciales

Per cent — *Pourcentage*

INCOME STATEMENT ANALYSIS — **ANALYSE DU COMPTE DE RESULTATS**

	1992	1993	1994	1995	1996	1997	1998	1999	2000	2001	
% of average balance sheet total											**% du total moyen du bilan**
40. Interest income	11.10	9.08	6.80	7.26	6.60	5.67	6.62	6.66	7.22	7.75	40. Produits financiers
41. Interest expenses	8.18	6.00	3.96	4.50	4.02	3.48	4.46	4.72	5.20	5.71	41. Frais financiers
42. Net interest income	2.93	3.08	2.84	2.76	2.58	2.19	2.16	1.94	2.02	2.03	42. Produits financiers nets
43. Non-interest income (net)	1.10	1.51	0.97	1.26	1.17	1.09	0.87	0.84	1.18	1.01	43. Produits non financiers (nets)
a. Fees and commissions receivable	0.61	0.61	0.72	0.82	0.83	0.79	0.72	0.58	0.68	0.69	a. Frais et commissions à recevoir
b. Fees and commissions payable	-	-	-	0.01	0.07	0.09	0.12	0.10	0.10	0.14	b. Frais et commissions à payer
c. Net profits or loss on financial operations	0.32	0.71	0.10	0.30	0.26	0.30	0.18	0.29	0.33	0.22	c. Profits ou pertes nets sur opérations financières
d. Other	0.17	0.19	0.15	0.15	0.14	0.10	0.10	0.07	0.28	0.24	d. Autres
44. Gross income	4.03	4.58	3.82	4.02	3.75	3.28	3.02	2.79	3.20	3.04	44. Résultat brut
45. Operating expenses	2.48	2.38	2.57	3.02	2.73	2.40	2.18	1.74	1.99	1.93	45. Frais d'exploitation
a. Staff costs	1.24	1.22	1.07	1.25	1.24	1.16	1.10	0.95	1.04	1.00	a. Dépenses en personnel
b. Property costs	0.30	0.25	0.21	0.22	0.21	0.17	0.16	0.13	0.14	0.15	b. Dépenses en immobilier
c. Other	0.94	0.92	1.29	1.55	1.29	1.07	0.93	0.65	0.80	0.78	c. Autres
46. Net income	1.55	2.20	1.24	1.01	1.02	0.89	0.84	1.05	1.21	1.11	46. Résultat net
47. Provisions (net)	2.81	1.69	0.07	-0.28	-0.23	-0.07	0.10	0.02	0.10	0.36	47. Provisions (nettes)
a. Provisions on loans	2.23	1.34	-0.05	-0.31	-0.17	-0.08	0.13	0.03	0.12	0.30	a. Provisions sur prêts
b. Provisions on securities	..	..	..	..	..	0.01	0.01	..	..	-	b. Provisions sur titres
c. Other	..	..	..	..	-0.06	..	-0.03	-	-0.02	0.06	c. Autres
48. Profit before tax	-1.26	0.52	1.17	1.28	1.25	0.96	0.74	1.03	1.11	0.74	48. Bénéfices avant impôt
49. Income tax	0.02	0.07	0.09	0.06	0.09	0.07	0.05	0.16	0.24	0.03	49. Impôt sur le revenu
50. Profit after tax	-1.29	0.44	1.08	1.22	1.16	0.89	0.69	0.87	0.87	0.71	50. Bénéfices après impôt
51. Distributed profit	0.03	0.06	0.39	0.49	0.49	0.37	0.32	0.70	0.62	0.76	51. Bénéfices distribués
52. Retained profit	-1.32	0.39	0.70	0.73	0.67	0.53	0.37	0.16	0.25	-0.05	52. Bénéfices mis en réserve
% of gross income											**% du total du résultat brut**
53. Net interest income	72.66	67.16	74.47	68.57	68.87	66.66	71.28	69.76	63.25	66.87	53. Produits financiers nets
54. Non-interest income (net)	27.34	32.84	25.53	31.43	31.13	33.34	28.72	30.24	36.76	33.13	54. Produits non financiers (nets)
a. Fees and commissions receivable	15.14	13.32	18.81	20.47	22.20	24.10	23.71	20.83	21.19	22.66	a. Frais et commissions à recevoir
b. Fees and commissions payable	0.01	0.02	0.01	0.29	1.84	2.87	4.00	3.50	3.22	4.74	b. Frais et commissions à payer
c. Net profits or loss on financial operations	8.04	15.47	2.73	7.51	7.05	9.09	5.80	10.48	10.17	7.16	c. Profits ou pertes nets sur opérations financières
d. Other	4.17	4.07	3.99	3.74	3.73	3.02	3.20	2.43	8.60	8.05	d. Autres
55. Operating expenses	61.48	51.99	67.43	74.98	72.84	72.96	72.18	62.33	62.12	63.58	55. Frais d'exploitation
a. Staff costs	30.87	26.54	28.14	31.05	32.95	35.25	36.21	34.03	32.52	33.01	a. Dépenses en personnel
b. Property costs	7.36	5.42	5.40	5.43	5.48	5.08	5.30	4.84	4.50	4.93	b. Dépenses en immobilier
c. Other	23.25	20.02	33.90	38.51	34.42	32.65	30.66	23.46	25.10	25.64	c. Autres
56. Net income	38.52	48.01	32.57	25.02	27.16	27.04	27.82	37.67	37.88	36.42	56. Résultat net
57. Provisions (net)	69.88	36.76	1.91	-6.86	-6.13	-2.17	3.42	0.86	3.12	11.97	57. Provisions (nettes)
a. Provisions on loans	55.38	29.23	-1.22	-7.79	-4.62	-2.39	4.30	0.94	3.71	9.92	a. Provisions sur prêts
b. Provisions on securities	..	..	..	..	0.01	0.23	0.17	..	..	-	b. Provisions sur titres
c. Other	..	..	..	..	-1.51	..	-1.05	-0.08	-0.59	2.05	c. Autres
58. Profit before tax	-31.36	11.25	30.66	31.88	33.28	29.20	24.40	36.81	34.76	24.45	58. Bénéfices avant impôt
59. Income tax	0.55	1.58	2.26	1.55	2.27	2.07	1.63	5.66	7.59	0.99	59. Impôt sur le revenu
60. Profit after tax	-31.91	9.67	28.40	30.33	31.01	27.14	22.77	31.15	27.18	23.46	60. Bénéfices après impôt
% of net income											**% du total du résultat net**
61. Provisions (net)	181.42	76.56	5.88	-27.42	-22.55	-8.02	12.28	2.28	8.24	32.87	61. Provisions (nettes)
a. Provisions on loans	143.78	60.88	-3.74	-31.13	-16.99	-8.85	15.47	2.49	9.78	27.24	a. Provisions sur prêts
b. Provisions on securities	..	..	..	..	0.02	0.83	0.59	..	..	..	b. Provisions sur titres
c. Other	..	..	..	..	-5.56	..	-3.79	-0.21	-1.56	5.62	c. Autres
62. Profit before tax	-81.42	23.44	94.12	127.42	122.53	108.02	87.72	97.72	91.76	67.13	62. Bénéfices avant impôt
63. Income tax	1.42	3.30	6.93	6.19	8.36	7.64	5.85	15.03	20.03	2.71	63. Impôt sur le revenu
64. Profit after tax	-82.84	20.14	87.19	121.23	114.17	100.38	81.87	82.70	71.74	64.42	64. Bénéfices après impôt

Per cent

Pourcentage

	1992	1993	1994	1995	1996	1997	1998	1999	2000	2001	
BALANCE SHEET ANALYSIS											**ANALYSE DU BILAN**
% of year-end balance sheet total											**% du total du bilan en fin d'exercice**
Assets											**Actif**
65. Cash & balance with Central bank	0.68	0.32	0.53	0.66	4.54	1.96	1.17	3.90	2.34	2.49	65. Caisse & solde auprès de la Banque centrale
66. Interbank deposits	9.70	5.95	4.95	4.25	4.19	3.64	4.48	4.74	6.99	5.90	66. Dépôts interbancaires
67. Loans	73.44	76.09	74.57	73.99	68.85	74.29	75.67	73.79	73.97	75.06	67. Prêts
68. Securities	10.89	11.81	14.57	15.75	16.86	15.21	13.57	10.36	9.80	9.98	68. Valeurs mobilières
69. Other assets	5.28	5.82	5.37	5.34	5.55	4.90	5.11	7.20	6.90	6.56	69. Autres actifs
Liabilities											**Passif**
70. Capital & reserves	2.20	4.50	5.66	6.67	6.22	6.20	6.05	6.58	6.38	6.01	70. Capital et réserves
71. Borrowing from Central bank	7.67	2.45	0.57	1.29	0.06	1.05	1.62	2.89	2.42	1.26	71. Emprunts auprès de la Banque centrale
72. Interbank deposits	10.24	9.72	7.40	7.29	15.29	16.20	12.68	11.55	13.12	13.57	72. Dépôts interbancaires
73. Non-bank deposits	59.10	60.79	69.20	66.26	58.15	51.95	49.57	51.68	49.49	51.21	73. Dépôts non bancaires
74. Bonds	15.20	16.26	11.03	10.88	11.16	14.64	18.52	16.23	16.58	16.38	74. Obligations
75. Other liabilities	5.58	6.28	6.15	7.62	9.11	9.96	11.58	11.08	12.02	11.57	75. Autres engagements
Memorandum items											***Pour mémoire***
76. Short-term securities	*1.02*	*2.06*	*5.41*	*5.92*	*6.30*	*5.69*	*3.14*	*3.64*	*2.10*	*2.10*	*76. Titres à court terme*
77. Bonds	*8.02*	*7.81*	*7.32*	*7.89*	*8.17*	*6.88*	*7.88*	*5.57*	*6.53*	*6.61*	*77. Obligations*
78. Shares and participations	*1.85*	*1.94*	*1.84*	*1.94*	*2.39*	*2.65*	*2.55*	*1.16*	*1.17*	*1.27*	*78. Actions et participations*
79. Claims on non-residents	*19.75*	*13.51*	*9.89*	*10.07*	*10.35*	*10.38*	*12.47*	*13.10*	*16.09*	*14.54*	*79. Créances sur des non-résidents*
80. Liabilities to non-residents	*17.94*	*18.01*	*11.72*	*11.53*	*20.58*	*24.90*	*27.04*	*27.00*	*30.49*	*30.55*	*80. Engagements envers des non-résidents*

* See notes on previous pages.

* Voir les notes en pages précédentes.

NORWAY
Savings banks

NORVEGE
Caisses d'épargne

Million Norwegian kroner / *Millions de couronnes norvégiennes*

	1992	1993	1994	1995	1996	1997	1998	1999	2000	2001		
INCOME STATEMENT												**COMPTE DE RESULTATS**
1. Interest income	28849	25903	20762	21427	21519	20519	27059	34997	40818	49441	1.	Produits financiers
2. Interest expenses	18350	14169	9932	10788	11080	9917	15452	21255	25629	32921	2.	Frais financiers
3. Net interest income	10499	11734	10830	10639	10439	10601	11607	13742	15189	16520	3.	Produits financiers nets
4. Non-interest income (net)	1705	3343	1147	2521	2423	2738	2347	3660	3430	3378	4.	Produits non financiers (nets)
a. Fees and commissions receivable	*1278*	*1409*	*1624*	*1780*	*2124*	*2556*	*2716*	*3048*	*3598*	*3924*		*a. Frais et commissions à recevoir*
b. Fees and commissions payable	*22*	*26*	*36*	*43*	*457*	*557*	*589*	*661*	*784*	*925*		*b. Frais et commissions à payer*
c. Net profits or loss on financial operations	*222*	*1719*	*-668*	*556*	*496*	*498*	*-14*	*1063*	*443*	*198*		*c. Profits ou pertes nets sur opérations financières*
d. Other	*226*	*242*	*228*	*229*	*260*	*241*	*234*	*211*	*173*	*181*		*d. Autres*
5. Gross income	12204	15077	11977	13160	12862	13340	13954	17402	18620	19898	5.	Résultat brut
6. Operating expenses (1)	7200	7340	7593	8117	8330	8444	8691	9730	10475	11385	6.	Frais d'exploitation (1)
a. Staff costs	*3520*	*3370*	*3564*	*3774*	*3820*	*4198*	*4342*	*4875*	*5237*	*5608*		*a. Dépenses en personnel*
b. Property costs	*633*	*574*	*515*	*513*	*580*	*634*	*695*	*718*	*844*	*925*		*b. Dépenses en immobilier*
c. Other	*3047*	*3395*	*3513*	*3829*	*3930*	*3613*	*3654*	*4137*	*4393*	*4852*		*c. Autres*
7. Net income	5004	7737	4384	5044	4532	4895	5263	7672	8145	8512	7.	Résultat net
8. Provisions (net) (1)	1828	2740	796	391	95	252	430	481	-1325	1344	8.	Provisions (nettes) (1)
a. Provisions on loans	*3891*	*2500*	*883*	*435*	*244*	*293*	*767*	*1022*	*1226*	*1667*		*a. Provisions sur prêts*
b. Provisions on securities	..	..	..	..	*3*	..	..	..	*-*	*10*		*b. Provisions sur titres*
c. Other	..	..	..	..	*-151*	*-41*	*-337*	*-541*	*-2551*	*-333*		*c. Autres*
9. Profit before tax	3176	4997	3588	4652	4437	4643	4833	7191	9470	7168	9.	Bénéfices avant impôt
10. Income tax	327	655	781	996	1186	1285	1332	1598	2477	1988	10.	Impôt sur le revenu
11. Profit after tax	2849	4342	2807	3656	3251	3359	3500	5593	6993	5180	11.	Bénéfices après impôt
12. Distributed profit	17	420	650	818	886	987	1126	1363	1560	1471	12.	Bénéfices distribués
13. Retained profit	2832	3922	2157	2839	2364	2372	2374	4231	5434	3709	13.	Bénéfices mis en réserve
BALANCE SHEET												**BILAN**
Assets												**Actif**
14. Cash & balance with Central bank	2355	2072	2454	2671	4867	6112	5086	11848	9434	8660	14.	Caisse & solde auprès de la Banque centrale
15. Interbank deposits	5572	4060	5844	3635	5576	7306	9787	6543	10993	9923	15.	Dépôts interbancaires
16. Loans	195420	205142	219207	239213	271647	311677	345455	416259	481675	540136	16.	Prêts
17. Securities	26974	29968	28588	30485	30207	29017	33921	38037	40085	46980	17.	Valeurs mobilières
18. Other assets	8466	7934	8666	8285	7267	7904	9132	15723	17933	19485	18.	Autres actifs
Liabilities												**Passif**
19. Capital & reserves	13345	18746	20724	23405	26000	28617	33494	38698	44307	48455	19.	Capital et réserves
20. Borrowing from Central bank	10567	8712	2770	4870	147	1637	6403	6008	2578	5334	20.	Emprunts auprès de la Banque centrale
21. Interbank deposits	10387	5544	6085	7666	18170	31536	33136	46429	42683	38862	21.	Dépôts interbancaires
22. Non-bank deposits	189855	197262	208499	216058	230050	234870	251278	290002	323582	355548	22.	Dépôts non bancaires
23. Bonds	8238	9738	13911	14393	20372	34753	48013	56629	84015	109871	23.	Obligations
24. Other liabilities	6394	9173	12768	17897	24825	30604	31056	50644	62956	67113	24.	Autres engagements
Balance sheet total												**Total du bilan**
25. End-year total	238787	249176	264758	284289	319565	362016	403381	488411	560121	625183	25.	En fin d'exercice
26. Average total	241573	250961	261576	276702	302474	340481	383705	443618	522900	596754	26.	Moyen

NORWAY
Savings banks

Million Norwegian kroner

	1992	1993	1994	1995	1996	1997	1998	1999	2000	2001
Memorandum items										
27. Short-term securities	1613	3283	5316	7950	9889	7695	8286	16354	6504	3973
28. Bonds	22521	22471	18666	16900	14454	13829	17882	16417	25760	34214
29. Shares and participations	2841	4214	4605	5634	5864	7492	7753	5266	7821	8793
30. Claims on non-residents	6069	4547	7328	5007	6240	8392	10596	11248	12638	17561
31. Liabilities to non-residents	8701	9666	9816	8647	15479	36618	44964	69362	85951	99388
Capital adequacy										
32. Tier 1 Capital	15555	19751	20825	23420	25897	28472	33248	37749	42492	46716
33. Tier 2 Capital	4515	5793	7092	5985	6561	7590	7920	8723	11310	12247
34. Supervisory deductions	205	34	139	302	380	930	584	459	537	658
35. Total net capital resources	19865	25510	27779	29100	32078	35132	40585	46012	53264	58305
36. Risk-weighted assets	163288	166764	175644	189122	212586	244448	283932	337248	389219	423748
SUPPLEMENTARY INFORMATION										
37. Number of institutions	134	133	132	133	133	133	133	130	130	129
38. Number of branches	1105	1110	1090	1124	1160	1116	1074	1069	862	1002
39. Number of employees (x 1000)	13	13	13	11	11	11	11	11	11	11

1 Change in methodology

Change in methodology

. Due to methodological changes, write-downs are included under Operating expenses (item 6) and not under Provisions (net) (item 8) in the 1991 data.

Notes

. Average balance sheet totals (item 26) are based on thirteen end-month data.

NORVEGE
Caisses d'épargne

Millions de couronnes norvégiennes

Pour mémoire
27. Titres à court terme
28. Obligations
29. Actions et participations
30. Créances sur des non-résidents
31. Engagements envers des non-résidents

Solvabilité
32. Fonds propres de base
33. Fonds propres complémentaires
34. Eléments à déduire des fonds propres
35. Total net des ressources en capital
36. Actifs pondérés des risques

RENSEIGNEMENTS COMPLEMENTAIRES
37. Nombre d'institutions
38. Nombre de succursales
39. Nombre de salariés (x 1000)

1 Changement méthodologique.

Changement méthodologique.

. Suite aux changements méthodologiques, les dévaluations sont incluses sous la rubrique Frais d'exploitation (poste 6) et non sous la rubrique Provisions (nettes) (poste 8) pour les données de 1991.

Notes

. La moyenne du total des actifs/passifs (poste 26) est basée sur treize données de fin de mois.

	1992	1993	1994	1995	1996	1997	1998	1999	2000	2001	
Per cent											*Pourcentage*
INCOME STATEMENT ANALYSIS											**ANALYSE DU COMPTE DE RESULTATS**
% of average balance sheet total											**% du total moyen du bilan**
40. Interest income	11.94	10.32	7.94	7.74	7.11	6.03	7.05	7.89	7.81	8.28	40. Produits financiers
41. Interest expenses	7.60	5.65	3.80	3.90	3.66	2.91	4.03	4.79	4.90	5.52	41. Frais financiers
42. Net interest income	4.35	4.68	4.14	3.84	3.45	3.11	3.02	3.10	2.90	2.77	42. Produits financiers nets
43. Non-interest income (net)	0.71	1.33	0.44	0.91	0.80	0.80	0.61	0.83	0.66	0.57	43. Produits non financiers (nets)
a. Fees and commissions receivable	*0.53*	*0.56*	*0.62*	*0.64*	*0.70*	*0.75*	*0.71*	*0.69*	*0.69*	*0.66*	*a. Frais et commissions à recevoir*
b. Fees and commissions payable	*0.01*	*0.01*	*0.01*	*0.02*	*0.15*	*0.16*	*0.15*	*0.15*	*0.15*	*0.16*	*b. Frais et commissions à payer*
c. Net profits or loss on financial operations	*0.09*	*0.68*	*-0.26*	*0.20*	*0.16*	*0.15*	*-*	*0.24*	*0.08*	*0.03*	*c. Profits ou pertes nets sur opérations financières*
d. Other	*0.09*	*0.10*	*0.09*	*0.08*	*0.09*	*0.07*	*0.06*	*0.05*	*0.03*	*0.03*	*d. Autres*
44. Gross income	5.05	6.01	4.58	4.76	4.25	3.92	3.64	3.92	3.56	3.33	44. Résultat brut
45. Operating expenses	2.98	2.92	2.90	2.93	2.75	2.48	2.27	2.19	2.00	1.91	45. Frais d'exploitation
a. Staff costs	*1.46*	*1.34*	*1.36*	*1.36*	*1.26*	*1.23*	*1.13*	*1.10*	*1.00*	*0.94*	*a. Dépenses en personnel*
b. Property costs	*0.26*	*0.23*	*0.20*	*0.19*	*0.19*	*0.19*	*0.18*	*0.16*	*0.16*	*0.16*	*b. Dépenses en immobilier*
c. Other	*1.26*	*1.35*	*1.34*	*1.38*	*1.30*	*1.06*	*0.95*	*0.93*	*0.84*	*0.81*	*c. Autres*
46. Net income	2.07	3.08	1.68	1.82	1.50	1.44	1.37	1.73	1.56	1.43	46. Résultat net
47. Provisions (net)	0.76	1.09	0.30	0.14	0.03	0.07	0.11	0.11	-0.25	0.23	47. Provisions (nettes)
a. Provisions on loans	*1.61*	*1.00*	*0.34*	*0.16*	*0.08*	*0.09*	*0.20*	*0.23*	*0.23*	*0.28*	*a. Provisions sur prêts*
b. Provisions on securities	*..*	*..*	*..*	*..*	*-0.05*	*-0.01*	*-0.09*	*-0.12*	*-0.49*	*-0.06*	*b. Provisions sur titres*
c. Other	*1.31*	*1.99*	*1.37*	*1.68*	*1.47*	*1.36*	*1.26*	*1.62*	*1.81*	*1.20*	*c. Autres*
48. Profit before tax	0.14	0.26	0.30	0.36	0.39	0.38	0.35	0.36	0.47	0.33	48. Bénéfices avant impôt
49. Income tax	1.18	1.73	1.07	1.32	1.07	0.99	0.91	1.26	1.34	0.87	49. Impôt sur le revenu
50. Profit after tax	0.01	0.17	0.25	0.30	0.29	0.29	0.29	0.31	0.30	0.25	50. Bénéfices après impôt
51. Distributed profit	1.17	1.56	0.82	1.03	0.78	0.70	0.62	0.95	1.04	0.62	51. Bénéfices distribués
52. Retained profit											52. Bénéfices mis en réserve
% of gross income											**% du total du résultat brut**
53. Net interest income	86.03	77.83	90.42	80.84	81.16	79.47	83.18	78.97	81.57	83.02	53. Produits financiers nets
54. Non-interest income (net)	13.97	22.17	9.58	19.16	18.84	20.52	16.82	21.03	18.42	16.98	54. Produits non financiers (nets)
a. Fees and commissions receivable	*10.47*	*9.35*	*13.56*	*13.53*	*16.51*	*19.16*	*19.46*	*17.52*	*19.32*	*19.72*	*a. Frais et commissions à recevoir*
b. Fees and commissions payable	*0.18*	*0.17*	*0.30*	*0.33*	*3.55*	*4.18*	*4.22*	*3.80*	*4.21*	*4.65*	*b. Frais et commissions à payer*
c. Net profits or loss on financial operations	*1.82*	*11.40*	*-5.58*	*4.22*	*3.86*	*3.73*	*-0.10*	*6.11*	*2.38*	*1.00*	*c. Profits ou pertes nets sur opérations financières*
d. Other	*1.85*	*1.61*	*1.90*	*1.74*	*2.02*	*1.81*	*1.68*	*1.21*	*0.93*	*0.91*	*d. Autres*
55. Operating expenses	59.00	48.68	63.40	61.68	64.76	63.30	62.28	55.91	56.26	57.22	55. Frais d'exploitation
a. Staff costs	*28.84*	*22.35*	*29.76*	*28.68*	*29.70*	*31.47*	*31.12*	*28.01*	*28.13*	*28.18*	*a. Dépenses en personnel*
b. Property costs	*5.19*	*3.81*	*4.30*	*3.90*	*4.51*	*4.75*	*4.98*	*4.13*	*4.53*	*4.65*	*b. Dépenses en immobilier*
c. Other	*24.97*	*22.52*	*29.33*	*29.10*	*30.56*	*27.08*	*26.19*	*23.77*	*23.59*	*24.38*	*c. Autres*
56. Net income	41.00	51.32	36.60	38.33	35.24	36.69	37.72	44.09	43.74	42.78	56. Résultat net
57. Provisions (net)	14.98	18.17	6.65	2.97	0.74	1.89	3.08	2.76	-7.12	6.75	57. Provisions (nettes)
a. Provisions on loans	*31.88*	*16.58*	*7.37*	*3.31*	*1.90*	*2.20*	*5.50*	*5.87*	*6.58*	*8.38*	*a. Provisions sur prêts*
b. Provisions on securities	*..*	*..*	*..*	*..*	*0.02*	*1.81*	*1.68*	*1.21*	*0.93*	*0.05*	*b. Provisions sur titres*
c. Other	*..*	*..*	*..*	*..*	*-1.17*	*-0.31*	*-2.42*	*-3.11*	*-13.70*	*-1.67*	*c. Autres*
58. Profit before tax	26.02	33.14	29.96	35.35	34.50	34.81	34.64	41.32	50.86	36.02	58. Bénéfices avant impôt
59. Income tax	2.68	4.34	6.52	7.57	9.22	9.63	9.55	9.18	13.30	9.99	59. Impôt sur le revenu
60. Profit after tax	23.34	28.80	23.44	27.78	25.28	25.18	25.08	32.14	37.56	26.03	60. Bénéfices après impôt
% of net income											**% du total du résultat net**
61. Provisions (net)	36.53	35.41	18.16	7.75	2.10	5.15	8.17	6.27	-16.27	15.79	61. Provisions (nettes)
a. Provisions on loans	*77.76*	*32.31*	*20.14*	*8.62*	*5.38*	*5.99*	*14.57*	*13.32*	*15.05*	*19.58*	*a. Provisions sur prêts*
b. Provisions on securities	*..*	*..*	*..*	*..*	*0.07*					*0.12*	*b. Provisions sur titres*
c. Other	*..*	*..*	*..*	*..*	*-3.33*	*-0.84*	*-6.40*	*-7.05*	*-31.32*	*-3.91*	*c. Autres*
62. Profit before tax	63.47	64.59	81.84	92.23	97.90	94.85	91.83	93.73	116.27	84.21	62. Bénéfices avant impôt
63. Income tax	6.53	8.47	17.81	19.75	26.17	26.25	25.31	20.83	30.41	23.36	63. Impôt sur le revenu
64. Profit after tax	56.93	56.12	64.03	72.48	71.73	68.62	66.50	72.90	85.86	60.86	64. Bénéfices après impôt

Savings banks
Caisses d'épargne

Per cent — *Pourcentage*

BALANCE SHEET ANALYSIS — **ANALYSE DU BILAN**

% of year-end balance sheet total — % du total du bilan en fin d'exercice

	1992	1993	1994	1995	1996	1997	1998	1999	2000	2001		
Assets												**Actif**
65. Cash & balance with Central bank	0.99	0.83	0.93	0.94	1.52	1.69	1.26	2.43	1.68	1.39	65.	Caisse & solde auprès de la Banque centrale
66. Interbank deposits	2.33	1.63	2.21	1.28	1.74	2.02	2.43	1.34	1.96	1.59	66.	Dépôts interbancaires
67. Loans	81.84	82.33	82.80	84.14	85.01	86.09	85.64	85.23	85.99	86.40	67.	Prêts
68. Securities	11.30	12.03	10.80	10.72	9.45	8.02	8.41	7.79	7.16	7.51	68.	Valeurs mobilières
69. Other assets	3.55	3.18	3.27	2.91	2.27	2.18	2.26	3.22	3.20	3.12	69.	Autres actifs
Liabilities												**Passif**
70. Capital & reserves	5.59	7.52	7.83	8.23	8.14	7.90	8.30	7.92	7.91	7.75	70.	Capital et réserves
71. Borrowing from Central bank	4.43	3.50	1.05	1.71	0.05	0.45	1.59	1.23	0.46	0.85	71.	Emprunts auprès de la Banque centrale
72. Interbank deposits	4.35	2.22	2.30	2.70	5.69	8.71	8.21	9.51	7.62	6.22	72.	Dépôts interbancaires
73. Non-bank deposits	79.51	79.17	78.75	76.00	71.99	64.88	62.29	59.38	57.77	56.87	73.	Dépôts non bancaires
74. Bonds	3.45	3.91	5.25	5.06	6.37	9.60	11.90	11.59	15.00	17.57	74.	Obligations
75. Other liabilities	2.68	3.68	4.82	6.30	7.77	8.45	7.70	10.37	11.24	10.73	75.	Autres engagements
Memorandum items												*Pour mémoire*
76. Short-term securities	0.68	1.32	2.01	2.80	3.09	2.13	2.05	3.35	1.16	0.64	76.	Titres à court terme
77. Bonds	9.43	9.02	7.05	5.94	4.52	3.82	4.43	3.36	4.60	5.47	77.	Obligations
78. Shares and participations	1.19	1.69	1.74	1.98	1.83	2.07	1.92	1.08	1.40	1.41	78.	Actions et participations
79. Claims on non-residents	2.54	1.82	2.77	1.76	1.95	2.32	2.63	2.30	2.26	2.81	79.	Créances sur des non-résidents
80. Liabilities to non-residents	3.64	3.88	3.71	3.04	4.84	10.12	11.15	14.20	15.35	15.90	80.	Engagements envers des non-résidents

* See notes on previous pages.   * Voir les notes en pages précédentes.

POLAND
All banks

POLOGNE
Ensemble des banques

Million zlotys

Millions de zlotys

	1993	1994	1995	1996	1997	1998	1999	2000	2001	
INCOME STATEMENT										**COMPTE DE RESULTATS**
1. Interest income	13485	15990	21461	26182	32388	40013	36508	53084	51409	1. Produits financiers
2. Interest expenses	9546	10955	13814	15861	20577	26934	22744	36129	36027	2. Frais financiers
3. Net interest income	3939	5035	7647	10320	11812	13079	13764	16956	15382	3. Produits financiers nets
4. Non-interest income (net)	1639	1770	2464	3261	4566	5770	8505	10484	13877	4. Produits non financiers (nets)
a. Fees and commissions receivable	935	1186	1531	2091	3159	3686	5019	6551	7205	a. Frais et commissions à recevoir
b. Fees and commissions payable	231	146	222	212	347	459	647	915	989	b. Frais et commissions à payer
c. Net profits or loss on financial operations	885	939	1023	707	271	190	868	1335	1681	c. Profits ou pertes nets sur opérations financières
d. Other (1)	49	-209	132	674	1483	2353	3265	3513	5980	d. Autres (1)
5. Gross income	5578	6805	10111	13581	16378	18849	22269	27440	29259	5. Résultat brut
6. Operating expenses	2677	3594	4962	6922	9012	11723	14079	17350	18012	6. Frais d'exploitation
a. Staff costs	1320	1841	2716	3756	4778	6117	7080	8544	8646	a. Dépenses en personnel
b. Property costs	154	297	532	711	937	1255	1663	1924	2103	b. Dépenses en immobilier
c. Other	1203	1456	1715	2454	3297	4351	5336	6882	7263	c. Autres
7. Net income	2901	3211	5149	6660	7366	7126	8190	10090	11247	7. Résultat net
8. Provisions (net)	1974	2008	459	257	709	2470	3100	4482	5457	8. Provisions (nettes)
a. Provisions on loans	1819	1661	118	-12	675	2338	2808	3723	5135	a. Provisions sur prêts
b. Provisions on securities	25	170	71	-23	34	132	292	554	322	b. Provisions sur titres
c. Other	129	177	270	291	-	-	-	205	-	c. Autres
9. Profit before tax	927	1203	4690	6403	6657	4656	5090	5608	5790	9. Bénéfices avant impôt
10. Income tax (2)	1328	1081	1843	1983	2161	2831	1909	1792	1557	10. Impôt sur le revenu (2)
11. Profit after tax	-401	122	2847	4420	4496	1825	3181	3816	4233	11. Bénéfices après impôt
12. Distributed profit	..	..	..	..	738	595	553	662	1450	12. Bénéfices distribués
13. Retained profit (3)	..	..	..	..	3915	2658	2906	3648	2920	13. Bénéfices mis en réserve (3)
BALANCE SHEET										**BILAN**
Assets										**Actif**
14. Cash & balance with Central bank	8266	9799	13941	14423	18141	24906	16499	16313	28908	14. Caisse & solde auprès de la Banque centrale
15. Interbank deposits (4)	12708	19156	19997	25641	33689	42083	51703	78232	80028	15. Dépôts interbancaires (4)
16. Loans (5)	27083	31302	45762	77025	105303	136121	173788	193820	209195	16. Prêts (5)
17. Securities	19611	30978	46240	61942	65793	85791	86515	94960	95800	17. Valeurs mobilières
18. Other assets	15333	18441	23402	18046	24743	29826	34922	45162	55775	18. Autres actifs
Liabilities										**Passif**
19. Capital & reserves	7177	10194	13169	14142	20188	26778	30352	35772	42982	19. Capital et réserves
20. Borrowing from Central bank (6)	5053	5505	6031	9397	7914	6291	5736	5532	4487	20. Emprunts auprès de la Banque centrale (6)
21. Interbank deposits	5510	7541	11330	15666	16473	35262	33877	46372	35872	21. Dépôts interbancaires
22. Non-bank deposits	49275	69801	90759	118894	152719	197970	241426	277984	310113	22. Dépôts non bancaires
23. Bonds	326	627	1745	1156	2609	1666	1284	2081	2762	23. Obligations
24. Other liabilities	15660	16007	26309	37822	47766	50760	50752	60745	73490	24. Autres engagements
Balance sheet total										**Total du bilan**
25. End-year total	83001	109676	149342	197077	247669	318727	363427	428486	469706	25. En fin d'exercice
26. Average total	..	96338	129509	173210	222373	283198	341077	395960	449096	26. Moyen

POLAND
All banks

POLOGNE
Ensemble des banques

Million zlotys / *Millions de zlotys*

	1993	1994	1995	1996	1997	1998	1999	2000	2001		
Memorandum items											**Pour mémoire**
27. Short-term securities	..	..	..	..	..	..	..	..	..	27.	Titres à court terme
28. Bonds	..	..	..	..	..	..	..	..	..	28.	Obligations
29. Shares and participations	..	..	..	..	..	..	..	..	..	29.	Actions et participations
30. Claims on non-residents	..	..	..	..	25593	18941	32600	46310	60463	30.	Créances sur des non-résidents
31. Liabilities to non-residents	..	..	..	..	15070	18667	28087	27389	32206	31.	Engagements envers des non-résidents
Capital adequacy											**Solvabilité**
32. Tier 1 Capital (7)	5604	8234	10183	13444	17175	25173	29314	33606	39699	32.	Fonds propres de base (7)
33. Tier 2 Capital	878	1304	2345	3082	4044	1822	1632	1832	2185	33.	Fonds propres complémentaires
34. Supervisory deductions	3088	4281	4867	3999	3358	4527	5179	4749	4115	34.	Eléments à déduire des fonds propres
35. Total net capital resources	3394	5257	7661	12526	17861	22468	25767	30689	37769	35.	Total net des ressources en capital
36. Risk-weighted assets	37285	48067	67457	102924	143465	192516	196095	237237	251079	36.	Actifs pondérés des risques
SUPPLEMENTARY INFORMATION											**RENSEIGNEMENTS COMPLEMENTAIRES**
37. Number of institutions	1740	1694	1591	1475	1378	1272	858	753	713	37.	Nombre d'institutions
38. Number of branches	1436	1454	1501	2082	2210	2532	3283	3598	4079	38.	Nombre de succursales
39. Number of employees (x 1000)	120	129	136	144	172	174	175	170	165	39.	Nombre de salariés (x 1000)

1 Other non-interest income (item 4.d) includes investment income, foreign exchange gains or losses, other operating income and expense, and extraordinary items

2 Income tax (item 10) includes corporate income tax and other taxes

3 Retained profits (item 13) includes the part of profit allocated for banks capital raising, and coverage of previous years' losses.

4 Interbank deposits (item 15) cover operations with financial entities: term and demand due, and current accounts.

5 Loans (item 16) includes due from non-financial and government entities.

6 Borrowing from the Central bank (item 20): operations with the Central bank.

7 Change in methodology

Change in methodology

. Beginning 1997, data for Tier 1 Capital (item 32) are based on new banking regulations.

Notes

. All banks include Commercial banks and Co-operative banks.

. Until 1996, the data dor Number of branches and employees (item 38 and 39) does not include Co-operative banks

1 Les Autres produits non financier (poste 4.d.) incluent le revenu des investissements, les gains et pertes de change, les autres revenus et frais d'exploitation, ainsi que les éléments extraordinaires.

2 L'Impôt sur le revenu (poste 10) comprend l'impôt sur les bénéfices des sociétés et d'autres impôts.

3 Les bénéfices mis en réserve (poste 13) incluent la part des bénéfices affectée à la collecte de capitaux des banques et la couverture des pertes des années précédentes.

4 Les Dépôts interbancaires (poste 15) comprennent les créances à vue et à terme et les comptes courants sur des entités financières.

5 Les Prêts (poste 16) comprennent les créances sur des entités non financières et sur des administrations publiques

6 Les Emprunts auprès de la Banque centrale (poste 20) : les opérations avec la Banque centrale.

7 Changement méthodologique

Changement méthodologique

. A partir de 1997, les données pour les Fonds propres de base (poste 32) sont établies en tenant compte de la nouvelle reglementation bancaire.

Notes

. L'ensemble des banques comprennent les Banques commerciales et les Banques mutualistes.

. Jusqu'en 1996, les données pour le nombre de succursales (poste 38) e le nombre de salariés (poste39) ne comprennent pas les las banques mutualistes

POLAND
All banks

POLOGNE
Ensemble des banques

Per cent / *Pourcentage*

INCOME STATEMENT ANALYSIS / **ANALYSE DU COMPTE DE RESULTATS**

	1993	1994	1995	1996	1997	1998	1999	2000	2001	
% of average balance sheet total										**% du total moyen du bilan**
40. Interest income	..	16.60	16.57	15.12	14.56	14.13	10.70	13.41	11.45	40. Produits financiers
41. Interest expenses	..	11.37	10.67	9.16	9.25	9.51	6.67	9.12	8.02	41. Frais financiers
42. Net interest income	..	5.23	5.90	5.96	5.31	4.62	4.04	4.28	3.43	42. Produits financiers nets
43. Non-interest income (net)	..	1.84	1.90	1.88	2.05	2.04	2.49	2.65	3.09	43. Produits non financiers (nets)
a. Fees and commissions receivable	..	1.23	1.18	1.21	1.42	1.30	1.47	1.65	1.60	a. Frais et commissions à recevoir
b. Fees and commissions payable	..	0.15	0.17	0.12	0.16	0.16	0.19	0.23	0.22	b. Frais et commissions à payer
c. Net profits or loss on financial operations	..	0.97	0.79	0.41	0.12	0.07	0.25	0.34	0.37	c. Profits ou pertes nets sur opérations financières
d. Other	..	-0.22	0.10	0.39	0.67	0.83	0.96	0.89	1.33	d. Autres
44. Gross income	..	7.06	7.81	7.84	7.37	6.66	6.53	6.93	6.52	44. Résultat brut
45. Operating expenses	..	3.73	3.83	4.00	4.05	4.14	4.13	4.38	4.01	45. Frais d'exploitation
a. Staff costs	..	1.91	2.10	2.17	2.15	2.16	2.08	2.16	1.93	a. Dépenses en personnel
b. Property costs	..	0.31	0.41	0.41	0.42	0.44	0.49	0.49	0.47	b. Dépenses en immobilier
c. Other	..	1.51	1.32	1.42	1.48	1.54	1.56	1.74	1.62	c. Autres
46. Net income	..	3.33	3.98	3.85	3.31	2.52	2.40	2.55	2.50	46. Résultat net
47. Provisions (net)	..	2.08	0.35	0.15	0.32	0.87	0.91	1.13	1.22	47. Provisions (nettes)
a. Provisions on loans	..	1.72	0.09	-0.01	0.30	0.83	0.82	0.94	1.14	a. Provisions sur prêts
b. Provisions on securities	..	0.18	0.05	-0.01	0.02	0.05	0.09	0.14	0.07	b. Provisions sur titres
c. Other	..	0.18	0.21	0.17	-	-	-	0.05	-	c. Autres
48. Profit before tax	..	1.25	3.62	3.70	2.99	1.64	1.49	1.42	1.29	48. Bénéfices avant impôt
49. Income tax	..	1.12	1.42	1.14	0.97	1.00	0.56	0.45	0.35	49. Impôt sur le revenu
50. Profit after tax	..	0.13	2.20	2.55	2.02	0.64	0.93	0.96	0.94	50. Bénéfices après impôt
51. Distributed profit	..	..	..	..	0.33	0.21	0.16	0.17	0.32	51. Bénéfices distribués
52. Retained profit	..	..	..	..	1.76	0.94	0.85	0.92	0.65	52. Bénéfices mis en réserve
% of gross income										**% du total du résultat brut**
53. Net interest income	70.62	73.99	75.63	75.99	72.12	69.39	61.81	61.79	52.57	53. Produits financiers nets
54. Non-interest income (net)	29.38	26.01	24.37	24.01	27.88	30.61	38.19	38.21	47.43	54. Produits non financiers (nets)
a. Fees and commissions receivable	16.76	17.43	15.14	15.40	19.29	19.56	22.54	23.87	24.62	a. Frais et commissions à recevoir
b. Fees and commissions payable	4.14	2.15	2.20	1.56	2.12	2.44	2.91	3.33	3.38	b. Frais et commissions à payer
c. Net profits or loss on financial operations	15.87	13.80	10.12	5.21	1.65	1.01	3.90	4.87	5.75	c. Profits ou pertes nets sur opérations financières
d. Other	0.88	-3.07	1.31	4.96	9.05	12.48	14.66	12.80	20.44	d. Autres
55. Operating expenses	47.99	52.81	49.08	50.97	55.03	62.19	63.22	63.23	61.56	55. Frais d'exploitation
a. Staff costs	23.66	27.05	26.86	27.66	29.17	32.45	31.79	31.14	29.55	a. Dépenses en personnel
b. Property costs	2.76	4.36	5.26	5.24	5.72	6.66	7.47	7.01	7.19	b. Dépenses en immobilier
c. Other	21.57	21.40	16.96	18.07	20.13	23.08	23.96	25.08	24.82	c. Autres
56. Net income	52.01	47.19	50.92	49.04	44.97	37.81	36.78	36.77	38.44	56. Résultat net
57. Provisions (net)	35.39	29.51	4.54	1.89	4.33	13.10	13.92	16.33	18.65	57. Provisions (nettes)
a. Provisions on loans	32.61	24.41	1.17	-0.09	4.12	12.40	12.61	13.57	17.55	a. Provisions sur prêts
b. Provisions on securities	0.45	2.50	0.70	-0.17	0.21	0.70	1.31	2.02	1.10	b. Provisions sur titres
c. Other	2.31	2.60	2.67	2.14	-	-	-	0.75	-	c. Autres
58. Profit before tax	16.62	17.68	46.39	47.15	40.65	24.70	22.86	20.44	19.79	58. Bénéfices avant impôt
59. Income tax	23.81	15.89	18.23	14.60	13.19	15.02	8.57	6.53	5.32	59. Impôt sur le revenu
60. Profit after tax	-7.19	1.79	28.16	32.55	27.45	9.68	14.28	13.91	14.47	60. Bénéfices après impôt
% of net income										**% du total du résultat net**
61. Provisions (net)	68.05	62.54	8.91	3.86	9.63	34.66	37.85	44.42	48.52	61. Provisions (nettes)
a. Provisions on loans	62.70	51.73	2.29	-0.18	9.16	32.81	34.29	36.90	45.66	a. Provisions sur prêts
b. Provisions on securities	0.86	5.29	1.38	-0.35	0.46	1.85	3.57	5.49	2.86	b. Provisions sur titres
c. Other	4.45	5.51	5.24	4.37	-	-	-	2.03	-	c. Autres
62. Profit before tax	31.95	37.46	91.09	96.14	90.37	65.34	62.15	55.58	51.48	62. Bénéfices avant impôt
63. Income tax	45.78	33.67	35.79	29.77	29.34	39.73	23.31	17.76	13.84	63. Impôt sur le revenu
64. Profit after tax	-13.82	3.80	55.29	66.37	61.04	25.61	38.84	37.82	37.64	64. Bénéfices après impôt

POLAND
All banks

POLOGNE
Ensemble des banques

Per cent / *Pourcentage*

BALANCE SHEET ANALYSIS / **ANALYSE DU BILAN**
% of year-end balance sheet total / **% du total du bilan en fin d'exercice**

	1993	1994	1995	1996	1997	1998	1999	2000	2001	
Assets										**Actif**
65. Cash & balance with Central bank	9.96	8.93	9.33	7.32	7.32	7.81	4.54	3.81	6.15	65. Caisse & solde auprès de la Banque centrale
66. Interbank deposits	15.31	17.47	13.39	13.01	13.60	13.20	14.23	18.26	17.04	66. Dépôts interbancaires
67. Loans	32.63	28.54	30.64	39.08	42.52	42.71	47.82	45.23	44.54	67. Prêts
68. Securities	23.63	28.25	30.96	31.43	26.56	26.92	23.81	22.16	20.40	68. Valeurs mobilières
69. Other assets	18.47	16.81	15.67	9.16	9.99	9.36	9.61	10.54	11.87	69. Autres actifs
Liabilities										**Passif**
70. Capital & reserves	8.65	9.29	8.82	7.18	8.15	8.40	8.35	8.35	9.15	70. Capital et réserves
71. Borrowing from Central bank	6.09	5.02	4.04	4.77	3.20	1.97	1.58	1.29	0.96	71. Emprunts auprès de la Banque centrale
72. Interbank deposits	6.64	6.88	7.59	7.95	6.65	11.06	9.32	10.82	7.64	72. Dépôts interbancaires
73. Non-bank deposits	59.37	63.64	60.77	60.33	61.66	62.11	66.43	64.88	66.02	73. Dépôts non bancaires
74. Bonds	0.39	0.57	1.17	0.59	1.05	0.52	0.35	0.49	0.59	74. Obligations
75. Other liabilities	18.87	14.59	17.62	19.19	19.29	15.93	13.96	14.18	15.65	75. Autres engagements
Memorandum items										*Pour mémoire*
76. Short-term securities	..	..	..	..	..	..	..	..	..	*76. Titres à court terme*
77. Bonds	..	..	..	..	..	..	..	..	..	*77. Obligations*
78. Shares and participations	..	..	..	..	..	..	..	..	..	*78. Actions et participations*
79. Claims on non-residents	..	..	..	..	*10.33*	*5.94*	*8.97*	*10.81*	*12.87*	*79. Créances sur des non-résidents*
80. Liabilities to non-residents	..	..	..	..	*6.08*	*5.86*	*7.73*	*6.39*	*6.86*	*80. Engagements envers des non-résidents*

* See notes on previous pages.   * Voir les notes en pages précédentes.

210

POLAND
Commercial banks

Million zlotys

POLOGNE
Banques commerciales

Millions de zlotys

INCOME STATEMENT — COMPTE DE RESULTATS

	1993	1994	1995	1996	1997	1998	1999	2000	2001	
1. Interest income	12070	14680	20089	24615	30384	37769	34426	50237	48197	1. Produits financiers
2. Interest expenses	8743	10023	12955	14999	19512	25646	21703	34680	34383	2. Frais financiers
3. Net interest income	3327	4657	7134	9616	10872	12123	12723	15558	13814	3. Produits financiers nets
4. Non-interest income (net)	1569	1679	2331	3075	4335	5501	8133	10009	13333	4. Produits non financiers (nets)
a. Fees and commissions receivable	850	1071	1395	1909	2928	3417	4644	6053	6630	a. Frais et commissions à recevoir
b. Fees and commissions payable	212	126	209	199	337	449	630	888	954	b. Frais et commissions à payer
c. Net profits or loss on financial operations	884	938	1023	707	267	188	865	1332	1681	c. Profits ou pertes nets sur opérations financières
d. Other (1)	47	-205	122	658	1477	2345	3254	3512	5976	d. Autres (1)
5. Gross income	4896	6336	9465	12691	15207	17624	20856	25567	27147	5. Résultat brut
6. Operating expenses	2099	3157	4434	6263	8173	10803	13038	16053	16548	6. Frais d'exploitation
a. Staff costs	1120	1689	2344	3296	4189	5463	6349	7649	7652	a. Dépenses en personnel
b. Property costs	138	274	500	673	892	1203	1598	1839	2003	b. Dépenses en immobilier
c. Other	842	1193	1590	2295	3092	4137	5091	6565	6893	c. Autres
7. Net income	2797	3179	5031	6428	7034	6821	7818	9514	10599	7. Résultat net
8. Provisions (net)	1745	1824	480	290	726	2451	3052	4377	5298	8. Provisions (nettes)
a. Provisions on loans	1595	1479	144	26	693	2319	2760	3628	4976	a. Provisions sur prêts
b. Provisions on securities	25	170	71	-23	33	132	292	528	322	b. Provisions sur titres
c. Other	126	175	265	286	-	-	-	221	-	c. Autres
9. Profit before tax	1052	1355	4551	6138	6308	4370	4766	5137	5301	9. Bénéfices avant impôt
10. Income tax (2)	1267	1038	1789	1909	2036	2722	1794	1618	1383	10. Impôt sur le revenu (2)
11. Profit after tax	-215	317	2762	4229	4272	1648	2972	3519	3918	11. Bénéfices après impôt
12. Distributed profit (3)	225	462	600	833	734	572	538	630	1413	12. Bénéfices distribués (3)
13. Retained profit (4)	755	1355	2300	3396	3727	2456	2712	3367	2622	13. Bénéfices mis en réserve (4)

BALANCE SHEET — BILAN

Assets — Actif

	1993	1994	1995	1996	1997	1998	1999	2000	2001	
14. Cash & balance with Central bank	7595	9333	13502	13926	17451	24525	16106	15863	28317	14. Caisse & solde auprès de la Banque centrale
15. Interbank deposits (5)	11046	17200	17209	22797	30668	37255	47131	73527	73170	15. Dépôts interbancaires (5)
16. Loans (6)	25285	29240	43285	72543	99777	129731	165607	183495	197624	16. Prêts (6)
17. Securities	19430	30809	45879	61210	64631	84626	85281	93655	94718	17. Valeurs mobilières
18. Other assets	14152	17289	22291	17483	23888	28898	33908	43905	54372	18. Autres actifs

Liabilities — Passif

	1993	1994	1995	1996	1997	1998	1999	2000	2001	
19. Capital & reserves	6657	9648	12491	13502	19295	25641	29013	34185	41053	19. Capital et réserves
20. Borrowing from Central bank (7)	5052	5489	6011	9395	7909	6291	5736	5532	4487	20. Emprunts auprès de la Banque centrale (7)
21. Interbank deposits	5288	7325	11213	15512	16411	35215	33810	46278	35768	21. Dépôts interbancaires
22. Non-bank deposits	45218	65343	85203	111846	143807	187085	228593	263026	292121	22. Dépôts non bancaires
23. Bonds	326	626	1741	1120	2538	1606	1245	2078	2762	23. Obligations
24. Other liabilities	14968	15440	25507	36586	46455	49197	49636	59346	72010	24. Autres engagements

Balance sheet total — Total du bilan

	1993	1994	1995	1996	1997	1998	1999	2000	2001	
25. End-year total	77509	103870	142165	187960	236415	305035	348033	410445	448201	25. En fin d'exercice
26. Average total	..	90689	123018	165063	212187	270725	326534	379241	429323	26. Moyen

POLAND
Commercial banks

POLOGNE
Banques commerciales

Million zlotys / *Millions de zlotys*

	1993	1994	1995	1996	1997	1998	1999	2000	2001	
Memorandum items										**Pour mémoire**
27. Short-term securities	..	..	..	..	..	..	..	..	..	27. Titres à court terme
28. Bonds	..	..	..	..	..	..	..	..	..	28. Obligations
29. Shares and participations	..	..	..	..	..	..	..	..	..	29. Actions et participations
30. Claims on non-residents	..	..	..	..	25593	18941	32600	46310	60463	30. Créances sur des non-résidents
31. Liabilities to non-residents	..	..	..	..	15070	18707	28087	27388	32206	31. Engagements envers des non-résidents
Capital adequacy										**Solvabilité**
32. Tier 1 Capital (8)	5144	7758	9667	12794	16322	24096	28065	32142	37909	32. Fonds propres de base (8)
33. Tier 2 Capital	823	1241	2191	2930	3885	1700	1513	1696	2048	33. Fonds propres complémentaires
34. Supervisory deductions	2696	3805	4508	3699	3098	4295	5018	4614	4006	34. Éléments à déduire des fonds propres
35. Total net capital resources	3271	5194	7350	12024	17109	21501	24560	29224	35951	35. Total net des ressources en capital
36. Risk-weighted assets	34673	45119	63753	97469	136672	184328	186754	225802	237968	36. Actifs pondérés des risques
SUPPLEMENTARY INFORMATION										**RENSEIGNEMENTS COMPLEMENTAIRES**
37. Number of institutions	87	82	81	81	83	83	77	74	71	37. Nombre d'institutions
38. Number of branches	1436	1454	1501	1580	1629	1864	2236	2449	2878	38. Nombre de succursales
39. Number of employees (x 1000)	120	129	136	144	147	149	150	144	139	39. Nombre de salariés (x 1000)

1 Other non-interest income (item 4.d) includes investment income, foreign exchange gains or losses, other operating income and expense, and extraordinary items

2 Income tax (item 10) includes corporate income tax and other taxes

3 Distributed profit (item12) includes deductions for social funds.

4 Retained profits (item 13) includes the part of profit allocated for banks capital raising, and coverage of previous years' losses

5 Interbank deposits (item 15) cover operations with financial entities: term and demand due, and current accounts.

6 Loans (item 16) includes due from non-financial and government entities.

7 Borrowing from the Central bank (item 20): operations with the Central bank.

8 Change in methodology

Change in methodology

. Beginning 1997, data for Tier 1 Capital (item 32) are based on new banking regulations.

Notes

. Commercial banks include Polish commercial banks and Foreign commercial banks.

1 Les Autres produits non financier (poste 4.d) incluent le revenu des investissements, les gains et pertes de change, les autres revenus et frais d'exploitation, ainsi que les éléments extraordinaires.

2 L'Impôt sur le revenu (poste 10) comprend l'impôt sur les bénéfices des sociétés et d'autres impôts.

3 Les Bénéfices distribués (poste 12) incluent les déductions pour les fonds sociaux.

4 Les bénéfices mis en réserve (poste 13) incluent la part des bénéfices affectée à la collecte de capitaux des banques et la couverture des pertes des années précédentes.

5 Les Dépôts interbancaires (poste 15) comprennent les créances à vue et à terme et les comptes courants sur des entités financières.

6 Les Prêts (poste 16) comprennent les créances sur des entités non financières et sur des administrations publiques

7 Les Emprunts auprès de la Banque centrale (poste 20) : les opérations avec la Banque centrale.

8 Changement méthodologique

Changement méthodologique

. A partir de 1997, les données pour les Fonds propres de base (poste 32) sont établies en tenant compte de la nouvelle reglementation bancaire.

Notes

. Les Banques commerciales comprennent les Banques commerciales polonaises et les Banques commerciales étrangères.

Per cent — *Pourcentage*

INCOME STATEMENT ANALYSIS — ANALYSE DU COMPTE DE RESULTATS

% of average balance sheet total — % du total moyen du bilan

#	Item	1993	1994	1995	1996	1997	1998	1999	2000	2001	(français)
40.	Interest income	..	16.19	16.33	14.91	14.32	13.95	10.54	13.25	11.23	Produits financiers
41.	Interest expenses	..	11.05	10.53	9.09	9.20	9.47	6.65	9.14	8.01	Frais financiers
42.	Net interest income	..	5.14	5.80	5.83	5.12	4.48	3.90	4.10	3.22	Produits financiers nets
43.	Non-interest income (net)	..	1.85	1.89	1.86	2.04	2.03	2.49	2.64	3.11	Produits non financiers (nets)
	a. Fees and commissions receivable	..	1.18	1.13	1.16	1.38	1.26	1.42	1.60	1.54	a. Frais et commissions à recevoir
	b. Fees and commissions payable	..	0.14	0.17	0.12	0.16	0.17	0.19	0.23	0.22	b. Frais et commissions à payer
	c. Net profits or loss on financial operations	..	1.03	0.83	0.43	0.13	0.07	0.26	0.35	0.39	c. Profits ou pertes nets sur opérations financières
	d. Other	..	-0.23	0.10	0.40	0.70	0.87	1.00	0.93	1.39	d. Autres
44.	Gross income	..	6.99	7.69	7.69	7.17	6.51	6.39	6.74	6.32	Résultat brut
45.	Operating expenses	..	3.48	3.60	3.79	3.85	3.99	3.99	4.23	3.85	Frais d'exploitation
	a. Staff costs	..	1.86	1.91	2.00	1.97	2.02	1.94	2.02	1.78	a. Dépenses en personnel
	b. Property costs	..	0.30	0.41	0.41	0.42	0.44	0.49	0.48	0.47	b. Dépenses en immobilier
	c. Other	..	1.32	1.29	1.39	1.46	1.53	1.56	1.73	1.61	c. Autres
46.	Net income	..	3.51	4.09	3.89	3.32	2.52	2.39	2.51	2.47	Résultat net
47.	Provisions (net)	..	2.01	0.39	0.18	0.34	0.91	0.93	1.15	1.23	Provisions (nettes)
	a. Provisions on loans	..	1.63	0.12	0.02	0.33	0.86	0.85	0.96	1.16	a. Provisions sur prêts
	b. Provisions on securities	..	0.19	0.06	-0.01	0.02	0.05	0.09	0.14	0.08	b. Provisions sur titres
	c. Other	..	0.19	0.22	0.17	-	-	-	0.06	-	c. Autres
48.	Profit before tax	..	1.49	3.70	3.72	2.97	1.61	1.46	1.35	1.23	Bénéfices avant impôt
49.	Income tax	..	1.14	1.45	1.16	0.96	1.01	0.55	0.43	0.32	Impôt sur le revenu
50.	Profit after tax	..	0.35	2.25	2.56	2.01	0.61	0.91	0.93	0.91	Bénéfices après impôt
51.	Distributed profit	..	0.51	0.49	0.50	0.35	0.21	0.16	0.17	0.33	Bénéfices distribués
52.	Retained profit	..	1.49	1.87	2.06	1.76	0.91	0.83	0.89	0.61	Bénéfices mis en réserve

% of gross income — % du total du résultat brut

#	Item	1993	1994	1995	1996	1997	1998	1999	2000	2001	(français)
53.	Net interest income	67.95	73.50	75.37	75.77	71.49	68.79	61.00	60.85	50.89	Produits financiers nets
54.	Non-interest income (net)	32.05	26.50	24.63	24.23	28.51	31.21	39.00	39.15	49.11	Produits non financiers (nets)
	a. Fees and commissions receivable	17.36	16.90	14.74	15.04	19.25	19.39	22.27	23.68	24.42	a. Frais et commissions à recevoir
	b. Fees and commissions payable	4.33	1.99	2.21	1.57	2.22	2.55	3.02	3.47	3.51	b. Frais et commissions à payer
	c. Net profits or loss on financial operations	18.06	14.80	10.81	5.57	1.76	1.07	4.15	5.21	6.19	c. Profits ou pertes nets sur opérations financières
	d. Other	0.96	-3.24	1.29	5.18	9.71	13.31	15.60	13.74	22.01	d. Autres
55.	Operating expenses	42.87	49.83	46.85	49.35	53.74	61.30	62.51	62.79	60.96	Frais d'exploitation
	a. Staff costs	22.88	26.66	24.76	25.97	27.55	31.00	30.44	29.92	28.19	a. Dépenses en personnel
	b. Property costs	2.82	4.32	5.28	5.30	5.87	6.83	7.66	7.19	7.38	b. Dépenses en immobilier
	c. Other	17.20	18.83	16.80	18.08	20.33	23.47	24.41	25.68	25.39	c. Autres
56.	Net income	57.13	50.17	53.15	50.65	46.26	38.70	37.49	37.21	39.04	Résultat net
57.	Provisions (net)	35.64	28.79	5.07	2.29	4.77	13.91	14.63	17.12	19.52	Provisions (nettes)
	a. Provisions on loans	32.58	23.34	1.52	0.20	4.56	13.16	13.23	14.19	18.33	a. Provisions sur prêts
	b. Provisions on securities	0.51	2.68	0.75	-0.18	0.22	0.75	1.40	2.07	1.19	b. Provisions sur titres
	c. Other	2.57	2.76	2.80	2.25	-	-	-	0.86	-	c. Autres
58.	Profit before tax	21.49	21.39	48.08	48.36	41.48	24.80	22.85	20.09	19.53	Bénéfices avant impôt
59.	Income tax	25.88	16.38	18.90	15.04	13.39	15.44	8.60	6.33	5.09	Impôt sur le revenu
60.	Profit after tax	-4.39	5.00	29.18	33.32	28.09	9.35	14.25	13.76	14.43	Bénéfices après impôt

% of net income — % du total du résultat net

#	Item	1993	1994	1995	1996	1997	1998	1999	2000	2001	(français)
61.	Provisions (net)	62.39	57.38	9.54	4.51	10.32	35.93	39.04	46.01	49.99	Provisions (nettes)
	a. Provisions on loans	57.03	46.52	2.86	0.40	9.85	34.00	35.30	38.13	46.95	a. Provisions sur prêts
	b. Provisions on securities	0.89	5.35	1.41	-0.36	0.47	1.94	3.73	5.55	3.04	b. Provisions sur titres
	c. Other	4.50	5.50	5.27	4.45	-	-	-	2.32	-	c. Autres
62.	Profit before tax	37.61	42.62	90.46	95.49	89.68	64.07	60.96	53.99	50.01	Bénéfices avant impôt
63.	Income tax	45.30	32.65	35.56	29.70	28.95	39.91	22.95	17.01	13.05	Impôt sur le revenu
64.	Profit after tax	-7.69	9.97	54.90	65.79	60.73	24.16	38.01	36.99	36.97	Bénéfices après impôt

POLAND
Commercial banks

POLOGNE
Banques commerciales

Per cent — *Pourcentage*

BALANCE SHEET ANALYSIS — **ANALYSE DU BILAN**

% of year-end balance sheet total — % du total du bilan en fin d'exercice

	1993	1994	1995	1996	1997	1998	1999	2000	2001	
Assets										**Actif**
65. Cash & balance with Central bank	9.80	8.99	9.50	7.41	7.38	8.04	4.63	3.86	6.32	65. Caisse & solde auprès de la Banque centrale
66. Interbank deposits	14.25	16.56	12.10	12.13	12.97	12.21	13.54	17.91	16.33	66. Dépôts interbancaires
67. Loans	32.62	28.15	30.45	38.59	42.20	42.53	47.58	44.71	44.09	67. Prêts
68. Securities	25.07	29.66	32.27	32.57	27.34	27.74	24.50	22.82	21.13	68. Valeurs mobilières
69. Other assets	18.26	16.64	15.68	9.30	10.10	9.47	9.74	10.70	12.13	69. Autres actifs
Liabilities										**Passif**
70. Capital & reserves	8.59	9.29	8.79	7.18	8.16	8.41	8.34	8.33	9.16	70. Capital et réserves
71. Borrowing from Central bank	6.52	5.28	4.23	5.00	3.35	2.06	1.65	1.35	1.00	71. Emprunts auprès de la Banque centrale
72. Interbank deposits	6.82	7.05	7.89	8.25	6.94	11.54	9.71	11.28	7.98	72. Dépôts interbancaires
73. Non-bank deposits	58.34	62.91	59.93	59.51	60.83	61.33	65.68	64.08	65.18	73. Dépôts non bancaires
74. Bonds	0.42	0.60	1.22	0.60	1.07	0.53	0.36	0.51	0.62	74. Obligations
75. Other liabilities	19.31	14.86	17.94	19.46	19.65	16.13	14.26	14.46	16.07	75. Autres engagements
Memorandum items										***Pour mémoire***
76. Short-term securities	..	..	..	..	..	..	..	..	..	*76. Titres à court terme*
77. Bonds	..	..	..	..	..	..	..	..	..	*77. Obligations*
78. Shares and participations	..	..	..	..	..	..	..	..	..	*78. Actions et participations*
79. Claims on non-residents	..	..	..	..	10.83	6.21	9.37	11.28	13.49	*79. Créances sur des non-résidents*
80. Liabilities to non-residents	..	..	..	..	6.37	6.13	8.07	6.67	7.19	*80. Engagements envers des non-résidents*

* See notes on previous pages. — * Voir les notes en pages précédentes.

POLAND

Polish commercial banks

POLOGNE

Banques commerciales polonaises

Million zlotys / *Millions de zlotys*

	1993	1994	1995	1996	1997	1998	1999	2000	2001	
INCOME STATEMENT										**COMPTE DE RESULTATS**
1. Interest income	11822	14167	19112	20934	24994	30577	17529	15412	15920	1. Produits financiers
2. Interest expenses	8567	9687	12312	12812	16103	21062	11088	10103	10329	2. Frais financiers
3. Net interest income	3255	4480	6800	8121	8891	9515	6441	5309	5591	3. Produits financiers nets
4. Non-interest income (net)	1430	1500	2116	2479	3391	4098	4280	1921	2591	4. Produits non financiers (nets)
a. Fees and commissions receivable	*820*	*1025*	*1313*	*1508*	*2345*	*2671*	*2171*	*1566*	*1651*	*a. Frais et commissions à recevoir*
b. Fees and commissions payable	*206*	*115*	*175*	*157*	*253*	*333*	*332*	*255*	*296*	*b. Frais et commissions à payer*
c. Net profits or loss on financial operations	*770*	*791*	*868*	*516*	*245*	*106*	*469*	*327*	*134*	*c. Profits ou pertes nets sur opérations financières*
d. Other (1)	*46*	*-201*	*110*	*613*	*1054*	*1654*	*1972*	*283*	*1102*	*d. Autres (1)*
5. Gross income	4685	5980	8916	10600	12282	13613	10721	7230	8182	5. Résultat brut
6. Operating expenses	2034	3039	4186	5195	6548	8578	6503	4909	4934	6. Frais d'exploitation
a. Staff costs	*1097*	*1647*	*2257*	*2813*	*3485*	*4522*	*3191*	*2388*	*2453*	*a. Dépenses en personnel*
b. Property costs	*132*	*265*	*471*	*546*	*711*	*958*	*880*	*564*	*570*	*b. Dépenses en immobilier*
c. Other	*805*	*1128*	*1456*	*1835*	*2352*	*3098*	*2432*	*1957*	*1911*	*c. Autres*
7. Net income	2651	2941	4730	5405	5734	5035	4218	2321	3248	7. Résultat net
8. Provisions (net)	1736	1801	446	207	488	2124	1521	1426	1622	8. Provisions (nettes)
a. Provisions on loans	*1584*	*1465*	*126*	*4*	*467*	*2013*	*1364*	*1184*	*1552*	*a. Provisions sur prêts*
b. Provisions on securities	*25*	*170*	*72*	*-15*	*21*	*110*	*157*	*143*	*70*	*b. Provisions sur titres*
c. Other	*126*	*165*	*249*	*219*	*-*	*-*	*-*	*99*	*-*	*c. Autres*
9. Profit before tax	915	1140	4284	5198	5246	2911	2697	895	1626	9. Bénéfices avant impôt
10. Income tax (2)	1243	961	1674	1556	1623	2186	895	299	550	10. Impôt sur le revenu (2)
11. Profit after tax	-328	179	2610	3643	3623	725	1802	596	1076	11. Bénéfices après impôt
12. Distributed profit (3)	225	459	591	730	656	349	49	15	4	12. Bénéfices distribués (3)
13. Retained profit (4)	660	1224	2142	2914	3146	1311	818	1029	1166	13. Bénéfices mis en réserve (4)
BALANCE SHEET										**BILAN**
Assets										**Actif**
14. Cash & balance with Central bank	7435	9047	13074	11973	14998	21552	8796	4972	11289	14. Caisse & solde auprès de la Banque centrale
15. Interbank deposits (5)	10077	16043	15710	16611	22125	29175	22897	11054	17475	15. Dépôts interbancaires (5)
16. Loans (6)	24608	27895	40737	61002	81767	101722	79727	50028	52169	16. Prêts (6)
17. Securities	19218	30309	44652	55662	58767	74989	48023	39058	36626	17. Valeurs mobilières
18. Other assets	14023	17077	21792	15646	20957	24633	16928	7396	7694	18. Autres actifs
Liabilities										**Passif**
19. Capital & reserves	6439	9210	11451	9989	14156	18875	13351	6770	7818	19. Capital et réserves
20. Borrowing from Central bank (7)	5051	5486	6001	9261	7835	6240	901	89	64	20. Emprunts auprès de la Banque centrale (7)
21. Interbank deposits	4659	6476	9496	10945	10155	24315	17359	8538	10278	21. Dépôts interbancaires
22. Non-bank deposits	44219	63528	82575	97471	124595	160364	118731	86511	94303	22. Dépôts non bancaires
23. Bonds	270	607	1636	1075	1830	1316	380	731	707	23. Obligations
24. Other liabilities	14725	15063	24806	32152	40044	40961	25649	9869	12083	24. Autres engagements
Balance sheet total										**Total du bilan**
25. End-year total	75360	100370	135965	160892	198615	252071	176371	112508	125253	25. En fin d'exercice
26. Average total	..	87866	118168	148429	179754	225343	214221	144449	118881	26. Moyen

215

POLAND
Polish commercial banks

POLOGNE
Banques commerciales polonaises

Million zlotys / *Millions de zlotys*

	1993	1994	1995	1996	1997	1998	1999	2000	2001	
Memorandum items										**Pour mémoire**
27. Short-term securities	..	..	..	..	..	..	..	..	..	27. Titres à court terme
28. Bonds	..	..	..	..	..	..	..	..	..	28. Obligations
29. Shares and participations	..	..	..	..	..	..	..	..	..	29. Actions et participations
30. Claims on non-residents	..	..	..	..	19719	15006	14284	3320	9635	30. Créances sur des non-résidents
31. Liabilities to non-residents	..	..	..	..	9212	10732	10528	1605	1636	31. Engagements envers des non-résidents
Capital adequacy										**Solvabilité**
32. Tier 1 Capital (8)	5016	7468	8877	10095	12214	17919	13260	5841	5843	32. Fonds propres de base (8)
33. Tier 2 Capital	806	1179	2022	2167	2901	1237	778	506	524	33. Fonds propres complémentaires
34. Supervisory deductions	2694	3795	4433	3508	2880	4092	3946	1598	745	34. Eléments à déduire des fonds propres
35. Total net capital resources	3128	4852	6466	8754	12235	15064	10092	4749	5622	35. Total net des ressources en capital
36. Risk-weighted assets	33257	42356	59660	79185	106954	141290	90549	49165	48266	36. Actifs pondérés des risques
SUPPLEMENTARY INFORMATION										**RENSEIGNEMENTS COMPLÉMENTAIRES**
37. Number of institutions	77	71	63	56	54	52	38	27	23	37. Nombre d'institutions
38. Number of branches	1426	1441	1472	1437	1460	1572	1243	960	1090	38. Nombre de succursales
39. Number of employees (x 1000)	119	128	134	129	131	131	86	60	58	39. Nombre de salariés (x 1000)

1 Other non-interest income (item 4.d) includes investment income, foreign exchange gains or losses, other operating income and expense, and extraordinary items

2 Income tax (item 10) includes corporate income tax and other taxes

3 Distributed profit (item12) includes deductions for social funds.

4 Retained profits (item 13) includes the part of profit allocated for banks capital raising, and coverage of previous years' losses.

5 Interbank deposits (item 15) cover operations with financial entities: term and demand due, and current accounts.

6 Loans (item 16) includes due from non-financial and government entities.

7 Borrowing from the Central bank (item 20): operations with the Central bank.

8 Change in methodology

Change in methodology

. Beginning 1997, data for Tier 1 Capital (item 32) are based on new banking regulations.

Notes

Polish commercial banks: Banks with a majority of Polish capital.

1 Les Autres produits non financier (poste 4.d.) incluent le revenu des investissements, les gains et pertes de change, les autres revenus et frais d'exploitation, ainsi que les éléments extraordinaires.

2 L'Impôt sur le revenu (poste 10) comprend l'impôt sur les bénéfices des sociétés et d'autres impôts.

3 Les Bénéfices distribués (poste 12) incluent les déductions pour les fonds sociaux.

4 Les bénéfices mis en réserve (poste 13) incluent la part des bénéfices affectée à la collecte de capitaux des banques et la couverture des pertes des années précédentes.

5 Les Dépôts interbancaires (poste 15) comprennent les créances à vue et à terme et les comptes courants sur des entités financières.

6 Les Prêts (poste 16) comprennent les créances sur des entités non financières et sur des administrations publiques

7 Les Emprunts auprès de la Banque centrale (poste 20) : les opérations avec la Banque centrale.

8 Changement méthodologique

Changement méthodologique

. A partir de 1997, les données pour les Fonds propres de base (poste 32) sont établies en tenant compte de la nouvelle reglementation bancaire.

Notes

Banques commerciales polonaises : Banques ayant une majorité de capitaux polonais

POLAND
Polish commercial banks

POLOGNE
Banques commerciales polonaises

Per cent / *Pourcentage*

INCOME STATEMENT ANALYSIS / **ANALYSE DU COMPTE DE RESULTATS**

#	Item	1993	1994	1995	1996	1997	1998	1999	2000	2001	Libellé
	% of average balance sheet total										**% du total moyen du bilan**
40.	Interest income	..	16.12	16.17	14.10	13.90	13.57	8.18	10.67	13.39	Produits financiers
41.	Interest expenses	..	11.02	10.42	8.63	8.96	9.35	5.18	6.99	8.69	Frais financiers
42.	Net interest income	..	5.10	5.75	5.47	4.95	4.22	3.01	3.68	4.70	Produits financiers nets
43.	Non-interest income (net)	..	1.71	1.79	1.67	1.89	1.82	2.00	1.33	2.18	Produits non financiers (nets)
	a. Fees and commissions receivable	..	1.17	1.11	1.02	1.30	1.19	1.01	1.08	1.39	a. Frais et commissions à recevoir
	b. Fees and commissions payable	..	0.13	0.15	0.11	0.14	0.15	0.15	0.18	0.25	b. Frais et commissions à payer
	c. Net profits or loss on financial operations	..	0.90	0.73	0.35	0.14	0.05	0.22	0.23	0.11	c. Profits ou pertes nets sur opérations financières
	d. Other	..	-0.23	0.09	0.41	0.59	0.73	0.92	0.20	0.93	d. Autres
44.	Gross income	..	6.81	7.55	7.14	6.83	6.04	5.00	5.01	6.88	Résultat brut
45.	Operating expenses	..	3.46	3.54	3.50	3.64	3.81	3.04	3.40	4.15	Frais d'exploitation
	a. Staff costs	..	1.87	1.91	1.90	1.94	2.01	1.49	1.65	2.06	a. Dépenses en personnel
	b. Property costs	..	0.30	0.40	0.37	0.40	0.43	0.41	0.39	0.48	b. Dépenses en immobilier
	c. Other	..	1.28	1.23	1.24	1.31	1.37	1.14	1.35	1.61	c. Autres
46.	Net income	..	3.35	4.00	3.64	3.19	2.23	1.97	1.61	2.73	Résultat net
47.	Provisions (net)	..	2.05	0.38	0.14	0.27	0.94	0.71	0.99	1.36	Provisions (nettes)
	a. Provisions on loans	..	1.67	0.11	-	0.26	0.89	0.64	0.82	1.31	a. Provisions sur prêts
	b. Provisions on securities	..	0.19	0.06	-0.01	0.01	0.05	0.07	0.10	0.06	b. Provisions sur titres
	c. Other	..	0.19	0.21	0.15				0.07		c. Autres
48.	Profit before tax	..	1.30	3.63	3.50	2.92	1.29	1.26	0.62	1.37	Bénéfices avant impôt
49.	Income tax	..	1.09	1.42	1.05	0.90	0.97	0.42	0.21	0.46	Impôt sur le revenu
50.	Profit after tax	..	0.20	2.21	2.45	2.02	0.32	0.84	0.41	0.91	Bénéfices après impôt
51.	Distributed profit	..	0.52	0.50	0.49	0.36	0.15	0.02	0.01	-	Bénéfices distribués
52.	Retained profit	..	1.39	1.81	1.96	1.75	0.58	0.38	0.71	0.98	Bénéfices mis en réserve
	% of gross income										**% du total du résultat brut**
53.	Net interest income	69.48	74.92	76.27	76.61	72.39	69.90	60.08	73.43	68.33	Produits financiers nets
54.	Non-interest income (net)	30.52	25.08	23.73	23.39	27.61	30.10	39.92	26.57	31.67	Produits non financiers (nets)
	a. Fees and commissions receivable	17.50	17.14	14.73	14.23	19.09	19.62	20.25	21.66	20.18	a. Frais et commissions à recevoir
	b. Fees and commissions payable	4.40	1.92	1.96	1.48	2.06	2.45	3.10	3.53	3.62	b. Frais et commissions à payer
	c. Net profits or loss on financial operations	16.44	13.23	9.74	4.87	1.99	0.78	4.37	4.52	1.64	c. Profits ou pertes nets sur opérations financières
	d. Other	0.98	-3.36	1.23	5.78	8.58	12.15	18.39	3.91	13.47	d. Autres
55.	Operating expenses	43.42	50.82	46.95	49.01	53.31	63.01	60.66	67.90	60.30	Frais d'exploitation
	a. Staff costs	23.42	27.54	25.31	26.54	28.37	33.22	29.76	33.03	29.98	a. Dépenses en personnel
	b. Property costs	2.82	4.43	5.28	5.15	5.79	7.04	8.21	7.80	6.97	b. Dépenses en immobilier
	c. Other	17.18	18.86	16.33	17.31	19.15	22.76	22.68	27.07	23.36	c. Autres
56.	Net income	56.58	49.18	53.05	50.99	46.69	36.99	39.34	32.10	39.70	Résultat net
57.	Provisions (net)	37.05	30.12	5.00	1.95	3.97	15.60	14.19	19.72	19.82	Provisions (nettes)
	a. Provisions on loans	33.81	24.50	1.41	0.04	3.80	14.79	12.72	16.38	18.97	a. Provisions sur prêts
	b. Provisions on securities	0.53	2.84	0.81	-0.14	0.17	0.81	1.46	1.98	0.86	b. Provisions sur titres
	c. Other	2.69	2.76	2.79	2.07				1.37		c. Autres
58.	Profit before tax	19.53	19.06	48.05	49.04	42.71	21.38	25.16	12.38	19.87	Bénéfices avant impôt
59.	Income tax	26.53	16.07	18.78	14.68	13.21	16.06	8.35	4.14	6.72	Impôt sur le revenu
60.	Profit after tax	-7.00	2.99	29.27	34.37	29.50	5.33	16.81	8.24	13.15	Bénéfices après impôt
	% of net income										**% du total du résultat net**
61.	Provisions (net)	65.48	61.24	9.43	3.83	8.51	42.18	36.06	61.44	49.94	Provisions (nettes)
	a. Provisions on loans	59.75	49.81	2.66	0.07	8.14	39.98	32.34	51.01	47.78	a. Provisions sur prêts
	b. Provisions on securities	0.94	5.78	1.52	-0.28	0.37	2.18	3.72	6.16	2.16	b. Provisions sur titres
	c. Other	4.75	5.61	5.26	4.05				4.27		c. Autres
62.	Profit before tax	34.52	38.76	90.57	96.17	91.49	57.82	63.94	38.56	50.06	Bénéfices avant impôt
63.	Income tax	46.89	32.68	35.39	28.79	28.30	43.42	21.22	12.88	16.93	Impôt sur le revenu
64.	Profit after tax	-12.37	6.09	55.18	67.40	63.18	14.40	42.72	25.68	33.13	Bénéfices après impôt

POLAND
Polish commercial banks

POLOGNE
Banques commerciales polonaises

Per cent — *Pourcentage*

BALANCE SHEET ANALYSIS — **ANALYSE DU BILAN**

% of year-end balance sheet total — **% du total du bilan en fin d'exercice**

	1993	1994	1995	1996	1997	1998	1999	2000	2001	
Assets										**Actif**
65. Cash & balance with Central bank	9.87	9.01	9.62	7.44	7.55	8.55	4.99	4.42	9.01	65. Caisse & solde auprès de la Banque centrale
66. Interbank deposits	13.37	15.98	11.55	10.32	11.14	11.57	12.98	9.83	13.95	66. Dépôts interbancaires
67. Loans	32.65	27.79	29.96	37.91	41.17	40.35	45.20	44.47	41.65	67. Prêts
68. Securities	25.50	30.20	32.84	34.60	29.59	29.75	27.23	34.72	29.24	68. Valeurs mobilières
69. Other assets	18.61	17.01	16.03	9.72	10.55	9.77	9.60	6.57	6.14	69. Autres actifs
Liabilities										**Passif**
70. Capital & reserves	8.54	9.18	8.42	6.21	7.13	7.49	7.57	6.02	6.24	70. Capital et réserves
71. Borrowing from Central bank	6.70	5.47	4.41	5.76	3.94	2.48	0.51	0.08	0.05	71. Emprunts auprès de la Banque centrale
72. Interbank deposits	6.18	6.45	6.98	6.80	5.11	9.65	9.84	7.59	8.21	72. Dépôts interbancaires
73. Non-bank deposits	58.68	63.29	60.73	60.58	62.73	63.62	67.32	76.89	75.29	73. Dépôts non bancaires
74. Bonds	0.36	0.60	1.20	0.67	0.92	0.52	0.22	0.65	0.56	74. Obligations
75. Other liabilities	19.54	15.01	18.24	19.98	20.16	16.25	14.54	8.77	9.65	75. Autres engagements
Memorandum items										***Pour mémoire***
76. Short-term securities	..	..	..	..	..	..	..	..	..	*76. Titres à court terme*
77. Bonds	..	..	..	..	..	..	..	..	..	*77. Obligations*
78. Shares and participations	..	..	..	..	..	..	..	..	..	*78. Actions et participations*
79. Claims on non-residents	..	..	..	..	*9.93*	*5.95*	*8.10*	*2.95*	*7.69*	*79. Créances sur des non-résidents*
80. Liabilities to non-residents	..	..	..	..	*4.64*	*4.26*	*5.97*	*1.43*	*1.31*	*80. Engagements envers des non-résidents*

* See notes on previous pages. * Voir les notes en pages précédentes.

POLAND
Foreign commercial banks

POLOGNE
Banques commerciales étrangères

Million zlotys — *Millions de zlotys*

	1993	1994	1995	1996	1997	1998	1999	2000	2001	
INCOME STATEMENT										**COMPTE DE RESULTATS**
1. Interest income	248	513	977	3682	5390	7192	16897	34825	32277	1. Produits financiers
2. Interest expenses	176	337	643	2187	3409	4585	10616	24577	24054	2. Frais financiers
3. Net interest income	72	176	334	1495	1981	2607	6281	10248	8223	3. Produits financiers nets
4. Non-interest income (net)	139	179	215	596	943	1404	3854	8089	10742	4. Produits non financiers (nets)
a. Fees and commissions receivable	30	46	83	401	583	746	2473	4487	4979	a. Frais et commissions à recevoir
b. Fees and commissions payable	6	11	33	41	84	115	299	633	658	b. Frais et commissions à payer
c. Net profits or loss on financial operations	115	148	155	192	22	81	395	1004	1547	c. Profits ou pertes nets sur opérations financières
d. Other (1)	1	-4	11	45	422	692	1285	3231	4874	d. Autres (1)
5. Gross income	211	355	549	2091	2924	4011	10135	18337	18965	5. Résultat brut
6. Operating expenses	66	117	249	1068	1628	2225	6535	11143	11614	6. Frais d'exploitation
a. Staff costs	23	43	86	483	706	940	3158	5261	5199	a. Dépenses en personnel
b. Property costs	6	9	29	127	181	245	718	1276	1433	b. Dépenses en immobilier
c. Other	38	65	133	459	741	1039	2659	4606	4982	c. Autres
7. Net income	145	238	300	1023	1296	1786	3600	7194	7351	7. Résultat net
8. Provisions (net)	10	23	34	83	238	327	1530	2951	3676	8. Provisions (nettes)
a. Provisions on loans	10	13	18	23	226	305	1395	2444	3425	a. Provisions sur prêts
b. Provisions on securities	-	-	-	-7	12	21	135	385	251	b. Provisions sur titres
c. Other	-	10	16	68	-	-	-	122	-	c. Autres
9. Profit before tax	135	215	266	940	1058	1459	2070	4243	3675	9. Bénéfices avant impôt
10. Income tax (2)	23	78	115	354	413	536	899	1340	833	10. Impôt sur le revenu (2)
11. Profit after tax	112	137	151	586	645	923	1171	2903	2842	11. Bénéfices après impôt
12. Distributed profit (3)	-	4	10	103	78	223	489	615	1409	12. Bénéfices distribués (3)
13. Retained profit (4)	95	131	158	483	581	1145	1894	2338	1456	13. Bénéfices mis en réserve (4)
BALANCE SHEET										**BILAN**
Assets										**Actif**
14. Cash & balance with Central bank	160	286	428	1953	2453	2973	7310	10890	17028	14. Caisse & solde auprès de la Banque centrale
15. Interbank deposits (5)	969	1158	1499	6186	8543	8080	24234	62473	55695	15. Dépôts interbancaires (5)
16. Loans (6)	678	1345	2549	11541	18009	28009	85880	133467	145455	16. Prêts (6)
17. Securities	212	500	1226	5549	5864	9637	37258	54597	58092	17. Valeurs mobilières
18. Other assets	130	212	498	1838	2931	4265	16980	36510	46678	18. Autres actifs
Liabilities										**Passif**
19. Capital & reserves	218	438	1040	3513	5139	6766	15662	27415	33235	19. Capital et réserves
20. Borrowing from Central bank (7)	2	3	10	133	73	51	4835	5443	4423	20. Emprunts auprès de la Banque centrale (7)
21. Interbank deposits	630	850	1717	4567	6257	10900	16451	37740	25490	21. Dépôts interbancaires
22. Non-bank deposits	1000	1814	2627	14376	19212	26721	109862	176515	197818	22. Dépôts non bancaires
23. Bonds	56	20	106	45	707	290	865	1347	2055	23. Obligations
24. Other liabilities	243	377	701	4434	6411	8236	23987	49477	59927	24. Autres engagements
Balance sheet total										**Total du bilan**
25. End-year total	2149	3500	6201	27067	37800	52964	171662	297937	322948	25. En fin d'exercice
26. Average total	..	2824	4850	16634	32433	45382	112313	234792	310442	26. Moyen

POLAND
Foreign commercial banks

Million zlotys

	1993	1994	1995	1996	1997	1998	1999	2000	2001
Memorandum items									
27. Short-term securities	..	..	..	..	..	..	..	..	:
28. Bonds	..	..	..	..	..	..	..	..	:
29. Shares and participations	..	..	..	..	..	..	..	..	:
30. Claims on non-residents	..	..	..	..	5874	3934	18316	42990	50828
31. Liabilities to non-residents	..	..	..	..	5859	7975	17559	25783	30570
Capital adequacy									
32. Tier 1 Capital (8)	127	289	791	2700	4108	6177	14805	26301	32066
33. Tier 2 Capital	16	62	169	763	984	463	735	1190	1524
34. Supervisory deductions	3	10	74	193	218	203	1072	3016	3261
35. Total net capital resources	140	341	886	3270	4874	6437	14468	24475	30329
36. Risk-weighted assets	1416	2764	4093	18284	29718	43038	96205	176637	189702
SUPPLEMENTARY INFORMATION									
37. Number of institutions	10	11	18	25	29	31	39	47	48
38. Number of branches	10	13	29	143	169	292	992	1489	1788
39. Number of employees (x 1000)	1	1	2	15	16	18	63	84	81

1 Other non-interest income (item 4.d) includes investment income, foreign exchange gains or losses, other operating income and expense, and extraordinary items

2 Income tax (item 10) includes corporate income tax and other taxes

3 Distributed profit (item12) includes deductions for social funds.

4 Retained profits (item 13) includes the part of profit allocated for banks' capital raising, and coverage of previous years' losses

5 Interbank deposits (item 15) cover operations with financial entities: term and demand due, and current accounts.

6 Loans (item 16) includes due from non-financial and government entities.

7 Borrowing from the Central bank (item 20): operations with the Central bank.

8 Change in methodology

Change in methodology

. Beginning 1997, data for Tier 1 Capital (item 32) are based on new banking regulations.

Notes

Foreign commercial banks: Banks with a majority of foreign capital.

POLOGNE
Banques commerciales étrangères

Millions de zlotys

	1993	1994	1995	1996	1997	1998	1999	2000	2001
Pour mémoire									
27. Titres à court terme									
28. Obligations									
29. Actions et participations									
30. Créances sur des non-résidents									
31. Engagements envers des non-résidents									
Solvabilité									
32. Fonds propres de base (8)									
33. Fonds propres complémentaires									
34. Eléments à déduire des fonds propres									
35. Total net des ressources en capital									
36. Actifs pondérés des risques									
RENSEIGNEMENTS COMPLEMENTAIRES									
37. Nombre d'institutions									
38. Nombre de succursales									
39. Nombre de salariés (x 1000)									

1 Les Autres produits non financier (poste 4.d.) incluent le revenu des investissements, les gains et pertes de change, les autres revenus et frais d'exploitation, ainsi que les éléments extraordinaires.

2 L'Impôt sur le revenu (poste 10) comprend l'impôt sur les bénéfices des sociétés et d'autres impôts.

3 Les Bénéfices distribués (poste 12) incluent les déductions pour les fonds sociaux.

4 Les bénéfices mis en réserve (poste 13) incluent la part des bénéfices affectée à la collecte de capitaux des banques et la couverture des pertes des années précédentes.

5 Les Dépôts interbancaires (poste 15) comprennent les créances à vue et à terme et les comptes courants sur des entités financières.

6 Les Prêts (poste 16) comprennent les créances sur des entités non financières et sur des administrations publiques

7 Les Emprunts auprès de la Banque centrale (poste 20) : les opérations avec la Banque centrale.

8 Changement méthodologique

Changement méthodologique

. A partir de 1997, les données pour les Fonds propres de base (poste 32) sont établies en tenant compte de la nouvelle reglementation bancaire.

Notes

Banques commerciales étrangères : Banques ayant une majorité de capitaux etrangers.

POLAND

Foreign commercial banks

POLOGNE

Banques commerciales étrangères

Per cent — *Pourcentage*

INCOME STATEMENT ANALYSIS — ANALYSE DU COMPTE DE RESULTATS

No.	Item (EN)	Poste (FR)	1993	1994	1995	1996	1997	1998	1999	2000	2001
	% of average balance sheet total	**% du total moyen du bilan**									
40.	Interest income	Produits financiers	..	18.17	20.14	22.14	16.62	15.85	15.04	14.83	10.40
41.	Interest expenses	Frais financiers	..	11.93	13.26	13.15	10.51	10.10	9.45	10.47	7.75
42.	Net interest income	Produits financiers nets	..	6.23	6.89	8.99	6.11	5.74	5.59	4.36	2.65
43.	Non-interest income (net)	Produits non financiers (nets)	..	6.34	4.43	3.58	2.91	3.09	3.43	3.45	3.46
	a. Fees and commissions receivable	*a. Frais et commissions à recevoir*	..	*1.63*	*1.71*	*2.41*	*1.80*	*1.64*	*2.20*	*1.91*	*1.60*
	b. Fees and commissions payable	*b. Frais et commissions à payer*	..	*0.39*	*0.68*	*0.25*	*0.26*	*0.25*	*0.27*	*0.27*	*0.21*
	c. Net profits or loss on financial operations	*c. Profits ou pertes nets sur opérations financières*	..	*5.24*	*3.20*	*1.15*	*0.07*	*0.18*	*0.35*	*0.43*	*0.50*
	d. Other	*d. Autres*	..	*-0.14*	*0.23*	*0.27*	*1.30*	*1.52*	*1.14*	*1.38*	*1.57*
44.	Gross income	Résultat brut	..	12.57	11.32	12.57	9.02	8.84	9.02	7.81	6.11
45.	Operating expenses	Frais d'exploitation	..	4.14	5.13	6.42	5.02	4.90	5.82	4.75	3.74
	a. Staff costs	*a. Dépenses en personnel*	..	*1.52*	*1.77*	*2.90*	*2.18*	*2.07*	*2.81*	*2.24*	*1.67*
	b. Property costs	*b. Dépenses en immobilier*	..	*0.32*	*0.60*	*0.76*	*0.56*	*0.54*	*0.64*	*0.54*	*0.46*
	c. Other	*c. Autres*	..	*2.30*	*2.74*	*2.76*	*2.28*	*2.29*	*2.37*	*1.96*	*1.60*
46.	Net income	Résultat net	..	8.43	6.19	6.15	4.00	3.94	3.21	3.06	2.37
47.	Provisions (net)	Provisions (nettes)	..	0.81	0.70	0.50	0.73	0.72	1.36	1.26	1.18
	a. Provisions on loans	*a. Provisions sur prêts*	..	*0.46*	*0.37*	*0.14*	*0.70*	*0.67*	*1.24*	*1.04*	*1.10*
	b. Provisions on securities	*b. Provisions sur titres*	..			*-0.04*	*0.04*	*0.05*	*0.12*	*0.16*	*0.08*
	c. Other	*c. Autres*	..	*0.35*	*0.33*	*0.41*				*0.05*	
48.	Profit before tax	Bénéfices avant impôt	..	7.61	5.48	5.65	3.26	3.21	1.84	1.81	1.18
49.	Income tax	Impôt sur le revenu	..	2.76	2.37	2.13	1.27	1.18	0.80	0.57	0.27
50.	Profit after tax	Bénéfices après impôt	..	4.85	3.11	3.52	1.99	2.03	1.04	1.24	0.92
51.	Distributed profit	Bénéfices distribués	..	0.14	0.21	0.62	0.24	0.49	0.44	0.26	0.45
52.	Retained profit	Bénéfices mis en réserve	..	4.64	3.26	2.90	1.79	2.52	1.69	1.00	0.47
	% of gross income	**% du total du résultat brut**									
53.	Net interest income	Produits financiers nets	34.12	49.58	60.84	71.50	67.75	65.00	61.97	55.89	43.36
54.	Non-interest income (net)	Produits non financiers (nets)	65.88	50.42	39.16	28.50	32.25	35.00	38.03	44.11	56.64
	a. Fees and commissions receivable	*a. Frais et commissions à recevoir*	*14.22*	*12.96*	*15.12*	*19.18*	*19.94*	*18.60*	*24.40*	*24.47*	*26.25*
	b. Fees and commissions payable	*b. Frais et commissions à payer*	*2.84*	*3.10*	*6.01*	*1.96*	*2.87*	*2.87*	*2.95*	*3.45*	*3.47*
	c. Net profits or loss on financial operations	*c. Profits ou pertes nets sur opérations financières*	*54.50*	*41.69*	*28.23*	*9.18*	*0.75*	*2.02*	*3.90*	*5.48*	*8.16*
	d. Other	*d. Autres*	*0.47*	*-1.13*	*2.00*	*2.15*	*14.43*	*17.25*	*12.68*	*17.62*	*25.70*
55.	Operating expenses	Frais d'exploitation	31.28	32.96	45.36	51.08	55.68	55.47	64.48	60.77	61.24
	a. Staff costs	*a. Dépenses en personnel*	*10.90*	*12.11*	*15.66*	*23.10*	*24.15*	*23.44*	*31.16*	*28.69*	*27.41*
	b. Property costs	*b. Dépenses en immobilier*	*2.84*	*2.54*	*5.28*	*6.07*	*6.19*	*6.11*	*7.08*	*6.96*	*7.56*
	c. Other	*c. Autres*	*18.01*	*18.31*	*24.23*	*21.95*	*25.34*	*25.90*	*26.24*	*25.12*	*26.27*
56.	Net income	Résultat net	68.72	67.04	54.64	48.92	44.32	44.53	35.52	39.23	38.76
57.	Provisions (net)	Provisions (nettes)	4.74	6.48	6.19	3.97	8.14	8.15	15.10	16.09	19.38
	a. Provisions on loans	*a. Provisions sur prêts*	*4.74*	*3.66*	*3.28*	*1.10*	*7.73*	*7.60*	*13.76*	*13.33*	*18.06*
	b. Provisions on securities	*b. Provisions sur titres*				*-0.33*	*0.41*	*0.52*	*1.33*	*2.10*	*1.32*
	c. Other	*c. Autres*		*2.82*	*2.91*	*3.25*				*0.67*	
58.	Profit before tax	Bénéfices avant impôt	63.98	60.56	48.45	44.95	36.18	36.37	20.42	23.14	19.38
59.	Income tax	Impôt sur le revenu	10.90	21.97	20.95	16.93	14.12	13.36	8.87	7.31	4.39
60.	Profit after tax	Bénéfices après impôt	53.08	38.59	27.50	28.02	22.06	23.01	11.55	15.83	14.99
	% of net income	**% du total du résultat net**									
61.	Provisions (net)	Provisions (nettes)	6.90	9.66	11.33	8.11	18.36	18.31	42.50	41.02	50.01
	a. Provisions on loans	*a. Provisions sur prêts*	*6.90*	*5.46*	*6.00*	*2.25*	*17.44*	*17.08*	*38.75*	*33.97*	*46.59*
	b. Provisions on securities	*b. Provisions sur titres*				*-0.68*	*0.93*	*1.18*	*3.75*	*5.35*	*3.41*
	c. Other	*c. Autres*		*4.20*	*5.33*	*6.65*				*1.70*	
62.	Profit before tax	Bénéfices avant impôt	93.10	90.34	88.67	91.89	81.64	81.69	57.50	58.98	49.99
63.	Income tax	Impôt sur le revenu	15.86	32.77	38.33	34.60	31.87	30.01	24.97	18.63	11.33
64.	Profit after tax	Bénéfices après impôt	77.24	57.56	50.33	57.28	49.77	51.68	32.53	40.35	38.66

POLAND

Foreign commercial banks

POLOGNE

Banques commerciales étrangères

Per cent	1993	1994	1995	1996	1997	1998	1999	2000	2001		Pourcentage
BALANCE SHEET ANALYSIS											**ANALYSE DU BILAN**
% of year-end balance sheet total											**% du total du bilan en fin d'exercice**
Assets											**Actif**
65. Cash & balance with Central bank	7.45	8.17	6.90	7.22	6.49	5.61	4.26	3.66	5.27		65. Caisse & solde auprès de la Banque centrale
66. Interbank deposits	45.09	33.09	24.17	22.85	22.60	15.26	14.12	20.97	17.25		66. Dépôts interbancaires
67. Loans	31.55	38.43	41.11	42.64	47.64	52.88	50.03	44.80	45.04		67. Prêts
68. Securities	9.87	14.29	19.77	20.50	15.51	18.20	21.70	18.33	17.99		68. Valeurs mobilières
69. Other assets	6.05	6.06	8.03	6.79	7.75	8.05	9.89	12.25	14.45		69. Autres actifs
Liabilities											**Passif**
70. Capital & reserves	10.14	12.51	16.77	12.98	13.60	12.77	9.12	9.20	10.29		70. Capital et réserves
71. Borrowing from Central bank	0.09	0.09	0.16	0.49	0.19	0.10	2.82	1.83	1.37		71. Emprunts auprès de la Banque centrale
72. Interbank deposits	29.32	24.29	27.69	16.87	16.55	20.58	9.58	12.67	7.89		72. Dépôts interbancaires
73. Non-bank deposits	46.53	51.83	42.36	53.11	50.83	50.45	64.00	59.25	61.25		73. Dépôts non bancaires
74. Bonds	2.61	0.57	1.71	0.17	1.87	0.55	0.50	0.45	0.64		74. Obligations
75. Other liabilities	11.31	10.77	11.30	16.38	16.96	15.55	13.97	16.61	18.56		75. Autres engagements
Memorandum items											**Pour mémoire**
76. Short-term securities	::	::	::	::	::	::	::	::	::		76. Titres à court terme
77. Bonds	::	::	::	::	::	::	::	::	::		77. Obligations
78. Shares and participations	::	::	::	::	::	::	::	::	::		78. Actions et participations
79. Claims on non-residents	::	::	::	::	15.54	7.43	10.67	14.43	15.74		79. Créances sur des non-résidents
80. Liabilities to non-residents	::	::	::	::	15.50	15.06	10.23	8.65	9.47		80. Engagements envers des non-résidents

* See notes on previous pages.

* Voir les notes en pages précédentes.

POLAND
Co-operative banks

POLOGNE
Banques mutualistes

Million zlotys / *Millions de zlotys*

INCOME STATEMENT — COMPTE DE RESULTATS

	1993	1994	1995	1996	1997	1998	1999	2000	2001	
1. Interest income	1415	1310	1373	1567	2004	2245	2083	2847	3212	1. Produits financiers
2. Interest expenses	803	932	859	863	1065	1288	1042	1449	1644	2. Frais financiers
3. Net interest income	612	378	514	705	939	957	1041	1398	1568	3. Produits financiers nets
4. Non-interest income (net)	69	92	134	186	234	268	372	475	543	4. Produits non financiers (nets)
a. Fees and commissions receivable	*85*	*115*	*136*	*182*	*232*	*269*	*375*	*498*	*575*	*a. Frais et commissions à recevoir*
b. Fees and commissions payable	*19*	*21*	*13*	*13*	*10*	*10*	*16*	*27*	*35*	*b. Frais et commissions à payer*
c. Net profits or loss on financial operations	*1*	*1*	*-*	*-*	*5*	*2*	*3*	*3*	*-*	*c. Profits ou pertes nets sur opérations financières*
d. Other (1)	*2*	*-4*	*11*	*16*	*7*	*7*	*10*	*1*	*3*	*d. Autres (1)*
5. Gross income	681	470	648	891	1173	1225	1413	1873	2111	5. Résultat brut
6. Operating expenses	577	437	528	659	838	921	1041	1297	1464	6. Frais d'exploitation
a. Staff costs	*200*	*152*	*372*	*461*	*589*	*655*	*731*	*895*	*994*	*a. Dépenses en personnel*
b. Property costs	*16*	*23*	*32*	*39*	*45*	*53*	*65*	*85*	*100*	*b. Dépenses en immobilier*
c. Other	*361*	*263*	*125*	*160*	*204*	*214*	*245*	*317*	*370*	*c. Autres*
7. Net income	104	33	120	232	335	304	372	576	647	7. Résultat net
8. Provisions (net)	229	185	-21	-33	-17	19	48	105	158	8. Provisions (nettes)
a. Provisions on loans	*224*	*182*	*-26*	*-38*	*-18*	*19*	*48*	*94*	*158*	*a. Provisions sur prêts*
b. Provisions on securities	*-*	*1*	*5*	*5*	*1*	*-*	*-*	*-*	*-*	*b. Provisions sur titres*
c. Other	*4*	*2*	*5*	*5*	*-*	*-*	*-*	*11*	*-*	*c. Autres*
9. Profit before tax	-125	-152	141	265	352	285	324	471	489	9. Bénéfices avant impôt
10. Income tax (2)	61	43	54	73	125	109	115	175	174	10. Impôt sur le revenu (2)
11. Profit after tax	-186	-195	87	191	227	176	209	296	315	11. Bénéfices après impôt
12. Distributed profit (3)	..	..	..	..	4	23	20	32	37	12. Bénéfices distribués (3)
13. Retained profit (4)	..	..	..	..	188	202	190	281	298	13. Bénéfices mis en réserve (4)

BALANCE SHEET — BILAN

Assets — Actif

	1993	1994	1995	1996	1997	1998	1999	2000	2001	
14. Cash & balance with Central bank	670	466	439	497	690	381	393	450	591	14. Caisse & solde auprès de la Banque centrale
15. Interbank deposits (5)	1662	1955	2788	2844	3021	4829	4572	4705	6858	15. Dépôts interbancaires (5)
16. Loans (6)	1798	2063	2477	4483	5527	6390	8181	10324	11571	16. Prêts (6)
17. Securities	181	170	361	731	1162	1165	1234	1305	1082	17. Valeurs mobilières
18. Other assets	1181	1152	1111	562	855	927	1014	1257	1403	18. Autres actifs

Liabilities — Passif

	1993	1994	1995	1996	1997	1998	1999	2000	2001	
19. Capital & reserves	520	546	678	640	894	1137	1339	1587	1929	19. Capital et réserves
20. Borrowing from Central bank (7)	1	16	20	2	5	-	..	-	-	20. Emprunts auprès de la Banque centrale (7)
21. Interbank deposits	222	216	117	154	62	47	67	94	104	21. Dépôts interbancaires
22. Non-bank deposits	4057	4459	5557	7048	8913	10885	12833	14958	17992	22. Dépôts non bancaires
23. Bonds	-	1	4	37	71	60	39	3	-	23. Obligations
24. Other liabilities	692	567	802	1236	1311	1563	1116	1399	1480	24. Autres engagements

Balance sheet total — Total du bilan

	1993	1994	1995	1996	1997	1998	1999	2000	2001	
25. End-year total	5492	5805	7177	9117	11254	13692	15394	18041	21505	25. En fin d'exercice
26. Average total	..	5649	6491	8147	10186	12473	14543	16719	19773	26. Moyen

POLAND
Co-operative banks

POLOGNE
Banques mutualistes

Million zlotys / *Millions de zlotys*

	1993	1994	1995	1996	1997	1998	1999	2000	2001
Memorandum items / **Pour mémoire**									
27. Short-term securities / Titres à court terme	..	..	..	..	..	..	..	..	..
28. Bonds / Obligations	..	..	..	..	..	..	..	..	..
29. Shares and participations / Actions et participations	..	..	..	..	-	-	..	..	..
30. Claims on non-residents / Créances sur des non-résidents	..	..	..	..	-	-	..	-	..
31. Liabilities to non-residents / Engagements envers des non-résidents	..	..	..	..	-	-	..	1	-
Capital adequacy / **Solvabilité**									
32. Tier 1 Capital (8) / Fonds propres de base (8)	460	476	516	650	853	1077	1249	1464	1790
33. Tier 2 Capital / Fonds propres complémentaires	56	63	154	152	159	122	119	136	137
34. Supervisory deductions / Eléments à déduire des fonds propres	392	476	359	300	260	232	161	135	109
35. Total net capital resources / Total net des ressources en capital	124	63	311	502	752	967	1207	1465	1818
36. Risk-weighted assets / Actifs pondérés des risques	2612	2948	3704	5455	6793	8188	9341	11435	13111
SUPPLEMENTARY INFORMATION / **RENSEIGNEMENTS COMPLÉMENTAIRES**									
37. Number of institutions / Nombre d'institutions	1653	1612	1510	1394	1295	1189	781	680	642
38. Number of branches / Nombre de succursales	..	..	..	502	581	668	1048	1149	1201
39. Number of employees (x 1000) / Nombre de salariés (x 1000)	..	..	25	25	25	25	25	26	26

1 Other non-interest income (item 4.d) includes investment income, foreign exchange gains or losses, other operating income and expense, and extraordinary items

2 Income tax (item 10) includes corporate income tax and other taxes

3 Distributed profit (item12) includes deductions for social funds.

4 Retained profits (item 13) includes the part of profit allocated for banks capital raising, and coverage of previous years' losses.

5 Interbank deposits (item 15) cover operations with financial entities: term and demand due, and current accounts.

6 Loans (item 16) includes due from non-financial and government entities.

7 Borrowing from the Central bank (item 20): operations with the Central bank.

8 Change in methodology

Change in methodology

. Beginning 1997, data for Tier 1 Capital (item 32) are based on new banking regulations.

1 Les Autres produits non financier (poste 4.d.) incluent le revenu des investissements, les gains et pertes de change, les autres revenus et frais d'exploitation, ainsi que les éléments extraordinaires.

2 L'Impôt sur le revenu (poste 10) comprend l'impôt sur les bénéfices des sociétés et d'autres impôts.

3 Les Bénéfices distribués (poste 12) incluent les déductions pour les fonds sociaux.

4 Les bénéfices mis en réserve (poste 13) incluent la part des bénéfices affecté à la collecte de capitaux des banques et la couverture des pertes des années précédentes.

5 Les Dépôts interbancaires (poste 15) comprennent les créances à vue et à terme et les comptes courants sur des entités financières.

6 Les Prêts (poste 16) comprennent les créances sur des entités non financières et sur des administrations publiques

7 Les Emprunts auprès de la Banque centrale (poste 20) : les opérations avec la Banque centrale.

8 Changement méthodologique

Changement méthodologique

. A partir de 1997, les données pour les Fonds propres de base (poste 32) sont établies en tenant compte de la nouvelle reglementation bancaire.

POLAND
Co-operative banks

POLOGNE
Banques mutualistes

Per cent — *Pourcentage*

INCOME STATEMENT ANALYSIS — **ANALYSE DU COMPTE DE RESULTATS**

	1993	1994	1995	1996	1997	1998	1999	2000	2001	
% of average balance sheet total										**% du total moyen du bilan**
40. Interest income	..	23.19	21.15	19.23	19.67	18.00	14.32	17.03	16.24	Produits financiers
41. Interest expenses	..	16.50	13.23	10.59	10.46	10.33	7.16	8.67	8.31	Frais financiers
42. Net interest income	..	6.69	7.92	8.65	9.22	7.67	7.16	8.36	7.93	Produits financiers nets
43. Non-interest income (net)	..	1.63	2.06	2.28	2.30	2.15	2.56	2.84	2.75	Produits non financiers (nets)
a. Fees and commissions receivable	..	2.04	2.10	2.23	2.28	2.16	2.58	2.98	2.91	*Frais et commissions à recevoir*
b. Fees and commissions payable	..	0.37	0.20	0.16	0.10	0.08	0.11	0.16	0.18	*Frais et commissions à payer*
c. Net profits or loss on financial operations	..	0.02	-	-	0.05	0.02	0.02	0.02	-	*Profits ou pertes nets sur opérations financières*
d. Other	..	-0.07	0.17	0.20	0.07	0.06	0.07	0.01	0.02	*Autres*
44. Gross income	..	8.32	9.98	10.94	11.52	9.82	9.72	11.20	10.68	Résultat brut
45. Operating expenses	..	7.74	8.13	8.09	8.23	7.38	7.16	7.76	7.40	Frais d'exploitation
a. Staff costs	..	2.69	5.73	5.66	5.78	5.25	5.03	5.35	5.03	*Dépenses en personnel*
b. Property costs	..	0.41	0.49	0.48	0.44	0.42	0.45	0.51	0.51	*Dépenses en immobilier*
c. Other	..	4.66	1.93	1.96	2.00	1.72	1.68	1.90	1.87	*Autres*
46. Net income	..	0.58	1.85	2.85	3.29	2.44	2.56	3.45	3.27	Résultat net
47. Provisions (net)	..	3.27	-0.32	-0.41	-0.17	0.15	0.33	0.63	0.80	Provisions (nettes)
a. Provisions on loans	..	3.22	-0.40	-0.47	-0.18	0.15	0.33	0.56	0.80	*Provisions sur prêts*
b. Provisions on securities	..	0.02			0.01	-	-	-	-	*Provisions sur titres*
c. Other	..	0.04	0.08	0.06				0.07		*Autres*
48. Profit before tax	..	-2.69	2.17	3.25	3.46	2.28	2.23	2.82	2.47	Bénéfices avant impôt
49. Income tax	..	0.76	0.83	0.90	1.23	0.87	0.79	1.05	0.88	Impôt sur le revenu
50. Profit after tax	..	-3.45	1.34	2.34	2.23	1.41	1.44	1.77	1.59	Bénéfices après impôt
51. Distributed profit	..	..	..	..	0.04	0.18	0.14	0.19	0.19	Bénéfices distribués
52. Retained profit	..	..	..	..	1.85	1.62	1.31	1.68	1.51	Bénéfices mis en réserve
% of gross income										**% du total du résultat brut**
53. Net interest income	89.87	80.43	79.32	79.12	80.05	78.12	73.67	74.64	74.28	Produits financiers nets
54. Non-interest income (net)	10.13	19.57	20.68	20.88	19.95	21.88	26.33	25.36	25.72	Produits non financiers (nets)
a. Fees and commissions receivable	12.48	24.47	20.99	20.43	19.78	21.96	26.54	26.59	27.24	*Frais et commissions à recevoir*
b. Fees and commissions payable	2.79	4.47	2.01	1.46	0.85	0.82	1.13	1.44	1.66	*Frais et commissions à payer*
c. Net profits or loss on financial operations	0.15	0.21			0.43	0.16	0.21	0.16		*Profits ou pertes nets sur opérations financières*
d. Other	0.29	-0.85	1.70	1.80	0.60	0.57	0.71	0.05	0.14	*Autres*
55. Operating expenses	84.73	92.98	81.48	73.96	71.44	75.18	73.67	69.25	69.35	Frais d'exploitation
a. Staff costs	29.37	32.34	57.41	51.74	50.21	53.47	51.73	47.78	47.09	*Dépenses en personnel*
b. Property costs	2.35	4.89	4.94	4.38	3.84	4.33	4.60	4.54	4.74	*Dépenses en immobilier*
c. Other	53.01	55.96	19.29	17.96	17.39	17.47	17.34	16.92	17.53	*Autres*
56. Net income	15.27	7.02	18.52	26.04	28.56	24.82	26.33	30.75	30.65	Résultat net
57. Provisions (net)	33.63	39.36	-3.24	-3.70	-1.45	1.55	3.40	5.61	7.48	Provisions (nettes)
a. Provisions on loans	32.89	38.72	-4.01	-4.26	-1.53	1.55	3.40	5.02	7.48	*Provisions sur prêts*
b. Provisions on securities		0.21			0.09			0.59		*Provisions sur titres*
c. Other	0.59	0.43	0.77	0.56						*Autres*
58. Profit before tax	-18.36	-32.34	21.76	29.74	30.01	23.27	22.93	25.15	23.16	Bénéfices avant impôt
59. Income tax	8.96	9.15	8.33	8.19	10.66	8.90	8.14	9.34	8.24	Impôt sur le revenu
60. Profit after tax	-27.31	-41.49	13.43	21.44	19.35	14.37	14.79	15.80	14.92	Bénéfices après impôt
% of net income										**% du total du résultat net**
61. Provisions (net)	220.19	560.61	-17.50	-14.22	-5.07	6.25	12.90	18.23	24.42	Provisions (nettes)
a. Provisions on loans	215.38	551.52	-21.67	-16.38	-5.37	6.25	12.90	16.32	24.42	*Provisions sur prêts*
b. Provisions on securities		3.03			0.30			1.91		*Provisions sur titres*
c. Other	3.85	6.06	4.17	2.16						*Autres*
62. Profit before tax	-120.19	-460.61	117.50	114.22	105.07	93.75	87.10	81.77	75.58	Bénéfices avant impôt
63. Income tax	58.65	130.30	45.00	31.47	37.31	35.86	30.91	30.38	26.89	Impôt sur le revenu
64. Profit after tax	-178.85	-590.91	72.50	82.33	67.76	57.89	56.18	51.39	48.69	Bénéfices après impôt

POLAND
Co-operative banks

POLOGNE
Banques mutualistes

Per cent — *Pourcentage*

BALANCE SHEET ANALYSIS — **ANALYSE DU BILAN**

% of year-end balance sheet total — **% du total du bilan en fin d'exercice**

	1993	1994	1995	1996	1997	1998	1999	2000	2001	
Assets										**Actif**
65. Cash & balance with Central bank	12.20	8.03	6.12	5.45	6.13	2.78	2.55	2.49	2.75	65. Caisse & solde auprès de la Banque centrale
66. Interbank deposits	30.26	33.68	38.85	31.19	26.84	35.27	29.70	26.08	31.89	66. Dépôts interbancaires
67. Loans	32.74	35.54	34.51	49.17	49.11	46.67	53.14	57.23	53.81	67. Prêts
68. Securities	3.30	2.93	5.03	8.02	10.33	8.51	8.02	7.23	5.03	68. Valeurs mobilières
69. Other assets	21.50	19.84	15.48	6.16	7.60	6.77	6.59	6.97	6.52	69. Autres actifs
Liabilities										**Passif**
70. Capital & reserves	9.47	9.41	9.45	7.02	7.94	8.30	8.70	8.80	8.97	70. Capital et réserves
71. Borrowing from Central bank	0.02	0.28	0.28	0.02	0.04	-	..	-	-	71. Emprunts auprès de la Banque centrale
72. Interbank deposits	4.04	3.72	1.63	1.69	0.55	0.34	0.44	0.52	0.48	72. Dépôts interbancaires
73. Non-bank deposits	73.87	76.81	77.43	77.31	79.20	79.50	83.36	82.91	83.66	73. Dépôts non bancaires
74. Bonds	-	0.02	0.06	0.41	0.63	0.44	0.25	0.02	-	74. Obligations
75. Other liabilities	12.60	9.77	11.17	13.56	11.65	11.42	7.25	7.75	6.88	75. Autres engagements
Memorandum items										**Pour mémoire**
76. Short-term securities	..	..	..	..	..	..	..	..	..	76. Titres à court terme
77. Bonds	..	..	..	..	..	..	..	..	..	77. Obligations
78. Shares and participations	..	..	..	..	..	..	..	..	..	78. Actions et participations
79. Claims on non-residents	..	..	..	..	..	-	..	-	-	79. Créances sur des non-résidents
80. Liabilities to non-residents	..	..	..	..	-	-	..	0.01	-	80. Engagements envers des non-résidents

* See notes on previous pages. — * Voir les notes en pages précédentes.

PORTUGAL
Commercial banks

Million euros

PORTUGAL
Banques commerciales

Millions d'euros

	1992[1]	1993	1994	1995	1996	1997	1998	1999	2000	2001	
INCOME STATEMENT											**COMPTE DE RESULTATS**
1. Interest income	12026	12118	11859	12803	12696	12907	12859	12428	15799	17519	1. Produits financiers
2. Interest expenses	8553	8610	8428	9382	9280	8995	8638	7833	11102	12413	2. Frais financiers
3. Net interest income	3473	3507	3431	3421	3416	3912	4222	4595	4698	5106	3. Produits financiers nets
4. Non-interest income (net)	940	1108	972	1078	1543	1825	2256	2029	2333	2169	4. Produits non financiers (nets)
a. Fees and commissions receivable	424	505	508	525	591	823	1092	1232	1489	1463	a. Frais et commissions à recevoir
b. Fees and commissions payable	46	58	70	88	100	112	168	200	243	261	b. Frais et commissions à payer
c. Net profits or loss on financial operations	389	453	277	346	658	683	882	540	659	329	c. Profits ou pertes nets sur opérations financières
d. Other	173	208	257	295	394	432	449	457	429	638	d. Autres
5. Gross income	4414	4616	4404	4499	4959	5737	6478	6624	7031	7275	5. Résultat brut
6. Operating expenses	2360	2593	2720	2922	3188	3445	3590	3876	4156	4153	6. Frais d'exploitation
a. Staff costs	1342	1453	1512	1627	1734	1890	1856	1968	2124	1995	a. Dépenses en personnel
b. Property costs	330	353	364	360	360	386	418	457	446	448	b. Dépenses en immobilier
c. Other	689	788	845	935	1093	1169	1315	1451	1586	1710	c. Autres
7. Net income	2054	2022	1683	1578	1771	2292	2888	2748	2874	3122	7. Résultat net
8. Provisions (net)	1134	941	759	602	632	747	1227	951	257	998	8. Provisions (nettes)
a. Provisions on loans	1022	1175	897	682	774	787	1109	1011	1122	781	a. Provisions sur prêts
b. Provisions on securities	248	-38	64	59	-16	102	164	175	204	202	b. Provisions sur titres
c. Other	-136	-195	-203	-140	-125	-142	-46	-235	-1069	14	c. Autres
9. Profit before tax	919	1081	925	976	1139	1544	1661	1797	2618	2125	9. Bénéfices avant impôt
10. Income tax	199	228	198	199	237	313	330	262	306	301	10. Impôt sur le revenu
11. Profit after tax	721	853	726	777	902	1231	1331	1535	2312	1823	11. Bénéfices après impôt
12. Distributed profit	..	..	..	..	..	..	..	..	..	..	12. Bénéfices distribués
13. Retained profit	..	..	..	..	..	..	..	..	..	..	13. Bénéfices mis en réserve
BALANCE SHEET											**BILAN**
Assets											**Actif**
14. Cash & balance with Central bank	11721	10729	10764	10359	9490	8264	8789	9592	8296	8808	14. Caisse & solde auprès de la Banque centrale
15. Interbank deposits	13140	23309	29922	36696	47170	63557	66232	67935	59256	63823	15. Dépôts interbancaires
16. Loans	40201	44192	46094	51666	58298	69817	89639	115502	140232	157473	16. Prêts
17. Securities	24340	28210	32740	36016	38945	39457	37808	37182	39953	38632	17. Valeurs mobilières
18. Other assets	6258	16842	20097	20258	7315	8529	10130	12012	14531	15927	18. Autres actifs
Liabilities											**Passif**
19. Capital & reserves	10411	11687	12582	12751	14760	17003	21969	26003	29631	33651	19. Capital et réserves
20. Borrowing from Central bank	126	1178	2491	2998	1111	554	1413	2405	1800	597	20. Emprunts auprès de la Banque centrale
21. Interbank deposits	16577	24271	29549	37053	50126	59678	70664	79309	80349	85062	21. Dépôts interbancaires
22. Non-bank deposits	60389	67644	73744	81318	87222	95943	101562	113451	122520	129642	22. Dépôts non bancaires
23. Bonds	1185	1806	1614	1555	2729	9634	10309	14159	19564	27220	23. Obligations
24. Other liabilities	6973	16696	19638	19321	5269	6813	6683	6896	8403	8492	24. Autres engagements
Balance sheet total											**Total du bilan**
25. End-year total	95661	123281	139617	154996	161217	189624	212599	242223	262267	284663	25. En fin d'exercice
26. Average total	..	110040	130662	149861	148488	176073	201173	223602	255194	272669	26. Moyen

PORTUGAL
Commercial banks

PORTUGAL
Banques commerciales

Million euros

Millions d'euros

	1992¹	1993	1994	1995	1996	1997	1998	1999	2000	2001		
Memorandum items												**Pour mémoire**
27. Short-term securities	5034	4516	6134	4299	4501	3698	1076	147	53	4	27.	Titres à court terme
28. Bonds	14404	17204	18700	22495	23816	24943	25124	23451	24371	22498	28.	Obligations
29. Shares and participations	3363	4020	5099	6169	7733	9203	9970	11396	13362	13865	29.	Actions et participations
30. Claims on non-residents	14316	24396	29134	32849	37858	52747	53671	52909	56060	60079	30.	Créances sur des non-résidents
31. Liabilities to non-residents	14745	20377	25666	30148	38158	51671	59314	61450	81030	96646	31.	Engagements envers des non-résidents
Capital adequacy												**Solvabilité**
32. Tier 1 Capital	..	7111	8093	8469	9250	10223	13477	14136	15924	16920	32.	Fonds propres de base
33. Tier 2 Capital	..	1615	1780	2018	3194	4300	5080	6890	8420	10096	33.	Fonds propres complémentaires
34. Supervisory deductions	..	1822	2086	2775	3463	4253	4697	5036	6659	5983	34.	Eléments à déduire des fonds propres
35. Total net capital resources	..	6904	7788	7712	8982	10271	13860	15989	17685	21033	35.	Total net des ressources en capital
36. Risk-weighted assets	..	55310	60642	68499	80593	97155	111654	135713	165334	179337	36.	Actifs pondérés des risques
SUPPLEMENTARY INFORMATION												**RENSEIGNEMENTS COMPLEMENTAIRES**
37. Number of institutions	27	35	37	37	39	44	43	45	42	42	37.	Nombre d'institutions
38. Number of branches	2657	2936	3155	3447	3766	4121	4307	4735	4895	4804	38.	Nombre de succursales
39. Number of employees (x 1000)	63	61	61	60	60	60	57	57	54	52	39.	Nombre de salariés (x 1000)

1 Break in series due to changes in methodology.

1 Rupture de serie consecutive aux changements méthodologiques.

Changes in methodology

. As from 1990, data are based on the new accounting framework for the Portuguese banking sector, introduced in January 1990. Also from 1990, data were revised taking into account the European Directives regarding capital funds and reserves. In addition, branches in off-shore centres of Madeira and Santa Maria Islands are also included.

. As from 1992, data are consolidated world-wide.

. Until 1989, time deposits with the Central bank are included under Interbank deposits (item 15).

. As from 1993, average balance sheet totals (item 26) are based on quarterly data.

. As from 1997, Tier 2 Capital (item 33) includes Tier 3 Capital.

. As from 1997, Risk-weighted assets (item 36) are the global own funds requirements, i.e. own funds requirements x 12.5.

Changements méthodologiques.

. A partir de 1990, les données sont établies à l'aide du nouveau cadre comptable pour le secteur bancaire portugais introduit en janvier 1990. Egalement à partir de 1990, les données ont été révisées en prenant en compte les directives européennes concernant les capitaux et réserves. De plus, les succursales des centres extraterritoriaux des îles de Madère et Santa Maria sont également incluses.

. A partir de 1992, les données sont regroupées sur une base mondiale.

. Jusqu'en 1989, les dépôts à terme auprès de la Banque centrale sont inclus sous "Dépôts interbancaires" (poste 15).

. A partir de 1993, la moyenne du total des actifs/passifs (poste 26) est basée sur les données trimestrielles.

. A partir de 1997, les données de la rubrique Fonds propres complémentaires (poste 33) incluent les fonds propres surcomplémentaires.

. A partir de 1997, les Actifs pondérés des risques (poste 36) sont égaux au montant minimum du total des fonds propres, à savoir la norme de fonds propres, multiplié par 12.5.

PORTUGAL
Commercial banks

Per cent

INCOME STATEMENT ANALYSIS

PORTUGAL
Banques commerciales

Pourcentage

ANALYSE DU COMPTE DE RESULTATS

	1992[1]	1993	1994	1995	1996	1997	1998	1999	2000	2001	
% of average balance sheet total											**% du total moyen du bilan**
40. Interest income	..	11.01	9.08	8.54	8.55	7.33	6.39	5.56	6.19	6.43	40. Produits financiers
41. Interest expenses	..	7.82	6.45	6.26	6.25	5.11	4.29	3.50	4.35	4.55	41. Frais financiers
42. Net interest income	..	3.19	2.63	2.28	2.30	2.22	2.10	2.05	1.84	1.87	42. Produits financiers nets
43. Non-interest income (net)	..	1.01	0.74	0.72	1.04	1.04	1.12	0.91	0.91	0.80	43. Produits non financiers (nets)
a. Fees and commissions receivable	..	0.46	0.39	0.35	0.40	0.47	0.54	0.55	0.58	0.54	a. Frais et commissions à recevoir
b. Fees and commissions payable	..	0.05	0.05	0.06	0.07	0.06	0.08	0.09	0.10	0.10	b. Frais et commissions à payer
c. Net profits or loss on financial operations	..	0.41	0.21	0.23	0.44	0.39	0.44	0.24	0.26	0.12	c. Profits ou pertes nets sur opérations financières
d. Other	..	0.19	0.20	0.20	0.27	0.25	0.22	0.20	0.17	0.23	d. Autres
44. Gross income	..	4.19	3.37	3.00	3.34	3.26	3.22	2.96	2.76	2.67	44. Résultat brut
45. Operating expenses	..	2.36	2.08	1.95	2.15	1.96	1.78	1.73	1.63	1.52	45. Frais d'exploitation
a. Staff costs	..	1.32	1.16	1.09	1.17	1.07	0.92	0.88	0.83	0.73	a. Dépenses en personnel
b. Property costs	..	0.32	0.28	0.24	0.24	0.22	0.21	0.20	0.17	0.16	b. Dépenses en immobilier
c. Other	..	0.72	0.65	0.62	0.74	0.66	0.65	0.65	0.62	0.63	c. Autres
46. Net income	..	1.84	1.29	1.05	1.19	1.30	1.44	1.23	1.13	1.14	46. Résultat net
47. Provisions (net)	..	0.86	0.58	0.40	0.43	0.42	0.61	0.43	0.10	0.37	47. Provisions (nettes)
a. Provisions on loans	..	1.07	0.69	0.46	0.52	0.45	0.55	0.45	0.44	0.29	a. Provisions sur prêts
b. Provisions on securities	..	-0.03	0.05	0.04	-0.01	0.06	0.08	0.08	0.08	0.07	b. Provisions sur titres
c. Other	..	-0.18	-0.16	-0.09	-0.08	-0.08	-0.02	-0.11	-0.42	0.01	c. Autres
48. Profit before tax	..	0.98	0.71	0.65	0.77	0.88	0.83	0.80	1.03	0.78	48. Bénéfices avant impôt
49. Income tax	..	0.21	0.15	0.13	0.16	0.18	0.16	0.12	0.12	0.11	49. Impôt sur le revenu
50. Profit after tax	..	0.78	0.56	0.52	0.61	0.70	0.66	0.69	0.91	0.67	50. Bénéfices après impôt
51. Distributed profit	..	..	..	..	..	..	..	..	..	..	51. Bénéfices distribués
52. Retained profit	..	..	..	..	..	..	..	..	..	..	52. Bénéfices mis en réserve
% of gross income											**% du total du résultat brut**
53. Net interest income	78.68	75.97	77.91	76.04	68.88	68.19	65.17	69.37	66.82	70.19	53. Produits financiers nets
54. Non-interest income (net)	21.30	24.00	22.07	23.96	31.12	31.81	34.83	30.63	33.18	29.81	54. Produits non financiers (nets)
a. Fees and commissions receivable	9.61	10.94	11.53	11.67	11.92	14.35	16.86	18.60	21.18	20.11	a. Frais et commissions à recevoir
b. Fees and commissions payable	1.04	1.26	1.59	1.96	2.02	1.95	2.59	3.02	3.46	3.59	b. Frais et commissions à payer
c. Net profits or loss on financial operations	8.81	9.81	6.29	7.69	13.27	11.91	13.62	8.15	9.37	4.52	c. Profits ou pertes nets sur opérations financières
d. Other	3.92	4.51	5.84	6.56	7.95	7.53	6.93	6.90	6.10	8.77	d. Autres
55. Operating expenses	53.47	56.17	61.76	64.95	64.29	60.05	55.42	58.51	59.11	57.09	55. Frais d'exploitation
a. Staff costs	30.40	31.48	34.33	36.16	34.97	32.94	28.65	29.71	30.21	27.42	a. Dépenses en personnel
b. Property costs	7.48	7.65	8.27	8.00	7.26	6.73	6.45	6.90	6.34	6.16	b. Dépenses en immobilier
c. Other	15.61	17.07	19.19	20.78	22.04	20.38	20.30	21.91	22.56	23.51	c. Autres
56. Net income	46.53	43.80	38.22	35.07	35.71	39.95	44.58	41.49	40.88	42.91	56. Résultat net
57. Provisions (net)	25.69	20.39	17.23	13.38	12.74	13.02	18.94	14.36	3.66	13.72	57. Provisions (nettes)
a. Provisions on loans	23.15	25.45	20.37	15.16	15.61	13.72	17.12	15.26	15.96	10.74	a. Provisions sur prêts
b. Provisions on securities	5.62	-0.82	1.45	1.31	-0.32	1.78	2.53	2.64	2.90	2.78	b. Provisions sur titres
c. Other	-3.08	-4.22	-4.61	-3.11	-2.52	-2.48	-0.71	-3.55	-15.20	0.19	c. Autres
58. Profit before tax	20.82	23.42	21.00	21.69	22.97	26.91	25.64	27.13	37.24	29.21	58. Bénéfices avant impôt
59. Income tax	4.51	4.94	4.50	4.42	4.78	5.46	5.09	3.96	4.35	4.14	59. Impôt sur le revenu
60. Profit after tax	16.33	18.48	16.49	17.27	18.19	21.46	20.55	23.17	32.88	25.06	60. Bénéfices après impôt
% of net income											**% du total du résultat net**
61. Provisions (net)	55.21	46.54	45.10	38.15	35.69	32.59	42.49	34.61	8.94	31.97	61. Provisions (nettes)
a. Provisions on loans	49.76	58.11	53.30	43.22	43.70	34.34	38.40	36.79	39.04	25.02	a. Provisions sur prêts
b. Provisions on securities	12.07	-1.88	3.80	3.74	-0.90	4.45	5.68	6.37	7.10	6.47	b. Provisions sur titres
c. Other	-6.62	-9.64	-12.06	-8.87	-7.06	-6.20	-1.59	-8.55	-37.20	0.45	c. Autres
62. Profit before tax	44.74	53.46	54.96	61.85	64.31	67.36	57.51	65.39	91.09	68.07	62. Bénéfices avant impôt
63. Income tax	9.69	11.28	11.76	12.61	13.38	13.66	11.43	9.53	10.65	9.64	63. Impôt sur le revenu
64. Profit after tax	35.10	42.19	43.14	49.24	50.93	53.71	46.09	55.86	80.45	58.39	64. Bénéfices après impôt

PORTUGAL
Commercial banks

Per cent

BALANCE SHEET ANALYSIS

% of year-end balance sheet total

	1992[1]	1993	1994	1995	1996	1997	1998	1999	2000	2001
Assets										
65. Cash & balance with Central bank	12.25	8.70	7.71	6.68	5.89	4.36	4.13	3.96	3.16	3.09
66. Interbank deposits	13.74	18.91	21.43	23.68	29.26	33.52	31.15	28.05	22.59	22.42
67. Loans	42.02	35.85	33.01	33.33	36.16	36.82	42.16	47.68	53.47	55.32
68. Securities	25.44	22.88	23.45	23.24	24.16	20.81	17.78	15.35	15.23	13.57
69. Other assets	6.54	13.66	14.39	13.07	4.54	4.50	4.76	4.96	5.54	5.60
Liabilities										
70. Capital & reserves	10.88	9.48	9.01	8.23	9.16	8.97	10.33	10.74	11.30	11.82
71. Borrowing from Central bank	0.13	0.96	1.78	1.93	0.69	0.29	0.66	0.99	0.69	0.21
72. Interbank deposits	17.33	19.69	21.16	23.91	31.09	31.47	33.24	32.74	30.64	29.88
73. Non-bank deposits	63.13	54.87	52.82	52.46	54.10	50.60	47.77	46.84	46.72	45.54
74. Bonds	1.24	1.46	1.16	1.00	1.69	5.08	4.85	5.85	7.46	9.56
75. Other liabilities	7.29	13.54	14.07	12.47	3.27	3.59	3.14	2.85	3.20	2.98
Memorandum items										
76. Short-term securities	5.26	3.66	4.39	2.77	2.79	1.95	0.51	0.06	0.02	-
77. Bonds	15.06	13.96	13.39	14.51	14.77	13.15	11.82	9.68	9.29	7.90
78. Shares and participations	3.52	3.26	3.65	3.98	4.80	4.85	4.69	4.70	5.09	4.87
79. Claims on non-residents	14.97	19.79	20.87	21.19	23.48	27.82	25.25	21.84	21.38	21.11
80. Liabilities to non-residents	15.41	16.53	18.38	19.45	23.67	27.25	27.90	25.37	30.90	33.95

* See notes on previous pages.

PORTUGAL
Banques commerciales

Pourcentage

ANALYSE DU BILAN

% du total du bilan en fin d'exercice

Actif
65. Caisse & solde auprès de la Banque centrale
66. Dépôts interbancaires
67. Prêts
68. Valeurs mobilières
69. Autres actifs

Passif
70. Capital et réserves
71. Emprunts auprès de la Banque centrale
72. Dépôts interbancaires
73. Dépôts non bancaires
74. Obligations
75. Autres engagements

Pour mémoire
76. Titres à court terme
77. Obligations
78. Actions et participations
79. Créances sur des non-résidents
80. Engagements envers des non-résidents

* Voir les notes en pages précédentes.

230

SLOVAK REPUBLIC
All banks

Million slovak koruna

REBUBLIQUE SLOVAQUE
Ensemble des banques

Millions de couronnes slovaques

	1995	1996	1997	1998	1999	2000	2001	
INCOME STATEMENT								**COMPTE DE RESULTATS**
1. Interest income	57503596	57211992	81211953	88166012	75043622	72342079	61277634	1. Produits financiers
2. Interest expenses	39234674	44588548	59938512	70524402	62670815	50950818	37678282	2. Frais financiers
3. Net interest income	18268922	12623444	21273441	17641610	12372807	21391261	23599352	3. Produits financiers nets
4. Non-interest income (net)	2354077	2870439	10287937	14097371	12478914	10636182	10343262	4. Produits non financiers (nets)
a. Fees and commissions receivable	2612577	3537969	3861925	5075560	5069826	5213374	6482209	a. Frais et commissions à recevoir
b. Fees and commissions payable	258500	667530	707732	788250	849405	896580	1060852	b. Frais et commissions à payer
c. Net profits or loss on financial operations	..	..	6120982	8303734	7942288	4868837	4698648	c. Profits ou pertes nets sur opérations financières
d. Other	..	..	1012932	1506327	316205	1450551	223257	d. Autres
5. Gross income	20622999	15493883	31561378	31738981	24851721	32027443	33942614	5. Résultat brut
6. Operating expenses	..	..	20746284	21502515	27416717	32115451	35748033	6. Frais d'exploitation
a. Staff costs	..	..	6914998	7541901	7780754	8307141	8684729	a. Dépenses en personnel
b. Property costs	..	..	10896587	11967738	12146949	12456360	13207214	b. Dépenses en immobilier
c. Other	..	..	2934699	1992876	7489014	11351950	13856090	c. Autres
7. Net income	..	..	10815094	10236466	-2564996	-88008	-1805419	7. Résultat net
8. Provisions (net)	..	-	10730585	12076481	26166948	-5246640	-11113907	8. Provisions (nettes)
a. Provisions on loans	..	..	2586318	7351428	18898004	19342432	-12470011	a. Provisions sur prêts
b. Provisions on securities	..	..	..	..	..	..	..	b. Provisions sur titres
c. Other	..	..	8144267	4725053	7268944	-24589072	1356104	c. Autres
9. Profit before tax	..	..	84509	-1840015	-28731944	5158632	9308488	9. Bénéfices avant impôt
10. Income tax	..	..	1425023	1838300	789773	781072	237487	10. Impôt sur le revenu
11. Profit after tax	..	..	-1340514	-3678315	-29521717	4377560	9071001	11. Bénéfices après impôt
12. Distributed profit	..	..	..	..	..	..	..	12. Bénéfices distribués
13. Retained profit	..	..	2314941	3351215	5307678	5913259	7800859	13. Bénéfices mis en réserve
BALANCE SHEET								**BILAN**
Assets								**Actif**
14. Cash & balance with Central bank	..	..	102234551	75377504	89831353	87925500	110256444	14. Caisse & solde auprès de la Banque centrale
15. Interbank deposits	..	..	165171890	174714524	141403948	158141655	126834180	15. Dépôts interbancaires
16. Loans	..	..	355158540	365395702	360695715	338798712	277186990	16. Prêts
17. Securities	..	..	117838626	109238738	109883357	168439996	268914296	17. Valeurs mobilières
18. Other assets	..	..	36448940	71538592	67949672	93648799	145616712	18. Autres actifs
Liabilities								**Passif**
19. Capital & reserves	..	..	64212872	74312594	100444074	72808629	78150653	19. Capital et réserves
20. Borrowing from Central bank	..	..	33018695	30933093	28357446	24570475	21231981	20. Emprunts auprès de la Banque centrale
21. Interbank deposits	..	..	180165723	191327236	126064872	131642200	142144624	21. Dépôts interbancaires
22. Non-bank deposits	..	..	447728492	462281009	506989377	598997890	664469311	22. Dépôts non bancaires
23. Bonds	..	..	33829399	27703103	29520308	29691850	26352751	23. Obligations
24. Other liabilities	..	..	17897366	9708025	-21612032	-10756382	-3540698	24. Autres engagements
Balance sheet total								**Total du bilan**
25. End-year total	..	..	776852547	796265060	769764045	846954662	928808622	25. En fin d'exercice
26. Average total	..	..	757927211	812340773	739566238	815080464	888776510	26. Moyen

231

SLOVAK REPUBLIC

All banks

REPUBLIQUE SLOVAQUE

Ensemble des banques

Million slovak koruna

Millions de couronnes slovaques

	1995	1996	1997	1998	1999	2000	2001		
Memorandum items									***Pour mémoire***
27. Short-term securities	..	..	..	..	..	..	..	27.	Titres à court terme
28. Bonds	..	..	..	..	..	..	..	28.	Obligations
29. Shares and participations	..	..	3925784	37930797	35741330	60660022	114216366	29.	Actions et participations
30. Claims on non-residents	55598417	82194965	128197594	148046868	74900522	113940954	133608988	30.	Créances sur des non-résidents
31. Liabilities to non-residents	35497990	78617314	111030970	109292607	41719911	47115293	77582487	31.	Engagements envers des non-résidents
Capital adequacy									***Solvabilité***
32. Tier 1 Capital	..	..	43614124	47981969	68737247	70255359	74352472	32.	Fonds propres de base
33. Tier 2 Capital	..	..	10031128	13547281	25117843	5296973	22556635	33.	Fonds propres complémentaires
34. Supervisory deductions	..	..	34096659	48859632	61843555	67907960	56831075	34.	Eléments à déduire des fonds propres
35. Total net capital resources	..	..	19548593	12969618	32011535	7644372	40078032	35.	Total net des ressources en capital
36. Risk-weighted assets	..	..	406041585	406977680	364450506	314061252	299791432	36.	Actifs pondérés des risques
SUPPLEMENTARY INFORMATION									**RENSEIGNEMENTS COMPLEMENTAIRES**
37. Number of institutions	31	29	29	26	25	23	21	37.	Nombre d'institutions
38. Number of branches	9	5	4	2	2	2	2	38.	Nombre de succursales
39. Number of employees (x 1000)	21	23	23	23	22	21	20	39.	Nombre de salariés (x 1000)

232

SLOVAK REPUBLIC

All banks

REBUBLIQUE SLOVAQUE

Ensemble des banques

Per cent — *Pourcentage*

INCOME STATEMENT ANALYSIS — ANALYSE DU COMPTE DE RESULTATS

	1995	1996	1997	1998	1999	2000	2001	
% of average balance sheet total								**% du total moyen du bilan**
40. Interest income	..	..	10.72	10.85	10.15	8.88	6.89	40. Produits financiers
41. Interest expenses	..	..	7.91	8.68	8.47	6.25	4.24	41. Frais financiers
42. Net interest income	..	..	2.81	2.17	1.67	2.62	2.66	42. Produits financiers nets
43. Non-interest income (net)	..	..	1.36	1.74	1.69	1.30	1.16	43. Produits non financiers (nets)
a. Fees and commissions receivable	..	..	*0.51*	*0.62*	*0.69*	*0.64*	*0.73*	*a. Frais et commissions à recevoir*
b. Fees and commissions payable	..	..	*0.09*	*0.10*	*0.11*	*0.11*	*0.12*	*b. Frais et commissions à payer*
c. Net profits or loss on financial operations	..	..	*0.81*	*1.02*	*1.07*	*0.60*	*0.53*	*c. Profits ou pertes nets sur opérations financières*
d. Other	..	..	*0.13*	*0.19*	*0.04*	*0.18*	*0.03*	*d. Autres*
44. Gross income	..	..	4.16	3.91	3.36	3.93	3.82	44. Résultat brut
45. Operating expenses	..	..	2.74	2.65	3.71	3.94	4.02	45. Frais d'exploitation
a. Staff costs	..	..	*0.91*	*0.93*	*1.05*	*1.02*	*0.98*	*a. Dépenses en personnel*
b. Property costs	..	..	*1.44*	*1.47*	*1.64*	*1.53*	*1.49*	*b. Dépenses en immobilier*
c. Other	..	..	*0.39*	*0.25*	*1.01*	*1.39*	*1.56*	*c. Autres*
46. Net income	..	..	1.43	1.26	-0.35	-0.01	-0.20	46. Résultat net
47. Provisions (net)	..	..	1.42	1.49	3.54	-0.64	-1.25	47. Provisions (nettes)
a. Provisions on loans	..	..	*0.34*	*0.90*	*2.56*	*2.37*	*-1.40*	*a. Provisions sur prêts*
b. Provisions on securities	..	..	..	..	..	..	..	*b. Provisions sur titres*
c. Other	..	..	*1.07*	*0.58*	*0.98*	*-3.02*	*0.15*	*c. Autres*
48. Profit before tax	..	..	*0.01*	*-0.23*	*-3.88*	*0.63*	*1.05*	*48. Bénéfices avant impôt*
49. Income tax	..	..	*0.19*	*0.23*	*0.11*	*0.10*	*0.03*	*49. Impôt sur le revenu*
50. Profit after tax	..	..	*-0.18*	*-0.45*	*-3.99*	*0.54*	*1.02*	*50. Bénéfices après impôt*
51. Distributed profit	..	..	..	..	..	..	..	*51. Bénéfices distribués*
52. Retained profit	..	..	*0.31*	*0.41*	*0.72*	*0.73*	*0.88*	*52. Bénéfices mis en réserve*
% of gross income								**% du total du résultat brut**
53. Net interest income	88.59	81.47	67.40	55.58	49.79	66.79	69.53	53. Produits financiers nets
54. Non-interest income (net)	11.41	18.53	32.60	44.42	50.21	33.21	30.47	54. Produits non financiers (nets)
a. Fees and commissions receivable	*12.67*	*22.83*	*12.24*	*15.99*	*20.40*	*16.28*	*19.10*	*a. Frais et commissions à recevoir*
b. Fees and commissions payable	*1.25*	*4.31*	*2.24*	*2.48*	*3.42*	*2.80*	*3.13*	*b. Frais et commissions à payer*
c. Net profits or loss on financial operations	..	..	*19.39*	*26.16*	*31.96*	*15.20*	*13.84*	*c. Profits ou pertes nets sur opérations financières*
d. Other	..	..	*3.21*	*4.75*	*1.27*	*4.53*	*0.66*	*d. Autres*
55. Operating expenses	..	..	65.73	67.75	110.32	100.27	105.32	55. Frais d'exploitation
a. Staff costs	..	..	*21.91*	*23.76*	*31.31*	*25.94*	*25.59*	*a. Dépenses en personnel*
b. Property costs	..	..	*34.53*	*37.71*	*48.88*	*38.89*	*38.91*	*b. Dépenses en immobilier*
c. Other	..	..	*9.30*	*6.28*	*30.13*	*35.44*	*40.82*	*c. Autres*
56. Net income	..	..	34.27	32.25	-10.32	-0.27	-5.32	56. Résultat net
57. Provisions (net)	..	..	34.00	38.05	105.29	-16.38	-32.74	57. Provisions (nettes)
a. Provisions on loans	..	..	*8.19*	*23.16*	*76.04*	*60.39*	*-36.74*	*a. Provisions sur prêts*
b. Provisions on securities	..	..	..	..	..	..	..	*b. Provisions sur titres*
c. Other	..	..	*25.80*	*14.89*	*29.25*	*-76.78*	*4.00*	*c. Autres*
58. Profit before tax	..	..	*0.27*	*-5.80*	*-115.61*	*16.11*	*27.42*	*58. Bénéfices avant impôt*
59. Income tax	..	..	*4.52*	*5.79*	*3.18*	*2.44*	*0.70*	*59. Impôt sur le revenu*
60. Profit after tax	..	..	*-4.25*	*-11.59*	*-118.79*	*13.67*	*26.72*	*60. Bénéfices après impôt*
% of net income								**% du total du résultat net**
61. Provisions (net)	..	..	99.22	117.98	-1020.16	5961.55	615.59	61. Provisions (nettes)
a. Provisions on loans	..	..	*23.91*	*71.82*	*-736.77*	*-21978.04*	*690.70*	*a. Provisions sur prêts*
b. Provisions on securities	..	..	..	..	..	..	..	*b. Provisions sur titres*
c. Other	..	..	*75.30*	*46.16*	*-283.39*	*27939.59*	*-75.11*	*c. Autres*
62. Profit before tax	..	..	0.78	-17.98	1120.16	-5861.55	-515.59	62. Bénéfices avant impôt
63. Income tax	..	..	13.18	17.96	-30.79	-887.50	-13.15	63. Impôt sur le revenu
64. Profit after tax	..	..	-12.39	-35.93	1150.95	-4974.05	-502.43	64. Bénéfices après impôt

SLOVAK REPUBLIC
All banks

REBUBLIQUE SLOVAQUE
Ensemble des banques

Per cent / *Pourcentage*

BALANCE SHEET ANALYSIS / **ANALYSE DU BILAN**
% of year-end balance sheet total / **% du total du bilan en fin d'exercice**

	1995	1996	1997	1998	1999	2000	2001		
Assets								**Actif**	
65. Cash & balance with Central bank	..	..	13.16	9.47	11.67	10.38	11.87	65. Caisse & solde auprès de la Banque centrale	
66. Interbank deposits	..	..	21.26	21.94	18.37	18.67	13.66	66. Dépôts interbancaires	
67. Loans	..	..	45.72	45.89	46.86	40.00	29.84	67. Prêts	
68. Securities	..	..	15.17	13.72	14.27	19.89	28.95	68. Valeurs mobilières	
69. Other assets	..	..	4.69	8.98	8.83	11.06	15.68	69. Autres actifs	
Liabilities								**Passif**	
70. Capital & reserves	..	..	8.27	9.33	13.05	8.60	8.41	70. Capital et réserves	
71. Borrowing from Central bank	..	..	4.25	3.88	3.68	2.90	2.29	71. Emprunts auprès de la Banque centrale	
72. Interbank deposits	..	..	23.19	24.03	16.38	15.54	15.30	72. Dépôts interbancaires	
73. Non-bank deposits	..	..	57.63	58.06	65.86	70.72	71.54	73. Dépôts non bancaires	
74. Bonds	..	..	4.35	3.48	3.83	3.51	2.84	74. Obligations	
75. Other liabilities	..	..	2.30	1.22	-2.81	-1.27	-0.38	75. Autres engagements	
Memorandum items								***Pour mémoire***	
76. Short-term securities	..	..	..	..	..	..	..	*76. Titres à court terme*	
77. Bonds	..	..	..	..	..	..	..	*77. Obligations*	
78. Shares and participations	..	..	0.51	4.76	4.64	7.16	12.30	*78. Actions et participations*	
79. Claims on non-residents	..	..	16.50	18.59	9.73	13.45	14.38	*79. Créances sur des non-résidents*	
80. Liabilities to non-residents	..	..	14.29	13.73	5.42	5.56	8.35	*80. Engagements envers des non-résidents*	

SPAIN
All banks

ESPAGNE
Ensemble des banques

Million euros / *Millions d'euros*

	1992	1993[1]	1994[1]	1995	1996	1997	1998	1999	2000	2001	
INCOME STATEMENT											**COMPTE DE RESULTATS**
1. Interest income	53925	61484	55600	60660	60921	51343	47019	41442	50419	61765	1. Produits financiers
2. Interest expenses	35832	42666	35890	41511	41602	31562	26796	21024	28236	33966	2. Frais financiers
3. Net interest income	18093	18819	19710	19149	19319	19781	20224	20417	22183	27798	3. Produits financiers nets
4. Non-interest income (net)	4605	6549	5384	5766	7013	8174	9539	9481	12351	10629	4. Produits non financiers (nets)
a. Fees and commissions receivable	3770	4085	4482	4606	5001	5970	7057	7841	8747	9145	a. Frais et commissions à recevoir
b. Fees and commissions payable	619	679	787	869	943	1064	1163	1282	1477	1644	b. Frais et commissions à payer
c. Net profits or loss on financial operations	697	2575	613	1232	2667	2820	3258	2261	4410	2202	c. Profits ou pertes nets sur opérations financières
d. Other	751	574	1076	798	288	450	387	660	671	925	d. Autres
5. Gross income	22702	25367	25095	24914	26332	27956	29763	29898	34533	38427	5. Résultat brut
6. Operating expenses	13700	15133	14983	15751	16370	17177	18036	18867	21073	21336	6. Frais d'exploitation
a. Staff costs	8321	9376	9113	9669	10047	10550	11051	11667	13333	13066	a. Dépenses en personnel
b. Property costs	5199	5559	5680	5872	6109	6396	6748	6982	7519	8035	b. Dépenses en immobilier
c. Other	186	204	182	209	214	230	237	218	220	235	c. Autres
7. Net income	8999	10234	10113	9164	9962	10778	11727	11031	13461	17091	7. Résultat net
8. Provisions (net)	3599	8168	5079	3451	3622	3394	3689	2235	3659	7333	8. Provisions (nettes)
a. Provisions on loans	3148	6295	3318	2933	2219	1661	1363	1170	2116	3171	a. Provisions sur prêts
b. Provisions on securities	559	1169	1647	757	674	435	1357	801	551	3375	b. Provisions sur titres
c. Other	-102	698	114	-240	727	1297	971	264	991	786	c. Autres
9. Profit before tax	5400	2067	5034	5712	6341	7384	8037	8795	9800	9758	9. Bénéfices avant impôt
10. Income tax	1317	1369	1184	1290	1364	1524	1573	1876	1517	1171	10. Impôt sur le revenu
11. Profit after tax	4085	698	3849	4422	4977	5860	6465	6920	8285	8587	11. Bénéfices après impôt
12. Distributed profit	1895	1902	2079	2221	2196	2752	2960	3467	4108	4580	12. Bénéfices distribués
13. Retained profit	2191	-1205	1769	2201	2784	3108	3504	3452	4177	4007	13. Bénéfices mis en réserve
BALANCE SHEET											**BILAN**
Assets											**Actif**
14. Cash & balance with Central bank	29958	25879	25842	22255	19526	18528	17933	22398	13609	20539	14. Caisse & solde auprès de la Banque centrale
15. Interbank deposits	85989	116695	105179	115320	123326	139774	134952	129946	121274	131451	15. Dépôts interbancaires
16. Loans	245127	259188	292033	314671	340260	383746	436990	494615	575860	641105	16. Prêts
17. Securities	90850	105496	129471	140645	148983	148692	159473	185878	213933	246380	17. Valeurs mobilières
18. Other assets	70414	113874	112746	129651	126840	120344	123038	128906	152914	156345	18. Autres actifs
Liabilities											**Passif**
19. Capital & reserves	50655	55053	61415	62318	65253	69587	72634	76860	94469	105348	19. Capital et réserves
20. Borrowing from Central bank	25732	39221	36441	39926	26727	13611	26747	23689	16138	10547	20. Emprunts auprès de la Banque centrale
21. Interbank deposits	69562	101745	108009	117198	125632	140858	136013	131164	123568	126882	21. Dépôts interbancaires
22. Non-bank deposits	308180	338550	365446	406677	427387	448401	464378	520507	596022	680747	22. Dépôts non bancaires
23. Bonds	7669	10562	18455	19780	23268	27071	30362	58060	66267	83670	23. Obligations
24. Other liabilities	60539	76001	75505	76646	90665	111558	142252	151466	181126	188628	24. Autres engagements
Balance sheet total											**Total du bilan**
25. End-year total	522340	621131	665272	722544	758933	811086	872387	961746	1077589	1195821	25. En fin d'exercice
26. Average total	498179	571737	643201	693907	740739	785010	841736	917067	1019668	1136705	26. Moyen

235

SPAIN
All banks

ESPAGNE
Ensemble des banques

Million euros

Millions d'euros

	1992	1993[1]	1994[1]	1995	1996	1997	1998	1999	2000	2001		
Memorandum items												***Pour mémoire***
27. Short-term securities	38807	35093	38290	41106	38604	29029	26613	25723	23290	21978	27.	Titres à court terme
28. Bonds	34534	49878	69068	74166	82265	85907	93931	110074	115349	143878	28.	Obligations
29. Shares and participations	17513	20531	22117	25377	28114	33757	38929	50081	75294	80524	29.	Actions et participations
30. Claims on non-residents	47222	99281	87652	106582	102357	101364	108672	119355	146291	165761	30.	Créances sur des non-résidents
31. Liabilities to non-residents	56147	73973	79700	79714	97328	123103	153569	186301	232167	257319	31.	Engagements envers des non-résidents
Capital adequacy (2)												***Solvabilité (2)***
32. Tier 1 Capital	..	..	..	..	..	..	..	60076	72308	78653	32.	Fonds propres de base
33. Tier 2 Capital	..	..	..	..	..	..	..	21165	27855	36088	33.	Fonds propres complémentaires
34. Supervisory deductions	..	..	..	..	..	..	..	2540	5550	5741	34.	Eléments à déduire des fonds propres
35. Total net capital resources	..	..	..	..	..	..	..	78701	94613	109000	35.	Total net des ressources en capital
36. Risk-weighted assets	..	..	..	..	..	..	..	651216	813022	891792	36.	Actifs pondérés des risques
SUPPLEMENTARY INFORMATION												**RENSEIGNEMENTS COMPLEMENTAIRES**
37. Number of institutions	319	316	316	318	313	307	300	290	281	281	37.	Nombre d'institutions
38. Number of branches	35429	35193	35544	36251	37079	37634	38639	38986	38967	38676	38.	Nombre de succursales
39. Number of employees (x 1000)	253	247	246	245	242	242	242	242	244	246	39.	Nombre de salariés (x 1000)

1 Break in series in 1993 due to restructuring of a major bank.

Break in series in 1994. Three official credit banks were classified as Commercial banks and no longer as Official credit institutions.

2 Change in methodology.

Notes

. All banks include Commercial banks, Savings banks and Co-operative banks.

Change in methodology

. As from 1992, Income tax (item 10) includes tax on domestic activities of resident entities rather than total tax.

. As from 1993, credit entities' branches from the European Union (EU) are not subject to capital requirements. As from 1994, credit entities' from non-EU members are also not subject to capital requirements if these countries have similar legislation.

. As from 1993, the means of calculating capital adequacy requirements has changed, as the gearing ratio and the additional surcharges relating to concentration have disappeared.

. As from 1994, trading portfolio price risk became subject to a different treatment than that of credit risk.

1 Rupture dans les séries en 1993 suite à la restructuration de l'une des principales banques.

Rupture dans les séries en 1994. Trois banques publiques de crédit ont été classées dans les Banques commerciales et non plus dans les Institutions publiques de crédit.

2 Changement méthodologique.

Notes

. L'Ensemble des banques comprend les Banques commerciales, les Caisses d'épargne et les Banques mutualistes.

Changement méthodologique

. A partir de 1992, la rubrique Impôt sur le revenu (poste 10) inclut l'impôt sur les activités domestiques des entités résidentes plutôt que l'impôt total.

. A partir de 1993, les succursales des entités de crédit de l'Union Européenne (UE) ne sont pas soumises à des exigences de capital. A partir de 1994, les entités de crédit des pays non membres de l'UE ne sont pas non plus soumises à des exigences de capital si ces pays ont une législation semblable.

. A partir de 1993, les moyens de calcul pour la solvabilité exigée a changé, étant donné que le ratio d'effet de levier et les charges supplémentaires relatifs à la concentration ont disparus.

. A partir de 1994, le risque du prix du portefeuille de transactions a été sujet à une couverture différente que celle du risque de crédit.

SPAIN
All banks

Per cent

ESPAGNE
Ensemble des banques

Pourcentage

INCOME STATEMENT ANALYSIS / ANALYSE DU COMPTE DE RESULTATS

		1992	1993¹	1994¹	1995	1996	1997	1998	1999	2000	2001		
	% of average balance sheet total											**% du total moyen du bilan**	
40.	Interest income	10.82	10.75	8.64	8.74	8.22	6.54	5.59	4.52	4.94	5.43	Produits financiers	40.
41.	Interest expenses	7.19	7.46	5.58	5.98	5.62	4.02	3.18	2.29	2.77	2.99	Frais financiers	41.
42.	Net interest income	3.63	3.29	3.06	2.76	2.61	2.52	2.40	2.23	2.18	2.45	Produits financiers nets	42.
43.	Non-interest income (net)	0.92	1.15	0.84	0.83	0.95	1.04	1.13	1.03	1.21	0.94	Produits non financiers (nets)	43.
	a. Fees and commissions receivable	0.76	0.71	0.70	0.66	0.68	0.76	0.84	0.86	0.86	0.80	a. Frais et commissions à recevoir	
	b. Fees and commissions payable	0.12	0.12	0.12	0.13	0.13	0.14	0.14	0.14	0.14	0.14	b. Frais et commissions à payer	
	c. Net profits or loss on financial operations	0.14	0.45	0.10	0.18	0.36	0.36	0.39	0.25	0.43	0.19	c. Profits ou pertes nets sur opérations financières	
	d. Other	0.15	0.10	0.17	0.12	0.04	0.06	0.05	0.07	0.07	0.08	d. Autres	
44.	Gross income	4.56	4.44	3.90	3.59	3.55	3.56	3.54	3.26	3.39	3.38	Résultat brut	44.
45.	Operating expenses	2.75	2.65	2.33	2.27	2.21	2.19	2.14	2.06	2.07	1.88	Frais d'exploitation	45.
	a. Staff costs	1.67	1.64	1.42	1.39	1.36	1.34	1.31	1.27	1.31	1.15	a. Dépenses en personnel	
	b. Property costs	1.04	0.97	0.88	0.85	0.82	0.81	0.80	0.76	0.74	0.71	b. Dépenses en immobilier	
	c. Other	0.04	0.04	0.03	0.03	0.03	0.03	0.03	0.02	0.02	0.02	c. Autres	
46.	Net income	1.81	1.79	1.57	1.32	1.34	1.37	1.39	1.20	1.32	1.50	Résultat net	46.
47.	Provisions (net)	0.72	1.43	0.79	0.50	0.49	0.43	0.44	0.24	0.36	0.65	Provisions (nettes)	47.
	a. Provisions on loans	0.63	1.10	0.52	0.42	0.30	0.21	0.16	0.13	0.21	0.28	a. Provisions sur prêts	
	b. Provisions on securities	0.11	0.20	0.26	0.11	0.09	0.06	0.16	0.09	0.05	0.30	b. Provisions sur titres	
	c. Other	-0.02	0.12	0.02	-0.03	0.10	0.17	0.12	0.03	0.10	0.07	c. Autres	
48.	Profit before tax	1.08	0.36	0.78	0.82	0.86	0.94	0.95	0.96	0.96	0.86	Bénéfices avant impôt	48.
49.	Income tax	0.26	0.24	0.18	0.19	0.18	0.19	0.19	0.20	0.15	0.10	Impôt sur le revenu	49.
50.	Profit after tax	0.82	0.12	0.60	0.64	0.67	0.75	0.77	0.75	0.81	0.76	Bénéfices après impôt	50.
51.	Distributed profit	0.38	0.33	0.32	0.32	0.30	0.35	0.35	0.38	0.40	0.40	Bénéfices distribués	51.
52.	Retained profit	0.44	-0.21	0.28	0.32	0.38	0.40	0.42	0.38	0.41	0.35	Bénéfices mis en réserve	52.
	% of gross income											**% du total du résultat brut**	
53.	Net interest income	79.70	74.19	78.54	76.86	73.37	70.76	67.95	68.29	64.24	72.34	Produits financiers nets	53.
54.	Non-interest income (net)	20.28	25.82	21.45	23.14	26.63	29.24	32.05	31.71	35.77	27.66	Produits non financiers (nets)	54.
	a. Fees and commissions receivable	16.61	16.10	17.86	18.49	18.99	21.35	23.71	26.23	25.33	23.80	a. Frais et commissions à recevoir	
	b. Fees and commissions payable	2.73	2.68	3.14	3.49	3.58	3.81	3.91	4.29	4.28	4.28	b. Frais et commissions à payer	
	c. Net profits or loss on financial operations	3.07	10.15	2.44	4.95	10.13	10.09	10.95	7.56	12.77	5.73	c. Profits ou pertes nets sur opérations financières	
	d. Other	3.31	2.26	4.29	3.20	1.09	1.61	1.30	2.21	1.94	2.41	d. Autres	
55.	Operating expenses	60.35	59.66	59.71	63.22	62.17	61.44	60.60	63.10	61.02	55.52	Frais d'exploitation	55.
	a. Staff costs	36.65	36.96	36.31	38.81	38.16	37.74	37.13	39.02	38.61	34.00	a. Dépenses en personnel	
	b. Property costs	22.90	21.91	22.63	23.57	23.20	22.88	22.67	23.35	21.77	20.91	b. Dépenses en immobilier	
	c. Other	0.82	0.80	0.73	0.84	0.81	0.82	0.80	0.73	0.64	0.61	c. Autres	
56.	Net income	39.64	40.34	40.30	36.78	37.83	38.55	39.40	36.90	38.98	44.48	Résultat net	56.
57.	Provisions (net)	15.85	32.20	20.24	13.85	13.76	12.14	12.39	7.48	10.60	19.08	Provisions (nettes)	57.
	a. Provisions on loans	13.87	24.82	13.22	11.77	8.43	5.94	4.58	3.91	6.13	8.25	a. Provisions sur prêts	
	b. Provisions on securities	2.46	4.61	6.56	3.04	2.56	1.56	4.56	2.68	1.60	8.78	b. Provisions sur titres	
	c. Other	-0.45	2.75	0.45	-0.96	2.76	4.64	3.26	0.88	2.87	2.05	c. Autres	
58.	Profit before tax	23.79	8.15	20.06	22.93	24.08	26.41	27.00	29.42	28.38	25.39	Bénéfices avant impôt	58.
59.	Income tax	5.80	5.40	4.72	5.18	5.18	5.45	5.29	6.27	4.39	3.05	Impôt sur le revenu	59.
60.	Profit after tax	17.99	2.75	15.34	17.75	18.90	20.96	21.72	23.15	23.99	22.35	Bénéfices après impôt	60.
	% of net income											**% du total du résultat net**	
61.	Provisions (net)	39.99	79.81	50.22	37.66	36.36	31.49	31.46	20.26	27.18	42.91	Provisions (nettes)	61.
	a. Provisions on loans	34.98	61.51	32.81	32.01	22.27	15.41	11.62	10.61	15.72	18.55	a. Provisions sur prêts	
	b. Provisions on securities	6.21	11.42	16.29	8.26	6.77	4.04	11.57	7.26	4.09	19.75	b. Provisions sur titres	
	c. Other	-1.13	6.82	1.13	-2.62	7.30	12.03	8.28	2.39	7.36	4.60	c. Autres	
62.	Profit before tax	60.01	20.20	49.78	62.33	63.65	68.51	68.53	79.73	72.80	57.09	Bénéfices avant impôt	62.
63.	Income tax	14.63	13.38	11.71	14.08	13.69	14.14	13.41	17.01	11.27	6.85	Impôt sur le revenu	63.
64.	Profit after tax	45.39	6.82	38.06	48.25	49.96	54.37	55.13	62.73	61.55	50.24	Bénéfices après impôt	64.

SPAIN
All banks

ESPAGNE
Ensemble des banques

Per cent — *Pourcentage*

BALANCE SHEET ANALYSIS — **ANALYSE DU BILAN**
% of year-end balance sheet total — **% du total du bilan en fin d'exercice**

	1992	1993[1]	1994[1]	1995	1996	1997	1998	1999	2000	2001	
Assets											**Actif**
65. Cash & balance with Central bank	5.74	4.17	3.88	3.08	2.57	2.28	2.06	2.33	1.26	1.72	65. Caisse & solde auprès de la Banque centrale
66. Interbank deposits	16.46	18.79	15.81	15.96	16.25	17.23	15.47	13.51	11.25	10.99	66. Dépôts interbancaires
67. Loans	46.93	41.73	43.90	43.55	44.83	47.31	50.09	51.43	53.44	53.61	67. Prêts
68. Securities	17.39	16.98	19.46	19.47	19.63	18.33	18.28	19.33	19.85	20.60	68. Valeurs mobilières
69. Other assets	13.48	18.33	16.95	17.94	16.71	14.84	14.10	13.40	14.19	13.07	69. Autres actifs
Liabilities											**Passif**
70. Capital & reserves	9.70	8.86	9.23	8.62	8.60	8.58	8.33	7.99	8.77	8.81	70. Capital et réserves
71. Borrowing from Central bank	4.93	6.31	5.48	5.53	3.52	1.68	3.07	2.46	1.50	0.88	71. Emprunts auprès de la Banque centrale
72. Interbank deposits	13.32	16.38	16.24	16.22	16.55	17.37	15.59	13.64	11.47	10.61	72. Dépôts interbancaires
73. Non-bank deposits	59.00	54.51	54.93	56.28	56.31	55.28	53.23	54.12	55.31	56.93	73. Dépôts non bancaires
74. Bonds	1.47	1.70	2.77	2.74	3.07	3.34	3.48	6.04	6.15	7.00	74. Obligations
75. Other liabilities	11.59	12.24	11.35	10.61	11.95	13.75	16.31	15.75	16.81	15.77	75. Autres engagements
Memorandum items											*Pour mémoire*
76. Short-term securities	7.43	5.65	5.76	5.69	5.09	3.58	3.05	2.67	2.16	1.84	76. Titres à court terme
77. Bonds	6.61	8.03	10.38	10.26	10.84	10.59	10.77	11.45	10.70	12.03	77. Obligations
78. Shares and participations	3.35	3.31	3.32	3.51	3.70	4.16	4.46	5.21	6.99	6.73	78. Actions et participations
79. Claims on non-residents	9.04	15.98	13.18	14.75	13.49	12.50	12.46	12.41	13.58	13.86	79. Créances sur des non-résidents
80. Liabilities to non-residents	10.75	11.91	11.98	11.03	12.82	15.18	17.60	19.37	21.55	21.52	80. Engagements envers des non-résidents

* See notes on previous pages.

* Voir les notes en pages précédentes.

SPAIN

Commercial banks

Million euros

ESPAGNE

Banques commerciales

Millions d'euros

	1992	1993[1]	1994[1]	1995	1996	1997	1998	1999	2000	2001	
INCOME STATEMENT											**COMPTE DE RESULTATS**
1. Interest income	34041	38737	35317	38348	37534	30656	27913	24041	29239	36475	1. Produits financiers
2. Interest expenses	23355	28057	24130	28063	27598	20625	17561	13973	18332	21418	2. Frais financiers
3. Net interest income	10686	10680	11187	10285	9937	10031	10352	10068	10906	15057	3. Produits financiers nets
4. Non-interest income (net)	3289	4931	3760	4070	4775	5443	5969	5726	7764	6802	4. Produits non financiers (nets)
a. Fees and commissions receivable	2856	2987	3159	3167	3335	3925	4601	5078	5643	5731	a. Frais et commissions à recevoir
b. Fees and commissions payable	457	485	571	628	662	734	790	859	968	1049	b. Frais et commissions à payer
c. Net profits or loss on financial operations	463	2117	487	1036	2057	2108	2069	1238	2857	1478	c. Profits ou pertes nets sur opérations financières
d. Other	427	311	685	495	45	144	89	268	232	642	d. Autres
5. Gross income	13975	15611	14947	14355	14712	15474	16321	15794	18671	21858	5. Résultat brut
6. Operating expenses	8462	9291	8835	9198	9386	9794	9993	10167	11598	11339	6. Frais d'exploitation
a. Staff costs	5211	5872	5367	5671	5788	6157	6242	6330	7466	6987	a. Dépenses en personnel
b. Property costs	3089	3245	3312	3379	3459	3484	3599	3704	3999	4209	b. Dépenses en immobilier
c. Other	162	174	156	147	140	153	153	133	134	143	c. Autres
7. Net income	5513	6319	6112	5157	5326	5680	6328	5627	7072	10520	7. Résultat net
8. Provisions (net)	2054	6287	3230	1968	1956	1847	2265	1161	1743	5312	8. Provisions (nettes)
a. Provisions on loans	2012	4426	1974	1675	1113	772	712	642	1046	1599	a. Provisions sur prêts
b. Provisions on securities	276	1271	1292	678	532	293	1076	494	122	2898	b. Provisions sur titres
c. Other	-234	590	-36	-386	311	782	478	25	575	815	c. Autres
9. Profit before tax	3459	33	2882	3190	3370	3833	4063	4465	5329	5207	9. Bénéfices avant impôt
10. Income tax	873	879	716	701	656	715	710	937	742	527	10. Impôt sur le revenu
11. Profit after tax	2586	-846	2166	2489	2714	3118	3353	3529	4587	4681	11. Bénéfices après impôt
12. Distributed profit	1533	1471	1657	1740	1604	2052	2149	2598	3132	3531	12. Bénéfices distribués
13. Retained profit	1053	-2318	509	749	1110	1066	1204	930	1455	1149	13. Bénéfices mis en réserve
BALANCE SHEET											**BILAN**
Assets											**Actif**
14. Cash & balance with Central bank	15103	13105	12926	11267	9510	8742	8712	12093	6913	9616	14. Caisse & solde auprès de la Banque centrale
15. Interbank deposits	52155	75249	70891	76525	79042	95451	86826	89657	81214	88120	15. Dépôts interbancaires
16. Loans	150290	156221	175821	187602	198600	218525	242221	268977	304066	331207	16. Prêts
17. Securities	53325	69525	79827	83997	86136	84437	93402	110856	127971	152290	17. Valeurs mobilières
18. Other assets	50879	86852	83639	97114	95812	91378	91275	87038	103964	108132	18. Autres actifs
Liabilities											**Passif**
19. Capital & reserves	33890	36073	39911	39428	39410	40498	40879	42415	56131	62765	19. Capital et réserves
20. Borrowing from Central bank	15585	32557	28808	31382	20633	8310	19604	19574	9119	7433	20. Emprunts auprès de la Banque centrale
21. Interbank deposits	59384	89310	92707	99353	104962	118007	105869	95943	87664	91458	21. Dépôts interbancaires
22. Non-bank deposits	160164	173344	183141	207662	209896	218503	218968	248827	285205	327156	22. Dépôts non bancaires
23. Bonds	4252	6166	13869	14132	16783	18497	19053	39245	42953	51620	23. Obligations
24. Other liabilities	48477	63503	64669	64549	77414	94720	118062	122619	143054	148935	24. Autres engagements
Balance sheet total											**Total du bilan**
25. End-year total	321752	400953	423107	456505	469099	498535	522435	568623	624126	689366	25. En fin d'exercice
26. Average total	310194	361353	412028	439805	462802	483817	510485	545529	596375	656746	26. Moyen

Commercial banks

Banques commerciales

Million euros

Millions d'euros

	1992	1993¹	1994¹	1995	1996	1997	1998	1999	2000	2001		
Memorandum items												**Pour mémoire**
27. Short-term securities	20410	20056	20933	23804	20695	15550	17444	16938	13809	13495	27.	Titres à court terme
28. Bonds	19317	33651	41975	41379	45685	47182	51439	61517	61192	82065	28.	Obligations
29. Shares and participations	13601	15825	16918	18814	19756	21705	24519	32401	52970	56729	29.	Actions et participations
30. Claims on non-residents	40731	85368	73726	89588	87085	85828	87482	86240	105512	123404	30.	Créances sur des non-résidents
31. Liabilities to non-residents	51224	68077	73335	73187	88913	109099	132119	154347	184322	202609	31.	Engagements envers des non-résidents
Capital adequacy (2)												**Solvabilité (2)**
32. Tier 1 Capital	..	..	..	..	..	..	..	32958	40375	43534	32.	Fonds propres de base
33. Tier 2 Capital	..	..	..	..	..	..	..	13417	17831	22706	33.	Fonds propres complémentaires
34. Supervisory deductions	..	..	..	..	..	..	..	1637	3789	3360	34.	Eléments à déduire des fonds propres
35. Total net capital resources	..	..	..	..	..	..	..	44738	54417	62880	35.	Total net des ressources en capital
36. Risk-weighted assets	..	..	..	..	..	..	..	399296	502393	533211	36.	Actifs pondérés des risques
SUPPLEMENTARY INFORMATION												**RENSEIGNEMENTS COMPLEMENTAIRES**
37. Number of institutions	164	164	165	170	165	159	152	146	141	145	37.	Nombre d'institutions
38. Number of branches	18058	17636	17557	17842	17674	17530	17450	16905	15811	14756	38.	Nombre de succursales
39. Number of employees (x 1000)	159	153	151	149	143	139	135	131	128	124	39.	Nombre de salariés (x 1000)

1 Break in series in 1993 due to restructuring of a major bank.

Break in series in 1994. Three official credit banks were classified as Commercial banks and no longer as Official credit institutions.

2 Change in methodology.

Change in methodology

. As from 1992, Income tax (item 10) includes tax on domestic activities of resident entities rather than total tax.

. As from 1993, credit entities' branches from the European Union (EU) are not subject to capital requirements. As from 1994, credit entities' from non-EU members are also not subject to capital requirements if these countries have similar legislation.

. As from 1993, the means of calculating capital adequacy requirements has changed, as the gearing ratio and the additional surcharges relating to concentration have disappeared.

. As from 1994, trading portfolio price risk became subject to a different treatment than that of credit risk.

1 Rupture dans les séries en 1993 suite à la restructuration de l'une des principales banques.

Rupture dans les séries en 1994. Trois banques publiques de crédit ont été classées dans les Banques commerciales et non plus dans les Institutions publiques de crédit.

2 Changement méthodologique.

Changement méthodologique

. A partir de 1992, la rubrique Impôt sur le revenu (poste 10) inclut l'impôt sur les activités domestiques des entités résidentes plutôt que l'impôt total.

. A partir de 1993, les succursales des entités de crédit de l'Union Européenne (UE) ne sont pas soumises à des exigences de capital. A partir de 1994, les entités de crédit des pays non membres de l'UE ne sont pas non plus soumises à des exigences de capital si ces pays ont une législation semblable.

. A partir de 1993, les moyens de calcul pour la solvabilité exigée a changé, étant donné que le ratio d'effet de levier et les charges supplémentaires relatifs à la concentration ont disparus.

. A partir de 1994, le risque du prix du portefeuille de transactions a été sujet à une couverture différente que celle du risque de crédit.

SPAIN
Commercial banks

ESPAGNE
Banques commerciales

Per cent

INCOME STATEMENT ANALYSIS

	1992	1993¹	1994¹	1995	1996	1997	1998	1999	2000	2001		*Pourcentage*
												ANALYSE DU COMPTE DE RESULTATS
% of average balance sheet total												**% du total moyen du bilan**
40. Interest income	10.97	10.72	8.32	8.72	8.11	6.34	5.47	4.41	4.90	5.55	40.	Produits financiers
41. Interest expenses	7.53	7.76	5.68	6.38	5.96	4.26	3.44	2.56	3.07	3.26	41.	Frais financiers
42. Net interest income	3.44	2.96	2.64	2.34	2.15	2.07	2.03	1.85	1.83	2.29	42.	Produits financiers nets
43. Non-interest income (net)	1.06	1.36	0.89	0.93	1.03	1.13	1.17	1.05	1.30	1.04	43.	Produits non financiers (nets)
a. Fees and commissions receivable	0.92	0.83	0.74	0.72	0.72	0.81	0.90	0.93	0.95	0.87		*a. Frais et commissions à recevoir*
b. Fees and commissions payable	0.15	0.13	0.13	0.14	0.14	0.15	0.15	0.16	0.16	0.16		*b. Frais et commissions à payer*
c. Net profits or loss on financial operations	0.15	0.59	0.11	0.24	0.44	0.44	0.41	0.23	0.48	0.23		*c. Profits ou pertes nets sur opérations financières*
d. Other	0.14	0.09	0.16	0.11	0.01	0.03	0.02	0.05	0.04	0.10		*d. Autres*
44. Gross income	4.51	4.32	3.52	3.26	3.18	3.20	3.20	2.90	3.13	3.33	44.	Résultat brut
45. Operating expenses	2.73	2.57	2.08	2.09	2.03	2.02	1.96	1.86	1.94	1.73	45.	Frais d'exploitation
a. Staff costs	1.68	1.63	1.26	1.29	1.25	1.27	1.22	1.16	1.25	1.06		*a. Dépenses en personnel*
b. Property costs	1.00	0.90	0.78	0.77	0.75	0.72	0.71	0.68	0.67	0.64		*b. Dépenses en immobilier*
c. Other	0.05	0.05	0.04	0.03	0.03	0.03	0.03	0.02	0.02	0.02		*c. Autres*
46. Net income	1.78	1.75	1.44	1.17	1.15	1.17	1.24	1.03	1.19	1.60	46.	Résultat net
47. Provisions (net)	0.66	1.74	0.76	0.45	0.42	0.38	0.44	0.21	0.29	0.81	47.	Provisions (nettes)
a. Provisions on loans	0.65	1.22	0.47	0.38	0.24	0.16	0.14	0.12	0.18	0.24		*a. Provisions sur prêts*
b. Provisions on securities	0.09	0.35	0.30	0.15	0.11	0.06	0.21	0.09	0.02	0.44		*b. Provisions sur titres*
c. Other	-0.08	0.16	-0.01	-0.09	0.07	0.16	0.09	0.00	0.10	0.12		*c. Autres*
48. Profit before tax	1.12	0.01	0.68	0.73	0.73	0.79	0.80	0.82	0.89	0.79	48.	Bénéfices avant impôt
49. Income tax	0.29	0.25	0.17	0.16	0.15	0.15	0.14	0.17	0.12	0.08	49.	Impôt sur le revenu
50. Profit after tax	0.83	-0.25	0.51	0.56	0.58	0.64	0.66	0.65	0.77	0.71	50.	Bénéfices après impôt
51. Distributed profit	0.49	0.41	0.39	0.40	0.35	0.42	0.42	0.48	0.53	0.54	51.	Bénéfices distribués
52. Retained profit	0.33	-0.65	0.12	0.17	0.23	0.22	0.24	0.17	0.24	0.17	52.	Bénéfices mis en réserve
% of gross income												**% du total du résultat brut**
53. Net interest income	76.47	68.41	74.84	71.65	67.54	64.82	63.43	63.75	58.41	68.89	53.	Produits financiers nets
54. Non-interest income (net)	23.53	31.59	25.16	28.35	32.46	35.18	36.57	36.25	41.58	31.12	54.	Produits non financiers (nets)
a. Fees and commissions receivable	20.44	19.22	21.13	22.06	22.67	25.37	28.19	32.15	30.22	26.22		*a. Frais et commissions à recevoir*
b. Fees and commissions payable	3.27	3.12	3.82	4.37	4.50	4.74	4.84	5.44	5.18	4.80		*b. Frais et commissions à payer*
c. Net profits or loss on financial operations	3.31	13.55	3.26	7.22	13.98	13.62	12.68	7.84	15.30	6.76		*c. Profits ou pertes nets sur opérations financières*
d. Other	3.06	2.00	4.58	3.45	0.31	0.93	0.55	1.70	1.24	2.94		*d. Autres*
55. Operating expenses	60.55	59.52	59.11	64.08	63.80	63.29	61.23	64.37	62.12	51.88	55.	Frais d'exploitation
a. Staff costs	37.29	37.61	35.91	39.51	39.34	39.79	38.25	40.08	39.99	31.97		*a. Dépenses en personnel*
b. Property costs	22.10	20.79	22.16	23.54	23.51	22.52	22.05	23.45	21.42	19.26		*b. Dépenses en immobilier*
c. Other	1.16	1.11	1.04	1.02	0.95	0.99	0.94	0.84	0.72	0.65		*c. Autres*
56. Net income	39.45	40.48	40.89	35.92	36.20	36.71	38.77	35.63	37.88	48.13	56.	Résultat net
57. Provisions (net)	14.70	40.27	21.61	13.71	13.30	11.94	13.88	7.35	9.34	24.30	57.	Provisions (nettes)
a. Provisions on loans	14.40	28.33	13.21	11.67	7.57	4.99	4.36	4.06	5.60	7.32		*a. Provisions sur prêts*
b. Provisions on securities	1.97	8.12	8.64	4.72	3.62	1.89	6.59	3.13	0.65	13.26		*b. Provisions sur titres*
c. Other	-1.67	3.77	-0.24	-2.69	2.11	5.05	2.93	0.16	3.08	3.73		*c. Autres*
58. Profit before tax	24.75	0.21	19.28	22.22	22.91	24.77	24.89	28.27	28.54	23.82	58.	Bénéfices avant impôt
59. Income tax	6.39	5.89	4.84	4.99	4.68	4.81	4.35	5.93	3.97	2.41	59.	Impôt sur le revenu
60. Profit after tax	18.36	-5.68	14.44	17.23	18.22	19.97	20.54	22.34	24.57	21.42	60.	Bénéfices après impôt
% of net income												**% du total du résultat net**
61. Provisions (net)	37.26	99.49	52.85	38.16	36.73	32.52	35.79	20.63	24.65	50.49	61.	Provisions (nettes)
a. Provisions on loans	36.50	70.00	32.30	32.48	20.90	13.59	11.25	11.41	14.79	15.20		*a. Provisions sur prêts*
b. Provisions on securities	5.01	20.07	21.14	13.15	9.99	5.16	17.00	8.78	1.73	27.55		*b. Provisions sur titres*
c. Other	-4.24	9.32	-0.59	-7.48	5.84	13.77	7.55	0.44	8.13	7.75		*c. Autres*
62. Profit before tax	62.74	0.52	47.15	61.86	63.27	67.48	64.21	79.35	75.35	49.50	62.	Bénéfices avant impôt
63. Income tax	16.20	14.54	11.83	13.90	12.94	13.10	11.22	16.65	10.49	5.01	63.	Impôt sur le revenu
64. Profit after tax	46.54	-14.02	35.32	47.95	50.34	54.40	52.99	62.72	64.86	44.50	64.	Bénéfices après impôt

SPAIN

Commercial banks

ESPAGNE

Banques commerciales

Per cent — *Pourcentage*

BALANCE SHEET ANALYSIS — **ANALYSE DU BILAN**

% of year-end balance sheet total — **% du total du bilan en fin d'exercice**

	1992	1993[1]	1994[1]	1995	1996	1997	1998	1999	2000	2001	
Assets											**Actif**
65. Cash & balance with Central bank	4.69	3.27	3.06	2.47	2.03	1.75	1.67	2.13	1.11	1.39	65. Caisse & solde auprès de la Banque centrale
66. Interbank deposits	16.21	18.77	16.75	16.76	16.85	19.15	16.62	15.77	13.01	12.78	66. Dépôts interbancaires
67. Loans	46.71	38.96	41.55	41.10	42.34	43.83	46.36	47.30	48.72	48.05	67. Prêts
68. Securities	16.57	17.34	18.87	18.40	18.36	16.94	17.88	19.50	20.50	22.09	68. Valeurs mobilières
69. Other assets	15.81	21.66	19.77	21.27	20.42	18.33	17.47	15.31	16.66	15.69	69. Autres actifs
Liabilities											**Passif**
70. Capital & reserves	10.53	9.00	9.43	8.64	8.40	8.12	7.82	7.46	8.99	9.10	70. Capital et réserves
71. Borrowing from Central bank	4.84	8.12	6.81	6.87	4.40	1.67	3.75	3.44	1.46	1.08	71. Emprunts auprès de la Banque centrale
72. Interbank deposits	18.46	22.27	21.91	21.76	22.38	23.67	20.26	16.87	14.05	13.27	72. Dépôts interbancaires
73. Non-bank deposits	49.78	43.23	43.28	45.49	44.74	43.83	41.91	43.76	45.70	47.46	73. Dépôts non bancaires
74. Bonds	1.32	1.54	3.28	3.10	3.58	3.71	3.65	6.90	6.88	7.49	74. Obligations
75. Other liabilities	15.07	15.84	15.28	14.14	16.50	19.00	22.60	21.56	22.92	21.60	75. Autres engagements
Memorandum items											***Pour mémoire***
76. Short-term securities	6.34	5.00	4.95	5.21	4.41	3.12	3.34	2.98	2.21	1.96	76. Titres à court terme
77. Bonds	6.00	8.39	9.92	9.06	9.74	9.46	9.85	10.82	9.80	11.90	77. Obligations
78. Shares and participations	4.23	3.95	4.00	4.12	4.21	4.35	4.69	5.70	8.49	8.23	78. Actions et participations
79. Claims on non-residents	12.66	21.29	17.42	19.62	18.56	17.22	16.75	15.17	16.91	17.90	79. Créances sur des non-résidents
80. Liabilities to non-residents	15.92	16.98	17.33	16.03	18.95	21.88	25.29	27.14	29.53	29.39	80. Engagements envers des non-résidents

* See notes on previous pages.   * Voir les notes en pages précédentes.

SPAIN
Savings banks

ESPAGNE
Caisses d'épargne

Million euros

Millions d'euros

	1992	1993	1994	1995	1996	1997	1998	1999	2000	2001		
INCOME STATEMENT												**COMPTE DE RESULTATS**
1. Interest income	18195	20803	18504	20281	21188	18762	17316	15764	19230	22894	1.	Produits financiers
2. Interest expenses	11539	13513	10852	12371	12836	10070	8531	6553	9206	11590	2.	Frais financiers
3. Net interest income	6656	7290	7652	7910	8351	8692	8785	9210	10025	11304	3.	Produits financiers nets
4. Non-interest income (net)	1274	1551	1552	1640	2152	2593	3403	3519	4307	3541	4.	Produits non financiers (nets)
a. Fees and commissions receivable	*847*	*1010*	*1215*	*1318*	*1517*	*1866*	*2235*	*2516*	*2821*	*3099*		*a. Frais et commissions à recevoir*
b. Fees and commissions payable	*144*	*174*	*192*	*215*	*248*	*289*	*329*	*374*	*452*	*532*		*b. Frais et commissions à payer*
c. Net profits or loss on financial operations	*240*	*445*	*120*	*196*	*587*	*663*	*1139*	*976*	*1526*	*716*		*c. Profits ou pertes nets sur opérations financières*
d. Other	*331*	*276*	*409*	*341*	*296*	*354*	*358*	*402*	*413*	*258*		*d. Autres*
5. Gross income	7933	8841	9204	9549	10503	11286	12188	12729	14332	14845	5.	Résultat brut
6. Operating expenses	4745	5295	5571	5937	6310	6646	7248	7864	8575	8981	6.	Frais d'exploitation
a. Staff costs	*2822*	*3191*	*3410*	*3638*	*3867*	*3973*	*4357*	*4861*	*5352*	*5495*		*a. Dépenses en personnel*
b. Property costs	*1905*	*2086*	*2140*	*2243*	*2375*	*2604*	*2813*	*2925*	*3143*	*3400*		*b. Dépenses en immobilier*
c. Other	*18*	*24*	*20*	*56*	*67*	*70*	*77*	*79*	*80*	*86*		*c. Autres*
7. Net income	3185	3546	3634	3613	4193	4639	4941	4865	5757	5864	7.	Résultat net
8. Provisions (net)	1466	1717	1729	1393	1581	1485	1399	994	1746	1783	8.	Provisions (nettes)
a. Provisions on loans	*1052*	*1693*	*1242*	*1143*	*997*	*801*	*585*	*515*	*956*	*1380*		*a. Provisions sur prêts*
b. Provisions on securities	*276*	*-102*	*325*	*77*	*142*	*140*	*280*	*278*	*394*	*445*		*b. Provisions sur titres*
c. Other	*138*	*120*	*162*	*173*	*441*	*544*	*535*	*202*	*397*	*-42*		*c. Autres*
9. Profit before tax	1719	1830	1905	2219	2612	3154	3541	3871	4010	4081	9.	Bénéfices avant impôt
10. Income tax (1)	408	453	432	540	647	744	791	865	706	579	10.	Impôt sur le revenu (1)
11. Profit after tax	1313	1377	1473	1679	1965	2410	2750	3006	3304	3502	11.	Bénéfices après impôt
12. Distributed profit	302	373	358	407	515	616	722	773	868	937	12.	Bénéfices distribués
13. Retained profit	1011	1004	1114	1272	1453	1794	2028	2233	2437	2565	13.	Bénéfices mis en réserve
BALANCE SHEET												**BILAN**
Assets												**Actif**
14. Cash & balance with Central bank	13538	11588	11756	9857	8954	8778	8300	9409	6096	9448	14.	Caisse & solde auprès de la Banque centrale
15. Interbank deposits	29585	35370	28981	32458	37670	37615	41561	34964	34757	36904	15.	Dépôts interbancaires
16. Loans	87048	94503	106301	115598	128322	149225	175728	203113	245274	278905	16.	Prêts
17. Securities	36293	34817	47179	53540	59377	60888	62405	70602	81234	89416	17.	Valeurs mobilières
18. Other assets	18573	25964	27797	31187	29529	27494	30236	40225	46502	45714	18.	Autres actifs
Liabilities												**Passif**
19. Capital & reserves	14986	16925	19160	20292	22888	25741	28035	30318	33735	37436	19.	Capital et réserves
20. Borrowing from Central bank	10147	6473	7212	8186	5725	5030	6911	3992	6898	3114	20.	Emprunts auprès de la Banque centrale
21. Interbank deposits	9415	11720	14551	16878	19498	21078	28138	33670	34358	33423	21.	Dépôts interbancaires
22. Non-bank deposits	135413	150692	166066	180188	196684	207180	220159	243334	278363	316036	22.	Dépôts non bancaires
23. Bonds	3417	4393	4586	5646	6483	8571	11304	18801	23263	31749	23.	Obligations
24. Other liabilities	11660	12038	10440	11450	12573	16401	23684	28197	37245	38630	24.	Autres engagements
Balance sheet total												**Total du bilan**
25. End-year total	185040	202241	222014	242640	263851	284000	318231	358312	413862	460387	25.	En fin d'exercice
26. Average total	173134	193640	212127	232327	253246	273926	301115	338272	386087	437124	26.	Moyen

SPAIN
Savings banks

ESPAGNE
Caisses d'épargne

Million euros

Millions d'euros

	1992	1993	1994	1995	1996	1997	1998	1999	2000	2001		
Memorandum items												***Pour mémoire***
27. Short-term securities	17790	14508	16648	16433	17214	12893	8689	8245	8715	7846	27.	*Titres à court terme*
28. Bonds	14701	15741	25519	30896	34294	36354	39818	45155	50682	58320	28.	*Obligations*
29. Shares and participations	3804	4568	5018	6214	7868	11641	13898	17202	21837	23250	29.	*Actions et participations*
30. Claims on non-residents	6401	13751	13739	16918	15131	15426	21037	32649	39336	40859	30.	*Créances sur des non-résidents*
31. Liabilities to non-residents	4832	5776	6226	6373	8215	13765	21130	31540	47161	53963	31.	*Engagements envers des non-résidents*
Capital adequacy (1)												***Solvabilité (1)***
32. Tier 1 Capital	..	..	..	..	..	..	..	24091	28487	31278	32.	*Fonds propres de base*
33. Tier 2 Capital	..	..	..	..	..	..	..	7497	9629	12819	33.	*Fonds propres complémentaires*
34. Supervisory deductions	..	..	..	..	..	..	..	879	1716	2312	34.	*Eléments à déduire des fonds propres*
35. Total net capital resources	..	..	..	..	..	..	..	30709	36400	41785	35.	*Total net des ressources en capital*
36. Risk-weighted assets	..	..	..	..	..	..	..	228473	282100	325289	36.	*Actifs pondérés des risques*
SUPPLEMENTARY INFORMATION												**RENSEIGNEMENTS COMPLEMENTAIRES**
37. Number of institutions	54	52	52	51	51	51	51	50	48	47	37.	*Nombre d'institutions*
38. Number of branches	14291	14485	14880	15214	16094	16636	17582	18337	19268	19829	38.	*Nombre de succursales*
39. Number of employees (x 1000)	83	83	84	84	87	90	94	97	102	106	39.	*Nombre de salariés (x 1000)*

1 Change in methodology.

Change in methodology

. As from 1992, Income tax (item 10) includes tax on domestic activities of resident entities rather than total tax.

. As from 1993, credit entities' branches from the European Union (EU) are not subject to capital requirements. As from 1994, credit entities' from non-EU members are also not subject to capital requirements if these countries have similar legislation.

. As from 1993, the means of calculating capital adequacy requirements has changed, as the gearing ratio and the additional surcharges relating to concentration have disappeared.

. As from 1994, trading portfolio price risk became subject to a different treatment than that of credit risk.

1 Changement méthodologique.

Changement méthodologique

. A partir de 1992, la rubrique Impôt sur le revenu (poste 10) inclut l'impôt sur les activités domestiques des entités résidentes plutôt que l'impôt total.

. A partir de 1993, les succursales des entités de crédit de l'Union Européenne (UE) ne sont pas soumises à des exigences de capital. A partir de 1994, les entités de crédit des pays non membres de l'UE ne sont pas non plus soumises à des exigences de capital si ces pays ont une législation semblable.

. A partir de 1993, les moyens de calcul pour la solvabilité exigée a changé, étant donné que le ratio d'effets de levier et les charges supplémentaires relatifs à la concentration ont disparus.

. A partir de 1994, le risque du prix du portefeuille de transactions a été sujet à une couverture différente que celle du risque de crédit.

SPAIN
Savings banks

ESPAGNE
Caisses d'épargne

Per cent / *Pourcentage*

INCOME STATEMENT ANALYSIS / **ANALYSE DU COMPTE DE RESULTATS**

#	English	1992	1993	1994	1995	1996	1997	1998	1999	2000	2001	French
	% of average balance sheet total											**% du total moyen du bilan**
40.	Interest income	10.51	10.74	8.72	8.73	8.37	6.85	5.75	4.66	4.98	5.24	Produits financiers
41.	Interest expenses	6.66	6.98	5.12	5.32	5.07	3.68	2.83	1.94	2.38	2.65	Frais financiers
42.	Net interest income	3.84	3.76	3.61	3.40	3.30	3.17	2.92	2.72	2.60	2.59	Produits financiers nets
43.	Non-interest income (net)	0.74	0.80	0.73	0.71	0.85	0.95	1.13	1.04	1.12	0.81	Produits non financiers (nets)
	a. Fees and commissions receivable	0.49	0.52	0.57	0.57	0.60	0.68	0.74	0.74	0.73	0.71	*a. Frais et commissions à recevoir*
	b. Fees and commissions payable	0.08	0.09	0.09	0.09	0.10	0.11	0.11	0.11	0.12	0.12	*b. Frais et commissions à payer*
	c. Net profits or loss on financial operations	0.14	0.23	0.06	0.08	0.23	0.24	0.38	0.29	0.40	0.16	*c. Profits ou pertes nets sur opérations financières*
	d. Other	0.19	0.14	0.19	0.15	0.12	0.13	0.12	0.12	0.11	0.06	*d. Autres*
44.	Gross income	4.58	4.57	4.34	4.11	4.15	4.12	4.05	3.76	3.71	3.40	Résultat brut
45.	Operating expenses	2.74	2.73	2.63	2.56	2.49	2.43	2.41	2.32	2.22	2.05	Frais d'exploitation
	a. Staff costs	1.63	1.65	1.61	1.57	1.53	1.45	1.45	1.44	1.39	1.26	*a. Dépenses en personnel*
	b. Property costs	1.10	1.08	1.01	0.97	0.94	0.95	0.93	0.86	0.81	0.78	*b. Dépenses en immobilier*
	c. Other	0.01	0.01	0.01	0.02	0.03	0.03	0.03	0.02	0.02	0.02	*c. Autres*
46.	Net income	1.84	1.83	1.71	1.56	1.66	1.69	1.64	1.44	1.49	1.34	Résultat net
47.	Provisions (net)	0.85	0.89	0.82	0.60	0.62	0.54	0.46	0.29	0.45	0.41	Provisions (nettes)
	a. Provisions on loans	0.61	0.87	0.59	0.49	0.39	0.29	0.19	0.15	0.25	0.32	*a. Provisions sur prêts*
	b. Provisions on securities	0.16	-0.05	0.15	0.03	0.06	0.05	0.09	0.08	0.10	0.10	*b. Provisions sur titres*
	c. Other	0.08	0.06	0.08	0.07	0.17	0.20	0.18	0.06	0.10	-0.01	*c. Autres*
48.	Profit before tax	0.99	0.95	0.90	0.96	1.03	1.15	1.18	1.14	1.04	0.93	Bénéfices avant impôt
49.	Income tax	0.24	0.23	0.20	0.23	0.26	0.27	0.26	0.26	0.18	0.13	Impôt sur le revenu
50.	Profit after tax	0.76	0.71	0.69	0.72	0.78	0.88	0.91	0.89	0.86	0.80	Bénéfices après impôt
51.	Distributed profit	0.17	0.19	0.17	0.18	0.20	0.22	0.24	0.23	0.22	0.21	Bénéfices distribués
52.	Retained profit	0.58	0.52	0.53	0.55	0.57	0.65	0.67	0.66	0.63	0.59	Bénéfices mis en réserve
	% of gross income											**% du total du résultat brut**
53.	Net interest income	83.90	82.46	83.14	82.84	79.51	77.02	72.08	72.35	69.95	76.15	Produits financiers nets
54.	Non-interest income (net)	16.06	17.54	16.86	17.17	20.49	22.98	27.92	27.65	30.05	23.85	Produits non financiers (nets)
	a. Fees and commissions receivable	10.68	11.42	13.20	13.80	14.44	16.53	18.34	19.77	19.68	20.88	*a. Frais et commissions à recevoir*
	b. Fees and commissions payable	1.82	1.97	2.09	2.25	2.36	2.56	2.70	2.94	3.15	3.58	*b. Frais et commissions à payer*
	c. Net profits or loss on financial operations	3.03	5.03	1.30	2.05	5.59	5.87	9.35	7.67	10.65	4.82	*c. Profits ou pertes nets sur opérations financières*
	d. Other	4.17	3.12	4.44	3.57	2.82	3.14	2.94	3.16	2.88	1.74	*d. Autres*
55.	Operating expenses	59.81	59.89	60.53	62.17	60.08	58.89	59.47	61.78	59.83	60.50	Frais d'exploitation
	a. Staff costs	35.57	36.09	37.03	38.10	36.82	35.20	35.75	38.19	37.34	37.02	*a. Dépenses en personnel*
	b. Property costs	24.01	23.59	23.25	23.49	22.61	23.07	23.08	22.98	21.93	22.90	*b. Dépenses en immobilier*
	c. Other	0.23	0.27	0.20	0.59	0.64	0.62	0.63	0.62	0.56	0.58	*c. Autres*
56.	Net income	40.15	40.11	39.48	37.84	39.92	41.10	40.54	38.22	40.17	39.50	Résultat net
57.	Provisions (net)	18.48	19.42	18.79	14.59	15.05	13.16	11.48	7.81	12.18	12.01	Provisions (nettes)
	a. Provisions on loans	13.26	19.15	13.49	11.97	9.49	7.10	4.80	4.05	6.67	9.30	*a. Provisions sur prêts*
	b. Provisions on securities	3.48	-1.15	3.53	0.81	1.35	1.24	2.30	2.18	2.75	3.00	*b. Provisions sur titres*
	c. Other	1.74	1.36	1.76	1.81	4.20	4.82	4.39	1.59	2.77	-0.28	*c. Autres*
58.	Profit before tax	21.67	20.70	20.70	23.24	24.87	27.95	29.05	30.41	27.98	27.49	Bénéfices avant impôt
59.	Income tax	5.14	5.12	4.69	5.66	6.16	6.59	6.49	6.80	4.93	3.90	Impôt sur le revenu
60.	Profit after tax	16.55	15.58	16.00	17.58	18.71	21.35	22.56	23.62	23.05	23.59	Bénéfices après impôt
	% of net income											**% du total du résultat net**
61.	Provisions (net)	46.03	48.42	47.58	38.56	37.71	32.01	28.31	20.43	30.33	30.41	Provisions (nettes)
	a. Provisions on loans	33.03	47.74	34.18	31.64	23.78	17.27	11.84	10.59	16.61	23.53	*a. Provisions sur prêts*
	b. Provisions on securities	8.67	-2.88	8.94	2.13	3.39	3.02	5.67	5.71	6.84	7.59	*b. Provisions sur titres*
	c. Other	4.33	3.38	4.46	4.79	10.52	11.73	10.83	4.15	6.90	-0.72	*c. Autres*
62.	Profit before tax	53.97	51.61	52.42	61.42	62.29	67.99	71.67	79.57	69.65	69.59	Bénéfices avant impôt
63.	Income tax	12.81	12.77	11.89	14.95	15.43	16.04	16.01	17.78	12.26	9.87	Impôt sur le revenu
64.	Profit after tax	41.22	38.83	40.53	46.47	46.86	51.95	55.66	61.79	57.39	59.72	Bénéfices après impôt

SPAIN
Savings banks

ESPAGNE
Caisses d'épargne

Per cent — *Pourcentage*

BALANCE SHEET ANALYSIS — **ANALYSE DU BILAN**

% of year-end balance sheet total — **% du total du bilan en fin d'exercice**

	1992	1993	1994	1995	1996	1997	1998	1999	2000	2001	
Assets											**Actif**
65. Cash & balance with Central bank	7.32	5.73	5.30	4.06	3.39	3.09	2.61	2.63	1.47	2.05	65. Caisse & solde auprès de la Banque centrale
66. Interbank deposits	15.99	17.49	13.05	13.38	14.28	13.24	13.06	9.76	8.40	8.02	66. Dépôts interbancaires
67. Loans	47.04	46.73	47.88	47.64	48.63	52.54	55.22	56.69	59.26	60.58	67. Prêts
68. Securities	19.61	17.22	21.25	22.07	22.50	21.44	19.61	19.70	19.63	19.42	68. Valeurs mobilières
69. Other assets	10.04	12.84	12.52	12.85	11.19	9.68	9.50	11.23	11.24	9.93	69. Autres actifs
Liabilities											**Passif**
70. Capital & reserves	8.10	8.37	8.63	8.36	8.67	9.06	8.81	8.46	8.15	8.13	70. Capital et réserves
71. Borrowing from Central bank	5.48	3.20	3.25	3.37	2.17	1.77	2.17	1.11	1.67	0.68	71. Emprunts auprès de la Banque centrale
72. Interbank deposits	5.09	5.80	6.55	6.96	7.39	7.42	8.84	9.40	8.30	7.26	72. Dépôts interbancaires
73. Non-bank deposits	73.18	74.51	74.80	74.26	74.54	72.95	69.18	67.91	67.26	68.65	73. Dépôts non bancaires
74. Bonds	1.85	2.17	2.07	2.33	2.46	3.02	3.55	5.25	5.62	6.90	74. Obligations
75. Other liabilities	6.30	5.95	4.70	4.72	4.77	5.78	7.44	7.87	9.00	8.39	75. Autres engagements
Memorandum items											***Pour mémoire***
76. *Short-term securities*	*9.61*	*7.17*	*7.50*	*6.77*	*6.52*	*4.54*	*2.73*	*2.30*	*2.11*	*1.70*	76. *Titres à court terme*
77. *Bonds*	*7.94*	*7.78*	*11.49*	*12.73*	*13.00*	*12.80*	*12.51*	*12.60*	*12.25*	*12.67*	77. *Obligations*
78. *Shares and participations*	*2.06*	*2.26*	*2.26*	*2.56*	*2.98*	*4.10*	*4.37*	*4.80*	*5.28*	*5.05*	78. *Actions et participations*
79. *Claims on non-residents*	*3.46*	*6.80*	*6.19*	*6.97*	*5.73*	*5.43*	*6.61*	*9.11*	*9.50*	*8.87*	79. *Créances sur des non-résidents*
80. *Liabilities to non-residents*	*2.61*	*2.86*	*2.80*	*2.63*	*3.11*	*4.85*	*6.64*	*8.80*	*11.40*	*11.72*	80. *Engagements envers des non-résidents*

* See notes on previous pages.   * Voir les notes en pages précédentes.

SPAIN

Co-operative banks

Million euros

ESPAGNE

Banques mutualistes

Millions d'euros

	1992	1993	1994	1995	1996	1997	1998	1999	2000	2001	
INCOME STATEMENT											**COMPTE DE RESULTATS**
1. Interest income	1689	1944	1779	2031	2199	1925	1790	1637	1950	2396	1. Produits financiers
2. Interest expenses	938	1096	908	1077	1168	867	704	498	698	959	2. Frais financiers
3. Net interest income	751	849	871	954	1031	1058	1087	1139	1252	1437	3. Produits financiers nets
4. Non-interest income (net)	42	67	72	56	86	138	167	236	279	286	4. Produits non financiers (nets)
a. Fees and commissions receivable	*66*	*88*	*108*	*121*	*149*	*179*	*221*	*247*	*284*	*315*	*a. Frais et commissions à recevoir*
b. Fees and commissions payable	*18*	*19*	*24*	*26*	*33*	*41*	*44*	*49*	*57*	*62*	*b. Frais et commissions à payer*
c. Net profits or loss on financial operations	*-6*	*13*	*6*	*-*	*23*	*49*	*50*	*47*	*27*	*8*	*c. Profits ou pertes nets sur opérations financières*
d. Other	*-6*	*-14*	*-18*	*-38*	*-53*	*-48*	*-60*	*-10*	*26*	*25*	*d. Autres*
5. Gross income	793	915	944	1010	1117	1196	1254	1375	1531	1723	5. Résultat brut
6. Operating expenses	493	547	577	616	674	737	795	836	900	1017	6. Frais d'exploitation
a. Staff costs	*288*	*313*	*337*	*360*	*392*	*421*	*452*	*476*	*516*	*585*	*a. Dépenses en personnel*
b. Property costs	*204*	*228*	*228*	*250*	*275*	*308*	*336*	*354*	*378*	*426*	*b. Dépenses en immobilier*
c. Other	*6*	*6*	*6*	*6*	*7*	*7*	*7*	*6*	*6*	*7*	*c. Autres*
7. Net income	301	369	367	394	443	459	458	539	632	707	7. Résultat net
8. Provisions (net)	78	164	120	90	85	62	25	80	169	237	8. Provisions (nettes)
a. Provisions on loans	*84*	*176*	*102*	*115*	*109*	*88*	*66*	*13*	*114*	*192*	*a. Provisions sur prêts*
b. Provisions on securities	*6*	*-*	*30*	*2*	*-*	*2*	*1*	*29*	*35*	*32*	*b. Provisions sur titres*
c. Other	*-6*	*-12*	*-12*	*-27*	*-25*	*-29*	*-42*	*37*	*19*	*13*	*c. Autres*
9. Profit before tax	222	204	246	303	359	397	433	459	461	469	9. Bénéfices avant impôt
10. Income tax	36	37	36	49	61	65	72	74	69	65	10. Impôt sur le revenu
11. Profit after tax	186	167	210	254	298	332	362	385	394	405	11. Bénéfices après impôt
12. Distributed profit	60	58	64	74	77	84	89	96	108	112	12. Bénéfices distribués
13. Retained profit	126	109	146	180	221	248	272	289	286	293	13. Bénéfices mis en réserve
BALANCE SHEET											**BILAN**
Assets											**Actif**
14. Cash & balance with Central bank	1316	1186	1160	1131	1062	1008	921	896	600	1475	14. Caisse & solde auprès de la Banque centrale
15. Interbank deposits	4249	6076	5307	6337	6614	6708	6565	5325	5303	6427	15. Dépôts interbancaires
16. Loans	7789	8464	9911	11471	13338	15996	19041	22525	26521	30993	16. Prêts
17. Securities	1232	1154	2464	3108	3470	3367	3666	4420	4728	4674	17. Valeurs mobilières
18. Other assets	962	1058	1310	1350	1499	1472	1527	1643	2448	2500	18. Autres actifs
Liabilities											**Passif**
19. Capital & reserves	1779	2056	2344	2598	2955	3348	3720	4127	4603	5148	19. Capital et réserves
20. Borrowing from Central bank	-	192	421	358	369	271	232	123	120	-	20. Emprunts auprès de la Banque centrale
21. Interbank deposits	763	715	751	967	1172	1773	2006	1551	1546	2001	21. Dépôts interbancaires
22. Non-bank deposits	12603	14515	16239	18827	20807	22718	25251	28346	32454	37556	22. Dépôts non bancaires
23. Bonds	-	2	-	2	2	3	5	14	51	301	23. Obligations
24. Other liabilities	403	459	397	647	678	437	506	650	827	1063	24. Autres engagements
Balance sheet total											**Total du bilan**
25. End-year total	15548	17938	20152	23399	25983	28551	31721	34811	39601	46069	25. En fin d'exercice
26. Average total	14851	16744	19046	21775	24691	27267	30136	33266	37206	42835	26. Moyen

247

SPAIN
Co-operative banks

ESPAGNE
Banques mutualistes

Million euros / *Millions d'euros*

	1992	1993	1994	1995	1996	1997	1998	1999	2000	2001		
Memorandum items												**Pour mémoire**
27. Short-term securities	607	529	709	869	695	586	480	540	766	637	27.	Titres à court terme
28. Bonds	517	487	1575	1891	2286	2371	2674	3402	3476	3492	28.	Obligations
29. Shares and participations	108	138	180	349	490	411	512	478	487	545	29.	Actions et participations
30. Claims on non-residents	90	162	186	76	141	110	153	467	1443	1497	30.	Créances sur des non-résidents
31. Liabilities to non-residents	90	120	138	154	200	239	320	414	684	747	31.	Engagements envers des non-résidents
Capital adequacy (1)												**Solvabilité (1)**
32. Tier 1 Capital	..	..	..	..	..	..	..	3027	3446	3841	32.	Fonds propres de base
33. Tier 2 Capital	..	..	..	..	..	..	..	251	395	563	33.	Fonds propres complémentaires
34. Supervisory deductions	..	..	..	..	..	..	..	24	45	69	34.	Eléments à déduire des fonds propres
35. Total net capital resources	..	..	..	..	..	..	..	3254	3796	4335	35.	Total net des ressources en capital
36. Risk-weighted assets	..	..	..	..	..	..	..	23447	28529	33292	36.	Actifs pondérés des risques
SUPPLEMENTARY INFORMATION												**RENSEIGNEMENTS COMPLEMENTAIRES**
37. Number of institutions	101	100	99	97	97	97	97	94	92	89	37.	Nombre d'institutions
38. Number of branches	3080	3072	3107	3195	3311	3468	3607	3744	3888	4091	38.	Nombre de succursales
39. Number of employees (x 1000)	11	11	11	12	12	13	13	14	14	16	39.	Nombre de salariés (x 1000)

1 Change in methodology.

Change in methodology

. As from 1992, Income tax (item 10) includes tax on domestic activities of
resident entities rather than total tax.

. As from 1993, credit entities' branches from the European Union (EU) are not
subject to capital requirements. As from 1994, credit entities' from non-EU
members are also not subject to capital requirements if these countries have
similar legislation.

. As from 1993, the means of calculating capital adequacy requirements has
changed, as the gearing ratio and the additional surcharges relating to
concentration have disappeared.

. As from 1994, trading portfolio price risk became subject to a different treatment
than that of credit risk.

1 Changement méthodologique.

Changement méthodologique

. A partir de 1992, la rubrique Impôt sur le revenu (poste 10) inclut l'impôt sur les activités
domestiques des entités résidentes plutôt que l'impôt total.

. A partir de 1993, les succursales des entités de crédit de l'Union Européenne (UE)
ne sont pas soumises à des exigences de capital. A partir de 1994, les entités de crédit
des pays non membres de l'UE ne sont pas non plus soumises à des exigences
de capital si ces pays ont une législation semblable.

. A partir de 1993, les moyens de calcul pour la solvabilité exigée a changé, étant donné
que le ratio d'effets de levier et les charges supplémentaires relatifs à la concentration
ont disparus.

. A partir de 1994, le risque du prix du portefeuille de transactions a été sujet à une
couverture différente que celle du risque de crédit.

SPAIN
Co-operative banks

ESPAGNE
Banques mutualistes

Per cent / *Pourcentage*

INCOME STATEMENT ANALYSIS / **ANALYSE DU COMPTE DE RESULTATS**

		1992	1993	1994	1995	1996	1997	1998	1999	2000	2001
% of average balance sheet total	**% du total moyen du bilan**										
40. Interest income	40. Produits financiers	11.37	11.61	9.34	9.33	8.91	7.06	5.94	4.92	5.24	5.59
41. Interest expenses	41. Frais financiers	6.32	6.55	4.77	4.95	4.73	3.18	2.34	1.50	1.88	2.24
42. Net interest income	42. Produits financiers nets	5.06	5.07	4.57	4.38	4.18	3.88	3.61	3.42	3.37	3.35
43. Non-interest income (net)	43. Produits non financiers (nets)	0.28	0.40	0.38	0.26	0.35	0.51	0.55	0.71	0.75	0.67
a. Fees and commissions receivable	*a. Frais et commissions à recevoir*	*0.44*	*0.54*	*0.57*	*0.56*	*0.60*	*0.66*	*0.73*	*0.74*	*0.76*	*0.74*
b. Fees and commissions payable	*b. Frais et commissions à payer*	*0.12*	*0.11*	*0.13*	*0.12*	*0.13*	*0.15*	*0.15*	*0.15*	*0.15*	*0.14*
c. Net profits or loss on financial operations	*c. Profits ou pertes nets sur opérations financières*	*-0.04*	*0.07*	*0.03*	*-*	*0.09*	*0.18*	*0.17*	*0.14*	*0.07*	*0.02*
d. Other	*d. Autres*	*-0.04*	*-0.07*	*-0.09*	*-0.17*	*-0.21*	*-0.18*	*-0.20*	*-0.03*	*0.07*	*0.06*
44. Gross income	44. Résultat brut	5.34	5.46	4.96	4.64	4.52	4.39	4.16	4.13	4.11	4.02
45. Operating expenses	45. Frais d'exploitation	3.32	3.27	3.03	2.83	2.73	2.70	2.64	2.51	2.42	2.37
a. Staff costs	*a. Dépenses en personnel*	*1.94*	*1.87*	*1.77*	*1.65*	*1.59*	*1.54*	*1.50*	*1.43*	*1.39*	*1.37*
b. Property costs	*b. Dépenses en immobilier*	*1.37*	*1.36*	*1.20*	*1.15*	*1.11*	*1.13*	*1.11*	*1.06*	*1.02*	*0.99*
c. Other	*c. Autres*	*0.04*	*0.04*	*0.03*	*0.03*	*0.03*	*0.03*	*0.02*	*0.02*	*0.02*	*0.02*
46. Net income	46. Résultat net	2.03	2.20	1.93	1.81	1.79	1.68	1.52	1.62	1.70	1.65
47. Provisions (net)	47. Provisions (nettes)	0.53	0.98	0.63	0.41	0.34	0.23	0.08	0.24	0.45	0.55
a. Provisions on loans	*a. Provisions sur prêts*	*0.57*	*1.05*	*0.54*	*0.53*	*0.44*	*0.32*	*0.22*	*0.04*	*0.31*	*0.45*
b. Provisions on securities	*b. Provisions sur titres*	*0.04*	*-*	*0.16*	*0.01*	*-*	*0.01*	*-*	*0.09*	*0.09*	*0.07*
c. Other	*c. Autres*	*-0.04*	*-0.07*	*-0.06*	*-0.12*	*-0.10*	*-0.11*	*-0.14*	*0.11*	*0.05*	*0.03*
48. Profit before tax	48. Bénéfices avant impôt	1.49	1.22	1.29	1.39	1.45	1.46	1.44	1.38	1.24	1.09
49. Income tax	49. Impôt sur le revenu	0.24	0.22	0.19	0.23	0.25	0.24	0.24	0.22	0.19	0.15
50. Profit after tax	50. Bénéfices après impôt	1.25	1.00	1.10	1.17	1.21	1.22	1.20	1.16	1.06	0.95
51. Distributed profit	51. Bénéfices distribués	0.40	0.35	0.34	0.34	0.31	0.31	0.30	0.29	0.29	0.26
52. Retained profit	52. Bénéfices mis en réserve	0.85	0.65	0.77	0.83	0.90	0.91	0.90	0.87	0.77	0.68
% of gross income	**% du total du résultat brut**										
53. Net interest income	53. Produits financiers nets	94.70	92.79	92.27	94.46	92.30	88.46	86.68	82.84	81.78	83.40
54. Non-interest income (net)	54. Produits non financiers (nets)	5.30	7.32	7.63	5.54	7.70	11.54	13.32	17.16	18.22	16.60
a. Fees and commissions receivable	*a. Frais et commissions à recevoir*	*8.32*	*9.95*	*11.44*	*11.98*	*13.34*	*14.97*	*17.62*	*17.96*	*18.55*	*18.28*
b. Fees and commissions payable	*b. Frais et commissions à payer*	*2.27*	*1.97*	*2.54*	*2.57*	*2.95*	*3.43*	*3.51*	*3.56*	*3.72*	*3.60*
c. Net profits or loss on financial operations	*c. Profits ou pertes nets sur opérations financières*	*-0.76*	*1.31*	*0.64*	*-*	*2.06*	*4.10*	*3.99*	*3.42*	*1.76*	*0.46*
d. Other	*d. Autres*	*-0.76*	*-1.31*	*-1.91*	*-3.76*	*-4.74*	*-4.01*	*-4.78*	*-0.73*	*1.70*	*1.45*
55. Operating expenses	55. Frais d'exploitation	62.17	59.78	61.12	60.99	60.34	61.62	63.40	60.80	58.79	59.02
a. Staff costs	*a. Dépenses en personnel*	*36.32*	*34.21*	*35.70*	*35.64*	*35.09*	*35.20*	*36.04*	*34.62*	*33.70*	*33.95*
b. Property costs	*b. Dépenses en immobilier*	*25.73*	*24.92*	*24.15*	*24.75*	*24.62*	*25.75*	*26.79*	*25.75*	*24.69*	*24.72*
c. Other	*c. Autres*	*0.76*	*0.66*	*0.64*	*0.59*	*0.63*	*0.59*	*0.56*	*0.44*	*0.39*	*0.41*
56. Net income	56. Résultat net	37.96	40.33	38.88	39.01	39.66	38.38	36.52	39.20	41.28	41.03
57. Provisions (net)	57. Provisions (nettes)	9.84	17.92	12.71	8.91	7.61	5.18	1.99	5.82	11.04	13.76
a. Provisions on loans	*a. Provisions sur prêts*	*10.59*	*19.23*	*10.81*	*11.39*	*9.76*	*7.36*	*5.26*	*0.95*	*7.45*	*11.14*
b. Provisions on securities	*b. Provisions sur titres*	*0.76*	*-*	*3.18*	*0.20*	*-*	*0.17*	*0.08*	*2.11*	*2.29*	*1.86*
c. Other	*c. Autres*	*-0.76*	*-1.31*	*-1.27*	*-2.67*	*-2.24*	*-2.42*	*-3.35*	*2.69*	*1.24*	*0.75*
58. Profit before tax	58. Bénéfices avant impôt	27.99	22.30	26.06	30.00	32.14	33.19	34.53	33.38	30.11	27.22
59. Income tax	59. Impôt sur le revenu	4.54	4.04	3.81	4.85	5.46	5.43	5.74	5.38	4.51	3.77
60. Profit after tax	60. Bénéfices après impôt	23.46	18.25	22.25	25.15	26.68	27.76	28.87	28.00	25.73	23.51
% of net income	**% du total du résultat net**										
61. Provisions (net)	61. Provisions (nettes)	25.91	44.44	32.70	22.84	19.19	13.51	5.46	14.84	26.74	33.52
a. Provisions on loans	*a. Provisions sur prêts*	*27.91*	*47.70*	*27.79*	*29.19*	*24.60*	*19.17*	*14.41*	*2.41*	*18.04*	*27.16*
b. Provisions on securities	*b. Provisions sur titres*	*1.99*	*-*	*8.17*	*0.51*	*-*	*0.44*	*0.22*	*5.38*	*5.54*	*4.53*
c. Other	*c. Autres*	*-1.99*	*-3.25*	*-3.27*	*-6.85*	*-5.64*	*-6.32*	*-9.17*	*6.86*	*3.01*	*1.84*
62. Profit before tax	62. Bénéfices avant impôt	73.75	55.28	67.03	76.90	81.04	86.49	94.54	85.16	72.94	66.34
63. Income tax	63. Impôt sur le revenu	11.96	10.03	9.81	12.44	13.77	14.16	15.72	13.73	10.92	9.19
64. Profit after tax	64. Bénéfices après impôt	61.79	45.26	57.22	64.47	67.27	72.33	79.04	71.43	62.34	57.28

SPAIN

Co-operative banks

ESPAGNE

Banques mutualistes

Per cent	1992	1993	1994	1995	1996	1997	1998	1999	2000	2001		Pourcentage
BALANCE SHEET ANALYSIS												**ANALYSE DU BILAN**
% of year-end balance sheet total												**% du total du bilan en fin d'exercice**
Assets												**Actif**
65. Cash & balance with Central bank	8.46	6.60	5.76	4.83	4.09	3.53	2.90	2.57	1.52	3.20		65. Caisse & solde auprès de la Banque centrale
66. Interbank deposits	27.33	33.87	26.33	27.08	25.46	23.49	20.70	15.30	13.39	13.95		66. Dépôts interbancaires
67. Loans	50.10	47.17	49.18	49.02	51.33	56.03	60.03	64.71	66.97	67.28		67. Prêts
68. Securities	7.92	6.43	12.23	13.28	13.35	11.79	11.56	12.70	11.94	10.15		68. Valeurs mobilières
69. Other assets	6.19	5.90	6.50	5.77	5.77	5.16	4.81	4.72	6.18	5.43		69. Autres actifs
Liabilities												**Passif**
70. Capital & reserves	11.44	11.45	11.63	11.10	11.37	11.73	11.73	11.86	11.62	11.17		70. Capital et réserves
71. Borrowing from Central bank	-	1.07	2.09	1.53	1.42	0.95	0.73	0.35	0.30	-		71. Emprunts auprès de la Banque centrale
72. Interbank deposits	4.91	3.99	3.73	4.13	4.51	6.21	6.32	4.46	3.90	4.34		72. Dépôts interbancaires
73. Non-bank deposits	81.06	80.90	80.58	80.46	80.08	79.57	79.60	81.43	81.95	81.52		73. Dépôts non bancaires
74. Bonds	-	-	-	0.01	0.01	0.01	0.02	0.04	0.13	0.65		74. Obligations
75. Other liabilities	2.59	2.55	1.97	2.77	2.61	1.53	1.60	1.87	2.09	2.31		75. Autres engagements
Memorandum items												*Pour mémoire*
76. Short-term securities	*3.90*	*2.95*	*3.52*	*3.71*	*2.67*	*2.05*	*1.51*	*1.55*	*1.93*	*1.38*		*76. Titres à court terme*
77. Bonds	*3.33*	*2.71*	*7.82*	*8.08*	*8.80*	*8.30*	*8.43*	*9.77*	*8.78*	*7.47*		*77. Obligations*
78. Shares and participations	*0.69*	*0.77*	*0.89*	*1.49*	*1.89*	*1.44*	*1.61*	*1.37*	*1.23*	*1.18*		*78. Actions et participations*
79. Claims on non-residents	*0.58*	*0.90*	*0.92*	*0.32*	*0.54*	*0.39*	*0.48*	*1.34*	*3.64*	*3.25*		*79. Créances sur des non-résidents*
80. Liabilities to non-residents	*0.58*	*0.67*	*0.68*	*0.66*	*0.77*	*0.84*	*1.01*	*1.19*	*1.73*	*1.62*		*80. Engagements envers des non-résidents*

* See notes on previous pages.

* Voir les notes en pages précédentes.

SWEDEN
Commercial banks

SUEDE
Banques commerciales

Million Swedish Kroner / *Millions de couronnes suédoises*

	1992	1993	1994	1995	1996	1997	1998	1999	2000	2001	
INCOME STATEMENT											**COMPTE DE RESULTATS**
1. Interest income	122619	123005	101973	122322	106585	95113	109096	101401	127101	124202	1. Produits financiers
2. Interest expenses	96190	85426	66498	83939	71623	63943	81432	73802	99192	92014	2. Frais financiers
3. Net interest income	26429	37579	35475	38383	34962	31170	27664	27599	27909	32188	3. Produits financiers nets
4. Non-interest income (net)	17704	43796	20540	21246	26222	28461	40041	34612	40667	43834	4. Produits non financiers (nets)
a. Fees and commissions receivable	..	..	..	..	14547	17973	18568	19814	24406	21825	a. Frais et commissions à recevoir
b. Fees and commissions payable	..	..	..	..	2254	2809	2952	3085	3637	3930	b. Frais et commissions à payer
c. Net profits or loss on financial operations	..	..	..	..	9415	2819	5318	2510	7482	5634	c. Profits ou pertes nets sur opérations financières
d. Other	..	..	..	..	4514	10478	19108	15373	12415	20304	d. Autres
5. Gross income	44133	81375	56015	59629	61184	59630	67705	62211	68576	76022	5. Résultat brut
6. Operating expenses	64668	89359	45428	42665	39361	47203	46537	45587	45687	48910	6. Frais d'exploitation
a. Staff costs	10442	13327	14117	16581	17442	18806	19464	20046	21693	21952	a. Dépenses en personnel
b. Property costs	181	440	512	499	..	..	..	..	..	..	b. Dépenses en immobilier
c. Other	54045	75592	30799	25585	..	..	..	..	..	..	c. Autres
7. Net income	-20535	-7984	10587	16964	21823	12427	21169	16625	22889	27111	7. Résultat net
8. Provisions (net)	-23564	-10050	-2948	-2026	94	649	2123	-2891	-4127	-3686	8. Provisions (nettes)
a. Provisions on loans	..	..	..	..	..	..	..	..	..	..	a. Provisions sur prêts
b. Provisions on securities	..	..	..	..	..	..	..	..	..	..	b. Provisions sur titres
c. Other	..	..	..	..	..	..	..	..	..	..	c. Autres
9. Profit before tax	3029	2066	13535	18990	21729	11777	19046	19515	27015	30798	9. Bénéfices avant impôt
10. Income tax	510	1482	2120	3668	5004	3527	3157	4378	6540	5518	10. Impôt sur le revenu
11. Profit after tax	2519	584	11415	15322	16725	8250	15889	15137	20475	25280	11. Bénéfices après impôt
12. Distributed profit	1727	23	1076	4545	17356	6040	15278	9164	13836	9104	12. Bénéfices distribués
13. Retained profit	792	561	10339	10777	-631	2210	611	5973	6639	16176	13. Bénéfices mis en réserve
BALANCE SHEET											**BILAN**
Assets											**Actif**
14. Cash & balance with Central bank	20577	21982	7566	9192	18476	15128	13408	20125	14081	23623	14. Caisse & solde auprès de la Banque centrale
15. Interbank deposits	112209	127046	133139	219714	331813	400198	363322	389839	450018	465719	15. Dépôts interbancaires
16. Loans	670191	690861	644503	635926	650554	718030	785389	839797	955080	1059298	16. Prêts
17. Securities (1)	272689	431645	486676	520098	532871	635375	788870	752881	899153	979767	17. Valeurs mobilières (1)
18. Other assets	77890	82295	72731	74429	196668	218265	237580	230235	274336	283426	18. Autres actifs
Liabilities											**Passif**
19. Capital & reserves	52898	73313	72486	86006	84965	105631	109904	122291	138540	158129	19. Capital et réserves
20. Borrowing from Central bank	60279	644	8	256	9563	31146	17382	13657	27450	50706	20. Emprunts auprès de la Banque centrale
21. Interbank deposits	300599	298288	294934	341201	419539	466468	563700	498414	621069	694910	21. Dépôts interbancaires
22. Non-bank deposits	535982	717766	731913	754923	788295	860671	866045	893400	1014679	1071383	22. Dépôts non bancaires
23. Bonds	89829	112966	107374	88391	161975	231892	316505	377607	420863	483316	23. Obligations
24. Other liabilities	113968	150854	137900	188582	266046	291188	315034	327508	370067	353387	24. Autres engagements
Balance sheet total											**Total du bilan**
25. End-year total	1153554	1353830	1344615	1459359	1730382	1986996	2188569	2232877	2592668	2811832	25. En fin d'exercice
26. Average total	1209533	1383064	1383358	1431405	1670222	1897439	2143528	2237113	2434179	2865173	26. Moyen

SWEDEN
Commercial banks

SUEDE
Banques commerciales

Million Swedish Kroner — *Millions de couronnes suédoises*

	1992	1993	1994	1995	1996	1997	1998	1999	2000	2001	
Memorandum items											**Pour mémoire**
27. Short-term securities	136911	145151	153025	132114	91922	49841	123346	105944	119308	123269	27. Titres à court terme
28. Bonds	77073	156453	203784	262578	184562	136203	189257	210583	247508	275229	28. Obligations
29. Shares and participations	27575	39675	36584	42527	48542	68864	84391	95523	136763	147003	29. Actions et participations
30. Claims on non-residents	360649	380901	341671	482088	589093	595427	781377	793563	895115	1028143	30. Créances sur des non-résidents
31. Liabilities to non-residents	563031	616819	568206	612010	668431	736462	1156956	1067720	1275229	1216011	31. Engagements envers des non-résidents
Capital adequacy											**Solvabilité**
32. Tier 1 Capital	46540	68476	70224	82887	79975	86943	89888	112274	123754	134510	32. Fonds propres de base
33. Tier 2 Capital (2)	28617	42747	42920	43152	46689	57976	62426	64358	72939	87175	33. Fonds propres complémentaires (2)
34. Supervisory deductions	1098	1331	1978	2303	4562	16349	15000	13373	10811	15056	34. Eléments à déduire des fonds propres
35. Total net capital resources	74059	109892	111166	123736	122103	128570	137314	163259	185881	206629	35. Total net des ressources en capital
36. Risk-weighted assets	693748	735779	671509	644835	749638	822877	893341	934261	1030748	1123380	36. Actifs pondérés des risques
SUPPLEMENTARY INFORMATION											**RENSEIGNEMENTS COMPLÉMENTAIRES**
37. Number of institutions	8	9	10	13	15	15	18	19	23	27	37. Nombre d'institutions
38. Number of branches	1872	2474	2327	2239	2202	2165	1823	1793	1732	1730	38. Nombre de succursales
39. Number of employees (x 1000)	28	37	39	39	39	39	39	38	37	37	39. Nombre de salariés (x 1000)

1 Securities also include loans to credit institutions (other than banks).

2 Beginnning 1997, Tier 2 Capital (item 33) includes Tier 3 Capital.

Notes

. Average balance sheet totals (item 26) are based on thirteen end-month data.

Change in methodology

. For the year 1991, the Föreningsbankernas Bank is exceptionally included under Co-operative banks and not under Commercial banks.

. As from 1992, Co-operative banks, which merged into one single commercial bank, are included under Commercial banks.

. As from 1993, Commercial banks include what was formerly the largest savings bank.

. Beginning 1992, Provisions on loans (item 8.a) and Provisions on securities (item 8.b) are no longer available due to new accounting methods

1 Les valeurs mobilières incluent également les prêts aux institutions de crédit (autres que banques)

2 A partir de 1997, des données de la rubrique Fonds propres complémentaires (poste 33) incluent les fonds propres surcomplémentaires.

Notes

. La moyenne du total des actifs/passifs (poste 26) est basée sur treize données de fin de mois.

Changement méthodologique

. Pour l'année 1991, la Föreningsbankernas Bank est comprise exceptionnellement dans les Banques mutualistes et non pas dans les Banques commerciales.

. Depuis 1992, les Banques mutualistes, ayant fusionnées en une seule banque commerciale, sont classées dans les données concernant les Banques commerciales.

. Depuis 1993, les Banques commerciales incluent ce qui était précédément la caisse d'épargne la plus grande.

. A partir de 1992, Provisions sur prêts (poste 8.a) et Provisions sur titres (poste 8.b) ne sont plus disponibles du fait de nouvelles techniques comptables.

252

	1992	1993	1994	1995	1996	1997	1998	1999	2000	2001	
Per cent											*Pourcentage*
INCOME STATEMENT ANALYSIS											**ANALYSE DU COMPTE DE RESULTATS**
% of average balance sheet total											**% du total moyen du bilan**
40. Interest income	10.14	8.89	7.37	8.55	6.38	5.01	5.09	4.53	5.22	4.33	40. Produits financiers
41. Interest expenses	7.95	6.18	4.81	5.86	4.29	3.37	3.80	3.30	4.07	3.21	41. Frais financiers
42. Net interest income	2.19	2.72	2.56	2.68	2.09	1.64	1.29	1.23	1.15	1.12	42. Produits financiers nets
43. Non-interest income (net)	1.46	3.17	1.48	1.48	1.57	1.50	1.87	1.55	1.67	1.53	43. Produits non financiers (nets)
a. Fees and commissions receivable	..	..	..	..	*0.87*	*0.95*	*0.87*	*0.89*	*1.00*	*0.76*	*a. Frais et commissions à recevoir*
b. Fees and commissions payable	..	..	..	..	*0.13*	*0.15*	*0.14*	*0.14*	*0.15*	*0.14*	*b. Frais et commissions à payer*
c. Net profits or loss on financial operations	..	..	..	..	*0.56*	*0.15*	*0.25*	*0.11*	*0.31*	*0.20*	*c. Profits ou pertes nets sur opérations financières*
d. Other	..	..	..	..	*0.27*	*0.55*	*0.89*	*0.69*	*0.51*	*0.71*	*d. Autres*
44. Gross income	3.65	5.88	4.05	4.17	3.66	3.14	3.16	2.78	2.82	2.65	44. Résultat brut
45. Operating expenses	5.35	6.46	3.28	2.98	2.36	2.49	2.17	2.04	1.88	1.71	45. Frais d'exploitation
a. Staff costs	*0.86*	*0.96*	*1.02*	*1.16*	*1.04*	*0.99*	*0.91*	*0.90*	*0.89*	*0.77*	*a. Dépenses en personnel*
b. Property costs	*0.01*	*0.03*	*0.04*	*0.03*	*..*	*..*	*..*	*..*	*..*	*..*	*b. Dépenses en immobilier*
c. Other	*4.47*	*5.47*	*2.23*	*1.79*	*..*	*..*	*..*	*..*	*..*	*..*	*c. Autres*
46. Net income	-1.70	-0.58	0.77	1.19	1.31	0.65	0.99	0.74	0.94	0.95	46. Résultat net
47. Provisions (net)	-1.95	-0.73	-0.21	-0.14	0.01	0.03	0.10	-0.13	-0.17	-0.13	47. Provisions (nettes)
a. Provisions on loans	*..*	*..*	*..*	*..*	*..*	*..*	*..*	*..*	*..*	*..*	*a. Provisions sur prêts*
b. Provisions on securities	*..*	*..*	*..*	*..*	*..*	*..*	*..*	*..*	*..*	*..*	*b. Provisions sur titres*
c. Other	*..*	*..*	*..*	*..*	*..*	*..*	*..*	*..*	*..*	*..*	*c. Autres*
48. Profit before tax	0.25	0.15	0.98	1.33	1.30	0.62	0.89	0.87	1.11	1.07	48. Bénéfices avant impôt
49. Income tax	0.04	0.11	0.15	0.26	0.30	0.19	0.15	0.20	0.27	0.19	49. Impôt sur le revenu
50. Profit after tax	0.21	0.04	0.83	1.07	1.00	0.43	0.74	0.68	0.84	0.88	50. Bénéfices après impôt
51. Distributed profit	0.14	-	0.08	0.32	1.04	0.32	0.71	0.41	0.57	0.32	51. Bénéfices distribués
52. Retained profit	0.07	0.04	0.75	0.75	-0.04	0.12	0.03	0.27	0.27	0.56	52. Bénéfices mis en réserve
% of gross income											**% du total du résultat brut**
53. Net interest income	59.88	46.18	63.33	64.37	57.14	52.27	40.86	44.36	40.70	42.34	53. Produits financiers nets
54. Non-interest income (net)	40.12	53.82	36.67	35.63	42.86	47.73	59.14	55.64	59.30	57.66	54. Produits non financiers (nets)
a. Fees and commissions receivable	*..*	*..*	*..*	*..*	*23.78*	*30.14*	*27.42*	*31.85*	*35.59*	*28.71*	*a. Frais et commissions à recevoir*
b. Fees and commissions payable	*..*	*..*	*..*	*..*	*3.68*	*4.71*	*4.36*	*4.96*	*5.30*	*5.17*	*b. Frais et commissions à payer*
c. Net profits or loss on financial operations	*..*	*..*	*..*	*..*	*15.39*	*4.73*	*7.85*	*4.03*	*10.91*	*7.41*	*c. Profits ou pertes nets sur opérations financières*
d. Other	*..*	*..*	*..*	*..*	*7.38*	*17.57*	*28.22*	*24.71*	*18.10*	*26.71*	*d. Autres*
55. Operating expenses	146.53	109.81	81.10	71.55	64.33	79.16	68.73	73.28	66.62	64.34	55. Frais d'exploitation
a. Staff costs	*23.66*	*16.38*	*25.20*	*27.81*	*28.51*	*31.54*	*28.75*	*32.22*	*31.63*	*28.88*	*a. Dépenses en personnel*
b. Property costs	*0.41*	*0.54*	*0.91*	*0.84*	*..*	*..*	*..*	*..*	*..*	*..*	*b. Dépenses en immobilier*
c. Other	*122.46*	*92.89*	*54.98*	*42.91*	*..*	*..*	*..*	*..*	*..*	*..*	*c. Autres*
56. Net income	-46.53	-9.81	18.90	28.45	35.67	20.84	31.27	26.72	33.38	35.66	56. Résultat net
57. Provisions (net)	-53.39	-12.35	-5.26	-3.40	0.15	1.09	3.14	-4.65	-6.02	-4.85	57. Provisions (nettes)
a. Provisions on loans	*..*	*..*	*..*	*..*	*..*	*..*	*..*	*..*	*..*	*..*	*a. Provisions sur prêts*
b. Provisions on securities	*..*	*..*	*..*	*..*	*..*	*..*	*..*	*..*	*..*	*..*	*b. Provisions sur titres*
c. Other	*..*	*..*	*..*	*..*	*..*	*..*	*..*	*..*	*..*	*..*	*c. Autres*
58. Profit before tax	6.86	2.54	24.16	31.85	35.51	19.75	28.13	31.37	39.39	40.51	58. Bénéfices avant impôt
59. Income tax	1.16	1.82	3.78	6.15	8.18	5.91	4.66	7.04	9.54	7.26	59. Impôt sur le revenu
60. Profit after tax	5.71	0.72	20.38	25.70	27.34	13.84	23.47	24.33	29.86	33.25	60. Bénéfices après impôt
% of net income											**% du total du résultat net**
61. Provisions (net)	114.75	125.88	-27.85	-11.94	0.43	5.22	10.03	-17.39	-18.03	-13.60	61. Provisions (nettes)
a. Provisions on loans	*..*	*..*	*..*	*..*	*..*	*..*	*..*	*..*	*..*	*..*	*a. Provisions sur prêts*
b. Provisions on securities	*..*	*..*	*..*	*..*	*..*	*..*	*..*	*..*	*..*	*..*	*b. Provisions sur titres*
c. Other	*..*	*..*	*..*	*..*	*..*	*..*	*..*	*..*	*..*	*..*	*c. Autres*
62. Profit before tax	-14.75	-25.88	127.85	111.94	99.57	94.77	89.97	117.38	118.03	113.60	62. Bénéfices avant impôt
63. Income tax	-2.48	-18.56	20.02	21.62	22.93	28.38	14.91	26.33	28.57	20.35	63. Impôt sur le revenu
64. Profit after tax	-12.27	-7.31	107.82	90.32	76.64	66.39	75.06	91.05	89.45	93.25	64. Bénéfices après impôt

Per cent
Pourcentage

BALANCE SHEET ANALYSIS
ANALYSE DU BILAN

% of year-end balance sheet total
% du total du bilan en fin d'exercice

	1992	1993	1994	1995	1996	1997	1998	1999	2000	2001		
Assets												**Actif**
65. Cash & balance with Central bank	1.78	1.62	0.56	0.63	1.07	0.76	0.61	0.90	0.54	0.84	65.	Caisse & solde auprès de la Banque centrale
66. Interbank deposits	9.73	9.38	9.90	15.06	19.18	20.14	16.60	17.46	17.36	16.56	66.	Dépôts interbancaires
67. Loans	58.10	51.03	47.93	43.58	37.60	36.14	35.89	37.61	36.84	37.67	67.	Prêts
68. Securities	23.64	31.88	36.19	35.64	30.79	31.98	36.05	33.72	34.68	34.84	68.	Valeurs mobilières
69. Other assets	6.75	6.08	5.41	5.10	11.37	10.98	10.86	10.31	10.58	10.08	69.	Autres actifs
Liabilities												**Passif**
70. Capital & reserves	4.59	5.42	5.39	5.89	4.91	5.32	5.02	5.48	5.34	5.62	70.	Capital et réserves
71. Borrowing from Central bank	5.23	0.05	-	0.02	0.55	1.57	0.79	0.61	1.06	1.80	71.	Emprunts auprès de la Banque centrale
72. Interbank deposits	26.06	22.03	21.93	23.38	24.25	23.48	25.76	22.32	23.95	24.71	72.	Dépôts interbancaires
73. Non-bank deposits	46.46	53.02	54.43	51.73	45.56	43.32	39.57	40.01	39.14	38.10	73.	Dépôts non bancaires
74. Bonds	7.79	8.34	7.99	6.06	9.36	11.67	14.46	16.91	16.23	17.19	74.	Obligations
75. Other liabilities	9.88	11.14	10.26	12.92	15.37	14.65	14.39	14.67	14.27	12.57	75.	Autres engagements
Memorandum items												***Pour mémoire***
76. Short-term securities	*11.87*	*10.72*	*11.38*	*9.05*	*5.31*	*2.51*	*5.64*	*4.74*	*4.60*	*4.38*	*76.*	*Titres à court terme*
77. Bonds	*6.68*	*11.56*	*15.16*	*17.99*	*10.67*	*6.85*	*8.65*	*9.43*	*9.55*	*9.79*	*77.*	*Obligations*
78. Shares and participations	*2.39*	*2.93*	*2.72*	*2.91*	*2.81*	*3.47*	*3.86*	*4.28*	*5.27*	*5.23*	*78.*	*Actions et participations*
79. Claims on non-residents	*31.26*	*28.14*	*25.41*	*33.03*	*34.04*	*29.97*	*35.70*	*35.54*	*34.52*	*36.56*	*79.*	*Créances sur des non-résidents*
80. Liabilities to non-residents	*48.81*	*45.56*	*42.26*	*41.94*	*38.63*	*37.06*	*52.86*	*47.82*	*49.19*	*43.25*	*80.*	*Engagements envers des non-résidents*

* See notes on previous pages.

* *Voir les notes en pages précédentes.*

Million Swedish Kroner

Millions de couronnes suédoises

	1992	1993	1994	1995	1996	1997	1998	1999	2000	2001		
INCOME STATEMENT												**COMPTE DE RESULTATS**
1. Interest income	2541	2296	1680	3610	4169	5452	7421	6765	10328	14026	1.	Produits financiers
2. Interest expenses	2454	1978	1390	3240	3330	3873	4861	4662	7550	10293	2.	Frais financiers
3. Net interest income	87	318	290	370	839	1579	2560	2103	2778	3733	3.	Produits financiers nets
4. Non-interest income (net)	451	1394	127	100	428	947	1038	1211	3094	2319	4.	Produits non financiers (nets)
a. Fees and commissions receivable	..	..	..	..	192	501	739	998	1804	1808		a. Frais et commissions à recevoir
b. Fees and commissions payable	..	..	..	..	34	101	176	170	380	497		b. Frais et commissions à payer
c. Net profits or loss on financial operations	..	..	..	..	67	399	291	177	1293	622		c. Profits ou pertes nets sur opérations financières
d. Other	..	..	..	..	204	149	184	206	377	386		d. Autres
5. Gross income	538	1712	417	470	1267	2527	3598	3314	5872	6052	5.	Résultat brut
6. Operating expenses	1369	538	316	639	1186	2210	3463	2680	4129	4783	6.	Frais d'exploitation
a. Staff costs	171	172	152	268	293	677	938	1078	1574	1729		a. Dépenses en personnel
b. Property costs	1	4	2	2	..	..	..	..	..	..		b. Dépenses en immobilier
c. Other	1197	362	162	369	..	..	..	..	..	..		c. Autres
7. Net income	-831	1174	101	-169	81	317	135	634	1743	1269	7.	Résultat net
8. Provisions (net)	157	143	3	-74	85	108	-496	1	191	379	8.	Provisions (nettes)
a. Provisions on loans	..	..	..	..	..	..	..	..	..	..		a. Provisions sur prêts
b. Provisions on securities	..	..	..	..	..	..	..	..	..	..		b. Provisions sur titres
c. Other	..	..	..	..	..	..	..	..	..	..		c. Autres
9. Profit before tax	-988	1031	98	-95	-4	208	631	633	1552	890	9.	Bénéfices avant impôt
10. Income tax	42	35	19	1	-	46	308	157	237	445	10.	Impôt sur le revenu
11. Profit after tax	-1030	996	79	-96	-4	162	324	476	1315	446	11.	Bénéfices après impôt
12. Distributed profit	8	95	135	-	65	92	319	..	..	-	12.	Bénéfices distribués
13. Retained profit	-1038	901	-56	-96	-69	70	5	476	1315	446	13.	Bénéfices mis en réserve
BALANCE SHEET												**BILAN**
Assets												**Actif**
14. Cash & balance with Central bank	2794	147	1023	19	25	276	184	565	678	428	14.	Caisse & solde auprès de la Banque centrale
15. Interbank deposits	6362	9651	10463	14015	18139	16786	29158	28779	41934	31175	15.	Dépôts interbancaires
16. Loans	15732	11967	13416	15293	17333	44786	56071	75594	107998	151411	16.	Prêts
17. Securities	5111	6136	9271	13770	14477	14197	34417	30666	46562	46321	17.	Valeurs mobilières
18. Other assets	1991	1101	3490	6759	6313	8193	8134	6462	10354	16447	18.	Autres actifs
Liabilities												**Passif**
19. Capital & reserves	664	1647	1401	1096	1175	3207	4289	4016	6905	6461	19.	Capital et réserves
20. Borrowing from Central bank	5	-	7	3	961	3	10328	7873	13985	-	20.	Emprunts auprès de la Banque centrale
21. Interbank deposits	26951	22573	29637	39318	38456	44842	68089	76521	69607	98250	21.	Dépôts interbancaires
22. Non-bank deposits	2916	3223	3996	4094	11272	26560	26319	40973	62429	80432	22.	Dépôts non bancaires
23. Bonds	493	252	184	169	107	761	773	1833	1080	1356	23.	Obligations
24. Other liabilities	960	1305	2438	5177	4316	8865	18165	10850	53520	59283	24.	Autres engagements
Balance sheet total												**Total du bilan**
25. End-year total	31989	29000	37662	49857	56286	84239	127963	142066	207526	245782	25.	En fin d'exercice
26. Average total	25834	31936	30835	44586	58078	77155	123334	158379	162618	242397	26.	Moyen

SWEDEN / SUÈDE
Foreign commercial banks / Banques commerciales étrangères

Million Swedish Kroner / Millions de couronnes suédoises

	1992	1993	1994	1995	1996	1997	1998	1999	2000	2001	
Memorandum items											**Pour mémoire**
27. Short-term securities	10260	7393	10323	11655	7294	2902	6205	3662	3784	2152	27. Titres à court terme
28. Bonds	100	606	1069	3705	1270	1098	5688	1666	13312	27339	28. Obligations
29. Shares and participations	4	5	4	15	2955	4530	6621	7453	15187	14770	29. Actions et participations
30. Claims on non-residents	6736	11612	8145	13307	16349	10118	18940	19993	46332	35305	30. Créances sur des non-résidents
31. Liabilities to non-residents	27839	23285	26114	35970	32339	19765	37497	33570	69960	101020	31. Engagements envers des non-résidents
Capital adequacy											**Solvabilité**
32. Tier 1 Capital	1386	1429	789	763	1519	2323	2590	3213	4951	5368	32. Fonds propres de base
33. Tier 2 Capital	193	167	149	..	..	251	251	211	171	131	33. Fonds propres complémentaires
34. Supervisory deductions	..	..	..	..	..	..	..	..	..	..	34. Eléments à déduire des fonds propres
35. Total net capital resources	1579	1596	938	763	1519	2574	2841	3424	5122	5499	35. Total net des ressources en capital
36. Risk-weighted assets	17619	11912	4946	2590	3846	10123	7632	10211	22067	26449	36. Actifs pondérés des risques
SUPPLEMENTARY INFORMATION											**RENSEIGNEMENTS COMPLÉMENTAIRES**
37. Number of institutions	8	8	12	13	21	22	19	17	24	24	37. Nombre d'institutions
38. Number of branches	10	10	11	13	21	54	52	54	58	71	38. Nombre de succursales
39. Number of employees (x 1000)	-	-	-	-	-	1	1	2	2	2	39. Nombre de salariés (x 1000)

Notes

. Average balance sheet totals (item 26) are based on thirteen end-month data.

Notes

. La moyenne du total des actifs/passifs (poste 26) est basée sur treize données de fin de mois.

Foreign commercial banks

Banques commerciales étrangères

Per cent — *Pourcentage*

		1992	1993	1994	1995	1996	1997	1998	1999	2000	2001	
	INCOME STATEMENT ANALYSIS											**ANALYSE DU COMPTE DE RESULTATS**
	% of average balance sheet total											**% du total moyen du bilan**
40.	Interest income	9.84	7.19	5.45	8.10	7.18	7.07	6.02	4.27	6.35	5.79	Produits financiers
41.	Interest expenses	9.50	6.19	4.51	7.27	5.73	5.02	3.94	2.94	4.64	4.25	Frais financiers
42.	Net interest income	0.34	1.00	0.94	0.83	1.44	2.05	2.08	1.33	1.71	1.54	Produits financiers nets
43.	Non-interest income (net)	1.75	4.36	0.41	0.22	0.74	1.23	0.84	0.76	1.90	0.96	Produits non financiers (nets)
	a. Fees and commissions receivable	..	..	..	..	0.33	0.65	0.60	0.63	1.11	0.75	a. Frais et commissions à recevoir
	b. Fees and commissions payable	..	..	..	..	0.06	0.13	0.14	0.11	0.23	0.21	b. Frais et commissions à payer
	c. Net profits or loss on financial operations	..	..	..	..	0.12	0.52	0.24	0.11	0.80	0.26	c. Profits ou pertes nets sur opérations financières
	d. Other	..	..	..	..	0.35	0.19	0.15	0.13	0.23	0.16	d. Autres
44.	Gross income	2.08	5.36	1.35	1.05	2.18	3.28	2.92	2.09	3.61	2.50	Résultat brut
45.	Operating expenses	5.30	1.68	1.02	1.43	2.04	2.86	2.81	1.69	2.54	1.97	Frais d'exploitation
	a. Staff costs	0.66	0.54	0.49	0.60	0.50	0.88	0.76	0.68	0.97	0.71	a. Dépenses en personnel
	b. Property costs	-	0.01	0.01	-	..	..	..	..	..	..	b. Dépenses en immobilier
	c. Other	4.63	1.13	0.53	0.83	..	..	..	..	..	..	c. Autres
46.	Net income	-3.22	3.68	0.33	-0.38	0.14	0.41	0.11	0.40	1.07	0.52	Résultat net
47.	Provisions (net)	0.61	0.45	0.01	-0.17	0.15	0.14	-0.40	-	0.12	0.16	Provisions (nettes)
	a. Provisions on loans	..	..	..	..	..	..	..	..	..	..	a. Provisions sur prêts
	b. Provisions on securities	..	..	..	..	..	..	..	..	..	..	b. Provisions sur titres
	c. Other	..	..	..	..	..	..	..	..	..	..	c. Autres
48.	Profit before tax	-3.82	3.23	0.32	-0.21	-0.01	0.27	0.51	0.40	0.95	0.37	Bénéfices avant impôt
49.	Income tax	0.16	0.11	0.06	-	-	0.06	0.25	0.10	0.15	0.18	Impôt sur le revenu
50.	Profit after tax	-3.99	3.12	0.26	-0.22	-0.01	0.21	0.26	0.30	0.81	0.18	Bénéfices après impôt
51.	Distributed profit	0.03	0.30	0.44	-	0.11	0.12	0.26	-	-	-	Bénéfices distribués
52.	Retained profit	-4.02	2.82	-0.18	-0.22	-0.12	0.09	-	0.30	0.81	0.18	Bénéfices mis en réserve
	% of gross income											**% du total du résultat brut**
53.	Net interest income	16.17	18.57	69.54	78.72	66.22	62.49	71.15	63.46	47.31	61.68	Produits financiers nets
54.	Non-interest income (net)	83.83	81.43	30.46	21.28	33.78	37.48	28.85	36.54	52.69	38.32	Produits non financiers (nets)
	a. Fees and commissions receivable	..	..	..	..	15.15	19.83	20.54	30.11	30.72	29.87	a. Frais et commissions à recevoir
	b. Fees and commissions payable	..	..	..	..	2.68	4.00	4.89	5.13	6.47	8.21	b. Frais et commissions à payer
	c. Net profits or loss on financial operations	..	..	..	..	5.29	15.79	8.09	5.34	22.02	10.28	c. Profits ou pertes nets sur opérations financières
	d. Other	..	..	..	..	16.10	5.90	5.11	6.22	6.42	6.38	d. Autres
55.	Operating expenses	254.46	31.43	75.78	135.96	93.61	87.46	96.25	80.87	70.32	79.03	Frais d'exploitation
	a. Staff costs	31.78	10.05	36.45	57.02	23.13	26.79	26.07	32.53	26.81	28.57	a. Dépenses en personnel
	b. Property costs	0.19	0.23	0.48	0.43	..	..	..	..	..	..	b. Dépenses en immobilier
	c. Other	222.49	21.14	38.85	78.51	..	..	..	..	..	..	c. Autres
56.	Net income	-154.46	68.57	24.22	-35.96	6.39	12.54	3.75	19.13	29.68	20.97	Résultat net
57.	Provisions (net)	29.18	8.35	0.72	-15.74	6.71	4.27	-13.79	0.03	3.25	6.26	Provisions (nettes)
	a. Provisions on loans	..	..	..	..	..	..	..	..	..	..	a. Provisions sur prêts
	b. Provisions on securities	..	..	..	..	..	..	..	..	..	..	b. Provisions sur titres
	c. Other	..	..	..	..	..	..	..	..	..	..	c. Autres
58.	Profit before tax	-183.64	60.22	23.50	-20.21	-0.32	8.23	17.54	19.10	26.43	14.71	Bénéfices avant impôt
59.	Income tax	7.81	2.04	4.56	0.21	-	1.82	8.56	4.74	4.04	7.35	Impôt sur le revenu
60.	Profit after tax	-191.45	58.18	18.94	-20.43	-0.32	6.41	9.01	14.36	22.39	7.37	Bénéfices après impôt
	% of net income											**% du total du résultat net**
61.	Provisions (net)	-18.89	12.18	2.97	43.79	104.94	34.07	-367.41	0.16	10.96	29.87	Provisions (nettes)
	a. Provisions on loans	..	..	..	..	..	..	..	..	..	..	a. Provisions sur prêts
	b. Provisions on securities	..	..	..	..	..	..	..	..	..	..	b. Provisions sur titres
	c. Other	..	..	..	..	..	..	..	..	..	..	c. Autres
62.	Profit before tax	118.89	87.82	97.03	56.21	-4.94	65.62	467.41	99.84	89.04	70.13	Bénéfices avant impôt
63.	Income tax	-5.05	2.98	18.81	-0.59	-	14.51	228.15	24.76	13.60	35.07	Impôt sur le revenu
64.	Profit after tax	123.95	84.84	78.22	56.80	-4.94	51.10	240.00	75.08	75.44	35.15	Bénéfices après impôt

SWEDEN

Foreign commercial banks

SUEDE

Banques commerciales étrangères

Per cent	1992	1993	1994	1995	1996	1997	1998	1999	2000	2001	*Pourcentage*
BALANCE SHEET ANALYSIS											**ANALYSE DU BILAN**
% of year-end balance sheet total											% du total du bilan en fin d'exercice
Assets											**Actif**
65. Cash & balance with Central bank	8.73	0.51	2.72	0.04	0.04	0.33	0.14	0.40	0.33	0.17	65. Caisse & solde auprès de la Banque centrale
66. Interbank deposits	19.89	33.28	27.78	28.11	32.23	19.93	22.79	20.26	20.21	12.68	66. Dépôts interbancaires
67. Loans	49.18	41.27	35.62	30.67	30.79	53.17	43.82	53.21	52.04	61.60	67. Prêts
68. Securities	15.98	21.16	24.62	27.62	25.72	16.85	26.90	21.59	22.44	18.85	68. Valeurs mobilières
69. Other assets	6.22	3.80	9.27	13.56	11.22	9.73	6.36	4.55	4.99	6.69	69. Autres actifs
Liabilities											**Passif**
70. Capital & reserves	2.08	5.68	3.72	2.20	2.09	3.81	3.35	2.83	3.33	2.63	70. Capital et réserves
71. Borrowing from Central bank	0.02	-	0.02	0.01	1.71	-	8.07	5.54	6.74	-	71. Emprunts auprès de la Banque centrale
72. Interbank deposits	84.25	77.84	78.69	78.86	68.32	53.23	53.21	53.86	33.54	39.97	72. Dépôts interbancaires
73. Non-bank deposits	9.12	11.11	10.61	8.21	20.03	31.53	20.57	28.84	30.08	32.72	73. Dépôts non bancaires
74. Bonds	1.54	0.87	0.49	0.34	0.19	0.90	0.60	1.29	0.52	0.55	74. Obligations
75. Other liabilities	3.00	4.50	6.47	10.38	7.67	10.52	14.20	7.64	25.79	24.12	75. Autres engagements
Memorandum items											*Pour mémoire*
76. Short-term securities	*32.07*	*25.49*	*27.41*	*23.38*	*12.96*	*3.44*	*4.85*	*2.58*	*1.82*	*0.88*	*76. Titres à court terme*
77. Bonds	*0.31*	*2.09*	*2.84*	*7.43*	*2.26*	*1.30*	*4.45*	*1.17*	*6.41*	*11.12*	*77. Obligations*
78. Shares and participations	*0.01*	*0.02*	*0.01*	*0.03*	*5.25*	*5.38*	*5.17*	*5.25*	*7.32*	*6.01*	*78. Actions et participations*
79. Claims on non-residents	*21.06*	*40.04*	*21.63*	*26.69*	*29.05*	*12.01*	*14.80*	*14.07*	*22.33*	*14.36*	*79. Créances sur des non-résidents*
80. Liabilities to non-residents	*87.03*	*80.29*	*69.34*	*72.15*	*57.45*	*23.46*	*29.30*	*23.63*	*33.71*	*41.10*	*80. Engagements envers des non-résidents*

* See notes on previous pages.   * Voir les notes en pages précédentes.

SWEDEN
Savings banks

Million Swedish Kroner

SUEDE
Caisses d'épargne

Millions de couronnes suédoises

	1992	1993	1994	1995	1996	1997	1998	1999	2000	2001	
INCOME STATEMENT											**COMPTE DE RESULTATS**
1. Interest income	49806	7551	6716	7251	6286	4903	5620	4967	4821	4999	1. Produits financiers
2. Interest expenses	37020	3585	3123	3584	2902	1698	2055	1574	1622	1665	2. Frais financiers
3. Net interest income	12786	3966	3593	3667	3384	3205	3565	3393	3199	3334	3. Produits financiers nets
4. Non-interest income (net)	19752	860	1184	1475	1300	1753	1896	1583	1732	1376	4. Produits non financiers (nets)
a. Fees and commissions receivable	..	..	..	..	836	1000	1278	1369	1454	1355	a. Frais et commissions à recevoir
b. Fees and commissions payable	..	..	..	..	156	191	321	322	288	317	b. Frais et commissions à payer
c. Net profits or loss on financial operations	..	..	..	..	148	60	67	49	58	32	c. Profits ou pertes nets sur opérations financières
d. Other	..	..	..	..	472	884	872	487	509	305	d. Autres
5. Gross income	32538	4826	4777	5142	4684	4957	5461	4977	4931	4710	5. Résultat brut
6. Operating expenses	28310	3741	3241	3417	2608	2644	3700	3857	3658	3519	6. Frais d'exploitation
a. Staff costs	5203	1138	1154	1259	1261	1315	1481	1552	1466	1414	a. Dépenses en personnel
b. Property costs	480	93	94	97	..	..	..	..	..	..	b. Dépenses en immobilier
c. Other	22627	2510	1993	2061	..	..	..	..	..	..	c. Autres
7. Net income	4228	1085	1536	1725	2075	2313	1761	1120	1273	1191	7. Résultat net
8. Provisions (net)	-6458	-532	-583	41	304	250	397	49	-238	-232	8. Provisions (nettes)
a. Provisions on loans	..	..	..	..	..	..	..	..	..	..	a. Provisions sur prêts
b. Provisions on securities	..	..	..	..	..	..	..	..	..	..	b. Provisions sur titres
c. Other	..	..	..	..	..	..	..	..	..	..	c. Autres
9. Profit before tax	10686	1617	2119	1684	1771	2063	1365	1071	1511	1423	9. Bénéfices avant impôt
10. Income tax	549	485	510	510	446	560	344	261	377	315	10. Impôt sur le revenu
11. Profit after tax	10137	1132	1609	1174	1325	1503	1021	810	1134	1108	11. Bénéfices après impôt
12. Distributed profit	-	-	-	-	-	-	-	-	-	-	12. Bénéfices distribués
13. Retained profit	10137	1132	1609	1174	1325	1503	1021	810	1134	1108	13. Bénéfices mis en réserve
BALANCE SHEET											**BILAN**
Assets											**Actif**
14. Cash & balance with Central bank	16375	1168	998	1054	1056	972	1071	1366	898	1010	14. Caisse & solde auprès de la Banque centrale
15. Interbank deposits	22127	9173	5471	6228	9293	6858	8706	6337	3831	6228	15. Dépôts interbancaires
16. Loans	214186	43009	44419	46551	43531	48294	63555	67254	67079	69350	16. Prêts
17. Securities	61489	16042	20844	19289	18420	15279	15544	12402	8213	8132	17. Valeurs mobilières
18. Other assets	18925	2421	2698	2645	2667	2557	5072	4418	3296	3058	18. Autres actifs
Liabilities											**Passif**
19. Capital & reserves	21519	7885	8464	10231	11628	13330	14578	14941	13820	14258	19. Capital et réserves
20. Borrowing from Central bank	8623	-	-	-	-	-	-	-	170	5	20. Emprunts auprès de la Banque centrale
21. Interbank deposits	48931	2458	2493	1560	1768	2261	3886	3526	5848	5087	21. Dépôts interbancaires
22. Non-bank deposits	197526	58016	59836	59935	59573	56334	73233	70202	60853	65620	22. Dépôts non bancaires
23. Bonds	21055	543	709	845	419	387	531	592	1282	1399	23. Obligations
24. Other liabilities	35448	2909	2930	3196	1579	1647	1720	2515	1344	1410	24. Autres engagements
Balance sheet total											**Total du bilan**
25. End-year total	333101	71813	74431	75767	74967	73959	93948	91776	83317	87779	25. En fin d'exercice
26. Average total	303500	..	73280	74126	71142	72419	83612	90205	87252	85763	26. Moyen

Million Swedish Kroner / *Millions de couronnes suédoises*

	1992	1993	1994	1995	1996	1997	1998	1999	2000	2001		
Memorandum items												**Pour mémoire**
27. Short-term securities	38517	9783	10088	4044	..	..	..	..	..	..	27.	Titres à court terme
28. Bonds	24190	6088	9165	11052	..	..	..	..	..	..	28.	Obligations
29. Shares and participations	10920	1314	2640	1481	..	..	..	..	..	..	29.	Actions et participations
30. Claims on non-residents	35000	347	480	..	..	..	..	..	..	..	30.	Créances sur des non-résidents
31. Liabilities to non-residents	74580	10	10	..	..	..	..	..	..	..	31.	Engagements envers des non-résidents
Capital adequacy												**Solvabilité**
32. Tier 1 Capital	20213	6701	7540	9155	10469	12436	11892	12759	12304	13060	32.	Fonds propres de base
33. Tier 2 Capital	5676	476	437	216	186	128	262	242	250	229	33.	Fonds propres complémentaires
34. Supervisory deductions	1423	1392	1483	459	876	698	743	975	1274	1086	34.	Eléments à déduire des fonds propres
35. Total net capital resources	24466	5785	6494	8912	9779	11866	11412	12026	11280	12203	35.	Total net des ressources en capital
36. Risk-weighted assets	195636	38838	39582	39539	40177	43131	56614	58511	56473	59676	36.	Actifs pondérés des risques
SUPPLEMENTARY INFORMATION												**RENSEIGNEMENTS COMPLEMENTAIRES**
37. Number of institutions	91	90	90	90	88	87	85	84	79	77	37.	Nombre d'institutions
38. Number of branches	1028	351	352	349	307	303	322	293	269	239	38.	Nombre de succursales
39. Number of employees (x 1000)	15	4	4	4	3	3	4	4	3	3	39.	Nombre de salariés (x 1000)

Change in methodology

As from 1993, Commercial banks include what was formerly the largest savings bank.

Changement méthodologique

Depuis 1993, les Banques commerciales incluent ce qui était précedément la caisse d'épargne la plus grande.

SWEDEN
Savings banks

SUEDE
Caisses d'épargne

Per cent / *Pourcentage*

INCOME STATEMENT ANALYSIS / **ANALYSE DU COMPTE DE RESULTATS**

	1992	1993	1994	1995	1996	1997	1998	1999	2000	2001	
% of average balance sheet total											**% du total moyen du bilan**
40. Interest income	16.41	..	9.16	9.78	8.84	6.77	6.72	5.51	5.53	5.83	40. Produits financiers
41. Interest expenses	12.20	..	4.26	4.84	4.08	2.34	2.46	1.74	1.86	1.94	41. Frais financiers
42. Net interest income	4.21	..	4.90	4.95	4.76	4.43	4.26	3.76	3.67	3.89	42. Produits financiers nets
43. Non-interest income (net)	6.51	..	1.62	1.99	1.83	2.42	2.27	1.75	1.99	1.60	43. Produits non financiers (nets)
a. Fees and commissions receivable	..	..	..	..	*1.18*	*1.38*	*1.53*	*1.52*	*1.67*	*1.58*	*a. Frais et commissions à recevoir*
b. Fees and commissions payable	..	..	..	..	*0.22*	*0.26*	*0.38*	*0.36*	*0.33*	*0.37*	*b. Frais et commissions à payer*
c. Net profits or loss on financial operations	..	..	..	..	*0.21*	*0.08*	*0.08*	*0.05*	*0.07*	*0.04*	*c. Profits ou pertes nets sur opérations financières*
d. Other	..	..	..	..	*0.66*	*1.22*	*1.04*	*0.54*	*0.58*	*0.36*	*d. Autres*
44. Gross income	10.72	..	6.52	6.94	6.58	6.84	6.53	5.52	5.65	5.49	44. Résultat brut
45. Operating expenses	9.33	..	4.42	4.61	3.67	3.65	4.43	4.28	4.19	4.10	45. Frais d'exploitation
a. Staff costs	*1.71*	..	*1.57*	*1.70*	*1.77*	*1.82*	*1.77*	*1.72*	*1.68*	*1.65*	*a. Dépenses en personnel*
b. Property costs	*0.16*	..	*0.13*	*0.13*	..	..	..	..	..	..	*b. Dépenses en immobilier*
c. Other	*7.46*	..	*2.72*	*2.78*	..	..	..	..	..	..	*c. Autres*
46. Net income	1.39	..	2.10	2.33	2.92	3.19	2.11	1.24	1.46	1.39	46. Résultat net
47. Provisions (net)	-2.13	..	-0.80	0.06	0.43	0.35	0.47	0.05	-0.27	-0.27	47. Provisions (nettes)
a. Provisions on loans	..	..	..	..	..	..	..	..	..	..	*a. Provisions sur prêts*
b. Provisions on securities	..	..	..	..	..	..	..	..	..	..	*b. Provisions sur titres*
c. Other	..	..	..	..	..	..	..	..	..	..	*c. Autres*
48. Profit before tax	3.52	..	2.89	2.27	2.49	2.85	1.63	1.19	1.73	1.66	48. Bénéfices avant impôt
49. Income tax	0.18	..	0.70	0.69	0.63	0.77	0.41	0.29	0.43	0.37	49. Impôt sur le revenu
50. Profit after tax	3.34	..	2.20	1.58	1.86	2.08	1.22	0.90	1.30	1.29	50. Bénéfices après impôt
51. Distributed profit	..	..	..	..	..	..	..	..	..	-	51. Bénéfices distribués
52. Retained profit	3.34	..	2.20	1.58	1.86	2.08	1.22	0.90	1.30	1.29	52. Bénéfices mis en réserve
% of gross income											**% du total du résultat brut**
53. Net interest income	39.30	82.18	75.21	71.31	72.25	64.66	65.28	68.17	64.88	70.79	53. Produits financiers nets
54. Non-interest income (net)	60.70	17.82	24.79	28.69	27.75	35.36	34.72	31.81	35.12	29.21	54. Produits non financiers (nets)
a. Fees and commissions receivable	..	..	..	..	*17.85*	*20.17*	*23.40*	*27.51*	*29.49*	*28.77*	*a. Frais et commissions à recevoir*
b. Fees and commissions payable	..	..	..	..	*3.33*	*3.85*	*5.88*	*6.47*	*5.84*	*6.73*	*b. Frais et commissions à payer*
c. Net profits or loss on financial operations	..	..	..	..	*3.16*	*1.21*	*1.23*	*0.98*	*1.18*	*0.68*	*c. Profits ou pertes nets sur opérations financières*
d. Other	..	..	..	..	*10.08*	*17.83*	*15.97*	*9.79*	*10.32*	*6.48*	*d. Autres*
55. Operating expenses	87.01	77.52	67.85	66.45	55.68	53.34	67.75	77.50	74.18	74.71	55. Frais d'exploitation
a. Staff costs	*15.99*	*23.58*	*24.16*	*24.48*	*26.92*	*26.53*	*27.12*	*31.18*	*29.73*	*30.02*	*a. Dépenses en personnel*
b. Property costs	*1.48*	*1.93*	*1.97*	*1.89*	..	..	..	..	..	..	*b. Dépenses en immobilier*
c. Other	*69.54*	*52.01*	*41.72*	*40.08*	..	..	..	..	..	..	*c. Autres*
56. Net income	12.99	22.48	32.15	33.55	44.30	46.66	32.25	22.50	25.82	25.29	56. Résultat net
57. Provisions (net)	-19.85	-11.02	-12.20	0.80	6.49	5.04	7.27	0.98	-4.83	-4.93	57. Provisions (nettes)
a. Provisions on loans	..	..	..	..	..	..	..	..	..	..	*a. Provisions sur prêts*
b. Provisions on securities	..	..	..	..	..	..	..	..	..	..	*b. Provisions sur titres*
c. Other	..	..	..	..	..	..	..	..	..	..	*c. Autres*
58. Profit before tax	32.84	33.51	44.36	32.75	37.81	41.62	25.00	21.52	30.64	30.21	58. Bénéfices avant impôt
59. Income tax	1.69	10.05	10.68	9.92	9.52	11.30	6.30	5.24	7.65	6.69	59. Impôt sur le revenu
60. Profit after tax	31.15	23.46	33.68	22.83	28.29	30.32	18.70	16.27	23.00	23.52	60. Bénéfices après impôt
% of net income											**% du total du résultat net**
61. Provisions (net)	-152.74	-49.03	-37.96	2.38	14.65	10.81	22.54	4.38	-18.70	-19.48	61. Provisions (nettes)
a. Provisions on loans	..	..	..	..	..	..	..	..	..	..	*a. Provisions sur prêts*
b. Provisions on securities	..	..	..	..	..	..	..	..	..	..	*b. Provisions sur titres*
c. Other	..	..	..	..	..	..	..	..	..	..	*c. Autres*
62. Profit before tax	252.74	149.03	137.96	97.62	85.35	89.19	77.51	95.63	118.70	119.48	62. Bénéfices avant impôt
63. Income tax	12.98	44.70	33.20	29.57	21.49	24.21	19.53	23.30	29.62	26.45	63. Impôt sur le revenu
64. Profit after tax	239.76	104.33	104.75	68.06	63.86	64.98	57.98	72.32	89.08	93.03	64. Bénéfices après impôt

SWEDEN
Savings banks

Per cent

BALANCE SHEET ANALYSIS

% of year-end balance sheet total

	1992	1993	1994	1995	1996	1997	1998	1999	2000	2001	
Assets											**Actif**
65. Cash & balance with Central bank	4.92	1.63	1.34	1.39	1.41	1.31	1.14	1.49	1.08	1.15	65. Caisse & solde auprès de la Banque centrale
66. Interbank deposits	6.64	12.77	7.35	8.22	12.40	9.27	9.27	6.90	4.60	7.10	66. Dépôts interbancaires
67. Loans	64.30	59.89	59.68	61.44	58.07	65.30	67.65	73.28	80.51	79.01	67. Prêts
68. Securities	18.46	22.34	28.00	25.46	24.57	20.66	16.55	13.51	9.86	9.26	68. Valeurs mobilières
69. Other assets	5.68	3.37	3.62	3.49	3.56	3.46	5.40	4.81	3.96	3.48	69. Autres actifs
Liabilities											**Passif**
70. Capital & reserves	6.46	10.98	11.37	13.50	15.51	18.02	15.52	16.28	16.59	16.24	70. Capital et réserves
71. Borrowing from Central bank	2.59	-	-	-	-	-	-	-	0.20	0.01	71. Emprunts auprès de la Banque centrale
72. Interbank deposits	14.69	3.42	3.35	2.06	2.36	3.06	4.14	3.84	7.02	5.80	72. Dépôts interbancaires
73. Non-bank deposits	59.30	80.79	80.39	79.10	79.47	76.17	77.95	76.49	73.04	74.76	73. Dépôts non bancaires
74. Bonds	6.32	0.76	0.95	1.12	0.56	0.52	0.57	0.65	1.54	1.59	74. Obligations
75. Other liabilities	10.64	4.05	3.94	4.22	2.11	2.23	1.83	2.74	1.61	1.61	75. Autres engagements
Memorandum items											***Pour mémoire***
76. Short-term securities	11.56	13.62	13.55	5.34	..	..	..	..	..	..	76. Titres à court terme
77. Bonds	7.26	8.48	12.31	14.59	..	..	..	..	..	..	77. Obligations
78. Shares and participations	3.28	1.83	3.55	1.95	..	..	..	..	..	..	78. Actions et participations
79. Claims on non-residents	10.51	0.48	0.64	..	..	..	..	..	..	..	79. Créances sur des non-résidents
80. Liabilities to non-residents	22.39	0.01	0.01	..	..	..	..	..	..	..	80. Engagements envers des non-résidents

* See notes on previous pages.

SUEDE
Caisses d'épargne

Pourcentage

ANALYSE DU BILAN

% du total du bilan en fin d'exercice

* Voir les notes en pages précédentes.

SWITZERLAND
All banks

SUISSE
Ensemble des banques

Million Swiss francs / *Millions de francs suisses*

	1992	1993	1994	1995	1996	1997	1998	1999	2000	2001	
INCOME STATEMENT											**COMPTE DE RESULTATS**
1. Interest income	74255	68499	59284	58408	57324	65169	68494	66634	93277	90951	1. Produits financiers
2. Interest expenses	56246	47246	42638	41904	39990	45484	46789	43915	68014	65873	2. Frais financiers
3. Net interest income	18009	21253	16646	16504	17334	19685	21705	22719	25264	25078	3. Produits financiers nets
4. Non-interest income (net)	17301	20242	19528	21611	25618	30080	32042	37816	42485	35831	4. Produits non financiers (nets)
a. Fees and commissions receivable	10851	13666	13541	12845	15407	19914	21837	24140	29718	26011	a. Frais et commissions à recevoir
b. Fees and commissions payable	632	760	756	891	1263	1734	1904	2362	3313	3019	b. Frais et commissions à payer
c. Net profits or loss on financial operations	3992	4662	3169	5575	6832	7679	4434	10259	11946	8478	c. Profits ou pertes nets sur opérations financières
d. Other	3090	2675	3574	4083	4642	4221	7675	5779	4135	4361	d. Autres
5. Gross income	35310	41495	36174	38115	42952	49765	53747	60535	67749	60909	5. Résultat brut
6. Operating expenses	18408	20183	20124	21512	28407	31449	28200	33299	37898	36555	6. Frais d'exploitation
a. Staff costs	11947	13184	12861	13401	14653	16269	15432	19806	22680	22139	a. Dépenses en personnel
b. Property costs	..	..	..	..	..	..	..	..	..	..	b. Dépenses en immobilier
c. Other	..	..	..	..	..	..	..	..	..	..	c. Autres
7. Net income	16902	21312	16050	16603	14545	18316	25547	27236	29851	24354	7. Résultat net
8. Provisions (net)	11386	13270	10046	9641	13090	13663	10708	8150	8241	10894	8. Provisions (nettes)
a. Provisions on loans	..	..	..	..	..	..	..	..	..	..	a. Provisions sur prêts
b. Provisions on securities	..	..	..	..	..	..	..	..	..	..	b. Provisions sur titres
c. Other	..	..	..	..	..	..	..	..	..	..	c. Autres
9. Profit before tax	5516	8042	6004	6962	1455	4653	14839	19086	21609	13460	9. Bénéfices avant impôt
10. Income tax	1403	1752	1260	1219	1185	1022	1140	2844	3289	2169	10. Impôt sur le revenu
11. Profit after tax	4113	6290	4744	5743	270	3631	13699	16242	18321	11291	11. Bénéfices après impôt
12. Distributed profit	2829	3579	3396	3741	2652	5947	6176	8805	7853	4216	12. Bénéfices distribués
13. Retained profit	1284	2711	1348	2002	-2382	-2316	7523	7437	10467	7075	13. Bénéfices mis en réserve
BALANCE SHEET											**BILAN**
Assets											**Actif**
14. Cash & balance with Central bank	11818	11828	10996	11424	13255	14619	14314	19699	14978	33144	14. Caisse & solde auprès de la Banque centrale
15. Interbank deposits	196342	205946	196210	231577	287606	396740	503511	633228	521298	531668	15. Dépôts interbancaires
16. Loans	726741	738605	744490	730522	784362	827753	894960	915261	921633	943151	16. Prêts
17. Securities	121896	159059	164578	188218	234009	298402	354634	433019	414021	442693	17. Valeurs mobilières
18. Other assets	55417	62368	66507	138995	148227	209299	250224	205660	215682	242375	18. Autres actifs
Liabilities											**Passif**
19. Capital & reserves	72241	78005	80516	82893	87614	89686	91420	100959	125762	129563	19. Capital et réserves
20. Borrowing from Central bank (1)	..	..	..	..	..	..	..	..	..	..	20. Emprunts auprès de la Banque centrale (1)
21. Interbank deposits	211373	241193	231238	243249	298266	375317	501479	608918	586473	583504	21. Dépôts interbancaires
22. Non-bank deposits	557064	588258	613777	627153	713898	792987	886636	974947	871672	923867	22. Dépôts non bancaires
23. Bonds	194451	183602	174309	174346	167100	174893	168710	176170	184537	217886	23. Obligations
24. Other liabilities	77084	86747	82942	173094	200581	313932	369198	345873	319169	338210	24. Autres engagements
Balance sheet total											**Total du bilan**
25. End-year total	1112213	1177805	1182782	1300735	1467458	1746814	2017643	2206867	2087613	2193032	25. En fin d'exercice
26. Average total	1092767	1145009	1180294	1241759	1384097	1607136	1882229	2112255	2147240	2140323	26. Moyen

Million Swiss francs — *Millions de francs suisses*

	1992	1993	1994	1995	1996	1997	1998	1999	2000	2001	
Memorandum items											**Pour mémoire**
27. Short-term securities	34438	34822	38926	46850	50271	71706	57188	116959	103409	104647	27. Titres à court terme
28. Bonds	68459	92633	86619	95346	119551	134025	174934	165467	152211	124643	28. Obligations
29. Shares and participations	18999	31605	39034	46021	57570	83533	110859	139882	149659	204469	29. Actions et participations
30. Claims on non-residents	392649	428143	415068	501797	648481	880071	1132444	1263563	1177326	1284879	30. Créances sur des non-résidents
31. Liabilities to non-residents	325954	351526	349274	428910	556828	780554	1014978	1136308	1093583	1200708	31. Engagements envers des non-résidents
Capital adequacy											**Solvabilité**
32. Tier 1 Capital	..	..	..	87652	86263	83260	90192	97248	123434	122132	32. Fonds propres de base
33. Tier 2 Capital	..	..	..	21992	24892	32396	27677	27905	31887	34531	33. Fonds propres complémentaires
34. Supervisory deductions	..	..	..	13821	14979	13869	12894	17329	31991	35766	34. Eléments à déduire des fonds propres
35. Total net capital resources	91362	99302	101483	95822	96176	101787	104975	107824	123329	120897	35. Total net des ressources en capital
36. Risk-weighted assets	..	..	..	912456	937377	956459	929519	954841	972792	1022029	36. Actifs pondérés des risques
SUPPLEMENTARY INFORMATION											**RENSEIGNEMENTS COMPLEMENTAIRES**
37. Number of institutions	434	419	393	382	370	360	339	334	335	327	37. Nombre d'institutions
38. Number of branches	4111	3991	3807	3727	3600	3395	3147	2922	2849	2813	38. Nombre de succursales
39. Number of employees (x 1000) (2)	119	117	117	116	116	115	114	115	120	115	39. Nombre de salariés (x 1000) (2)

1 Borrowing from Central bank (item 20) is included under Interbank deposits (item 21).

2 From 2001, the part time work is weighted in terms of the percentage of time worked (item 39).

Notes

All banks include Large commercial banks, Cantonal banks, Regional and savings banks, Loan associations and agricultural co-operative banks and Other Swiss and foreign commercial banks.

1 Emprunts auprès de la Banque centrale (poste 20) sont inclus sous Dépôts interbancaires (poste 21).

2 A compter de 2001, le travail à temps partiel est pondéré par le pourcentage du temps travaillé (poste 39).

Notes

L'Ensemble des banques comprend les Grandes banques commerciales les Banques cantonales, les Banques régionales et caisses d'épargne, les Caisses de crédit mutuel et les banques mutualistes agricoles, et les Autres banques commerciales suisses et étrangères.

SWITZERLAND

All banks

SUISSE

Ensemble des banques

Per cent — *Pourcentage*

INCOME STATEMENT ANALYSIS — **ANALYSE DU COMPTE DE RESULTATS**

		1992	1993	1994	1995	1996	1997	1998	1999	2000	2001	
	% of average balance sheet total											**% du total moyen du bilan**
40.	Interest income	6.80	5.98	5.02	4.70	4.14	4.05	3.64	3.15	4.34	4.25	Produits financiers
41.	Interest expenses	5.15	4.13	3.61	3.37	2.89	2.83	2.49	2.08	3.17	3.08	Frais financiers
42.	Net interest income	1.65	1.86	1.41	1.33	1.25	1.22	1.15	1.08	1.18	1.17	Produits financiers nets
43.	Non-interest income (net)	1.58	1.77	1.65	1.74	1.85	1.87	1.70	1.79	1.98	1.67	Produits non financiers (nets)
	a. Fees and commissions receivable	*0.99*	*1.19*	*1.15*	*1.03*	*1.11*	*1.24*	*1.16*	*1.14*	*1.38*	*1.22*	*a. Frais et commissions à recevoir*
	b. Fees and commissions payable	*0.06*	*0.07*	*0.06*	*0.07*	*0.09*	*0.11*	*0.10*	*0.11*	*0.15*	*0.14*	*b. Frais et commissions à payer*
	c. Net profits or loss on financial operations	*0.37*	*0.41*	*0.27*	*0.45*	*0.49*	*0.48*	*0.24*	*0.49*	*0.56*	*0.40*	*c. Profits ou pertes nets sur opérations financières*
	d. Other	*0.28*	*0.23*	*0.30*	*0.33*	*0.34*	*0.26*	*0.41*	*0.27*	*0.19*	*0.20*	*d. Autres*
44.	Gross income	3.23	3.62	3.06	3.07	3.10	3.10	2.86	2.87	3.16	2.85	Résultat brut
45.	Operating expenses	1.68	1.76	1.70	1.73	2.05	1.96	1.50	1.58	1.76	1.71	Frais d'exploitation
	a. Staff costs	*1.09*	*1.15*	*1.09*	*1.08*	*1.06*	*1.01*	*0.82*	*0.94*	*1.06*	*1.03*	*a. Dépenses en personnel*
	b. Property costs	:	:	:	:	:	:	:	:	:	:	*b. Dépenses en immobilier*
	c. Other											*c. Autres*
46.	Net income	1.55	1.86	1.36	1.34	1.05	1.14	1.36	1.29	1.39	1.14	Résultat net
47.	Provisions (net)	1.04	1.16	0.85	0.78	0.95	0.85	0.57	0.39	0.38	0.51	Provisions (nettes)
	a. Provisions on loans	:	:	:	:	:	:	:	:	:	:	*a. Provisions sur prêts*
	b. Provisions on securities	:	:	:	:	:	:	:	:	:	:	*b. Provisions sur titres*
	c. Other											*c. Autres*
48.	Profit before tax	0.50	0.70	0.51	0.56	0.11	0.29	0.79	0.90	1.01	0.63	Bénéfices avant impôt
49.	Income tax	0.13	0.15	0.11	0.10	0.09	0.06	0.06	0.13	0.15	0.10	Impôt sur le revenu
50.	Profit after tax	0.38	0.55	0.40	0.46	0.02	0.23	0.73	0.77	0.85	0.53	Bénéfices après impôt
51.	Distributed profit	0.26	0.31	0.29	0.30	0.19	0.37	0.33	0.42	0.37	0.20	Bénéfices distribués
52.	Retained profit	0.12	0.24	0.11	0.16	-0.17	-0.14	0.40	0.35	0.49	0.33	Bénéfices mis en réserve
	% of gross income											**% du total du résultat brut**
53.	Net interest income	51.00	51.22	46.02	43.30	40.36	39.56	40.38	37.53	37.29	41.17	Produits financiers nets
54.	Non-interest income (net)	49.00	48.78	53.98	56.70	59.64	60.44	59.62	62.47	62.71	58.83	Produits non financiers (nets)
	a. Fees and commissions receivable	*30.73*	*32.93*	*37.43*	*33.70*	*35.87*	*40.02*	*40.63*	*39.88*	*43.86*	*42.70*	*a. Frais et commissions à recevoir*
	b. Fees and commissions payable	*1.79*	*1.83*	*2.09*	*2.34*	*2.94*	*3.48*	*3.54*	*3.90*	*4.89*	*4.96*	*b. Frais et commissions à payer*
	c. Net profits or loss on financial operations	*11.31*	*11.24*	*8.76*	*14.63*	*15.91*	*15.43*	*8.25*	*16.95*	*17.63*	*13.92*	*c. Profits ou pertes nets sur opérations financières*
	d. Other	*8.75*	*6.45*	*9.88*	*10.71*	*10.81*	*8.48*	*14.28*	*9.55*	*6.10*	*7.16*	*d. Autres*
55.	Operating expenses	52.13	48.64	55.63	56.44	66.14	63.20	52.47	55.01	55.94	60.02	Frais d'exploitation
	a. Staff costs	*33.83*	*31.77*	*35.55*	*35.16*	*34.11*	*32.69*	*28.71*	*32.72*	*33.48*	*36.35*	*a. Dépenses en personnel*
	b. Property costs	:	:	:	:	:	:	:	:	:	:	*b. Dépenses en immobilier*
	c. Other											*c. Autres*
56.	Net income	47.87	51.36	44.37	43.56	33.86	36.80	47.53	44.99	44.06	39.98	Résultat net
57.	Provisions (net)	32.25	31.98	27.77	25.29	30.48	27.46	19.92	13.46	12.16	17.89	Provisions (nettes)
	a. Provisions on loans	:	:	:	:	:	:	:	:	:	:	*a. Provisions sur prêts*
	b. Provisions on securities	:	:	:	:	:	:	:	:	:	:	*b. Provisions sur titres*
	c. Other											*c. Autres*
58.	Profit before tax	15.62	19.38	16.60	18.27	3.39	9.35	27.61	31.53	31.90	22.10	Bénéfices avant impôt
59.	Income tax	3.97	4.22	3.48	3.20	2.76	2.05	2.12	4.70	4.85	3.56	Impôt sur le revenu
60.	Profit after tax	11.65	15.16	13.11	15.07	0.63	7.30	25.49	26.83	27.04	18.54	Bénéfices après impôt
	% of net income											**% du total du résultat net**
61.	Provisions (net)	67.36	62.27	62.59	58.07	90.00	74.60	41.91	29.92	27.61	44.73	Provisions (nettes)
	a. Provisions on loans	:	:	:	:	:	:	:	:	:	:	*a. Provisions sur prêts*
	b. Provisions on securities	:	:	:	:	:	:	:	:	:	:	*b. Provisions sur titres*
	c. Other											*c. Autres*
62.	Profit before tax	32.64	37.73	37.41	41.93	10.00	25.40	58.09	70.08	72.39	55.27	Bénéfices avant impôt
63.	Income tax	8.30	8.22	7.85	7.34	8.15	5.58	4.46	10.44	11.02	8.91	Impôt sur le revenu
64.	Profit after tax	24.33	29.51	29.56	34.59	1.86	19.82	53.62	59.63	61.37	46.36	Bénéfices après impôt

SWITZERLAND

All banks

SUISSE

Ensemble des banques

Per cent — *Pourcentage*

BALANCE SHEET ANALYSIS — ANALYSE DU BILAN

% of year-end balance sheet total — % du total du bilan en fin d'exercice

	1992	1993	1994	1995	1996	1997	1998	1999	2000	2001	
Assets											**Actif**
65. Cash & balance with Central bank	1.06	1.00	0.93	0.88	0.90	0.84	0.71	0.89	0.72	1.51	65. Caisse & solde auprès de la Banque centrale
66. Interbank deposits	17.65	17.49	16.59	17.80	19.60	22.71	24.96	28.69	24.97	24.24	66. Dépôts interbancaires
67. Loans	65.34	62.71	62.94	56.16	53.45	47.39	44.36	41.47	44.15	43.01	67. Prêts
68. Securities	10.96	13.50	13.91	14.47	15.95	17.08	17.58	19.62	19.83	20.19	68. Valeurs mobilières
69. Other assets	4.98	5.30	5.62	10.69	10.10	11.98	12.40	9.32	10.33	11.05	69. Autres actifs
Liabilities											**Passif**
70. Capital & reserves	6.50	6.62	6.81	6.37	5.97	5.13	4.53	4.57	6.02	5.91	70. Capital et réserves
71. Borrowing from Central bank	::	::	::	::			::	::	::	::	71. Emprunts auprès de la Banque centrale
72. Interbank deposits	19.00	20.48	19.55	18.70	20.33	21.49	24.85	27.59	28.09	26.61	72. Dépôts interbancaires
73. Non-bank deposits	50.09	49.95	51.89	48.22	48.65	45.40	43.95	44.18	41.75	42.13	73. Dépôts non bancaires
74. Bonds	17.48	15.59	14.74	13.40	11.39	10.01	8.36	7.98	8.84	9.94	74. Obligations
75. Other liabilities	6.93	7.37	7.01	13.31	13.67	17.97	18.30	15.67	15.29	15.42	75. Autres engagements
Memorandum items											*Pour mémoire*
76. Short-term securities	3.10	2.96	3.29	3.60	3.43	4.10	2.83	5.30	4.95	4.77	76. Titres à court terme
77. Bonds	6.16	7.86	7.32	7.33	8.15	7.67	8.67	7.50	7.29	5.68	77. Obligations
78. Shares and participations	1.71	2.68	3.30	3.54	3.92	4.78	5.49	6.34	7.17	9.32	78. Actions et participations
79. Claims on non-residents	35.30	36.35	35.09	38.58	44.19	50.38	56.13	57.26	56.40	58.59	79. Créances sur des non-résidents
80. Liabilities to non-residents	29.31	29.85	29.53	32.97	37.95	44.68	50.31	51.49	52.38	54.75	80. Engagements envers des non-résidents

* See notes on previous pages.   * Voir les notes en pages précédentes.

SWITZERLAND
Large commercial banks

SUISSE
Grandes banques commerciales

Million Swiss francs / *Millions de francs suisses*

	1992	1993	1994	1995	1996	1997	1998	1999	2000	2001	
INCOME STATEMENT											**COMPTE DE RESULTATS**
1. Interest income	37330	34051	30069	30007	31022	39176	43407	41760	62911	59858	1. Produits financiers
2. Interest expenses	27990	22748	21186	21786	21946	28430	30955	28904	48909	46444	2. Frais financiers
3. Net interest income	9340	11303	8883	8221	9076	10745	12452	12856	14002	13414	3. Produits financiers nets
4. Non-interest income (net)	9326	11508	10678	13143	15914	17436	18880	23214	24577	20531	4. Produits non financiers (nets)
a. Fees and commissions receivable	5950	7438	7495	7230	8767	11293	11940	12927	15764	14255	a. Frais et commissions à recevoir
b. Fees and commissions payable	255	272	266	369	603	828	860	1129	1725	1658	b. Frais et commissions à payer
c. Net profits or loss on financial operations	2720	3214	2028	4136	4855	5142	1876	7295	8995	6959	c. Profits ou pertes nets sur opérations financières
d. Other	912	1128	1421	2147	2895	1829	5925	4121	1544	975	d. Autres
5. Gross income	18666	22811	19561	21364	24990	28181	31332	36070	38579	33945	5. Résultat brut
6. Operating expenses	9765	11168	11085	12386	18219	19738	16233	19937	21819	20753	6. Frais d'exploitation
a. Staff costs	6455	7506	7164	7667	8668	9908	8733	12345	14018	13308	a. Dépenses en personnel
b. Property costs	..	..	..	..	..	..	..	..	..	..	b. Dépenses en immobilier
c. Other	..	..	..	..	..	..	..	..	..	..	c. Autres
7. Net income	8901	11643	8476	8978	6772	8444	15099	16133	16760	13192	7. Résultat net
8. Provisions (net)	5650	7384	5112	5545	9037	9119	6768	3585	3732	5653	8. Provisions (nettes)
a. Provisions on loans	..	..	..	..	..	..	..	..	..	..	a. Provisions sur prêts
b. Provisions on securities	..	..	..	..	..	..	..	..	..	..	b. Provisions sur titres
c. Other	..	..	..	..	..	..	..	..	..	..	c. Autres
9. Profit before tax	3251	4259	3364	3433	-2265	-675	8331	12548	13029	7539	9. Bénéfices avant impôt
10. Income tax	795	881	592	520	396	4	48	1503	1490	1029	10. Impôt sur le revenu
11. Profit after tax	2456	3378	2772	2913	-2661	-679	8283	11045	11539	6510	11. Bénéfices après impôt
12. Distributed profit	1584	1959	1955	2088	821	3086	2960	5336	3874	1160	12. Bénéfices distribués
13. Retained profit	872	1419	817	825	-3482	-3766	5323	5709	7665	5350	13. Bénéfices mis en réserve
BALANCE SHEET											**BILAN**
Assets											**Actif**
14. Cash & balance with Central bank	4889	4635	4478	4338	5897	6976	4835	6253	4614	22617	14. Caisse & solde auprès de la Banque centrale
15. Interbank deposits	103289	105729	101679	133775	181078	284325	387868	513811	391803	381989	15. Dépôts interbancaires
16. Loans	353135	356268	362606	344282	385678	413376	471547	460238	440280	451359	16. Prêts
17. Securities	73671	105712	109562	132430	173924	233984	285203	347938	321534	349864	17. Valeurs mobilières
18. Other assets	32297	39496	43664	115761	122794	182572	224095	176518	182077	210153	18. Autres actifs
Liabilities											**Passif**
19. Capital & reserves	35218	39452	42328	43926	41788	42422	42934	49605	68639	70128	19. Capital et réserves
20. Borrowing from Central bank (1)	..	..	..	..	..	..	..	..	..	..	20. Emprunts auprès de la Banque centrale (1)
21. Interbank deposits	128867	157226	147503	160358	209022	284892	407619	487461	449483	433948	21. Dépôts interbancaires
22. Non-bank deposits	303465	314050	335948	341877	404538	458373	535838	601465	490790	528741	22. Dépôts non bancaires
23. Bonds	59262	53765	52501	55074	56093	69762	66065	72334	67970	96540	23. Obligations
24. Other liabilities	40470	47347	43709	129351	157928	265783	321092	293891	263427	286626	24. Autres engagements
Balance sheet total											**Total du bilan**
25. End-year total	567281	611841	621989	730587	869370	1121233	1373548	1504760	1340310	1415981	25. En fin d'exercice
26. Average total	555234	589561	616915	676288	799979	995302	1247391	1439154	1422535	1378146	26. Moyen

SWITZERLAND

Large commercial banks

Million Swiss francs

	1992	1993	1994	1995	1996	1997	1998	1999	2000	2001
Memorandum items										
27. Short-term securities	26889	28279	30596	37617	39677	59849	45205	96879	88345	84418
28. Bonds	33756	53544	48148	57070	81185	97469	138450	124829	99207	74928
29. Shares and participations	13026	23889	30819	37744	47091	70271	92574	118057	127723	183952
30. Claims on non-residents	282046	308989	299813	386906	514175	735296	976418	1082279	983062	1066428
31. Liabilities to non-residents	248042	266879	266182	346690	456308	662478	887584	970407	916591	1008244
Capital adequacy										
32. Tier 1 Capital	..	..	..	43786	41053	35561	40514	44600	66775	63453
33. Tier 2 Capital	..	..	..	16369	19143	26292	21315	21101	23595	25426
34. Supervisory deductions	..	..	..	12139	12894	11652	10123	14289	28152	31206
35. Total net capital resources	47643	53224	55194	48015	47302	50201	51706	51412	62219	57673
36. Risk-weighted assets	..	..	..	540686	558415	564447	534225	518352	519935	551368
SUPPLEMENTARY INFORMATION										
37. Number of institutions	4	4	4	4	4	4	3	3	3	3
38. Number of branches	969	923	955	943	935	840	778	665	630	604
39. Number of employees (x 1000) (2)	62	61	62	63	64	63	61	59	56	56

1 Borrowing from Central bank (item 20) is included under Interbank deposits (item 21)

2 From 2001 on part time work is weighted in terms of the percentage of time worked (item 39).

SUISSE

Grandes banques commerciales

Millions de francs suisses

Pour mémoire
27. Titres à court terme
28. Obligations
29. Actions et participations
30. Créances sur des non-résidents
31. Engagements envers des non-résidents

Solvabilité
32. Fonds propres de base
33. Fonds propres complémentaires
34. Eléments à déduire des fonds propres
35. Total net des ressources en capital
36. Actifs pondérés des risques

RENSEIGNEMENTS COMPLÉMENTAIRES
37. Nombre d'institutions
38. Nombre de succursales
39. Nombre de salariés (x 1000) (2)

1 Emprunts auprès de la Banque centrale (poste 20) sont inclus sous Dépôts interbancaires (poste 21).

2 A compter de 2001, le travail à temps partiel est pondéré par le pourcentage du temps travaillé (poste39).

SWITZERLAND

Large commercial banks

SUISSE

Grandes banques commerciales

Per cent — *Pourcentage*

INCOME STATEMENT ANALYSIS — **ANALYSE DU COMPTE DE RESULTATS**

	1992	1993	1994	1995	1996	1997	1998	1999	2000	2001	
% of average balance sheet total											**% du total moyen du bilan**
40. Interest income	6.72	5.78	4.87	4.44	3.88	3.94	3.48	2.90	4.42	4.34	40. Produits financiers
41. Interest expenses	5.04	3.86	3.43	3.22	2.74	2.86	2.48	2.01	3.44	3.37	41. Frais financiers
42. Net interest income	1.68	1.92	1.44	1.22	1.13	1.08	1.00	0.89	0.98	0.97	42. Produits financiers nets
43. Non-interest income (net)	1.68	1.95	1.73	1.94	1.99	1.75	1.51	1.61	1.73	1.49	43. Produits non financiers (nets)
a. Fees and commissions receivable	*1.07*	*1.26*	*1.21*	*1.07*	*1.10*	*1.13*	*0.96*	*0.90*	*1.11*	*1.03*	*a. Frais et commissions à recevoir*
b. Fees and commissions payable	*0.05*	*0.05*	*0.04*	*0.05*	*0.08*	*0.08*	*0.07*	*0.08*	*0.12*	*0.12*	*b. Frais et commissions à payer*
c. Net profits or loss on financial operations	*0.49*	*0.55*	*0.33*	*0.61*	*0.61*	*0.52*	*0.15*	*0.51*	*0.63*	*0.50*	*c. Profits ou pertes nets sur opérations financières*
d. Other	*0.16*	*0.19*	*0.23*	*0.32*	*0.36*	*0.18*	*0.47*	*0.29*	*0.11*	*0.07*	*d. Autres*
44. Gross income	3.36	3.87	3.17	3.16	3.12	2.83	2.51	2.51	2.71	2.46	44. Résultat brut
45. Operating expenses	1.76	1.89	1.80	1.83	2.28	1.98	1.30	1.39	1.53	1.51	45. Frais d'exploitation
a. Staff costs	*1.16*	*1.27*	*1.16*	*1.13*	*1.08*	*1.00*	*0.70*	*0.86*	*0.99*	*0.97*	*a. Dépenses en personnel*
b. Property costs	..	..	..	..	..	..	..	..	..	..	*b. Dépenses en immobilier*
c. Other	..	..	..	..	..	..	..	..	..	..	*c. Autres*
46. Net income	1.60	1.97	1.37	1.33	0.85	0.85	1.21	1.12	1.18	0.96	46. Résultat net
47. Provisions (net)	1.02	1.25	0.83	0.82	1.13	0.92	0.54	0.25	0.26	0.41	47. Provisions (nettes)
a. Provisions on loans	..	..	..	..	..	..	..	..	..	..	*a. Provisions sur prêts*
b. Provisions on securities	..	..	..	..	..	..	..	..	..	..	*b. Provisions sur titres*
c. Other	..	..	..	..	..	..	..	..	..	..	*c. Autres*
48. Profit before tax	0.59	0.72	0.55	0.51	-0.28	-0.07	0.67	0.87	0.92	0.55	48. Bénéfices avant impôt
49. Income tax	0.14	0.15	0.10	0.08	0.05	0.00	0.00	0.10	0.10	0.07	49. Impôt sur le revenu
50. Profit after tax	0.44	0.57	0.45	0.43	-0.33	-0.07	0.66	0.77	0.81	0.47	50. Bénéfices après impôt
51. Distributed profit	0.29	0.33	0.32	0.31	0.10	0.31	0.24	0.37	0.27	0.08	51. Bénéfices distribués
52. Retained profit	0.16	0.24	0.13	0.12	-0.44	-0.38	0.43	0.40	0.54	0.39	52. Bénéfices mis en réserve
% of gross income											**% du total du résultat brut**
53. Net interest income	50.04	49.55	45.41	38.48	36.32	38.13	39.74	35.64	36.29	39.52	53. Produits financiers nets
54. Non-interest income (net)	49.96	50.45	54.59	61.52	63.68	61.87	60.26	64.36	63.71	60.48	54. Produits non financiers (nets)
a. Fees and commissions receivable	*31.88*	*32.61*	*38.32*	*33.84*	*35.08*	*40.07*	*38.11*	*35.84*	*40.86*	*41.99*	*a. Frais et commissions à recevoir*
b. Fees and commissions payable	*1.37*	*1.19*	*1.36*	*1.73*	*2.41*	*2.94*	*2.74*	*3.13*	*4.47*	*4.88*	*b. Frais et commissions à payer*
c. Net profits or loss on financial operations	*14.57*	*14.09*	*10.37*	*19.36*	*19.43*	*18.25*	*5.99*	*20.22*	*23.32*	*20.50*	*c. Profits ou pertes nets sur opérations financières*
d. Other	*4.89*	*4.94*	*7.26*	*10.05*	*11.58*	*6.49*	*18.91*	*11.43*	*4.00*	*2.87*	*d. Autres*
55. Operating expenses	52.31	48.96	56.67	57.98	72.91	70.04	51.81	55.27	56.56	61.14	55. Frais d'exploitation
a. Staff costs	*34.58*	*32.91*	*36.62*	*35.89*	*34.69*	*35.16*	*27.87*	*34.23*	*36.34*	*39.20*	*a. Dépenses en personnel*
b. Property costs	..	..	..	..	..	..	..	..	..	..	*b. Dépenses en immobilier*
c. Other	..	..	..	..	..	..	..	..	..	..	*c. Autres*
56. Net income	47.69	51.04	43.33	42.02	27.10	29.96	48.19	44.73	43.44	38.86	56. Résultat net
57. Provisions (net)	30.27	32.37	26.13	25.95	36.16	32.36	21.60	9.94	9.67	16.65	57. Provisions (nettes)
a. Provisions on loans	..	..	..	..	..	..	..	..	..	..	*a. Provisions sur prêts*
b. Provisions on securities	..	..	..	..	..	..	..	..	..	..	*b. Provisions sur titres*
c. Other	..	..	..	..	..	..	..	..	..	..	*c. Autres*
58. Profit before tax	17.42	18.67	17.20	16.07	-9.06	-2.40	26.59	34.79	33.77	22.21	58. Bénéfices avant impôt
59. Income tax	4.26	3.86	3.03	2.43	1.58	0.01	0.15	4.17	3.86	3.03	59. Impôt sur le revenu
60. Profit after tax	13.16	14.81	14.17	13.64	-10.65	-2.41	26.44	30.62	29.91	19.18	60. Bénéfices après impôt
% of net income											**% du total du résultat net**
61. Provisions (net)	63.48	63.42	60.31	61.76	133.45	107.99	44.82	22.22	22.27	42.85	61. Provisions (nettes)
a. Provisions on loans	..	..	..	..	..	..	..	..	..	..	*a. Provisions sur prêts*
b. Provisions on securities	..	..	..	..	..	..	..	..	..	..	*b. Provisions sur titres*
c. Other	..	..	..	..	..	..	..	..	..	..	*c. Autres*
62. Profit before tax	36.52	36.58	39.69	38.24	-33.45	-7.99	55.18	77.78	77.74	57.15	62. Bénéfices avant impôt
63. Income tax	8.93	7.57	6.98	5.79	5.85	0.05	0.32	9.32	8.89	7.80	63. Impôt sur le revenu
64. Profit after tax	27.59	29.01	32.70	32.45	-39.29	-8.04	54.86	68.46	68.85	49.35	64. Bénéfices après impôt

SWITZERLAND

Large commercial banks

Per cent — *Pourcentage*

BALANCE SHEET ANALYSIS — ANALYSE DU BILAN

% of year-end balance sheet total — % du total du bilan en fin d'exercice

	1992	1993	1994	1995	1996	1997	1998	1999	2000	2001	
Assets											**Actif**
65. Cash & balance with Central bank	0.86	0.76	0.72	0.59	0.68	0.62	0.35	0.42	0.34	1.60	65. Caisse & solde auprès de la Banque centrale
66. Interbank deposits	18.21	17.28	16.35	18.31	20.83	25.36	28.24	34.15	29.23	26.98	66. Dépôts interbancaires
67. Loans	62.25	58.23	58.30	47.12	44.36	36.87	34.33	30.59	32.85	31.88	67. Prêts
68. Securities	12.99	17.28	17.61	18.13	20.01	20.87	20.76	23.12	23.99	24.71	68. Valeurs mobilières
69. Other assets	5.69	6.46	7.02	15.84	14.12	16.28	16.32	11.73	13.58	14.84	69. Autres actifs
Liabilities											**Passif**
70. Capital & reserves	6.21	6.45	6.81	6.01	4.81	3.78	3.13	3.30	5.12	4.95	70. Capital et réserves
71. Borrowing from Central bank	..	..	..	..	..	..	..	..	..	..	71. Emprunts auprès de la Banque centrale
72. Interbank deposits	22.72	25.70	23.71	21.95	24.04	25.41	29.68	32.39	33.54	30.65	72. Dépôts interbancaires
73. Non-bank deposits	53.49	51.33	54.01	46.79	46.53	40.88	39.01	39.97	36.62	37.34	73. Dépôts non bancaires
74. Bonds	10.45	8.79	8.44	7.54	6.45	6.22	4.81	4.81	5.07	6.82	74. Obligations
75. Other liabilities	7.13	7.74	7.03	17.71	18.17	23.70	23.38	19.53	19.65	20.24	75. Autres engagements
Memorandum items											***Pour mémoire***
76. Short-term securities	4.74	4.62	4.92	5.15	4.56	5.34	3.29	6.44	6.59	5.96	76. Titres à court terme
77. Bonds	5.95	8.75	7.74	7.81	9.34	8.69	10.08	8.30	7.40	5.29	77. Obligations
78. Shares and participations	2.30	3.90	4.95	5.17	5.42	6.27	6.74	7.85	9.53	12.99	78. Actions et participations
79. Claims on non-residents	49.72	50.50	48.20	52.96	59.14	65.58	71.09	71.92	73.35	75.31	79. Créances sur des non-résidents
80. Liabilities to non-residents	43.72	43.62	42.80	47.45	52.49	59.08	64.62	64.49	68.39	71.20	80. Engagements envers des non-résidents

* See notes on previous pages.   * Voir les notes en pages précédentes.

SWITZERLAND

Other Swiss and foreign commercial banks

Million Swiss francs

SUISSE

Autres banques commerciales suisses et étrangères

Millions de francs suisses

INCOME STATEMENT — COMPTE DE RESULTATS

		1992	1993	1994	1995	1996	1997	1998	1999	2000	2001
1. Interest income	1. Produits financiers	12771	11989	9874	9967	8905	9587	9471	9564	12999	12643
2. Interest expenses	2. Frais financiers	9054	7480	6565	6455	5806	6228	6115	5940	8555	8223
3. Net interest income	3. Produits financiers nets	3717	4509	3309	3512	3099	3360	3356	3624	4444	4420
4. Non-interest income (net)	4. Produits non financiers (nets)	5722	6602	6356	6192	7263	9596	10323	11524	13743	11699
a. Fees and commissions receivable	a. Frais et commissions à recevoir	3916	5063	4959	4659	5500	7104	8131	9264	11594	9755
b. Fees and commissions payable	b. Frais et commissions à payer	332	430	425	436	548	738	852	1002	1304	1115
c. Net profits or loss on financial operations	c. Profits ou pertes nets sur opérations financières	1021	1179	911	1069	1470	1930	2063	2292	2317	1291
d. Other	d. Autres	1117	790	911	900	841	1301	981	970	1137	1768
5. Gross income	5. Résultat brut	9439	11111	9665	9704	10361	12956	13678	15148	18187	16119
6. Operating expenses	6. Frais d'exploitation	5135	5430	5394	5511	5959	6796	6958	7955	9303	9554
a. Staff costs	a. Dépenses en personnel	3246	3415	3412	3477	3646	3957	4225	4830	5632	5686
b. Property costs	b. Dépenses en immobilier	..	..	..	..	..	..	..	..	..	..
c. Other	c. Autres	..	..	..	..	..	..	..	..	..	..
7. Net income	7. Résultat net	4304	5681	4271	4193	4402	6160	6720	7193	8884	6565
8. Provisions (net)	8. Provisions (nettes)	2624	2859	2285	1703	1737	2102	1605	1721	2297	2009
a. Provisions on loans	a. Provisions sur prêts	..	..	..	..	..	..	..	..	..	..
b. Provisions on securities	b. Provisions sur titres	..	..	..	..	..	..	..	..	..	..
c. Other	c. Autres	..	..	..	..	..	..	..	..	..	..
9. Profit before tax	9. Bénéfices avant impôt	1680	2822	1986	2490	2665	4058	5115	5472	6587	4556
10. Income tax	10. Impôt sur le revenu	454	723	536	566	643	852	904	1121	1446	923
11. Profit after tax	11. Bénéfices après impôt	1226	2099	1450	1924	2022	3206	4211	4351	5141	3633
12. Distributed profit	12. Bénéfices distribués	673	1018	862	1039	1203	2157	2460	2643	3154	2337
13. Retained profit	13. Bénéfices mis en réserve	553	1081	588	885	819	1049	1751	1708	1987	1296

BALANCE SHEET — BILAN

Assets — Actif

		1992	1993	1994	1995	1996	1997	1998	1999	2000	2001
14. Cash & balance with Central bank	14. Caisse & solde auprès de la Banque centrale	3046	3267	3150	3331	3454	3587	3655	5935	4976	4625
15. Interbank deposits	15. Dépôts interbancaires	61590	64281	63189	64199	73157	81723	89078	88768	98874	114691
16. Loans	16. Prêts	77108	80898	78090	76700	81899	88643	85328	104695	114441	115857
17. Securities	17. Valeurs mobilières	26448	29945	31201	32428	36581	39463	43760	51250	54168	59002
18. Other assets	18. Autres actifs	8532	8455	8486	9833	12526	15127	14699	15645	18509	18004

Liabilities — Passif

		1992	1993	1994	1995	1996	1997	1998	1999	2000	2001
19. Capital & reserves	19. Capital et réserves	21770	22887	22637	23130	25049	25315	25431	27114	29567	31312
20. Borrowing from Central bank (1)	20. Emprunts auprès de la Banque centrale (1)	..	..	..	..	..	..	..	..	..	..
21. Interbank deposits	21. Dépôts interbancaires	59295	61617	60336	59609	65053	65929	65330	77008	89233	103495
22. Non-bank deposits	22. Dépôts non bancaires	69333	75551	76069	77913	90913	106380	115314	130832	135414	142554
23. Bonds	23. Obligations	13158	11853	10488	9549	8175	7217	6591	6613	7935	8350
24. Other liabilities	24. Autres engagements	13167	14937	14586	16289	18426	23701	23853	24726	28819	26467

Balance sheet total — Total du bilan

		1992	1993	1994	1995	1996	1997	1998	1999	2000	2001
25. End-year total	25. En fin d'exercice	176723	186845	184116	186490	207617	228542	236521	266293	290968	312180
26. Average total	26. Moyen	174479	181784	185481	185303	197054	218080	232532	251407	278631	301574

SWITZERLAND

Other Swiss and foreign commercial banks

Million Swiss francs

	1992	1993	1994	1995	1996	1997	1998	1999	2000	2001		
Memorandum items												*Millions de francs suisses*
												Pour mémoire
27. Short-term securities	6420	4825	6331	6540	7770	8826	8417	13827	10235	16332		27. Titres à court terme
28. Bonds	16689	20368	19548	20536	21021	19700	19897	23160	30804	28994		28. Obligations
29. Shares and participations	3339	4752	5321	5353	7495	10420	15020	13865	12777	13385		29. Actions et participations
30. Claims on non-residents	99193	105648	102717	100443	117911	128448	137994	158437	172436	192351		30. Créances sur des non-résidents
31. Liabilities to non-residents	71069	77797	76145	74396	91159	106148	113473	138032	147374	161418		31. Engagements envers des non-résidents
Capital adequacy												**Solvabilité**
32. Tier 1 Capital	..	..	..	23534	23871	24607	25244	26758	29242	30622		32. Fonds propres de base
33. Tier 2 Capital	..	..	..	2433	2340	2107	2554	3169	4146	5100		33. Fonds propres complémentaires
34. Supervisory deductions	..	..	..	1353	1655	1720	2011	2229	2610	3139		34. Eléments à déduire des fonds propres
35. Total net capital resources	..	..	..	24613	24556	24994	25787	27697	30778	32583		35. Total net des ressources en capital
36. Risk-weighted assets	..	..	..	127210	130947	139605	136796	165348	176129	188381		36. Actifs pondérés des risques
SUPPLEMENTARY INFORMATION												**RENSEIGNEMENTS COMPLÉMENTAIRES**
37. Number of institutions	227	230	226	225	222	214	203	200	204	205		37. Nombre d'institutions
38. Number of branches	592	578	561	564	553	550	509	527	544	551		38. Nombre de succursales
39. Number of employees (x 1000) (2)	27	27	27	26	26	26	27	29	31	31		39. Nombre de salariés (x 1000) (2)

1 Borrowing from Central bank (item 20) is included under Interbank deposits (item 21).

2 From 2001 on part time work is weighted in terms of the percentage of time worked (item 39).

Notes

Other Swiss and foreign commercial banks include Other Swiss commercial banks and Foreign commercial banks.

1 Emprunts auprès de la Banque centrale (poste 20) sont inclus sous Dépôts interbancaires (poste 21).

2 A compter de 2001, le travail à temps partiel est pondéré par le pourcentage du temps travaillé (poste 39).

Notes

Les Autres banques commerciales suisses et étrangères comprennent les Autres banques commerciales suisses et les Banques commerciales étrangères.

SWITZERLAND

Other Swiss and foreign commercial banks

Per cent — *Pourcentage*

INCOME STATEMENT ANALYSIS — ANALYSE DU COMPTE DE RESULTATS

	1992	1993	1994	1995	1996	1997	1998	1999	2000	2001	
% of average balance sheet total											**% du total moyen du bilan**
40. Interest income	7.32	6.60	5.32	5.38	4.52	4.40	4.07	3.80	4.67	4.19	40. Produits financiers
41. Interest expenses	5.19	4.11	3.54	3.48	2.95	2.86	2.63	2.36	3.07	2.73	41. Frais financiers
42. Net interest income	2.13	2.48	1.78	1.90	1.57	1.54	1.44	1.44	1.59	1.47	42. Produits financiers nets
43. Non-interest income (net)	3.28	3.63	3.43	3.34	3.69	4.40	4.44	4.58	4.93	3.88	43. Produits non financiers (nets)
a. Fees and commissions receivable	2.24	2.79	2.67	2.51	2.79	3.26	3.50	3.68	4.16	3.23	a. Frais et commissions à recevoir
b. Fees and commissions payable	0.19	0.24	0.23	0.24	0.28	0.34	0.37	0.40	0.47	0.37	b. Frais et commissions à payer
c. Net profits or loss on financial operations	0.59	0.65	0.49	0.58	0.75	0.88	0.89	0.91	0.83	0.43	c. Profits ou pertes nets sur opérations financières
d. Other	0.64	0.43	0.49	0.49	0.43	0.60	0.42	0.39	0.41	0.59	d. Autres
44. Gross income	5.41	6.11	5.21	5.24	5.26	5.94	5.88	6.03	6.53	5.34	44. Résultat brut
45. Operating expenses	2.94	2.99	2.91	2.97	3.02	3.12	2.99	3.16	3.34	3.17	45. Frais d'exploitation
a. Staff costs	1.86	1.88	1.84	1.88	1.85	1.81	1.82	1.92	2.02	1.89	a. Dépenses en personnel
b. Property costs	..	..	..	..	..	..	..	..	..	..	b. Dépenses en immobilier
c. Other	..	..	..	..	..	..	..	..	..	..	c. Autres
46. Net income	2.47	3.13	2.30	2.26	2.23	2.82	2.89	2.86	3.19	2.18	46. Résultat net
47. Provisions (net)	1.50	1.57	1.23	0.92	0.88	0.96	0.69	0.68	0.82	0.67	47. Provisions (nettes)
a. Provisions on loans	..	..	..	..	..	..	..	..	..	..	a. Provisions sur prêts
b. Provisions on securities	..	..	..	..	..	..	..	..	..	..	b. Provisions sur titres
c. Other	..	..	..	..	..	..	..	..	..	..	c. Autres
48. Profit before tax	0.96	1.55	1.07	1.34	1.35	1.86	2.20	2.18	2.36	1.51	48. Bénéfices avant impôt
49. Income tax	0.26	0.40	0.29	0.31	0.33	0.39	0.39	0.45	0.52	0.31	49. Impôt sur le revenu
50. Profit after tax	0.70	1.15	0.78	1.04	1.03	1.47	1.81	1.73	1.85	1.20	50. Bénéfices après impôt
51. Distributed profit	0.39	0.56	0.46	0.56	0.61	0.99	1.06	1.05	1.13	0.77	51. Bénéfices distribués
52. Retained profit	0.32	0.59	0.32	0.48	0.42	0.48	0.75	0.68	0.71	0.43	52. Bénéfices mis en réserve
% of gross income											**% du total du résultat brut**
53. Net interest income	39.38	40.58	34.24	36.19	29.91	25.93	24.54	23.92	24.44	27.42	53. Produits financiers nets
54. Non-interest income (net)	60.62	59.42	65.76	63.81	70.10	74.07	75.47	76.08	75.56	72.58	54. Produits non financiers (nets)
a. Fees and commissions receivable	41.49	45.57	51.31	48.01	53.08	54.83	59.45	61.16	63.75	60.52	a. Frais et commissions à recevoir
b. Fees and commissions payable	3.52	3.87	4.40	4.49	5.29	5.70	6.23	6.61	7.17	6.92	b. Frais et commissions à payer
c. Net profits or loss on financial operations	10.82	10.61	9.43	11.02	14.19	14.90	15.08	15.13	12.74	8.01	c. Profits ou pertes nets sur opérations financières
d. Other	11.83	7.11	9.43	9.27	8.12	10.04	7.17	6.40	6.25	10.97	d. Autres
55. Operating expenses	54.40	48.87	55.81	56.79	57.51	52.45	50.87	52.52	51.15	59.27	55. Frais d'exploitation
a. Staff costs	34.39	30.74	35.30	35.83	35.19	30.54	30.89	31.89	30.97	35.28	a. Dépenses en personnel
b. Property costs	..	..	..	..	..	..	..	..	..	..	b. Dépenses en immobilier
c. Other	..	..	..	..	..	..	..	..	..	..	c. Autres
56. Net income	45.60	51.13	44.19	43.21	42.49	47.55	49.13	47.48	48.85	40.73	56. Résultat net
57. Provisions (net)	27.80	25.73	23.64	17.55	16.76	16.22	11.73	11.36	12.63	12.46	57. Provisions (nettes)
a. Provisions on loans	..	..	..	..	..	..	..	..	..	..	a. Provisions sur prêts
b. Provisions on securities	..	..	..	..	..	..	..	..	..	..	b. Provisions sur titres
c. Other	..	..	..	..	..	..	..	..	..	..	c. Autres
58. Profit before tax	17.80	25.40	20.55	25.66	25.72	31.32	37.40	36.12	36.22	28.26	58. Bénéfices avant impôt
59. Income tax	4.81	6.51	5.55	5.83	6.21	6.58	6.61	7.40	7.95	5.73	59. Impôt sur le revenu
60. Profit after tax	12.99	18.89	15.00	19.83	19.52	24.75	30.79	28.72	28.27	22.54	60. Bénéfices après impôt
% of net income											**% du total du résultat net**
61. Provisions (net)	60.97	50.33	53.50	40.62	39.46	34.12	23.88	23.93	25.86	30.60	61. Provisions (nettes)
a. Provisions on loans	..	..	..	..	..	..	..	..	..	..	a. Provisions sur prêts
b. Provisions on securities	..	..	..	..	..	..	..	..	..	..	b. Provisions sur titres
c. Other	..	..	..	..	..	..	..	..	..	..	c. Autres
62. Profit before tax	39.03	49.67	46.50	59.38	60.54	65.88	76.12	76.07	74.14	69.40	62. Bénéfices avant impôt
63. Income tax	10.55	12.73	12.55	13.50	14.61	13.83	13.45	15.58	16.28	14.06	63. Impôt sur le revenu
64. Profit after tax	28.49	36.95	33.95	45.89	45.93	52.05	62.66	60.49	57.87	55.34	64. Bénéfices après impôt

SWITZERLAND
Other Swiss and foreign commercial banks

SUISSE
Autres banques commerciales suisses et étrangères

Per cent — *Pourcentage*

	1992	1993	1994	1995	1996	1997	1998	1999	2000	2001	
BALANCE SHEET ANALYSIS											**ANALYSE DU BILAN**
% of year-end balance sheet total											*% du total du bilan en fin d'exercice*
Assets											**Actif**
65. Cash & balance with Central bank	1.72	1.75	1.71	1.79	1.66	1.57	1.55	2.23	1.71	1.48	65. Caisse & solde auprès de la Banque centrale
66. Interbank deposits	34.85	34.40	34.32	34.42	35.24	35.76	37.66	33.33	33.98	36.74	66. Dépôts interbancaires
67. Loans	43.63	43.30	42.41	41.13	39.45	38.79	36.08	39.32	39.33	37.11	67. Prêts
68. Securities	14.97	16.03	16.95	17.39	17.62	17.27	18.50	19.25	18.62	18.90	68. Valeurs mobilières
69. Other assets	4.83	4.53	4.61	5.27	6.03	6.62	6.21	5.88	6.36	5.77	69. Autres actifs
Liabilities											**Passif**
70. Capital & reserves	12.32	12.25	12.29	12.40	12.07	11.08	10.75	10.18	10.16	10.03	70. Capital et réserves
71. Borrowing from Central bank	..	..	..	..	..	..		..	..	..	71. Emprunts auprès de la Banque centrale
72. Interbank deposits	33.55	32.98	32.77	31.96	31.33	28.85	27.62	28.92	30.67	33.15	72. Dépôts interbancaires
73. Non-bank deposits	39.23	40.44	41.32	41.78	43.79	46.55	48.75	49.13	46.54	45.66	73. Dépôts non bancaires
74. Bonds	7.45	6.34	5.70	5.12	3.94	3.16	2.79	2.48	2.73	2.67	74. Obligations
75. Other liabilities	7.45	7.99	7.92	8.73	8.87	10.37	10.08	9.29	9.90	8.48	75. Autres engagements
Memorandum items											***Pour mémoire***
76. Short-term securities	*3.63*	*2.58*	*3.44*	*3.51*	*3.74*	*3.86*	*3.56*	*5.19*	*3.52*	*5.23*	*76. Titres à court terme*
77. Bonds	*9.44*	*10.90*	*10.62*	*11.01*	*10.12*	*8.62*	*8.41*	*8.70*	*10.59*	*9.29*	*77. Obligations*
78. Shares and participations	*1.89*	*2.54*	*2.89*	*2.87*	*3.61*	*4.56*	*6.35*	*5.21*	*4.39*	*4.29*	*78. Actions et participations*
79. Claims on non-residents	*56.13*	*56.54*	*55.79*	*53.86*	*56.79*	*56.20*	*58.34*	*59.50*	*59.26*	*61.62*	*79. Créances sur des non-résidents*
80. Liabilities to non-residents	*40.21*	*41.64*	*41.36*	*39.89*	*43.91*	*46.45*	*47.98*	*51.83*	*50.65*	*51.71*	*80. Engagements envers des non-résidents*

* See notes on previous pages.   * Voir les notes en pages précédentes.

SWITZERLAND
Other Swiss commercial banks

SUISSE
Autres banques commerciales suisses

Million Swiss francs / Millions de francs suisses

INCOME STATEMENT / COMPTE DE RESULTATS

	1992	1993	1994	1995	1996	1997	1998	1999	2000	2001	
1. Interest income	5737	5548	4509	4798	4216	4227	3684	3867	5190	5106	1. Produits financiers
2. Interest expenses	3817	3189	2809	2884	2469	2502	2195	2208	3201	2999	2. Frais financiers
3. Net interest income	1920	2359	1700	1914	1747	1724	1489	1659	1988	2107	3. Produits financiers nets
4. Non-interest income (net)	2574	2934	3042	3021	3353	4819	4644	5353	6338	4913	4. Produits non financiers (nets)
a. Fees and commissions receivable	1874	2318	2422	2195	2558	3347	3581	4102	5141	4409	a. Frais et commissions à recevoir
b. Fees and commissions payable	191	212	229	221	253	320	377	439	594	552	b. Frais et commissions à payer
c. Net profits or loss on financial operations	465	553	414	560	773	1071	954	1271	1261	453	c. Profits ou pertes nets sur opérations financières
d. Other	426	275	435	487	275	720	486	419	529	603	d. Autres
5. Gross income	4494	5293	4742	4935	5100	6543	6133	7012	8326	7020	5. Résultat brut
6. Operating expenses	2400	2467	2502	2604	2758	3125	2925	3511	4125	4133	6. Frais d'exploitation
a. Staff costs	1510	1556	1573	1602	1671	1773	1750	2080	2469	2497	a. Dépenses en personnel
b. Property costs	:	:	:	:	:	:	:	:	:	:	b. Dépenses en immobilier
c. Other	:	:	:	:	:	:	:	:	:	:	c. Autres
7. Net income	2094	2826	2240	2331	2341	3418	3208	3501	4201	2887	7. Résultat net
8. Provisions (net)	1216	1351	1132	829	883	957	581	739	1042	699	8. Provisions (nettes)
a. Provisions on loans	:	:	:	:	:	:	:	:	:	:	a. Provisions sur prêts
b. Provisions on securities	:	:	:	:	:	:	:	:	:	:	b. Provisions sur titres
c. Other	:	:	:	:	:	:	:	:	:	:	c. Autres
9. Profit before tax	878	1475	1108	1502	1458	2461	2627	2762	3160	2188	9. Bénéfices avant impôt
10. Income tax	235	400	290	354	357	444	446	565	665	398	10. Impôt sur le revenu
11. Profit after tax	643	1075	818	1148	1101	2017	2181	2197	2495	1790	11. Bénéfices après impôt
12. Distributed profit	390	608	539	651	749	1443	1571	1634	1749	1280	12. Bénéfices distribués
13. Retained profit	253	467	279	497	353	573	610	563	746	510	13. Bénéfices mis en réserve

BALANCE SHEET / BILAN

Assets / Actif

	1992	1993	1994	1995	1996	1997	1998	1999	2000	2001	
14. Cash & balance with Central bank	1083	1361	1341	1500	1578	1467	1625	2970	2522	2213	14. Caisse & solde auprès de la Banque centrale
15. Interbank deposits	22526	23528	23920	25032	30205	33397	32666	35660	35262	34829	15. Dépôts interbancaires
16. Loans	42436	44418	43969	45241	46831	48862	41940	49552	54801	56310	16. Prêts
17. Securities	12212	12010	12493	14052	14665	16635	16702	25169	28066	24115	17. Valeurs mobilières
18. Other assets	4343	4300	4283	4591	5854	7007	5651	7264	8583	7747	18. Autres actifs

Liabilities / Passif

	1992	1993	1994	1995	1996	1997	1998	1999	2000	2001	
19. Capital & reserves	8574	8607	8601	9110	9918	9923	8993	10154	11027	11730	19. Capital et réserves
20. Borrowing from Central bank (1)	:	:	:	:	:	:	:	:	:	:	20. Emprunts auprès de la Banque centrale (1)
21. Interbank deposits	17215	17087	16927	18536	18899	18744	15876	20123	24831	22153	21. Dépôts interbancaires
22. Non-bank deposits	40147	43370	44920	47280	54148	60597	58534	71600	71213	71251	22. Dépôts non bancaires
23. Bonds	10476	9512	8528	7883	6769	5998	5015	6024	7679	8087	23. Obligations
24. Other liabilities	6189	7040	7030	7608	9399	12104	10165	12714	14483	11994	24. Autres engagements

Balance sheet total / Total du bilan

	1992	1993	1994	1995	1996	1997	1998	1999	2000	2001	
25. End-year total	82600	85616	86007	90416	99134	107366	98585	120615	129234	125213	25. En fin d'exercice
26. Average total	81281	84108	85812	88212	94775	103250	102976	109600	124925	127224	26. Moyen

SWITZERLAND
Other Swiss commercial banks

SUISSE
Autres banques commerciales suisses

Million Swiss francs
Millions de francs suisses

	1992	1993	1994	1995	1996	1997	1998	1999	2000	2001		
Memorandum items												**Pour mémoire**
27. Short-term securities	4315	2771	4056	4009	4852	5640	4331	7432	4771	3653	27.	Titres à court terme
28. Bonds	5858	7110	6232	7245	6416	6694	7745	10758	15129	10923	28.	Obligations
29. Shares and participations	2039	2128	2205	2797	3212	3958	4356	6728	7914	9312	29.	Actions et participations
30. Claims on non-residents	34826	36166	35054	33769	40515	42911	43580	54183	57434	57100	30.	Créances sur des non-résidents
31. Liabilities to non-residents	26160	27918	27093	26542	31026	33225	30504	41654	43477	43617	31.	Engagements envers des non-résidents
Capital adequacy												**Solvabilité**
32. Tier 1 Capital	..	..	..	9378	8977	9372	8752	10050	10781	11426	32.	Fonds propres de base
33. Tier 2 Capital	..	..	..	1374	1441	1153	1584	2071	2288	2298	33.	Fonds propres complémentaires
34. Supervisory deductions	..	..	..	656	848	931	1091	1339	1445	1402	34.	Eléments à déduire des fonds propres
35. Total net capital resources	..	..	..	10096	9570	9595	9245	10781	11625	12322	35.	Total net des ressources en capital
36. Risk-weighted assets	..	..	..	59351	56503	59914	55094	71407	77407	77275	36.	Actifs pondérés des risques
SUPPLEMENTARY INFORMATION												**RENSEIGNEMENTS COMPLEMENTAIRES**
37. Number of institutions	93	87	86	84	81	80	75	77	76	80	37.	Nombre d'institutions
38. Number of branches	317	289	277	277	262	241	199	220	222	227	38.	Nombre de succursales
39. Number of employees (x 1000) (2)	13	13	13	13	12	12	11	12	14	14	39.	Nombre de salariés (x 1000) (2)

1 Borrowing from Central bank (item 20) is included under Interbank deposits (item 21).

2 From 2001 on part time work is weighted in terms of the percentage of time worked (item 39).

Notes

. Other Swiss commercial banks are sub-group of Other Swiss and Foreign commercial banks.

1 Emprunts auprès de la Banque centrale (poste 20) sont inclus sous Dépôts interbancaires (poste 21).

2 A compter de 2001, le travail à temps partiel est pondéré par le pourcentage du temps travaillé (poste 39).

Notes

. Les autres banques commerciales suisses sont un sous-groupe des autres banques commerciales suisses et étrangères.

SWITZERLAND

Other Swiss commercial banks

SUISSE

Autres banques commerciales suisses

Per cent — *Pourcentage*

	1992	1993	1994	1995	1996	1997	1998	1999	2000	2001		
INCOME STATEMENT ANALYSIS												**ANALYSE DU COMPTE DE RESULTATS**
% of average balance sheet total												**% du total moyen du bilan**
40. Interest income	7.06	6.60	5.25	5.44	4.45	4.09	3.58	3.53	4.15	4.01	40.	Produits financiers
41. Interest expenses	4.70	3.79	3.27	3.27	2.61	2.42	2.13	2.01	2.56	2.36	41.	Frais financiers
42. Net interest income	2.36	2.80	1.98	2.17	1.84	1.67	1.45	1.51	1.59	1.66	42.	Produits financiers nets
43. Non-interest income (net)	3.17	3.49	3.54	3.42	3.54	4.67	4.51	4.88	5.07	3.86	43.	Produits non financiers (nets)
a. Fees and commissions receivable	2.31	2.76	2.82	2.49	2.70	3.24	3.48	3.74	4.12	3.47		a. Frais et commissions à recevoir
b. Fees and commissions payable	0.23	0.25	0.27	0.25	0.27	0.31	0.37	0.40	0.48	0.43		b. Frais et commissions à payer
c. Net profits or loss on financial operations	0.57	0.66	0.48	0.63	0.82	1.04	0.93	1.16	1.01	0.36		c. Profits ou pertes nets sur opérations financières
d. Other	0.52	0.33	0.51	0.55	0.29	0.70	0.47	0.38	0.42	0.47		d. Autres
44. Gross income	5.53	6.29	5.53	5.59	5.38	6.34	5.96	6.40	6.66	5.52	44.	Résultat brut
45. Operating expenses	2.95	2.93	2.92	2.95	2.91	3.03	2.84	3.20	3.30	3.25	45.	Frais d'exploitation
a. Staff costs	1.86	1.85	1.83	1.82	1.76	1.72	1.70	1.90	1.98	1.96		a. Dépenses en personnel
b. Property costs	..	..	..	..	..	..	..	..	..	..		b. Dépenses en immobilier
c. Other	..	..	..	..	..	..	..	..	..	..		c. Autres
46. Net income	2.58	3.36	2.61	2.64	2.47	3.31	3.12	3.19	3.36	2.27	46.	Résultat net
47. Provisions (net)	1.50	1.61	1.32	0.94	0.93	0.93	0.56	0.67	0.83	0.55	47.	Provisions (nettes)
a. Provisions on loans	..	..	..	..	..	..	..	..	..	..		a. Provisions sur prêts
b. Provisions on securities	..	..	..	..	..	..	..	..	..	..		b. Provisions sur titres
c. Other	..	..	..	..	..	..	..	..	..	..		c. Autres
48. Profit before tax	1.08	1.75	1.29	1.70	1.54	2.38	2.55	2.52	2.53	1.72	48.	Bénéfices avant impôt
49. Income tax	0.29	0.48	0.34	0.40	0.38	0.43	0.43	0.52	0.53	0.31	49.	Impôt sur le revenu
50. Profit after tax	0.79	1.28	0.95	1.30	1.16	1.95	2.12	2.00	2.00	1.41	50.	Bénéfices après impôt
51. Distributed profit	0.48	0.72	0.63	0.74	0.79	1.40	1.53	1.49	1.40	1.01	51.	Bénéfices distribués
52. Retained profit	0.31	0.56	0.33	0.56	0.37	0.55	0.59	0.51	0.60	0.40	52.	Bénéfices mis en réserve
% of gross income												**% du total du résultat brut**
53. Net interest income	42.72	44.57	35.85	38.78	34.25	26.35	24.28	23.66	23.88	30.01	53.	Produits financiers nets
54. Non-interest income (net)	57.28	55.43	64.15	61.22	65.75	73.65	75.72	76.34	76.12	69.99	54.	Produits non financiers (nets)
a. Fees and commissions receivable	41.70	43.79	51.08	44.48	50.16	51.15	58.39	58.50	61.75	62.81		a. Frais et commissions à recevoir
b. Fees and commissions payable	4.25	4.01	4.83	4.48	4.96	4.89	6.15	6.26	7.13	7.86		b. Frais et commissions à payer
c. Net profits or loss on financial operations	10.35	10.45	8.73	11.35	15.16	16.37	15.56	18.13	15.15	6.45		c. Profits ou pertes nets sur opérations financières
d. Other	9.48	5.20	9.17	9.87	5.39	11.00	7.92	5.98	6.35	8.59		d. Autres
55. Operating expenses	53.40	46.61	52.76	52.77	54.08	47.76	47.69	50.07	49.54	58.87	55.	Frais d'exploitation
a. Staff costs	33.60	29.40	33.17	32.46	32.76	27.10	28.53	29.66	29.65	35.57		a. Dépenses en personnel
b. Property costs	..	..	..	..	..	..	..	..	..	..		b. Dépenses en immobilier
c. Other	..	..	..	..	..	..	..	..	..	..		c. Autres
56. Net income	46.60	53.39	47.24	47.23	45.90	52.24	52.31	49.93	50.46	41.13	56.	Résultat net
57. Provisions (net)	27.06	25.52	23.87	16.80	17.31	14.63	9.47	10.54	12.52	9.96	57.	Provisions (nettes)
a. Provisions on loans	..	..	..	..	..	..	..	..	..	..		a. Provisions sur prêts
b. Provisions on securities	..	..	..	..	..	..	..	..	..	..		b. Provisions sur titres
c. Other	..	..	..	..	..	..	..	..	..	..		c. Autres
58. Profit before tax	19.54	27.87	23.37	30.44	28.59	37.61	42.83	39.39	37.95	31.17	58.	Bénéfices avant impôt
59. Income tax	5.23	7.56	6.12	7.17	7.00	6.79	7.27	8.06	7.99	5.67	59.	Impôt sur le revenu
60. Profit after tax	14.31	20.31	17.25	23.26	21.59	30.83	35.56	31.33	29.97	25.50	60.	Bénéfices après impôt
% of net income												**% du total du résultat net**
61. Provisions (net)	58.07	47.81	50.54	35.56	37.72	28.00	18.11	21.11	24.80	24.21	61.	Provisions (nettes)
a. Provisions on loans	..	..	..	..	..	..	..	..	..	..		a. Provisions sur prêts
b. Provisions on securities	..	..	..	..	..	..	..	..	..	..		b. Provisions sur titres
c. Other	..	..	..	..	..	..	..	..	..	..		c. Autres
62. Profit before tax	41.93	52.19	49.46	64.44	62.28	72.00	81.89	78.89	75.22	75.79	62.	Bénéfices avant impôt
63. Income tax	11.22	14.15	12.95	15.19	15.25	12.99	13.90	16.14	15.83	13.79	63.	Impôt sur le revenu
64. Profit after tax	30.71	38.04	36.52	49.25	47.03	59.01	67.99	62.75	59.39	62.00	64.	Bénéfices après impôt

SWITZERLAND

Other Swiss commercial banks

SUISSE

Autres banques commerciales suisses

Per cent — *Pourcentage*

BALANCE SHEET ANALYSIS — **ANALYSE DU BILAN**

% of year-end balance sheet total — % du total du bilan en fin d'exercice

	1992	1993	1994	1995	1996	1997	1998	1999	2000	2001	
Assets											**Actif**
65. Cash & balance with Central bank	1.31	1.59	1.56	1.66	1.59	1.37	1.65	2.46	1.95	1.77	65. Caisse & solde auprès de la Banque centrale
66. Interbank deposits	27.27	27.48	27.81	27.69	30.47	31.11	33.13	29.57	27.29	27.82	66. Dépôts interbancaires
67. Loans	51.38	51.88	51.12	50.04	47.24	45.51	42.54	41.08	42.40	44.97	67. Prêts
68. Securities	14.78	14.03	14.53	15.54	14.79	15.49	16.94	20.87	21.72	19.26	68. Valeurs mobilières
69. Other assets	5.26	5.02	4.98	5.08	5.91	6.53	5.73	6.02	6.64	6.19	69. Autres actifs
Liabilities											**Passif**
70. Capital & reserves	10.38	10.05	10.00	10.08	10.00	9.24	9.12	8.42	8.53	9.37	70. Capital et réserves
71. Borrowing from Central bank	..	..	..	..	..	..	..	..	..	..	71. Emprunts auprès de la Banque centrale
72. Interbank deposits	20.84	19.96	19.68	20.50	19.06	17.46	16.10	16.68	19.21	17.69	72. Dépôts interbancaires
73. Non-bank deposits	48.60	50.66	52.23	52.29	54.62	56.44	59.37	59.36	55.10	56.90	73. Dépôts non bancaires
74. Bonds	12.68	11.11	9.92	8.72	6.83	5.59	5.09	4.99	5.94	6.46	74. Obligations
75. Other liabilities	7.49	8.22	8.17	8.41	9.48	11.27	10.31	10.54	11.21	9.58	75. Autres engagements
Memorandum items											**Pour mémoire**
76. Short-term securities	5.22	3.24	4.72	4.43	4.89	5.25	4.39	6.16	3.69	2.92	76. Titres à court terme
77. Bonds	7.09	8.30	7.25	8.01	6.47	6.23	7.86	8.92	11.71	8.72	77. Obligations
78. Shares and participations	2.47	2.49	2.56	3.09	3.24	3.69	4.42	5.58	6.12	7.44	78. Actions et participations
79. Claims on non-residents	42.16	42.24	40.76	37.35	40.87	39.97	44.21	44.92	44.44	45.60	79. Créances sur des non-résidents
80. Liabilities to non-residents	31.67	32.61	31.50	29.36	31.30	30.95	30.94	34.53	33.64	34.83	80. Engagements envers des non-résidents

* See notes on previous pages. — * Voir les notes en pages précédentes.

SWITZERLAND

Foreign commercial banks

Million Swiss francs

SUISSE

Banques commerciales étrangères

Millions de francs suisses

	1992	1993	1994	1995	1996	1997	1998	1999	2000	2001	
INCOME STATEMENT											**COMPTE DE RESULTATS**
1. Interest income	7034	6442	5365	5169	4689	5360	5787	5697	7809	7537	1. Produits financiers
2. Interest expenses	5237	4291	3756	3571	3337	3725	3920	3733	5354	5224	2. Frais financiers
3. Net interest income	1797	2151	1609	1598	1351	1635	1866	1964	2455	2313	3. Produits financiers nets
4. Non-interest income (net)	3148	3666	3312	3170	3910	4778	5679	6171	7406	6786	4. Produits non financiers (nets)
a. Fees and commissions receivable	2042	2745	2538	2465	2942	3757	4550	5162	6453	5346	a. Frais et commissions à recevoir
b. Fees and commissions payable	142	218	197	215	295	418	476	563	710	563	b. Frais et commissions à payer
c. Net profits or loss on financial operations	557	625	496	509	697	859	1110	1021	1055	838	c. Profits ou pertes nets sur opérations financières
d. Other	691	514	475	412	566	580	495	551	607	1165	d. Autres
5. Gross income	4945	5817	4921	4768	5261	6413	7546	8135	9861	9099	5. Résultat brut
6. Operating expenses	2734	2963	2891	2907	3201	3671	4033	4444	5178	5421	6. Frais d'exploitation
a. Staff costs	1736	1859	1839	1875	1976	2184	2475	2750	3163	3189	a. Dépenses en personnel
b. Property costs	..	..	..	..	..	..	..	..	..	..	b. Dépenses en immobilier
c. Other	..	..	..	..	..	..	..	..	..	..	c. Autres
7. Net income	2211	2854	2030	1861	2060	2742	3513	3691	4683	3678	7. Résultat net
8. Provisions (net)	1408	1508	1153	874	854	1145	1024	982	1256	1310	8. Provisions (nettes)
a. Provisions on loans	..	..	..	..	..	..	..	..	..	..	a. Provisions sur prêts
b. Provisions on securities	..	..	..	..	..	..	..	..	..	..	b. Provisions sur titres
c. Other	..	..	..	..	..	..	..	..	..	..	c. Autres
9. Profit before tax	803	1346	877	987	1206	1597	2489	2709	3427	2368	9. Bénéfices avant impôt
10. Income tax	219	323	247	212	286	408	458	557	781	525	10. Impôt sur le revenu
11. Profit after tax	584	1023	630	775	920	1189	2031	2152	2646	1843	11. Bénéfices après impôt
12. Distributed profit	283	409	323	387	455	714	889	1009	1405	1057	12. Bénéfices distribués
13. Retained profit	301	614	307	388	465	475	1142	1143	1241	786	13. Bénéfices mis en réserve
BALANCE SHEET											**BILAN**
Assets											**Actif**
14. Cash & balance with Central bank	1963	1906	1809	1830	1875	2120	2030	2965	2454	2412	14. Caisse & solde auprès de la Banque centrale
15. Interbank deposits	39064	40752	39269	39167	42951	48326	56411	53108	63612	79862	15. Dépôts interbancaires
16. Loans	34672	36481	34121	31459	35068	39781	43388	55143	59640	59547	16. Prêts
17. Securities	14236	17935	18708	18376	21916	22828	27058	26081	26102	34887	17. Valeurs mobilières
18. Other assets	4189	4155	4203	5242	6673	8120	9048	8381	9926	10257	18. Autres actifs
Liabilities											**Passif**
19. Capital & reserves	13197	14281	14036	14020	15131	15392	16439	16960	18540	19582	19. Capital et réserves
20. Borrowing from Central bank (1)											20. Emprunts auprès de la Banque centrale (1)
21. Interbank deposits	42081	44529	43409	41073	46154	47185	49454	56885	64403	81342	21. Dépôts interbancaires
22. Non-bank deposits	29186	32181	31149	30634	36765	45783	56780	59231	64201	71303	22. Dépôts non bancaires
23. Bonds	2682	2340	1959	1667	1406	1219	1576	589	256	263	23. Obligations
24. Other liabilities	6978	7897	7556	8681	9028	11596	13685	12013	14334	14473	24. Autres engagements
Balance sheet total											**Total du bilan**
25. End-year total	94124	101229	98109	96074	108483	121175	137936	145678	161734	186967	25. En fin d'exercice
26. Average total	93198	97677	99669	97092	102279	114829	129556	141807	153706	174351	26. Moyen

SWITZERLAND
Foreign commercial banks

Million Swiss francs / *Millions de francs suisses*

	1992	1993	1994	1995	1996	1997	1998	1999	2000	2001		
Memorandum items												**Pour mémoire**
27. Short-term securities	2105	2054	2275	2531	2918	3185	4086	6395	5464	12679	27.	Titres à court terme
28. Bonds	10831	13257	13317	13291	14605	13007	12153	12403	15675	18071	28.	Obligations
29. Shares and participations	1300	2623	3116	2555	4283	6463	10664	7137	4863	4073	29.	Actions et participations
30. Claims on non-residents	64367	69482	67663	66674	77395	85538	94414	104254	115002	135251	30.	Créances sur des non-résidents
31. Liabilities to non-residents	44909	49879	49052	47855	60132	72923	82969	96378	103897	117801	31.	Engagements envers des non-résidents
Capital adequacy												**Solvabilité**
32. Tier 1 Capital	..	..	..	14156	14894	15235	16492	16708	18461	19196	32.	Fonds propres de base
33. Tier 2 Capital	..	..	..	1059	899	954	970	1098	1858	2802	33.	Fonds propres complémentaires
34. Supervisory deductions	..	..	..	697	807	789	920	890	1165	1737	34.	Eléments à déduire des fonds propres
35. Total net capital resources	..	..	..	14517	14986	15399	16542	16916	19153	20261	35.	Total net des ressources en capital
36. Risk-weighted assets	..	..	..	67859	74444	79691	81702	93941	98722	111106	36.	Actifs pondérés des risques
SUPPLEMENTARY INFORMATION												**RENSEIGNEMENTS COMPLEMENTAIRES**
37. Number of institutions	134	143	140	141	141	134	128	123	127	125	37.	Nombre d'institutions
38. Number of branches	275	289	284	287	291	309	310	307	322	324	38.	Nombre de succursales
39. Number of employees (x 1000) (2)	14	14	14	14	14	15	16	16	17	17	39.	Nombre de salariés (x 1000) (2)

1 Borrowing from Central bank (item 20) is included under Interbank deposits (item 21).

2 From 2001 on part time work is weighted in terms of the percentage of time worked (item 39).

Notes

. Foreign commercial banks are a sub-group of other Swiss anc foreign comemrcial banks.

1 Emprunts auprès de la Banque centrale (poste 20) sont inclus sous Dépôts interbancaires (poste 21).

2 A compter de 2001, le travail à temps partiel est pondéré par le pourcentage du temps travaillé (poste 39).

Notes

. Les banques commerciales étrangères sont un sous-groupe des autres banques commerciales suisses et étrangères.

Per cent — *Pourcentage*

INCOME STATEMENT ANALYSIS — ANALYSE DU COMPTE DE RESULTATS

% of average balance sheet total — **% du total moyen du bilan**

		1992	1993	1994	1995	1996	1997	1998	1999	2000	2001	
40.	Interest income	7.55	6.60	5.38	5.32	4.58	4.67	4.47	4.02	5.08	4.32	Produits financiers
41.	Interest expenses	5.62	4.39	3.77	3.68	3.26	3.24	3.03	2.63	3.48	3.00	Frais financiers
42.	Net interest income	1.93	2.20	1.61	1.65	1.32	1.42	1.44	1.38	1.60	1.33	Produits financiers nets
43.	Non-interest income (net)	3.38	3.75	3.32	3.26	3.82	4.16	4.38	4.35	4.82	3.89	Produits non financiers (nets)
	a. Fees and commissions receivable	2.19	2.81	2.55	2.54	2.88	3.27	3.51	3.64	4.20	3.07	a. Frais et commissions à recevoir
	b. Fees and commissions payable	0.15	0.22	0.20	0.22	0.29	0.36	0.37	0.40	0.46	0.32	b. Frais et commissions à payer
	c. Net profits or loss on financial operations	0.60	0.64	0.50	0.52	0.68	0.75	0.86	0.72	0.69	0.48	c. Profits ou pertes nets sur opérations financières
	d. Other	0.74	0.53	0.48	0.42	0.55	0.51	0.38	0.39	0.39	0.67	d. Autres
44.	Gross income	5.31	5.96	4.94	4.91	5.14	5.58	5.82	5.74	6.42	5.22	Résultat brut
45.	Operating expenses	2.93	3.03	2.90	2.99	3.13	3.20	3.11	3.13	3.37	3.11	Frais d'exploitation
	a. Staff costs	1.86	1.90	1.85	1.93	1.93	1.90	1.91	1.94	2.06	1.83	a. Dépenses en personnel
	b. Property costs	..	..	..	..	..	..	..	..	..	..	b. Dépenses en immobilier
	c. Other	..	..	..	..	..	..	..	..	..	..	c. Autres
46.	Net income	2.37	2.92	2.04	1.92	2.01	2.39	2.71	2.60	3.05	2.11	Résultat net
47.	Provisions (net)	1.51	1.54	1.16	0.90	0.83	1.00	0.79	0.69	0.82	0.75	Provisions (nettes)
	a. Provisions on loans	..	..	..	..	..	..	..	..	..	..	a. Provisions sur prêts
	b. Provisions on securities	..	..	..	..	..	..	..	..	..	..	b. Provisions sur titres
	c. Other	..	..	..	..	..	..	..	..	..	..	c. Autres
48.	Profit before tax	0.86	1.38	0.88	1.02	1.18	1.39	1.92	1.91	2.23	1.36	Bénéfices avant impôt
49.	Income tax	0.23	0.33	0.25	0.22	0.28	0.36	0.35	0.39	0.51	0.30	Impôt sur le revenu
50.	Profit after tax	0.63	1.05	0.63	0.80	0.90	1.04	1.57	1.52	1.72	1.06	Bénéfices après impôt
51.	Distributed profit	0.30	0.42	0.32	0.40	0.44	0.62	0.69	0.71	0.91	0.61	Bénéfices distribués
52.	Retained profit	0.32	0.63	0.31	0.40	0.45	0.41	0.88	0.81	0.81	0.45	Bénéfices mis en réserve

% of gross income — **% du total du résultat brut**

		1992	1993	1994	1995	1996	1997	1998	1999	2000	2001	
53.	Net interest income	36.34	36.98	32.70	33.52	25.68	25.50	24.73	24.14	24.90	25.42	Produits financiers nets
54.	Non-interest income (net)	63.66	63.02	67.30	66.48	74.32	74.50	75.26	75.86	75.10	74.58	Produits non financiers (nets)
	a. Fees and commissions receivable	41.29	47.19	51.57	51.70	55.92	58.58	60.30	63.45	65.44	58.75	a. Frais et commissions à recevoir
	b. Fees and commissions payable	2.87	3.75	4.00	4.51	5.61	6.52	6.31	6.92	7.20	6.19	b. Frais et commissions à payer
	c. Net profits or loss on financial operations	11.26	10.74	10.08	10.68	13.25	13.39	14.71	12.55	10.70	9.21	c. Profits ou pertes nets sur opérations financières
	d. Other	13.97	8.84	9.65	8.64	10.76	9.04	6.56	6.77	6.16	12.80	d. Autres
55.	Operating expenses	55.29	50.94	58.75	60.97	60.84	57.24	53.45	54.63	52.51	59.58	Frais d'exploitation
	a. Staff costs	35.11	31.96	37.37	39.32	37.56	34.06	32.80	33.80	32.08	35.05	a. Dépenses en personnel
	b. Property costs	..	..	..	..	..	..	..	..	..	..	b. Dépenses en immobilier
	c. Other	..	..	..	..	..	..	..	..	..	..	c. Autres
56.	Net income	44.71	49.06	41.25	39.03	39.16	42.76	46.55	45.37	47.49	40.42	Résultat net
57.	Provisions (net)	28.47	25.92	23.43	18.33	16.23	17.85	13.57	12.07	12.74	14.40	Provisions (nettes)
	a. Provisions on loans	..	..	..	..	..	..	..	..	..	..	a. Provisions sur prêts
	b. Provisions on securities	..	..	..	..	..	..	..	..	..	..	b. Provisions sur titres
	c. Other	..	..	..	..	..	..	..	..	..	..	c. Autres
58.	Profit before tax	16.24	23.14	17.82	20.70	22.92	24.90	32.98	33.30	34.75	26.02	Bénéfices avant impôt
59.	Income tax	4.43	5.55	5.02	4.45	5.44	6.36	6.07	6.85	7.92	5.77	Impôt sur le revenu
60.	Profit after tax	11.81	17.59	12.80	16.25	17.49	18.54	26.91	26.45	26.83	20.25	Bénéfices après impôt

% of net income — **% du total du résultat net**

		1992	1993	1994	1995	1996	1997	1998	1999	2000	2001	
61.	Provisions (net)	63.68	52.84	56.80	46.96	41.46	41.76	29.15	26.61	26.82	35.62	Provisions (nettes)
	a. Provisions on loans	..	..	..	..	..	..	..	..	..	..	a. Provisions sur prêts
	b. Provisions on securities	..	..	..	..	..	..	..	..	..	..	b. Provisions sur titres
	c. Other	..	..	..	..	..	..	..	..	..	..	c. Autres
62.	Profit before tax	36.32	47.16	43.20	53.04	58.54	58.24	70.85	73.39	73.18	64.38	Bénéfices avant impôt
63.	Income tax	9.91	11.32	12.17	11.39	13.88	14.88	13.04	15.09	16.68	14.27	Impôt sur le revenu
64.	Profit after tax	26.41	35.84	31.03	41.64	44.66	43.36	57.81	58.30	56.50	50.11	Bénéfices après impôt

SWITZERLAND

Foreign commercial banks

SUISSE

Banques commerciales étrangères

Per cent — *Pourcentage*

BALANCE SHEET ANALYSIS — ANALYSE DU BILAN

% of year-end balance sheet total — % du total du bilan en fin d'exercice

	1992	1993	1994	1995	1996	1997	1998	1999	2000	2001	
Assets											**Actif**
65. Cash & balance with Central bank	2.09	1.88	1.84	1.90	1.73	1.75	1.47	2.04	1.52	1.29	65. Caisse & solde auprès de la Banque centrale
66. Interbank deposits	41.50	40.26	40.03	40.77	39.59	39.88	40.90	36.46	39.33	42.71	66. Dépôts interbancaires
67. Loans	36.84	36.04	34.78	32.74	32.33	32.83	31.46	37.85	36.88	31.85	67. Prêts
68. Securities	15.12	17.72	19.07	19.13	20.20	18.84	19.62	17.90	16.14	18.66	68. Valeurs mobilières
69. Other assets	4.45	4.10	4.28	5.46	6.15	6.70	6.56	5.75	6.14	5.49	69. Autres actifs
Liabilities											**Passif**
70. Capital & reserves	14.02	14.11	14.31	14.59	13.95	12.70	11.92	11.64	11.46	10.47	70. Capital et réserves
71. Borrowing from Central bank	..	..	..	..	..	..	..	..	..	..	71. Emprunts auprès de la Banque centrale
72. Interbank deposits	44.71	43.99	44.25	42.75	42.54	38.94	35.85	39.05	39.82	43.51	72. Dépôts interbancaires
73. Non-bank deposits	31.01	31.79	31.75	31.89	33.89	37.78	41.16	40.66	39.70	38.14	73. Dépôts non bancaires
74. Bonds	2.85	2.31	2.00	1.74	1.30	1.01	1.14	0.40	0.16	0.14	74. Obligations
75. Other liabilities	7.41	7.80	7.70	9.04	8.32	9.57	9.92	8.25	8.86	7.74	75. Autres engagements
Memorandum items											*Pour mémoire*
76. Short-term securities	2.24	2.03	2.32	2.63	2.69	2.63	2.96	4.39	3.38	6.78	76. Titres à court terme
77. Bonds	11.51	13.10	13.57	13.83	13.46	10.73	8.81	8.51	9.69	9.67	77. Obligations
78. Shares and participations	1.38	2.59	3.18	2.66	3.95	5.33	7.73	4.90	3.01	2.18	78. Actions et participations
79. Claims on non-residents	68.39	68.64	68.97	69.40	71.34	70.59	68.45	71.56	71.11	72.34	79. Créances sur des non-résidents
80. Liabilities to non-residents	47.71	49.27	50.00	49.81	55.43	60.18	60.15	66.16	64.24	63.01	80. Engagements envers des non-résidents

* See notes on previous pages.

* Voir les notes en pages précédentes.

Cantonal banks / Banques cantonales

Million Swiss francs / Millions de francs suisses

INCOME STATEMENT / COMPTE DE RESULTATS

	Item	1992	1993	1994	1995	1996	1997	1998	1999	2000	2001
1.	Interest income / Produits financiers	15597	14889	13316	12367	11653	10966	10357	10117	11383	11979
2.	Interest expenses / Frais financiers	12456	11241	10259	9193	8293	7414	6639	6146	7095	7404
3.	Net interest income / Produits financiers nets	3141	3648	3057	3174	3361	3551	3718	3971	4289	4575
4.	Non-interest income (net) / Produits non financiers (nets)	1616	1546	1818	1728	1825	2445	2237	2403	3382	2935
	a. Fees and commissions receivable / Frais et commissions à recevoir	689	874	829	712	909	1197	1407	1563	1838	1581
	b. Fees and commissions payable / Frais et commissions à payer	33	45	52	64	90	131	145	177	241	210
	c. Net profits or loss on financial operations / Profits ou pertes nets sur opérations financières	183	203	175	306	413	510	415	577	504	127
	d. Other / Autres	776	514	866	774	593	869	560	440	1281	1437
5.	Gross income / Résultat brut	4757	5194	4875	4902	5186	5996	5955	6374	7671	7510
6.	Operating expenses / Frais d'exploitation	2312	2430	2594	2529	2966	3556	3563	3864	4996	4309
	a. Staff costs / Dépenses en personnel	1516	1576	1665	1619	1676	1702	1745	1851	2048	2076
	b. Property costs / Dépenses en immobilier	:	:	:	:	:	:	:	:	:	:
	c. Other / Autres	:	:	:	:	:	:	:	:	:	:
7.	Net income / Résultat net	2445	2764	2281	2373	2220	2440	2392	2510	2676	3201
8.	Provisions (net) / Provisions (nettes)	2236	2186	1779	1700	1539	1621	1494	2005	1650	2641
	a. Provisions on loans / Provisions sur prêts	:	:	:	:	:	:	:	:	:	:
	b. Provisions on securities / Provisions sur titres	:	:	:	:	:	:	:	:	:	:
	c. Other / Autres	:	:	:	:	:	:	:	:	:	:
9.	Profit before tax / Bénéfices avant impôt	209	578	502	673	681	819	898	505	1026	560
10.	Income tax / Impôt sur le revenu	46	42	39	36	41	45	57	60	103	97
11.	Profit after tax / Bénéfices après impôt	163	536	463	637	640	774	841	445	922	463
12.	Distributed profit / Bénéfices distribués	418	468	484	501	511	563	596	662	685	585
13.	Retained profit / Bénéfices mis en réserve	-255	68	-21	136	129	211	245	-217	237	-122

BALANCE SHEET / BILAN

Assets / Actif

	Item	1992	1993	1994	1995	1996	1997	1998	1999	2000	2001
14.	Cash & balance with Central bank / Caisse & solde auprès de la Banque centrale	2311	2500	2136	2408	2456	2471	4084	4904	3331	3661
15.	Interbank deposits / Dépôts interbancaires	22311	25069	22802	24134	25162	23211	19556	22883	23185	25798
16.	Loans / Prêts	189022	198362	205616	207095	209883	214577	221178	228487	234723	238203
17.	Securities / Valeurs mobilières	15414	17221	18212	17926	18602	19903	20804	29118	30553	26172
18.	Other assets / Autres actifs	9773	9928	10515	9965	9754	8831	8701	10802	11594	10945

Liabilities / Passif

	Item	1992	1993	1994	1995	1996	1997	1998	1999	2000	2001
19.	Capital & reserves / Capital et réserves	9827	10471	10825	10917	15281	16351	17147	17950	19171	19087
20.	Borrowing from Central bank (1) / Emprunts auprès de la Banque centrale (1)										
21.	Interbank deposits / Dépôts interbancaires	17065	17171	18328	18023	19017	18942	20610	34243	35728	34303
22.	Non-bank deposits / Dépôts non bancaires	117334	127706	131878	133061	139538	144734	149385	152497	152679	154767
23.	Bonds / Obligations	77677	79506	78954	77944	73237	70109	68572	69974	74654	77034
24.	Other liabilities / Autres engagements	16927	18226	19296	21582	18785	18858	18609	21531	21152	19588

Balance sheet total / Total du bilan

	Item	1992	1993	1994	1995	1996	1997	1998	1999	2000	2001
25.	End-year total / En fin d'exercice	238830	253080	259281	261527	265858	268994	274323	296193	303385	304779
26.	Average total / Moyen	233556	245955	256181	260404	263693	267426	271659	285258	299789	304082

SWITZERLAND
Cantonal banks

SUISSE
Banques cantonales

Million Swiss francs / *Millions de francs suisses*

	1992	1993	1994	1995	1996	1997	1998	1999	2000	2001	
Memorandum items											**Pour mémoire**
27. Short-term securities	992	1602	1896	2593	2741	2831	3299	5994	4398	3602	27. Titres à court terme
28. Bonds	12635	13480	14180	13129	13233	12820	12809	13910	15690	14186	28. Obligations
29. Shares and participations	1786	2139	2136	2204	2299	2286	2727	7388	8710	6676	29. Actions et participations
30. Claims on non-residents	10673	12763	11780	13754	15823	15800	17518	22306	18843	22555	30. Créances sur des non-résidents
31. Liabilities to non-residents	5854	5947	6139	7040	8457	10539	12237	25877	24981	25897	31. Engagements envers des non-résidents
Capital adequacy											**Solvabilité**
32. Tier 1 Capital	..	..	..	14445	14912	16293	17089	17896	19079	18991	32. Fonds propres de base
33. Tier 2 Capital	..	..	..	1677	1629	2134	1855	1615	1716	1459	33. Fonds propres complémentaires
34. Supervisory deductions	..	..	..	282	309	400	653	706	1072	1245	34. Eléments à déduire des fonds propres
35. Total net capital resources	11535	12601	13399	15840	16231	18028	18291	18805	19723	19205	35. Total net des ressources en capital
36. Risk-weighted assets	..	..	..	167741	170791	173249	176220	186080	187647	190883	36. Actifs pondérés des risques
SUPPLEMENTARY INFORMATION											**RENSEIGNEMENTS COMPLEMENTAIRES**
37. Number of institutions	28	28	27	25	24	24	24	24	24	24	37. Nombre d'institutions
38. Number of branches	779	826	761	759	737	713	744	754	748	752	38. Nombre de succursales
39. Number of employees (x 1000) (2)	19	20	20	19	18	18	18	18	19	18	39. Nombre de salariés (x 1000) (2)

1 Borrowing from Central bank (item 20) is included under Interbank deposits (item 21)

2 From 2001 on part time work is weighted in terms of the percentage of time worked (item 39).

1 Emprunts auprès de la Banque centrale (poste 20) sont inclus sous Dépôts interbancaires (poste 21).

2 A compter de 2001, le travail à temps partiel est pondéré par le pourcentage du temps travaillé (poste 39).

SWITZERLAND
Cantonal banks

Per cent

INCOME STATEMENT ANALYSIS

SUISSE
Banques cantonales

Pourcentage

ANALYSE DU COMPTE DE RESULTATS

% of average balance sheet total — % du total moyen du bilan

	1992	1993	1994	1995	1996	1997	1998	1999	2000	2001	
40. Interest income	6.68	6.05	5.20	4.75	4.42	4.10	3.81	3.55	3.80	3.94	40. Produits financiers
41. Interest expenses	5.33	4.57	4.00	3.53	3.14	2.77	2.44	2.15	2.37	2.43	41. Frais financiers
42. Net interest income	1.34	1.48	1.19	1.22	1.27	1.33	1.37	1.39	1.43	1.50	42. Produits financiers nets
43. Non-interest income (net)	0.69	0.63	0.71	0.66	0.69	0.91	0.82	0.84	1.13	0.97	43. Produits non financiers (nets)
a. Fees and commissions receivable	0.30	0.36	0.32	0.27	0.34	0.45	0.52	0.55	0.61	0.52	a. Frais et commissions à recevoir
b. Fees and commissions payable	0.01	0.02	0.02	0.02	0.03	0.05	0.05	0.06	0.08	0.07	b. Frais et commissions à payer
c. Net profits or loss on financial operations	0.08	0.08	0.07	0.12	0.16	0.19	0.15	0.20	0.17	0.04	c. Profits ou pertes nets sur opérations financières
d. Other	0.33	0.21	0.34	0.30	0.22	0.32	0.21	0.15	0.43	0.47	d. Autres
44. Gross income	2.04	2.11	1.90	1.88	1.97	2.24	2.19	2.23	2.56	2.47	44. Résultat brut
45. Operating expenses	0.99	0.99	1.01	0.97	1.12	1.33	1.31	1.35	1.67	1.42	45. Frais d'exploitation
a. Staff costs	0.65	0.64	0.65	0.62	0.64	0.64	0.64	0.65	0.68	0.68	a. Dépenses en personnel
b. Property costs	..	..	..	..	..	..	..	..	..	..	b. Dépenses en immobilier
c. Other	..	..	..	..	..	..	..	..	..	..	c. Autres
46. Net income	1.05	1.12	0.89	0.91	0.84	0.91	0.88	0.88	0.89	1.05	46. Résultat net
47. Provisions (net)	0.96	0.89	0.69	0.65	0.58	0.61	0.55	0.70	0.55	0.87	47. Provisions (nettes)
a. Provisions on loans	..	..	..	..	..	..	..	..	..	..	a. Provisions sur prêts
b. Provisions on securities	..	..	..	..	..	..	..	..	..	..	b. Provisions sur titres
c. Other	..	..	..	..	..	..	..	..	..	..	c. Autres
48. Profit before tax	0.09	0.24	0.20	0.26	0.26	0.31	0.33	0.18	0.34	0.18	48. Bénéfices avant impôt
49. Income tax	0.02	0.02	0.02	0.01	0.02	0.02	0.02	0.02	0.03	0.03	49. Impôt sur le revenu
50. Profit after tax	0.07	0.22	0.18	0.24	0.24	0.29	0.31	0.16	0.31	0.15	50. Bénéfices après impôt
51. Distributed profit	0.18	0.19	0.19	0.19	0.19	0.21	0.22	0.23	0.23	0.19	51. Bénéfices distribués
52. Retained profit	-0.11	0.03	-0.01	0.05	0.05	0.08	0.09	-0.08	0.08	-0.04	52. Bénéfices mis en réserve

% of gross income — % du total du résultat brut

	1992	1993	1994	1995	1996	1997	1998	1999	2000	2001	
53. Net interest income	66.03	70.23	62.71	64.75	64.81	59.22	62.43	62.30	55.91	60.92	53. Produits financiers nets
54. Non-interest income (net)	33.97	29.77	37.29	35.25	35.19	40.78	37.57	37.70	44.09	39.08	54. Produits non financiers (nets)
a. Fees and commissions receivable	14.48	16.83	17.01	14.52	17.53	19.96	23.63	24.52	23.96	21.05	a. Frais et commissions à recevoir
b. Fees and commissions payable	0.69	0.87	1.07	1.31	1.74	2.18	2.43	2.78	3.14	2.80	b. Frais et commissions à payer
c. Net profits or loss on financial operations	3.85	3.91	3.59	6.24	7.96	8.51	6.97	9.05	6.57	1.69	c. Profits ou pertes nets sur opérations financières
d. Other	16.31	9.90	17.76	15.79	11.43	14.49	9.40	6.90	16.70	19.13	d. Autres
55. Operating expenses	48.60	46.78	53.21	51.59	57.19	59.31	59.83	60.62	65.13	57.38	55. Frais d'exploitation
a. Staff costs	31.87	30.34	34.15	33.03	32.32	28.39	29.30	29.04	26.70	27.64	a. Dépenses en personnel
b. Property costs	..	..	..	..	..	..	..	..	..	..	b. Dépenses en immobilier
c. Other	..	..	..	..	..	..	..	..	..	..	c. Autres
56. Net income	51.40	53.22	46.79	48.41	42.81	40.69	40.17	39.38	34.88	42.62	56. Résultat net
57. Provisions (net)	47.00	42.09	36.49	34.68	29.68	27.03	25.09	31.46	21.51	35.17	57. Provisions (nettes)
a. Provisions on loans	..	..	..	..	..	..	..	..	..	..	a. Provisions sur prêts
b. Provisions on securities	..	..	..	..	..	..	..	..	..	..	b. Provisions sur titres
c. Other	..	..	..	..	..	..	..	..	..	..	c. Autres
58. Profit before tax	4.39	11.13	10.30	13.73	13.13	13.66	15.08	7.92	13.38	7.46	58. Bénéfices avant impôt
59. Income tax	0.97	0.81	0.80	0.73	0.79	0.75	0.96	0.94	1.34	1.29	59. Impôt sur le revenu
60. Profit after tax	3.43	10.32	9.50	12.99	12.34	12.91	14.12	6.98	12.02	6.17	60. Bénéfices après impôt

% of net income — % du total du résultat net

	1992	1993	1994	1995	1996	1997	1998	1999	2000	2001	
61. Provisions (net)	91.45	79.09	77.99	71.64	69.32	66.43	62.46	79.88	61.66	82.51	61. Provisions (nettes)
a. Provisions on loans	..	..	..	..	..	..	..	..	..	..	a. Provisions sur prêts
b. Provisions on securities	..	..	..	..	..	..	..	..	..	..	b. Provisions sur titres
c. Other	..	..	..	..	..	..	..	..	..	..	c. Autres
62. Profit before tax	8.55	20.91	22.01	28.36	30.68	33.57	37.54	20.12	38.34	17.49	62. Bénéfices avant impôt
63. Income tax	1.88	1.52	1.71	1.52	1.85	1.84	2.38	2.39	3.85	3.03	63. Impôt sur le revenu
64. Profit after tax	6.67	19.39	20.30	26.84	28.83	31.72	35.16	17.73	34.45	14.46	64. Bénéfices après impôt

SWITZERLAND
Cantonal banks

SUISSE
Banques cantonales

Per cent — *Pourcentage*

BALANCE SHEET ANALYSIS — **ANALYSE DU BILAN**

% of year-end balance sheet total — **% du total du bilan en fin d'exercice**

	1992	1993	1994	1995	1996	1997	1998	1999	2000	2001	
Assets											**Actif**
65. Cash & balance with Central bank	0.97	0.99	0.82	0.92	0.92	0.92	1.49	1.66	1.10	1.20	65. Caisse & solde auprès de la Banque centrale
66. Interbank deposits	9.34	9.91	8.79	9.23	9.46	8.63	7.13	7.73	7.64	8.46	66. Dépôts interbancaires
67. Loans	79.14	78.38	79.30	79.19	78.95	79.77	80.63	77.14	77.37	78.16	67. Prêts
68. Securities	6.45	6.80	7.02	6.85	7.00	7.40	7.58	9.83	10.07	8.59	68. Valeurs mobilières
69. Other assets	4.09	3.92	4.06	3.81	3.67	3.28	3.17	3.65	3.82	3.59	69. Autres actifs
Liabilities											**Passif**
70. Capital & reserves	4.11	4.14	4.18	4.17	5.75	6.08	6.25	6.06	6.32	6.26	70. Capital et réserves
71. Borrowing from Central bank	..	..	..	..	..	..	..	..	..	..	71. Emprunts auprès de la Banque centrale
72. Interbank deposits	7.15	6.78	7.07	6.89	7.15	7.04	7.51	11.56	11.78	11.26	72. Dépôts interbancaires
73. Non-bank deposits	49.13	50.46	50.86	50.88	52.49	53.81	54.46	51.49	50.33	50.78	73. Dépôts non bancaires
74. Bonds	32.52	31.42	30.45	29.80	27.55	26.06	25.00	23.62	24.61	25.28	74. Obligations
75. Other liabilities	7.09	7.20	7.44	8.25	7.07	7.01	6.78	7.27	6.97	6.43	75. Autres engagements
Memorandum items											***Pour mémoire***
76. Short-term securities	*0.42*	*0.63*	*0.73*	*0.99*	*1.03*	*1.05*	*1.20*	*2.02*	*1.45*	*1.18*	*76. Titres à court terme*
77. Bonds	*5.29*	*5.33*	*5.47*	*5.02*	*4.98*	*4.77*	*4.67*	*4.70*	*5.17*	*4.65*	*77. Obligations*
78. Shares and participations	*0.75*	*0.85*	*0.82*	*0.84*	*0.86*	*0.85*	*0.99*	*2.49*	*2.87*	*2.19*	*78. Actions et participations*
79. Claims on non-residents	*4.47*	*5.04*	*4.54*	*5.26*	*5.95*	*5.87*	*6.39*	*7.53*	*6.21*	*7.40*	*79. Créances sur des non-résidents*
80. Liabilities to non-residents	*2.45*	*2.35*	*2.37*	*2.69*	*3.18*	*3.92*	*4.46*	*8.74*	*8.23*	*8.50*	*80. Engagements envers des non-résidents*

* See notes on previous pages.   * Voir les notes en pages précédentes.

Regional and savings banks

Banques régionales et caisses d'épargne

Million Swiss francs / *Millions de francs suisses*

	1992	1993	1994	1995	1996	1997	1998	1999	2000	2001	
INCOME STATEMENT											**COMPTE DE RESULTATS**
1. Interest income	6053	5104	3761	3655	3343	3050	2882	2790	3070	3232	1. Produits financiers
2. Interest expenses	4677	3799	2828	2616	2238	1873	1646	1536	1756	1898	2. Frais financiers
3. Net interest income	1376	1305	933	1039	1105	1177	1236	1254	1314	1334	3. Produits financiers nets
4. Non-interest income (net)	510	467	546	393	432	413	391	421	471	387	4. Produits non financiers (nets)
a. Fees and commissions receivable	259	248	208	186	189	256	271	280	358	285	a. Frais et commissions à recevoir
b. Fees and commissions payable	8	8	6	10	13	19	22	26	33	27	b. Frais et commissions à payer
c. Net profits or loss on financial operations	56	55	43	51	74	81	60	67	78	49	c. Profits ou pertes nets sur opérations financières
d. Other	203	172	300	166	182	95	82	100	67	80	d. Autres
5. Gross income	1886	1772	1479	1432	1536	1590	1627	1675	1784	1721	5. Résultat brut
6. Operating expenses	871	796	672	672	799	834	865	888	944	993	6. Frais d'exploitation
a. Staff costs	558	500	424	427	431	442	437	451	489	512	a. Dépenses en personnel
b. Property costs	:	:	:	:	:	:	:	:	:	:	b. Dépenses en immobilier
c. Other	:	:	:	:	:	:	:	:	:	:	c. Autres
7. Net income	1015	976	807	760	737	756	762	787	841	728	7. Résultat net
8. Provisions (net)	704	662	726	476	465	431	407	388	363	287	8. Provisions (nettes)
a. Provisions on loans	:	:	:	:	:	:	:	:	:	:	a. Provisions sur prêts
b. Provisions on securities	:	:	:	:	:	:	:	:	:	:	b. Provisions sur titres
c. Other	:	:	:	:	:	:	:	:	:	:	c. Autres
9. Profit before tax	311	314	81	284	272	326	355	399	477	441	9. Bénéfices avant impôt
10. Income tax	87	83	67	69	63	66	70	85	108	93	10. Impôt sur le revenu
11. Profit after tax	224	231	14	215	209	260	285	314	369	348	11. Bénéfices après impôt
12. Distributed profit	149	128	88	106	109	132	151	153	128	120	12. Bénéfices distribués
13. Retained profit	75	103	-74	109	100	128	134	161	242	228	13. Bénéfices mis en réserve
BALANCE SHEET											**BILAN**
Assets											**Actif**
14. Cash & balance with Central bank	1142	943	759	806	858	856	968	1563	1153	1206	14. Caisse & solde auprès de la Banque centrale
15. Interbank deposits	4185	5516	3723	4027	3055	2460	1852	2229	2892	3727	15. Dépôts interbancaires
16. Loans	75047	67931	59348	60288	60881	61184	62900	64435	65907	66910	16. Prêts
17. Securities	6120	5938	5346	5169	4636	4716	4523	4362	4388	4458	17. Valeurs mobilières
18. Other assets	3447	3132	2473	1974	1841	1535	1476	1476	1468	1381	18. Autres actifs
Liabilities											**Passif**
19. Capital & reserves	4454	4164	3645	3749	4281	4306	4521	4800	4864	5156	19. Capital et réserves
20. Borrowing from Central bank (1)	:	:	:	:	:	:	:	:	:	:	20. Emprunts auprès de la Banque centrale (1)
21. Interbank deposits	3873	2745	2256	2414	2384	2348	3731	5239	5761	5631	21. Dépôts interbancaires
22. Non-bank deposits	43445	43414	38964	40103	41258	42700	43023	43965	43599	44912	22. Dépôts non bancaires
23. Bonds	33125	28362	22782	21603	19591	17663	16885	16654	17971	18643	23. Obligations
24. Other liabilities	5044	4775	4003	4394	3757	3732	3560	3405	3612	3340	24. Autres engagements
Balance sheet total											**Total du bilan**
25. End-year total	89941	83460	71650	72264	71271	70750	71718	74067	75808	77682	25. En fin d'exercice
26. Average total	91341	86701	77555	71957	71768	71011	71234	72893	74938	76745	26. Moyen

SWITZERLAND
Regional and savings banks

SUISSE
Banques régionales et caisses d'épargne

Million Swiss francs

Millions de francs suisses

	1992	1993	1994	1995	1996	1997	1998	1999	2000	2001	
Memorandum items											**Pour mémoire**
27. Short-term securities	109	90	76	71	54	170	246	241	398	270	27. Titres à court terme
28. Bonds	5359	5225	4731	4599	4101	4023	3766	3558	3390	3625	28. Obligations
29. Shares and participations	652	623	539	499	459	328	310	340	361	332	29. Actions et participations
30. Claims on non-residents	738	743	758	694	571	503	485	507	604	834	30. Créances sur des non-résidents
31. Liabilities to non-residents	990	903	808	784	904	951	1122	1315	1378	1518	31. Engagements envers des non-résidents
Capital adequacy											**Solvabilité**
32. Tier 1 Capital	..	..	..	4216	4215	4284	4517	4792	4830	5150	32. Fonds propres de base
33. Tier 2 Capital	..	..	..	601	674	605	539	420	676	587	33. Fonds propres complémentaires
34. Supervisory deductions	..	..	..	47	104	79	78	79	80	80	34. Eléments à déduire des fonds propres
35. Total net capital resources	..	..	..	4770	4785	4809	4978	5133	5426	5657	35. Total net des ressources en capital
36. Risk-weighted assets	..	..	..	45546	44614	43880	44348	44919	46039	46488	36. Actifs pondérés des risques
SUPPLEMENTARY INFORMATION											**RENSEIGNEMENTS COMPLEMENTAIRES**
37. Number of institutions	174	155	135	127	119	117	108	106	103	94	37. Nombre d'institutions
38. Number of branches	602	525	444	427	413	400	394	394	390	387	38. Nombre de succursales
39. Number of employees (x 1000) (2)	8	7	6	5	5	5	5	5	5	5	39. Nombre de salariés (x 1000) (2)

1   Borrowing from Central bank (item 20) is included under Interbank deposits (item 21)

2   From 2001 on part time work is weighted in terms of
    the percentage of time worked (item 39).

1   Emprunts auprès de la Banque centrale (poste 20) sont inclus sous Dépôts
    interbancaires (poste 21).

2   A compter de 2001, le travail à temps partiel est pondéré par
    le pourcentage du temps travaillé (poste 39).

Regional and savings banks
Banques régionales et caisses d'épargne

Per cent / Pourcentage	1992	1993	1994	1995	1996	1997	1998	1999	2000	2001
INCOME STATEMENT ANALYSIS / **ANALYSE DU COMPTE DE RESULTATS**										
% of average balance sheet total / **% du total moyen du bilan**										
40. Interest income / Produits financiers	6.63	5.89	4.85	5.08	4.66	4.30	4.05	3.83	4.10	4.21
41. Interest expenses / Frais financiers	5.12	4.38	3.65	3.64	3.12	2.64	2.31	2.11	2.34	2.47
42. Net interest income / Produits financiers nets	1.51	1.51	1.20	1.44	1.54	1.66	1.74	1.72	1.75	1.74
43. Non-interest income (net) / Produits non financiers (nets)	0.56	0.54	0.70	0.55	0.60	0.58	0.55	0.58	0.63	0.50
a. Fees and commissions receivable / Frais et commissions à recevoir	0.28	0.29	0.27	0.26	0.26	0.36	0.38	0.38	0.48	0.37
b. Fees and commissions payable / Frais et commissions à payer	0.01	0.01	0.01	0.01	0.02	0.03	0.03	0.04	0.04	0.04
c. Net profits or loss on financial operations / Profits ou pertes nets sur opérations financières	0.06	0.06	0.06	0.07	0.10	0.11	0.08	0.09	0.10	0.06
d. Other / Autres	0.22	0.20	0.39	0.23	0.25	0.13	0.12	0.14	0.09	0.10
44. Gross income / Résultat brut	2.06	2.04	1.91	1.99	2.14	2.24	2.28	2.30	2.38	2.24
45. Operating expenses / Frais d'exploitation	0.95	0.92	0.87	0.93	1.11	1.17	1.21	1.22	1.26	1.29
a. Staff costs / Dépenses en personnel	0.61	0.58	0.55	0.59	0.60	0.62	0.61	0.62	0.65	0.67
b. Property costs / Dépenses en immobilier	..	..	..	..	..	..	..	..	..	..
c. Other / Autres	..	..	..	..	..	..	..	..	..	..
46. Net income / Résultat net	1.11	1.13	1.04	1.06	1.03	1.06	1.07	1.08	1.12	0.95
47. Provisions (net) / Provisions (nettes)	0.77	0.76	0.94	0.66	0.65	0.61	0.57	0.53	0.48	0.37
a. Provisions on loans / Provisions sur prêts	..	..	..	..	..	..	..	..	..	..
b. Provisions on securities / Provisions sur titres	..	..	..	..	..	..	..	..	..	..
c. Other / Autres	..	..	..	..	..	..	..	..	..	..
48. Profit before tax / Bénéfices avant impôt	0.34	0.36	0.10	0.39	0.38	0.46	0.50	0.55	0.64	0.57
49. Income tax / Impôt sur le revenu	0.10	0.10	0.09	0.10	0.09	0.09	0.10	0.12	0.14	0.12
50. Profit after tax / Bénéfices après impôt	0.25	0.27	0.02	0.30	0.29	0.37	0.40	0.43	0.49	0.45
51. Distributed profit / Bénéfices distribués	0.16	0.15	0.11	0.15	0.15	0.19	0.21	0.21	0.17	0.16
52. Retained profit / Bénéfices mis en réserve	0.08	0.12	-0.10	0.15	0.14	0.18	0.19	0.22	0.32	0.30
% of gross income / **% du total du résultat brut**										
53. Net interest income / Produits financiers nets	72.96	73.65	63.08	72.56	71.94	74.03	75.97	74.87	73.65	77.51
54. Non-interest income (net) / Produits non financiers (nets)	27.04	26.35	36.92	27.44	28.13	25.97	24.03	25.13	26.40	22.49
a. Fees and commissions receivable / Frais et commissions à recevoir	13.73	14.00	14.06	12.99	12.30	16.10	16.66	16.72	20.07	16.56
b. Fees and commissions payable / Frais et commissions à payer	0.42	0.45	0.41	0.70	0.85	1.19	1.35	1.55	1.85	1.57
c. Net profits or loss on financial operations / Profits ou pertes nets sur opérations financières	2.97	3.10	2.91	3.56	4.82	5.09	3.69	4.00	4.37	2.85
d. Other / Autres	10.76	9.71	20.28	11.59	11.85	5.97	5.04	5.97	3.76	4.65
55. Operating expenses / Frais d'exploitation	46.18	44.92	45.44	46.93	52.02	52.45	53.17	53.01	52.91	57.70
a. Staff costs / Dépenses en personnel	29.59	28.22	28.67	29.82	28.06	27.80	26.86	26.93	27.41	29.75
b. Property costs / Dépenses en immobilier	..	..	..	..	..	..	..	..	..	..
c. Other / Autres	..	..	..	..	..	..	..	..	..	..
56. Net income / Résultat net	53.82	55.08	54.56	53.07	47.98	47.55	46.83	46.99	47.14	42.30
57. Provisions (net) / Provisions (nettes)	37.33	37.36	49.09	33.24	30.27	27.11	25.02	23.16	20.35	16.68
a. Provisions on loans / Provisions sur prêts	..	..	..	..	..	..	..	..	..	..
b. Provisions on securities / Provisions sur titres	..	..	..	..	..	..	..	..	..	..
c. Other / Autres	..	..	..	..	..	..	..	..	..	..
58. Profit before tax / Bénéfices avant impôt	16.49	17.72	5.48	19.83	17.71	20.50	21.82	23.82	26.74	25.62
59. Income tax / Impôt sur le revenu	4.61	4.68	4.53	4.82	4.10	4.15	4.30	5.07	6.05	5.40
60. Profit after tax / Bénéfices après impôt	11.88	13.04	0.95	15.01	13.61	16.35	17.52	18.75	20.68	20.22
% of net income / **% du total du résultat net**										
61. Provisions (net) / Provisions (nettes)	69.36	67.83	89.96	62.63	63.09	57.01	53.41	49.30	43.16	39.42
a. Provisions on loans / Provisions sur prêts	..	..	..	..	..	..	..	..	..	..
b. Provisions on securities / Provisions sur titres	..	..	..	..	..	..	..	..	..	..
c. Other / Autres	..	..	..	..	..	..	..	..	..	..
62. Profit before tax / Bénéfices avant impôt	30.64	32.17	10.04	37.37	36.91	43.12	46.59	50.70	56.72	60.58
63. Income tax / Impôt sur le revenu	8.57	8.50	8.30	9.08	8.55	8.73	9.19	10.80	12.84	12.77
64. Profit after tax / Bénéfices après impôt	22.07	23.67	1.73	28.29	28.36	34.39	37.40	39.90	43.88	47.80

SWITZERLAND

Regional and savings banks

SUISSE

Banques régionales et caisses d'épargne

Per cent — *Pourcentage*

	1992	1993	1994	1995	1996	1997	1998	1999	2000	2001		
BALANCE SHEET ANALYSIS												**ANALYSE DU BILAN**
% of year-end balance sheet total												**% du total du bilan en fin d'exercice**
Assets												**Actif**
65. Cash & balance with Central bank	1.27	1.13	1.06	1.12	1.20	1.21	1.35	2.11	1.52	1.55	65.	Caisse & solde auprès de la Banque centrale
66. Interbank deposits	4.65	6.61	5.20	5.57	4.29	3.48	2.58	3.01	3.81	4.80	66.	Dépôts interbancaires
67. Loans	83.44	81.39	82.83	83.43	85.42	86.48	87.70	87.00	86.94	86.13	67.	Prêts
68. Securities	6.80	7.11	7.46	7.15	6.50	6.67	6.31	5.89	5.79	5.74	68.	Valeurs mobilières
69. Other assets	3.83	3.75	3.45	2.73	2.58	2.17	2.06	1.99	1.94	1.78	69.	Autres actifs
Liabilities												**Passif**
70. Capital & reserves	4.95	4.99	5.09	5.19	6.01	6.09	6.30	6.48	6.42	6.64	70.	Capital et réserves
71. Borrowing from Central bank	..	..	..	..	..	..	..	..	..	..	71.	Emprunts auprès de la Banque centrale
72. Interbank deposits	4.31	3.29	3.15	3.34	3.34	3.32	5.20	7.07	7.60	7.25	72.	Dépôts interbancaires
73. Non-bank deposits	48.30	52.02	54.38	55.50	57.89	60.35	59.99	59.36	57.51	57.82	73.	Dépôts non bancaires
74. Bonds	36.83	33.98	31.80	29.89	27.49	24.97	23.54	22.49	23.71	24.00	74.	Obligations
75. Other liabilities	5.61	5.72	5.59	6.08	5.27	5.27	4.96	4.60	4.76	4.30	75.	Autres engagements
Memorandum items												*Pour mémoire*
76. Short-term securities	*0.12*	*0.11*	*0.11*	*0.10*	*0.08*	*0.24*	*0.34*	*0.33*	*0.53*	*0.35*	*76.*	*Titres à court terme*
77. Bonds	*5.96*	*6.26*	*6.60*	*6.36*	*5.75*	*5.69*	*5.25*	*4.80*	*4.47*	*4.67*	*77.*	*Obligations*
78. Shares and participations	*0.72*	*0.75*	*0.75*	*0.69*	*0.64*	*0.46*	*0.43*	*0.46*	*0.48*	*0.43*	*78.*	*Actions et participations*
79. Claims on non-residents	*0.82*	*0.89*	*1.06*	*0.96*	*0.80*	*0.71*	*0.68*	*0.68*	*0.80*	*1.07*	*79.*	*Créances sur des non-résidents*
80. Liabilities to non-residents	*1.10*	*1.08*	*1.13*	*1.08*	*1.27*	*1.34*	*1.56*	*1.78*	*1.82*	*1.95*	*80.*	*Engagements envers des non-résidents*

* See notes on previous pages. * Voir les notes en pages précédentes.

SWITZERLAND

Loan associations and agricultural co-operatives

Million Swiss francs

SUISSE

Caisses de crédit mutuel et banques mutualistes agricoles

Millions de francs suisses

	1992	1993	1994	1995	1996	1997	1998	1999	2000	2001	
INCOME STATEMENT											**COMPTE DE RESULTATS**
1. Interest income	2504	2466	2265	2411	2401	2390	2377	2402	2915	3240	1. Produits financiers
2. Interest expenses	2070	1978	1799	1854	1707	1539	1434	1388	1699	1904	2. Frais financiers
3. Net interest income	434	488	466	557	694	852	943	1014	1216	1336	3. Produits financiers nets
4. Non-interest income (net)	128	121	131	155	185	190	211	255	311	279	4. Produits non financiers (nets)
a. Fees and commissions receivable	38	43	50	57	41	64	88	107	164	135	a. Frais et commissions à recevoir
b. Fees and commissions payable	3	5	8	12	8	18	25	28	11	9	b. Frais et commissions à payer
c. Net profits or loss on financial operations	12	12	13	13	21	16	21	28	53	52	c. Profits ou pertes nets sur opérations financières
d. Other	82	71	76	96	132	128	127	148	106	101	d. Autres
5. Gross income	562	609	597	712	879	1041	1154	1269	1527	1615	5. Résultat brut
6. Operating expenses	325	359	380	415	464	525	580	655	837	947	6. Frais d'exploitation
a. Staff costs	173	187	197	211	233	259	292	330	493	556	a. Dépenses en personnel
b. Property costs	:	:	:	:	:	:	:	:	:	:	b. Dépenses en immobilier
c. Other	:	:	:	:	:	:	:	:	:	:	c. Autres
7. Net income	237	250	217	297	415	516	574	614	690	668	7. Résultat net
8. Provisions (net)	172	179	143	218	312	390	435	451	199	305	8. Provisions (nettes)
a. Provisions on loans	:	:	:	:	:	:	:	:	:	:	a. Provisions sur prêts
b. Provisions on securities	:	:	:	:	:	:	:	:	:	:	b. Provisions sur titres
c. Other	:	:	:	:	:	:	:	:	:	:	c. Autres
9. Profit before tax	65	71	74	79	103	126	140	163	491	363	9. Bénéfices avant impôt
10. Income tax	21	24	27	27	42	55	61	74	142	27	10. Impôt sur le revenu
11. Profit after tax	44	47	47	52	61	71	79	89	349	336	11. Bénéfices après impôt
12. Distributed profit	5	6	6	7	8	8	10	11	12	14	12. Bénéfices distribués
13. Retained profit	39	41	41	45	53	63	69	78	337	322	13. Bénéfices mis en réserve
BALANCE SHEET											**BILAN**
Assets											**Actif**
14. Cash & balance with Central bank	431	482	472	541	590	730	771	1044	904	1036	14. Caisse & solde auprès de la Banque centrale
15. Interbank deposits	4967	5351	4817	5442	5154	5022	5157	5537	4544	5463	15. Dépôts interbancaires
16. Loans	32429	35145	38831	42157	46020	49972	54007	57406	66281	70821	16. Prêts
17. Securities	244	244	257	265	267	337	343	351	3378	3196	17. Valeurs mobilières
18. Other assets	1368	1356	1369	1462	1311	1235	1253	1219	2034	1893	18. Autres actifs
Liabilities											**Passif**
19. Capital & reserves	964	1019	1067	1139	1214	1292	1386	1490	3521	3881	19. Capital et réserves
20. Borrowing from Central bank (1)	:	:	:	:	:	:	:	:	:	:	20. Emprunts auprès de la Banque centrale (1)
21. Interbank deposits	2273	2434	2816	2844	2790	3206	4189	4967	6267	6127	21. Dépôts interbancaires
22. Non-bank deposits	23487	27537	30919	34198	37651	40799	43277	46188	49190	52893	22. Dépôts non bancaires
23. Bonds	11229	10116	9584	10175	10004	10141	10598	10594	16007	17320	23. Obligations
24. Other liabilities	1485	1474	1360	1511	1684	1858	2082	2317	2158	2188	24. Autres engagements
Balance sheet total											**Total du bilan**
25. End-year total	39438	42579	45747	49868	53343	57296	61530	65558	77142	82409	25. En fin d'exercice
26. Average total	38157	41009	44163	47808	51606	55320	59413	63544	71350	79776	26. Moyen

SWITZERLAND

SUISSE

Loan associations and agricultural co-operatives

Caisses de crédit mutuel et banques mutualistes agricoles

Million Swiss francs / *Millions de francs suisses*

	1992	1993	1994	1995	1996	1997	1998	1999	2000	2001	
Memorandum items											**Pour mémoire**
27. Short-term securities	28	25	27	31	28	29	21	18	33	25	27. Titres à court terme
28. Bonds	20	16	11	12	11	13	12	10	3120	2910	28. Obligations
29. Shares and participations	197	203	219	222	225	227	228	232	87	124	29. Actions et participations
30. Claims on non-residents	..	..	..	..	..	24	29	33	2381	2712	30. Créances sur des non-résidents
31. Liabilities to non-residents	..	..	..	..	..	438	561	676	3260	3631	31. Engagements envers des non-résidents
Capital adequacy											**Solvabilité**
32. Tier 1 Capital	..	..	..	1671	2212	2515	2827	3203	3507	3916	32. Fonds propres de base
33. Tier 2 Capital	..	..	..	912	1106	1258	1414	1601	1754	1958	33. Fonds propres complémentaires
34. Supervisory deductions	..	..	..	0	16	18	29	26	78	96	34. Eléments à déduire des fonds propres
35. Total net capital resources	..	..	..	2584	3301	3756	4212	4778	5184	5778	35. Total net des ressources en capital
36. Risk-weighted assets	..	..	..	31272	32610	35279	37930	40141	43043	44909	36. Actifs pondérés des risques
SUPPLEMENTARY INFORMATION											**RENSEIGNEMENTS COMPLEMENTAIRES**
37. Number of institutions	2	2	1	1	1	1	1	1	1	1	37. Nombre d'institutions
38. Number of branches	1169	1139	1086	1034	962	892	722	582	537	519	38. Nombre de succursales
39. Number of employees (x 1000) (2)	3	3	3	3	3	3	3	4	5	5	39. Nombre de salariés (x 1000) (2)

1 Borrowing from Central bank (item 20) is included under Interbank deposits (item 21)

2 From 2001 on part time work is weighted in terms of the percentage of time worked (item 39).

1 Emprunts auprès de la Banque centrale (poste 20) sont inclus sous Dépôts interbancaires (poste 21).

2 A compter de 2001, le travail à temps partiel est pondéré par le pourcentage du temps travaillé (poste 39).

292

SWITZERLAND / SUISSE

Loan associations and agricultural co-operatives / Caisses de crédit mutuel et banques mutualistes agricoles

Per cent / Pourcentage

INCOME STATEMENT ANALYSIS / ANALYSE DU COMPTE DE RESULTATS

		1992	1993	1994	1995	1996	1997	1998	1999	2000	2001		
% of average balance sheet total												**% du total moyen du bilan**	
40.	Interest income	6.56	6.01	5.13	5.04	4.65	4.32	4.00	3.78	4.09	4.06	Produits financiers	40.
41.	Interest expenses	5.42	4.82	4.07	3.88	3.31	2.78	2.41	2.18	2.38	2.39	Frais financiers	41.
42.	Net interest income	1.14	1.19	1.06	1.17	1.34	1.54	1.59	1.60	1.70	1.67	Produits financiers nets	42.
43.	Non-interest income (net)	0.34	0.30	0.30	0.32	0.36	0.34	0.36	0.40	0.44	0.35	Produits non financiers (nets)	43.
	a. Fees and commissions receivable	0.10	0.10	0.11	0.12	0.08	0.12	0.15	0.17	0.23	0.17	*a. Frais et commissions à recevoir*	
	b. Fees and commissions payable	0.01	0.01	0.02	0.03	0.02	0.03	0.04	0.04	0.02	0.01	*b. Frais et commissions à payer*	
	c. Net profits or loss on financial operations	0.03	0.03	0.03	0.03	0.04	0.03	0.04	0.04	0.07	0.07	*c. Profits ou pertes nets sur opérations financières*	
	d. Other	0.21	0.17	0.17	0.20	0.26	0.23	0.21	0.23	0.15	0.13	*d. Autres*	
44.	Gross income	1.47	1.49	1.35	1.49	1.70	1.88	1.94	2.00	2.14	2.02	Résultat brut	44.
45.	Operating expenses	0.85	0.88	0.86	0.87	0.90	0.95	0.98	1.03	1.17	1.19	Frais d'exploitation	45.
	a. Staff costs	0.45	0.46	0.45	0.44	0.45	0.47	0.49	0.52	0.69	0.70	*a. Dépenses en personnel*	
	b. Property costs	..	..	..	..	..	..	..	..	..	..	*b. Dépenses en immobilier*	
	c. Other											*c. Autres*	
46.	Net income	0.62	0.61	0.49	0.62	0.80	0.93	0.97	0.97	0.97	0.84	Résultat net	46.
47.	Provisions (net)	0.45	0.44	0.32	0.46	0.60	0.70	0.73	0.71	0.28	0.38	Provisions (nettes)	47.
	a. Provisions on loans	..	..	..	..	..	..	..	..			*a. Provisions sur prêts*	
	b. Provisions on securities	..	..	..	..	..	..	..	..			*b. Provisions sur titres*	
	c. Other	..	..	..	..	..	..	..	..			*c. Autres*	
48.	Profit before tax	0.17	0.17	0.17	0.17	0.20	0.23	0.24	0.26	0.69	0.46	Bénéfices avant impôt	48.
49.	Income tax	0.06	0.06	0.06	0.06	0.08	0.10	0.10	0.12	0.20	0.03	Impôt sur le revenu	49.
50.	Profit after tax	0.12	0.11	0.11	0.11	0.12	0.13	0.13	0.14	0.49	0.42	Bénéfices après impôt	50.
51.	Distributed profit	0.01	0.01	0.01	0.01	0.02	0.01	0.02	0.02	0.02	0.02	Bénéfices distribués	51.
52.	Retained profit	0.10	0.10	0.09	0.09	0.10	0.11	0.12	0.12	0.47	0.40	Bénéfices mis en réserve	52.
% of gross income												**% du total du résultat brut**	
53.	Net interest income	77.22	80.13	78.06	78.23	78.95	81.84	81.72	79.91	79.63	82.72	Produits financiers nets	53.
54.	Non-interest income (net)	22.78	19.87	21.94	21.77	21.05	18.25	18.28	20.09	20.37	17.28	Produits non financiers (nets)	54.
	a. Fees and commissions receivable	6.76	7.06	8.38	8.01	4.66	6.15	7.63	8.43	10.74	8.36	*a. Frais et commissions à recevoir*	
	b. Fees and commissions payable	0.53	0.82	1.34	1.69	0.91	1.73	2.17	2.21	0.72	0.56	*b. Frais et commissions à payer*	
	c. Net profits or loss on financial operations	2.14	1.97	2.18	1.83	2.39	1.54	1.82	2.21	3.47	3.22	*c. Profits ou pertes nets sur opérations financières*	
	d. Other	14.59	11.66	12.73	13.48	15.02	12.30	11.01	11.66	6.94	6.25	*d. Autres*	
55.	Operating expenses	57.83	58.95	63.65	58.29	52.79	50.43	50.26	51.62	54.81	58.64	Frais d'exploitation	55.
	a. Staff costs	30.78	30.71	33.00	29.63	26.51	24.88	25.30	26.00	32.29	34.43	*a. Dépenses en personnel*	
	b. Property costs	..	..	..	..	..	..	..	..	..	..	*b. Dépenses en immobilier*	
	c. Other											*c. Autres*	
56.	Net income	42.17	41.05	36.35	41.71	47.21	49.57	49.74	48.38	45.19	41.36	Résultat net	56.
57.	Provisions (net)	30.60	29.39	23.95	30.62	35.49	37.46	37.69	35.54	13.03	18.89	Provisions (nettes)	57.
	a. Provisions on loans	..	..	..	..	..	..	..	..			*a. Provisions sur prêts*	
	b. Provisions on securities	..	..	..	..	..	..	..	..			*b. Provisions sur titres*	
	c. Other	..	..	..	..	..	..	..	..			*c. Autres*	
58.	Profit before tax	11.57	11.66	12.40	11.10	11.72	12.10	12.13	12.84	32.15	22.48	Bénéfices avant impôt	58.
59.	Income tax	3.74	3.94	4.52	3.79	4.78	5.28	5.29	5.83	9.30	1.67	Impôt sur le revenu	59.
60.	Profit after tax	7.83	7.72	7.87	7.30	6.94	6.82	6.85	7.01	22.86	20.80	Bénéfices après impôt	60.
% of net income												**% du total du résultat net**	
61.	Provisions (net)	72.57	71.60	65.90	73.40	75.18	75.58	75.78	73.45	28.84	45.66	Provisions (nettes)	61.
	a. Provisions on loans	..	..	..	..	..	..	..	..			*a. Provisions sur prêts*	
	b. Provisions on securities	..	..	..	..	..	..	..	..			*b. Provisions sur titres*	
	c. Other	..	..	..	..	..	..	..	..			*c. Autres*	
62.	Profit before tax	27.43	28.40	34.10	26.60	24.82	24.42	24.39	26.55	71.16	54.34	Bénéfices avant impôt	62.
63.	Income tax	8.86	9.60	12.44	9.09	10.12	10.66	10.63	12.05	20.58	4.04	Impôt sur le revenu	63.
64.	Profit after tax	18.57	18.80	21.66	17.51	14.70	13.76	13.76	14.50	50.58	50.30	Bénéfices après impôt	64.

SWITZERLAND

Loan associations and agricultural co-operatives

SUISSE

Caisses de crédit mutuel et banques mutualistes agricoles

Per cent — *Pourcentage*

	1992	1993	1994	1995	1996	1997	1998	1999	2000	2001	
BALANCE SHEET ANALYSIS											**ANALYSE DU BILAN**
% of year-end balance sheet total											**% du total du bilan en fin d'exercice**
Assets											**Actif**
65. Cash & balance with Central bank	1.09	1.13	1.03	1.08	1.11	1.27	1.25	1.59	1.17	1.26	65. Caisse & solde auprès de la Banque centrale
66. Interbank deposits	12.59	12.57	10.53	10.91	9.66	8.77	8.38	8.45	5.89	6.63	66. Dépôts interbancaires
67. Loans	82.23	82.54	84.88	84.54	86.27	87.22	87.77	87.57	85.92	85.94	67. Prêts
68. Securities	0.62	0.57	0.56	0.53	0.50	0.59	0.56	0.54	4.38	3.88	68. Valeurs mobilières
69. Other assets	3.47	3.18	2.99	2.93	2.46	2.16	2.04	1.86	2.64	2.30	69. Autres actifs
Liabilities											**Passif**
70. Capital & reserves	2.44	2.39	2.33	2.28	2.28	2.25	2.25	2.27	4.56	4.71	70. Capital et réserves
71. Borrowing from Central bank	..	..	..	..	..	..	..	..	..	..	71. Emprunts auprès de la Banque centrale
72. Interbank deposits	5.76	5.72	6.16	5.70	5.23	5.60	6.81	7.58	8.12	7.43	72. Dépôts interbancaires
73. Non-bank deposits	59.55	64.67	67.59	68.58	70.58	71.21	70.33	70.45	63.77	64.18	73. Dépôts non bancaires
74. Bonds	28.47	23.76	20.95	20.40	18.75	17.70	17.22	16.16	20.75	21.02	74. Obligations
75. Other liabilities	3.77	3.46	2.97	3.03	3.16	3.24	3.38	3.53	2.80	2.66	75. Autres engagements
Memorandum items											**Pour mémoire**
76. Short-term securities	0.07	0.06	0.06	0.06	0.05	0.05	0.03	0.03	0.04	0.03	76. Titres à court terme
77. Bonds	0.05	0.04	0.02	0.02	0.02	0.02	0.02	0.02	4.04	3.53	77. Obligations
78. Shares and participations	0.50	0.48	0.48	0.45	0.42	0.40	0.37	0.35	0.11	0.15	78. Actions et participations
79. Claims on non-residents	..	..	..	..	..	0.04	0.05	0.05	3.09	3.29	79. Créances sur des non-résidents
80. Liabilities to non-residents	..	..	..	..	..	0.76	0.91	1.03	4.23	4.41	80. Engagements envers des non-résidents

* See notes on previous pages.   * Voir les notes en pages précédentes.

TURKEY
Commercial banks

Billion Turkish liras

TURQUIE
Banques commerciales

Milliards de livres turques

	1992	1993	1994	1995	1996	1997	1998	1999	2000	2001	
INCOME STATEMENT											**COMPTE DE RESULTATS**
1. Interest income	117540	207330	514052	885708	2101034	4808925	10676924	21475809	22185265	45582136	1. Produits financiers
2. Interest expenses	78163	121951	339317	628951	1433562	3344226	7249447	16827693	17544641	30883784	2. Frais financiers
3. Net interest income	39377	85379	174735	256757	667472	1464699	3427477	4648116	4640624	14698352	3. Produits financiers nets
4. Non-interest income (net) (1)	-2471	-14022	-50508	11521	-95019	-11728	-80058	876540	494509	-7178890	4. Produits non financiers (nets) (1)
a. Fees and commissions receivable (2)	22002	47349	279493	329669	783875	1635959	3486701	10089599	13169809	80452309	a. Frais et commissions à recevoir (2)
b. Fees and commissions payable (2)	25086	62359	329816	349996	849730	1883809	4057768	11674340	14227645	86645804	b. Frais et commissions à payer (2)
c. Net profits or loss on financial operations	4886	12131	14938	59403	91560	136275	327449	1972889	771331	-237119	c. Profits ou pertes nets sur opérations financières
d. Other	-4273	-11143	-15123	-27555	-120724	99847	163560	488392	781014	-748276	d. Autres
5. Gross income	36906	71357	124227	268278	572453	1452971	3347419	5524656	5135133	7519462	5. Résultat brut
6. Operating expenses (1)	20146	34504	60869	109526	217151	727099	1598925	3108023	5180704	3967201	6. Frais d'exploitation (1)
a. Staff costs	15507	24943	42159	80914	163073	353052	764183	1375383	2015138	2563364	a. Dépenses en personnel
b. Property costs	1790	3245	6082	14048	27672	29327	66072	137931	246672	535431	b. Dépenses en immobilier
c. Other	2849	6316	12628	14564	26406	344720	768670	1594709	2918894	868406	c. Autres
7. Net income	16760	36853	63358	158752	355302	725872	1748494	2416633	-45571	3552261	7. Résultat net
8. Provisions (net) (1)	2073	6785	21187	28849	62563	90132	589413	1829051	2669352	6270990	8. Provisions (nettes) (1)
a. Provisions on loans	1438	3647	10954	12338	28406	71204	416480	1334938	2141662	5318436	a. Provisions sur prêts
b. Provisions on securities	40	331	92	108	6007	3386	116136	56502	431274	84402	b. Provisions sur titres
c. Other	595	2807	10141	16403	28150	15542	56797	437611	96416	868152	c. Autres
9. Profit before tax	14687	30068	42171	129903	292739	635740	1159081	587582	-2714923	-2718729	9. Bénéfices avant impôt
10. Income tax	2134	6254	8765	11802	25620	180390	495206	1087586	648833	827154	10. Impôt sur le revenu
11. Profit after tax	12553	23814	33406	118101	267119	455350	663875	-500004	-3363756	-3545883	11. Bénéfices après impôt
12. Distributed profit	3848	9907	17719	32854	32269	153805	206973	353618	268204	223068	12. Bénéfices distribués
13. Retained profit	8705	13907	15687	85247	234850	301545	456902	-853622	-3631960	-3768951	13. Bénéfices mis en réserve
BALANCE SHEET											**BILAN**
Assets											**Actif**
14. Cash & balance with Central bank	29766	54533	104892	199906	285441	577679	930460	2017117	2278481	4806514	14. Caisse & solde auprès de la Banque centrale
15. Interbank deposits	85047	201809	316511	590727	1099571	2566086	4367147	8836263	15815770	25601824	15. Dépôts interbancaires
16. Loans	206434	388218	693028	1552477	3469960	7826158	12363852	18528491	29816204	32848125	16. Prêts
17. Securities	60357	112829	218776	421401	1375558	2908041	6019343	15692529	22218182	64814226	17. Valeurs mobilières
18. Other assets	128810	216203	521056	1038898	2174259	4457829	11407172	23608264	29324445	35717221	18. Autres actifs
Liabilities											**Passif**
19. Capital & reserves	23960	46326	83617	164774	340722	1600329	2976309	3582937	6070605	15183331	19. Capital et réserves
20. Borrowing from Central bank	8003	16969	12319	12303	8619	63771	164235	320247	588288	184011	20. Emprunts auprès de la Banque centrale
21. Interbank deposits	20435	78412	50306	181551	491220	3301434	6115906	13207230	23462114	22196068	21. Dépôts interbancaires
22. Non-bank deposits	285234	466751	1224806	2486483	5653896	11374578	21774578	43378444	58900061	109512216	22. Dépôts non bancaires
23. Bonds	6187	24525	16615	39686	28998	176314	172796	214594	221172	447125	23. Obligations
24. Other liabilities	166595	340609	466600	918612	1881334	1819575	3884150	7979212	10210842	16265158	24. Autres engagements
Balance sheet total											**Total du bilan**
25. End-year total	510414	973592	1854263	3803409	8404789	18335793	35087974	68682664	99453082	163787909	25. En fin d'exercice
26. Average total	390186	742003	1413928	2828836	6104099	13370291	26711884	51885319	84067873	131620496	26. Moyen

TURKEY
Commercial banks

TURQUE
Banques commerciales

Billion Turkish liras — *Milliards de livres turques*

	1992	1993	1994	1995	1996	1997	1998	1999	2000	2001	
Memorandum items											**Pour mémoire**
27. Short-term securities (3)	..	..	..	..	..	674401	1718503	1659651	985546	5041831	27. Titres à court terme (3)
28. Bonds	41965	90302	106754	209567	720312	1943489	3639491	11399036	16426497	59575497	28. Obligations
29. Shares and participations	11096	18116	34325	59410	123881	290152	661343	2633840	4806131	5238729	29. Actions et participations
30. Claims on non-residents	81980	162573	393540	678256	1600055	2491477	4210584	9754002	10746512	21077048	30. Créances sur des non-résidents
31. Liabilities to non-residents	55466	144014	126322	329517	936479	3014155	4978251	10556681	15384778	21102494	31. Engagements envers des non-résidents
Capital adequacy											**Solvabilité**
32. Tier 1 Capital	..	64589	107703	256125	575104	1278674	2326586	2426692	3011597	10933465	32. Fonds propres de base
33. Tier 2 Capital	..	10769	21804	83170	162040	301347	662755	1250773	4307682	3870408	33. Fonds propres complémentaires
34. Supervisory deductions	..	6096	14874	31069	79071	197551	508451	1310900	2219656	2642668	34. Eléments à déduire des fonds propres
35. Total net capital resources	..	69262	114633	308226	658073	1382470	2480890	2366565	3788230	11866010	35. Total net des ressources en capital
36. Risk-weighted assets	..	628831	1202608	2365808	5387488	11569773	20321282	33964247	49874833	131719330	36. Actifs pondérés des risques
SUPPLEMENTARY INFORMATION											**RENSEIGNEMENTS COMPLEMENTAIRES**
37. Number of institutions	58	59	55	55	55	59	60	62	61	46	37. Nombre d'institutions
38. Number of branches	6188	6208	6085	6196	6385	6763	7272	7626	7812	6854	38. Nombre de succursales
39. Number of employees (x 1000)	145	142	137	139	141	150	163	169	165	133	39. Nombre de salariés (x 1000)

1   Change in methodology

2   Fees and commissions receivable (item 4.a) includes gains on foreign-exchange claims and operations. Fees and commissions payable (item 4.b) includes losses on foreign-exchange liabilities and operations.

3   The Gold is included in Short-term securities (item 27).

Notes

. The category Commercial banks covers all commercial banks operating in Turkey including foreign branches of domestic banks and foreign banks established in Turkey.

Change in methodology

• Iller Bankasi, although not being a full commercial bank, is included in the data until end-1988.

. Until 1992, the sub-items (a., b., c. and d.) of Non-interest income (item 4), Operating expenses (item 6) and net Provisions (item 8), exclude activities of foreign branches of domestic banks. These activities are included in the total item figure.

1   Changement méthodologique

2   Les frais et commissions à recevoir (poste 4.a) comprennent les gains au titre de créances et d'opérations en devises. Les frais et commissions à payer (poste 4.b) comprennent les pertes au titre d'engagements et d'opérations en devises.

3   L'or est inclus dans les Titres à court terme (poste 27).

Notes

. La catégorie "Banques commerciales" regroupe toutes les banques commerciales en activité en Turquie y compris les succursales étrangères des banques domestiques ainsi que les banques étrangères basées en Turquie.

Changement méthodologique

• Iller Bankasi, bien que celle-ci ne soit pas à tous égards une banque commerciale, est incluse dans les données jusqu'en fin 1988.

. Jusqu'en 1992, les sous-catégories (a., b., c., et d.) des Produits non financiers (poste 4), des Frais d'exploitation (poste 6) et des Provisions nettes (poste 8) excluent les activités des succursales étrangères des banques locales. Ces activités sont incluses dans le résultat total.

Per cent / *Pourcentage*

INCOME STATEMENT ANALYSIS / ANALYSE DU COMPTE DE RESULTATS

% of average balance sheet total / **% du total moyen du bilan**

	1992	1993	1994	1995	1996	1997	1998	1999	2000	2001	
40. Interest income	30.12	27.94	36.36	31.31	34.42	35.97	39.97	41.39	26.39	34.63	40. Produits financiers
41. Interest expenses	20.03	16.44	24.00	22.23	23.49	25.01	27.14	32.43	20.87	23.46	41. Frais financiers
42. Net interest income	10.09	11.51	12.36	9.08	10.93	10.95	12.83	8.96	5.52	11.17	42. Produits financiers nets
43. Non-interest income (net)	-0.63	-1.89	-3.57	0.41	-1.56	-0.09	-0.30	1.69	0.59	-5.45	43. Produits non financiers (nets)
a. Fees and commissions receivable	5.64	6.38	19.77	11.65	12.84	12.24	13.05	19.45	15.67	61.12	a. Frais et commissions à recevoir
b. Fees and commissions payable	6.43	8.40	23.33	12.37	13.92	14.09	15.19	22.50	16.92	65.83	b. Frais et commissions à payer
c. Net profits or loss on financial operations	1.25	1.63	1.06	2.10	1.50	1.02	1.23	3.80	0.92	-0.18	c. Profits ou pertes nets sur opérations financières
d. Other	-1.10	-1.50	-1.07	-0.97	-1.98	0.75	0.61	0.94	0.93	-0.57	d. Autres
44. Gross income	9.46	9.62	8.79	9.48	9.38	10.87	12.53	10.65	6.11	5.71	44. Résultat brut
45. Operating expenses	5.16	4.65	4.30	3.87	3.56	5.44	5.99	5.99	6.16	3.01	45. Frais d'exploitation
a. Staff costs	3.97	3.36	2.98	2.86	2.67	2.64	2.86	2.65	2.40	1.95	a. Dépenses en personnel
b. Property costs	0.46	0.44	0.43	0.50	0.45	0.22	0.25	0.27	0.29	0.41	b. Dépenses en immobilier
c. Other	0.73	0.85	0.89	0.51	0.43	2.58	2.88	3.07	3.47	0.66	c. Autres
46. Net income	4.30	4.97	4.48	5.61	5.82	5.43	6.55	4.66	-0.05	2.70	46. Résultat net
47. Provisions (net)	0.53	0.91	1.50	1.02	1.02	0.67	2.21	3.53	3.18	4.76	47. Provisions (nettes)
a. Provisions on loans	0.37	0.49	0.77	0.44	0.47	0.53	1.56	2.57	2.55	4.04	a. Provisions sur prêts
b. Provisions on securities	0.01	0.04	0.01	-	0.10	0.03	0.43	0.11	0.51	0.06	b. Provisions sur titres
c. Other	0.15	0.38	0.72	0.58	0.46	0.12	0.21	0.84	0.11	0.66	c. Autres
48. Profit before tax	3.76	4.05	2.98	4.59	4.80	4.75	4.34	1.13	-3.23	-2.07	48. Bénéfices avant impôt
49. Income tax	0.55	0.84	0.62	0.42	0.42	1.35	1.85	2.10	0.77	0.63	49. Impôt sur le revenu
50. Profit after tax	3.22	3.21	2.36	4.17	4.38	3.41	2.49	-0.96	-4.00	-2.69	50. Bénéfices après impôt
51. Distributed profit	0.99	1.34	1.25	1.16	0.53	1.15	0.77	0.68	0.32	0.17	51. Bénéfices distribués
52. Retained profit	2.23	1.87	1.11	3.01	3.85	2.26	1.71	-1.65	-4.32	-2.86	52. Bénéfices mis en réserve

% of gross income / **% du total du résultat brut**

	1992	1993	1994	1995	1996	1997	1998	1999	2000	2001	
53. Net interest income	106.70	119.65	140.66	95.71	116.60	100.81	102.39	84.13	90.37	195.47	53. Produits financiers nets
54. Non-interest income (net)	-6.70	-19.65	-40.66	4.29	-16.60	-0.81	-2.39	15.87	9.63	-95.47	54. Produits non financiers (nets)
a. Fees and commissions receivable	59.62	66.36	224.99	122.88	136.93	112.59	104.16	182.63	256.46	1069.92	a. Frais et commissions à recevoir
b. Fees and commissions payable	67.97	87.39	265.49	130.46	148.44	129.65	121.22	211.31	277.06	1152.29	b. Frais et commissions à payer
c. Net profits or loss on financial operations	13.24	17.00	12.02	22.14	15.99	9.38	9.78	35.71	15.02	-3.15	c. Profits ou pertes nets sur opérations financières
d. Other	-11.58	-15.62	-12.17	-10.27	-21.09	6.87	4.89	8.84	15.21	-9.95	d. Autres
55. Operating expenses	54.59	48.35	49.00	40.83	37.93	50.04	47.77	56.26	100.89	52.76	55. Frais d'exploitation
a. Staff costs	42.02	34.96	33.94	30.16	28.49	24.30	22.83	24.90	39.24	34.09	a. Dépenses en personnel
b. Property costs	4.85	4.55	4.90	5.24	4.83	2.02	1.97	2.50	4.80	7.12	b. Dépenses en immobilier
c. Other	7.72	8.85	10.17	5.43	4.61	23.73	22.96	28.87	56.84	11.55	c. Autres
56. Net income	45.41	51.65	51.00	59.17	62.07	49.96	52.23	43.74	-0.89	47.24	56. Résultat net
57. Provisions (net)	5.62	9.51	17.06	10.75	10.93	6.20	17.61	33.11	51.98	83.40	57. Provisions (nettes)
a. Provisions on loans	3.90	5.11	8.82	4.60	4.96	4.90	12.44	24.16	41.71	70.73	a. Provisions sur prêts
b. Provisions on securities	0.11	0.46	0.07	0.04	1.05	0.23	3.47	1.02	8.40	1.12	b. Provisions sur titres
c. Other	1.61	3.93	8.16	6.11	4.92	1.07	1.70	7.92	1.88	11.55	c. Autres
58. Profit before tax	39.80	42.14	33.95	48.42	51.14	43.75	34.63	10.64	-52.87	-36.16	58. Bénéfices avant impôt
59. Income tax	5.78	8.76	7.06	4.40	4.48	12.42	14.79	19.69	12.64	11.00	59. Impôt sur le revenu
60. Profit after tax	34.01	33.37	26.89	44.02	46.66	31.34	19.83	-9.05	-65.50	-47.16	60. Bénéfices après impôt

% of net income / **% du total du résultat net**

	1992	1993	1994	1995	1996	1997	1998	1999	2000	2001	
61. Provisions (net)	12.37	18.41	33.44	18.17	17.61	12.42	33.71	75.69	-5857.57	176.54	61. Provisions (nettes)
a. Provisions on loans	8.58	9.90	17.29	7.77	7.99	9.81	23.82	55.24	-4699.62	149.72	a. Provisions sur prêts
b. Provisions on securities	0.24	0.90	0.15	0.07	1.69	0.47	6.64	2.34	-946.38	2.38	b. Provisions sur titres
c. Other	3.55	7.62	16.01	10.33	7.92	2.14	3.25	18.11	-211.57	24.44	c. Autres
62. Profit before tax	87.63	81.59	66.56	81.83	82.39	87.58	66.29	24.31	5957.57	-76.54	62. Bénéfices avant impôt
63. Income tax	12.73	16.97	13.83	7.43	7.21	24.85	28.32	45.00	-1423.78	23.29	63. Impôt sur le revenu
64. Profit after tax	74.90	64.62	52.73	74.39	75.18	62.73	37.97	-20.69	7381.35	-99.82	64. Bénéfices après impôt

TURKEY

Commercial banks

TURQUIE

Banques commerciales

Per cent / *Pourcentage*

BALANCE SHEET ANALYSIS — **ANALYSE DU BILAN**

% of year-end balance sheet total / % du total du bilan en fin d'exercice

	1992	1993	1994	1995	1996	1997	1998	1999	2000	2001	
Assets											**Actif**
65. Cash & balance with Central bank	5.83	5.60	5.66	5.26	3.40	3.15	2.65	2.94	2.29	2.93	65. Caisse & solde auprès de la Banque centrale
66. Interbank deposits	16.66	20.73	17.07	15.53	13.08	13.99	12.45	12.87	15.90	15.63	66. Dépôts interbancaires
67. Loans	40.44	39.87	37.37	40.82	41.29	42.68	35.24	26.98	29.98	20.06	67. Prêts
68. Securities	11.83	11.59	11.80	11.08	16.37	15.86	17.16	22.85	22.34	39.57	68. Valeurs mobilières
69. Other assets	25.24	22.21	28.10	27.31	25.87	24.31	32.51	34.37	29.49	21.81	69. Autres actifs
Liabilities											**Passif**
70. Capital & reserves	4.69	4.76	4.51	4.33	4.05	8.73	8.48	5.22	6.10	9.27	70. Capital et réserves
71. Borrowing from Central bank	1.57	1.74	0.66	0.32	0.10	0.35	0.47	0.47	0.59	0.11	71. Emprunts auprès de la Banque centrale
72. Interbank deposits	4.00	8.05	2.71	4.77	5.84	18.01	17.43	19.23	23.59	13.55	72. Dépôts interbancaires
73. Non-bank deposits	55.88	47.94	66.05	65.38	67.27	62.03	62.06	63.16	59.22	66.86	73. Dépôts non bancaires
74. Bonds	1.21	2.52	0.90	1.04	0.35	0.96	0.49	0.31	0.22	0.27	74. Obligations
75. Other liabilities	32.64	34.98	25.16	24.15	22.38	9.92	11.07	11.62	10.27	9.93	75. Autres engagements
Memorandum items											***Pour mémoire***
76. Short-term securities (3)	*..*	*..*	*..*	*5.51*	*8.57*	*3.68*	*4.90*	*2.42*	*0.99*	*3.08*	*76. Titres à court terme (3)*
77. Bonds	*8.22*	*9.28*	*5.76*	*5.51*	*8.57*	*10.60*	*10.37*	*16.60*	*16.52*	*36.37*	*77. Obligations*
78. Shares and participations	*2.17*	*1.86*	*1.85*	*1.56*	*1.47*	*1.58*	*1.88*	*3.83*	*4.83*	*3.20*	*78. Actions et participations*
79. Claims on non-residents	*16.06*	*16.70*	*21.22*	*17.83*	*19.04*	*13.59*	*12.00*	*14.20*	*10.81*	*12.87*	*79. Créances sur des non-résidents*
80. Liabilities to non-residents	*10.87*	*14.79*	*6.81*	*8.66*	*11.14*	*16.44*	*14.19*	*15.37*	*15.47*	*12.88*	*80. Engagements envers des non-résidents*

* See notes on previous pages. / * Voir les notes en pages précédentes.

UNITED KINGDOM
Commercial banks

ROYAUME-UNI
Banques commerciales

Million pounds sterling / *Millions de livres*

		1992	1993	1994	1995	1996	1997	1998	1999	2000	2001	
INCOME STATEMENT												**COMPTE DE RESULTATS**
1. Interest income		52004	44836	41577	48897	55421	62079	71026	66285	79153	80235	1. Produits financiers
2. Interest expenses		36550	28463	24970	31135	34459	39282	46934	40421	52090	50392	2. Frais financiers
3. Net interest income		15454	16372	16606	17762	20961	22797	24092	25864	27063	29843	3. Produits financiers nets
4. Non-interest income (net)		11267	13113	12426	13239	13494	14201	15608	17779	20577	23095	4. Produits non financiers (nets)
a. Fees and commissions receivable		..	..	10472	10707	12380	13347	13441	14808	16301	18343	a. Frais et commissions à recevoir
b. Fees and commissions payable		..	..	1097	1254	1557	1982	2077	2459	2787	3398	b. Frais et commissions à payer
c. Net profits or loss on financial operations		..	..	3051	3786	2671	2837	4244	5430	7063	8150	c. Profits ou pertes nets sur opérations financières
d. Other		..	..	..	..	..	..	..	..	..	..	d. Autres
5. Gross income		26721	29485	29033	31001	34455	36998	39701	43643	47640	52938	5. Résultat brut
6. Operating expenses		17621	18622	18599	19757	21394	22515	22433	23812	26459	30379	6. Frais d'exploitation
a. Staff costs		9704	10272	10434	11055	11580	11944	11638	12506	13130	14851	a. Dépenses en personnel
b. Property costs		..	..	4114	4255	4701	5016	4215	5089	6361	7721	b. Dépenses en immobilier
c. Other		..	..	4051	4447	5114	5555	6580	6217	6968	7807	c. Autres
7. Net income		9100	10863	10433	11244	13061	14482	17267	19832	21180	22560	7. Résultat net
8. Provisions (net)		7298	5814	2349	2304	1937	1970	2823	2862	3123	4189	8. Provisions (nettes)
a. Provisions on loans		..	..	..	..	..	..	..	..	..	..	a. Provisions sur prêts
b. Provisions on securities		..	..	..	..	..	..	..	..	..	..	b. Provisions sur titres
c. Other		..	..	..	..	..	..	..	..	..	..	c. Autres
9. Profit before tax		1802	5049	8085	8940	11125	12512	14445	16970	18058	18370	9. Bénéfices avant impôt
10. Income tax		997	1847	2709	3037	3893	3892	4247	5145	5498	5707	10. Impôt sur le revenu
11. Profit after tax		805	3202	5376	5903	7232	8620	10198	11824	12560	12663	11. Bénéfices après impôt
12. Distributed profit		1238	1838	2188	3615	2933	4411	5263	5674	6985	8544	12. Bénéfices distribués
13. Retained profit		-433	1364	3188	2288	4299	4209	4935	6151	5574	4120	13. Bénéfices mis en réserve
BALANCE SHEET (1)												**BILAN (1)**
Assets												**Actif**
14. Cash & balance with Central bank		5191	5252	5152	5614	5771	5959	6224	8798	9070	9145	14. Caisse & solde auprès de la Banque centrale
15. Interbank deposits		87921	102950	113393	111545	121256	143759	140106	139140	148495	160988	15. Dépôts interbancaires
16. Loans		376505	376115	375285	419637	561512	610591	632814	726043	877772	935876	16. Prêts
17. Securities		84290	110735	126055	148818	187550	227836	242425	265898	321160	375540	17. Valeurs mobilières
18. Other assets		92946	95074	102008	120554	138963	157199	177493	182788	273043	299421	18. Autres actifs
Liabilities												**Passif**
19. Capital & reserves		24518	26228	29520	31267	42570	47712	51026	56270	84045	91605	19. Capital et réserves
20. Borrowing from Central bank		-	-								-	20. Emprunts auprès de la Banque centrale
21. Interbank deposits (1)		..	..	123328	131288	130571	142039	148303	159552	198715	219316	21. Dépôts interbancaires (1)
22. Non-bank deposits		476173	493912	379619	420525	548559	604594	627554	682961	807602	859612	22. Dépôts non bancaires
23. Bonds		62101	75112	82619	90451	131452	158998	168228	210110	257255	300171	23. Obligations
24. Other liabilities		84062	94875	106806	132637	161900	192000	203951	213773	281922	310264	24. Autres engagements
Balance sheet total												**Total du bilan**
25. End-year total		646854	690127	721892	806168	1015053	1145343	1199062	1322665	1629540	1780968	25. En fin d'exercice
26. Average total		589603	668491	706010	764030	975230	1088107	1172203	1234358	1388891	1687486	26. Moyen

UNITED KINGDOM
Commercial banks

ROYAUME-UNI
Banques commerciales

Million pounds sterling / *Millions de livres*

	1992	1993	1994	1995	1996	1997	1998	1999	2000	2001	
Memorandum items											**Pour mémoire**
27. Short-term securities	24263	21699	25498	29845	17373	22787	22348	21117	21105	31780	27. Titres à court terme
28. Bonds	..	..	..	..	..	..	..	..	..	:	28. Obligations
29. Shares and participations	..	..	..	..	..	..	..	..	..	:	29. Actions et participations
30. Claims on non-residents	..	..	..	..	..	..	..	..	..	:	30. Créances sur des non-résidents
31. Liabilities to non-residents	..	..	..	..	..	..	..	..	..	:	31. Engagements envers des non-résidents
Capital adequacy											**Solvabilité**
32. Tier 1 Capital	..	..	..	32291	43026	47739	50654	54399	59122	68276	32. Fonds propres de base
33. Tier 2 Capital	..	..	..	23010	25234	27246	28961	37144	44049	49845	33. Fonds propres complémentaires
34. Supervisory deductions	..	..	..	4636	5873	6196	7072	8844	15960	19517	34. Eléments à déduire des fonds propres
35. Total net capital resources	..	..	..	50665	62387	68789	72543	82699	87211	98605	35. Total net des ressources en capital
36. Risk-weighted assets	..	..	..	464098	541409	582568	616622	648437	780519	879732	36. Actifs pondérés des risques
SUPPLEMENTARY INFORMATION											**RENSEIGNEMENTS COMPLEMENTAIRES**
37. Number of institutions	39	37	37	40	44	45	45	41	44	42	37. Nombre d'institutions
38. Number of branches	11751	11445	11075	10601	12070	11863	11501	11271	11427	10899	38. Nombre de succursales
39. Number of employees (x 1000)	401	372	387	382	416	419	409	409	407	437	39. Nombre de salariés (x 1000)

1 Change in methodology
1 Changement méthodologique

Notes

. Commercial banks comprises the world-wide operations of nine major British banking groups:

Until 1996, the Standard Chartered Group was included in the coverage

Change in methodology

. Until 1994, Interbank deposits (item 21) are included under Non-bank deposits (item 22).

. As from 1992, due to revised reporting requirements, balance-sheet data include long-term assurance funds.

Notes

. Les "Banques commerciales" regroupent les activités mondiales des neuf grandes banques britanniques :

Jusqu'en 1996, les activités du Standard Chartered Group ont été incluses

Changement méthodologique

. Jusqu'en 1994, les Dépôts interbancaires (poste 21) sont inclus sous la rubrique Dépôts non bancaires (poste 22).

. A compter de 1992, suite aux révisions du règlement en vigueur, les données de bilan comprennent les fonds d'assurance à long terme.

UNITED KINGDOM

Commercial banks

ROYAUME-UNI

Banques commerciales

Per cent / *Pourcentage*

	1992	1993	1994	1995	1996	1997	1998	1999	2000	2001		
INCOME STATEMENT ANALYSIS												**ANALYSE DU COMPTE DE RESULTATS**
% of average balance sheet total												**% du total moyen du bilan**
40. Interest income	8.82	6.71	5.89	6.40	5.68	5.71	6.06	5.37	5.70	4.75	40.	Produits financiers
41. Interest expenses	6.20	4.26	3.54	4.08	3.53	3.61	4.00	3.27	3.75	2.99	41.	Frais financiers
42. Net interest income	2.62	2.45	2.35	2.32	2.15	2.10	2.06	2.10	1.95	1.77	42.	Produits financiers nets
43. Non-interest income (net)	1.91	1.96	1.76	1.73	1.38	1.31	1.33	1.44	1.48	1.37	43.	Produits non financiers (nets)
a. Fees and commissions receivable	:	:	*1.48*	*1.40*	*1.27*	*1.23*	*1.15*	*1.20*	*1.17*	*1.09*		*a. Frais et commissions à recevoir*
b. Fees and commissions payable	:	:	*0.16*	*0.16*	*0.16*	*0.18*	*0.18*	*0.20*	*0.20*	*0.20*		*b. Frais et commissions à payer*
c. Net profits or loss on financial operations	:	:	*0.43*	*0.50*	*0.27*	*0.26*	*0.36*	*0.44*	*0.51*	*0.48*		*c. Profits ou pertes nets sur opérations financières*
d. Other												*d. Autres*
44. Gross income	4.53	4.41	4.11	4.06	3.53	3.40	3.39	3.54	3.43	3.14	44.	Résultat brut
45. Operating expenses	2.99	2.79	2.63	2.59	2.19	2.07	1.91	1.93	1.91	1.80	45.	Frais d'exploitation
a. Staff costs	*1.65*	*1.54*	*1.48*	*1.45*	*1.19*	*1.10*	*0.99*	*1.01*	*0.95*	*0.88*		*a. Dépenses en personnel*
b. Property costs	:	:	*0.58*	*0.56*	*0.48*	*0.46*	*0.36*	*0.41*	*0.46*	*0.46*		*b. Dépenses en immobilier*
c. Other	:	:	*0.57*	*0.58*	*0.52*	*0.51*	*0.56*	*0.50*	*0.50*	*0.46*		*c. Autres*
46. Net income	1.54	1.63	1.48	1.47	1.34	1.33	1.47	1.61	1.52	1.34	46.	Résultat net
47. Provisions (net)	1.24	0.87	0.33	0.30	0.20	0.18	0.24	0.23	0.22	0.25	47.	Provisions (nettes)
a. Provisions on loans	:	:	:	:	:	:	:	:	:	:		*a. Provisions sur prêts*
b. Provisions on securities	:	:	:	:	:	:	:	:	:	:		*b. Provisions sur titres*
c. Other	:	:	:	:	:	:	:	:	:	:		*c. Autres*
48. Profit before tax	0.31	0.76	1.15	1.17	1.14	1.15	1.23	1.37	1.30	1.09	48.	Bénéfices avant impôt
49. Income tax	0.17	0.28	0.38	0.40	0.40	0.36	0.36	0.42	0.40	0.34	49.	Impôt sur le revenu
50. Profit after tax	0.14	0.48	0.76	0.77	0.74	0.79	0.87	0.96	0.90	0.75	50.	Bénéfices après impôt
51. Distributed profit	0.21	0.27	0.31	0.47	0.30	0.41	0.45	0.46	0.50	0.51	51.	Bénéfices distribués
52. Retained profit	-0.07	0.20	0.45	0.30	0.44	0.39	0.42	0.50	0.40	0.24	52.	Bénéfices mis en réserve
% of gross income												**% du total du résultat brut**
53. Net interest income	57.83	55.53	57.20	57.29	60.84	61.62	60.68	59.26	56.81	56.37	53.	Produits financiers nets
54. Non-interest income (net)	42.17	44.47	42.80	42.71	39.16	38.38	39.31	40.74	43.19	43.63	54.	Produits non financiers (nets)
a. Fees and commissions receivable	:	:	*36.07*	*34.54*	*35.93*	*36.07*	*33.86*	*33.93*	*34.22*	*34.65*		*a. Frais et commissions à recevoir*
b. Fees and commissions payable	:	:	*3.78*	*4.05*	*4.52*	*5.36*	*5.23*	*5.63*	*5.85*	*6.42*		*b. Frais et commissions à payer*
c. Net profits or loss on financial operations	:	:	*10.51*	*12.21*	*7.75*	*7.67*	*10.69*	*12.44*	*14.83*	*15.40*		*c. Profits ou pertes nets sur opérations financières*
d. Other												*d. Autres*
55. Operating expenses	65.94	63.16	64.06	63.73	62.09	60.85	56.50	54.56	55.54	57.39	55.	Frais d'exploitation
a. Staff costs	*36.32*	*34.84*	*35.94*	*35.66*	*33.61*	*32.28*	*29.31*	*28.66*	*27.56*	*28.05*		*a. Dépenses en personnel*
b. Property costs	:	:	*14.17*	*13.73*	*13.64*	*13.56*	*10.62*	*11.66*	*13.35*	*14.58*		*b. Dépenses en immobilier*
c. Other	:	:	*13.95*	*14.34*	*14.84*	*15.01*	*16.57*	*14.25*	*14.63*	*14.75*		*c. Autres*
56. Net income	34.06	36.84	35.93	36.27	37.91	39.14	43.49	45.44	44.46	42.62	56.	Résultat net
57. Provisions (net)	27.31	19.72	8.09	7.43	5.62	5.32	7.11	6.56	6.56	7.91	57.	Provisions (nettes)
a. Provisions on loans	:	:	:	:	:	:	:	:	:	:		*a. Provisions sur prêts*
b. Provisions on securities	:	:	:	:	:	:	:	:	:	:		*b. Provisions sur titres*
c. Other	:	:	:	:	:	:	:	:	:	:		*c. Autres*
58. Profit before tax	6.74	17.12	27.85	28.84	32.29	33.82	36.38	38.88	37.91	34.70	58.	Bénéfices avant impôt
59. Income tax	3.73	6.26	9.33	9.80	11.30	10.52	10.70	11.79	11.54	10.78	59.	Impôt sur le revenu
60. Profit after tax	3.01	10.86	18.52	19.04	20.99	23.30	25.69	27.09	26.36	23.92	60.	Bénéfices après impôt
% of net income												**% du total du résultat net**
61. Provisions (net)	80.20	53.52	22.52	20.49	14.83	13.60	16.35	14.43	14.75	18.57	61.	Provisions (nettes)
a. Provisions on loans	:	:	:	:	:	:	:	:	:	:		*a. Provisions sur prêts*
b. Provisions on securities	:	:	:	:	:	:	:	:	:	:		*b. Provisions sur titres*
c. Other	:	:	:	:	:	:	:	:	:	:		*c. Autres*
62. Profit before tax	19.80	46.48	77.49	79.51	85.18	86.40	83.66	85.57	85.26	81.43	62.	Bénéfices avant impôt
63. Income tax	10.96	17.00	25.97	27.01	29.81	26.87	24.60	25.94	25.96	25.30	63.	Impôt sur le revenu
64. Profit after tax	8.85	29.48	51.53	52.50	55.37	59.52	59.06	59.62	59.30	56.13	64.	Bénéfices après impôt

Per cent / *Pourcentage*

BALANCE SHEET ANALYSIS / **ANALYSE DU BILAN**

% of year-end balance sheet total / **% du total du bilan en fin d'exercice**

Assets / **Actif**

	1992	1993	1994	1995	1996	1997	1998	1999	2000	2001	
65. Cash & balance with Central bank	0.80	0.76	0.71	0.70	0.57	0.52	0.52	0.67	0.56	0.51	65. Caisse & solde auprès de la Banque centrale
66. Interbank deposits	13.59	14.92	15.71	13.84	11.95	12.55	11.68	10.52	9.11	9.04	66. Dépôts interbancaires
67. Loans	58.21	54.50	51.99	52.05	55.32	53.31	52.78	54.89	53.87	52.55	67. Prêts
68. Securities	13.03	16.05	17.46	18.46	18.48	19.89	20.22	20.10	19.71	21.09	68. Valeurs mobilières
69. Other assets	14.37	13.78	14.13	14.95	13.69	13.73	14.80	13.82	16.76	16.81	69. Autres actifs
Liabilities											**Passif**
70. Capital & reserves	3.79	3.80	4.09	3.88	4.19	4.17	4.26	4.25	5.16	5.14	70. Capital et réserves
71. Borrowing from Central bank	-	-			-	-	-	-	-	-	71. Emprunts auprès de la Banque centrale
72. Interbank deposits	‥	‥	17.08	16.29	12.86	12.40	12.37	12.06	12.19	12.31	72. Dépôts interbancaires
73. Non-bank deposits	73.61	71.57	52.59	52.16	54.04	52.79	52.34	51.64	49.56	48.27	73. Dépôts non bancaires
74. Bonds	9.60	10.88	11.44	11.22	12.95	13.88	14.03	15.89	15.79	16.85	74. Obligations
75. Other liabilities	13.00	13.75	14.80	16.45	15.95	16.76	17.01	16.16	17.30	17.42	75. Autres engagements
Memorandum items											***Pour mémoire***
76. *Short-term securities*	*3.75*	*3.14*	*3.53*	*3.70*	*1.71*	*1.99*	*1.86*	*1.60*	*1.30*	*1.78*	76. *Titres à court terme*
77. *Bonds*	‥	‥	‥	‥	‥	‥	‥	‥	‥	‥	77. *Obligations*
78. *Shares and participations*	‥	‥	‥	‥	‥	‥	‥	‥	‥	‥	78. *Actions et participations*
79. *Claims on non-residents*	‥	‥	‥	‥	‥	‥	‥	‥	‥	‥	79. *Créances sur des non-résidents*
80. *Liabilities to non-residents*	‥	‥	‥	‥	‥	‥	‥	‥	‥	‥	80. *Engagements envers des non-résidents*

* See notes on previous pages. * Voir les notes en pages précédentes.

UNITED STATES
Commercial banks

ETATS-UNIS
Banques commerciales

Million US dollars / *Millions de dollars des EU*

	1992	1993	1994	1995	1996	1997	1998	1999	2000	2001	
INCOME STATEMENT											**COMPTE DE RESULTATS**
1. Interest income	256415	244742	257065	302376	313248	338224	359179	366177	424443	406662	1. Produits financiers
2. Interest expenses	122517	105615	110850	147960	150101	164514	178000	174903	222113	189418	2. Frais financiers
3. Net interest income	133899	139127	146215	154418	163147	173710	181179	191274	202328	217243	3. Produits financiers nets
4. Non-interest income (net)	71402	80986	76639	84360	96519	107646	127083	144617	150086	164042	4. Produits non financiers (nets)
a. Fees and commissions receivable	:	:	:	:	:	:	:	:	:	60489	a. Frais et commissions à recevoir
b. Fees and commissions payable (1)	:	:	:	:	:	:	:	:	:	:	b. Frais et commissions à payer (1)
c. Net profits or loss on financial operations	10230	12292	5681	6818	8648	9844	10795	10728	10156	17199	c. Profits ou pertes nets sur opérations financières
d. Other	:	:	:	:	:	:	:	:	:	86354	d. Autres
5. Gross income	205301	220113	222854	238778	259666	281356	308262	335591	352414	381285	5. Résultat brut
6. Operating expenses	132815	140523	144905	151141	162456	170988	193702	204403	215789	225957	6. Frais d'exploitation
a. Staff costs	55484	58507	60904	64014	67800	72342	79506	86151	89031	94523	a. Dépenses en personnel
b. Property costs	18152	18578	18978	19760	20889	22082	24161	25864	26764	28027	b. Dépenses en immobilier
c. Other	59181	63439	65023	67366	73766	76563	90036	92389	99995	103406	c. Autres
7. Net income	72486	79590	77949	87637	97210	110368	114560	131488	136625	155328	7. Résultat net
8. Provisions (net)	26813	16841	10991	12632	16211	19176	21222	21121	29789	43447	8. Provisions (nettes)
a. Provisions on loans	26813	16841	10991	12632	16211	19176	21222	21121	29789	43447	a. Provisions sur prêts
b. Provisions on securities (2)	:	:	:	:	:	:	:	:	:	:	b. Provisions sur titres (2)
c. Other	-	-	-	-	-	-	-	-	-	-	c. Autres
9. Profit before tax	45673	62749	66958	75005	80999	91192	93338	110367	106836	111881	9. Bénéfices avant impôt
10. Income tax	14450	19861	22429	26222	28448	31986	31892	39263	37367	37358	10. Impôt sur le revenu
11. Profit after tax	31224	42886	44528	48783	52551	59206	61447	71104	69470	74524	11. Bénéfices après impôt
12. Distributed profit	14226	22068	28165	31106	39419	42752	41206	51955	52547	55045	12. Bénéfices distribués
13. Retained profit	16997	20816	16362	17678	13131	16454	20241	19149	16923	19478	13. Bénéfices mis en réserve
BALANCE SHEET											**BILAN**
Assets											**Actif**
14. Cash & balance with Central bank	138712	133256	151760	161565	162511	169647	164255	166278	173609	212489	14. Caisse & solde auprès de la Banque centrale
15. Interbank deposits	158476	138952	150903	143937	173203	184879	190763	198381	191380	173823	15. Dépôts interbancaires
16. Loans	2129905	2241078	2443128	2718622	2903625	3147327	3420547	3621978	3992164	4104965	16. Prêts
17. Securities	846728	950578	911227	916391	924232	1006031	1090563	1146296	1219183	1314348	17. Valeurs mobilières
18. Other assets	218947	227303	331803	349298	388013	463803	515719	541183	595267	699388	18. Autres actifs
Liabilities											**Passif**
19. Capital & reserves	262440	295448	310923	348218	375167	414350	454151	472045	522484	589861	19. Capital et réserves
20. Borrowing from Central bank	47968	45588	39102	44153	56718	50970	54588	49242	57142	56682	20. Emprunts auprès de la Banque centrale
21. Interbank deposits											21. Dépôts interbancaires
22. Non-bank deposits	2634891	2692515	2814639	2961755	3118225	3347971	3600350	3753916	4090446	4310526	22. Dépôts non bancaires
23. Bonds	33521	37148	40580	43261	50938	61661	72144	75805	86397	94664	23. Obligations
24. Other liabilities	513952	620468	783623	892426	950536	1096735	1200615	1323107	1415134	1453279	24. Autres engagements
Balance sheet total											**Total du bilan**
25. End-year total	3492768	3691167	3988821	4289813	4551584	4971687	5381847	5674116	6171603	6505013	25. En fin d'exercice
26. Average total	3441557	3565707	3863406	4147649	4376036	4733178	5144295	5438619	5905234	6335324	26. Moyen

303

UNITED STATES
Commercial banks

ETATS-UNIS
Banques commerciales

Million US dollars / *Millions de dollars des EU*

	1992	1993	1994	1995	1996	1997	1998	1999	2000	2001		
Memorandum items												**Pour mémoire**
27. Short-term securities	..	..	..	..	..	..	..	..	..	..	27.	*Titres à court terme*
28. Bonds	..	..	..	..	..	..	..	..	..	..	28.	*Obligations*
29. Shares and participations	..	..	..	..	..	..	..	..	..	..	29.	*Actions et participations*
30. Claims on non-residents	..	..	..	..	..	..	..	..	..	..	30.	*Créances sur des non-résidents*
31. Liabilities to non-residents	..	..	..	..	..	..	..	..	..	..	31.	*Engagements envers des non-résidents*
Capital adequacy												**Solvabilité**
32. Tier 1 Capital	236533	266816	291740	311709	331223	355031	380096	408985	443865	473251	32.	*Fonds propres de base*
33. Tier 2 Capital	56950	64689	68634	74790	82346	92223	112100	117276	125930	137021	33.	*Fonds propres complémentaires*
34. Supervisory deductions	..	..	..	..	..	..	..	..	..	..	34.	*Eléments à déduire des fonds propres*
35. Total net capital resources	293482	331505	360374	386499	413569	447253	492196	526261	569795	610271	35.	*Total net des ressources en capital*
36. Risk-weighted assets	2541125	2571692	2732794	3003045	3251021	3584701	4005211	4285419	4686074	4936078	36.	*Actifs pondérés des risques*
SUPPLEMENTARY INFORMATION												**RENSEIGNEMENTS COMPLEMENTAIRES**
37. Number of institutions	11495	11001	10489	9983	9576	9187	8815	8623	8361	8130	37.	*Nombre d'institutions*
38. Number of branches	..	..	..	..	..	..	..	..	..	..	38.	*Nombre de succursales*
39. Number of employees (x 1000)	1475	1490	1483	1479	1484	1530	1613	1644	1658	1695	39.	*Nombre de salariés (x 1000)*

Notes

1 Fees and commissions payable (item 4.b.) are included under Fees and commissions receivable (item 4.a.).

2 Provisions on securities (item 8.b.) are included under Provisions on loans (item 8.a.)

. Income data have been adjusted to account for the effects of mergers on reported earnings.

. Non-interest income (item 4) includes extraordinary items and realized gains on investment account securities.

. Loans (item 16) are reported net of loss reserves and include federal funds sold and reverse repurchase agreements.

. Bonds (item 23) include subordinated notes and debentures and exclude senior debt.

. Average balance sheet totals (item 26) are based on the quarterly average levels.

Notes

1 Les Frais et commissions à payer (poste 4.b.) sont inclus sous Frais et commissions à recevoir (poste 4.a.).

2 Les Provisions sur titres (poste 8.b.) sont incluses sous Provisions sur prêts (poste 8.a.)

. Les données sur le revenu ont été ajustées pour rendre compte des effets de fusion en ce qui concerne les gains rapportés.

. La rubrique Produits non-financiers (item 4) comprend les profits exceptionnels et les revenus provenant des ventes de titres de placement

. Les données publiées dans la rubrique Prêts (items 16) sont nettes de réserves pour pertes et comprennent le solde des fonds fédéraux et les opérations de mise en pension.

. La rubrique Obligations (item23) regroupe les créances et les certificats de dettes subordonnées et ne comprend pas la dette de premier rang

. Le total moyen du bilan (item 26) est basé sur les moyennes trimestrielles

UNITED STATES
Commercial banks

ETATS-UNIS
Banques commerciales

Per cent   *Pourcentage*

	1992	1993	1994	1995	1996	1997	1998	1999	2000	2001	
INCOME STATEMENT ANALYSIS											**ANALYSE DU COMPTE DE RESULTATS**
% of average balance sheet total											**% du total moyen du bilan**
40. Interest income	7.45	6.86	6.65	7.29	7.16	7.15	6.98	6.73	7.19	6.42	40. Produits financiers
41. Interest expenses	3.56	2.96	2.87	3.57	3.43	3.48	3.46	3.22	3.76	2.99	41. Frais financiers
42. Net interest income	3.89	3.90	3.78	3.72	3.73	3.67	3.52	3.52	3.43	3.43	42. Produits financiers nets
43. Non-interest income (net)	2.07	2.27	1.98	2.03	2.21	2.27	2.47	2.66	2.54	2.59	43. Produits non financiers (nets)
a. Fees and commissions receivable	*..*	*..*	*..*	*..*	*..*	*..*	*..*	*..*	*..*	*0.95*	*a. Frais et commissions à recevoir*
b. Fees and commissions payable	*..*	*..*	*..*	*..*	*..*	*..*	*..*	*..*	*..*	*..*	*b. Frais et commissions à payer*
c. Net profits or loss on financial operations	*0.30*	*0.34*	*0.15*	*0.16*	*0.20*	*0.21*	*0.21*	*0.20*	*0.17*	*0.27*	*c. Profits ou pertes nets sur opérations financières*
d. Other	*..*	*..*	*..*	*..*	*..*	*..*	*..*	*..*	*..*	*1.36*	*d. Autres*
44. Gross income	5.97	6.17	5.77	5.76	5.93	5.94	5.99	6.18	5.97	6.02	44. Résultat brut
45. Operating expenses	3.86	3.94	3.75	3.64	3.71	3.61	3.77	3.76	3.65	3.57	45. Frais d'exploitation
a. Staff costs	*1.61*	*1.64*	*1.58*	*1.54*	*1.55*	*1.53*	*1.55*	*1.58*	*1.51*	*1.49*	*a. Dépenses en personnel*
b. Property costs	*0.53*	*0.52*	*0.49*	*0.48*	*0.48*	*0.47*	*0.47*	*0.48*	*0.45*	*0.44*	*b. Dépenses en immobilier*
c. Other	*1.72*	*1.78*	*1.68*	*1.62*	*1.69*	*1.62*	*1.75*	*1.70*	*1.69*	*1.63*	*c. Autres*
46. Net income	2.11	2.23	2.02	2.11	2.22	2.33	2.23	2.42	2.31	2.45	46. Résultat net
47. Provisions (net)	0.78	0.47	0.28	0.30	0.37	0.41	0.41	0.39	0.50	0.69	47. Provisions (nettes)
a. Provisions on loans	*0.78*	*0.47*	*0.28*	*0.30*	*0.37*	*0.41*	*0.41*	*0.39*	*0.50*	*0.69*	*a. Provisions sur prêts*
b. Provisions on securities	*..*	*..*	*..*	*..*	*..*	*..*	*..*	*..*	*..*	*-*	*b. Provisions sur titres*
c. Other	*..*	*..*	*..*	*..*	*..*	*..*	*..*	*..*	*..*	*-*	*c. Autres*
48. Profit before tax	1.33	1.76	1.73	1.81	1.85	1.93	1.81	2.03	1.81	1.77	48. Bénéfices avant impôt
49. Income tax	0.42	0.56	0.58	0.63	0.65	0.68	0.62	0.72	0.63	0.59	49. Impôt sur le revenu
50. Profit after tax	0.91	1.20	1.15	1.18	1.20	1.25	1.19	1.31	1.18	1.18	50. Bénéfices après impôt
51. Distributed profit	0.41	0.62	0.73	0.75	0.90	0.90	0.80	0.96	0.89	0.87	51. Bénéfices distribués
52. Retained profit	0.49	0.58	0.42	0.43	0.30	0.35	0.39	0.35	0.29	0.31	52. Bénéfices mis en réserve
% of gross income											**% du total du résultat brut**
53. Net interest income	65.22	63.21	65.61	64.67	62.83	61.74	58.77	56.95	57.41	56.98	53. Produits financiers nets
54. Non-interest income (net)	34.78	36.79	34.39	35.33	37.17	38.26	41.23	43.05	42.59	43.02	54. Produits non financiers (nets)
a. Fees and commissions receivable	*..*	*..*	*..*	*..*	*..*	*..*	*..*	*..*	*..*	*15.86*	*a. Frais et commissions à recevoir*
b. Fees and commissions payable	*..*	*..*	*..*	*..*	*..*	*..*	*..*	*..*	*..*	*..*	*b. Frais et commissions à payer*
c. Net profits or loss on financial operations	*4.98*	*5.58*	*2.55*	*2.86*	*3.33*	*3.50*	*3.50*	*3.19*	*2.88*	*4.51*	*c. Profits ou pertes nets sur opérations financières*
d. Other	*..*	*..*	*..*	*..*	*..*	*..*	*..*	*..*	*..*	*22.65*	*d. Autres*
55. Operating expenses	64.69	63.84	65.02	63.30	62.56	60.77	62.84	60.85	61.23	59.26	55. Frais d'exploitation
a. Staff costs	*27.03*	*26.58*	*27.33*	*26.81*	*26.11*	*25.71*	*25.79*	*25.65*	*25.26*	*24.79*	*a. Dépenses en personnel*
b. Property costs	*8.84*	*8.44*	*8.52*	*8.28*	*8.04*	*7.85*	*7.84*	*7.70*	*7.59*	*7.35*	*b. Dépenses en immobilier*
c. Other	*28.83*	*28.82*	*29.18*	*28.21*	*28.41*	*27.21*	*29.21*	*27.51*	*28.37*	*27.12*	*c. Autres*
56. Net income	35.31	36.16	34.98	36.70	37.44	39.23	37.16	39.15	38.77	40.74	56. Résultat net
57. Provisions (net)	13.06	7.65	4.93	5.29	6.24	6.82	6.88	6.29	8.45	11.39	57. Provisions (nettes)
a. Provisions on loans	*13.06*	*7.65*	*4.93*	*5.29*	*6.24*	*6.82*	*6.88*	*6.29*	*8.45*	*11.39*	*a. Provisions sur prêts*
b. Provisions on securities	*..*	*..*	*..*	*..*	*..*	*..*	*..*	*..*	*..*	*..*	*b. Provisions sur titres*
c. Other	*..*	*..*	*..*	*..*	*..*	*..*	*..*	*..*	*..*	*..*	*c. Autres*
58. Profit before tax	22.25	28.51	30.05	31.41	31.19	32.41	30.28	32.86	30.32	29.34	58. Bénéfices avant impôt
59. Income tax	7.04	9.02	10.06	10.98	10.96	11.37	10.35	11.69	10.60	9.80	59. Impôt sur le revenu
60. Profit after tax	15.21	19.48	19.98	20.43	20.24	21.04	19.93	21.17	19.71	19.55	60. Bénéfices après impôt
% of net income											**% du total du résultat net**
61. Provisions (net)	36.99	21.16	14.10	14.41	16.68	17.37	18.52	16.06	21.80	27.97	61. Provisions (nettes)
a. Provisions on loans	*36.99*	*21.16*	*14.10*	*14.41*	*16.68*	*17.37*	*18.52*	*16.06*	*21.80*	*27.97*	*a. Provisions sur prêts*
b. Provisions on securities	*..*	*..*	*..*	*..*	*..*	*..*	*..*	*..*	*..*	*..*	*b. Provisions sur titres*
c. Other	*..*	*..*	*..*	*..*	*..*	*..*	*..*	*..*	*..*	*..*	*c. Autres*
62. Profit before tax	63.01	78.84	85.90	85.59	83.32	82.63	81.48	83.94	78.20	72.03	62. Bénéfices avant impôt
63. Income tax	19.93	24.95	28.77	29.92	29.26	28.98	27.84	29.86	27.35	24.05	63. Impôt sur le revenu
64. Profit after tax	43.08	53.88	57.12	55.66	54.06	53.64	53.64	54.08	50.85	47.98	64. Bénéfices après impôt

UNITED STATES
Commercial banks

ETATS-UNIS
Banques commerciales

Per cent — *Pourcentage*

BALANCE SHEET ANALYSIS — **ANALYSE DU BILAN**

% of year-end balance sheet total — **% du total du bilan en fin d'exercice**

	1992	1993	1994	1995	1996	1997	1998	1999	2000	2001	
Assets											**Actif**
65. Cash & balance with Central bank	3.97	3.61	3.80	3.77	3.57	3.41	3.05	2.93	2.81	3.27	65. Caisse & solde auprès de la Banque centrale
66. Interbank deposits	4.54	3.76	3.78	3.36	3.81	3.72	3.54	3.50	3.10	2.67	66. Dépôts interbancaires
67. Loans	60.98	60.71	61.25	63.37	63.79	63.31	63.56	63.83	64.69	63.10	67. Prêts
68. Securities	24.24	25.75	22.84	21.36	20.31	20.24	20.26	20.20	19.75	20.21	68. Valeurs mobilières
69. Other assets	6.27	6.16	8.32	8.14	8.52	9.33	9.58	9.54	9.65	10.75	69. Autres actifs
Liabilities											**Passif**
70. Capital & reserves	7.51	8.00	7.79	8.12	8.24	8.33	8.44	8.32	8.47	9.07	70. Capital et réserves
71. Borrowing from Central bank	..	..	..	..	..	..	..	..	..	..	71. Emprunts auprès de la Banque centrale
72. Interbank deposits	1.37	1.24	0.98	1.03	1.25	1.03	1.01	0.87	0.93	0.87	72. Dépôts interbancaires
73. Non-bank deposits	75.44	72.94	70.56	69.04	68.51	67.34	66.90	66.16	66.28	66.26	73. Dépôts non bancaires
74. Bonds	0.96	1.01	1.02	1.01	1.12	1.24	1.34	1.34	1.40	1.46	74. Obligations
75. Other liabilities	14.71	16.81	19.65	20.80	20.88	22.06	22.31	23.32	22.93	22.34	75. Autres engagements
Memorandum items											**Pour mémoire**
76. Short-term securities	..	..	..	..	..	..	..	..	..	..	76. Titres à court terme
77. Bonds	..	..	..	..	..	..	..	..	..	..	77. Obligations
78. Shares and participations	..	..	..	..	..	..	..	..	..	..	78. Actions et participations
79. Claims on non-residents	..	..	..	..	..	..	..	..	..	..	79. Créances sur des non-résidents
80. Liabilities to non-residents	..	..	..	..	..	..	..	..	..	..	80. Engagements envers des non-résidents

* See notes on previous pages. * Voir les notes en pages précédentes.

UNITED STATES
Large commercial banks

ETATS-UNIS
Grandes banques commerciales

Million US dollars / *Millions de dollars des EU*

	1992	1993	1994	1995	1996	1997	1998	1999	2000	2001
INCOME STATEMENT / **COMPTE DE RESULTATS**										
1. Interest income / Produits financiers	130968	130319	138252	166497	179355	212103	237988	247565	296002	284707
2. Interest expenses / Frais financiers	67889	62847	65521	87700	91103	108455	123538	122573	160857	135234
3. Net interest income / Produits financiers nets	63077	67472	72731	78798	88254	103649	114450	124991	135144	149472
4. Non-interest income (net) / Produits non financiers (nets)	45222	52627	49316	55149	66623	77931	95212	112689	118543	130374
a. Fees and commissions receivable / Frais et commissions à recevoir	..	..	..	..	..	..	..	..	..	46238
b. Fees and commissions payable (1) / Frais et commissions à payer (1)	..	..	..	..	..	..	..	..	..	..
c. Net profits or loss on financial operations / Profits ou pertes nets sur opérations financières	8358	10956	6165	6543	8199	9423	10109	10656	10478	16480
d. Other / Autres	..	..	..	..	..	..	..	..	..	67656
5. Gross income / Résultat brut	108299	120099	122047	133947	154877	181580	209662	237680	253687	279846
6. Operating expenses / Frais d'exploitation	69786	76503	80265	85595	98329	110932	133478	144110	154411	162804
a. Staff costs / Dépenses en personnel	29152	31857	33710	36330	40615	46126	53123	59147	61691	66221
b. Property costs / Dépenses en immobilier	9981	10527	10897	11509	12823	14430	16625	18138	19046	20184
c. Other / Autres	30655	34119	35657	37756	44891	50376	63727	66823	73673	76399
7. Net income / Résultat net	38513	43596	41782	48352	56548	70648	76184	93570	99276	117042
8. Provisions (net) / Provisions (nettes)	16463	10323	6324	6335	9137	12052	14917	15304	22232	34422
a. Provisions on loans / Provisions sur prêts	16463	10323	6324	6335	9137	12052	14917	15304	22232	34422
b. Provisions on securities (2) / Provisions sur titres (2)	-	-	-	-	-	-	-	-	-	-
c. Other / Autres	-	-	-	-	-	-	-	-	-	-
9. Profit before tax / Bénéfices avant impôt	22050	33273	35458	42017	47411	58596	61267	78266	77044	82620
10. Income tax / Impôt sur le revenu	6898	10427	12061	15218	17091	21103	21630	28970	27757	28028
11. Profit after tax / Bénéfices après impôt	15150	22846	23398	26800	30322	37494	39639	49299	49289	54591
12. Distributed profit / Bénéfices distribués	6009	10549	15906	17418	23954	27403	26472	37206	38345	37274
13. Retained profit / Bénéfices mis en réserve	9140	12297	7492	9383	6368	10092	13168	12093	10943	17318
BALANCE SHEET / **BILAN**										
Assets / **Actif**										
14. Cash & balance with Central bank / Caisse & solde auprès de la Banque centrale	87177	85257	98331	107163	116808	132419	133251	129570	141139	159927
15. Interbank deposits / Dépôts interbancaires	94393	84408	98254	88206	114705	135911	140023	152875	142764	143420
16. Loans / Prêts	1109360	1201840	1346936	1541373	1772315	2111099	2378999	2538248	2873314	2955101
17. Securities / Valeurs mobilières	375440	458419	438566	461164	495883	599081	676151	726448	819518	899756
18. Other assets / Autres actifs	141106	153676	252389	269103	309639	387623	436705	456332	508406	599663
Liabilities / **Passif**										
19. Capital & reserves / Capital et réserves	123521	147015	158195	180622	210899	258690	297976	316292	359233	415039
20. Borrowing from Central bank / Emprunts auprès de la Banque centrale										
21. Interbank deposits / Dépôts interbancaires	27070	25373	23022	26842	38818	37828	41490	36863	44926	41753
22. Non-bank deposits / Dépôts non bancaires	1252106	1326240	1448839	1547985	1763736	2082856	2333485	2477304	2785874	2968929
23. Bonds / Obligations	30722	33887	36889	38903	46796	58584	68640	72304	83300	90914
24. Other liabilities / Autres engagements	374057	451085	567532	672657	749101	928174	1023537	1100710	1211808	1241232
Balance sheet total / **Total du bilan**										
25. End-year total / En fin d'exercice	1807476	1983600	2234476	2467009	2809350	3366133	3765129	4003473	4485141	4757867
26. Average total / Moyen	1777490	1900706	2152902	2389212	2639565	3118494	3565371	3814981	4263559	4656388

Large commercial banks

Grandes banques commerciales

Million US dollars

Millions de dollars des EU

	1992	1993	1994	1995	1996	1997	1998	1999	2000	2001		
Memorandum items												***Pour mémoire***
27. Short-term securities	..	..	..	..	..	..	..	..	..	..	27.	*Titres à court terme*
28. Bonds	..	..	..	..	..	..	..	..	..	..	28.	*Obligations*
29. Shares and participations	..	..	..	..	..	..	..	..	..	..	29.	*Actions et participations*
30. Claims on non-residents	..	..	..	..	..	..	..	..	..	..	30.	*Créances sur des non-résidents*
31. Liabilities to non-residents	..	..	..	..	..	..	..	..	..	..	31.	*Engagements envers des non-résidents*
Capital adequacy												***Solvabilité***
32. Tier 1 Capital	105946	127613	144290	157880	177241	209952	237494	262895	295946	321444	32.	*Fonds propres de base*
33. Tier 2 Capital	41859	49222	52251	57428	65131	76795	95834	101313	110378	120874	33.	*Fonds propres complémentaires*
34. Supervisory deductions											34.	*Eléments à déduire des fonds propres*
35. Total net capital resources	147805	176835	196541	215308	242372	286747	333328	364208	406324	442318	35.	*Total net des ressources en capital*
36. Risk-weighted assets	1473085	1523372	1637900	1841934	2092638	2505698	2936885	3170631	3534157	3754714	36.	*Actifs pondérés des risques*
SUPPLEMENTARY INFORMATION												**RENSEIGNEMENTS COMPLEMENTAIRES**
37. Number of institutions	100	100	100	100	100	100	100	100	100	100	37.	*Nombre d'institutions*
38. Number of branches	..	..	..	..	..	..	..	..	..	..	38.	*Nombre de succursales*
39. Number of employees (x 1000)	668	693	696	721	781	879	990	1028	1068	1107	39.	*Nombre de salariés (x 1000)*

1 Fees and commissions payable (item 4.b.) are included under Fees and commissions receivable (item 4.a.).

2 Provisions on securities (item 8.b.) are included under Provisions on loans (item 8.a.)

Notes

. Large commercial banks refer to the 100 largest Commercial banks.

. Income data have been adjusted to account for the effects of mergers on reported earnings.

. Non-interest income (item 4) includes extraordinary items and realized gains on investment account securities.

. Loans (item 16) are reported net of loss reserves and include federal funds sold and reverse repurchase agreements.

. Bonds (item 23) include subordinated notes and debentures and exclude senior debt.

. Average balance sheet totals (item 26) are based on the quarterly average levels.

1 Les Frais et commissions à payer (poste 4.b.) sont inclus sous Frais et commissions à recevoir (poste 4.a.).

2 Les Provisions sur titres (poste 8.b.) sont incluses sous Provisions sur prêts (poste 8.a.)

Notes

. Les "Grandes banques commerciales" font référence aux 100 plus grandes Banques commerciales.

. Les données sur le revenu ont été ajustées pour rendre compte des effets de fusion en ce qui concerne les gains rapportés.

. La rubrique Produits non-financiers (item 4) comprend les profits exceptionnels et les revenus provenant des ventes de titres de placement

. Les données publiées dans la rubrique Prêts (items 16) sont nettes de réserves pour pertes et comprennent le solde des fonds fédéraux et les opérations de mise en pension.

. La rubrique Obligations (item23) regroupe les créances et les certificats de dettes subordonnées et ne comprend pas la dette de premier rang

. Le total moyen du bilan (item 26) est basé sur les moyennes trimestrielles

Per cent — *Pourcentage*

INCOME STATEMENT ANALYSIS — ANALYSE DU COMPTE DE RESULTATS

% of average balance sheet total — % du total moyen du bilan

	1992	1993	1994	1995	1996	1997	1998	1999	2000	2001	
40. Interest income	7.37	6.86	6.42	6.97	6.79	6.80	6.67	6.49	6.94	6.11	40. Produits financiers
41. Interest expenses	3.82	3.31	3.04	3.67	3.45	3.48	3.46	3.21	3.77	2.90	41. Frais financiers
42. Net interest income	3.55	3.55	3.38	3.30	3.34	3.32	3.21	3.28	3.17	3.21	42. Produits financiers nets
43. Non-interest income (net)	2.54	2.77	2.29	2.31	2.52	2.50	2.67	2.95	2.78	2.80	43. Produits non financiers (nets)
a. Fees and commissions receivable	*..*	*..*	*..*	*..*	*..*	*..*	*..*	*..*	*..*	*0.99*	*a. Frais et commissions à recevoir*
b. Fees and commissions payable	*..*	*..*	*..*	*..*	*..*	*..*	*..*	*..*	*..*	*..*	*b. Frais et commissions à payer*
c. Net profits or loss on financial operations	*0.47*	*0.58*	*0.29*	*0.27*	*0.31*	*0.30*	*0.28*	*0.28*	*0.25*	*0.35*	*c. Profits ou pertes nets sur opérations financières*
d. Other	*..*	*..*	*..*	*..*	*..*	*..*	*..*	*..*	*..*	*1.45*	*d. Autres*
44. Gross income	6.09	6.32	5.67	5.61	5.87	5.82	5.88	6.23	5.95	6.01	44. Résultat brut
45. Operating expenses	3.93	4.02	3.73	3.58	3.73	3.56	3.74	3.78	3.62	3.50	45. Frais d'exploitation
a. Staff costs	*1.64*	*1.68*	*1.57*	*1.52*	*1.54*	*1.48*	*1.49*	*1.55*	*1.45*	*1.42*	*a. Dépenses en personnel*
b. Property costs	*0.56*	*0.55*	*0.51*	*0.48*	*0.49*	*0.46*	*0.47*	*0.48*	*0.45*	*0.43*	*b. Dépenses en immobilier*
c. Other	*1.72*	*1.80*	*1.66*	*1.58*	*1.70*	*1.62*	*1.79*	*1.75*	*1.73*	*1.64*	*c. Autres*
46. Net income	2.17	2.29	1.94	2.02	2.14	2.27	2.14	2.45	2.33	2.51	46. Résultat net
47. Provisions (net)	0.93	0.54	0.29	0.27	0.35	0.39	0.42	0.40	0.52	0.74	47. Provisions (nettes)
a. Provisions on loans	*0.93*	*0.54*	*0.29*	*0.27*	*0.35*	*0.39*	*0.42*	*0.40*	*0.52*	*0.74*	*a. Provisions sur prêts*
b. Provisions on securities	*..*	*..*	*..*	*..*	*..*	*..*	*..*	*..*	*..*	*..*	*b. Provisions sur titres*
c. Other	*-*	*-*	*-*	*-*	*-*	*-*	*-*	*-*	*-*	*-*	*c. Autres*
48. Profit before tax	1.24	1.75	1.65	1.76	1.80	1.88	1.72	2.05	1.81	1.77	48. Bénéfices avant impôt
49. Income tax	0.39	0.55	0.56	0.64	0.65	0.68	0.61	0.76	0.65	0.60	49. Impôt sur le revenu
50. Profit after tax	0.85	1.20	1.09	1.12	1.15	1.20	1.11	1.29	1.16	1.17	50. Bénéfices après impôt
51. Distributed profit	0.34	0.56	0.74	0.73	0.91	0.88	0.74	0.98	0.90	0.80	51. Bénéfices distribués
52. Retained profit	0.51	0.65	0.35	0.39	0.24	0.32	0.37	0.32	0.26	0.37	52. Bénéfices mis en réserve

% of gross income — % du total du résultat brut

	1992	1993	1994	1995	1996	1997	1998	1999	2000	2001	
53. Net interest income	58.24	56.18	59.59	58.83	56.98	57.08	54.59	52.59	53.27	53.41	53. Produits financiers nets
54. Non-interest income (net)	41.76	43.82	40.41	41.17	43.02	42.92	45.41	47.41	46.73	46.59	54. Produits non financiers (nets)
a. Fees and commissions receivable	*..*	*..*	*..*	*..*	*..*	*..*	*..*	*..*	*..*	*16.52*	*a. Frais et commissions à recevoir*
b. Fees and commissions payable	*..*	*..*	*..*	*..*	*..*	*..*	*..*	*..*	*..*	*..*	*b. Frais et commissions à payer*
c. Net profits or loss on financial operations	*7.72*	*9.12*	*5.05*	*4.88*	*5.29*	*5.19*	*4.82*	*4.48*	*4.13*	*5.89*	*c. Profits ou pertes nets sur opérations financières*
d. Other	*..*	*..*	*..*	*..*	*..*	*..*	*..*	*..*	*..*	*24.18*	*d. Autres*
55. Operating expenses	64.44	63.70	65.77	63.90	63.49	61.09	63.66	60.63	60.87	58.18	55. Frais d'exploitation
a. Staff costs	*26.92*	*26.53*	*27.62*	*27.12*	*26.22*	*25.40*	*25.34*	*24.89*	*24.32*	*23.66*	*a. Dépenses en personnel*
b. Property costs	*9.22*	*8.77*	*8.93*	*8.59*	*8.28*	*7.95*	*7.93*	*7.63*	*7.51*	*7.21*	*b. Dépenses en immobilier*
c. Other	*28.31*	*28.41*	*29.22*	*28.19*	*28.98*	*27.74*	*30.40*	*28.11*	*29.04*	*27.30*	*c. Autres*
56. Net income	35.56	36.30	34.23	36.10	36.51	38.91	36.34	39.37	39.13	41.82	56. Résultat net
57. Provisions (net)	15.20	8.60	5.18	4.73	5.90	6.64	7.11	6.44	8.76	12.30	57. Provisions (nettes)
a. Provisions on loans	*15.20*	*8.60*	*5.18*	*4.73*	*5.90*	*6.64*	*7.11*	*6.44*	*8.76*	*12.30*	*a. Provisions sur prêts*
b. Provisions on securities	*..*	*..*	*..*	*..*	*..*	*..*	*..*	*..*	*..*	*..*	*b. Provisions sur titres*
c. Other	*-*	*-*	*-*	*-*	*-*	*-*	*-*	*-*	*-*	*-*	*c. Autres*
58. Profit before tax	20.36	27.70	29.05	31.37	30.61	32.27	29.22	32.93	30.37	29.52	58. Bénéfices avant impôt
59. Income tax	6.37	8.68	9.88	11.36	11.04	11.62	10.32	12.19	10.94	10.02	59. Impôt sur le revenu
60. Profit after tax	13.99	19.02	19.17	20.01	19.58	20.65	18.91	20.74	19.43	19.51	60. Bénéfices après impôt

% of net income — % du total du résultat net

	1992	1993	1994	1995	1996	1997	1998	1999	2000	2001	
61. Provisions (net)	42.75	23.68	15.14	13.10	16.16	17.06	19.58	16.36	22.39	29.41	61. Provisions (nettes)
a. Provisions on loans	*42.75*	*23.68*	*15.14*	*13.10*	*16.16*	*17.06*	*19.58*	*16.36*	*22.39*	*29.41*	*a. Provisions sur prêts*
b. Provisions on securities	*..*	*..*	*..*	*..*	*..*	*..*	*..*	*..*	*..*	*..*	*b. Provisions sur titres*
c. Other	*-*	*-*	*-*	*-*	*-*	*-*	*-*	*-*	*-*	*-*	*c. Autres*
62. Profit before tax	57.25	76.32	84.86	86.90	83.84	82.94	80.42	83.64	77.61	70.59	62. Bénéfices avant impôt
63. Income tax	17.91	23.92	28.87	31.47	30.22	29.87	28.39	30.96	27.96	23.95	63. Impôt sur le revenu
64. Profit after tax	39.34	52.40	56.00	55.43	53.62	53.07	52.03	52.69	49.65	46.64	64. Bénéfices après impôt

UNITED STATES
Large commercial banks

ETATS-UNIS
Grandes banques commerciales

Per cent — *Pourcentage*

BALANCE SHEET ANALYSIS — **ANALYSE DU BILAN**

% of year-end balance sheet total — **% du total du bilan en fin d'exercice**

		1992	1993	1994	1995	1996	1997	1998	1999	2000	2001		
	Assets												**Actif**
65.	Cash & balance with Central bank	4.82	4.30	4.40	4.34	4.16	3.93	3.54	3.24	3.15	3.36	65.	Caisse & solde auprès de la Banque centrale
66.	Interbank deposits	5.22	4.26	4.40	3.58	4.08	4.04	3.72	3.82	3.18	3.01	66.	Dépôts interbancaires
67.	Loans	61.38	60.59	60.28	62.48	63.09	62.72	63.19	63.40	64.06	62.11	67.	Prêts
68.	Securities	20.77	23.11	19.63	18.69	17.65	17.80	17.96	18.15	18.27	18.91	68.	Valeurs mobilières
69.	Other assets	7.81	7.75	11.30	10.91	11.02	11.52	11.60	11.40	11.34	12.60	69.	Autres actifs
	Liabilities												**Passif**
70.	Capital & reserves	6.83	7.41	7.08	7.32	7.51	7.69	7.91	7.90	8.01	8.72	70.	Capital et réserves
71.	Borrowing from Central bank	..	..	..	..	..	..	..	..	..	..	71.	Emprunts auprès de la Banque centrale
72.	Interbank deposits	1.50	1.28	1.03	1.09	1.38	1.12	1.10	0.92	1.00	0.88	72.	Dépôts interbancaires
73.	Non-bank deposits	69.27	66.86	64.84	62.75	62.78	61.88	61.98	61.88	62.11	62.40	73.	Dépôts non bancaires
74.	Bonds	1.70	1.71	1.65	1.58	1.67	1.74	1.82	1.81	1.86	1.91	74.	Obligations
75.	Other liabilities	20.69	22.74	25.40	27.27	26.66	27.57	3.28	27.49	27.02	26.09	75.	Autres engagements
	Memorandum items												***Pour mémoire***
76.	Short-term securities	..	..	..	..	..	..	..	..	..	..	76.	Titres à court terme
77.	Bonds	..	..	..	..	..	..	..	..	..	..	77.	Obligations
78.	Shares and participations	..	..	..	..	..	..	..	..	..	..	78.	Actions et participations
79.	Claims on non-residents	..	..	..	..	..	..	..	..	..	..	79.	Créances sur des non-résidents
80.	Liabilities to non-residents	..	..	..	..	..	..	..	..	..	..	80.	Engagements envers des non-résidents

* See notes on previous pages.   * Voir les notes en pages précédentes.

310

UNITED STATES
Savings banks

ETATS-UNIS
Caisses d'épargne

Million US dollars / *Millions de dollars des EU*

		1992	1993	1994	1995	1996	1997	1998	1999	2000	2001		
INCOME STATEMENT													**COMPTE DE RESULTATS**
1. Interest income		117208	97635	77652	66138	63470	70995	72270	69174	71085	74203	1.	Produits financiers
2. Interest expenses		90942	69492	45852	34518	33411	42529	42171	40559	41902	42880	2.	Frais financiers
3. Net interest income		26266	28143	31800	31620	30059	28466	30099	28615	29183	31323	3.	Produits financiers nets
4. Non-interest income (net)		7319	6646	6311	6416	6123	7121	7493	7029	9200	9789	4.	Produits non financiers (nets)
a. Fees and commissions receivable		5066	5318	4737	4741	4838	5032	4845	4990	5556	6928		a. Frais et commissions à recevoir
b. Fees and commissions payable		..	..	..	..	..	..	..	..	..	..		b. Frais et commissions à payer
c. Net profits or loss on financial operations		..	..	..	..	..	..	..	..	..	..		c. Profits ou pertes nets sur opérations financières
d. Other		2255	1327	1574	1675	1285	2088	2647	2039	3643	2860		d. Autres
5. Gross income		33585	34789	38111	38036	36182	35587	37592	35644	38383	41112	5.	Résultat brut
6. Operating expenses		28474	26462	25232	24898	23231	21835	25700	21072	23570	23993	6.	Frais d'exploitation
a. Staff costs		10811	9838	9612	9964	9756	9586	10140	9937	10868	11084		a. Dépenses en personnel
b. Property costs		5052	4554	4276	4080	3968	4006	4097	3791	4283	4401		b. Dépenses en immobilier
c. Other		12612	12070	11342	10854	9507	8242	11464	7344	8416	8508		c. Autres
7. Net income		5111	8327	12879	13138	12951	13752	11892	14572	14813	17119	7.	Résultat net
8. Provisions (net)		9267	6999	5176	4312	2481	2117	2534	2186	1772	1563	8.	Provisions (nettes)
a. Provisions on loans		9267	6999	5176	4312	2481	2117	2534	2186	1772	1563		a. Provisions sur prêts
b. Provisions on securities (1)		-	-	-	-	-	-	-	-	-	-		b. Provisions sur titres (1)
c. Other		-	-	-	-	-	-	-	-	-	-		c. Autres
9. Profit before tax		-4156	1328	7703	8826	10470	11635	9358	12386	13041	15556	9.	Bénéfices avant impôt
10. Income tax		1360	2812	3755	3858	3780	4159	3037	4852	5269	6125	10.	Impôt sur le revenu
11. Profit after tax (2)		-5516	-1482	3948	4968	6690	7476	6321	7534	7772	9431	11.	Bénéfices après impôt (2)
12. Distributed profit		1288	1818	2107	2293	2598	4083	5810	4906	6566	6100	12.	Bénéfices distribués
13. Retained profit		-6804	-3300	1841	2675	4092	3393	511	2628	1206	3331	13.	Bénéfices mis en réserve
BALANCE SHEET													**BILAN**
Assets													**Actif**
14. Cash & balance with Central bank		-	-	-	-	-	-	-	-	-	-	14.	Caisse & solde auprès de la Banque centrale
15. Interbank deposits		15081	13431	12230	10060	6179	11228	10102	9237	14780	10595	15.	Dépôts interbancaires
16. Loans		812146	723734	647917	626380	635061	647908	681328	691760	714241	754781	16.	Prêts
17. Securities		285320	252942	267585	275773	290276	288582	262356	248679	269377	291451	17.	Valeurs mobilières
18. Other assets		146631	122895	102482	88674	77048	78023	74503	76510	89840	92107	18.	Autres actifs
Liabilities													**Passif**
19. Capital & reserves		67535	68628	74350	78421	79934	86063	85790	89332	94509	94971	19.	Capital et réserves
20. Borrowing from Central bank		-	-	-	-	-	-	-	-	-	-	20.	Emprunts auprès de la Banque centrale
21. Interbank deposits		46966	25964	26585	33767	52809	55288	52248	50713	62857	82074	21.	Dépôts interbancaires
22. Non-bank deposits		964667	881972	801071	774157	737180	741907	727920	704136	704859	707261	22.	Dépôts non bancaires
23. Bonds		4331	3524	3056	2533	2395	2581	2401	2935	2812	3019	23.	Obligations
24. Other liabilities		175679	132914	125152	112009	136246	139902	159930	179069	223201	261609	24.	Autres engagements
Balance sheet total													**Total du bilan**
25. End-year total		1259178	1113002	1030214	1000887	1008564	1025741	1028289	1026185	1088238	1148934	25.	En fin d'exercice
26. Average total		1343345	1186090	1071608	1015551	1004726	1017153	1027015	1027237	1057212	1118349	26.	Moyen

UNITED STATES
Savings banks

ETATS-UNIS
Caisses d'épargne

Million US dollars / *Millions de dollars des EU*

	1992	1993	1994	1995	1996	1997	1998	1999	2000	2001		
Memorandum items												**Pour mémoire**
27. Short-term securities	..	..	..	..	..	..	..	..	..	..	27.	Titres à court terme
28. Bonds	..	..	..	..	..	..	..	..	..	..	28.	Obligations
29. Shares and participations	..	..	..	..	..	..	..	..	..	..	29.	Actions et participations
30. Claims on non-residents	..	..	..	..	..	..	..	..	..	..	30.	Créances sur des non-résidents
31. Liabilities to non-residents	..	..	..	..	..	..	..	..	..	..	31.	Engagements envers des non-résidents
Capital adequacy												**Solvabilité**
32. Tier 1 Capital	58341	61819	70034	74252	76979	79337	79250	80542	83997	89582	32.	Fonds propres de base
33. Tier 2 Capital	9507	9106	8696	7891	7487	7759	7796	7931	8645	8265	33.	Fonds propres complémentaires
34. Supervisory deductions	-	-	-	-	-	-	-	-	-	-	34.	Eléments à déduire des fonds propres
35. Total net capital resources	67848	70925	78730	82143	84466	87096	87046	88473	92642	97847	35.	Total net des ressources en capital
36. Risk-weighted assets	773376	673237	576129	544492	542416	556747	575681	584756	615113	675029	36.	Actifs pondérés des risques
SUPPLEMENTARY INFORMATION												**RENSEIGNEMENTS COMPLEMENTAIRES**
37. Number of institutions	2815	2561	2390	2262	2152	2030	1924	1780	1684	1641	37.	Nombre d'institutions
38. Number of branches	18792	17016	15407	14599	14644	13436	13740	12656	12451	13070	38.	Nombre de succursales
39. Number of employees (x 1000)	345	305	296	287	262	250	253	245	237	244	39.	Nombre de salariés (x 1000)

1 Provisions on securities (item 8.b.) are included under Provisions on loans (item 8.a.)

2 Change in methodology.

Notes

. Savings institutions include Savings banks and Savings and loan associations.

Change in methodology

. Until 1996, Profit after tax (item 11) reflects extraordinary items and realized gains on assets and securities taken into account when calculating net income.

1 Les Provisions sur titres (poste 8.b.) sont incluses sous Provisions sur prêts (poste 8.a.)

2 Changement méthodologique.

Notes

. Les "Institutions d'épargne" comprennent les Caisses d'épargne et les Associations d'épargne et de prêts.

Changement méthodologique

. Jusqu'en 1996, la rubrique Bénéfices après impôts (poste 11) représente les profits exceptionnels et les revenus provenant des actifs et valeurs mobilières pris en compte lors du calcul du résultat net.

UNITED STATES

Savings banks

ETATS-UNIS

Caisses d'épargne

Per cent / *Pourcentage*

INCOME STATEMENT ANALYSIS / **ANALYSE DU COMPTE DE RESULTATS**

	1992	1993	1994	1995	1996	1997	1998	1999	2000	2001		
% of average balance sheet total												**% du total moyen du bilan**
40. Interest income	8.73	8.23	7.25	6.51	6.32	6.98	7.04	6.73	6.72	6.64	40.	Produits financiers
41. Interest expenses	6.77	5.86	4.28	3.40	3.33	4.18	4.11	3.95	3.96	3.83	41.	Frais financiers
42. Net interest income	1.96	2.37	2.97	3.11	2.99	2.80	2.93	2.79	2.76	2.80	42.	Produits financiers nets
43. Non-interest income (net)	0.54	0.56	0.59	0.63	0.61	0.70	0.73	0.68	0.87	0.88	43.	Produits non financiers (nets)
a. Fees and commissions receivable	0.38	0.45	0.44	0.47	0.48	0.49	0.47	0.49	0.53	0.62		a. Frais et commissions à recevoir
b. Fees and commissions payable												b. Frais et commissions à payer
c. Net profits or loss on financial operations												c. Profits ou pertes nets sur opérations financières
d. Other	0.17	0.11	0.15	0.16	0.13	0.21	0.26	0.20	0.34	0.26		d. Autres
44. Gross income	2.50	2.93	3.56	3.75	3.60	3.50	3.66	3.47	3.63	3.68	44.	Résultat brut
45. Operating expenses	2.12	2.23	2.35	2.45	2.31	2.15	2.50	2.05	2.23	2.15	45.	Frais d'exploitation
a. Staff costs	0.80	0.83	0.90	0.98	0.97	0.94	0.99	0.97	1.03	0.99		a. Dépenses en personnel
b. Property costs	0.38	0.38	0.40	0.40	0.39	0.39	0.40	0.37	0.41	0.39		b. Dépenses en immobilier
c. Other	0.94	1.02	1.06	1.07	0.95	0.81	1.12	0.71	0.80	0.76		c. Autres
46. Net income	0.38	0.70	1.20	1.29	1.29	1.35	1.16	1.42	1.40	1.53	46.	Résultat net
47. Provisions (net)	0.69	0.59	0.48	0.42	0.25	0.21	0.25	0.21	0.17	0.14	47.	Provisions (nettes)
a. Provisions on loans	0.69	0.59	0.48	0.42	0.25	0.21	0.25	0.21	0.17	0.14		a. Provisions sur prêts
b. Provisions on securities												b. Provisions sur titres
c. Other												c. Autres
48. Profit before tax	-0.31	0.11	0.72	0.87	1.04	1.14	0.91	1.21	1.23	1.39	48.	Bénéfices avant impôt
49. Income tax	0.10	0.24	0.35	0.38	0.38	0.41	0.30	0.47	0.50	0.55	49.	Impôt sur le revenu
50. Profit after tax	-0.41	-0.12	0.37	0.49	0.67	0.73	0.62	0.73	0.74	0.84	50.	Bénéfices après impôt
51. Distributed profit	0.10	0.15	0.20	0.23	0.26	0.40	0.57	0.48	0.62	0.55	51.	Bénéfices distribués
52. Retained profit	-0.51	-0.28	0.17	0.26	0.41	0.33	0.05	0.26	0.11	0.30	52.	Bénéfices mis en réserve
% of gross income												**% du total du résultat brut**
53. Net interest income	78.21	80.90	83.44	83.13	83.08	79.99	80.07	80.28	76.03	76.19	53.	Produits financiers nets
54. Non-interest income (net)	21.79	19.10	16.56	16.87	16.92	20.01	19.93	19.72	23.97	23.81	54.	Produits non financiers (nets)
a. Fees and commissions receivable	15.08	15.29	12.43	12.46	13.37	14.14	12.89	14.00	14.48	16.85		a. Frais et commissions à recevoir
b. Fees and commissions payable												b. Frais et commissions à payer
c. Net profits or loss on financial operations												c. Profits ou pertes nets sur opérations financières
d. Other	6.71	3.81	4.13	4.40	3.55	5.87	7.04	5.72	9.49	6.96		d. Autres
55. Operating expenses	84.78	76.06	66.21	65.46	64.21	61.36	68.37	59.12	61.41	58.36	55.	Frais d'exploitation
a. Staff costs	32.19	28.28	25.22	26.20	26.96	26.94	26.97	27.88	28.31	26.96		a. Dépenses en personnel
b. Property costs	15.04	13.09	11.22	10.73	10.97	11.26	10.90	10.64	11.16	10.70		b. Dépenses en immobilier
c. Other	37.55	34.69	29.76	28.54	26.28	23.16	30.50	20.60	21.93	20.69		c. Autres
56. Net income	15.22	23.94	33.79	34.54	35.79	38.64	31.63	40.88	38.59	41.64	56.	Résultat net
57. Provisions (net)	27.59	20.12	13.58	11.34	6.86	5.95	6.74	6.13	4.62	3.80	57.	Provisions (nettes)
a. Provisions on loans	27.59	20.12	13.58	11.34	6.86	5.95	6.74	6.13	4.62	3.80		a. Provisions sur prêts
b. Provisions on securities												b. Provisions sur titres
c. Other												c. Autres
58. Profit before tax	-12.37	3.82	20.21	23.20	28.94	32.69	24.89	34.75	33.98	37.84	58.	Bénéfices avant impôt
59. Income tax	4.05	8.08	9.85	10.14	10.45	11.69	8.08	13.61	13.73	14.90	59.	Impôt sur le revenu
60. Profit after tax	-16.42	-4.26	10.36	13.06	18.49	21.01	16.81	21.14	20.25	22.94	60.	Bénéfices après impôt
% of net income												**% du total du résultat net**
61. Provisions (net)	181.31	84.05	40.19	32.82	19.16	15.39	21.31	15.00	11.96	9.13	61.	Provisions (nettes)
a. Provisions on loans	181.31	84.05	40.19	32.82	19.16	15.39	21.31	15.00	11.96	9.13		a. Provisions sur prêts
b. Provisions on securities												b. Provisions sur titres
c. Other												c. Autres
62. Profit before tax	-81.31	15.95	59.81	67.18	80.84	84.61	78.69	85.00	88.04	90.87	62.	Bénéfices avant impôt
63. Income tax	26.61	33.77	29.16	29.37	29.19	30.24	25.54	33.30	35.57	35.78	63.	Impôt sur le revenu
64. Profit after tax	-107.92	-17.80	30.65	37.81	51.66	54.36	53.15	51.70	52.47	55.09	64.	Bénéfices après impôt

UNITED STATES
Savings banks

ETATS-UNIS
Caisses d'épargne

Per cent — *Pourcentage*

BALANCE SHEET ANALYSIS — **ANALYSE DU BILAN**

% of year-end balance sheet total — % du total du bilan en fin d'exercice

	1992	1993	1994	1995	1996	1997	1998	1999	2000	2001	
Assets											**Actif**
65. Cash & balance with Central bank	-	-	-	-	-	-	-	-	-	-	65. Caisse & solde auprès de la Banque centrale
66. Interbank deposits	1.20	1.21	1.19	1.01	0.61	1.09	0.98	0.90	1.36	0.92	66. Dépôts interbancaires
67. Loans	64.50	65.03	62.89	62.58	62.97	63.16	66.26	67.41	65.63	65.69	67. Prêts
68. Securities	22.66	22.73	25.97	27.55	28.78	28.13	25.51	24.23	24.75	25.37	68. Valeurs mobilières
69. Other assets	11.64	11.04	9.95	8.86	7.64	7.61	7.25	7.46	8.26	8.02	69. Autres actifs
Liabilities											**Passif**
70. Capital & reserves	5.36	6.17	7.22	7.84	7.93	8.39	8.34	8.71	8.68	8.27	70. Capital et réserves
71. Borrowing from Central bank	-	-	-	-	-	-	-	-	-	-	71. Emprunts auprès de la Banque centrale
72. Interbank deposits	3.73	2.33	2.58	3.37	5.24	5.39	5.08	4.94	5.78	7.14	72. Dépôts interbancaires
73. Non-bank deposits	76.61	79.24	77.76	77.35	73.09	72.33	70.79	68.62	64.77	61.56	73. Dépôts non bancaires
74. Bonds	0.34	0.32	0.30	0.25	0.24	0.25	0.23	0.29	0.26	0.26	74. Obligations
75. Other liabilities	13.95	11.94	12.15	11.19	13.51	13.64	15.55	17.45	20.51	22.77	75. Autres engagements
Memorandum items											***Pour mémoire***
76. Short-term securities	..	..	..	..	..	..	..	..	..	..	76. Titres à court terme
77. Bonds	..	..	..	..	..	..	..	..	..	..	77. Obligations
78. Shares and participations	..	..	..	..	..	..	..	..	..	..	78. Actions et participations
79. Claims on non-residents	..	..	..	..	..	..	..	..	..	..	79. Créances sur des non-résidents
80. Liabilities to non-residents	..	..	..	..	..	..	..	..	..	..	80. Engagements envers des non-résidents

* See notes on previous pages.   * Voir les notes en pages précédentes.

Part II

GENERAL TABLES

TABLEAUX GÉNÉRAUX

STRUCTURE OF THE FINANCIAL SYSTEM
STRUCTURE DU SYSTEME FINANCIER
end-June 2000 - fin juin 2000

	Number of institutions / Nombre d'institutions	Number of branches / Nombre de succursales	Number of employees / Nombre de salariés	Total assets or liabilities / Total des actifs ou des passifs _million A$ / $A_	Total financial assets / Total des actifs financiers _million A$ / $A_	%	
Central bank	1	2	807	55694	55402	..	_Banque centrale_
Other monetary institutions	50	5005	..	735378	731659	..	_Autres institutions monétaires_
Commercial banks (1)	25	4934	..	663297	659669	..	Banques commerciales (1)
Foreign-owned banks (2)	25	71	..	72081	71991	..	Banques étrangères (2)
Other financial institutions	559		..	176627	..	..	_Autres institutions financières_
Mortgage credit institutions (3)	19	310	2654	12723	12548	..	Institutions de crédit hypothécaire (3)
Credit co-operatives	215	898	8501	21509	21024	..	Coopératives de crédit
Finance companies (4)	211	..	..	70854	..	..	Sociétés financières (4)
Others (5)	114	..	..	71541	..	..	Autres (5)
Insurance institutions	210076	..	..	735280	..	..	_Institutions d'assurance_
Insurance companies (6)	207	..	..	244845	..	..	Sociétés d'assurance (6)
Pension funds and foundations (7)	214296		..	278307	..	..	Fonds de pension et fondations (7)
Others (8)	755	..	..	212128	..	..	Autres (8)
All financial institutions	210686	..	..	1701401	..	..	_Ensemble des institutions financières_

1 Includes 11 banks authorised as subsidiaries of foreign banks. Total assets of foreign subsidiary banks was $A 44 729
  million at June 2000. Data refers to Australian operations of banks.
2 Refers to banks authorised as foreign branch banks. Data refers to the Australian operations of these banks.
3 Co-operative building societies.
4 General financiers and other finance companies.
5 Other companies registered under Financial Corporations Act.
6 Life and General Insurance companies.
7 Non-life superannuation.
8 Public unit trusts, trustee companies and friendly societies.

1 Y compris 11 banques agréées comme filiales de banques étrangères. Le total des actifs des filiales bancaires
  étrangères était de 44 729 millions de $A en juin 2000. Les données se réfèrent aux transactions australiennes des banques.
2 Comprend les banques agréées comme succursales bancaires étrangères.   Les données se réfèrent aux
  opérations australiennes de ces banques.
3 Mutuelles de crédit immobilier.
4 Financiers et autres sociétés financières.
5 Autres sociétés enregistrées sous la loi de finance des sociétés.
6 Compagnies d'assurance et d'assurance vie.
7 Cotisations non-vie.
8 Fonds commun de placement, compagnies fiduciaires et sociétés de prévoyance.

**RESIDENT/NON-RESIDENT AND DOMESTIC/FOREIGN CURRENCY
CLASSIFICATION OF BANK ASSETS AND LIABILITIES (1)
end-June 2000
RESIDENT/NON RESIDENT ET MONNAIE NATIONALE/ETRANGERE
CLASSIFICATION DE L'ACTIF ET DU PASSIF DES BANQUES (1)
fin juin 2000**

Million Australian dollars   *Millions de dollars australiens*

	Residents / Résidents	Non-residents / Non résidents	Total / Total	
Assets				*Actif*
Domestic currency	671517	16512	688029	Monnaie nationale
Foreign currencies	*27818*	*19530*	*47349*	Monnaies étrangères
Total	699336	36042	735378	Total
Liabilities (2)				*Passif (2)*
Domestic currency	508096	27909	536005	Monnaie nationale
Foreign currencies	*23572*	*86282*	*109855*	Monnaies étrangères
Total	531668	114191	645859	Total

1 Figures refer to balances reported on banks' Australian books. They exclude banks' overseas branch and overseas
  bank subsidiary operations and domestic and overseas non-bank subsidiaries.
2 Liabilities exclude shareholders' funds of banks.

1 Les chiffres se réfèrent aux bilans présentés dans les comptes australiens des banques. Ils excluent les opérations des
  succursales étrangères et celles des filiales bancaires étrangères ainsi que les filiales non bancaires étrangères.
2 Les fonds des actionnaires des banques sont exclus du passif.

STRUCTURE OF THE FINANCIAL SYSTEM
STRUCTURE DU SYSTEME FINANCIER
end-June 2001 - fin juin 2001

	Number of institutions / Nombre d'institutions	Number of branches / Nombre de succursales	Number of employees / Nombre de salariés	Total assets or liabilities / Total des actifs ou des passifs million A$ / $A	Total financial assets / Total des actifs financiers million A$ / $A	%	
Central bank	1	2	800	58113	57833	..	Banque centrale
Other monetary institutions	51	4711	..	807699	803594	..	Autres institutions monétaires
Commercial banks (1)	26	4696	..	726226	722205	..	Banques commerciales (1)
Foreign-owned banks (2)	25	15	..	81473	81389	..	Banques étrangères (2)
						..	
Other financial institutions	523	..	..	203622	..	..	Autres institutions financières
Mortgage credit institutions (3)	18	308	2762	13073	12920	..	Institutions de crédit hypothécaire (3)
Credit co-operatives	205	903	8217	23945	23456		Coopératives de crédit
Finance companies (4)	203	..	..	82340	..	..	Sociétés financières (4)
Others (5)	97	..	..	84264	..	..	Autres (5)
Insurance institutions	227419	..	..	798166	..	..	Institutions d'assurance
Insurance companies (6)	213	..	..	251601	..	..	Sociétés d'assurance (6)
Pension funds and foundations (7)	226480	..	..	298917	..	..	Fonds de pension et fondations (7)
	..	..	..	..	..	..	
Others (8)	726	..	..	247648	..	..	Autres (8)
All financial institutions	227994	..	..	1867600	..	..	Ensemble des institutions financières

1 Includes 13 banks authorised as subsidiaries of foreign banks. Total assets of foreign subsidiary banks was $A 54 100 million at June 2001. Data refers to Australian operations of banks.
2 Refers to banks authorised as foreign branch banks. Data refers to the Australian operations of these banks.
3 Co-operative building societies.
4. General financiers and other finance companies.
5. Other companies registered under Financial Corporations Act)
6 Life and General Insurance companies.
7 Non-life superannuation.
8 Public unit trusts, trustee companies and friendly societies.

1 Y compris 13 banques agréées comme filiales de banques étrangères. Le total des actifs des filiales bancaires étrangères était de 54 100 millions de $A en juin 2001. Les données se réfèrent aux transactions australiennes des banques.
2 Comprend les banques agréées comme succursales bancaires étrangères. Les données se réfèrent aux opérations australiennes de ces banques.
3 Mutuelles de crédit immobilier.
4 Financiers et autres sociétés financières.
5 Autres sociétés enregistrées sous la loi de finance des sociétés.
6 Compagnies d'assurance et d'assurance vie.
7 Cotisations non-vie.
8 Fonds commun de placement, compagnies fiduciaires et sociétés de prévoyance.

**RESIDENT/NON-RESIDENT AND DOMESTIC/FOREIGN CURRENCY
CLASSIFICATION OF BANK ASSETS AND LIABILITIES (1)
end-June 2001
RESIDENT/NON RESIDENT ET MONNAIE NATIONALE/ETRANGERE
CLASSIFICATION DE L'ACTIF ET DU PASSIF DES BANQUES (1)
fin juin 2001**

Million Australian dollars   *Millions de dollars australiens*

	Residents / Résidents	Non-residents / Non résidents	Total / Total	
Assets				*Actif*
Domestic currency	727615	17898	745512	Monnaie nationale
Foreign currencies	32720	29467	62187	Monnaies étrangères
Total	760334	47365	807699	Total
Liabilities (2)				*Passif (2)*
Domestic currency	531395	27977	559372	Monnaie nationale
Foreign currencies	28064	133039	161103	Monnaies étrangères
Total	559459	161016	720475	Total

1 Figures refer to balances reported on banks' Australian books. They exclude banks' overseas branch and overseas
   bank subsidiary operations and domestic and overseas non-bank subsidiaries.
2 Liabilities exclude shareholders' funds of banks.

1 Les chiffres se réfèrent aux bilans présentés dans les comptes australiens des banques. Ils excluent les opérations des
   succursales étrangères et celles des filiales bancaires étrangères ainsi que les filiales non bancaires étrangères.
2 Les fonds des actionnaires des banques sont exclus du passif.

STRUCTURE OF THE FINANCIAL SYSTEM
STRUCTURE DU SYSTEME FINANCIER

1999

	Number of institutions / Nombre d'institutions	Number of branches / Nombre de succursales	Number of employees / Nombre de salariés	Total assets or liabilities / Total des actifs ou des passifs	Total financial assets / Total des actifs financiers		
				million EUR	million EUR	%	
Central bank	1	8	..	37845	33964	5	Banque centrale
Other monetary institutions	853	4379	..	441261	436874	65	Autres institutions monétaires
Commercial banks	36	746	..	111249	110378	16	Banques commerciales
Foreign-owned banks (1)	28		..	13858	13683	2	Banques étrangères (1)
Savings banks	71	1421	..	190029	188779	28	Caisses d'épargne
Co-operative banks	718	2212	..	126125	124035	18	Banques mutualistes
Other financial institutions	93	160	..	65653	65147	10	Autres institutions financières
Mortgage credit institutions	9	155	..	28684	28506	4	Institutions de crédit hypothécaire
Development credit institutions				-	-	-	Institutions de crédit de développement
Finance companies				-	-	-	Sociétés financières
Others (2)	84	5	..	36969	36641	5	Autres (2)
Insurance institutions	1235	..	..	138639	134848	20	Institutions d'assurance
Insurance companies	70	..	..	51157	47398	7	Sociétés d'assurance
Pension funds and foundations	17	..	..	7141	7109	1	Fonds de pension et fondations
Others (3)	1148	..	..	80341	80341	12	Autres (3)
All financial institutions	2182	4547	..	683397	670833	100	Ensemble des institutions financières

1 Foreign-owned bank branches are included with those of Commercial banks
2 Special purpose credit institutions.
3 The item "others" includes all kinds of Investment funds existing in Austria.

1 Les succursales des Banques étrangères sont incluses avec celles des Banques commerciales
2 Institutions de crédit specialisées.
3 Le poste "autres" inclut tous les types de fonds d'investissements existants en Autriche

RESIDENT/NON-RESIDENT AND DOMESTIC/FOREIGN CURRENCY
CLASSIFICATION OF BANK ASSETS AND LIABILITIES

RESIDENT/NON RESIDENT ET MONNAIE NATIONALE/ETRANGERE
CLASSIFICATION DE L'ACTIF ET DU PASSIF DES BANQUES

1999

Million euros   *Millions d'euros*

	Residents / Résidents	Non-residents / Non résidents	Total / Total	
Assets				Actif
Domestic currency	321975	63867	385842	Monnaie nationale
Foreign currencies	70964	67828	138793	Monnaies étrangères
Total	392939	131695	524635	Total
Liabilities				Passif
Domestic currency	332527	51979	384506	Monnaie nationale
Foreign currencies	44993	95135	140128	Monnaies étrangères
Total	377520	147115	524635	Total

STRUCTURE OF THE FINANCIAL SYSTEM
STRUCTURE DU SYSTEME FINANCIER

2000

	Number of institutions / Nombre d'institutions	Number of branches / Nombre de succursales	Number of employees / Nombre de salariés	Total assets or liabilities / Total des actifs ou des passifs	Total financial assets / Total des actifs financiers		
				million EUR	million EUR	%	
Central bank	1	8	..	36186	36076	..	Banque centrale
Other monetary institutions	827	4361	..	469714	466865	..	Autres institutions monétaires
Commercial banks	32	751	..	103372	104059	..	Banques commerciales
Foreign-owned banks (1)	29		..	14687	14574	..	Banques étrangères (1)
Savings banks	70	1397	..	213218	211916	..	Caisses d'épargne
Co-operative banks	696	2213	..	138437	136316	..	Banques mutualistes
Other financial institutions	91	161	..	73013	72538	..	Autres institutions financières
Mortgage credit institutions	9	154	..	31919	31742	..	Institutions de crédit hypothécaire
Development credit institutions				-	-	-	Institutions de crédit de développement
Finance companies				-	-	-	Sociétés financières
Others (2)	82	7	..	41094	40797	..	Autres (2)
Insurance institutions	1539	-	..	145521	141723	..	Institutions d'assurance
Insurance companies	68	-	..	54134	50365	..	Sociétés d'assurance
Pension funds and foundations	19	-	..	7848	7819	..	Fonds de pension et fondations
Others (3)	1452	-	..	83539	83539	..	Autres (3)
All financial institutions	2458	4369	..	724434	717202	..	Ensemble des institutions financières

1 Foreign-owned bank branches are included with those of Commercial banks
2 Special purpose credit institutions.
3 The item "others" includes all kinds of Investment funds existing in Austria.

1 Les succursales des Banques étrangères sont incluses avec celles des Banques commerciales
2 Institutions de crédit specialisées.
3 Le poste "autres" inclut tous les types de fonds d'investissements existants en Autriche

RESIDENT/NON-RESIDENT AND DOMESTIC/FOREIGN CURRENCY
CLASSIFICATION OF BANK ASSETS AND LIABILITIES

RESIDENT/NON RESIDENT ET MONNAIE NATIONALE/ETRANGERE
CLASSIFICATION DE L'ACTIF ET DU PASSIF DES BANQUES

2000

Million euros   Millions d'euros

	Residents / Résidents	Non-residents / Non résidents	Total / Total	
Assets				Actif
Domestic currency	331167	80771	411938	Monnaie nationale
Foreign currencies	73272	77490	150762	Monnaies étrangères
Total	404438	158261	562700	Total
Liabilities				Passif
Domestic currency	345765	65955	411721	Monnaie nationale
Foreign currencies	42257	108722	150979	Monnaies étrangères
Total	388023	174677	562700	Total

STRUCTURE OF THE FINANCIAL SYSTEM
STRUCTURE DU SYSTEME FINANCIER

2001

	Number of institutions / Nombre d'institutions	Number of branches / Nombre de succursales	Number of employees / Nombre de salariés	Total assets or liabilities / Total des actifs ou des passifs million EUR	Total financial assets / Total des actifs financiers million EUR	%	
Central bank	1	8	..	31301	31165	..	Banque centrale
Other monetary institutions	815	4318	..	487602	483198	..	Autres institutions monétaires
Commercial banks	33	738	..	13103	12562	..	Banques commerciales
Foreign-owned banks (1)	28		..	116161	115802	..	Banques étrangères (1)
Savings banks	67	1380	..	203214	201914	..	Caisses d'épargne
Co-operative banks	687	2200	..	155123	152920	..	Banques mutualistes
Other financial institutions	87	169	..	81081	80628	..	Autres institutions financières
Mortgage credit institutions	9	164	..	35821	35646	..	Institutions de crédit hypothécaire
Development credit institutions	..	..	..	-	-	-	Institutions de crédit de développement
Finance companies	..	..	..	-	-	-	Sociétés financières
Others (2)	78	5	..	45259	44982	..	Autres (2)
Insurance institutions	1800	-	..	152333	148464	..	Institutions d'assurance
Insurance companies	65	-	..	57471	53637	..	Sociétés d'assurance
Pension funds and foundations	19	-	..	8048	8013	..	Fonds de pension et fondations
Others (3)	1716	-	..	86814	86814	..	Autres (3)
All financial institutions	2703	4495	..	752316	743455	..	Ensemble des institutions financières

1 Foreign-owned bank branches are included with those of Commercial banks
2 Special purpose credit institutions.
3 The item "others" includes all kinds of Investment funds existing in Austria.

1 Les succursales des Banques étrangères sont incluses avec celles des Banques commerciales
2 Institutions de crédit specialisées.
3 Le poste "autres" inclut tous les types de fonds d'investissements existants en Autriche

RESIDENT/NON-RESIDENT AND DOMESTIC/FOREIGN CURRENCY
CLASSIFICATION OF BANK ASSETS AND LIABILITIES
RESIDENT/NON RESIDENT ET MONNAIE NATIONALE/ETRANGERE
CLASSIFICATION DE L'ACTIF ET DU PASSIF DES BANQUES

2001

Million euros   Millions d'euros

	Residents / Résidents	Non-residents / Non résidents	Total / Total	
Assets				Actif
Domestic currency	351931	90321	442252	Monnaie nationale
Foreign currencies	78920	66568	145488	Monnaies étrangères
Total	430851	156890	587741	Total
Liabilities				Passif
Domestic currency	366996	64866	431861	Monnaie nationale
Foreign currencies	46613	109266	155879	Monnaies étrangères
Total	413609	174132	587741	Total

STRUCTURE OF THE FINANCIAL SYSTEM
STRUCTURE DU SYSTEME FINANCIER

2000

	Number of institutions / Nombre d'institutions	Number of branches / Nombre de succursales	Number of employees / Nombre de salariés	Total assets or liabilities / Total des actifs ou des passifs million EUR	Total financial assets / Total des actifs financiers million EUR	%	
Central bank	1	13	2672	36515	..	..	Banque centrale
Credit institutions	118	13696	76364	778063	..	..	Etablissements de crédit
Largest credit institutions governed by Belgian law	5	..	..	599559	..	..	Principaux établissements de crédit de droit belge
Other credit institutions governed by Belgian law	67	..	..	125570	..	..	Autres établissements de crédit de droit belge
Branches of credit institutions governed by foreign law	46	..	..	52935	..	..	Succursales d'établissements de crédit de droit étranger
Collective investment institutions	392	..	..	138230	..	..	Organismes de placement collectif
Securities dealers	46	..	..	6990	6905	..	Sociétés de bourse
Mortgage companies	..	..	..	..	..	..	Sociétés hypothécaires
Insurance institutions	517	..	..	122958	107534	..	Entreprises d'assurance
Insurance companies	210	..	..	108350	93015	..	Compagnies d'assurance
Pension funds	307	..	..	14608	14519	..	Fonds de pension
All financial institutions	..	..	..	..	..	..	Ensemble des institutions financières

RESIDENT/NON-RESIDENT AND DOMESTIC/FOREIGN CURRENCY
CLASSIFICATION OF CREDIT INSTITUTIONS ASSETS AND LIABILITIES

RESIDENT/NON RESIDENT ET MONNAIE NATIONALE/ETRANGERE
CLASSIFICATION DE L'ACTIF ET DU PASSIF DES ETABLISSEMENTS DE CREDIT

2000

Million euros   *Millions d'euros*

	Residents / Résidents	Non-residents / Non résidents	Total / Total	
Assets				Actif
Domestic currency	372853	203185	576038	Monnaie nationale
Foreign currencies	21471	180554	202026	Monnaies étrangères
Total	394324	383739	778063	Total
Liabilities				Passif
Domestic currency	385029	182988	568017	Monnaie nationale
Foreign currencies	22647	187399	210046	Monnaies étrangères
Total	407676	370388	778063	Total

STRUCTURE OF THE FINANCIAL SYSTEM
STRUCTURE DU SYSTEME FINANCIER

2001

	Number of institutions / Nombre d'institutions	Number of branches / Nombre de succursales	Number of employees / Nombre de salariés	Total assets or liabilities / Total des actifs ou des passifs million EUR	Total financial assets / Total des actifs financiers million EUR	%	
Central bank	1	12	2652	31203	..	..	Banque centrale
Credit institutions	112	12173	75843	846329	..	..	Etablissements de crédit
Largest credit institutions governed by Belgian law	5	..	..	672155	..	..	Principaux établissements de crédit de droit belge
Other credit institutions governed by Belgian law	62	..	..	131221	..	..	Autres établissements de crédit de droit belge
Branches of credit institutions governed by foreign law	45	..	..	42953	..	..	Succursales d'établis- sements de crédit de droit étranger
Collective investment institutions	406 (*)	..	..	143700	..	..	Organismes de placement collectif
Securities dealers	43	..	..	9711	9597	..	Sociétés de bourse
Mortgage companies		..	..	..	..	..	Sociétés hypothécaires
Insurance institutions	523	..	..	132943	116159	..	Entreprises d'assurance
Insurance companies	204	..	..	118720	102004	..	Compagnies d'assurance
Pension funds	319	..	..	14223	14155	..	Fonds de pension
All financial institutions	..	..	..	..	..	..	Ensemble des institutions financières

* Number of institutions at 30/06/2001
* Nombre arrêté au 30/06/2001.

RESIDENT/NON-RESIDENT AND DOMESTIC/FOREIGN CURRENCY
CLASSIFICATION OF CREDIT INSTITUTIONS ASSETS AND LIABILITIES

RESIDENT/NON RESIDENT ET MONNAIE NATIONALE/ETRANGERE
CLASSIFICATION DE L'ACTIF ET DU PASSIF DES ETABLISSEMENTS DE CREDIT

2001

Million euros   *Millions d'euros*

	Residents / Résidents	Non-residents / Non résidents	Total / Total	
Assets				*Actif*
Domestic currency	386609	248912	635521	Monnaie nationale
Foreign currencies	24263	186545	210808	Monnaies étrangères
Total	410873	435457	846329	Total
Liabilities				*Passif*
Domestic currency	411859	218121	629980	Monnaie nationale
Foreign currencies	20573	198776	219349	Monnaies étrangères
Total	432432	416897	849329	Total

STRUCTURE OF THE FINANCIAL SYSTEM (1)
STRUCTURE DU SYSTEME FINANCIER (1)

2000

	Number of institutions / Nombre d'institutions	Number of branches / Nombre de succursales	Number of employees / Nombre de salariés	Total assets or liabilities / Total des actifs ou des passifs	Total financial assets / Total des actifs financiers		
				million C$ / $ can	million C$ / $ can	%	
Central bank	1	1	..	39352	39114	1	Banque centrale
Other monetary institutions	..	..	..	1145870	1126375	35	Autres institutions monétaires
Commercial banks (2)	53	..	..	1015483	998520	31	Banques commerciales (2)
Co-operative banks	..	..	..	130387	127855	4	Banques mutualistes
Other financial institutions	..	..	..	1284487	1258475	39	Autres institutions financières
Mortgage credit institutions	..	..	..	10751	10621	0	Institutions de crédit hypothécaire
Development credit institutions	..	..	..	60015	56065	2	Institutions de crédit de développement
Finance companies	..	..	..	72218	71972	2	Sociétés financières
Others	..	..	..	1141503	1119817	35	Autres
Insurance institutions	..	..	..	835832	820531	25	Institutions d'assurance
Insurance companies	..	..	..	321892	306591	9	Sociétés d'assurance
Pension funds and foundations	..	..	..	513940	513940	16	Fonds de pension et fondations
All financial institutions	..	..	..	3305541	3244495	100	Ensemble des institutions financières

1 Data are taken from Canada's National Balance Sheet Accounts for the period ending 31 December and cover only booked-in Canada business.
2 Data include Foreign-owned banks

1 Les données se rapportent au Comptes du bilan national du Canada à la fin du 31 décembre et concernent uniquement les opérations enregistrées au Canada.
2 Les données incluent les Banques étrangères

RESIDENT/NON-RESIDENT AND DOMESTIC/FOREIGN CURRENCY
CLASSIFICATION OF BANK ASSETS AND LIABILITIES

RESIDENT/NON RESIDENT ET MONNAIE NATIONALE/ETRANGERE
CLASSIFICATION DE L'ACTIF ET DU PASSIF DES BANQUES

2000

Million canadian dollars

Millions de dollars canadiens

	Residents / Résidents	Non-residents / Non résidents	Total / Total	
Assets				Actif
Domestic currency	..	..	904971	Monnaie nationale
Foreign currencies	..	..	599092	Monnaies étrangères
Total	..	..	1504063	Total
Liabilities				Passif
Domestic currency	..	..	881311	Monnaie nationale
Foreign currencies	..	..	622752	Monnaies étrangères
Total	..	..	1504063	Total

STRUCTURE OF THE FINANCIAL SYSTEM (1)
STRUCTURE DU SYSTEME FINANCIER (1)

2001

	Number of institutions / Nombre d'institutions	Number of branches / Nombre de succursales	Number of employees / Nombre de salariés	Total assets or liabilities / Total des actifs ou des passifs	Total financial assets / Total des actifs financiers		
				million C$ / $ can	million C$ / $ can	%	
Central bank	1	1	..	43400	43153	1	Banque centrale
Other monetary institutions	..	..	..	1239415	1217936	35	Autres institutions monétaires
Commercial banks (2)	48	..	..	1094876	1076207	31	Banques commerciales (2)
Co-operative banks	..	..	..	144539	141729	4	Banques mutualistes
Other financial institutions	..	..	..	1364231	1336217	39	Autres institutions financières
Mortgage credit institutions	..	..	..	9640	9494	0	Institutions de crédit hypothécaire
Development credit institutions	..	..	..	65545	61693	2	Institutions de crédit de développement
Finance companies	..	..	..	73863	73590	2	Sociétés financières
Others	..	..	..	1215183	1191440	35	Autres
Insurance institutions	..	..	..	860697	844501	25	Institutions d'assurance
Insurance companies	..	..	..	333716	317520	9	Sociétés d'assurance
Pension funds and foundations	..	..	..	526981	526981	15	Fonds de pension et fondations
All financial institutions	..	..	..	3507743	3441807	100	Ensemble des institutions financières

1 Data are taken from Canada's National Balance Sheet Accounts for the period ending 31 December and cover only booked-in Canada business.
2 Data include Foreign-owned banks

1 Les données se rapportent au Comptes du bilan national du Canada à la fin du 31 décembre et concernent uniquement les opérations enregistrées au Canada.
2 Les données incluent les Banques étrangères

RESIDENT/NON-RESIDENT AND DOMESTIC/FOREIGN CURRENCY CLASSIFICATION OF BANK ASSETS AND LIABILITIES
RESIDENT/NON RESIDENT ET MONNAIE NATIONALE/ETRANGERE CLASSIFICATION DE L'ACTIF ET DU PASSIF DES BANQUES

2001

Million canadian dollars   *Millions de dollars canadiens*

	Residents / Résidents	Non-residents / Non résidents	Total / Total	
Assets				Actif
Domestic currency	..	..	987736	Monnaie nationale
Foreign currencies	..	..	659850	Monnaies étrangères
Total	..	..	1647586	Total
Liabilities				Passif
Domestic currency	..	..	932232	Monnaie nationale
Foreign currencies	..	..	714354	Monnaies étrangères
Total	..	..	1647586	Total

STRUCTURE OF THE FINANCIAL SYSTEM
STRUCTURE DU SYSTEME FINANCIER

2000

	Number of institutions / Nombre d'institutions	Number of branches / Nombre de succursales	Number of employees / Nombre de salariés	Total assets or liabilities / Total des actifs ou des passifs million Ck / KC	Total financial assets / Total des actifs financiers million Ck / KC	%	
Central bank	1	7	1460	616017	..	..	Banque centrale
Other monetary institutions	40	1809	45512	2717232	..	..	Autres institutions monétaires
Commercial banks (1)	11	1210	27684	1274263	..	..	Banques commerciales(1)
Foreign-owned banks(2)	23	590	16202	1313446	..	..	Banques étrangères (2)
Savings banks (3)	6	9	1626	129524	..	..	Caisses d'épargne (3)
Co-operative banks	-	-	-	-	..	..	Banques mutualistes
Other financial institutions	415	-	1626	-	-	-	Autres institutions financières
Mortgage credit institutions	..	..	..	..	..	..	Institutions de crédit hypothécaire
Development credit institutions	..	..	..	..	..	..	Institutions de crédit de développement
Finance companies	415		2311	..	..	..	Sociétés financières
Insurance institutions	98	1091	19756	..	..	..	Institutions d'assurance
Insurance companies	40	1068	19226	..	..	..	Sociétés d'assurance
Pension funds and foundations	18	-	240	..	..	..	Fonds de pension et fondations
Others (4)	40	23	290	..	..	..	Autres (4)
All financial institutions	554	2907	68358	3481165	..	..	Ensemble des institutions financières

1 Includes 1 bank with special statute.
2 Banks with more than 50% foreign capital and branches of foreign banks.
3 Building savings institutions.
4 Assistance companies in the Insurance sector.

1 Inclus 1 banque de régime spécial.
2 Banques avec plus de 50 % de capital étranger et succursales de banques étrangères
3 Institutions d'épargne immobilière.
4 Compagnies d'assistance dans le secteur de l'Assurance

RESIDENT/NON-RESIDENT AND DOMESTIC/FOREIGN CURRENCY
CLASSIFICATION OF BANK ASSETS AND LIABILITIES

RESIDENT/NON RESIDENT ET MONNAIE NATIONALE/ETRANGERE
CLASSIFICATION DE L'ACTIF ET DU PASSIF DES BANQUES

2000

Million Czech koruna   *Millions de couronnes tchèques*

	Residents / Résidents	Non-residents / Non résidents	Total / Total	
Assets				Actif
Domestic currency	2142759	186083	2328842	Monnaie nationale
Foreign currencies	222040	337445	559486	Monnaies étrangères
Total	2364799	523528	2717232 [1]	Total
Liabilities				Passif
Domestic currency	2144133	86882	2231014	Monnaie nationale
Foreign currencies	236029	250189	486218	Monnaies étrangères
Total	2380162	337071	2717232	Total

1 Includes adjustments and depreciation in the amount of Ck 171095 million, for which the breakdown by currencies and resident/non-resident is not available.

1 Inclus des ajustements et des dépréciations d'un montant de 171095 millions de Ck, pour lequel la ventilation par monnaie nationale/étrangère et par résident/non-résident n'est pas disponible.

STRUCTURE OF THE FINANCIAL SYSTEM
STRUCTURE DU SYSTEME FINANCIER

2001

	Number of institutions / Nombre d'institutions	Number of branches / Nombre de succursales	Number of employees / Nombre de salariés	Total assets or liabilities / Total des actifs ou des passifs	Total financial assets / Total des actifs financiers		
				million Ck / KC	million Ck / KC	%	
Central bank	1	7	1459	629214	..	..	Banque centrale
Other monetary institutions	38	1800	40871	2766858.86	..	..	Autres institutions monétaires
Commercial banks (1)	10	1189	23711	1193395	..	..	Banques commerciales(1)
Foreign-owned banks(2)	22	601	15482	1414353	..	..	Banques étrangères (2)
Savings banks (3)	6	10	1678	159111	..	..	Caisses d'épargne (3)
Co-operative banks	-	-	-	-	..	..	Banques mutualistes
Other financial institutions	473	-	-	-	-	-	Autres institutions financières
Mortgage credit institutions	..	..	..	..	..	..	Institutions de crédit hypothécaire
Development credit institutions	..	..	..	..	..	..	Institutions de crédit de développement
Finance companies	473	..	..	..	..	..	Sociétés financières
Insurance institutions	58	-	-	-	..	..	Institutions d'assurance
Insurance companies	43	..	..	..	..	..	Sociétés d'assurance
Pension funds and foundations	15	..	..	..	..	..	Fonds de pension et fondations
Others (4)	..	..	..	..	..	..	Autres (4)
All financial institutions	570	1807	42330	3396073	..	..	Ensemble des institutions financières

1 Includes 1 bank with special statute.
2 Banks with more than 50% foreign capital and branches of foreign banks.
3 Building savings institutions.
4 Assistance companies in the Insurance sector.

1 Inclus 1 banque de régime spécial.
2 Banques avec plus de 50 % de capital étranger et succursales de banques étrangères
3 Institutions d'épargne immobilière.
4 Compagnies d'assistance dans le secteur de l'Assurance.

RESIDENT/NON-RESIDENT AND DOMESTIC/FOREIGN CURRENCY
CLASSIFICATION OF BANK ASSETS AND LIABILITIES
RESIDENT/NON RESIDENT ET MONNAIE NATIONALE/ETRANGERE
CLASSIFICATION DE L'ACTIF ET DU PASSIF DES BANQUES

2001

Million Czech koruna   *Millions de couronnes tchèques*

	Residents / Résidents	Non-residents / Non résidents	Total / Total	
Assets				Actif
Domestic currency	2078442	210721	2289163	Monnaie nationale
Foreign currencies	186496	395571	582067	Monnaies étrangères
Total	2264938	606292	2766859 [1]	Total
Liabilities				Passif
Domestic currency	2205058	82277	2287335	Monnaie nationale
Foreign currencies	242153	237371	479524	Monnaies étrangères
Total	2447211	319648	2766859	Total

1 Includes adjustments and depreciation in the amount of Ck 104371 million, for which the breakdown by currencies and resident/non-resident is not available.

1 Inclus des ajustements et des dépréciations d'un montant de 104371 millions de Ck, pour lequel la ventilation par monnaie nationale / étrangère et par résident/non-résident n'est pas disponible.

STRUCTURE OF THE FINANCIAL SYSTEM
STRUCTURE DU SYSTEME FINANCIER

2000

	Number of institutions / Nombre d'institutions	Number of branches / Nombre de succursales	Number of employees / Nombre de salariés	Total assets or liabilities / Total des actifs ou des passifs million DKr/KrD	Total financial assets / Total des actifs financiers million DKr/KrD	%	
Central bank	1	-	550	237000	..	..	Banque centrale
Other monetary institutions	117	..	..	..	..	..	Autres institutions monétaires
Commercial banks (1)	99	2258	43431	1745377	..	..	Banques commerciales (1)
Foreign-owned banks	18	-	-				Banques étrangères
Other financial institutions	..	..	..	..	..	..	Autres institutions financières
Mortgage credit institutions	10	-	4075	1378053	..	..	Institutions de crédit hypothécaire
Development credit institutions	..	..	..	..	..	..	Institutions de crédit de développement
Finance companies	..	..	..	..	..	..	Sociétés financières
Insurance institutions	282		13646	1067065	..	..	Institutions d'assurance
Insurance companies	230	-	13604	1023750	..	..	Sociétés d'assurance
Pension funds and foundations	52	-	42	43315	..	..	Fonds de pension et fondations
All financial institutions	..	..	..	..	..	..	Ensemble des institutions financières

1 Includes banks, savings banks, and credit co-operatives with a minimum working capital of DKr 250 million.

1 Comprend les banques, les caisses d'épargne et les institutions coopératives de crédit disposant d'un fond de roulement minimum de 250 millions de DKr.

RESIDENT/NON-RESIDENT AND DOMESTIC/FOREIGN CURRENCY
CLASSIFICATION OF CREDIT INSTITUTIONS ASSETS AND LIABILITIES

RESIDENT/NON RESIDENT ET MONNAIE NATIONALE/ETRANGERE
CLASSIFICATION DE L'ACTIF ET DU PASSIF DES ETABLISSEMENTS DE CREDIT

2000

Million Danish kroner   *Millions de couronnes danoises*

	Residents / Résidents	Non-residents / Non résidents	Total / Total	
Assets				Actif
Domestic currency	920459	164184	1084643	Monnaie nationale
Foreign currencies	133130	468198	601329	Monnaies étrangères
Total	1053589	632383	1685972	Total
Liabilities				Passif
Domestic currency	943563	112367	1055930	Monnaie nationale
Foreign currencies	76395	553654	630049	Monnaies étrangères
Total	1019958	666021	1685979	Total

STRUCTURE OF THE FINANCIAL SYSTEM
STRUCTURE DU SYSTEME FINANCIER

2001

	Number of institutions / Nombre d'institutions	Number of branches / Nombre de succursales	Number of employees / Nombre de salariés	Total assets or liabilities / Total des actifs ou des passifs _million DKr/KrD_	Total financial assets / Total des actifs financiers _million DKr/KrD_	%	
Central bank	1	..	558	295286	..	..	Banque centrale
Other monetary institutions	..	..	..	..	..	..	Autres institutions monétaires
Commercial banks (1)	99	2103	43653	1979421	..	..	Banques commerciales (1)
Foreign-owned banks	21	-	-	..	..	..	Banques étrangères
Other financial institutions	..	..	..	..	..	..	Autres institutions financières
Mortgage credit institutions	8	-	3924	1616933	..	..	Institutions de crédit hypothécaire
Development credit institutions	..	..	..	..	..	..	Institutions de crédit de développement
Finance companies	..	..	..	..	..	..	Sociétés financières
Insurance institutions	270	..	13499	1068538	..	..	Institutions d'assurance
Insurance companies	220	-	13460	1028554	..	..	Sociétés d'assurance
Pension funds and foundations	50	-	39	39984	..	..	Fonds de pension et fondations
All financial institutions	..	..	..	..	..	..	Ensemble des institutions financières

1 Includes banks, savings banks, and credit co-operatives with a minimum working capital of DKr 250 million.

1 Comprend les banques, les caisses d'épargne et les institutions coopératives de crédit disposant d'un fond de roulement minimum de 250 millions de DKr.

RESIDENT/NON-RESIDENT AND DOMESTIC/FOREIGN CURRENCY
CLASSIFICATION OF CREDIT INSTITUTIONS ASSETS AND LIABILITIES

RESIDENT/NON RESIDENT ET MONNAIE NATIONALE/ETRANGERE
CLASSIFICATION DE L'ACTIF ET DU PASSIF DES ETABLISSEMENTS DE CREDIT

2001

Million Danish kroner   _Millions de couronnes danoises_

	Residents / Résidents	Non-residents / Non résidents	Total / Total	
Assets				Actif
Domestic currency	1084422	135113	1219535	Monnaie nationale
Foreign currencies	157292	421953	579246	Monnaies étrangères
Total	1241715	557066	1798781	Total
Liabilities				Passif
Domestic currency	1035604	93488	1129092	Monnaie nationale
Foreign currencies	73423	596274	669697	Monnaies étrangères
Total	1109027	689762	1798789	Total

STRUCTURE OF THE FINANCIAL SYSTEM
STRUCTURE DU SYSTEME FINANCIER

2000

	Number of institutions / Nombre d'institutions	Number of branches / Nombre de succursales	Number of employees / Nombre de salariés	Total assets or liabilities / Total des actifs ou des passifs	Total financial assets / Total des actifs financiers		
				million EUR	million EUR	%	
Central bank	1	4	768	11610	11610	4	Banque centrale
Other monetary institutions	342	1,221	24,625	137809	137188	46	Autres institutions monétaires
Commercial banks	9	485	15,423	99748	99300	33	Banques commerciales
Foreign-owned banks	6	19	647	9537	9522	3	Banques étrangères
Savings banks	40	212	1,858	6251	6157	2	Caisses d'épargne
Co-operative banks	287	505	6,697	22273	22209	7	Banques mutualistes
Other financial institutions					40343	14	Autres institutions financières
Other credit institutions	16	11	1281	11667	11643	4	Autres établissements de crédit
Mutual funds and fund companies	230			14333	14333	5	Fonds commun de placement et entreprises de placement
Investment firms	47		1430	1082	1035	0	Sociétés d'investissement
Financial auxiliaries	..	..	..	..	1509	1	Auxiliaires financiers
Insurance institutions	..	..	..	..	107602	36	Institutions d'assurance
Employment pension schemes*	..	..	..	..	61960	21	Fonds de pension *
Insurance corporations	..	..	..	..	45642	15	Sociétés d'assurance
All financial institutions	..	..	..	..	298252	100	Ensemble des institutions financières

1 Employement pension schemes are nowadays a part of social security funds.

1 Les régimes de retraites font de nos jours partie de la Sécurité Sociale.

RESIDENT/NON-RESIDENT AND DOMESTIC/FOREIGN CURRENCY
CLASSIFICATION OF BANK ASSETS AND LIABILITIES

RESIDENT/NON RESIDENT ET MONNAIE NATIONALE/ETRANGERE
CLASSIFICATION DE L'ACTIF ET DU PASSIF DES BANQUES

2000

Million euros   Millions d'euros

	Residents / Résidents	Non-residents / Non résidents	Total / Total	
Assets				Actif
Domestic currency	94137	15637	109773	Monnaie nationale
Foreign currencies	3156	24880	28036	Monnaies étrangères
Total	97293	40516	137809	Total
Liabilities				Passif
Domestic currency	97354	9073	106427	Monnaie nationale
Foreign currencies	1704	29678	31382	Monnaies étrangères
Total	99058	38752	137809	Total

STRUCTURE OF THE FINANCIAL SYSTEM
STRUCTURE DU SYSTEME FINANCIER

2001

	Number of institutions / Nombre d'institutions	Number of branches / Nombre de succursales	Number of employees / Nombre de salariés	Total assets or liabilities / Total des actifs ou des passifs million EUR	Total financial assets / Total des actifs financiers million EUR	%	
Central bank	1	4	764	2240	2240	4	Banque centrale
Other monetary institutions	342	1,282	24,652	26142	25749	49	Autres institutions monétaires
Commercial banks	9	505	15,146	19377	19203	37	Banques commerciales
Foreign-owned banks	7	62	718	1572	1571	3	Banques étrangères
Savings banks	40	213	1,918	1173	1136	2	Caisses d'épargne
Co-operative banks	286	502	6,870	4020	3840	7	Banques mutualistes
Other financial institutions					6964	13	Autres institutions financières
Other credit institutions	28	6	1304	2886	2542	5	Autres établissements de crédit
Mutual funds and fund companies	279				2635	5	Fonds commun de placement et entreprises de placement
Investment firms	50	8	1209	218	212	0	Sociétés d'investissement
Financial auxiliaries	..	..	..	..	268	10	Auxiliaires financiers
Insurance institutions	..	..	..	..	17377	33	Institutions d'assurance
Employment pension schemes*	..	..	..	..	10730	20	Fonds de pension *
Insurance corporations	..	..	..	..	6646	13	Sociétés d'assurance
All financial institutions	..	..	..	..	52598	100	Ensemble des institutions financières

1 Employement pension schemes are nowadays a part of social security funds.

1 Les régimes de retraites font de nos jours partie de la Sécurité Sociale.

RESIDENT/NON-RESIDENT AND DOMESTIC/FOREIGN CURRENCY
CLASSIFICATION OF BANK ASSETS AND LIABILITIES

RESIDENT/NON RESIDENT ET MONNAIE NATIONALE/ETRANGERE
CLASSIFICATION DE L'ACTIF ET DU PASSIF DES BANQUES

2001

Million euros   *Millions d'euros*

	Residents / Résidents	Non-residents / Non résidents	Total / Total	
Assets				Actif
Domestic currency	16541	2647	19188	Monnaie nationale
Foreign currencies	558	6395	6953	Monnaies étrangères
Total	17099	9043	26142	Total
Liabilities				Passif
Domestic currency	17553	2181	19733	Monnaie nationale
Foreign currencies	371	6038	6409	Monnaies étrangères
Total	17924	8218	26142	Total

STRUCTURE OF THE FINANCIAL SYSTEM (1)
STRUCTURE DU SYSTEME FINANCIER (1)

2000

	Number of institutions / Nombre d'institutions (2)	Number of branches / Nombre de succursales (2)	Number of employees / Nombre de salariés (3)	Total assets or liabilities / Total des actifs ou des passifs million EUR	Total financial assets / Total des actifs financiers million EUR	%	
Central bank	1	211	16393	125288	..	..	Banque centrale
Other monetary institutions	518	25574	352550	2615978	..	..	Autres institutions monétaires
Commercial banks	365	10140	188493	1765868	..	..	Banques commerciales
Foreign-owned banks(4)	..	..	..	..	..	..	Banques étrangères (4)
Savings banks (5)	..	..	..	..	..	..	Caisses d'épargne (5)
Co-operative banks	153	15434	164057	850110	..	..	Banques mutualistes
Other financial institutions	598	83	31276	447435	..	..	Autres institutions financières
Finance companies of which: Security houses	557 ..	.. ..	24694 ..	399255 ..	.. ..	.. ..	Sociétés financières dont : Maisons de titres
Specialised financial institutions	19	..	5346	46363	..	..	Institutions financières spécialisées
Municipal credit institutions	22	83	1236	1816	..	..	Caisses de crédit municipal
Insurance institutions	..	..	..	..	..	..	Institutions d'assurance
All financial institutions (6)	1117	25868	400219	3188701	..	..	Ensemble des institutions financières (6)

1 The data provided cover exclusively activities in France, including the overseas departments and territories.
2 Number of institutions and branches are taken from the "Rapport annuel du Comité des établissements de crédit".
3 Number of employees encompasses all staff, without deductions in the case of part-time staff
4 Data for Foreign-owned banks is included in Commercial banks figures.
5 On 1 January 2000, savings banks adopted the status of co-operative banks
6 All credit institutions.

1 Les données répertoriées concernent uniquement l'activité en métropole et dans les départements et territoires d'Outre-Mer.
2 Le nombre d'établissements et de guichets sont repris dans le "Rapport annuel du Comité des établissements de crédit".
3 En ce qui concerne les effectifs, il s'agit des effectifs sans déduction éventuelle des temps partiels
4 Les données pour les Banques étrangères sont comprises dans celles des Banques commerciales.
5 Depuis le 1er janvier 2000, les caisses d'épargne ont le statut de banques mutualistes.
6 Ensemble des institutions de crédit.

RESIDENT/NON-RESIDENT AND DOMESTIC/FOREIGN CURRENCY
CLASSIFICATION OF BANK ASSETS AND LIABILITIES (1)

RESIDENT/NON RESIDENT ET MONNAIE NATIONALE/ETRANGERE
CLASSIFICATION DE L'ACTIF ET DU PASSIF DES BANQUES (1)

2000

Million euros   Millions d'euros

	Residents / Résidents	Non-residents / Non résidents	Total / Total	
Assets				Actif
Domestic currency	2156131	425345	2581476	Monnaie nationale
Foreign currencies	119844	362093	481937	Monnaies étrangères
Total	2275975	787438	3063413	Total
Liabilities				Passif
Domestic currency	2133382	400210	2533592	Monnaie nationale
Foreign currencies	109443	420378	529821	Monnaies étrangères
Total	2242825	820588	3063413	Total

1 Data are for activities in France and its overseas departments and territories as of 31 December 2000

1 Il s'agit de données relatives à l'activité en métropole, dans les départements et territoires d'Outre-Mer au 31 décembre 2000.

STRUCTURE OF THE FINANCIAL SYSTEM (1)
STRUCTURE DU SYSTEME FINANCIER (1)

2001

	Number of institutions / Nombre d'institutions (2)	Number of branches / Nombre de succursales (2)	Number of employees / Nombre de salariés (3)	Total assets or liabilities / Total des actifs ou des passifs million EUR	Total financial assets / Total des actifs financiers million EUR	%	
Central bank	1	211	16323	127726	..	..	Banque centrale
Other monetary institutions	507	26049	364510	2856850	..	..	Autres institutions monétaires
Commercial banks	360	10200	195520	1996299	..	..	Banques commerciales
Foreign-owned banks(4)	..	..	..	..	..	..	Banques étrangères (4)
Savings banks (5)	..	..	..	..	..	..	Caisses d'épargne (5)
Co-operative banks	147	15770	168990	860551	..	..	Banques mutualistes
Other financial institutions	561	79	30185	508119	..	..	Autres institutions financières
Finance companies of which:	523	..	23657	459460	..	..	Sociétés financières dont :
Security houses	..	..	..	..	..	..	Maisons de titres
Specialised financial institutions	17	..	5276	46778	..	..	Institutions financières spécialisées
Municipal credit institutions	21	79	1252	1881	..	..	Caisses de crédit municipal
Insurance institutions	..	..	..	..	..	..	Institutions d'assurance
All financial institutions (6)	1069	26339	411018	3492695	..	..	Ensemble des institutions financières (6)

1 The data provided cover exclusively activities in France, including the overseas departments and territories.
2 Number of institutions and branches are taken from the "Rapport annuel du Comité des établissements de crédit".
3 Number of employees encompasses all staff, without deductions in the case of part-time staff
4 Data for Foreign-owned banks is included in Commercial banks figures.
5 On 1 January 2000, saving banks adopted the status of co-operative banks
6 All credit institutions.

1 Les données répertoriées concernent uniquement l'activité en métropole et dans les départements et territoires d'Outre-Mer.
2 Le nombre d'établissements et de guichets sont repris dans le "Rapport annuel du Comité des établissements de crédit".
3 En ce qui concerne les effectifs, il s'agit des effectifs sans déduction éventuelle des temps partiels
4 Les données pour les Banques étrangères sont comprises dans celles des Banques commerciales.
5 Depuis le 1er janvier 2000, les caisses d'épargne ont le statut de banques mutualistes.
6 Ensemble des institutions de crédit.

RESIDENT/NON-RESIDENT AND DOMESTIC/FOREIGN CURRENCY
CLASSIFICATION OF BANK ASSETS AND LIABILITIES (1)

RESIDENT/NON RESIDENT ET MONNAIE NATIONALE/ETRANGERE
CLASSIFICATION DE L'ACTIF ET DU PASSIF DES BANQUES (1)

2001

Million euros / Millions d'euros

	Residents / Résidents	Non-residents / Non résidents	Total / Total	
Assets				Actif
Domestic currency	2333027	482179	2815206	Monnaie nationale
Foreign currencies	151977	397786	549763	Monnaies étrangères
Total	2485004	879965	3364969	Total
Liabilities				Passif
Domestic currency	2285373	461037	2746410	Monnaie nationale
Foreign currencies	123715	494844	618559	Monnaies étrangères
Total	2409088	955881	3364969	Total

1 Data are for activities in France and its overseas departments and territories as of 31 December 2001

1 Il s'agit de données relatives à l'activité en métropole, dans les départements et territoires d'Outre-Mer au 31 décembre 2001.

STRUCTURE OF THE FINANCIAL SYSTEM
STRUCTURE DU SYSTEME FINANCIER

2000

	Number of institutions / Nombre d'institutions	Number of branches / Nombre de succursales	Number of employees / Nombre de salariés (x 1000)	Total assets or liabilities / Total des actifs ou des passifs bil / mlds EUR	Total financial assets / Total des actifs financiers bil / mlds EUR	%	
Central bank	1	128	16	257	255	..	Banque centrale
Other monetary institutions	2645	38744	..	..	..	..	Autres institutions monétaires
Commercial banks	204	6440	221	2147	2139	..	Banques commerciales
Foreign-owned banks (1)	87	80	..	..	..	..	Banques étrangères (1)
Savings banks	562	16892	283	954	939	..	Caisses d'épargne
Co-operative banks	1792	15332	171	534	524	..	Banques mutualistes
Other financial institutions	..	..	..	..	..	..	Autres institutions financières
Mortgage credit institutions	31	192	11	897	896	..	Institutions de crédit hypothécaire
Development credit institutions	..	..	..	..	..	..	Institutions de crédit de développement
Finance companies	..	..	..	..	..	..	Sociétés financières
Others	..	..	..	..	..	..	Autres
Insurance institutions	..	..	..	..	..	..	Institutions d'assurance
All financial institutions	..	..	..	..	..	..	Ensemble des institutions financières

1 Only domestic branches of foreign banks, excluding banks majority-owned by foreign banks, which are part of the commercial banks

1 Seules les succursales des banques étrangères sont incluses, sont exclues les banques détenues majoritairement par des banques étrangères, lesquelles font partie des banques commerciales

RESIDENT/NON-RESIDENT AND DOMESTIC/FOREIGN CURRENCY CLASSIFICATION OF BANK ASSETS AND LIABILITIES

RESIDENT/NON RESIDENT ET MONNAIE NATIONALE/ETRANGERE CLASSIFICATION DE L'ACTIF ET DU PASSIF DES BANQUES

2000

Billion euros   Milliards d'euros

	Residents / Résidents	Non-residents / Non résidents	Total / Total	
Assets				Actif
Domestic currency	3722	560	4282	Monnaie nationale
Foreign currencies	111	1032	1143	Monnaies étrangères
Total	3833	1592	5425	Total
Liabilities				Passif
Domestic currency	4109	403	4512	Monnaie nationale
Foreign currencies	64	849	913	Monnaies étrangères
Total	4173	1252	5425	Total

STRUCTURE OF THE FINANCIAL SYSTEM
STRUCTURE DU SYSTEME FINANCIER

2001

	Number of institutions / Nombre d'institutions	Number of branches / Nombre de succursales	Number of employees / Nombre de salariés (x 1000)	Total assets or liabilities / Total des actifs ou des passifs bil / mlds EUR	Total financial assets / Total des actifs financiers bil / mlds EUR	%	
Central bank	1	125	16	240	238	..	Banque centrale
Other monetary institutions	2434	36651	..	..	..	..	Autres institutions monétaires
Commercial banks	199	5563	215	2338	2330	..	Banques commerciales
Foreign-owned banks (1)	79	13	..	..	..	..	Banques étrangères (1)
Savings banks	537	16491	282	986	971	..	Caisses d'épargne
Co-operative banks	1619	14584	170	552	542	..	Banques mutualistes
Other financial institutions	..	..	..	..	..	..	Autres institutions financières
Mortgage credit institutions	28	136	11	922	921	..	Institutions de crédit hypothécaire
Development credit institutions	..	..	..	..	..	..	Institutions de crédit de développement
Finance companies	..	..	..	..	..	..	Sociétés financières
Others	..	..	..	..	..	..	Autres
Insurance institutions	..	..	..	..	..	..	Institutions d'assurance
All financial institutions	..	..	..	..	..	..	Ensemble des institutions financières

1 Only domestic branches of foreign banks, excluding banks majority-owned by foreign banks, which are part of the commercial banks

1 Seules les succursales des banques étrangères sont incluses, sont exclues les banques détenues majoritairement par des banques étrangères, lesquelles font partie des banques commerciales

RESIDENT/NON-RESIDENT AND DOMESTIC/FOREIGN CURRENCY
CLASSIFICATION OF BANK ASSETS AND LIABILITIES

RESIDENT/NON RESIDENT ET MONNAIE NATIONALE/ETRANGERE
CLASSIFICATION DE L'ACTIF ET DU PASSIF DES BANQUES

2001

Billion euros   Milliards d'euros

	Residents / Résidents	Non-residents / Non résidents	Total / Total	
Assets				Actif
Domestic currency	3720	692	4412	Monnaie nationale
Foreign currencies	123	1180	1303	Monnaies étrangères
Total	3843	1872	5715	Total
Liabilities				Passif
Domestic currency	4304	437	4741	Monnaie nationale
Foreign currencies	64	910	974	Monnaies étrangères
Total	4368	1347	5715	Total

STRUCTURE OF THE FINANCIAL SYSTEM
STRUCTURE DU SYSTEME FINANCIER

1999

	Number of institutions / Nombre d'institutions	Number of branches / Nombre de succursales (1)	Number of employees / Nombre de salariés	Total assets or liabilities / Total des actifs ou des passifs million EUR	Total financial assets / Total des actifs financiers million EUR	%	
Central bank	1	28	3212	37667	37553	16	*Banque centrale*
Other monetary institutions	53	2613	57879	145432	143840	61	*Autres institutions monétaires*
Commercial banks (2)	39	2444	56407	135756	134197	57	Banques commerciales (2)
Foreign-owned banks (3)	22	130	4144	17893	17748	8	Banques étrangères (3)
Savings banks	1	131	1155	9247	9224	4	Caisses d'épargne
Co-operative banks	13	38	317	429	419	0	Banques mutualistes
Other financial institutions	251	19	1074	48333	48010	20	*Autres institutions financières*
Mortgage credit institutions (4)	1	20	259	662	653	0	Institutions de crédit hypothécaire (4)
Development credit institutions (4)	2	15	667	4228	4004	2	Institutions de crédit de développement (4)
Deposits and loan fund (4)	1	4	407	2989	2974	1	Dépôts et prêts (4)
Others (5)	248	na	na	40453	40379	17	Autres (5)
Insurance institutions	114	na	na	7238	6871	3	*Institutions d'assurance*
Insurance companies	114	na	na	7238	6871	3	Sociétés d'assurance
Pension funds and foundations	..	..	..	..	..	..	Fonds de pension et fondations
All financial institutions	419	2660	62165	238670	236273	100	*Ensemble des institutions financières*

1 Including head office.
2 Including the Agricultural Bank of Greece.
3 Foreign-owned banks are a subgroup of commercial banks.
4 These institutions are monetary institutions
5 Not including venture capital companies for which data are not available.

1 Y compris le siege central.
2 Y compris la Banque Agricole de Grece.
3 Les banques etrangeres sont un sous-groupe des banques commerciales.
4 Cettes institutions sont des institutions monetaires
5 Non inclues les sociétés de capital-risque pour lesquelles il n' y a pas de donnees disponibles.

RESIDENT/NON-RESIDENT AND DOMESTIC/FOREIGN CURRENCY
CLASSIFICATION OF BANK ASSETS AND LIABILITIES (1)

RESIDENT/NON RESIDENT ET MONNAIE NATIONALE/ETRANGERE
CLASSIFICATION DE L'ACTIF ET DU PASSIF DES BANQUES (1)

1999

Million euros   *Millions d'euros*

	Residents / Résidents	Non-residents / Non résidents	Total / Total	
Assets				*Actif*
Domestic currency	..	..	97316	Monnaie nationale
Foreign currencies	..	..	38441	Monnaies étrangères
Total	..	..	135756	Total
Liabilities				*Passif*
Domestic currency	..	..	96023	Monnaie nationale
Foreign currencies	..	..	39734	Monnaies étrangères
Total	..	..	135756	Total

1 Data refer to commercial banks (including the Agricultural Bank of Greece).

1 Les données concernent les banques commerciales (y compris la Banque Agricole de Grèce).

STRUCTURE OF THE FINANCIAL SYSTEM
STRUCTURE DU SYSTEME FINANCIER

2000

	Number of institutions / Nombre d'institutions	Number of branches / Nombre de succursales (1)	Number of employees / Nombre de salariés	Total assets or liabilities / Total des actifs ou des passifs *million EUR*	Total financial assets / Total des actifs financiers *million EUR*	%	
Central bank	1	28	3172	34146	34003	14	*Banque centrale*
Other monetary institutions	54	2817	59628	171312	166473	66	*Autres institutions monétaires*
Commercial banks (2)	39	2637	57922	160939	156137	62	Banques commerciales (2)
Foreign-owned banks (3)	22	164	4739	22332	22170	9	Banques étrangères (3)
Savings banks	1	134	1319	9829	9805	4	Caisses d'épargne
Co-operative banks	14	46	387	544	531	0	Banques mutualistes
Other financial institutions	309	19	1094	43978	43549	17	*Autres institutions financières*
Mortgage credit institutions (4)	..	..	..	..	..	..	Institutions de crédit hypothécaire (4)
Development credit institutions (4)	2	15	672	4212	3969	2	Institutions de crédit de développement (4)
Deposits and loan fund (4)	1	4	422	3244	3233	1	Dépôts et prêts (4)
Others (5)	306	na	na	36522	36347	14	Autres (5)
Insurance institutions	110	na	na	7839	7325	3	*Institutions d'assurance*
Insurance companies	110	na	na	7839	7325	3	Sociétés d'assurance
Pension funds and foundations	..	..	..	..	..	..	Fonds de pension et fondations
All financial institutions	474	2864	63894	257276	251351	100	*Ensemble des institutions financières*

1 Including head office.
2 Including the Agricultural Bank of Greece and, as from 2000, mortgage credit institutions.
3 Foreign-owned banks are a subgroup of commercial banks.
4 These institutions are monetary institutions
5 Not including venture capital companies for which data are not available.

1 Y compris le siege central.
2 Y compris la Banque Agricole de Grece.
3 Les banques etrangeres sont un sous-groupe des banques commerciales.
4 Cettes institutions sont des institutions monetaires
5 Non inclues les sociétés de capital-risque pour lesquelles il n' y a pas de donnees disponibles.

RESIDENT/NON-RESIDENT AND DOMESTIC/FOREIGN CURRENCY
CLASSIFICATION OF BANK ASSETS AND LIABILITIES (1)

RESIDENT/NON RESIDENT ET MONNAIE NATIONALE/ETRANGERE
CLASSIFICATION DE L'ACTIF ET DU PASSIF DES BANQUES (1)

2000

Million euros   *Millions d'euros*

	Residents / Résidents	Non-residents / Non résidents	Total / Total	
Assets				*Actif*
Domestic currency	..	..	123696	Monnaie nationale
Foreign currencies	..	..	37243	Monnaies étrangères
Total	..	..	160939	Total
Liabilities				*Passif*
Domestic currency	..	..	113803	Monnaie nationale
Foreign currencies	..	..	47137	Monnaies étrangères
Total	..	..	160939	Total

1 Data refer to commercial banks (including the Agricultural Bank of Greece and mortgage credit institutions).

1 Les données concernent les banques commerciales (y compris la Banque Agricole de Grèce et les institutions de credit hypothecaire).

STRUCTURE OF THE FINANCIAL SYSTEM
STRUCTURE DU SYSTEME FINANCIER

2001

	Number of institutions / Nombre d'institutions	Number of branches / Nombre de succursales (1)	Number of employees / Nombre de salariés	Total assets or liabilities / Total des actifs ou des passifs *million EUR*	Total financial assets / Total des actifs financiers *million EUR*	%	
Central bank	1	28	3090	32572	32346	13	*Banque centrale*
Other monetary institutions	58	3156	59111	181046	177704	69	*Autres institutions monetaires*
Commercial banks	42	2965	57341	169708	166411	65	Banques commerciales
Foreign-owned banks (2)	21	188	4835	17845	17660	7	Banques etrangeres (2)
Savings banks	1	135	1286	10604	10580	4	Caisses d'epargne
Co-operative banks	15	56	484	734	714	0	Banques mutualistes
Other financial institutions	318	21	1086	40759	40359	16	*Autres institutions financieres*
Mortgage credit institutions (3)	..	..	..	..	..	..	Institutions de credit hypothecaire (3)
Development credit institutions (3)	2	17	656	3773	3511	1	Institutions de credit de developpement (3)
Deposits and loan fund (3)	1	4	430	3885	3880	2	Depots et prets (3)
Others (4)	315	na	na	33102	32968	13	Autres (4)
Insurance institutions	107	na	na	7939	7445	3	*Institutions d'assurance*
Insurance companies	107	na	na	7939	7445	3	Societes d'assurance
Pension funds and foundations	..	..	..	..	..	..	Fonds de pension et fondations
All financial institutions	484	3205	63287	262316	257854	100	*Ensemble des institutions financieres*

1 Including head office.
2 Foreign-owned banks are a subgroup of commercial banks.
3 These institutions are monetary institutions
4 Not including venture capital companies for which data are not available.

1 Y compris le siege central.
2 Les banques etrangeres sont un sous-groupe des banques commerciales.
3 Cettes institutions sont des institutions monetaires
4 Non inclues les sociétés de capital-risque pour lesquelles il n' y a pas de donnees disponibles.

RESIDENT/NON-RESIDENT AND DOMESTIC/FOREIGN CURRENCY
CLASSIFICATION OF BANK ASSETS AND LIABILITIES (1)
RESIDENT/NON RESIDENT ET MONNAIE NATIONALE/ETRANGERE
CLASSIFICATION DE L'ACTIF ET DU PASSIF DES BANQUES (1)

2001

Million euros   *Millions d'euros*

	Residents / Résidents	Non-residents / Non résidents	Total / Total	
Assets				*Actif*
Domestic currency	na	na	85466	Monnaie nationale
Foreign currencies	na	na	84241	Monnaies etrangeres
Total	na	na	169708	Total
Liabilities				*Passif*
Domestic currency	na	na	94722	Monnaie nationale
Foreign currencies	na	na	74986	Monnaies etrangeres
Total	na	na	169708	Total

1 Data refer to commercial banks.

1 Les données concernent les banques commerciales.

STRUCTURE OF THE FINANCIAL SYSTEM
STRUCTURE DU SYSTEME FINANCIER

2000

	Number of institutions / Nombre d'institutions	Number of branches / Nombre de succursales	Number of employees / Nombre de salariés (x 1000)	Total assets or liabilities / Total des actifs ou des passifs[1] million Ft	Total financial assets / Total des actifs financiers million Ft	%	
Central bank	1	4	1	6509350	..	..	Banque centrale
Other monetary institutions(2)	..	..	..	7336081	..	..	Autres institutions monétaires(2)
Commercial banks	34	1129	26	8025683	7666751	0.96	Banques commerciales
Specialized banks	4	7	-	322324	310786	0.96	Banques spécialisées
Home savings and loan associations	4	6	-	79564	75522	0.95	Caisses d'épargne et associations de prêt
Co-operative banks	195	..	..	532311	498376	0.94	Banques mutualistes
Other financial institutions	..	..	..	..	..	..	Autres institutions financières
Insurance institutions	61	..	..	..	..	..	Institutions d'assurance
Insurance companies	23			708541	..	..	Sociétés d'assurance
Pension funds and foundations	198	..	-	1424200	..	..	Fonds de pension et fondations
Others (3)	..	..	..	..	..	..	Autres (3)
All financial institutions	..	..	..	..	..	..	Ensemble des institutions financières

1 Excluding National Bank of Hungary bond buy-backs.
2 Excluding Co-operative banks.
3 Insurance associations.

1 Hors opérations de rachat d'obligations de la Banque nationale de Hongrie.
2 Hors banques mutualistes.
3 Associations d'assurance.

RESIDENT/NON-RESIDENT AND DOMESTIC/FOREIGN CURRENCY
CLASSIFICATION OF BANK ASSETS AND LIABILITIES
RESIDENT/NON RESIDENT ET MONNAIE NATIONALE/ETRANGERE
CLASSIFICATION DE L'ACTIF ET DU PASSIF DES BANQUES

2000

Million forints   *Millions de forints*

	Residents / Résidents	Non-residents / Non résidents	Total / Total	
Assets				Actif
Domestic currency	5353389	7067	5360456	Monnaie nationale
Foreign currencies	2305232	761883	3067115	Monnaies étrangères
Total	7658621	768950	8427571	Total
Liabilities				Passif
Domestic currency	5269765	79719	5349484	Monnaie nationale
Foreign currencies	1560954	1517133	3078087	Monnaies étrangères
Total	6830719	1596852	8427571	Total

341

STRUCTURE OF THE FINANCIAL SYSTEM
STRUCTURE DU SYSTEME FINANCIER

2001

	Number of institutions / Nombre d'institutions	Number of branches / Nombre de succursales	Number of employees / Nombre de salariés (x 1000)	Total assets or liabilities / Total des actifs ou des passifs[1] million Ft	Total financial assets / Total des actifs financiers[2] million Ft	%	
Central bank	1	4	1	5453364	..	..	Banque centrale
Other monetary institutions(3)	..	..	..	7336081	..	..	Autres institutions monétaires(3)
Commercial banks	33	1109	25	8885062	8521670	0.96	Banques commerciales
Specialized banks	4	8	-	500225	486820	0.97	Banques spécialisées
Home savings and loan associations	4	8	-	114066	109751	0.96	Caisses d'épargne et associations de prêt
Co-operative banks	189	..	..	638600	600041	0.94	Banques mutualistes
Other financial institutions	..	..	..	..	..	..	Autres institutions financières
Insurance institutions	..	..	..	..	..	..	Institutions d'assurance
Insurance companies	26	..	..	850892	..	..	Sociétés d'assurance
Pension funds and foundations	138	..	-	2057800	..	..	Fonds de pension et fondations
Others (4)	..	..	..	..	..	..	Autres (4)
All financial institutions	..	..	..	..	..	..	Ensemble des institutions financières

1 Excluding National Bank of Hungary bond buy-backs.
2 cash and balances with central bank + loans + debt securities+ shares and other equity
3 Excluding Co-operative banks.
4. Insurance associations.

1 Hors opérations de rachat d'obligations de la Banque nationale de Hongrie.
2 Caisse et solde auprès de la banque centrale+prets+titres de créance+parts et autres avoirs nets
3 Hors banques mutualistes.
4. Associations d'assurance.

RESIDENT/NON-RESIDENT AND DOMESTIC/FOREIGN CURRENCY CLASSIFICATION OF BANK ASSETS AND LIABILITIES
RESIDENT/NON RESIDENT ET MONNAIE NATIONALE/ETRANGERE CLASSIFICATION DE L'ACTIF ET DU PASSIF DES BANQUES

2001

Million forints   *Millions de forints*

	Residents / Résidents	Non-residents / Non résidents	Total / Total	
Assets				Actif
Domestic currency	6,143,836	87,783	6,231,619	Monnaie nationale
Foreign currencies	2,132,039	1,135,695	3,267,734	Monnaies étrangères
Total	8,275,875	1,223,478	9,499,353	Total
Liabilities				Passif
Domestic currency	6,116,430	80,173	6,196,603	Monnaie nationale
Foreign currencies	1,711,592	1,591,158	3,302,750	Monnaies étrangères
Total	7,828,022	1,671,331	9,499,353	Total

STRUCTURE OF THE FINANCIAL SYSTEM
STRUCTURE DU SYSTEME FINANCIER

2000

	Number of institutions / Nombre d'institutions	Number of branches / Nombre de succursales (1)	Number of employees / Nombre de salariés	Total assets or liabilities / Total des actifs ou des passifs million IKr / Krl	Total financial assets / Total des actifs financiers million IKr / Krl	%	
Central bank	1	1	113	102076	102076	5	Banque centrale
Other monetary institutions	29	180	3046	862252	848888	40	Autres institutions monétaires
Commercial banks	4	122	2395	720721	709841	34	Banques commerciales
Foreign-owned banks	-	-	-	-	-	-	Banques étrangères
Savings banks	25	58	651	141531	139047	7	Caisses d'épargne
Co-operative banks	-	-	-	-	-	-	Banques mutualistes
Other financial institutions	16	17	573	526764	524294	25	Autres institutions financières
Mortgage credit institutions	1	1	62	311036	310950	15	Institutions de crédit hypothécaire
Development credit institutions	1	2	20	10467	10328	0	Institutions de crédit de développement
Finance companies	13	13	469	158220	156041	7	Sociétés financières
Others	1	1	22	47041	46975	2	Autres
Insurance institutions	70	70	645	635970	631467	30	Institutions d'assurance
Insurance companies	14	14	491	69882	66550	3	Sociétés d'assurance
Pension funds and foundations	56	56	154	566088	564917	27	Fonds de pension et fondations
Others	-	-	-	-	-	-	Autres
All financial institutions	116	268	4377	2127062	2106725	100	Ensemble des institutions financières

1 The number of branches includes the number of head offices shown in the first column

1 Le nombre de filiales comprend le nombre de sièges sociaux apparaissant dans la première colonne

RESIDENT/NON-RESIDENT AND DOMESTIC/FOREIGN CURRENCY CLASSIFICATION OF BANK ASSETS AND LIABILITIES (1)

RESIDENT/NON RESIDENT ET MONNAIE NATIONALE/ETRANGERE CLASSIFICATION DE L'ACTIF ET DU PASSIF DES BANQUES (1)

Million Icelandic krónur   *Millions de couronnes islandaises*

	Residents / Résidents	Non-residents / Non résidents	Total / Total	
Assets				Actif
Domestic currency	784738	143	784881	Monnaie nationale
Foreign currencies	54918	22453	77371	Monnaies étrangères
Total	839656	22596	862252	Total
Liabilities				Passif
Domestic currency	618941	279	619220	Monnaie nationale
Foreign currencies	-105627	348659	243032	Monnaies étrangères
Total	513314	348938	862252	Total

1 Commercial and savings banks.

1 Banques commerciales et caisses d'épargne.

STRUCTURE OF THE FINANCIAL SYSTEM
STRUCTURE DU SYSTEME FINANCIER

2001

	Number of institutions / Nombre d'institutions	Number of branches / Nombre de succursales (1)	Number of employees / Nombre de salariés	Total assets or liabilities / Total des actifs ou des passifs million IKr / Krl	Total financial assets / Total des actifs financiers million IKr / Krl	%	
Central bank	1	1	116	116144	116144	5	Banque centrale
Other monetary institutions	28	180	3194	1013986	1001035	40	Autres institutions monétaires
Commercial banks	4	118	2509	852014	841923	34	Banques commerciales
Foreign-owned banks	-	-	-	-	-	-	Banques étrangères
Savings banks	24	62	685	161972	159112	6	Caisses d'épargne
Co-operative banks	-	-	-	-	-	-	Banques mutualistes
Other financial institutions	14	15	575	641072	638882	26	Autres institutions financières
Mortgage credit institutions	1	1	60	362263	362173	15	Institutions de crédit hypothécaire
Development credit institutions	1	2	20	13073	12985	1	Institutions de crédit de développement
Finance companies	11	11	473	212489	210546	9	Sociétés financières
Others	1	1	22	53247	53178	2	Autres
Insurance institutions	68	68	570	723394	716623	29	Institutions d'assurance
Insurance companies	14	14	510	78637	73154	3	Sociétés d'assurance
Pension funds and foundations	54	54	60	644757	643469	26	Fonds de pension et fondations
Others	-	-	-	-	-	-	Autres
All financial institutions	111	264	4455	2494596	2472684	100	Ensemble des institutions financières

1 The number of branches includes the number of head offices shown in the first column

1 Le nombre de filiales comprend le nombre de sièges sociaux apparaissant dans la première colonne

RESIDENT/NON-RESIDENT AND DOMESTIC/FOREIGN CURRENCY
CLASSIFICATION OF BANK ASSETS AND LIABILITIES (1)

RESIDENT/NON RESIDENT ET MONNAIE NATIONALE/ETRANGERE
CLASSIFICATION DE L'ACTIF ET DU PASSIF DES BANQUES (1)

Million Icelandic krónur   Millions de couronnes islandaises

	Residents / Résidents	Non-residents / Non résidents	Total / Total	
Assets				Actif
Domestic currency	680553	27	680579	Monnaie nationale
Foreign currencies	300074	33333	333407	Monnaies étrangères
Total	980626	33360	1013986	Total
Liabilities				Passif
Domestic currency	560576	454	561030	Monnaie nationale
Foreign currencies	37490	415466	452956	Monnaies étrangères
Total	598066	415920	1013986	Total

1 Commercial and savings banks.

1 Banques commerciales et caisses d'épargne.

STRUCTURE OF THE FINANCIAL SYSTEM
STRUCTURE DU SYSTEME FINANCIER

1999

	Number of institutions / Nombre d'institutions	Number of branches / Nombre de succursales	Number of employees / Nombre de salariés	Total assets or liabilities / Total des actifs ou des passifs million EUR	Total financial assets / Total des actifs financiers million EUR	%	
Central bank	1	2	668	14772	14715	..	Banque centrale
Credit institutions (1)	82 [2]	977	37,667	302751	301102	..	Institutions de crédit (1)
Other financial institutions	..	..	..	..	..	..	Autres institutions financières
Mortgage credit institutions	..	..	..	..	..		Institutions de crédit hypothécaire
Development credit institutions	..	..	..	..	..		Institutions de crédit de développement
Finance companies	..	..	..	..	..		Sociétés financières
Others	..	..	..	..	..	..	Autres
Insurance institutions							Institutions d'assurance
Life insurance (3)	..	..	..	36684	36206	..	Assurance vie (3)
Industrial insurance (4)	..	..	..	8935	8714	..	Assurance des entreprises (4)
Pension funds and foundations	..	..	..	..	..	..	Fonds de pension et fondations
Others							Autres
All financial institutions	..	..	..	..	..	..	Ensemble des institutions financières

1 Data refer to within-the-State offices of credit institutions and domestic interbank positions are not netted out
2 Includes 26 EU branches.
3 Data refer to life assurance undertakings with their head offices in Ireland
4 Data refer to non-life insurance undertakings with their head offices in Ireland

1 Les données font référence aux agences sur le territoire de la République d'Irlande des établissements de crédit et les positions interbancaires intérieures sont indiquées en chiffres bruts.
2 Inclut 26 succursales appartenant à l'Union Européenne.
3 Les données font référence aux sociétés d'assurance vie dont le siège social est en Irlande.
4 Les données font référence aux sociétés d'assurance non-vie dont le siège social est en Irlande.

RESIDENT/NON-RESIDENT AND DOMESTIC/FOREIGN CURRENCY CLASSIFICATION OF BANK ASSETS AND LIABILITIES (1)

RESIDENT/NON RESIDENT ET MONNAIE NATIONALE/ETRANGERE CLASSIFICATION DE L'ACTIF ET DU PASSIF DES BANQUES (1)

1999

Million euros   Millions d'euros

	Residents / Résidents	Non-residents / Non résidents	Total / Total	
Assets				Actif
Domestic currency	108974	69603	178577	Monnaie nationale
Foreign currencies	27518	96656	124174	Monnaies étrangères
Total	136492	166259	302751	Total
Liabilities				Passif
Domestic currency	97810	75316	173126	Monnaie nationale
Foreign currencies	29397	100228	129625	Monnaies étrangères
Total	127207	175544	302751	Total

1 Data refer to within-the-State offices of credit institutions. Domestic interbank positions are not netted out.

1 Les données font référence aux agences sur le territoire de la République d'Irlande des établissements de crédit. Les positions interbancaires nationales sont indiquées en chiffres bruts.

STRUCTURE OF THE FINANCIAL SYSTEM
STRUCTURE DU SYSTEME FINANCIER

2000

	Number of institutions / Nombre d'institutions	Number of branches / Nombre de succursales	Number of employees / Nombre de salariés	Total assets or liabilities / Total des actifs ou des passifs	Total financial assets / Total des actifs financiers		
				million EUR	million EUR	%	
Central bank	1	2	707	17927	17870	..	Banque centrale
Credit institutions (1)	82 [2]	880	34,770	355341	353634	..	Institutions de crédit (1)
Other financial institutions	..	..	..	..	..	..	Autres institutions financières
Mortgage credit institutions	..	..	..	..	..	..	Institutions de crédit hypothécaire
Development credit institutions	..	..	..	..	..	..	Institutions de crédit de développement
Finance companies	..	..	..	..	..	..	Sociétés financières
Others							Autres
Insurance institutions	..	..	..	..	..	..	Institutions d'assurance
Life insurance (3)	..	..	..	..	..	..	Assurance vie (3)
Industrial insurance (4)	..	..	..	..	..	..	Assurance des entreprises (4)
Pension funds and foundations	..	..	..				Fonds de pension et fondations
Others	..	..	..				Autres
All financial institutions	..	..	..	..	..	..	Ensemble des institutions financières

1 Data refer to within-the-State offices of credit institutions and domestic interbank positions are not netted out.
2 Includes 28 EU branches.
3 Data refer to life assurance undertakings with their head offices in Ireland
4 Data refer to non-life insurance undertakings with their head offices in Ireland

1 Les données font référence aux agences sur le territoire de la République d'Irlande des établissements de crédit et les positions interbancaires intérieures sont indiquées en chiffres bruts.
2 Inclut 28 succursales appartenant à l'Union Européenne.
3 Les données font référence aux sociétés d'assurance vie dont le siège social est en Irlande.
4 Les données font référence aux sociétés d'assurance non-vie dont le siège social est en Irlande.

RESIDENT/NON-RESIDENT AND DOMESTIC/FOREIGN CURRENCY
CLASSIFICATION OF BANK ASSETS AND LIABILITIES (1)
RESIDENT/NON RESIDENT ET MONNAIE NATIONALE/ETRANGERE
CLASSIFICATION DE L'ACTIF ET DU PASSIF DES BANQUES (1)

2000

Million euros   Millions d'euros

	Residents / Résidents	Non-residents / Non résidents	Total / Total	
Assets				Actif
Domestic currency	121494	86441	207935	Monnaie nationale
Foreign currencies	33646	113759	147406	Monnaies étrangères
Total	155141	200200	355341	Total
Liabilities				Passif
Domestic currency	109315	88410	197725	Monnaie nationale
Foreign currencies	37334	120282	157616	Monnaies étrangères
Total	146649	208691	355341	Total

1 Data refer to within-the-State offices of credit institutions. Domestic interbank positions are not netted out.

1 Les données font référence aux agences sur le territoire de la République d'Irlande des établissements de crédit. Les positions interbancaires nationales sont indiquées en chiffres bruts.

IRELAND   IRLANDE

STRUCTURE OF THE FINANCIAL SYSTEM
STRUCTURE DU SYSTEME FINANCIER

2001

	Number of institutions / Nombre d'institutions	Number of branches / Nombre de succursales	Number of employees / Nombre de salariés	Total assets or liabilities / Total des actifs ou des passifs	Total financial assets / Total des actifs financiers		
				million EUR	million EUR	%	
Central bank	1	2	-	,,	,,		Banque centrale
Credit institutions (1)	87²	970	40,928	,,	,,		Institutions de crédit (1)
Other financial institutions	,,	,,	,,	,,	,,		Autres institutions financières
Mortgage credit institutions	,,	,,	,,	,,	,,		Institutions de crédit hypothécaire
Development credit institutions	,,	,,	,,	,,	,,		Institutions de crédit de développement
Finance companies	,,	,,	,,	,,	,,		Sociétés financières
Others							Autres
Insurance institutions	,,	,,	,,	,,	,,		Institutions d'assurance
Life insurance (3)	,,	,,	,,	,,	,,		Assurance vie (3)
Industrial insurance (4)	,,	,,	,,	,,	,,		Assurance des entreprises (4)
Pension funds and foundations	,,	,,	,,	,,	,,		Fonds de pension et fondations
Others	,,	,,	,,	,,	,,		Autres
All financial institutions	,,	,,	,,	,,	,,		Ensemble des institutions financières

1 Data refer to within-the-State offices of credit institutions and domestic interbank positions are not netted out.
2 Includes 32 EU branches.
3 Data refer to life assurance undertakings with their head offices in Ireland
4 Data refer to non-life insurance undertakings with their head offices in Ireland

1 Les données font référence aux agences sur le territoire de la République d'Irlande des établissements de crédit et les positions interbancaires intérieures sont indiquées en chiffres bruts.
2 Inclut 32 succursales appartenant à l'Union Européenne.
3 Les données font référence aux sociétés d'assurance vie dont le siège social est en Irlande.
4 Les données font référence aux sociétés d'assurance non-vie dont le siège social est en Irlande.

STRUCTURE OF THE FINANCIAL SYSTEM
STRUCTURE DU SYSTEME FINANCIER

2000

	Number of institutions / Nombre d'institutions	Number of branches / Nombre de succursales	Number of employees / Nombre de salariés	Total assets or liabilities / Total des actifs ou des passifs million / millions EUR	Total financial assets / Total des actifs financiers mill / mill EUR	%	
Central bank	1	99	8647	180795			Banque centrale
Other monetary institutions	841	28177	344305	1898428	-	-	Autres institutions monétaires
Commercial banks (1)	240	20338	264495	1496692	-	-	Banques commerciales (1)
Foreign-owned banks	58	99	3322	82406	-	-	Banques étrangères
Co-operative banks (2)	543	7740	76488	319330	-	-	Banques mutualistes (2)
Other financial institutions (3)	453	-	36717	150552	-	-	Autres institutions financières(3)
Insurance institutions	904	-	-	328799	-	-	Institutions d'assurance
Insurance companies	200	-	-	250979	-	-	Sociétés d'assurance
Pension funds and foundations	704	-	-	77820	-	-	Fonds de pension et fondations
All financial institutions	2199	-	-	2558575	-	-	Ensemble des institutions financières

1 Including Central credit and refinancing institutions (istituti centrali di categoria e di rifinanziamento)
2 Co-operative banks (banche popolari) and mutual banks (banche di credito cooperativo)
3 Leasing and factoring companies, consumer credit, securities firms and other financial institutions.

1 Sont inclus les institutions centrales de categorie et de refinancemant (istituti centrali di categoria e di rifinanziamento)
2 Banques coopératives (banche popolari) et mutuelles (banche di credito cooperativo)
3 Sociétés de crédit-bail et d'affacturage, crédit à la consommation, maisons de titres et autres institutions financières

RESIDENT/NON-RESIDENT AND DOMESTIC/FOREIGN CURRENCY
CLASSIFICATION OF BANK ASSETS AND LIABILITIES

RESIDENT/NON RESIDENT ET MONNAIE NATIONALE/ETRANGERE
CLASSIFICATION DE L'ACTIF ET DU PASSIF DES BANQUES

2000

Million euros   Millions d'euros

	Residents / Résidents	Non-residents / Non résidents	Total / Total	
Assets				Actif
Domestic currency	1848403	148586	1996989	Monnaie nationale
Foreign currencies	62423	58974	121397	Monnaies étrangères
Total	1910826	207559	2118385	Total
Liabilities				Passif
Domestic currency	1770597	195962	1966559	Monnaie nationale
Foreign currencies	46267	105451	151719	Monnaies étrangères
Total	1816864	301413	2118277	Total

STRUCTURE OF THE FINANCIAL SYSTEM
STRUCTURE DU SYSTEME FINANCIER

2001

	Number of institutions / Nombre d'institutions	Number of branches / Nombre de succursales	Number of employees / Nombre de salariés	Total assets or liabilities / Total des actifs ou des passifs million / millions EUR	Total financial assets / Total des actifs financiers mill / mill EUR	%	
Central bank	1	99	8560	179099			Banque centrale
Other monetary institutions	830	29270	343846	1960514	-	-	Autres institutions monétaires
Commercial banks (1)	252	21081	262621	1515535	-		Banques commerciales (1)
Foreign-owned banks	60	109	3806	77338	-		Banques étrangères
Co-operative banks (2)	518	8080	77419	367641	-		Banques mutualistes (2)
Other financial institutions (3)	469	-	33268	154452	-		Autres institutions financières(3)
Insurance institutions	918	-	-	358662	-	-	Institutions d'assurance
Insurance companies	202	-	-	279185	-	-	Sociétés d'assurance
Pension funds and foundations	716	-	-	79477	-	-	Fonds de pension et fondations
All financial institutions	2218	-	-	2652727	-	-	Ensemble des institutions financières

1 Including Central credit and refinancing institutions (istituti centrali di categoria e di rifinanziamento)
2 Co-operative banks (banche popolari) and mutual banks (banche di credito cooperativo)
3 Leasing and factoring companies, consumer credit, securities firms and other financial institutions.

1 Sont inclus les institutions centrales de categorie et de refinancemant (istituti centrali di categoria e di rifinanziamento)
2 Banques coopératives (banche popolari) et mutuelles (banche di credito cooperativo)
3 Sociétés de crédit-bail et d'affacturage, crédit à la consommation, maisons de titres et autres institutions financières

RESIDENT/NON-RESIDENT AND DOMESTIC/FOREIGN CURRENCY CLASSIFICATION OF BANK ASSETS AND LIABILITIES

RESIDENT/NON RESIDENT ET MONNAIE NATIONALE/ETRANGERE CLASSIFICATION DE L'ACTIF ET DU PASSIF DES BANQUES

2001

Million euros   *Millions d'euros*

	Residents / Résidents	Non-residents / Non résidents	Total / Total	
Assets				Actif
Domestic currency	1973966	140196	2114162	Monnaie nationale
Foreign currencies	58499	52117	110616	Monnaies étrangères
Total	2032466	192313	2224779	Total
Liabilities				Passif
Domestic currency	1863710	209206	2072916	Monnaie nationale
Foreign currencies	45594	106271	151865	Monnaies étrangères
Total	1909304	315478	2224782	Total

STRUCTURE OF THE FINANCIAL SYSTEM
STRUCTURE DU SYSTEME FINANCIER

2000

(fiscal year ending 31 March 2001)
(exercice financier se terminant le 31 mars 2001)

	Number of institutions / Nombre d'institutions	Number of branches / Nombre de succursales	Number of employees / Nombre de salariés (x 1000)	Total assets or liabilities / Total des actifs ou des passifs 100 million ¥	Total financial assets / Total des actifs financiers 100 million ¥	%	
Ordinary Banks	127	13342	324	6935020	6852178		Banques ordinaires
City Banks	9	2556	113	4271620	4229283		City banks
Regional Banks	64	7067	148	2058302	2028242		Banques régionales
Regional Banks II	54	3719	63	60597	594653		Banques Sogo
Long-Term Credit Banks	1	23	4	437156	434806		Banques de crédit à long terme
Banking Departments of Trust Banks	8	367	24	670728	663778		Départements bancaires des banques de gestion de patrimoine
Trust Departments of Banks	51	..	..	3449750	3395174		Départements de gestion de patrimoine des banques
Credit Associations (Shinkin Banks)	370	8025	133	1112063	1092529		Associations de crédit (Shinkin banks)
Labor Credit Associations	39	643	11	130226	128736		Associations de crédit aux travailleurs
Credit Co-operatives	280	2151	30	201114	196724		Coopératives de crédit
Agricultural Co-operatives	1303	..	..	..	739403		Coopératives agricoles
Fishery Co-operatives	778	..	..	..	18528		Coopératives de la pêche
Central Co-operative Bank for Agriculture & Forestry (Norinchukin Bank)	1	..	..	600358	598241		Banque centrale coopérative pour l'agriculture et la sylvi-culture (Norinchukin Bank)
Central Bank for Commercial & Industrial Co-operatives (Shoko Chukin Bank)	1	..	..	138869	138296		Banque centrale des coopéra-tives commerciales et indus-trielles (Shoko chukin Bank)
Insurance institutions Insurance companies	77	..	..	2179940	2080301		Institutions d'assurance Compagnies d'assurance
Postal saving system	1	24819	63	2528907	2528907		Système d'épargne postale
Government financial Institutions	8	259	11	1692028	1690162		Institutions financières gouvernementales
All financial institutions	3045	..	..	..	20557763		Ensemble des institutions financières

p: provisional figures
p: données provisoires

STRUCTURE OF THE FINANCIAL SYSTEM
STRUCTURE DU SYSTEME FINANCIER

2001

(fiscal year ending 31 March 2002)
(exercice financier se terminant le 31 mars 2002)

	Number of institutions / Nombre d'institutions	Number of branches / Nombre de succursales	Number of employees / Nombre de salariés (x 1000)	Total assets or liabilities / Total des actifs ou des passifs 100 million ¥	Total financial assets / Total des actifs financiers 100 million ¥	%	
Ordinary Banks	*124*	*12892*	*306*	*6525450*	*6445458*		*Banques ordinaires*
City Banks	7	2472	105	3861455	3820970		City banks
Regional Banks	64	6933	141	2062552	2033214		Banques régionales
Regional Banks II	53	3611	60	601443	591274		Banques Sogo
Long-Term Credit Banks	*1*	*34*	*4*	*390601*	*388052*		*Banques de crédit à long terme*
Banking Departments of Trust Banks	*8*	*330*	*23*	*644779*	*638860*		*Départements bancaires des banques de gestion de patrimoine*
Trust Departments of Banks	*49*	..	..	*3929199*	*3855892*		*Départements de gestion de patrimoine des banques*
Credit Associations (Shinkin Banks)	p *349*	p *8051*	p *130*	p *1121379*	p *1101635*		*Associations de crédit (Shinkin banks)*
Labor Credit Associations	*21*	*658*	*11*	*138424*	*137042*		*Associations de crédit aux travailleurs*
Credit Co-operatives	*247*	*2012*	*28*	*180795*	*176825*		*Coopératives de crédit*
Agricultural Co-operatives	*1140*	..	..	..	*752252*		*Coopératives agricoles*
Fishery Co-operatives	*609*	*373*	*9*	..	*16482*		*Coopératives de la pêche*
Central Co-operative Bank for Agriculture & Forestry (Norinchukin Bank)	*1*	*30*	*3*	*567196*	*565084*		*Banque centrale coopérative pour l'agriculture et la sylviculture (Norinchukin Bank)*
Central Bank for Commercial & Industrial Co-operatives (Shoko Chukin Bank)	*1*	*101*	*5*	*136969*	*136425*		*Banque centrale des coopératives commerciales et industrielles (Shoko chukin Bank)*
Insurance institutions Insurance companies	*71*	..	..	*2178310*	*2080535*		*Institutions d'assurance* Compagnies d'assurance
Postal saving system	*1*	*24813*	*62*	*2957835*	*2957835*		*Système d'épargne postale*
Government financial Institutions	*8*	*259*	*11*	*1651322*	*1649448*		*Institutions financières gouvernementales*
All financial institutions	p *2630*	..	..	..	p *20901825*		*Ensemble des institutions financières*

p: provisional figures
p: données provisoires

STRUCTURE OF THE FINANCIAL SYSTEM
STRUCTURE DU SYSTEME FINANCIER

2000

	Number of institutions / Nombre d'institutions	Number of branches / Nombre de succursales	Number of employees / Nombre de salariés	Total assets or liabilities / Total des actifs ou des passifs billion / milliards W	Total financial assets / Total des actifs financiers bl / mlds W	%	
Central bank	..	..	..	..	..	..	Banque centrale
Other monetary institutions	63	5268	92883	781327.9	767960.5	..	Autres institutions monétaires
Commercial banks	17	4085	70559	580999.9	569898.8	..	Banques commerciales
Foreign-owned banks	43	62	2829	47618.3	47392.4	..	Banques étrangères
Specialized banks	3	1121	19495	152709.7	150669.3	..	Banques spécialisées
Development credit institutions	2	42	2506	95624.5	94835.5	..	Institutions de développement
Investment institutions	..	..	..	..	..	..	Institutions d'investissement
Savings institutions	..	..	..	..	..	..	Institutions d'épargne
Insurance institutions	..	..	..	..	..	..	Institutions d'assurance
All financial institutions	..	..	..	..	..	..	Ensemble des institutions financières

Note: Total assets exclude guarantees and the accounts of their overseas branches.

Note : L'ensemble des actifs exclut les garanties et les comptes de leurs succursales étrangères.

STRUCTURE OF THE FINANCIAL SYSTEM
STRUCTURE DU SYSTEME FINANCIER

2001

	Number of institutions / Nombre d'institutions	Number of branches / Nombre de succursales	Number of employees / Nombre de salariés	Total assets or liabilities / Total des actifs ou des passifs billion / milliards W	Total financial assets / Total des actifs financiers bl / mlds W	%	
Central bank	..	..	..	..	..	..	Banque centrale
Other monetary institutions	60	5294	90260	873663.6	859901.5	..	Autres institutions monétaires
Commercial banks	15	4131	68377	641419.8	629803.9	..	Banques commerciales
Foreign-owned banks	42	62	3036	57998	57855.6	..	Banques étrangères
Specialized banks	3	1101	18847	174245.8	172242	..	Banques spécialisées
Development credit institutions	2	44	2522	99469.5	98692.1	..	Institutions de développement
Investment institutions	..	..	..	..	..	..	Institutions d'investissement
Savings institutions	..	..	..	..	..	..	Institutions d'épargne
Insurance institutions	..	..	..	..	..	..	Institutions d'assurance
All financial institutions	..	..	..	..	..	..	Ensemble des institutions financières

Note: Total assets exclude guarantees and the accounts of their overseas branches.

Note : L'ensemble des actifs exclut les garanties et les comptes de leurs succursales étrangères.

STRUCTURE OF THE FINANCIAL SYSTEM
STRUCTURE DU SYSTEME FINANCIER

2000

	Number of institutions / Nombre d'institutions	Number of branches / Nombre de succursales	Number of employees / Nombre de salariés	Total assets or liabilities / Total des actifs ou des passifs million / millions EUR	Total financial assets / Total des actifs financiers mill / mill EUR	%	
Banks and savings institutions of which:	202	303	23,035	647,749	..	..	Établissements bancaires et d'épargne dont :
Bodies set up under Luxembourg public law	2	100	1,787	33,783	..	..	Établissements de droit public luxembourgeois
Sociétés anonymes set up under Luxembourg law	135	203	20,243	486,960	..	..	Sociétés anonymes de droit luxembourgeois
Foreign companies	61	..	1,005	127,006	..	..	Sociétés de droit étranger
Savings banks and credit unions organised in the form of agricultural associations or co-operative societies of which:	53	..	..	..	..	..	Caisses d'épargne et de crédit organisées sous forme d'associations agricoles ou de sociétés coopératives dont :
Co-operative societies set up under Luxembourg law	1	..	..	..	..	..	Sociétés coopératives de droit luxembourgeois
Central savings banks	1	..	..	..	..	..	Caisses centrales
Local rural savings banks	35				..	..	Caisses rurales locales
Non-bank financial institutions	113		3,499	1,990	..	..	Établissements financiers non bancaires

RESIDENT/NON-RESIDENT AND DOMESTIC/FOREIGN CURRENCY CLASSIFICATION OF BANK ASSETS AND LIABILITIES

RESIDENT/NON RESIDENT ET MONNAIE NATIONALE/ETRANGERE CLASSIFICATION DE L'ACTIF ET DU PASSIF DES BANQUES

2000

Million Euros   *Millions d'euros*

	Residents / Résidents	Non-residents / Non résidents	Total / Total	
Assets				Actif
Domestic currency	52,985	293,409	346,394	Monnaie nationale
Foreign currencies	46,484	254,871	301,355	Monnaies étrangères
Total	99,470	548,279	647,749	Total
Liabilities				Passif
Domestic currency	115,226	220,045	335,271	Monnaie nationale
Foreign currencies	80,206	232,273	312,478	Monnaies étrangères
Total	195,431	452,318	647,749	Total

Note: Local rural savings banks not included in this table.

Note : Les caisses ruarles locales ne sont pas pris en compte dans ce tableau.

STRUCTURE OF THE FINANCIAL SYSTEM
STRUCTURE DU SYSTEME FINANCIER

2001

	Number of institutions / Nombre d'institutions	Number of branches / Nombre de succursales	Number of employees / Nombre de salariés	Total assets or liabilities / Total des actifs ou des passifs million / millions EUR	Total financial assets / Total des actifs financiers mill / mill EUR	%	
Banks and savings institutions of which:	189	260	23,894	721,000	..	..	Établissements bancaires et d'épargne dont :
Bodies set up under Luxembourg public law	2	89	1,796	36,981	..	..	Établissements de droit public luxembourgeois
Sociétés anonymes set up under Luxembourg law	124	169	20,857	544,960	..	..	Sociétés anonymes de droit luxembourgeois
Foreign companies	61	2	1,241	139,059	..	..	Sociétés de droit étranger
Savings banks and credit unions organised in the form of agricultural associations or co-operative societies of which:	53	..	..	..	..	..	Caisses d'épargne et de crédit organisées sous forme d'associations agricoles ou de sociétés coopératives dont :
Co-operative societies set up under Luxembourg law	1	..	..	..	..	..	Sociétés coopératives de droit luxembourgeois
Central savings banks	1	..	..	..	..	..	Caisses centrales
Local rural savings banks	35				..	..	Caisses rurales locales
Non-bank financial institutions	145		4176	2479	..	..	Établissements financiers non bancaires

RESIDENT/NON-RESIDENT AND DOMESTIC/FOREIGN CURRENCY
CLASSIFICATION OF BANK ASSETS AND LIABILITIES

RESIDENT/NON RESIDENT ET MONNAIE NATIONALE/ETRANGERE
CLASSIFICATION DE L'ACTIF ET DU PASSIF DES BANQUES

2001

Million Euros   *Millions d'euros*

	Residents / Résidents	Non-residents / Non résidents	Total / Total	
Assets				Actif
Domestic currency	52,985	293,409	346,394	Monnaie nationale
Foreign currencies	46,484	254,871	301,355	Monnaies étrangères
Total	99,470	548,279	647,749	Total
Liabilities				Passif
Domestic currency	115,226	220,045	335,271	Monnaie nationale
Foreign currencies	80,206	232,273	312,478	Monnaies étrangères
Total	195,431	452,318	647,749	Total

Note: Local rural savings banks not included in this table.

Note : Les caisses rurales locales ne sont pas prises en compte dans ce tableau.

STRUCTURE OF THE FINANCIAL SYSTEM
STRUCTURE DU SYSTEME FINANCIER

2000

	Number of institutions / Nombre d'institutions	Number of branches / Nombre de succursales	Number of employees / Nombre de salariés	Total assets or liabilities / Total des actifs ou des passifs	Total financial assets / Total des actifs financiers		
				million Mex$ / $Mex	million Mex$ / $Mex	%	
Central bank	1	..	..	..	..	..	Banque centrale
Other monetary institutions	42	7039	109568	1479963	-	-	Autres institutions monétaires
Commercial banks	18	6110	93974	1176852			Banques commerciales
Foreign-owned banks	18	929	15594	301470			Banques étrangères
Savings banks (+)	6	-	-	1642			Caisses d'épargne (+)
Co-operative banks							Banques mutualistes
Other financial institutions							Autres institutions financières
Mortgage credit institutions	22	-	-	30246			Institutions de crédit hypothécaire
Development credit institutions	5	404	10916	499606			Institutions de crédit de développement
Finance companies							Sociétés financières
Others (1)	285	-	-	34876			Autres (1)
Insurance institutions							Institutions d'assurance
Insurance companies	70	-	-	150311			Sociétés d'assurance
All financial institutions							Ensemble des institutions financières

1 Includes leasing companies, factoring companies, foreign exchange houses and credit unions.

1 Y compris les sociétés de crédit-bail, les sociétés d'affacturage, les sociétés de change et les caisses de crédit mutuel.

STRUCTURE OF THE FINANCIAL SYSTEM
STRUCTURE DU SYSTEME FINANCIER

2001

	Number of institutions / Nombre d'institutions	Number of branches / Nombre de succursales	Number of employees / Nombre de salariés	Total assets or liabilities / Total des actifs ou des passifs _million Mex$ / $Mex_	Total financial assets / Total des actifs financiers _million Mex$ / $Mex_	%	
Central bank	1	..	..	..	..	..	_Banque centrale_
Other monetary institutions	39	6511	99659	1586942	-	-	_Autres institutions monétaires_
Commercial banks	18	5770	87858	1310572			Banques commerciales
Foreign-owned banks	15	741	11801	274288			Banques étrangères
Savings banks (+)	6	..	..	2083			Caisses d'épargne (+)
Co-operative banks							Banques mutualistes
Other financial institutions							_Autres institutions financières_
Mortgage credit institutions	22	..	..	43496			Institutions de crédit hypothécaire
Development credit institutions	5	390	10443	530204			Institutions de crédit de développement
Finance companies							Sociétés financières
Others (1)	252	..	..	38853			Autres (1)
Insurance institutions							_Institutions d'assurance_
Insurance companies	70	-	-	181161			Sociétés d'assurance
All financial institutions							_Ensemble des institutions financières_

1 Includes leasing companies, factoring companies, foreign exchange houses and credit unions.

1 Y compris les sociétés de crédit-bail, les sociétés d'affacturage, les sociétés de change et les caisses de crédit mutuel.

STRUCTURE OF THE FINANCIAL SYSTEM
STRUCTURE DU SYSTEME FINANCIER
1999

	Number of institutions / Nombre d'institutions	Number of branches / Nombre de succursales (1)	Number of employees / Nombre de salariés (1)	Total assets or liabilities / Total des actifs ou des passifs Million Eur	Total financial assets / Total des actifs financiers Million Eur	%	
Central bank	1	5	1799	53365	53183	..	Banque centrale
Other monetary institutions (2)	94	6258	147566	982616	977080	..	Autres institut. monétaires(2)
Universal banks (3)	86	4450	99007	..	..	..	Banques universelles (3)
Co-operative banks(4)	1	1795	47908	304940	302989	..	Banques mutualistes (4)
Savings banks	1	3	12	..	..	..	Caisses d'épargne
Security credit institutions	6	10	639	..	..	..	Institutions de crédit de valeurs mobilières
Other financial institutions	1	1	25	..	..	..	Autres institutions financières
Mortgage credit institutions (2)	1	1	25	..	..	..	Institutions de crédit hypothécaire (2)
Insurance institutions	1421	..	..			..	Institutions d'assurance
Insurance companies	382	..	..	243952	232063	..	Sociétés d'assurance
Pension funds and foundations	1039	..	..	436264	410716	..	Fonds de pension et fondations
Mutual funds	457	..	..	98289	80001		Fonds commun de placement
All financial institutions	1974	..	..	..	..	..	Ensemble des institutions financières

1 The figures for number of branches and employees are from *Banks and Brokers in the Netherlands, 2000/2001*, Netherlands Institute
  for the Banking and Stockbroking Industry. The branch figures except for Co-operative banks (Rabobank) are estimates.
2 Data reflect the credit institutions which have consolidated their domestic bank (and non-bank) subsidiaries. This implies that
  the data of universal banks, savings banks, security credit institutions and mortgage credit institutions do not
  correspond to the groups as registered in the Register of the Act on the Supervision of the Credit System 1992. For example,
  a large number of savings banks have merged - or been taken over - and the parent saving bank has become a universal bank.
3 Branch figures include local post offices which are jointly owned by the Royal Dutch Post and the ING Bank.
4 The Rabobanken comprises 1 central institution, which reports as a group, with 424 members and a total of 1795 offices .

1 Les chiffres pour le nombre de succursales et de salariés proviennent de "Les banques et courtiers dans les Pays-Bas, 2000/2001",
  Institut néerlandais pour la banque et l'industrie du commerce des valeurs en Bourse. Les chiffres qui se réfèrent aux succursales sont
  des estimations, sauf dans le cas des Banques mutualistes (Rabobank).
2 Les données reflètent les institutions de crédit qui ont consolidé leurs filiales bancaires (et non-bancaires) nationales. Ceci implique
  que les données des banques universelles, des banques d'épargne, des institutions de crédit et de crédit hypothécaire ne correspondent pas aux groupes répertoriés en tant que tel dans le Register of the Act on the Supervision of the Credit System de 1992.
  Par exemple, un grand nombre de banques d'épargne ont fusionné - ou ont été absorbées - et la banque d'épargne mère est
  devenue une banque universelle.
3 Les chiffres pour les succursales comprennent les bureaux de poste locaux appartenant conjointement à la Royal Dutch Pos
  et à la banque ING.
4 La Rabobanken comprend 1 institution centrale, qui en tant que groupe comprend 424 membres et a au total 1795 agences.

RESIDENT/NON-RESIDENT AND DOMESTIC/FOREIGN CURRENCY
CLASSIFICATION OF BANK ASSETS AND LIABILITIES(1)

RESIDENT/NON RESIDENT ET MONNAIE NATIONALE/ETRANGERE(1)
CLASSIFICATION DE L'ACTIF ET DU PASSIF DES BANQUES

1999

Million Euros   *Millions d'euros*

	Residents / Résidents	Non-residents / Non résidents	Total / Total	
Assets(2)				*Actif (2)*
National currency	667828	150383	818211	Monnaie nationale
Non-MU currencies	50415	113990	164405	Monnaies hors Union Monétaire
Total	718243	264372	982616	Total
Liabilities(2)				*Passif (2)*
National currency	460587	295275	755862	Monnaie nationale
Non-MU currencies	25775	200979	226754	Monnaies hors Union Monétaire
Total	486362	496254	982616	Total

1 Monetary institutions, excluding the Central bank.

2 The figures concerning the assets / liabilities are based on returns submitted by monetary financial institutions respresenting about 96 % of the aggregate balance sheet total of all Dutch monetary financial institutions. These data have been grossed up to 100%

1 Institutions monétaires à l'exclusion de la Banque centrale.

2 Les chiffres concernant les actifs/passifs sont basés sur les rapports envoyés par les Institutions monétaires et financière représentant environ 96% du total du bilan de toutes les institutions financières monétaires. Ces données ont ete arrondies a 100%

STRUCTURE OF THE FINANCIAL SYSTEM
STRUCTURE DU SYSTEME FINANCIER
2000

	Number of institutions / Nombre d'institutions	Number of branches / Nombre de succursales (1)	Number of employees / Nombre de salariés (1)	Total assets or liabilities / Total des actifs ou des passifs Million Eur	Total financial assets / Total des actifs financiers Million Eur	%	
Central bank	1	5	1641	42882	42701	..	Banque centrale
Other monetary institutions (2)	93	5974	153976	1148926	1142982	..	Autres institut. monétaires(2)
Universal banks (3)	87	4241	102562	..	..	..	Banques universelles (3)
Co-operative banks(4)	1	1727	50119	372871	370784	..	Banques mutualistes (4)
Savings banks				..	..	..	Caisses d'épargne
Security credit institutions	5	6	1295	..	..	..	Institutions de crédit de valeurs mobilières
Other financial institutions	2	10	113	..	..	..	Autres institutions financières
Mortgage credit institutions (2)	2	10	113	..	..	..	Institutions de crédit hypothécaire (2)
Insurance institutions	1325	..	..	..	..	..	Institutions d'assurance
Insurance companies (5)	339	..	..	263556	249035	..	Sociétés d'assurance (5)
Pension funds and foundations	986	..	..	444932	421017	..	Fonds de pension et fondations
Mutual funds (6)	368	..	..	118028	88850		Fonds commun de placement (6)
All financial institutions	1884	..	..	..	..	..	Ensemble des institutions financières

1 The figures for number of branches and employees are from *Banks and Brokers in the Netherlands, 2001/2002*, Netherlands Institute for the Banking and Stockbroking Industry. The branch figures except for Co-operative banks (Rabobank) are estimates.
2 Data reflect the credit institutions which have consolidated their domestic bank (and non-bank) subsidiaries. This implies that the data of universal banks, savings banks, security credit institutions and mortgage credit institutions do not correspond to the groups as registered in the Register of the Act on the Supervision of the Credit System 1992. For example, a large number of savings banks have merged - or been taken over - and the parent saving bank has become a universal bank.
3 Branch figures include local post offices which are jointly owned by the Royal Dutch Post and the ING Bank.
4 The Rabobanken comprises 1 central institution, which reports as a group, with 397 members and a total of 1727 offices .
5 The number of institutions are excluding: foreign companies (Dutch representatives of companies whose head office is abroad; 19 institutions and the institutions by virtue of a completed notification (688).
6 The number of institutions concerns the number of entries in the register under the Act on the Supervision of Collective Investment Schemes Including the number of subfunds, the total number of funds is 558

1 Les chiffres pour le nombre de succursales et de salariés proviennent de "Les banques et courtiers dans les Pays-Bas, 2001/2002", Institut néerlandais pour la banque et l'industrie du commerce des valeurs en Bourse. Les chiffres qui se réfèrent aux succursales sont des estimations, sauf dans le cas des Banques mutualistes (Rabobank).
2 Les données reflètent les institutions de crédit qui ont consolidé leurs filiales bancaires (et non-bancaires) nationales. Ceci implique que les données des banques universelles, des banques d'épargne, des institutions de crédit et de crédit hypothécaire ne correspondent pas aux groupes répertoriés en tant que tel dans le Register of the Act on the Supervision of the Credit System de 1992. Par exemple, un grand nombre de banques d'épargne ont fusionné - ou ont été absorbées - et la banque d'épargne mère est devenue une banque universelle.
3 Les chiffres pour les succursales comprennent les bureaux de poste locaux appartenant conjointement à la Royal Dutch Post et à la banque ING.
4 La Rabobanken comprend 1 institution centrale, qui en tant que groupe comprend 397 membres et a au total 1727 agences.
5 Le nombre d'institutions exclut : les sociétés étrangères (des filiales néerlandaises de sociétés dont la maison mère se trouve à l'étranger :19 institutions et les établissements en cours de notification (688)
6 Le nombre d'institutions concerne le nombre d'entrées au registre suivant la loi sur la Supervision des plans d'investissements collectifs Ce qui inclut aussi les sous catégories de fonds, le nombre total de fonds se monte à 558

RESIDENT/NON-RESIDENT AND DOMESTIC/FOREIGN CURRENCY
CLASSIFICATION OF BANK ASSETS AND LIABILITIES (1)
RESIDENT/NON RESIDENT ET MONNAIE NATIONALE/ETRANGERE
CLASSIFICATION DE L'ACTIF ET DU PASSIF DES BANQUES (1)

2000

Million Euros   *Millions d'euros*

	Residents / Résidents	Non-residents / Non résidents	Total / Total	
Assets(2)				*Actif (2)*
National currency	789986	159050	949036	Monnaie nationale
Non-MU currencies	36484	163406	199890	Monnaies hors Union Monétaire
Total	826470	322456	1148926	Total
Liabilities(2)				*Passif (2)*
National currency	560101	254525	814626	Monnaie nationale
Non-MU currencies	27045	307255	334300	Monnaies hors Union Monétaire
Total	587146	561780	1148926	Total

1 Monetary institutions, excluding the Central bank.

2 The figures concerning the assets / liabilities are based on returns submitted by monetary financial institutions respresenting about 96 % of the aggregate balance sheet total of all Dutch monetary financial institutions. These data have been grossed up to 100%

1 Institutions monétaires à l'exclusion de la Banque centrale.

2 Les chiffres concernant les actifs/passifs sont basés sur les rapports envoyés par les Institutions monétaires et financière représentant environ 96% du total du bilan de toutes les institutions financières monétaires. Ces données ont ete arrondies a 100%

STRUCTURE OF THE FINANCIAL SYSTEM
STRUCTURE DU SYSTEME FINANCIER

2001

	Number of institutions / Nombre d'institutions	Number of branches / Nombre de succursales	Number of employees / Nombre de salariés	Total assets or liabilities / Total des actifs ou des passifs	Total financial assets / Total des actifs financiers		
				million NZ$ / $ NZ	million NZ$ / $ NZ	%	
Central bank	1	1	189	10855	10809		Banque centrale
Other monetary institutions(1)	17	858	22417	189797	..		Autres institutions monétaires(1)
Other financial institutions(2)	130	..	..	10400	..		Autres institutions financières(2)
Insurance institutions							Institutions d'assurance
Insurance companies(3)	90	..	..	12930	..		Sociétés d'assurance(3)
Pension funds and foundations(4)	30	..	..	19918	..		Fonds de pension et fondations(4)
Others(5)	54	..	..	24740			Autres(5)
All financial institutions	322	..	..	268640	..		Ensemble des institutions financières

1 Data for registered banks.
2 all other deposit-taking financial institutions.
3 Life company funds under management and general insurance company assets
4 Funds under management of superannuation funds and unit trusts
5 Unit trusts and other managed funds.

Sources: Total assets and number of institutions: Reserve Bank of New Zealand; employee and branch numbers, Statistics New Zealand

1 Données concernant les banques répertoriées.
2 Tout autre banque de dépôt.
3 Les companies d'assurance-vie et les actifs des companies d'assurance générales
4 Les fonds sous la gestion des caisses de retraite et des sociétés d'investissement
5 Sociétés d'investissement et autres fonds gérés.

Sources: Le total des actifs et le nombre d'institutions, Reserve Bank de Nouvelle Zélande; nombre d'employés et de succursales, les statistiques de Nouvelle Zélande.

RESIDENT/NON-RESIDENT AND DOMESTIC/FOREIGN CURRENCY
CLASSIFICATION OF BANK ASSETS AND LIABILITIES (1)

RESIDENT/NON RESIDENT ET MONNAIE NATIONALE/ETRANGERE
CLASSIFICATION DE L'ACTIF ET DU PASSIF DES BANQUES (1)

2001

Million New Zealand dollars

Millions de dollars de Nouvelle-Zélande

	Residents / Résidents	Non-residents / Non résidents	Total / Total	
Assets				Actif
Domestic currency	163075	11709	174784	Monnaie nationale
Foreign currencies	5123	9890	15013	Monnaies étrangères
Total	168198	21598	189797	Total
Liabilities				Passif
Domestic currency	120398	26522	146920	Monnaie nationale
Foreign currencies	3194	39682	42876	Monnaies étrangères
Total	123593	66204	189797	Total

1 Data are based on the Reserve Bank of New Zealand's quarterly survey of M3 institutions. The data cover local activities of banks registered in New Zealand and exclude business conducted from their non New Zealand operations

1 Les données se réfèrent à l'enquête trimestrielle des institutions de M3. Il s'agit des données relatives aux activités locales des banques répertoriées en Nouvelle-Zélande, sont exclues les activités de leurs agences à l'étranger

STRUCTURE OF THE FINANCIAL SYSTEM
STRUCTURE DU SYSTEME FINANCIER

2000

	Number of institutions / Nombre d'institutions	Number of branches / Nombre de succursales	Number of employees Nombre de salariés (1)	Total assets or liabilities / Total des actifs ou des passifs million NKr / KrN	Total financial assets / Total des actifs financiers million NKr / KrN	%	
Central bank	1	12	1086	809684	807745	26	Banque centrale
Other monetary institutions	152	1273	22885	1334522	1324679	42	Autres institutions monétaires
Commercial banks	11	322	10445	626172	620674	20	Banques commerciales
Foreign-owned banks	11	89	1856	148229	147743	5	Banques étrangères
Savings banks	130	862	10584	560121	556262	18	Caisses d'épargne
Co-operative banks	..	..	..	..	..	..	Banques mutualistes
Other financial institutions	69	34	2203	465754	465279	15	Autres institutions financières
Mortgage credit institutions	12	6	274	211740	211589	7	Institutions de crédit hypothécaire
Development credit institutions	..	..	..	..	..	..	Institutions de crédit de développement
Finance companies	54	28	1929	74064	73849	2	Sociétés financières
Others (2)	3	..	..	179950	179841	6	Autres (2)
Insurance institutions	267	..	8657	580756	537516	17	Institutions d'assurance
Insurance companies	115	..	8657	479081	439194	14	Sociétés d'assurance
Pension funds and foundations	150	..	..	99870	96517	3	Fonds de pension et fondations
Others (3)	2	..	..	1805	1805	0	Autres (3)
All financial institutions	489	1319	34831	3190716	3135219	100	Ensemble des institutions financières

1 Man-labour years, except for the central bank.
2 State lending institutions exclusive of the Guarantee Institute for Export Credit (GIEK).
3 Joint scheme for collective agreement-based pensions (FTP) and Agreement-based pensions (AFP).

1 Travail-années, sauf pour la banque centrale.
2 Institutions de prêts de l'état à l'exclusion de l'Institut de garantie pour le crédit à l'exportation (GIEK)
3 FTP et AFP.

RESIDENT/NON-RESIDENT AND DOMESTIC/FOREIGN CURRENCY CLASSIFICATION OF BANK ASSETS AND LIABILITIES

RESIDENT/NON RESIDENT ET MONNAIE NATIONALE/ETRANGERE CLASSIFICATION DE L'ACTIF ET DU PASSIF DES BANQUES

2000

Million Norwegian kroner   Millions de couronnes norvégiennes

	Residents / Résidents	Non-residents / Non résidents	Total / Total	
				Actif
Assets				
Domestic currency	1099191	19353	1118544	Monnaie nationale
Foreign currencies	98561	117417	215978	Monnaies étrangères
Total	1197752	136770	1334522	Total
				Passif
Liabilities				
Domestic currency	969919	56941	1026860	Monnaie nationale
Foreign currencies	36671	270992	307663	Monnaies étrangères
Total	1006588	327934	1334522	Total

STRUCTURE OF THE FINANCIAL SYSTEM
STRUCTURE DU SYSTEME FINANCIER

2001

	Number of institutions / Nombre d'institutions	Number of branches / Nombre de succursales	Number of employees Nombre de salariés (1)	Total assets or liabilities / Total des actifs ou des passifs million NKr / KrN	Total financial assets / Total des actifs financiers million NKr / KrN	%	
Central bank	1	-	662	987693	985861	28	Banque centrale
Other monetary institutions	151	1390	23367	1451435	1441777	41	Autres institutions monétaires
Commercial banks	12	165	6782	451209	448328	13	Banques commerciales
Foreign-owned banks	10	223	5468	375043	372119	11	Banques étrangères
Savings banks	129	1002	11117	625183	621330	18	Caisses d'épargne
Co-operative banks	..	..	..	..	..	..	Banques mutualistes
Other financial institutions	71	39	2415	527785	527317	15	Autres institutions financières
Mortgage credit institutions	11	6	282	250263	250091	7	Institutions de crédit hypothécaire
Development credit institutions	..	..	..	..	..	..	Institutions de crédit de développement
Finance companies	57	33	2133	87603	87408	2	Sociétés financières
Others (2)	3	..	..	189919	189818	5	Autres (2)
Insurance institutions	266	..	9473	600762	552940	16	Institutions d'assurance
Insurance companies	116	..	9473	513527	469055	13	Sociétés d'assurance
Pension funds and foundations	148	..	..	85800	82450	2	Fonds de pension et fondations
Others (3)	2	..	..	1435	1435	-	Autres (3)
All financial institutions	489	1429	35917	3567675	3507895	100	Ensemble des institutions financières

1 Man-labour years, except for the central bank.
2 State lending institutions exclusive of the Guarantee Institute for Export Credit (GIEK).
3 Joint scheme for collective agreement-based pensions (FTP) and Agreement-based pensions (AFP).

1 Travail-années, sauf pour la banque centrale.
2 Institutions de prêts de l'état à l'exclusion de l'Institut de garantie pour le crédit à l'exportation (GIEK)
3 FTP et AFP.

RESIDENT/NON-RESIDENT AND DOMESTIC/FOREIGN CURRENCY
CLASSIFICATION OF BANK ASSETS AND LIABILITIES

RESIDENT/NON RESIDENT ET MONNAIE NATIONALE/ETRANGERE
CLASSIFICATION DE L'ACTIF ET DU PASSIF DES BANQUES

2001

Million Norwegian kroner   *Millions de couronnes norvégiennes*

	Residents / Résidents	Non-residents / Non résidents	Total / Total	
Assets				Actif
Domestic currency	1201432	30046	1231478	Monnaie nationale
Foreign currencies	112988	106969	219957	Monnaies étrangères
Total	1314420	137015	1451435	Total
Liabilities				Passif
Domestic currency	1053748	61824	1115572	Monnaie nationale
Foreign currencies	39254	296609	335863	Monnaies étrangères
Total	1093002	358433	1451435	Total

STRUCTURE OF THE FINANCIAL SYSTEM
STRUCTURE DU SYSTEME FINANCIER

2000

	Number of institutions / Nombre d'institutions	Number of branches / Nombre de succursales	Number of employees / Nombre de salariés (1)	Total assets or liabilities / Total des actifs ou des passifs million PLN	Total financial assets / Total des actifs financiers million PLN	%	
Central bank (2)							*Banque centrale (2)*
Other monetary institutions							*Autres institutions monétaires*
Commercial banks	73	2,406	145,541	410,449			Banques commerciales
Banks with a majority of Polish capital	27	960	60,714	112,527			- Banques ayant une majorité de capitaux polonais
Banks with a majority of foreign capital	46	1,446	84,827	297,922			- Banques ayant une majorité de capitaux étrangers
Co-operative banks	680	1,148	25,694	18,044			Banques mutualistes
Other financial institutions							*Autres institutions financières*
Finance companies (3)	81			9,451	9,451		Sociétés financières (3)
Insurance institutions							*Institutions d'assurance*
Insurance companies (4)	66	-	30,573	37,927	32,217		Sociétés d'assurance (4)
All financial institutions							*Ensemble des institutions financières*

1 Number of full-time contracts.
2 Central bank branches: 13 regional branches, 1 chief branch of foreign exchange.
3 Finance company figures refer to open-end (trust) funds. Data are for end-June 1999
4 Data refer to insurance companies submitting financial statements to the supervisory office.
  Number of employees: average employment excluding brokers.
  Figures are for end-September 1999.

1 Nombre de contrats à plein temps.
2 Succursales de la Banque centrale : 13 succursales régionales, 1 succursale principale de change.
3 Les données pour les Sociétés financières concernent les fonds à capital. Les chiffres se rapportent à fin juin 1999.
4 Les données se réfèrent aux compagnies d'assurance qui soumettent leurs comptes au bureau de surveillance.
  Le nombre d'employés : nombre moyen excluant les courtiers.
  Les chiffres se rapportent à fin septembre 1999.

RESIDENT/NON-RESIDENT AND DOMESTIC/FOREIGN CURRENCY
CLASSIFICATION OF BANK ASSETS AND LIABILITIES

RESIDENT/NON RESIDENT ET MONNAIE NATIONALE/ETRANGERE
CLASSIFICATION DE L'ACTIF ET DU PASSIF DES BANQUES

2000

Million zlotys   *Millions de zlotys*

	Residents / Résidents	Non-residents / Non résidents	Total / Total	
Assets				*Actif*
Domestic currency	344841	4053	348894	Monnaie nationale
Foreign currencies	56976	42257	99233	Monnaies étrangères
Total	401817	46310	448127(1)	Total
Liabilities				*Passif*
Domestic currency	349444	5599	355043	Monnaie nationale
Foreign currencies	51660	21790	73450	Monnaies étrangères
Total	401104	27389	428493	Total

1 Includes provisions, accumulated depreciation and valuation allowances in the amount of ZL 19 634 million, for which
  the breakdown by currencies and resident/non-resident is not available.

1 Y compris les provisions, l'amortissement cumulé et les dotations de réévaluation d'un montant de 19 634 millions de ZL,
  pour lequel la ventilation par monnaie et par résident/non-résident n'est pas disponible.

STRUCTURE OF THE FINANCIAL SYSTEM
STRUCTURE DU SYSTEME FINANCIER

2001

	Number of institutions / Nombre d'institutions	Number of branches / Nombre de succursales	Number of employees / Nombre de salariés (1)	Total assets or liabilities / Total des actifs ou des passifs million PLN	Total financial assets / Total des actifs financiers million PLN	%	
Central bank (2)	1	14	6,377	138,358	-		Banque centrale (2)
Other monetary institutions							Autres institutions monétaires
Commercial banks							Banques commerciales
Banks with a majority of Polish capital	23	1,090	57,774	125,253			- Banques ayant une majorité de capitaux polonais
Banks with a majority of foreign capital	48	1,788	81,050	322,948			- Banques ayant une majorité de capitaux étrangers
Co-operative banks	642	1,201	26,405	21,505			Banques mutualistes
Other financial institutions							Autres institutions financières
Finance companies (3)	92	-	-	12,886	12,886		Sociétés financières (3)
Insurance institutions							Institutions d'assurance
Insurance companies (4)	70	2	30,437	47,258	41,082		Sociétés d'assurance (4)
All financial institutions							Ensemble des institutions financières

1 Number of full-time contracts.
2 Central bank branches: 13 regional branches, 1 chief branch of foreign exchange.
3 Finance company figures refer to open-end (trust) funds
4 Data refer to insurance companies submitting financial statements to the supervisory office.
  Number of employees: average employment excluding brokers.

1 Nombre de contrats à plein temps.
2 Succursales de la Banque centrale : 13 succursales régionales, 1 succursale principale de change.
3 Les données pour les Sociétés financières concernent les fonds à capital.
4 Les données se réfèrent aux compagnies d'assurance qui soumettent leurs comptes au bureau de surveillance.
  Le nombre d'employés : nombre moyen excluant les courtiers.

RESIDENT/NON-RESIDENT AND DOMESTIC/FOREIGN CURRENCY CLASSIFICATION OF BANK ASSETS AND LIABILITIES

RESIDENT/NON RESIDENT ET MONNAIE NATIONALE/ETRANGERE CLASSIFICATION DE L'ACTIF ET DU PASSIF DES BANQUES

2001

Million zlotys   *Millions de zlotys*

	Residents / Résidents	Non-residents / Non résidents	Total / Total	
Assets				Actif
Domestic currency	366,057	7,298	373,355	Monnaie nationale
Foreign currencies	69,094	53,165	122,259	Monnaies étrangères
Total	435,151	60,463	495614 (1)	Total
Liabilities				Passif
Domestic currency	374,720	10,294	385,014	Monnaie nationale
Foreign currencies	62,750	21,942	84,692	Monnaies étrangères
Total	437,470	32,236	469,706	Total

1 Includes provisions, accumulated depreciation and valuation allowances in the amount of ZL 19 634 million, for which the breakdown by currencies and resident/non-resident is not available.

1 Y compris les provisions, l'amortissement cumulé et les dotations de réévaluation d'un montant de 19 634 millions de ZL, pour lequel la ventilation par monnaie et par résident/non-résident n'est pas disponible.

STRUCTURE OF THE FINANCIAL SYSTEM
STRUCTURE DU SYSTEME FINANCIER

2000

	Number of institutions / Nombre d'institutions	Number of branches / Nombre de succursales	Number of employees / Nombre de salariés	Total assets or liabilities / Total des actifs ou des passifs _million Eur_	Total financial assets / Total des actifs financiers (1) _million Eur_	%	
Central bank	_1_	_11_	_1832_	_27130_	_26187_	..	_Banque centrale_
Other monetary institutions (2)	_218_	_5662_	_58097_	_281005_	_262596_	..	_Autres institutions monétaires (2)_
Commercial banks (3)	42	4895	53843	262267	244754	..	Banques commerciales (3)
Foreign-owned banks (4)	25	95	1083	8793	8476	..	Banques étrangères (4)
Savings banks	5	20	145	314	282	..	Caisses d'épargne
Co-operative banks	146	652	3026	9631	9083	..	Banques mutualistes
Other financial instit. (5)	_268_	..	..	..	..	..	_Autres instit. financières (5)_
Insurance institutions	_124_	..	..	_40307_	_38320_	..	_Institutions d'assurance_
Insurance companies	93	777	13251	26541	25248	..	Sociétés d'assurance
Pension funds and foundations (6)	31	..	..	13767	13072	..	Fonds de pension et fondations (6)
All financial institutions	..	..	..	..	..	..	_Ensemble des institutions financières_

1 Financial assets are net of provisions.
2 The number mentioned at the table does not include Money Market Funds
3 Banks with head-offices in Portuguese territory.
4 Branches of foreign banks located in Portuguese territory.
5 Other financial institutions registered at the Banco de Portugal.
6 The number mentioned at the table refers to the number of entities (pension funds managing companies and insurance companies)
that are currently managing pension funds. That number is being provided because pension funds cannot be clearly considered
as legal entities. The number of Portuguese pension funds is 244.

1 Actifs financiers sont net de provisions.
2 Le nombre mentionné dans le tableau n'inclut pas les organismes de placement collectif monétaires
3 Banques dont le siège social se situe en territoire portugais.
4 Filiales de banques étrangères situées en territoire portugais.
5 Autres institutions financières répertoriées à la Banco de Portugal.
6 Le nombre mentionné dans le tableau se réfère au nombre d'entités (fonds de pension gérant des sociétés et des
companies d'assurance), qui gèrent actuellement des fonds de pension. Le nombre de fonds de pension portugais est de 244

RESIDENT/NON-RESIDENT AND DOMESTIC/FOREIGN CURRENCY CLASSIFICATION OF BANK ASSETS AND LIABILITIES (1)

RESIDENT/NON RESIDENT ET MONNAIE NATIONALE/ETRANGERE CLASSIFICATION DE L'ACTIF ET DU PASSIF DES BANQUES (1)

2000

Million euros   _Millions d'euros_

	Residents / Résidents	Non-residents / Non résidents	Total / Total	
Assets				_Actif_
Domestic currency	..	..	..	Monnaie nationale
Foreign currencies	..	..	..	Monnaies étrangères
Total	206207	56060	262267	Total
Liabilities				_Passif_
Domestic currency	..	..	..	Monnaie nationale
Foreign currencies	..	..	..	Monnaies étrangères
Total	181236	81030	262267	Total

1 Domestic/foreign currency breakdown not available.

1 La ventilation par monnaie nationale/étrangère n'est pas disponible

STRUCTURE OF THE FINANCIAL SYSTEM
STRUCTURE DU SYSTEME FINANCIER

2001

	Number of institutions / Nombre d'institutions	Number of branches / Nombre de succursales	Number of employees / Nombre de salariés	Total assets or liabilities / Total des actifs ou des passifs million Eur	Total financial assets / Total des actifs financiers (1) million Eur	%	
Central bank	1	11	1814	27439	26462	..	Banque centrale
Other monetary institutions (2)	209	5596	56213	307045	286950	..	Autres institutions monétaires (2)
Commercial banks (3)	42	4804	51537	284663	265409	..	Banques commerciales (3)
Foreign-owned banks (4)	25	108	1154	11223	10929	..	Banques étrangères (4)
Savings banks	5	20	145	339	311	..	Caisses d'épargne
Co-operative banks	137	664	3377	10820	10300	..	Banques mutualistes
Other financial institutions (5)	254	..	..	..	..	..	Autres institutions financières (5)
Insurance institutions	117	..	..	43330	41142	..	Institutions d'assurance
Insurance companies	86	767	13413	28503	27186	..	Sociétés d'assurance
Pension funds and foundations (6)	31	..	..	14826	13956	..	Fonds de pension et fondations (6)
All financial institutions	..	..	..	..	..	..	Ensemble des institutions financières

1 Financial assets are net of provisions.
2 The number mentioned at the table does not include Money Market Funds
3 Banks with head-offices in Portuguese territory.
4 Branches of foreign banks located in Portuguese territory.
5 Other financial institutions registered at the Banco de Portugal.
6 The number mentioned at the table refers to the number of entities (pension funds managing companies and insurance companies) that are currently managing pension funds. That number is being provided because pension funds cannot be clearly considered as legal entities. The number of Portuguese pension funds is 236.

1 Actifs financiers sont net de provisions.
2 Le nombre mentionné dans le tableau n'inclut pas les organismes de placement collectif monétaires
3 Banques dont le siège social se situe en territoire portugais.
4 Filiales de banques étrangères situées en territoire portugais.
5 Autres institutions financières répertoriées à la Banco de Portugal.
6 Le nombre mentionné dans le tableau se réfère au nombre d'entités (fonds de pension gérant des sociétés et des companies d'assurance), qui gèrent actuellement des fonds de pension. Le nombre de fonds de pension portugais est de 236

RESIDENT/NON-RESIDENT AND DOMESTIC/FOREIGN CURRENCY CLASSIFICATION OF BANK ASSETS AND LIABILITIES (1)

RESIDENT/NON RESIDENT ET MONNAIE NATIONALE/ETRANGERE CLASSIFICATION DE L'ACTIF ET DU PASSIF DES BANQUES (1)

2001

Million euros   Millions d'euros

	Residents / Résidents	Non-residents / Non résidents	Total / Total	
Assets				Actif
Domestic currency	..	..	..	Monnaie nationale
Foreign currencies	..	..	..	Monnaies étrangères
Total	224584	60079	284663	Total
Liabilities				Passif
Domestic currency	..	..	..	Monnaie nationale
Foreign currencies	..	..	..	Monnaies étrangères
Total	188017	96646	284663	Total

1 Domestic/foreign currency breakdown not available.

1 La ventilation par monnaie nationale/étrangère n'est pas disponible

STRUCTURE OF THE FINANCIAL SYSTEM
STRUCTURE DU SYSTEME FINANCIER
1995

	Number of institutions / Nombre d'institutions	Number of branches / Nombre de succursales	Number of employees / Nombre de salariés	Total assets or liabilities / Total des actifs ou des passifs million SKK	Total financial assets / Total des actifs financiers million SKK	%	
Central bank	1	3	1230	222236	220207	99	Banque centrale
Other monetary institutions	33	894	21976	313999	258409	82	Autres institutions monétaires
Commercial banks	14	852	19365	227738	174440	77	Banques commerciales
Foreign-owned banks (1)	17	42	2302	53602	52257	97	Banques étrangères (1)
Savings banks	..	..	..	..	..	..	Caisses d'épargne
Co-operative banks	..	..	..	..	..	..	Banques mutualistes
Building savings banks	2	-	309	32659	31712	97	Caisses d'épargne pour le batiment
Other financial institutions	..	..	..	..	..	..	Autres institutions financières
Mortgage credit institutions (2)	..	..	..	..	..	..	Institutions de crédit hypothécaire (2)
Development credit institutions	..	..	..	..	..	..	Institutions de crédit de développement
Finance companies	..	..	..	..	..	..	Sociétés financières
Others	..	..	..	..	..	..	Autres
Insurance institutions	17	513	5109	32537	28074	..	Institutions d'assurance
Insurance companies (3)	17	513	5109	32537	28074	..	Sociétés d'assurance (3)
Pension funds and foundations	..	..	..	..	..	..	Fonds de pension et fondations
Others	..	..	..	..	..	..	Autres
All financial institutions	..	..	..	..	..	..	Ensemble des institutions financières

1 Banks with more than 50% of capital and branches of foreign banks
2 There are no special mortgage credit institutions in Slovak Republic. Several commercial banks have licences serving mortgage cr
3 Data are without health and social insurance companies

1 Il s'agit de banques détenant plus de 50% du capital et de succursales de banques étrangères.
2 Il n'y a pas d'institutions de crédit hypothécaire spéciales en République Slovaque. Plusieurs banques commerciales ont des licences pour délivrer les crédits hypothécaires.
3 Ces données n'incluent pas les companies d'assurance sociale et d'assurance-maladie

RESIDENT/NON-RESIDENT AND DOMESTIC/FOREIGN CURRENCY
CLASSIFICATION OF BANK ASSETS AND LIABILITIES
RESIDENT/NON RESIDENT ET MONNAIE NATIONALE/ETRANGERE
CLASSIFICATION DE L'ACTIF ET DU PASSIF DES BANQUES
1995

Million Slovak Kroner   *Millions de couronnes slovaques*

	Residents / Résidents	Non-residents / Non résidents	Total / Total	
Assets (4)				Actif (4)
Domestic currency	543406	4381	547787	Monnaie nationale
Foreign currencies	30416	51216	81632	Monnaies étrangères
Total	573822	55597	629419	Total
Liabilities (4)				Passif (4)
Domestic currency	514105	5089	519194	Monnaie nationale
Foreign currencies	48418	30409	78827	Monnaies étrangères
Total	562523	35498	598021	Total

4 Assets and liabilities are not balanced, provisions are not included

4 Les actifs et les passifs ne sont pas équilibrés, les provisions ne sont pas comprises

STRUCTURE OF THE FINANCIAL SYSTEM
STRUCTURE DU SYSTEME FINANCIER
1996

	Number of institutions / Nombre d'institutions	Number of branches / Nombre de succursales	Number of employees / Nombre de salariés	Total assets or liabilities / Total des actifs ou des passifs million SKK	Total financial assets / Total des actifs financiers million SKK	%	
Central bank	1	3	1278	208838	203125	97	Banque centrale
Other monetary institutions	29	868	23947	416301	329263	79	Autres institutions monétaires
Commercial banks	14	841	20986	295673	211689	72	Banques commerciales
Foreign-owned banks (1)	13	27	2573	95712	93754	93	Banques étrangères (1)
Savings banks	..	..	..	..	..	..	Caisses d'épargne
Co-operative banks	..	..	..	..	..	..	Banques mutualistes
Building saving banks	2	-	388	24 916	23820	96	Caisses d'épargne pour le batiment
Other financial institutions	-	-	-	..	..	..	Autres institutions financières
Mortgage credit institutions (2)	..	..	..	..	..	..	Institutions de crédit hypothécaire (2)
Development credit institutions	..	..	..	..	..	..	Institutions de crédit de développement
Finance companies	..	..	..	..	..	..	Sociétés financières
Others	..	..	..	..	..	..	Autres
Insurance institutions	21	594	5832	38096	32432	..	Institutions d'assurance
Insurance companies (3)	21	594	5832	38096	32432	..	Sociétés d'assurance (3)
Pension funds and foundations	..	..	..	..	..	..	Fonds de pension et fondations
Others	..	..	..	..	..	..	Autres
All financial institutions	..	..	..	..	..	..	Ensemble des institutions financières

1 Banks with more than 50% of capital and branches of foreign banks
2 There are no special mortgage credit institutions in Slovak Republic. Several commercial banks have licences serving mortgage cr
3 Data are without health and social insurance companies

1 Il s'agit de banques détenant plus de 50% du capital et de succursales de banques étrangères.
2 Il n'y a pas d'institutions de crédit hypothécaire spéciales en République Slovaque. Plusieurs banques commerciales ont des licences pour délivrer les crédits hypothécaires.
3 Ces données n'incluent pas les companies d'assurance sociale et d'assurance-maladie

RESIDENT/NON-RESIDENT AND DOMESTIC/FOREIGN CURRENCY
CLASSIFICATION OF BANK ASSETS AND LIABILITIES
RESIDENT/NON RESIDENT ET MONNAIE NATIONALE/ETRANGERE
CLASSIFICATION DE L'ACTIF ET DU PASSIF DES BANQUES
1996

Million Slovak Kroner   *Millions de couronnes slovaques*

	Residents / Résidents	Non-residents / Non résidents	Total / Total	
Assets (4)				Actif (4)
Domestic currency	641012	5043	646055	Monnaie nationale
Foreign currencies	35020	77152	112172	Monnaies étrangères
Total	676032	82195	758227	Total
Liabilities (4)				Passif (4)
Domestic currency	589370	9156	589526	Monnaie nationale
Foreign currencies	48609	69461	118070	Monnaies étrangères
Total	637979	78617	716596	Total

4 Assets and liabilities are not balanced, provisions are not included

4 Les actifs et les passifs ne sont pas équilibrés, les provisions ne sont pas comprises.

STRUCTURE OF THE FINANCIAL SYSTEM
STRUCTURE DU SYSTEME FINANCIER
1997

	Number of institutions / Nombre d'institutions	Number of branches / Nombre de succursales	Number of employees Nombre de salariés	Total assets or liabilities / Total des actifs ou des passifs million SKK	Total financial assets / Total des actifs financiers million SKK	%	
Central bank	1	3	1302	197602	189043	96	Banque centrale
Other monetary institutions	29	861	23768	482306	358523	74	Autres institutions monétaires
Commercial banks	15	824	20446	286894	166670	58	Banques commerciales
Foreign-owned banks (1)	12	37	2777	156269	153689	98	Banques étrangères (1)
Savings banks	..	..	..	..	..	..	Caisses d'épargne
Co-operative banks	..	..	..	..	..	..	Banques mutualistes
Building saving banks	2	-	545	39143	38164	98	Caisses d'épargne pour le batiment
Other financial institutions	-	-	-	..	..	..	Autres institutions financières
Mortgage credit institutions (2)	..	..	..	..	..	..	Institutions de crédit hypothécaire (2)
Development credit institutions	..	..	..	..	..	..	Institutions de crédit de développement
Finance companies	..	..	..	..	..	..	Sociétés financières
Others	..	..	..	..	..	..	Autres
Insurance institutions	22	676	6368	41895	34745	..	Institutions d'assurance
Insurance companies (3)	22	676	6368	41895	34745	..	Sociétés d'assurance (3)
Pension funds and foundations	..	..	..	..	..	..	Fonds de pension et fondations
Others	..	..	..	..	..	..	Autres
All financial institutions	..	..	..	..	..	..	Ensemble des institutions financières

1 Banks with more than 50% of capital and branches of foreign banks
2 There are no special mortgage credit institutions in Slovak Republic. Several commercial banks have licences serving mortgage cr
3 Data are without health and social insurance companies

1 Il s'agit de banques détenant plus de 50% du capital et de succursales de banques étrangères.
2 Il n'y a pas d'institutions de crédit hypothécaire spéciales en République Slovaque. Plusieurs banques commerciales
  ont des licences pour délivrer les crédits hypothécaires.
3 Ces données n'incluent pas les companies d'assurance sociale et d'assurance-maladie

RESIDENT/NON-RESIDENT AND DOMESTIC/FOREIGN CURRENCY
CLASSIFICATION OF BANK ASSETS AND LIABILITIES
RESIDENT/NON RESIDENT ET MONNAIE NATIONALE/ETRANGERE
CLASSIFICATION DE L'ACTIF ET DU PASSIF DES BANQUES
1997

Million Slovak Kroner   *Millions de couronnes slovaques*

	Residents / Résidents	Non-residents / Non résidents	Total / Total	
Assets (4)				Actif (4)
Domestic currency	658119	8989	667108	Monnaie nationale
Foreign currencies	38767	119209	157976	Monnaies étrangères
Total	696886	128198	825084	Total
Liabilities (4)				Passif (4)
Domestic currency	613860	10909	624769	Monnaie nationale
Foreign currencies	51962	100122	152084	Monnaies étrangères
Total	665822	111031	776853	Total

4 Assets and liabilities are not balanced, provisions are not included

4 Les actifs et les passifs ne sont pas équilibrés, les provisions ne sont pas comprises

STRUCTURE OF THE FINANCIAL SYSTEM
STRUCTURE DU SYSTEME FINANCIER
1998

	Number of institutions / Nombre d'institutions	Number of branches / Nombre de succursales	Number of employees / Nombre de salariés	Total assets or liabilities / Total des actifs ou des passifs million SKK	Total financial assets / Total des actifs financiers million SKK	%	
Central bank	1	3	1312	206117	185794	90	Banque centrale
Other monetary institutions	26	918	23815	599906	436059	73	Autres institutions monétaires
Commercial banks	15	869	20160	358 020	198462	55	Banques commerciales
Foreign-owned banks (1)	9	49	3042	193452	190296	98	Banques étrangères (1)
Savings banks	..	..	..	..	..	..	Caisses d'épargne
Co-operative banks	..	..	..	..	..	..	Banques mutualistes
Building saving banks	2	-	613	48532	47301	98	Caisses d'épargne pour le batiment
Other financial institutions	-	-	-	..	..	..	Autres institutions financières
Mortgage credit institutions (2)	..	..	..	..	..	..	Institutions de crédit hypothécaire (2)
Development credit institutions	..	..	..	..	..	..	Institutions de crédit de développement
Finance companies	..	..	..	..	..	..	Sociétés financières
Others	..	..	..	..	..	..	Autres
Insurance institutions	27	611	7615	47198	39366	..	Institutions d'assurance
Insurance companies (3)	27	611	7615	47198	39366	..	Sociétés d'assurance (3)
Pension funds and foundations	..	..	..	..	..	..	Fonds de pension et fondations
Others	..	..	..	..	..	..	Autres
All financial institutions	..	..	..	..	..	..	Ensemble des institutions financières

1 Banks with more than 50% of capital and branches of foreign banks
2 There are no special mortgage credit institutions in Slovak Republic. Several commercial banks have licences serving mortgage cr
3 Data are without health and social insurance companies

1 Il s'agit de banques détenant plus de 50% du capital et de succursales de banques étrangères.
2 Il n'y a pas d'institutions de crédit hypothécaire spéciales en République Slovaque. Plusieurs banques commerciales
   ont des licences pour délivrer les crédits hypothécaires.
3 Ces données n'incluent pas les companies d'assurance sociale et d'assurance-maladie

RESIDENT/NON-RESIDENT AND DOMESTIC/FOREIGN CURRENCY
CLASSIFICATION OF BANK ASSETS AND LIABILITIES
RESIDENT/NON RESIDENT ET MONNAIE NATIONALE/ETRANGERE
CLASSIFICATION DE L'ACTIF ET DU PASSIF DES BANQUES
1998

Million Slovak Kroner   Millions de couronnes slovaques

	Residents / Résidents	Non-residents / Non résidents	Total / Total	
Assets (4)				Actif (4)
Domestic currency	657461	50748	708209	Monnaie nationale
Foreign currencies	21956	126091	148047	Monnaies étrangères
Total	679417	176849	856256	Total
Liabilities (4)				Passif (4)
Domestic currency	610974	75998	686972	Monnaie nationale
Foreign currencies	10898	98395	109293	Monnaies étrangères
Total	621872	174393	796265	Total

4 Assets and liabilities are not balanced, provisions are not included

4 Les actifs et les passifs ne sont pas équilibrés, les provisions ne sont pas comprises

STRUCTURE OF THE FINANCIAL SYSTEM
STRUCTURE DU SYSTEME FINANCIER
1999

	Number of institutions / Nombre d'institutions	Number of branches / Nombre de succursales	Number of employees Nombre de salariés	Total assets or liabilities / Total des actifs ou des passifs million SKK	Total financial assets / Total des actifs financiers million SKK	%	
Central bank	1	3	1308	247453	226061	91	Banque centrale
Other monetary institutions	25	905	23984	896440	657833	73	Autres institutions monétaires
Commercial banks	14	836	19909	653362	420072	64	Banques commerciales
Foreign-owned banks (1)	9	69	3388	185688	181784	98	Banques étrangères (1)
Savings banks	..	..	..	..	..	..	Caisses d'épargne
Co-operative banks	..	..	..	..	..	..	Banques mutualistes
Building saving banks	2	-	687	57390	55977	98	Caisses d'épargne pour le batiment
Other financial institutions	-	-	-	..	..	..	Autres institutions financières
Mortgage credit institutions (2)	..	..	..	..	..	..	Institutions de crédit hypothécaire (2)
Development credit institutions	..	..	..	..	..	..	Institutions de crédit de développement
Finance companies	..	..	..	..	..	..	Sociétés financières
Others	..	..	..	..	..	..	Autres
Insurance institutions	30	614	7763	51650	43391	..	Institutions d'assurance
Insurance companies (3)	27	614	7763	50003	41775	..	Sociétés d'assurance (3)
Pension funds and foundations	3			1647	1616	..	Fonds de pension et fondations
Others	..	..	..	..	..	..	Autres
All financial institutions	..	..	..	..	..	..	Ensemble des institutions financières

1 Banks with more than 50% of capital and branches of foreign banks
2 There are no special mortgage credit institutions in Slovak Republic. Several commercial banks have licences serving mortgage cr
3 Data are without health and social insurance companies

1 Il s'agit de banques détenant plus de 50% du capital et de succursales de banques étrangères.
2 Il n'y a pas d'institutions de crédit hypothécaire spéciales en République Slovaque. Plusieurs banques commerciales
  ont des licences pour délivrer les crédits hypothécaires.
3 Ces données n'incluent pas les companies d'assurance sociale et d'assurance-maladie

RESIDENT/NON-RESIDENT AND DOMESTIC/FOREIGN CURRENCY
CLASSIFICATION OF BANK ASSETS AND LIABILITIES
RESIDENT/NON RESIDENT ET MONNAIE NATIONALE/ETRANGERE
CLASSIFICATION DE L'ACTIF ET DU PASSIF DES BANQUES
1999

Million Slovak Kroner   *Millions de couronnes slovaques*

	Residents / Résidents	Non-residents / Non résidents	Total / Total	
Assets (4)				Actif (4)
Domestic currency	716642	19901	736543	Monnaie nationale
Foreign currencies	67865	55000	122865	Monnaies étrangères
Total	784507	74901	859408	Total
Liabilities (4)				Passif (4)
Domestic currency	639321	12090	651411	Monnaie nationale
Foreign currencies	88724	29630	118354	Monnaies étrangères
Total	728045	41720	769765	Total

4 Assets and liabilities are not balanced, provisions are not included

4 Les actifs et les passifs ne sont pas équilibrés, les provisions ne sont pas comprises

STRUCTURE OF THE FINANCIAL SYSTEM
STRUCTURE DU SYSTEME FINANCIER

2000

	Number of institutions / Nombre d'institutions	Number of branches / Nombre de succursales	Number of employees / Nombre de salariés	Total assets or liabilities / Total des actifs ou des passifs — million SKK	Total financial assets / Total des actifs financiers — million SKK	%	
Central bank	1	3	1314	282755	251375	89	Banque centrale
Other monetary institutions	23	766	22266	1075762	837161	78	Autres institutions monétaires
Commercial banks	9	619	15683	712688	491247	69	Banques commerciales
Foreign-owned banks (1)	11	147	5716	290988	284080	98	Banques étrangères (1)
Savings banks	..	..	..	..	..	..	Caisses d'épargne
Co-operative banks	..	..	..	..	..	..	Banques mutualistes
Building saving banks	3	-	867	72086	61834	86	Caisses d'épargne pour le batiment
Other financial institutions	-	-	-	..	..	..	Autres institutions financières
Mortgage credit institutions (2)	..	..	..	..	..	..	Institutions de crédit hypothécaire (2)
Development credit institutions	..	..	..	..	..	..	Institutions de crédit de développement
Finance companies	..	..	..	..	..	..	Sociétés financières
Others	..	..	..	..	..	..	Autres
Insurance institutions	32	690	8074	57772	49423	..	Institutions d'assurance
Insurance companies (3)	28	690	8074	54702	46397	..	Sociétés d'assurance (3)
Pension funds and foundations	4			3070	3026	..	Fonds de pension et fondations
Others	..	..	..	..	..	..	Autres
All financial institutions	..	..	..	..	..	..	Ensemble des institutions financières

1 Banks with more than 50% of capital and branches of foreign banks
2 There are no special mortgage credit institutions in Slovak Republic. Several commercial banks have licences serving mortgage cr
3 Data are without health and social insurance companies

1 Il s'agit de banques détenant plus de 50% du capital et de succursales de banques étrangères.
2 Il n'y a pas d'institutions de crédit hypothécaire spéciales en République Slovaque. Plusieurs banques commerciales
  ont des licences pour délivrer les crédits hypothécaires.
3 Ces données n'incluent pas les companies d'assurance sociale et d'assurance-maladie

RESIDENT/NON-RESIDENT AND DOMESTIC/FOREIGN CURRENCY
CLASSIFICATION OF BANK ASSETS AND LIABILITIES

RESIDENT/NON RESIDENT ET MONNAIE NATIONALE/ETRANGERE
CLASSIFICATION DE L'ACTIF ET DU PASSIF DES BANQUES
2000

Million Slovak Kroner   *Millions de couronnes slovaques*

	Residents / Résidents	Non-residents / Non résidents	Total / Total	
Assets (4)				Actif (4)
Domestic currency	768246	31139	799385	Monnaie nationale
Foreign currencies	72344	82802	155146	Monnaies étrangères
Total	840590	113941	954531	Total
Liabilities (4)				Passif (4)
Domestic currency	693890	14969	708859	Monnaie nationale
Foreign currencies	105949	32147	138096	Monnaies étrangères
Total	799839	46816	846955	Total

4 Assets and liabilities are not balanced, provisions are not included

4 Les actifs et les passifs ne sont pas équilibrés, les provisions ne sont pas comprises

STRUCTURE OF THE FINANCIAL SYSTEM
STRUCTURE DU SYSTEME FINANCIER

2001

	Number of institutions / Nombre d'institutions	Number of branches / Nombre de succursales	Number of employees / Nombre de salariés	Total assets or liabilities / Total des actifs ou des passifs million SKK	Total financial assets / Total des actifs financiers million SKK	%	
Central bank	1	3	1316	283424	269513	95	Banque centrale
Other monetary institutions	21	724	21265	962062	758189	79	Autres institutions monétaires
Commercial banks	6	62	2759	375188	189272	50	Banques commerciales
Foreign-owned banks (1)	12	662	17590	517457	501017	97	Banques étrangères (1)
Savings banks	..	..	..	..	..	..	Caisses d'épargne
Co-operative banks							Banques mutualistes
Building saving banks	3	-	916	69857	67900	97	Caisses d'épargne pour le batiment
Other financial institutions	-	-	-	..	..	..	Autres institutions financières
Mortgage credit institutions (2)	..	..	..	..	..	..	Institutions de crédit hypothécaire (2)
Development credit institutions	..	..	..	..	..	..	Institutions de crédit de développement
Finance companies	..	..	..	..	..	..	Sociétés financières
Others	..	..	..	..	..	..	Autres
Insurance institutions	32	758	8809	71603	64079	..	Institutions d'assurance
Insurance companies (3)	28	758	8809	66637	59337	..	Sociétés d'assurance (3)
Pension funds and foundations	4			4966	4742	..	Fonds de pension et fondations
Others	..	..	..	..	..	..	Autres
All financial institutions	..	..	..	..	..	..	Ensemble des institutions financières

1 Banks with more than 50% of capital and branches of foreign banks
2 There are no special mortgage credit institutions in Slovak Republic. Several commercial banks have licences serving mortgage cr
3 Data are without health and social insurance companies

1 Il s'agit de banques détenant plus de 50% du capital et de succursales de banques étrangères.
2 Il n'y a pas d'institutions de crédit hypothécaire spéciales en République Slovaque. Plusieurs banques commerciales
  ont des licences pour délivrer les crédits hypothécaires.
3 Ces données n'incluent pas les companies d'assurance sociale et d'assurance-maladie

RESIDENT/NON-RESIDENT AND DOMESTIC/FOREIGN CURRENCY
CLASSIFICATION OF BANK ASSETS AND LIABILITIES

RESIDENT/NON RESIDENT ET MONNAIE NATIONALE/ETRANGERE
CLASSIFICATION DE L'ACTIF ET DU PASSIF DES BANQUES
2001

Million Slovak Kroner   *Millions de couronnes slovaques*

	Residents / Résidents	Non-residents / Non résidents	Total / Total	
Assets (4)				Actif (4)
Domestic currency	808593	44495	853088	Monnaie nationale
Foreign currencies	82813	89114	171927	Monnaies étrangères
Total	891406	133609	1025015	Total
Liabilities (4)				Passif (4)
Domestic currency	729069	38989	768058	Monnaie nationale
Foreign currencies	122157	38594	160701	Monnaies étrangères
Total	851226	77583	928809	Total

4 Assets and liabilities are not balanced, provisions are not included

4 Les actifs et les passifs ne sont pas équilibrés, les provisions ne sont pas comprises

STRUCTURE OF THE FINANCIAL SYSTEM
STRUCTURE DU SYSTEME FINANCIER

2000

	Number of institutions Nombre d'institutions	Number of branches Nombre de succursale	Number of employees Nombre de salariés	Total assets or liabilities / Total des actifs ou des passifs Millions EUR	Total financial assets / Total des actifs financiers (1) Millions EUR	%	
Central bank	1	53	3032	118124	117898	10	Banque centrale
Other monetary institutions	281	38967	243795	1077589	1057054	85	Autres institutions monétaire
Commercial banks	89	15687	124137	578526	569865	46	Banques commerciales
Foreign-owned banks(2)	52	124	3445	45600	45349	4	Banques étrangères (2)
Savings banks	48	19268	101718	413862	403228	33	Caisses d'épargne
Co-operative banks	92	3888	14495	39601	38612	3	Banques mutualistes
Other financial institutions	87	344	5156	62203	61829	5	Autres institutions financière
Development credit institutions	1	1	267	31421	31290	3	Institutions de crédit de développement
Specialised credit institutions	86	343	4889	30782	30539	2	Institutions spécialisées de crédit
Finance companies							Sociétés financières
Others							Autres
Insurance institutions (3)	...	...	...	...	...	...	Institutions d'assurance (3)
Insurance companies	...	...	...	...	...	...	Sociétés d'assurance
Pension funds and foundations							Fonds de pension et fondations
Others							Autres
All financial institutions	369	39364	251983	1257916	1236781	100	Ensemble des institutions financières

1. Total assets minus real assets
2. Only branches of foreign banks (subsidiaries not included).
3. Insurance institutions are included in "Other resident sectors" in the Spanish money and banking statistics
1. Total des actifs moins actifs nets.
2. Seules les succursales des banques étrangères sont compris (pas les filiales).
3. Les institutions d'assurance sont inclus dans "Autres secteurs résidents" dans les statistiques monétaires et bancaires espagi

RESIDENT/NON-RESIDENT AND DOMESTIC/FOREIGN CURRENCY
CLASSIFICATION OF BANK ASSETS AND LIABILITIES

RESIDENT/NON RESIDENT ET MONNAIE NATIONALE/ETRANGERE
CLASSIFICATION DE L'ACTIF ET DU PASSIF DES BANQUES

2000

Euro millions   Millions d'euros

	Residents / Résidents	Non-residents / Non résidents	Total / Total	
Assets				Actif
Domestic currency (1)	906170	77605	983775	Monnaie nationale (1)
Foreign currencies	25129	68686	93814	Monnaies étrangères
Total	931299	146291	1077589	Total
Liabilities				Passif
Domestic currency (1)	839887	124209	964096	Monnaie nationale (1)
Foreign currencies	5535	107958	113493	Monnaies étrangères
Total	845422	232167	1077589	Total

1. Euros (Pesetas and other EU currencies)
1. Euros (pesetas et les autres monnaies de l'Union Européenne)

STRUCTURE OF THE FINANCIAL SYSTEM
STRUCTURE DU SYSTEME FINANCIER

2001

	Number of institutions / Nombre d'institutions	Number of branches / Nombre de succursales	Number of employees / Nombre de salariés	Total assets or liabilities / Total des actifs ou des passifs euro millions	Total financial assets / Total des actifs financiers (1) euro millions	%	
Central bank	1	53	3079	96401	96167	7	Banque centrale
Other monetary institutions	281	38676	244786	1195821	1175052	88	Autres institutions monétaires
Commercial banks	89	14618	119918	635868	627299	47	Banques commerciales
Foreign-owned banks(2)	56	138	3695	53497	53170	4	Banques étrangères (2)
Savings banks	47	19829	105593	460387	449594	34	Caisses d'épargne
Co-operative banks	89	4091	15580	46069	44989	3	Banques mutualistes
Other financial institutions	86	348	5333	69704	69300	5	Autres institutions financières
Development credit institutions	1	1	271	32914	32792	2	Institutions de crédit de développement
Specialised credit institutions	85	347	5062	36790	36508	3	Institutions spécialisées de crédit
Finance companies							Sociétés financières
Others							Autres
Insurance institutions (3)	...	...	...	...	...	...	Institutions d'assurance (3)
Insurance companies	...	...	...	...	...	...	Sociétés d'assurance
Pension funds and foundations							Fonds de pension et fondations
Others							Autres
All financial institutions	368	39077	253198	1361926	1340519	100	Ensemble des institutions financières

1 Total assets minus real assets
2 Only branches of foreign banks (subsidiaries not included).
3 Insurance institutions are included in "Other resident sectors" in the Spanish money and banking statistics
1 Total des actifs moins actifs nets.
2 Seules les succursales des banques étrangères sont compris (pas les filiales).
3 Les institutions d'assurance sont inclus dans "Autres secteurs résidents" dans les statistiques monétaires et bancaires espagnoles

RESIDENT/NON-RESIDENT AND DOMESTIC/FOREIGN CURRENCY
CLASSIFICATION OF BANK ASSETS AND LIABILITIES
RESIDENT/NON RESIDENT ET MONNAIE NATIONALE/ETRANGERE
CLASSIFICATION DE L'ACTIF ET DU PASSIF DES BANQUES

2001

Euro millions   Millions d'euros

	Residents / Résidents	Non-residents / Non résidents	Total / Total	
Assets				Actif
Domestic currency (1)	1005848	98577	1104425	Monnaie nationale (1)
Foreign currencies	24212	67184	91396	Monnaies étrangères
Total	1030060	165761	1195821	Total
Liabilities				Passif
Domestic currency (1)	921550	162694	1084244	Monnaie nationale (1)
Foreign currencies	16952	94625	111577	Monnaies étrangères
Total	938502	257319	1195821	Total

1 Euros (Pesetas and other EU currencies)
1 Euros (pesetas et les autres monnaies de l'Union Européenne)

STRUCTURE OF THE FINANCIAL SYSTEM
STRUCTURE DU SYSTEME FINANCIER

2000

	Number of institutions / Nombre d'institutions	Number of branches / Nombre de succursales	Number of employees Nombre de salariés	Total assets or liabilities / Total des actifs ou des passifs million SKr / KrS	Total financial assets / Total des actifs financiers million SKr / KrS	%	
Central bank	1	1	408	233255	232833		Banque centrale
Other monetary institutions	126	2059	41995	2883511	2860863		Autres institutions monétaires
Commercial banks	23	1732	37072	2592668	2574846		Banques commerciales
Foreign-owned banks	24	58	1743	207526	204997		Banques étrangères
Savings banks	79	269	3180	83317	81020		Caisses d'épargne
Co-operative banks							Banques mutualistes
Other financial institutions	195	..	6997	1676802	1673873		Autres institutions financières
Mortgage credit institutions	13	..	699	1169498	1169428		Institutions de crédit hypothécaire
Development credit institutions	10	..	228	276710	275882		Institutions de crédit de développement
Finance companies	64	..	2604	184762	184203		Sociétés financières
Securities brokerage companies	108	..	3466	45832	44360		Sociétés de courtage
Mutual funds	544	..	..	767331	767331		Fonds communs de placement
Others	32	..	..	175210	175149		Autres
Insurance institutions	156	..	..	2611750	2515297		Institutions d'assurance
Insurance companies	155	..	..	1827756	1731303		Sociétés d'assurance
Pension funds and foundations* Others	1	..	..	783994	783994		Fonds de pension et fondations* Autres
All financial institutions	1054	..	..	8347859	8225346		Ensemble des institutions financières

* Including National Pension Insurance Fund (1-6); at market value
* Y compris le Fond de pension national d'assurance (1-6)

RESIDENT/NON-RESIDENT AND DOMESTIC/FOREIGN CURRENCY
CLASSIFICATION OF BANK ASSETS AND LIABILITIES (1)

RESIDENT/NON RESIDENT ET MONNAIE NATIONALE/ETRANGERE
CLASSIFICATION DE L'ACTIF ET DU PASSIF DES BANQUES (1)

2000

Million Swedish kroner   *Millions de couronnes suèdoises*

	Residents / Résidents	Non-residents / Non résidents	Total / Total	
Assets				Actif
Domestic currency	1498182	184992	1683174	Monnaie nationale
Foreign currencies	282658	710123	992781	Monnaies étrangères
Total	1780840	895115	2675955	Total
Liabilities				Passif
Domestic currency	1325702	185250	1510952	Monnaie nationale
Foreign currencies	75024	1089979	1165003	Monnaies étrangères
Total	1400726	12752229	2675955	Total

1 Swedish banks.

STRUCTURE OF THE FINANCIAL SYSTEM
STRUCTURE DU SYSTEME FINANCIER

2001

	Number of institutions / Nombre d'institutions	Number of branches / Nombre de succursales	Number of employees / Nombre de salariés	Total assets or liabilities / Total des actifs ou des passifs million SKr / KrS	Total financial assets / Total des actifs financiers million SKr / KrS	%	
Central bank	1	1	427	235532	235126		Banque centrale
Other monetary institutions	129	2040	41635	3145393	3120991		Autres institutions monétaires
Commercial banks	27	1730	37095	2811832	2792398		Banques commerciales
Foreign-owned banks	25	71	1997	245782	242584		Banques étrangères
Savings banks	77	239	2543	87779	86009		Caisses d'épargne
Co-operative banks							Banques mutualistes
Other financial institutions	191	..	7805	1724047	1721994		Autres institutions financières
Mortgage credit institutions	13	..	533	1211737	1211683		Institutions de crédit hypothécaire
Development credit institutions	9	..	237	257503	257128		Institutions de crédit de développement
Finance companies	64	..	3111	207679	206998		Sociétés financières
Securities brokerage companies	105	..	3924	47128	46185		Sociétés de courtage
Mutual funds	557	..	..	731852	731852		Fonds communs de placement
Others	28	..	..	153798	153741		Autres
Insurance institutions	159	..	..	2416329	2348377		Institutions d'assurance
Insurance companies	158	..	..	1781544	1713592		Sociétés d'assurance
Pension funds and foundations*	1	..	..	634785	634785		Fonds de pension et fondations*
Others							Autres
All financial institutions	1065	..	..	8406951	8312081		Ensemble des institutions financières

* Including National Pension Insurance Fund (1-6); at market value
* Y compris le Fond de pension national d'assurance (1-6)

RESIDENT/NON-RESIDENT AND DOMESTIC/FOREIGN CURRENCY
CLASSIFICATION OF BANK ASSETS AND LIABILITIES (1)

RESIDENT/NON RESIDENT ET MONNAIE NATIONALE/ETRANGERE
CLASSIFICATION DE L'ACTIF ET DU PASSIF DES BANQUES (1)

2001

Million Swedish kroner   *Millions de couronnes suèdoises*

	Residents / Résidents	Non-residents / Non résidents	Total / Total	
Assets				Actif
Domestic currency	1703820	174867	1878687	Monnaie nationale
Foreign currencies	157648	853276	1010924	Monnaies étrangères
Total	1861468	1028143	2889611	Total
Liabilities				Passif
Domestic currency	1402921	166509	1569430	Monnaie nationale
Foreign currencies	270679	1049502	1320181	Monnaies étrangères
Total	1673600	1216011	2889611	Total

1 Swedish banks.
1 Banques suèdoises.

STRUCTURE OF THE FINANCIAL SYSTEM
STRUCTURE DU SYSTEME FINANCIER

2000

	Number of institutions / Nombre d'institutions	Number of branches / Nombre de succursales (1)	Number of employees / Nombre de salariés	Total assets or liabilities / Total des actifs ou des passifs million SF / FS	
1. Central bank	1	8	575	119098	1. Banque centrale
2. Other monetary institutions					2. Autres institutions monétaires
2.1 Banks Total of which:	375	2903	124998	2124880	2.1 Banques - total dont :
2.1.1 Cantonal banks	24	748	19190	303385	2.1.1 Banques cantonales
2.1.2 Large banks (2)	3	630	59114	1340310	2.1.2 Grandes banques (2)
2.1.3 Regional and Savings Banks	103	390	5451	75808	2.1.3 Banques régionales et caisses d'épargne
2.1.4 Loan Associations and Agricultural Credit Co operatives	1	537	4999	77142	2.1.4 Caisses de crédit mutuel et caisses Raiffeisen
2.1.5 Other banks	204	544	30912	290968	2.1.5 Autres banques
of which: Swiss	77	222	13629	129234	dont : en mains suisse
of which: foreign controlled	127	322	17283	161734	dont : en mains étrangères
2.1.6 Branches of foreign banks	23	27	1243	18843	2.1.6 Succursales de banques étrangères
2.1.7 Private bankers	17	27	4089	18424	2.1.7 Banquiers privés
2.2 Post Office System	1				2.2 Services postaux
3. Other financial institutions					3. Autres institutions financières
4. Memorandum: Banks with special statute					4. Pour mémoire: Banques à statut particulier
4.1 Central mortgage bond issuing houses of Swiss cantonal banks	1			26837	4.1 Centrales de lettres de gage des banques cantonales suisses
4.2 Mortgage bond issuing houses of Swiss mortgage loan banks	1		7	20524	4.2 Banques des lettres de gage d'Etablissements suisses de Crédit hypothécaire
4.3 Central bank of the Swiss Union of agricultural credit banks	..	..	..	..	4.3 Banque centrale de l'Union suisse des Caisses Raiffeisen
4.4 Clearing centre of regional banks and savings banks	1		46	2829	4.4 Centrale de Clearing des Banques Régionales et Caisses d'Epargne suisses
4.5 SIS Segaintersettle AG	1		459	1032	4.5 SIS Segaintersettle AG

1. Excluding receiving outlets and representative offices.
2. Balance Sheet Total (SF million)

Union de Banques Suisses	320633
Société de Banques Suisses	308253
Crédit Suisse	203892
Banque Populaire Suisse	36592

1. Sans les bureaux de recettes et représentations.
2. Total du bilan (millions de francs suisses)

Union de Banques Suisses	320633
Société de Banques Suisses	308253
Crédit Suisse	203892
Banque Populaire Suisse	36592

RESIDENT/NON-RESIDENT AND DOMESTIC/FOREIGN CURRENCY CLASSIFICATION OF BANK ASSETS AND LIABILITIES

RESIDENT/NON RESIDENT ET MONNAIE NATIONALE/ETRANGERE CLASSIFICATION DE L'ACTIF ET DU PASSIF DES BANQUES

2000

Million Swiss francs   *Millions de francs suisses*

	Residents / Résidents	Non-residents / Non résidents	Total / Total	
Assets				*Actif*
Domestic currency	862957	98180	961137	Monnaie nationale
Foreign currencies	65733	1098010	1163743	Monnaies étrangères
Total	928690	1196190	2124880	Total
Liabilities				*Passif*
Domestic currency	878653	108285	986938	Monnaie nationale
Foreign currencies	134847	1003095	1137942	Monnaies étrangères
Total	1013500	1111380	2124880	Total

SWITZERLAND

SUISSE

STRUCTURE OF THE FINANCIAL SYSTEM
STRUCTURE DU SYSTEME FINANCIER

2001

	Number of institutions / Nombre d'institutions	Number of branches / Nombre de succursales (1)	Number of employees / Nombre de salariés	Total assets or liabilities / Total des actifs ou des passifs million SF / FS	
1. Central bank	1	8	585	120153	1. Banque centrale
2. Other monetary institutions					2. Autres institutions monétaires
2.1 Banks Total of which:	369	2877	120414	2227416	2.1 Banques - total dont :
2.1.1 Cantonal banks	24	752	17677	304779	2.1.1 Banques cantonales
2.1.2 Large banks (2)	3	604	55991	1415981	2.1.2 Grandes banques (2)
2.1.3 Regional and Savings Banks	94	387	4697	77682	2.1.3 Banques régionales et caisses d'épargne
2.1.4 Loan Associations and Agricultural Credit Co operatives	1	519	5466	82409	2.1.4 Caisses de crédit mutuel et caisses Raiffeisen
2.1.5 Other banks	205	551	30761	312180	2.1.5 Autres banques
of which: Swiss	80	227	13564	125213	dont : en mains suisse
of which: foreign controlled	125	324	17197	186967	dont : en mains étrangères
2.1.6 Branches of foreign banks	25	37	1320	17010	2.1.6 Succursales de banques étrangères
2.1.7 Private bankers	17	27	4503	17374	2.1.7 Banquiers privés
2.2 Post Office System	1				2.2 Services postaux
3. Other financial institutions					3. Autres institutions financières
4. Memorandum: Banks with special statute					4. Pour mémoire: Banques à statut particulier
4.1 Central mortgage bond issuing houses of Swiss cantonal banks	1			26837	4.1 Centrales de lettres de gage des banques cantonales suisses
4.2 Mortgage bond issuing houses of Swiss mortgage loan banks	1		7	21432	4.2 Banques des lettres de gage d'Etablissements suisses de Crédit hypothécaire
4.3 Central bank of the Swiss Union of agricultural credit banks	..	..	..	..	4.3 Banque centrale de l'Union suisse des Caisses Raiffeisen
4.4 Clearing centre of regional banks and savings banks	1		40	3439	4.4 Centrale de Clearing des Banques Régionales et Caisses d'Epargne suisses
4.5 Intersettle	1		585	1103	4.5 Intersettle

1. Excluding receiving outlets and representative offices.
2. Balance Sheet Total (SF million)

Union de Banques Suisses	320633
Société de Banques Suisses	308253
Crédit Suisse	203892
Banque Populaire Suisse	36592

1. Sans les bureaux de recettes et représentations.
2. Total du bilan (millions de francs)

Union de Banques Suisses	320633
Société de Banques Suisses	308253
Crédit Suisse	203892
Banque Populaire Suisse	36592

RESIDENT/NON-RESIDENT AND DOMESTIC/FOREIGN CURRENCY
CLASSIFICATION OF BANK ASSETS AND LIABILITIES

RESIDENT/NON RESIDENT ET MONNAIE NATIONALE/ETRANGERE
CLASSIFICATION DE L'ACTIF ET DU PASSIF DES BANQUES

2001

Million Swiss francs   *Millions de francs suisses*

	Residents / Résidents	Non-residents / Non résidents	Total / Total	
				Actif
Assets				
Domestic currency	847939	106102	954041	Monnaie nationale
Foreign currencies	74467	1198906	1273373	Monnaies étrangères
Total	922406	1305008	2227414	Total
				Passif
Liabilities				
Domestic currency	875376	121195	996571	Monnaie nationale
Foreign currencies	133747	1097096	1230843	Monnaies étrangères
Total	1009123	1218291	2227414	Total

STRUCTURE OF THE FINANCIAL SYSTEM
STRUCTURE DU SYSTEME FINANCIER

2000

	Number of institutions / Nombre d'institutions	Number of branches / Nombre de succursales	Number of employees / Nombre de salariés	Total assets or liabilities / Total des actifs ou des passifs bln / mlds TL / LT	Total financial assets / Total des actifs financiers bln / mlds TL / LT	%	
Central bank	1	21	5550	30894507	..	..	Banque centrale
Other monetary institutions	..	..	..	..	..	..	Autres institutions monétaires
Commercial banks	61	7812	165224	99453082	..	..	Banques commerciales
Foreign-owned banks (1)	..	..	..	..	..	..	Banques étrangères (1)
Savings banks	..	..	..	..	..	..	Caisses d'épargne
Co-operative banks	..	..	..	..	..	..	Banques mutualistes
Other financial institutions(2)	..	..	..	..	..	..	Autres institutions financières(2)
Insurance institutions	..	..	..	..	..	..	Institutions d'assurance
Insurance companies (3)	..	..	..	..	..	..	Sociétés d'assurance (3)
Pension funds and foundations	..	..	..	..	..	..	Fonds de pension et fondations
All financial institutions	..	..	..	..	..	..	Ensemble des institutions financières

1 Data for Foreign-owned banks is included in Commercial bank figures.
2 Incudes Reinsurance companies.
3 Includes Special finance houses, Leasing companies and Factoring companies.

1 Les données pour les Banques étrangères sont comprises dans celles des Banques commerciales.
2 Y compris les sociétés de réassurance.
3 Y compris les sociétés de financement spécialisées, les sociétés de crédit-bail et les sociétés d'affacturage

RESIDENT/NON-RESIDENT AND DOMESTIC/FOREIGN CURRENCY CLASSIFICATION OF BANK ASSETS AND LIABILITY

RESIDENT/NON RESIDENT ET MONNAIE NATIONALE/ETRANGER CLASSIFICATION DE L'ACTIF ET DU PASSIF DES BANQUES

2000

Billion Turkish liras   *Milliards de livres turques*

	Residents / Résidents	Non-residents / Non résidents	Total / Total	
Assets				Actif
Domestic currency	..	..	64941298	Monnaie nationale
Foreign currencies	..	..	34511784	Monnaies étrangères
Total	..	..	99453082	Total
Liabilities				Passif
Domestic currency	..	..	53129582	Monnaie nationale
Foreign currencies	..	..	46323500	Monnaies étrangères
Total	..	..	99453082	Total

STRUCTURE OF THE FINANCIAL SYSTEM
STRUCTURE DU SYSTEME FINANCIER

2000

	Number of institutions / Nombre d'institutions	Number of branches / Nombre de succursales	Number of employees / Nombre de salariés	Total assets or liabilities / Total des actifs ou des passifs bln / mlds £	Total financial assets / Total des actifs financiers bln / mlds £	%	
Central bank	1	..	2500	39.8	..	..	Banque centrale
Other monetary institutions	409	12700	479100	3144.6	..	..	Autres institutions monétaires
Commercial banks	..	11600	388600	1404.0	..	..	Banques commerciales
Foreign-owned banks	..	1000	90500	1740.9	..	..	Banques étrangères
Savings banks	..	..	..	..	..	..	Caisses d'épargne
Co-operative banks	..	..	..	..	..	..	Banques mutualistes
Other financial institutions	..	..	..	..	..	..	Autres institutions financières
Mortgage credit institutions	..	2100	..	158.6	..	..	Institutions de crédit hypothécaire
Development credit institutions	..	..	..	60.9	..	..	Institutions de crédit de développement
Finance companies	..	..	..	35.2	..	..	Sociétés financières
Others	..	..	..	..	..	..	Autres
Insurance institutions	..	..	..	1786.9	..	..	Institutions d'assurance
Insurance companies	..	..	..	932.7	..	..	Sociétés d'assurance
Pension funds and foundations	..	..	..	765.5	..	..	Fonds de pension et fondations
Others	..	..	..	89	..	..	Autres
All financial institutions	..	..	..	..	..	..	Ensemble des institutions financières

RESIDENT/NON-RESIDENT AND DOMESTIC/FOREIGN CURRENCY
CLASSIFICATION OF BANK ASSETS AND LIABILITIES

RESIDENT/NON RESIDENT ET MONNAIE NATIONALE/ETRANGERE
CLASSIFICATION DE L'ACTIF ET DU PASSIF DES BANQUES
2000

Million pounds sterling Millions de livres

	Residents / Résidents	Non-residents / Non résidents	Total (1)/ Total (1)	
Assets				Actif
Domestic currency	1262449	147516	1468527	Monnaie nationale
Foreign currencies	343225	1241175	1676109	Monnaies étrangères
Total	1605674	1388691	3144636	Total
Liabilities				Passif
Domestic currency	936010	200182	1484130	Monnaie nationale
Foreign currencies	255629	1054544	1660506	Monnaies étrangères
Total	1191639	1254726	3144636	Total

1 Includes capital and unclassified (net), for which breakdown by resident/non-resident is not available
1 Y compris le Capital et le non classé (net),pour lequel la ventilation par monnaie et par résident/non-résident n'est pas disponible

STRUCTURE OF THE FINANCIAL SYSTEM
STRUCTURE DU SYSTEME FINANCIER

2001

	Number of institutions / Nombre d'institutions	Number of branches / Nombre de succursales	Number of employees Nombre de salariés	Total assets or liabilities / Total des actifs ou des passifs bln / mlds £	Total financial assets / Total des actifs financiers bln / mlds £	%	
Central bank	1	..	2300	28.0	..	..	Banque centrale
Other monetary institutions	385	12400	459400	3426.7	..	..	Autres institutions monétaires
Commercial banks	..	11400	372600	1610.1	..	..	Banques commerciales
Foreign-owned banks	..	1000	86800	1816.5	..	..	Banques étrangères
Savings banks	..	..	..	..	..	..	Caisses d'épargne
Co-operative banks	..	..	..	..	..	..	Banques mutualistes
Other financial institutions	..	..	273500	..	..	..	Autres institutions financières
Mortgage credit institutions	..	..	75400	173.7	..	..	Institutions de crédit hypothécaire
Development credit institutions	..	..	..	..	..	..	Institutions de crédit de développement
Finance companies	..	..	..	35.3	..	..	Sociétés financières
Others	..	..	..	..	..	..	Autres
Insurance institutions	..	..	357500	..	..	..	Institutions d'assurance
Insurance companies	..	..	..	..	..	..	Sociétés d'assurance
Pension funds and foundations	..	..	..	..	..	..	Fonds de pension et fondations
Others	..	..	..	..	..	..	Autres
All financial institutions	..	..	1092700	..	..	..	Ensemble des institutions financières

RESIDENT/NON-RESIDENT AND DOMESTIC/FOREIGN CURRENCY CLASSIFICATION OF BANK ASSETS AND LIABILITIES

RESIDENT/NON RESIDENT ET MONNAIE NATIONALE/ETRANGERE CLASSIFICATION DE L'ACTIF ET DU PASSIF DES BANQUES
2001

Million pounds sterling   *Millions de livres*

	Residents / Résidents	Non-residents / Non résidents	Total (1)/ Total (1)	
Assets				Actif
Domestic currency	1374647	163738	1595380	Monnaie nationale
Foreign currencies	400832	1326579	1831322	Monnaies étrangères
Total	1775479	1490317	3426702	Total
Liabilities				Passif
Domestic currency	1013050	215444	1588618	Monnaie nationale
Foreign currencies	310177	1156370	1838090	Monnaies étrangères
Total	1323227	1371814	3426708	Total

1 Includes capital and unclassified (net), for which breakdown by resident/non-resident is not available
1 Y compris le Capital et le non classé (net),pour lequel la ventilation par monnaie et par résident/non-résident n'est pas disponible